THE PALACE OF NESTOR
AT PYLOS
IN WESTERN MESSENIA

THE PALACE OF NESTOR
AT PYLOS
IN WESTERN MESSENIA

❖

Excavations Conducted by
the University of Cincinnati
1939, 1952-1965

❖

Edited by
Carl W. Blegen and Marion Rawson

❖

Published with a Grant from
The Classics Fund
of the University of Cincinnati,
a Gift of Louise Taft Semple
in Memory of Charles Phelps Taft

THRONE ROOM OF THE MEGARON

Reconstruction in water color by Piet de Jong. 1956

THE PALACE OF NESTOR AT PYLOS
IN WESTERN MESSENIA

VOLUME I

THE BUILDINGS

AND THEIR CONTENTS

PART 1 · TEXT

BY CARL W. BLEGEN AND MARION RAWSON

1966

PUBLISHED FOR THE UNIVERSITY OF CINCINNATI

BY PRINCETON UNIVERSITY PRESS

TO THE MEMORY OF

KONSTANTINOS KOUROUNIOTIS

FOREWORD

ACKNOWLEDGMENTS

IN THE COURSE OF the many seasons of excavation in and about the Palace of Nestor at Pylos, the Cincinnati Expedition has incurred countless heavy debts which are owed to generous colleagues and friends who have given us invaluable counsel and aid. It is a pleasant duty to acknowledge these obligations and to offer our warmest thanks to those who have helped us and facilitated our work.

First and foremost we wish to pay a tribute of deep respect and affection to the late Konstantinos Kourouniotis, our original colleague and the proposer of the joint Helleno-American archaeological exploration of Mycenaean settlements and cemeteries in Western Messenia. To his memory we gratefully dedicate this volume.

It was with the enthusiastic encouragement and generous financial support of Professor and Mrs. William T. Semple that we were enabled while our benefactors still lived to carry the project almost to completion through twelve of the fifteen seasons required. After the death of Mrs. Semple, followed by that of her husband, a grant for the concluding campaigns of 1963, 1964, and 1965 was provided by the Classics Fund of the University of Cincinnati, a gift of Louise Taft Semple in memory of Charles Phelps Taft. To the Board of Trustees of the Fund we offer our grateful thanks.

We are also deeply indebted to Professor Spyridon Marinatos, both as a colleague in succession to Dr. Kourouniotis, and for some years as Director General of the Greek Archaeological Service under which we worked. We tender our warm thanks likewise to the succeeding Directors, Professor Anastasios K. Orlandos, the late Dr. John Papademetriou, and Dr. John Kontis, all of whom lent us a helping hand and extended unfailing courtesies, as well as to Dr. Nikolaos Yalouris, Ephor of our district.

With great pleasure we acknowledge the friendly cooperation of the many residents in Chora who owned the land on which we excavated. We are particularly grateful to Mr. Konstantinos P. Tsakonas, a distinguished lawyer representing the Tsakonas family, to which the site belonged; he had long before informed the Archaeological Service that there were antiquities underneath the olive trees on the Englianos hill. We extend warm thanks also to George Petropoulos, the Andreas Anastasopoulos family, and Nikos Antonopoulos who allowed us to dig in their fields below the acropolis. Similar generous courtesy was shown us by Mr. and Mrs. P. Kanakaris, Evstathis Vayenas, and Nikolaos Gliatas who permitted us to wreck their currant-drying-beds superposed over tholos tombs; and by Dem. Paraskevopoulos, Evstathis Deriziotis, Panagiotis Tsakalis, Aristomenos Kontos, Nikos Charalambopoulos, and the Kokkevis family who gave us like facilities in the course of our wide search for chamber tombs.

We owe a special debt to the Greek Archaeological Service which in 1960 erected a lofty metal roof over the Main Building of the palace. Since that time, whatever the weather, it has been possible for the benefit of visitors to leave most of the interior of the building exposed to view: the hearths, the bathroom with the bathtub, the stairways, parts of the floors, the oil magazines, and other interesting remains. Almost all those who now visit the site express their cordial satisfaction with this manner of protecting the antiquities. Dr. Papademetriou and Dr. E. Stikas, Director of Reconstruction and Protection of Monuments, deserve great credit for carrying this project to completion.

Many of the objects found in the palace and in tombs were sent to the National Museum in Athens for cleaning and repair. We are greatly indebted to the Director, Dr. Christos Karouzos, for giving us space in the Museum's laboratory and for the services of a technician. All the Linear B tablets from Englianos have been entered in the accession records of the National Museum and will presumably be kept permanently in Athens where a representative selection has long been on display in a case of its own in the Mycenaean Room. Some other items of gold and ivory and of other materials from the palace and from tombs are also displayed in the same room, but the objects recovered from Tholos 5 have been returned to the new Museum in Chora.

Dr. Bert Hodge Hill, who participated in the initial campaign in 1939 and paid many visits to the site in later seasons, rendered invaluable assistance to the Expedition in many ways, especially in the somewhat complicated and long-drawn-out negotiations that led to the ultimate acquisition of ownership of the hill in the name of the Greek Government. Several journeys to Englianos were necessary and Dr. Hill blithely ventured to set forth, despite the hazards that were sometimes met with in that region during the unsettled times after World War II. Mr. Aristides Kyriakides, our legal counsellor, also gave indispensable help in Athens in conducting this same transaction to its conclusion, properly conveying to the State the title to the hill called Englianos.

Words are inadequate to express our thanks to Professor George E. Mylonas, who as a colleague in 1952 opened the initial exploratory trench across the Main Building of the palace and ultimately uncovered the entire Throne Room with its imposing hearth.

To Miss Alison Frantz the Expedition owes a great debt. It is with much pride that we are able to publish so many of her matchless photographs of the palace taken in 1952, 1953, 1955, 1956, and 1960. In addition she photographed nearly all the Linear B tablets from the site, as well as numerous seals and sealings, other objects, and many pots from the pantries in the Main Building.

Professor John L. Caskey has also rendered service of inestimable value to the Expedition not only in photographing hundreds of pots from the palace and the tombs but also in dealing with the practical business of negotiating with the publishers and of meeting the financial requirements.

Professor Mabel Lang too has taken innumerable photographs, not only general views and details of the palace itself but also of all the frescoes worth recording and likewise many inscribed tablets and sealings and vast numbers of miscellaneous objects and potsherds.

Lord William Taylour has provided us with photographs of the palace in addition to those recording his excavation of tholoi and chamber tombs.

Emile Saraphis of Athens came to Chora and photographed all the pots in room- and tomb-groups and also many separately. Kosta Kostantopoulos, photographer of the National Museum in Athens, took pictures of the small objects deposited in the Museum.[1]

Special acknowledgment is due to Dr. Demetrios Theocharis, who worked with us through the four early campaigns from 1952 to 1955: he surveyed the site and drew the first plans of the palace which formed the basis for all subsequent drawings. George Papathanasopoulos, who joined us in 1958, participated in three seasons and paid several visits later. He measured and drew plans of the walls and buildings uncovered in those years and they were duly added to the general plan. In 1957 Lloyd Cotsen, who was serving as architect at the excavations at Lerna, spent a few days at Englianos, during which he measured, drew, and added to the general plan the various elements brought to light in that season.

Dr. John Travlos, architect of the American School's Excavations, in 1960 made a new survey of the palace and the whole site; the resulting plans appear in Figures 416 and 417. We are greatly indebted to Dr. Travlos for coming to our assistance.

Our warm thanks are owed to David French, who supervised the clearing of the Wine Magazine, surveyed it, and drew a detailed plan of the building and the wine jars in position on the floor.

With cordial gratitude we own our weighty obligation to the American School of Classical Studies at Athens. Professor Lamar Crosby, Acting Director in 1939 and, after World War II, the successive Directors John L. Caskey and Henry S. Robinson were always ready to come to our help when needed. We remember too with deep pleasure the timely and expert aid given us by Professor Eugene Vanderpool, who in 1952 supervised the excavation of the Vestibule and the Portico that led into the Throne Room.

It is a great satisfaction to have an opportunity in behalf of the Expedition to ex-

[1] Photographs of details of excavation and of views (except those from the air), which are not specifically attributed to others, were taken by C. W. Blegen.

press heartfelt thanks to the members of the staff who toiled diligently and devotedly in the excavation and in the study of the remains uncovered and the objects found. Although some of these associates were not free to stay more than one season, others were able to return year after year. Continuity of method and supervision was thus maintained so far as possible from the beginning to the end of our activities, largely through the indispensable participation of Marion Rawson from 1953 to 1965 and of Mabel Lang from 1957 to 1965.

Special mention should also be made of Piet de Jong, our artist, whose constructive imagination recreated and brought to vivid perception the lingering aura of the royal Mycenaean rulers who dwelt in this palace.

All who took part, whether for a long or a shorter period, were conscientious workers whose industry and cooperation are gratefully acknowledged and their names are recorded in the following list: Dr. and Mrs. Hill, Mrs. Blegen, Dr. William A. McDonald, Professor Mylonas, Dr. Theocharis, Professor Vanderpool, Marion Rawson, Rosemary Hope, Lord William Taylour, Piet de Jong, Watson Smith, Robert J. Buck, Emmett L. Bennett, Jr., Rolf Hubbe, Mr. and Mrs. William P. Donovan, Professor Lang, George Papathanasopoulos, David French, Mr. and Mrs. William G. Kittredge, Peter Smith, John Pedley.

In the actual labor of digging we benefited substantially from a similar continuity in the roster of our workmen. All were residents of Chora or other nearby villages. Many quickly learned the aim of our digging and the need of care to avoid damaging delicate fragile objects. This continuity was mainly assured through the competent management of our Foreman, Dionysios Androutsakis, who was a good teacher, skilled in training his men. He also shared fully our feelings of responsibility for protecting and safeguarding the antiquities that were being recovered.

During the many campaigns the Expedition kept an established base of operations in Chora. The people of the village have been very friendly and have done all in their power to make our sojourn among them as pleasant and comfortable as possible. Thanks to the initiative of Dr. Charalambos Panagopoulos, who in 1954 was president of the Village Council, a house in an attractive garden in the upper edge of the community was put at our disposal. With the addition of several rooms and a kitchen, built by us, it has served admirably as headquarters and as a home for the staff. We are deeply beholden to Dr. Panagopoulos and the people of Chora for their hospitality. No account of the work done by the expedition would be complete without giving honorable mention to Mrs. Antonia Th. Matzaka, who with her two daughters took charge of the housekeeping in 1952 and has since then devotedly looked out for our comfort and welfare.

On the western side of the Atlantic we owe much to the University of Cincinnati for its constant encouragement and support of the Expedition in the field. It is with special pleasure that we take this occasion to offer our cordial thanks to President Walter Langsam and the other administrative officers of the University for numerous courtesies and favors, particularly for the granting of leaves of absence from the campus.

For their assistance in the preparation of the material for this volume acknowledgments are due to Hero Athanasiades, William B. Dinsmoor, Jr., Roger Holzen, Lewey T. Lands, and Mrs. Edward Wolfley, Jr., who provided plans and drawings; to Mrs. Donald Bradeen and Aziza Kokkoni for typing; to Carolyn Fishback and Mrs. Alfred Osborne for pasting up the illustrations; to Barbara Reinders and Michele Vogt for typing and other help; to Mrs. Harvey Deal and Mrs. John Coleman for reading proof and helping with the indexes.

Warm thanks are also tendered to Mrs. Blegen for critical reading of most of the manuscript, to Miss Anne Blegen for much typing and for editorial checking of the entire text, and to Mrs. John L. Caskey, Mrs. Kittredge, and Miss Lang for assisting with the indexes.

Much of the photographic work and especially the enlargements were done by Emile Saraphis of Athens, Alan Wright, the Photographic Laboratories of the College of Medicine of the University of Cincinnati and of the Agora Excavations in Athens.

The *American Journal of Archaeology* has been very generous to the Expedition in allotting space for the publication year after year of the annual preliminary reports on the progress of the excavations. We are deeply grateful to the Editor, Professor Richard Stillwell, and to the Assistant Editor, Mrs. E. Baldwin Smith, for their unfailing courtesy and help.

Princeton University Press has done its best to make this volume handsome in design and typography. Our thanks are due to the Trustees of the Press, to the Director, Herbert Bailey, to the Chief Typographer, P. J. Conkwright, and to the Fine Arts Editor, Harriet Anderson; to the latter we are especially grateful for her careful scrutiny of the manuscript. For their painstaking care in the production of the illustrations, we are greatly indebted to E. Harold Hugo and John Peckham of the Meriden Gravure Company.

PLAN OF PUBLICATION

From beginning to end the excavation of the Palace of Nestor has had fairly widespread mention in public print. The discovery in 1939 of hundreds of clay tablets bearing inscriptions in Linear B script—the first of their kind to be found on the Greek mainland—attracted much attention. The gradual uncovering of the buildings furnished topics for frequent stories in the newspapers and periodicals. Moreover, a provisional report presenting the results of each campaign was duly published in the *American Journal of Archaeology*. These reports were drawn up promptly at the close of the season before the material recovered had been cleaned and fully studied; some errors and mistakes were thus inevitable; but all these preliminary publications and press accounts are superseded by this concluding work which is a product of much labor, thought, and study.

Volume I contains a description of the palace, room by room, in each instance (where anything was found) accompanied by a descriptive catalogue of the objects from the room. The book includes also a detailed analytical classification of the pottery and the shapes noted.

Volume II by Professor Lang presents the abundant remains of the frescoes found in the palace and outside it.

Volume III deals with the walls, pottery, and other objects of earlier periods discovered underneath the palace as well as outside it in all parts of the hilltop; also with the ruins of the lower town below the acropolis; it offers too an account of the three tholos tombs excavated in the neighborhood of the citadel as well as the chamber tombs investigated along a ridge to the west of the palace site, and some similar sepulchers at Kato Englianos.

Volume IV will provide a complete set of photographs of all the tablets found at Nestor's Pylos with text and comment by Professor Emmett L. Bennett, Jr.

The palace and the tombs yielded 10 seals and 130 seal impressions in clay, the latter representing 91 different seals. While we were preparing the present volume Mrs. Agnes Sakellariou was compiling for the *Corpus der minoischen und mykenischen Siegel*, sponsored by the Akademie der Wissenschaften und der Literatur at Mainz, a descriptive catalogue of the seals and sealings in the National Museum in Athens. For inclusion in that work and to avoid repeating in duplicate a long catalogue we were happy to turn over all our pertinent material—which was already in the National Museum—to Mrs. Sakellariou. In our Volume I the glyptic items from the palace are briefly described in the lists of objects found, many are illustrated, and references to the *Corpus* are given.

Chora, Triphylias
May 1965

Athens
April 1966

C. W. B.

CONTENTS

[xiii]

CONTENTS

ILLUSTRATIONS

Frontispieces: Reconstructions in water color by Piet de Jong. 1956
(The designs and patterns above the level of the dado are hypothetical)

Part 1 Throne Room of the Megaron

Part 2 Court of the Megaron

[xv]

[xxiii]

MAPS, PLANS, AND SECTIONS

ABBREVIATIONS

AA	*Archäologischer Anzeiger* (in *Jahrbuch des deutschen archäologischen Instituts.* Berlin)
AJA	*American Journal of Archaeology*
AM	*Mitteilungen des deutschen archäologischen Instituts, athenische Abteilung* (Athens)
Asine	Frödin, O., and A. W. Persson, *Asine: Results of the Swedish Excavations 1922-1930* (Stockholm, 1938)
BCH	*Bulletin de correspondance hellénique. École française d'Athènes* (Paris)
BMC I, I	Forsdyke, E. J., *Catalogue of the Greek and Etruscan Vases in the British Museum,* Vol. I Part I: *Prehistoric Aegean Pottery* (London, 1925)
BSA	*The Annual of the British School at Athens* (London)
ChT	Wace, A. J. B., *Chamber Tombs at Mycenae* (*Archaeologia* 82. Oxford, 1932)
CMMS	*Corpus of Minoan Mycenaean Seals*
CVA	*Corpus Vasorum Antiquorum*
Deltion	Ἀρχαιολογικὸν Δελτίον
Docs.	Ventris, M., and J. Chadwick, *Documents in Mycenaean Greek* (Cambridge, 1956)
EphArch	Ἐφημερὶς Ἀρχαιολογική
Ergon	Τὸ Ἔργον τῆς Ἀρχαιολογικῆς Ἑταιρείας (Athens)
Etudes crétoises	*Études crétoises. École française d'Athènes* (Paris)
Eutresis	Goldman, H., *Excavations at Eutresis in Boeotia* (Cambridge, Mass., 1931)
Festos	Pernier, L., *Il palazzo minoico di Festos. Scavi e studi della missione archeologica italiana a Creta dal 1900 al 1934* (Rome, 1935)
Hesperia	*Hesperia. Journal of the American School of Classical Studies at Athens*
Jhb	*Jahrbuch des deutschen archäologischen Instituts* (Berlin)
Korakou	Blegen, C. W., *Korakou: A Prehistoric Settlement near Corinth* (Boston and New York, 1921)
MonAnt	*Monumenti Antichi pubblicati per cura della Reale Accademia dei Lincei* (Rome)
MP	Furumark, A., *The Mycenaean Pottery: Analysis and Classification* (Stockholm, 1941)
MV	Furtwaengler, A., and G. Loeschcke, *Mykenische Vasen* (Berlin, 1886)
Mykenai	Tsountas, C., Μυκῆναι καὶ Μυκηναῖος πολιτισμός (Athens)
NT, Dendra	Persson, A. W., *New Tombs at Dendra near Midea* (Lund, 1942)

[xxix]

NM	Inventory number, National Museum, Athens
OOT	Bennett, E. L., Jr., *Minos* 5 (1957): *The Olive Oil Tablets of Pylos, 1939-1956*
PM	Evans, Sir Arthur, *The Palace of Minos* (London, 1921-1936)
Praktika	Πρακτικὰ τῆς ἐν ᾿Αθήναις ᾿Αρχαιολογικῆς ῾Εταιρείας
Prosymna	Blegen, C. W., *Prosymna: The Helladic Settlement Preceding the Argive Heraeum* (Cambridge, 1937)
PT I	Bennett, E. L., Jr., *The Pylos Tablets: A Preliminary Transcription* (Princeton, 1951)
PT II	Bennett, E. L., Jr., *The Pylos Tablets: Texts of the Inscriptions Found, 1939-1954* (Princeton, 1955)
RT, Dendra	Persson, A. W., *The Royal Tombs at Dendra near Midea* (Lund, 1931)
TI	Dörpfeld, W., *Troja und Ilion: Ergebnisse der Ausgrabungen in den vorhistorischen und historischen Schichten von Ilion* (Athens, 1902)
Tiryns	*Deutsches archaeologisches Institut in Athen, Die Ergebnisse der Ausgrabungen des Instituts.* II: G. Rodenwaldt, *Die Fresken des Palastes* (Berlin, 1912). III: K. Müller, *Die Architektur der Burg und Palastes* (Augsburg, 1930)
Troy	*Troy, Excavations Conducted by the University of Cincinnati, 1932-1938.* I: C. W. Blegen, J. L. Caskey, M. Rawson, J. Sperling, *General Introduction, The First and Second Settlements* (Princeton, 1950); III: C. W. Blegen, J. L. Caskey, M. Rawson, *The Sixth Settlement* (Princeton, 1953)
Zygouries	Blegen, C. W., *Zygouries: A Prehistoric Settlement in the Valley of Cleonae* (Cambridge, Mass., 1928)

THE PALACE OF NESTOR

THE BUILDINGS

AND THEIR CONTENTS

HISTORY OF THE EXCAVATION

WESTERN MESSENIA was long neglected as a region deserving intensive archaeological exploration. The Bay of Navarino, the island of Sphacteria, and the fortress crowning the rocky promontory, called Koryphasion or Pylos, were often visited by early travelers and historians, who were mainly interested in following Thucydides' account of the campaign of 425 B.C. in the Peloponnesian War when the Athenians won a notable triumph over the Spartans, capturing 292 of them alive.

In 1874, among the first of the exploring archaeologists, Schliemann visited the region, looked at the "Cave of Nestor" on the steep northeast slope of the citadel and collected prehistoric sherds within it. Fourteen years later he returned, toward the end of November 1888, and made numerous soundings throughout the high acropolis, where he found rock at a depth of 0.60 m. to 1.50 m., some late pottery, but no fragments of classical or Mycenaean wares.[1] He had observed, however, that many sherds from the "Cave of Nestor" were of the "so-called Mycenaean type." This was apparently the first discovery of Mycenaean pottery on the west coast of the Peloponnesos. In 1896 a French expedition undertook brief explorations in the cave, and reported the finding of various kinds of pottery ranging from pre-Geometric to Roman wares.[2] Some of the pieces recovered were recognized by Tsountas as pre-Mycenaean (Mattpainted Ware).

In 1909 the Ephor A. Skias conducted a small excavation below the village of Tragana (Fig. 400), where traces of a tomb had been found and reported. Lack of time and of funds restricted the investigation to a brief period: it was determined, however, that the remains were of Mycenaean date, and the Ephor believed that it was a stone-lined shaft grave similar to those in the grave circle at Mycenae.[3] Following further activities of enterprising local amateur archaeologists, the Ephor K. Kourouniotis was sent to Messenia in 1912 to continue the excavation. He discovered that the presumed shaft was part of the dromos of a tholos tomb, the contents of which indicated that it was in use through a long period from early to late Mycenaean times.[4] The vault had collapsed causing much disturbance in the burial deposits. Among the objects recovered were some items of gold jewelry and many fine vases, including three large jars, decorated in what Evans had first called the "Palace Style," much like those found in tholos tombs at Kakovatos (Fig. 399).

At that site some 50 km. to the north of Navarino Bay, in the district which after Mycenaean times came to be called Triphylia, Professor W. Dörpfeld in 1907 discovered and excavated three tholos tombs. On a low hill above them he found ruins

[1] *AM* XIV (1889), 132f.
[2] Laurent, *BCH* XX (1896), 388ff.
[3] *Praktika* 1909, 274ff.
[4] *EphArch* 1914, 99ff.

of stone walls of a building which he conjectured had been a palace. Although they had been robbed in ancient times, the tombs still retained many valuable objects of gold, bronze, amber, paste, stone, bone and other material, which the looters had missed. Notable among the finds is a magnificent series of large jars bearing painted decoration in the Palace Style. Dörpfeld concluded that the site must be that of Nestor's Pylos, which many Alexandrian scholars, followed by Strabo, had postulated must lie in Triphylia. This view, which had not hitherto found general favor among scholars of modern times, was henceforth accepted by many.[5]

In 1926 Kourouniotis was again dispatched to western Messenia to deal with the discovery of yet another tholos tomb. This lay under the remnants of a tumulus in the middle of a flat field some ten minutes to the south of the village formerly known as Osman Aga, but now renamed Koryphasion (Fig. 400). The chamber, ca. 6 m. in diameter, was filled with stones that fell in the collapse of the vault. Tomb robbers had also apparently been active here, and the interments were all disturbed.[6] Several pots could nonetheless be put together from the fragments collected from the debris. Most of these vases are of Middle Helladic types with linear decoration executed in dull paint, evidence which suggests that this is probably the earliest of all the tholoi that have yet been excavated. During his campaign Kourouniotis and his assistant Ph. Stavropoulos along with Charalambos Christophilopoulos, owner of half the ground on which the tholos tomb lay, carried out explorations in the general neighborhood and observed traces of several additional tholoi, which had not been opened.

It was shortly after this—in 1927 and 1928—that, on the initiative of Kourouniotis, a joint Hellenic-American Expedition was formed, Kourouniotis representing the Greek Archaeological Service and C. W. Blegen the University of Cincinnati. The purpose of the enterprise, as formulated by Kourouniotis, was to explore western Messenia in a search for Mycenaean settlements, tholos tombs, and cemeteries. Because of previous commitments on the part of the two colleagues, a good many years were to pass before the undertaking could be actually inaugurated in the chosen field. Both partners, however, found an opportunity to do some exploring and had visited Epano Englianos in the late nineteen-twenties. In 1938 they made another tour, this time together, saw that site again and looked at several other possibilities, as well as at signs of additional tholos tombs; but it was only in 1939 that it at last became feasible to start a campaign of actual exploratory digging. The necessary funds for the expedition were generously provided by Professor and Mrs. W. T. Semple of Cincinnati.

The two colleagues agreed in believing that the Mycenaean tholoi, widely dis-

[5] *AM* XXXIII (1908), Dörpfeld, 295-317, pls. XV-XVII; XXXIV (1909), Müller, 269-325, pls. XII-XXIV.

[6] *Praktika* 1925-1926, 140f.; *AA* 1926-1927, col. 384; *Hesperia* XXIII (1954), 158-162.

tributed throughout Greece from the Peloponnesos to Thessaly, were royal sepulchers, made for kings, great and small, along with their families, the rulers of the principal centers, such as Mycenae and Thebes, as well as those of the more modest and even little kingdoms of the kind recorded in the Catalogue of Ships.[7] We believed also that the evident concentration of so many tholoi around the northerly border of the Bay of Navarino must indicate the presence, somewhere in that vicinity, of an important palace in which some of those royal families lived before they died and were buried. It was this hypothetical palace that was the first object of the expedition's search, and neither colleague had any preconceived theory about whose palace it might turn out to be, if actually found.

In the spring of 1939 Kourouniotis, then Director of the National Museum in Athens, was unable to be absent for long periods from his duties. The junior colleague was therefore deputed to initiate the trial excavations. Accompanied by Dr. Bert Hodge Hill, he reached modern Pylos on March 25. The two carried out some further preliminary exploring in the hills to the northeast of Koryphasion village and a few days later they were joined in continued activity of the same kind by William A. McDonald, a student at the American School of Classical Studies at Athens, who joined our staff.

As acting foreman we employed Charalambos Christophilopoulos, who had become deeply interested in archaeological matters when he worked under Kourouniotis in the excavation of a beehive tomb in 1926. Since then he had devoted much of his time to peregrinations about the countryside looking for remains of ancient towns or tombs. He was therefore extremely useful to us in our search for Mycenaean settlements. He conducted us to many places where he had observed walls or pottery of earlier eras; and when we passed through villages we always inquired if there were old ruins anywhere in the neighborhood. A friendly reception invariably awaited us and the villagers were ready and eager to show us what they thought might be remains of the past. In the course of eight or ten days six or seven possible Mycenaean sites were noted and recorded; but one stood out conspicuously above all the others as the most promising. That was the hill called Englianos or Epano Englianos (Fig. 400), where we had decided to begin our trial excavations.

This elevation (Fig. 1), which was occupied by a handsome olive orchard, was owned by the Tsakonas family of Chora. Perikles Tsakonas, the elderly survivor of two brothers who had held the property together, represented the family and very kindly gave us permission to dig exploratory trenches, provided that due care should be taken to avoid causing serious damage to the olives.

The first trench was laid out early on April 4, and by mid-morning even the rosiest expectations had been surpassed: substantial stone walls, more than 1 m.

---

[7] *Iliad* II, 484ff.

thick, had been exposed to view; fragments of plaster retaining vestiges of painted decoration had been recovered; a cement-like lime floor had been reached; and five clay tablets bearing inscribed signs in the Linear B script had come virtually undamaged, though lime-coated, out of the soil, the first of their kind to be found in mainland Greece. It was at once obvious that a palatial building occupied the hill.

During the following weeks until May 10, under the supervision of Mr. McDonald, Trench I was excavated to the level of the floors, and seven further trenches were opened in order to ascertain the limits of the structure (Figs. 401, 402) so that plans might be made for excavation on a full scale the next year. A small chamber, which was cleared at the southern end of Trench I, came to be known as the Archives Room, since it yielded more than 600 tablets and fragments of tablets. So far as possible, all were exposed to view and photographed (Figs. 78, 79), and were then taken up by Messrs. McDonald and Blegen.

About one kilometer to the south of the site and close to the western side of the highroad a large lintel block still in its place indicated the presence of a tholos tomb under an *aloni*, or drying bed for currants, belonging to Nikolaos Gliatas of Chora. With the kind permission of the owner, this tomb was excavated under the supervision of Mrs. C. W. Blegen, who was assisted by Mrs. B. H. Hill. Although it had been robbed and thoroughly disturbed in ancient times, after which the vault had collapsed, the tomb was found still to contain many objects of gold, bronze, stone, ivory, and pottery which had been overlooked by the looters.[8]

At the end of the season the trenches on the site were refilled with earth so that the land could be cultivated again. All items of gold, bronze, stone, and ivory from the tomb and from the palace, and all the tablets recovered, along with some sample pots, were taken to the National Museum in Athens to be cleaned and mended. The bulk of the pottery was left in a storeroom in Koryphasion village. In Athens the tablets were carefully cleaned and fitted together during the autumn and winter of 1939-1940 by Andreas Mavraganis under the supervision of Dr. Hill. The latter, assisted by Miss Margaret MacVeagh (Mrs. Samuel Thorne), from attached labels and wrappings transferred to the tablets themselves the original inventory numbers assigned at the excavations. Photographs were taken by Miss Alison Frantz and in 1940 a complete set of prints of all tablets and fragments reached Cincinnati. They provided material for an intensive study of the contents of the documents, mainly by Emmett L. Bennett, Jr., who in 1951 published a preliminary transcription and made the texts available to all scholars interested in the problem of solving the language.[9]

As for the continuation of future work in the field, untoward circumstances, be-

---

[8] A report on the results of the campaign was published in *AJA* XLIII (1939), 557-576.

[9] *The Pylos Tablets: A Preliminary Transcription* (Princeton, 1951).

yond our control, soon intervened to give us abundant time to consider the problems of the systematic excavation of the palace which we were eager to undertake. The outbreak of World War II, its long duration, and its lingering aftermath in Messenia left no early opportunity for peaceful archaeological research. It was not until 1952—more than a dozen years after the exploratory soundings—that the task of uncovering the palace could be begun. Following the auspicious results of the trial campaign, Kourouniotis promptly applied for the expropriation of the site in accordance with the provisions of the Greek law. During the war and the invasion and occupation of Greece, no progress could be made; but in the period of reconstruction after hostilities had ceased and order was restored, the normal tenure of life was gradually reestablished. In this interval, with the effective help of Dr. Hill and with the generous and able legal aid of Aristides Kyriakides, the somewhat complex formalities of acquiring in the name of the Greek State the title to the ground to be excavated were ultimately overcome. In the meantime, however, the expedition suffered a great loss in the death of the senior colleague and the initiator of the joint undertaking, Konstantinos Kourouniotis, to whose memory this volume is dedicated. As his successor Professor Spyridon Marinatos of the University of Athens was appointed by the Archaeological Council. Professor Marinatos proposed that, while continuing the joint sponsorship, each colleague should have independent authority and responsibility for his own part in the project; and he chose to leave the area about the palace to the Cincinnati Expedition while he himself turned to settlements and cemeteries in other parts of western Messenia.

The systematic excavation of the palace began May 30, 1952, and the work of the first season[10] was continued until July 19 with an average number of 23 workmen. The regular staff comprised Professor George E. Mylonas, Demetrios Theocharis, C. W. Blegen, and Eugene Vanderpool from July 2 to 20. We had no foreman. Professor Mylonas laid out a long exploratory trench from southwest to northeast, discovered and cleared the Throne Room (Fig. 65), revealed its hearth, and began to uncover the Vestibule. After his departure Mr. Vanderpool completed removing the debris from the Vestibule and exposed to view the greater part of the Portico (Fig. 50). Mr. Theocharis dug several trenches to determine the northeastern and southeastern limits of the building (Fig. 404) and commenced investigations in what later proved to be the Propylon; he also measured the whole site and drew the plan of it and of all the remains that had been brought to light (Fig. 403). In the outer annex (7) to the Archives Room (8 on Key Plan)[11] which was

[10] A report on the results of the campaign appeared in *AJA* 57 (1953), 59-64.

[11] This Key Plan, which bears the identifying numbers of all rooms and areas in the palace, is printed for the convenience of the reader on the fold-in page at the back of this volume.

discovered in 1939, 468 inscribed tablets and fragments were recovered: almost all of them—after having been recorded in plans and photographed in place, as found—were lifted, numbered, and wrapped up in paper by the three regular members of the staff, working together. When the campaign ended, all the tablets, as wrapped, were taken to Athens for cleaning and mending.[12] At the close of the season a protective covering of earth was spread over the hearth and the floors of the Throne Room, Vestibule, Portico and Archives Rooms to prevent damage during our long absence through the autumn and winter until we returned in the spring of 1953. While all that had been exposed to view was still visible, Miss Frantz spent two days at the excavations and took numerous photographs in color as well as in black and white, providing us with a wealth of illustrations of details and of general views.

The second campaign was carried out in ten weeks from May 21 to July 29, 1953.[13] The members of the staff were Marion Rawson, Rosemary Hope, D. Theocharis, Lord William Taylour, W. A. McDonald, Piet de Jong, and C. W. Blegen. The number of workmen ranged from 10 to 35, averaging 30; and Dionysios Androutsakis was appointed Acting Foreman. Work was concentrated chiefly on the area directly to the southwest of the Throne Room. Miss Rawson took charge of clearing six small rooms (16 to 21 on Key Plan), four of which (18, 19, 20, 21) proved to be pantries or storerooms for pottery (Fig. 64). They contained a large assortment of predominantly plain undecorated household pots of many shapes, the great majority badly shattered in their fall from the wooden shelves on which they were stored on the day the palace was destroyed by fire. Some 6,000 vessels were represented in the wreckage. One of the three inscribed tablets found in 1953 came from Room 20.

Under the supervision of Miss Hope part of Court 88 and Rooms 89 and 90 were cleared; she also uncovered the spacious Entrance Hall 64, which proved to lead into the Southwestern Building (Fig. 194) and to retain many remains of the frescoes that once decorated its walls. Mr. McDonald completed the excavation of the areas numbered 89 and 90—after Miss Hope's departure—and of Room 67 (which he had first exposed at the end of Trench v in 1939), and recovered a great number of tripod cooking pots and other vessels in coarse domestic ware. He likewise opened numerous exploratory trenches at intervals on all sides around the steep edge of the acropolis in search of a possible circuit wall. No certain remains of a fortification were found, but this work revealed a deep habitation deposit along the abrupt northwestern bank of the hill, containing in the lower levels potsherds which may be assigned to early Mycenaean and Middle Helladic times; and remnants of house walls near the eastern angle of the hill.

[12] *PT II*, Nos. 621-994.   [13] Preliminary report in *AJA* 58 (1954), 27-32.

Projecting at the top of a slope, less than 100 m. to the northeast of the acropolis, a huge block of conglomerate, which had long been known and was recognized as part of a lintel, betrayed the presence of a tholos tomb. The threshing floor that covered it was the property of Mr. and Mrs. P. Kanakaris, who very generously permitted us to destroy the greater part of the *aloni* and to open the tomb. It was excavated under the supervision of Lord William Taylour. Although the tomb had been plundered in ancient times, many objects had eluded the attention of the robbers and had also escaped serious damage when the stones of the dome fell into the chamber. More than 900 items of gold, silver, bronze, stone, ivory, amber, paste, and clay were recovered and inventoried by Lord William. The oldest burials go back to the early Mycenaean Period, long before the neighboring palace was built, and even the latest elements in the tomb probably antedate the construction of the megaron.

Mr. Theocharis cleared to the level of its pavement the greater part of the Court (3 on Key Plan) on which the Portico of the Main Building faced. The southeastern limit of the Court was found to be formed by a wall that had a dado course of large squared blocks of poros. In addition to his excavating, Theocharis made a survey of all the remains of the buildings exposed and drew up a plan of the palace as it appeared at the end of the season (Fig. 405). He also prepared a plan and a section of the large tholos tomb that has been mentioned.

Mr. de Jong made a close detailed study, square by square, of the painted decoration on the floor of the Throne Room and on the border of the hearth, all of which were reproduced in a water-color drawing (Fig. 73). This season too Miss Frantz assisted us generously, staying two days at the excavations and taking many photographs of all areas before the winter cover of earth was laid over the floors.

Zacharias Kanakis, formerly Chief Technician in the Museum at Herakleion, assisted materially in mending a good many pots, and especially in lifting and cleaning numerous fragments of frescoes.

During the season Messrs. McDonald and Theocharis undertook a brief exploration in the "Cave of Nestor," the open entrance of which is conspicuous in the sheer northeastern face of Koryphasion which overlooks the Osman Aga Lagoon (Fig. 400). No architectural remains were found, but a trench sunk through a deep stratified deposit yielded potsherds ranging from Neolithic through Early, Middle, and Late Helladic and later periods.

The campaign of 1954 was conducted from April 30 to July 31.[14] The month of May was devoted mainly to the study and mending of pottery and the cleaning of frescoes in the workroom at Chora, and actual excavations were not begun until the

[14] Preliminary report: *AJA* 59 (1955), 31-37.

end of May. The members of the staff were M. Rawson, Watson Smith, D. Theocharis, P. de Jong, Robert J. Buck, Lord William Taylour, Mrs. Blegen, Mrs. Hill, Emmett L. Bennett, Jr., and C. W. Blegen. Dionysios Androutsakis was Foreman, and the number of workmen employed ranged from 12 to 27, averaging 21.

Mr. Smith, who took charge of the cleaning of the numerous fragments of frescoes found in the two preceding seasons, rendered able assistance also in organizing and recording the growing collection of this material. Thanks to the friendly courtesy of Dr. Platon, Director of the Herakleion Museum, we again profited greatly from the services of Z. Kanakis, who removed for preservation many remains of frescoes which still adhered more or less precariously to the walls in various rooms, and who took a full share in the cleaning operation.

Miss Rawson directed the excavation of an area some 11 m. wide and 30 m. long, to the northeast of the Throne Room, where, separated from the latter by a lengthy narrow corridor, was uncovered a complex of nearly a dozen rooms, passages, cubicles, and a stairway which had once led to an upper story (25 to 36 on Key Plan). Rooms 27 (the clearing of which was completed by Mr. Bennett) and 32 were oil magazines, containing—in addition to many smaller pots—numerous large jars which had evidently been full of oil on the day the palace was burned and thus contributed fuel to the fire. The stairway (36) was found to retain in place eight of its stone steps. This group of rooms lay along the northeastern side of the Main Building, where the only surviving section of the outside wall is preserved (Fig. 27), illustrating the technique of construction with an outer face of large squared blocks of poros and an inner backing of rubble which was coated with plaster.

Under the supervision of Mr. Theocharis, in the southeastern quarter of the building, alongside the Archives Rooms, the main entrance to the palace was found, a Propylon (1 and 2) built with the plan of a capital letter H, having a doorway in the crossbar, and a single column in each façade between the lateral walls (Fig. 46). Scattered about in the gateway and in Ramp 59 beyond the Archives Rooms were found fragments of a silver cup decorated in the main zone with bearded human heads inlaid in gold and niello. Many fragments of plaster bearing remains of frescoes were recovered, and a heap of inscribed tablets came to light in the southwestern side of the inner Portico, presumably having fallen from Archives Room 8.

To the southwest of the latter Mrs. Blegen, assisted by Mrs. Hill, uncovered what later proved to be a ramp paved with stucco (59), which led to the Southwestern Building, and beside the ramp, a storeroom (60) filled with pottery. More than 500 pots of many different shapes were salvaged in the part of the room that was cleared in 1954. One additional gold head and a socket for another belonging to the silver cup were found in the surface soil above the ramp. Mr. Bennett took over responsibility for this area when Mrs. Blegen was obliged to leave before the end of the season. He exposed the greater part of the ramp and investigated an underground drain that carried rain water and waste from the palace to the low area beyond the southwestern edge of the hill.

Farther to the northwest, alongside the Portico and the Vestibule of the Throne Room, Mr. Buck cleared a rectangular room (12) with a good stucco floor on which lay badly damaged remains of frescoes. Some slight evidence suggested that this was an entrance lobby containing a doorway through which one could enter from the Southwestern Court (63). Adjoining this room, to the northwest, Mr. Buck recognized scanty ruins of a stairway (14 and 15)—marked by remnants of two steps—which had apparently ascended in three short flights and two right-angled turns to the floor above. The lobby and the staircase extended to the exterior southwestern wall of the Main Building; but the wall was found to be missing, all its stones, except in the lowest foundations, having been removed by seekers of building material. Mr. Buck also uncovered Corridor 13, and outside the building exposed the northeastern part of Court 63.

During the campaign 46 inscribed tablets and fragments were found, mainly in the Propylon (2) and in the oil magazine (32).

All the new architectural elements uncovered in 1954 were measured and drawn by Mr. Theocharis and added to the general plan (Fig. 406). Mr. de Jong spent the greater part of July at Chora studying the frescoes and recording many in watercolor drawings. Lord William Taylour was able to devote ten days in July to a detailed examination of the pottery he had found in the tholos tomb in 1953.

After a preliminary week in Chora occupied with cleaning, mending, and study of the pottery and frescoes from earlier campaigns, the excavations of 1955 were begun on May 23 and were continued until July 30.[15] The staff was made up of M. Rawson, Mrs. Blegen, Rolf Hubbe, P. de Jong, D. Theocharis, Lord William Taylour, and C. W. Blegen. Under our regular Foreman, D. Androutsakis, the workmen engaged ranged in number from 10 to 35, with an average of 20.

Mr. de Jong resumed his work on the frescoes, fitting fragments together and reconstructing on paper some of the compositions that could be worked out; among them remnants of a design of griffins and lions that occupied the wall directly behind the throne. He also drew profiles of many pots, and reproduced in water color numerous vases decorated with painted patterns.

In the course of the season considerable progress was made in the task of uncovering the Main Building. Miss Rawson extended her work along the northeastern side of this unit (Fig. 36), exposing to view four further rooms, a passage, a gateway

---

15 Preliminary report: *AJA* 60 (1956), 95-101.

opening into a small walled court (37 to 43 on Key Plan), and a two-columned porch facing the interior court in front of the megaron (44). Especially noteworthy was the discovery of a bathroom (43) well-preserved, the first of its kind to be found almost intact on the Greek Mainland. It contained a terracotta larnax, decorated with painted patterns, which was set in a tublike base of clay (Fig. 139), while a tall stuccoed clay stand in a corner held two large jars, perhaps for water and oil. The lobby (38) and the bathroom (43) were filled with wreckage and the broken and burned remains of many capacious oil-jars which had apparently fallen from the upper story and poured their inflammable contents into the rooms below.

To the northwest of Pantry 18 and the Throne Room, excavations under the supervision of Mr. Hubbe revealed another small pottery storeroom (22) which yielded more than 600 shallow bowls, shallow cups and dippers, the latter perhaps for use in dipping out oil from deep jars; and farther northeastward, directly behind the Throne Room, two long narrow oil magazines (23 and 24), containing respectively 17 and 16 large pithoi set in stucco-coated stands that were built up against the walls on all sides (Fig. 22). Scattered about on the stand and the floor in Magazine 23 lay some 60 inscribed tablets and fragments, which, when fitted and joined together, were reduced to 33 in number; they have been found to deal with various kinds and flavors of olive oil. The northwestern wall of the two magazines is also the exterior wall of the Main Building on this side: only its foundations are preserved, the superstructure having been carried away by looters.

In the southwestern part of the central unit Lord William Taylour excavated the area between the Archives Rooms (7 and 8) and what we have called the Entrance Lobby 12; he discovered here a suite of two chambers (Fig. 80 and 9 and 10 on Key Plan), apparently a waiting room, with a bench on which visitors could sit and a stand enclosing two pithoi for water or wine, and an adjoining pantry where drinking cups—kylikes—were kept in abundant numbers on wooden shelves, and presumably also refreshments.

Outside the Main Building, toward the southwest (Fig. 178), Mrs. Blegen completed the clearing of Ramp 59 and Pottery Storeroom 60, raising the total yield of pots from the latter to some 800. Among these vessels were many large, deep, spouted "milk-bowls" introducing a new shape, in handmade ware. Lord William, farther to the northwestward, opened a considerable area in the stucco-paved Court 63 in front of Entrance Hall 64 of the Southwestern Building.

In the latter structure, behind Hall 64, Mrs. Blegen uncovered a complex of rooms and passages: remnants of a staircase which led to an upper floor (69), another pottery storeroom (68) which contained many cooking pots, small storage jars, and at least three large, flat circular baking pans, and two further chambers

(71 and 72) of unknown use, though five inscribed tablets were recovered in the doorway between the two.

The yield of inscribed tablets and fragments in 1955 reached a total of 85, most of them from Magazine 23, some from Lobby 38 and neighborhood, and a few from the doorway between Rooms 71 and 72 in the Southwestern Building.

The architectural remains uncovered during the season were measured by Mr. Theocharis who also carried out a fresh survey of all the walls that had hitherto been exposed and drew a new plan of the entire complex at the end of the campaign (Fig. 407). It had now become clear that the palace comprised at least two separate residential buildings.

Miss Frantz once again came to our aid, devoting an arduous day to taking many photographs which showed the new elements of the palace that had just been brought to light, in their proper setting and relationship with what had previously been unearthed.

The campaign of 1956 was begun May 8 and continued to July 31.[16] The staff comprised M. Rawson, Mrs. Blegen, Mr. and Mrs. William P. Donovan, P. de Jong, and C. W. Blegen. D. Androutsakis was Foreman and the number of the workmen employed ranged from 15 to 41 with an average of 18.

Miss Rawson resumed operations in the eastern corner of the Main Building (Fig. 143) and exposed to view a large room with a central hearth (46 on Key Plan); a doorway giving access to another closed, unroofed court (47) on the northeast, and another door for communication through corridors (48, 49, 51, and 52) to two small chambers (50 and 53). This suite was tentatively regarded as the Queen's quarters, comprising a reception hall, court, boudoir, and a washroom. The fire had caused great havoc here, but numerous fragments of frescoes—many apparently fallen from an upper story—were recovered in a fairly good state of preservation. Between this section and the Propylon Miss Rawson uncovered a rectangular area, surrounded by thick walls or foundations, within which illicit digging before our time had caused some disturbance; the remains, including three steps and a landing of a staircase, were conjectured to be possibly those of a tower beside the chief gateway.

With this excavation the whole of the Main Building of the palace had been cleared, though much work was still needed to clean the floors and to examine details in almost all the rooms. Only six fragments of inscribed tablets were found in 1956.

To the southwest, outside the Main Building, Mrs. Blegen laid bare the lime pavement in the northwestern part of Court 88. She also extended her investigations in the

---

[16] Preliminary report: *AJA* 61 (1957), 129-135.

Southwestern Building, uncovering Rooms 73, 75, 76, 78, and 82 (Fig. 217). The latter, first thought to be part of the large building, was subsequently found to be a separate structure, perhaps earlier than the palace, and it was replaced by an overlying house (83, 84, 85, and 86) before the destruction of the entire palatial complex. Room 78 was believed to be a bathroom, on the scanty evidence of a single stone drain-section.

In a search for chamber tombs, under the supervision of Mr. Donovan, widespread exploratory trenches were dug on the neighboring hillocks to the northeast and to the west and southwest of the acropolis. On a ridge in the northeastern region, 350 m. or more distant from the palace, ground belonging to Demetrios Paraskevopoulos yielded Middle Helladic and Mycenaean sherds, but no trace of tombs. Some 250 m. and more to the westward, however, a Mycenaean cemetery of chamber tombs was discovered. Several dromoi were noted along a boundary ledge between properties of the Vayenas and Tsakalis families of Chora; and one chamber was partially excavated with results of considerable promise for further investigation. Mrs. Donovan assisted in inventorying numerous pots from the palace and tombs which were stored in the workroom in Chora.

Mr. de Jong during June and July reproduced in water colors many of the pots recovered from the palace, including most of those bearing decoration in a late local version of the Palace Style. He also made drawings in color of the hearth in the Queen's Hall, the floor designs in Rooms 49 and 50 (Figs. 163-167); and he likewise with creative imagination drew detailed perspective restorations of the Throne Room (Frontispiece) and the Court of the Megaron (Part 2, Frontispiece). In addition to this work Mr. de Jong measured all the new architectural elements of the buildings exposed during the season and added them to the plan which was made by Mr. Theocharis in 1955 (Fig. 408).

In mid-July when the whole Main Building was free of protective earth and tidily swept, Miss Frantz put us under ever-deepening obligation, giving two whole days to the task of photographing—from a high ladder and from the ground—all the various sections of the excavated areas, as well as the whole ensemble from many points of view.

In 1957 work in and about the palace was carried on from May 21 to August 3.[17] Members of the staff were M. Rawson, Professor Mabel Lang, W. P. Donovan, Lord William Taylour, and C. W. Blegen. Dr. J. Lawrence Angel spent 12 days at Chora in July, studying the skulls and skeletal remains which were recovered in 1956 and 1957. Our regular Foreman, D. Androutsakis, had charge of the workmen,

[17] Preliminary report: *AJA* 62 (1958), Part I, 175-181; Part II, M. Lang, on the Linear B Tablets, *ibid.*, 181-191.

varying from 8 to 18 in number, and averaging 14, all veterans of many campaigns.

Opening exploratory trenches to the northeast of the Main Building, Miss Rawson discovered and cleared a third separate unit belonging to the palace complex (Fig. 234). This was evidently the laboratory or the repair shop of the establishment, comprising seven rooms of various sizes (92-100 on Key Plan), some very large, in addition to a roofed porch (94) facing a court (92). In the latter a stone altar was found standing directly in front of the façade of a small chamber (93), apparently a shrine. A rectangular room (98) and a very large hall (99) may have been used for storage of materials needed in the Workshop: Room 98 contained many pots, large and small; on the floor were found more than 20 clay sealings. Room 99 had been lined with wooden shelves, supported by posts resting on flat stones; scattered about on the earth floor were found nearly 100 fragments of inscribed tablets (many dealing with bronze, leather, and other materials), and 15 further clay sealings.

The total number of tablets and fragments recovered in 1957 reached 131.

Outside the palace site, some 150 m. distant toward the south, Lord William uncovered the scanty remains of another tholos tomb, traces of which were visible in the *aloni*, or drying bed for currants, owned by E. Vayenas. The tumulus that once rose above the grave had been cut away and the stone vault itself had also been razed except for a remnant less than a half circle in extent and preserved only to a height of one or two courses of flat stones at the level of the currant bed. Just 0.25 m. beneath the latter, part of the floor of the tomb was found undisturbed, along with six burial pits. What was left of the grave was relatively rich, producing fragments of a gold diadem, some objects of silver; 24 swords and daggers, two caldrons, a mirror, and the bar and two scale pans of a balance, all of bronze; numerous stone arrowheads, two fine seal stones, and many vases, ranging from early Mycenaean I (two at least of Cretan origin) to late Mycenaean III A.

Continuing his excavation in the cemetery of chamber tombs discovered in 1956, Mr. Donovan cleared two chambers, E 4 and E 6, which yielded a great deal of pottery and a considerable amount of simple jewelry, including 15 gold beads. Farther down the slope Lord William opened yet another chamber tomb, K 4, the roof of which had not collapsed. Though small, it contained many burials along with which were recovered numerous pots, intact and remarkably well preserved.

In 1957 Miss Lang undertook the task of cleaning and studying the formidable accumulations of fresco fragments collected in 1956 and earlier years; this was the beginning of a fruitful labor of inestimable value to the expedition continuing through all the subsequent campaigns of excavation. In this first season she succeeded in fitting together numerous pieces and reconstituting the head of a griffin, the head of a lion or panther, and parts of other animals from the Queen's Hall. Besides cleaning all the sealings recovered during the season, she likewise cleaned and prepared for publication in the preliminary report all the inscribed tablets found in 1957 as well as the small bits from 1956.

Mr. Lloyd Cotsen, architect and draftsman for the excavations at Lerna, kindly measured and added to the general plan the newly uncovered walls of the Northeastern Building (Fig. 409). All the sealings, tablets and fragments of tablets were photographed by Miss Frantz.

For the seventh campaign, which was carried out from May 9 to August 3, 1958,[18] the staff consisted of M. Rawson, Mrs. Blegen, M. Lang, David French, George Papathanasopoulos, Lord William Taylour, and C. W. Blegen. John Travlos, Architect of the American School Excavations, surveyed the walls uncovered during the season and incorporated them in the plan of the entire complex of buildings (Fig. 410). Under our Foreman D. Androutsakis we employed trained workmen ranging from 9 to 24 in number and averaging 18.

Miss Rawson, investigating the extensive unexcavated area to the northeast of the Main Building between the Palace Workshop and the abrupt northwestern edge of the acropolis, discovered a hitherto unknown structure (104-105 on Key Plan), some 18.40 m. long and 8.50 m. wide, which was soon identified as a wine magazine (Fig. 254). It was cleared under the supervision of Mr. French, who drew a detailed plan of the structure and the numerous pithoi or wine jars it contained (Fig. 428). In the vestibule and the principal room he recovered some 60 or more clay sealings which had presumably been attached to the containers in which wine was brought to the magazine. Four of the sealings were found to bear on the obverse the sign 131, which Professor Sundwall had first identified as meaning wine (*Docs.*, 50).

Miss Rawson resumed her investigations in the northeastern area between the Wine Magazine and the Workshop, uncovering numerous foundation walls of houses that had apparently been demolished when the site was being cleared for the palace of Mycenaean III B (Fig. 410). She also recognized ruins of some small rooms which were in use during the latest phases of that palace (103), perhaps for housing servants or slaves. Miss Rawson extended her operations along the northwestern end of the Workshop, where she exposed remains of a distributing system for water brought to the spot in an aqueduct coming from the northeast. The channel was traced by means of several soundings to the northeastern end of the hill. In the steep northeastern scarp of the Englianos ridge Miss Rawson exposed a descending roadway, paved with stones (Fig. 259): it seemed to pass through a

[18] Preliminary report: *AJA* 63 (1959), Part I, 121-127; Part II, on inscribed tablets by M. Lang, *ibid.*, 128-137.

gateway in a circuit wall of early Mycenaean times which did not survive into the period of the palace of Mycenaean III B.

Mr. Papathanasopoulos conducted a thorough examination of the North Magazine (27 on Key Plan, and Fig. 421), emptying all the pithoi. Next he began the excavation of a deep habitation deposit in the area behind the central unit of the palace. Here he uncovered a small circular building (87) and a fairly large house of several rooms (83, 84, 85, 86) which he believed must have been erected in one of the latest phases of the palace before the final catastrophe and burning of the entire establishment. These buildings too presumably served as the abode of the servants and retainers who looked after the royal residence. In deeper digging Mr. Papathanasopoulos tested the accumulated underlying strata, reaching a depth of more than 3 m. He found here what seemed to be a regular sequence of deposits that produced pottery ranging from Middle Helladic in the bottom layer through Late Helladic I and II in the intermediate levels, still well below the floors belonging to Mycenaean III B.

Mrs. Blegen continued the investigation of the Southwestern Building, bringing to light the outside wall of large rough stones that formed the substructure of the tower-like western corner of this unit. She also traced the exterior southwestern foundation of the building some 20 m. southeastward from the corner. The floors of the rooms in this section were found to have been destroyed by erosion, probably after the walls had been pillaged by quarrying activities through centuries; but almost all the internal divisions can still be recognized and the plan of the Southwestern Building began to emerge with some approach to clarity.

In July Lord William extended his explorations in a search for further tombs. Soundings in two threshing floors—or drying beds for currants—yielded only scanty remains of small buildings: in one *aloni*, owned by E. Vayenas, apparently a house with rectangular rooms, and associated late Mycenaean pottery; in the other, belonging to E. Deriziotis, remnants of two apsidal or circular huts, possibly of yet earlier date. Much farther southward, not far from the village of Koryphasion, Lord William cleared half of a small tholos in which were found bones representing several burials, bits of iron, and fragments of pottery from which four or five Protogeometric vases were put together. The other half of the tomb had been dug away in the eighteen-nineties when the carriage road from Kyparissia to Pylos was being built. In that long span of more than half a century no one had ventured to disturb the remaining visible half. On the hillside, high above the little tholos in land owned by the Kokkevi family of Chora, Lord William found a Mycenaean chamber tomb. The time available permitted only the excavation of the dromos, which yielded fragments of two large kraters. One had been decorated with a hunting scene, in which a stag, the head of a man, and a dog pursuing a lion are recognizable.

Miss Lang patiently cleaned and joined together many fragments of frescoes as she worked through the great assemblages of material from 1955 and 1956. Beside this major occupation she cleaned, mended, catalogued, and photographed some 65 clay sealings, and dealt in a similar manner with 30 or more inscribed tablets and fragments found during the current season, which she prepared for prompt publication in the annual report.

The excavations of 1959 were carried out from May 10 to August 3.[19] Members of the staff were M. Rawson, Mrs. Blegen, M. Lang, G. Papathanasopoulos, C. W. Blegen, and for a short time Lord William Taylour. The architectural remains uncovered during the campaign were surveyed by Mr. Papathanasopoulos and added to the general plan (Fig. 411). D. Androutsakis was Foreman and we employed experienced workmen, ranging from 9 to 18 in number and averaging 14.

Considerable progress was made in exposing the remains of the Southwestern Building under the supervision of Mrs. Blegen. The massive exterior southwest wall was followed in its surviving foundations some 25 m. southeastward beyond the point previously reached. The great hall (65 on Key Plan) which opens off the entrance hall (64) was found to be much larger than hitherto recognized, extending southwestward to the outside wall (Fig. 193). In this spacious room one column base of stone had been exposed in 1939, and the substantial circular substructures of three further bases were now uncovered, suggesting a quadruple arrangement of columns like that in the Throne Room (6). But the spacing did not fit the room symmetrically; it left a large empty area at the back of the hall ample enough to hold two additional columns. Whether the number was originally four or six could not be determined, for erosion along the southwestern edge of the hill has eaten away in the crucial part of the hall not only the floor, but the underlying deposit to a depth far below the foundations of the columns. Within the square formed by the one preserved base and the three substructures no surviving trace of a hearth was found; but beneath the floor level of the hall a good many potsherds assignable to Mycenaean III A were recovered.

Throughout the northeasterly area of the acropolis Miss Rawson conducted extensive explorations. In a slight hollow near the steep edge of the eastern angle, where some stone walls had been exposed in 1953 by Mr. McDonald, she uncovered remains of drains and a narrow street, bordered on each side by house-walls, apparently of early Mycenaean times (Figs. 257, 416). Some scanty superposed walls could be attributed, on the evidence of the accompanying potsherds, to Mycenaean III B. A small kiln, perhaps belonging to a potter's establishment, contained a few sherds

---

[19] Preliminary report: *AJA* 64 (1960), Part I, 153-160; Part II, M. Lang, on inscribed tablets, *ibid.*, 160-164.

of the same late period. At the northeastern end of the citadel, where a stone-paved street had been discovered in 1958, Miss Rawson widened her excavation and revealed the ruins of the gateway and scanty remnants of the thick wall through which it led (Fig. 259). Soundings to the northwestward along the steep bank disclosed some crumbling vestiges of what was evidently a circuit wall but not a single stone was found to mark a continuation to the southeastward. The gateway itself (Figs. 259, 416) and the wall, which was in some places covered by a sterile stratum of yellow clay, could be dated by the associated pottery to Late Helladic I, if not earlier. It was clear in any event that the wall and gateway had been destroyed and covered before the palace of Mycenaean III B was built.

Under the supervision of Mr. Papathanasopoulos exploratory trenches were dug in the olive grove of N. Antonopoulos, just below the southwest end of the acropolis. Stone walls of houses appeared in all these trenches, and it became clear that the lower town was of considerable extent (Figs. 258, 411). Three periods were recognizable: in the uppermost stratum, just below the plowed soil, ruins of dwellings destroyed by fire, and characterized by potsherds of Mycenaean III B; next below, another complex of house-walls also wrecked by fire, and marked by a fairly large deposit of pottery of Mycenaean III A; and finally, still deeper, remains of an earlier settlement which used pottery of Late Helladic II and I, and, presumably in its early phases, some wares of Middle Helladic types. In the surface layer of cultivated soil were found eight fragments of tablets inscribed in Linear B, evidently washed down from the citadel.

Below the opposite end of the site, on the northwestern side of the hill, under the *aloni* belonging to George Petropoulos of Chora, Miss Rawson uncovered stone foundations of houses at three levels (Fig. 260), obviously representing as many phases, all datable, as indicated by the pottery, to the Middle Helladic era.

In July Lord William completed the excavation of the small chamber tomb, the dromos of which had been found in 1958, in a locality called Mavroudia, or Kato Englianos, some 3 kilometers south of the palace site and not far above the stream that separates Triphylia from Pylia (Fig. 400). Some gold beads, a shallow bronze vessel, a mirror, and several implements also of bronze, and a score of pots were recovered in the chamber. Many of the vases seem to be of Mycenaean III B, others evidently of III C. Whether this tomb was probably connected with a small Mycenaean settlement (at a site called Portes) not far below the village of Koryphasion rather than with the palace at Epano Englianos, which is much farther away, could not be determined.

During the month of July Miss Lang concentrated her attention on the task of cleaning innumerable fragments of frescoes and joining together as many as possible. In addition she cleaned all the clay sealings found in 1959 as well as some 30 fragments of new tablets inscribed in Linear B, and took many photographs of these objects and of interesting frescoes and selected potsherds. She also prepared the publication of the tablets in the annual report.

The ninth campaign of excavations occupied some 14 weeks from April 23 to August 1, 1960.[20] Members of the staff were M. Rawson, Mrs. Blegen, M. Lang, P. de Jong, G. Papathanasopoulos, and C. W. Blegen. D. Androutsakis was Foreman and the number of our workmen varied, according to need, from 9 to 27 with an average of 15.

Mr. Travlos made a fresh survey of the site and drew up a plan of the entire acropolis (Fig. 416) and a detailed new plan of the palace itself (Fig. 417). In preparation for this work all parts of the palace were cleared of protecting earth and swept clean. Miss Frantz spent three days with us and took numerous photographs, both general views and innumerable details in all parts of the buildings, many of which are gratefully used in this publication. The Greek Archaeological Service had long wished to erect a roof over the central building so that floors, hearths, stands, benches, stairways, bath and other details of interest might be left open to view by visitors, instead of being covered with earth for protection during the winter. The Director of the Service had, however, consented to wait until after the season of 1960 so that the new plan could be made and the photographs needed could be taken before the light was shut off by the roof.

In the excavations of 1960 our chief efforts were concentrated along the southwestern edge of the hill, Mr. Papathanasopoulos supervising operations in the northwestern sector (Fig. 202), and Mrs. Blegen in the southeastern (Fig. 204). The general plan of the Southwestern Building from its northwestern limits (81 on Key Plan) to the entrance hall (64) and the ceremonial hall (65) was to a considerable extent clarified: no floors and no floor deposits had survived but the foundations of the partition walls marked the lines of the internal divisions. Walls of earlier structures were exposed at lower levels, accompanied by pottery of Mycenaean III A, though no connected plan of an older building could be recognized.

Farther southeastward the fire and subsequent quarrying operations of plunderers in search of building material had caused much greater havoc, and we were only able to conjecture that three or more phases are represented. The line of the original exterior wall, which is laid out in re-entrant angles, could be followed most of the way to the southeastern end of the building, and two possible later replacements of the wall were distinguished. An examination of the main drain, which carried water away from the central building to the low ground beyond the South-

[20] Preliminary report: *AJA* 65 (1961), Part I, 153-158; Part II, M. Lang, on inscribed tablets, *ibid.*, 158-163.

western Building, offered modest help in determining the relative sequence of some foundation walls: for one or two of the latter had been broken through for the underground drain, while others had evidently been superposed over it after its installation. Thirty fragments of inscribed tablets were recovered, mainly from the surface soil in this area, and 13 clay sealings were found, almost all in the underlying burned debris.

Investigation by Miss Rawson below the southeastern edge of the site, in land owned by the Anastasopoulos family of Chora, revealed, beneath a deposit of the Geometric period (e.g., Fig. 347 No. 982), remains of house-walls which could be assigned on the evidence of the associated pottery to Mycenaean III B; it thus became clear that the lower town of that period extended around the southeast side of the acropolis.

By numerous soundings and probings Miss Rawson was able to carry out a detailed study of many problems, chiefly in the Main Building, but spreading also over into the Palace Workshop. Stone walls and foundations of earlier structures were exposed in many places underneath the level of the floors of Mycenaean III B (Fig. 108). But, without destroying lime pavements—which was precluded—it was not possible to uncover enough connected remains to form any idea of the plan of the antecedent building or buildings. It was obvious, however, that the site was occupied before the palace was built.

Through June and July Miss Lang continued her work on the frescoes, dealing not only with the current influx of material, but making good progress in her scrutiny of the fragments assembled in the collections of earlier years. She organized the whole bulky accumulation of plaster from nine seasons of excavation, classified all the pieces by place of discovery, and drew up descriptions of the varieties that occur in different parts of the palace. She succeeded in finding many fragments which joined others and became worthy of reconstruction in water colors. Miss Lang also cleaned some remains of wall paintings that still clung to their original places on walls in various parts of the palace. In addition to these activities she cleaned the clay sealings recovered in 1960 and the fragments of inscribed tablets, which she likewise prepared for publication in the annual report. To her, moreover, we owe the photographs of tablets, sealings, many fragments of frescoes, and details of the palace.

Mr. de Jong spent a fortnight at the excavations in June, collaborating with Miss Lang in the study of the frescoes, before being recalled to England for an emergency; he was able to return to Chora in August to complete drawing the compositions that were ready for his attention.

In the autumn of 1960 the Greek Archaeological Service enclosed the entire acropolis at Englianos in a sturdy wire fence and during the following winter erected a high, protective, metal roof over the whole central building (Figs. 6, 7, 8). Henceforth the hearths, parts of the floors, the stairways, the bath, the oil magazines and many other items of interest could be left open through all seasons for visitors to see.

The campaign of 1961 was continued from May 12 to July 30.[21] The staff comprised M. Rawson, Mrs. Blegen, M. Lang, G. Papathanasopoulos, P. de Jong, and C. W. Blegen. D. Androutsakis, our Foreman, enlisted a force of workmen numbering 6 to 13, with an average of 11. Relatively little was undertaken in the way of new digging, chiefly in the southern sector along the southwestern edge of the site.

Here, under the supervision of Mrs. Blegen, the massive foundation of a small building, part of which had been exposed in 1960, was laid bare. In this place too erosion and the removal of building material had made away with the walls and the floor, and nothing could be definitely concluded about the character and use of the structure. It appears in any event to be earlier than the palace of Mycenaean III B, and it was probably destroyed and covered over before the palace was built. Mr. Papathanasopoulos measured the walls exposed and drew a plan (Fig. 412). From the plowed earth here and in a small area farther northwestward 19 fragments of inscribed tablets were recovered.

A chance intrusion by outsiders led to the discovery of a great heap of broken plaster which had evidently been removed from the palace in the course of renovations and thrown over the northwestern edge of the acropolis. Under the direction of Miss Rawson the deposit was systematically excavated and some 3,000 fragments of varying sizes were recovered. Miss Lang cleaned and classified them and fitted together parts of many different compositions, some of which were drawn in water colors by Mr. de Jong.

Much time was devoted by Miss Rawson to a searching study of details in the Main Building: walls, floors, stairways, doorways, hearths, courts, bath; and with the cooperation of Miss Lang all the plaster still adhering to walls was examined and cleaned (e.g., Fig. 90), and a good many remains of frescoes—almost all badly damaged by fire—were revealed. Renewed soundings in some areas below the level of the floors disclosed further stone walls of earlier structures in addition to those seen in the campaign of 1960. In connection with this detailed study considerable progress was made in drafting a methodical description of the palace, room by room, in preparation for the ultimate publication.

Over and above her major work on the frescoes, Miss Lang cleaned the clay seal impressions and the 19 tablets of the season, photographed them all as well as many

---

[21] Preliminary report: *AJA* 66 (1962), Part I, 145-149; Part II, M. Lang, on inscribed tablets, *ibid.*, 149-152.

of the frescoes, and prepared for publication in the annual report the texts of the inscriptions with photographs, line drawings, and commentary.

The eleventh annual campaign was conducted from May 2 to July 31, 1962.[22] The members of the staff were M. Rawson, Mrs. Blegen, M. Lang, Mr. and Mrs. William G. Kittredge, P. de Jong, and C. W. Blegen. D. Androutsakis was our Foreman and the workmen employed varied from 9 to 15, with an average of 14. Although considerable new digging was undertaken, our chief attention was directed, as in the preceding year, to study and writing in the task of drawing up the final publication.

Under the supervision of Mrs. Kittredge some 20 exploratory trenches were dug to test the southeastern and northeastern slopes of the hill. Almost everywhere only a shallow accumulation of soil was found covering *stereo* (firm undisturbed ground), and few traces of building activity of the late Mycenaean Period—or any other period—were revealed. This evidence confirmed the conclusion drawn from similar tests in preceding campaigns that the northeastern part of the acropolis in the time of the palace was kept free of intrusive structures of any consequence. Along the crest of the elevation Mrs. Kittredge exposed to its whole length the aqueduct (Fig. 416), running from northeast to southwest (Fig. 243), which Miss Rawson had traced in 1958. It was a ditch-like open channel cut in *stereo*, lined in some places with a stone wall on one side, in one stretch walled on both sides, elsewhere unlined, sloping gently toward the southwest. The source of the water was probably a copious spring, now called Rouvelli, which still pours out a steady stream beside the highroad some 1,360 m. to the northeast of Englianos. Professor Jesse E. Fant of the University of Minnesota in a provisional survey very kindly determined for us that the spring is 20.92 m. higher than the discharging area beside the palace, and he judged that this difference in level was sufficient for the water to flow in an open channel—provided that the aqueduct was carried by a bridge across intervening hollows. The exact line followed by the conduit from the spring to the site has not been identified.

Mrs. Kittredge likewise conducted some further investigations along the bottom of the scarp that forms the northwestern edge of the citadel, where she discovered some house walls and a small group of Middle Helladic pots. In addition to this work she also rendered valuable assistance in inventorying pottery.

Behind the Main Building of the palace Mr. Kittredge supervised an extensive examination of the deep accumulation of habitation deposit known to lie in this area. He found a sequence of walls, one above another, representing eight building levels, all lying below the final stratum of occupation of the palace. The walls in

22 Preliminary report: *AJA* 67 (1963), Part I, 155-160; Part II, M. Lang, on inscribed tablets, *ibid.*, 160-162.

the four deepest levels were found to be oriented from north to south and east to west, the four in the upper series followed a different system, being laid out from northwest to southeast and northeast to southwest. Abundant pottery was recovered of types indicating that the settlement on the hill existed from Middle Helladic times through Late Helladic I and II to the end of III B.

In the southernmost area of the hill some remains of the lower town were uncovered under Mrs. Blegen's care. The houses here had apparently been built directly against the rising scarp of the acropolis; erosion, however, had carried away almost everything except the inner ends of the rooms protected by the vertical bank. The evidence of the pottery suggested that some of these buildings must be attributed to Mycenaean III A; above them lay a deposit of burnt rubbish, perhaps the wreckage removed from the top of the hill when the ground was being cleared for the palace of Mycenaean III B.

Much detailed investigation was carried out in the Main Building by Miss Rawson. The northerly part of the stucco floor of the Portico was cleaned and remains of the painted decoration were revealed. Several layers could be differentiated, one bearing representations of some odd-looking fish. The Southwestern Building was likewise re-examined, with special attention to the floors and doorways. The Palace Workshop too was subjected to supplementary probing and study: Miss Rawson reopened the stone-lined pit beneath Room 97, which had been discovered in 1957. The removal of some splinters of stone slabs wedged in at the floor level along one side led to the recovery of two gold, ten amethyst, and a few crumbling amber beads as well as some bits of bones, not identified as human. The structure was, in any event, clearly a shaft grave antedating the building of the palace, but how much earlier could not be determined.

Miss Lang continued her work on the frescoes through June and July. During the season she concentrated in the storerooms of the new Museum in Chora—not yet in a finished state—all the plaster that had been stowed away at Englianos and in our workroom in the old schoolhouse at Chora. This material was sorted out (by place of discovery) and recorded room by room, and was divided into three categories: one comprising all pieces worthy of being placed on exhibition; another constituting a study collection to be stored on shelves or in drawers in a workroom; and the third lot, all fragments, judged to be worth keeping merely as corroborative material, was repacked in wooden boxes. Miss Lang also made great progress in finding more and more joins among the fragments and in identifying further scenes and compositions. She likewise continued her task of photographing typical, or characteristic, or notable pieces and schemes of decoration. Only three small fragments of tablets came to light in 1962: they were cleaned, photographed and prepared by Miss Lang, as usual, for publication in the annual report.

Mr. de Jong during July and the early part of August devoted his attention to the reconstruction in water color of the most important compositions, many of which had been studied in collaboration with Miss Lang. The collection of frescoes had been growing through the years and was becoming notable in quality and variety.

Professor John L. Caskey rendered invaluable assistance by photographing for us more than 300 pots, and also by providing us with a potmender, Sotiris Maras, who during the digging season and later made gratifying progress in joining together and repairing great numbers of vases from the palace.

A twelfth campaign began on May 3 and was continued until August 1, 1963.[23] Members of the staff were M. Rawson, M. Lang, Mrs. Blegen, Peter Smith, C. W. Blegen, Hero Athanasiades during the month of May, and P. de Jong in July. In May Mrs. William F. Wyatt assisted in inventorying pottery; in June Miss Beatrix Preyer gave useful general help in typing and other ways. Professor Frederick Matson, of Pennsylvania State University, a specialist in ceramics, visited the excavations for a few days and began a technical examination of some of the pottery found in the palace. The expedition directed its efforts mainly to the task of completing a systematic and comprehensive description of the palace and the objects found in it for the general publication; but some supplementary excavations were undertaken with a small force of workmen, ranging from five to eight in number, under our competent Foreman, D. Androutsakis.

Under the supervision of Mr. Smith a considerable part of the precipitous scarp that forms the northwestern edge of the acropolis was cleared of shrubbery and vegetation. A watchful eye was kept—unfortunately in vain—for heaps of fresco fragments, which, like those found in 1961, might have been thrown out from the palace; and Mr. Smith also studied the stratification of the deposit that had accumulated on this slope of the hill. To the northeast of the Wine Magazine, between two walls and under a floor of Mycenaean III A, he dug a test pit which reached native rock and yielded early Mycenaean pottery. Mr. Smith also opened further exploratory trenches near the southernmost angle of the site which added a little to our knowledge of that region. In the Museum he measured hundreds of pots for our records.

Just before the end of the campaign Mr. Papathanasopoulos resumed his examination of the deep habitation deposit directly behind the Main Building of the palace. This work, though not yet completed, revealed stratigraphic evidence indicating that Englianos was already occupied at least as early as the later phases of the Middle Helladic Period.

---

[23] Preliminary report: *AJA* 68 (1964), Part I, 95-98; Part II, M. Lang, on Pylos Pots and the Mycenaean Units of Capacity, *ibid.*, 99-105.

In the Main Building, under the direction of Miss Rawson, the cleaning of the floors of the Portico and the Vestibule was continued and completed. Although badly damaged by fire and perhaps other causes, these pavements had somehow managed to retain here and there scanty recognizable vestiges of the painted patterns that once decorated them. As in the Throne Room, the design was laid out in large rectangles, separated from one another by paired parallel lines enclosing between them a band of red paint. The surviving remnants were measured, traced and drawn by Mr. de Jong. Miss Rawson also exposed again and restudied many of the doorways in the Main and the Southwestern Buildings: details were checked against the earlier drawings, which were corrected wherever needed; and plans were made by Miss Athanasiades of thresholds and jamb bases which had not hitherto been drawn by Mr. de Jong.

Progress was made by Miss Rawson and Mr. Blegen in the task of preparing for the final publication a systematic description of the palace, room by room, accompanied by catalogues of all the objects found in each. The first draft, which was drawn up in 1961 and 1962, was read over on the spot, revised and rephrased in the interest of clarity as well as brevity, and supplemented wherever new information was available.

During the winter of 1962-1963 Miss Rawson devoted much time and thought to a searching study of the pottery found in the palace. She worked out an orderly classification of the many shapes and variations represented in the abundant material at her disposal. Her methodical arrangement, tested with C. W. Blegen, category by category, in the workroom at Chora in the presence of the pots themselves, proved to be practicable and it is in the main followed in this publication. Miss Rawson also selected for the present publication examples of each type which are described in detail and illustrated in profile drawings and in photographs in this work. Profiles of characteristic shapes were drawn by Miss Athanasiades, in supplement to those previously provided by Mr. de Jong, and photographs were taken by Emile Saraphis of Athens to complete the series made by Professor Caskey in 1962.

The great number of intact or nearly whole pots recovered from the palace and the numerous different sizes that occur in some categories of shapes offered an unusual opportunity for investigating the capacities of ordinary Mycenaean household vessels. This task was carried out with great efficiency by our Foreman, D. Androutsakis, who with containers of certified metric content measured the capacities in grams of 778 vessels. The results, though not pretending to claim absolute accuracy, were studied by Professor Lang, who discussed in the report of the season of 1963 the conclusions that may be drawn and the possible correlations with the measures recorded on the Linear B tablets.

The pottery, the inscribed tablets, the sealings, and the scanty items of terracotta that chanced to be in the palace on the day of the destruction came through the fire with relatively little damage. The objects of gold, silver, bronze, stone, ivory, bone, paste, wood, and other perishable material, however, were found in most instances in a miserable state, melted, warped, twisted, misshapen, if not burned to ashes. It was nonetheless our duty to collect and record these remnants and to make what we could of them. After they had been cleaned they were worked over by Miss Rawson who sorted and recorded them. Most of these fragments were in a wretched state of preservation and intrinsically worthless; but it seemed to us that it might be useful to illustrate typical examples in our publication, as well as in the Museum, to give a vivid idea of the devastating power of a great fire in a Mycenaean palace. Miss Lang photographed the pieces selected by Miss Rawson.

Professor Lang, in addition to her generous assistance in arranging and typing the classification and description of the pottery, in photographing the miscellaneous objects and in meeting other problems, continued industriously her major work on the frescoes. She devoted countless hours to the cleaning, study, and joining of innumerable fragments of plaster. Before the end of the season she was able to draw up a catalogue of 150 items bearing recognizable scenes and decorative motives. These were built up from some one thousand fragments which she succeeded in joining or associating together. As in previous campaigns, she discovered several hitherto unrecognized compositions, added many pieces to groups which had been assembled earlier, and corrected not a few interpretations which her recent discoveries had shown must be changed.

Mr. de Jong spent the month of July at the excavations, collaborating with Miss Lang in work on the frescoes and making many drawings of the new discoveries and of others from past seasons which had not yet been drawn. He also finished the drawing of the surviving floor patterns in the Portico and the Vestibule of the Throne Room, which were later rendered in water color at a smaller scale (Fig. 56); and to him we owe likewise drawings of a few more decorated vases.

A thirteenth and concluding campaign[24] in and about the palace was carried out from May 7 to July 31, 1964. Members of the staff in addition to Mr. and Mrs. Blegen, were M. Rawson, M. Lang, P. de Jong, and John Pedley. D. Androutsakis was Foreman.

Attention was concentrated mainly on a detailed study of the pottery, the frescoes, and the other objects found in the palace, all needed for the preparation of a full publication of the results reached in this excavation, which has been continued annually through the years since 1952.

[24] *AJA* 69 (1965), 95-101.

During the winter of 1963-1964 Miss Rawson had arranged the illustrations in a logical order and laid out the plates for this volume. At Chora she and Mr. Blegen looked through a vast collection of potsherds from all parts of the palace and site and summarized the evidence that could be gleaned. Miss Rawson also finished examining the miscellaneous objects of metal, stone, bone and ivory, terracotta, etc., many of which she selected for publication and illustration. She also completed the catalogues of all things found, room by room.

Miss Lang continued her work on the frescoes, completing the catalogue of the 206 items to be published, some of which are made up of nearly 100 fragments joined or associated together. She studied in detail the technique and subject matter of the wall paintings, examined comparative material from other sites and wrote a first draft of more than half the book on the frescoes which is to be issued as Volume II of our publication on the Palace of Nestor. In addition to the foregoing Miss Lang took numerous photographs of frescoes, miscellaneous objects and views, cleaned and prepared for publication two fragments of inscribed tablets (which Miss Rawson found in the material from Room 99) and assisted valiantly in typing and in other ways.

Mr. de Jong drew in water color a good many not yet recorded frescoes and revised some earlier drawings of others that had been changed and expanded by the addition of new fragments. The total number of drawings reached 96, ranging from small pieces to large compositions of almost two square meters. Mr. de Jong also drew in color several pots, and provided plans and sections of the Throne Room, as well as Halls 64 and 65 (Figs. 418, 419) and reconstructed in black and white the coping bordering the clerestory above the hearth in Room 46 (Fig. 423).

In the way of actual digging our most spectacular feat was certainly the removal in three days—with the help of a mechanical "digger"—of 1,017 tons of earth which had originally covered the palace, and which in the course of the excavations had been heaped up into a high mound along the northwestern edge of the site in an area beyond the buildings of Mycenaean III B. The heavy rains of the past winter had opened a crevasse in the mound threatening a landslide which might cause damage to a vineyard below. That danger is now gone. No objects were found in this earth.

Under the supervision of Mr. Pedley several small trial trenches were opened in the ground to the northeast of the Wine Magazine (105), and also alongside the outer wall of the North Oil Magazine (27), as well as between the Main and Southwestern Buildings where remains of a wall separating Room 83 from Court 88 were re-exposed. In addition to two or three small probings elsewhere, 14 soundings were sunk in an effort to seek evidence which might determine the sequence of some at least of the numerous dilapidated walls and foundations which form a confused maze on the southwestern slope of the hill. The results permitted the attribution of some of these structures to three or four successive phases (Fig. 412). The latest and the next in order apparently represent Mycenaean III B; an earlier system III A, and the earliest Late Helladic I and Middle Helladic. Some interesting fragments of frescoes, antedating the late palace, were recovered and also a good deal of fine pottery of early Mycenaean date.

Along the southwestern edge of the acropolis a substantial wall built of small field stones, and probably of the same early period, was seen to resemble closely a comparable wall which was discovered in 1959, so far as could be determined, in association with a gateway, at the northeastern end of the hill (Fig. 416). Our conjecture that the citadel was enclosed by a protecting wall in early Mycenaean times thus seems to be confirmed.

C. W. B.

THE SITE

THE elevation called Epano Englianos (sometimes abbreviated to Ano Englianos) rises slightly above the neighboring hillocks (Fig. 1) some 9 km. to the north-northeast of the nearest point on the Bay of Navarino (Fig. 400). By the highway, which has to run around the eastern shore of the Bay, the distance from the modern town of Pylos to the site is about 17 km. The road, continuing northward to Kyparissia and beyond, swings in an easterly bend to pass through the village of Chora, almost 4 km. from Englianos.[1] The sea lies only some 5.7 km.—as the crow flies—to the westward; but, owing to the irregular conformation of the ground, the path for walkers who wish to visit the sandy beaches, is a good deal longer. The site lay far enough from the coast to be reasonably safe from sudden attacks by pirates, but near enough to maintain convenient landing-places both on the west and in the Bay of Navarino.

The plateau forming the top of Epano Englianos offers a splendid view of the encircling countryside. To the south is the sparkling Bay of Navarino, protected from the sea on the west by the rocky island Sphacteria, bordered on the south by the pointed peak of Mount St. Nicholas and modern Pylos (Fig. 3), on the southeast by the foothills rising toward the bare heights of the more remote Mount Lykodemos. Looking northward from our point of vantage we see in the foreground a succession of rugged ridges and deep ravines and, more distantly, the long lofty range of Mount Aigaleon (Fig. 2), a massif which is mentioned on the Linear B tablets found in the palace as an important landmark in the realm of Pylos. Toward the east the eye rests on a series of precipitous gullies and high separating ridges (Fig. 1), all beautifully green in spring and summer when the vineyards flourish in companionship with venerable gray-green olive trees. To the west one views further waves of abrupt crests and hollows and, beyond low bordering hills, the blue Ionian Sea. For quiet, peaceful charm and beauty western Messenia holds a notable place among the attractive provinces of Greece. It was probably not for this natural allure, but rather for the dominating position, giving a commanding view of the possible approaches from all sides, that the first settlers chose this hill for the town that later became the seat and the capital of kings who ruled over a broad region of Messenia.

Epano Englianos is a ridge-like acropolis running from northeast to southwest (Figs. 4, 5), with a maximum length of 170 m. and a width of some 90 m. at its broadest (Fig. 416). The hill rises from the surrounding ground in steep scarps,

---

[1] In Chora a museum has been built by the Greek Archaeological Service to house the frescoes, the pottery, and other objects found in the palace and the material recovered from many Mycenaean tombs in the surrounding region.

especially on the northwest and the northeast, but somewhat less precipitously on the southeast and the southwest. The only relatively easy way of access now is from the east, where an entrance-way was made by digging in 1952. On this side the hill descends in an inclined almost steplike terrace which at the bottom drops off in an abrupt bank, from 1 to 2 or 3 m. high above the modern highroad. The uppermost part of the citadel, parallel to and not far from the northwestern edge, has an altitude of approximately 146 m. above sea level,[2] about 8.80 m. higher than the motor road at the place where the latter passes the entrance to the site.

When we first visited the hill it was an attractive olive orchard belonging to the families of Perikles and Panagiotis Tsakonas of Chora, who kindly permitted us to open seven exploratory trenches in the broad lanes between the rows of olive trees. These spaces too were cultivated and had been planted to wheat by a tenant farmer, who was duly compensated for the damage done to his crop. After the war title to the property, of approximately 13 *stremmata*, or about four acres, was acquired and conveyed to the Greek State as a permanent archaeological area.

As already mentioned (p. 21) a protective fence was set up around the site in 1960 and in the following winter a lofty metal roof was built over the Main Building (Figs. 6-8). This work was done by and at the expense of the Greek Archaeological Service, and has been a great boon to many visitors in the hot season and in inclement weather.

The acropolis itself was occupied by habitations before the Palace of Nestor was built. In a slight hollow near the easternmost angle of the hilltop, foundation walls of stone, apparently belonging to houses bordering a narrow street, came to light (Figs. 257, 416). The accompanying pottery indicated an early Mycenaean date in Late Helladic I. In a deep stratified deposit behind the late palace, along the northwestern edge of the citadel, a maze of superposed foundation walls was exposed, revealing a sequence of eight building periods, all antedating the last phases of occupation. The associated ceramic evidence pointed to a long era of habitation beginning in Middle Helladic times.

At the northeastern end of the hill ruins of a gateway have been uncovered (Figs. 259, 416), comprising a stone-paved roadway that ascended between two flanking bastions or towers. Disconnected remnants of walls have been observed extending southwestward along the northwestern brow of the ridge, presumably marking the original course of a defensive work. This and the gateway—on the testimony of the pottery—must be attributed to the same early Mycenaean stage. No certain vestiges of the wall seem to have survived along the eastern edge of the site, or at any rate, none have been seen. At the bottom of the southwestern slope, however, two or

---

2 We owe this figure to the kindness of Professor Jesse E. Fant of the University of Minnesota, who worked out the measurement with an aneroid barometer.

more sectors of a wall have been recognized which in its construction exhibits the same technique and a similar use of relatively thin flattish field stones as noted in the remains connected with the northeastern gateway. Here too pottery of Late Helladic I gives evidence for the early date. It is thus safe to conclude that the citadel was surrounded by a circuit wall in the sixteenth century. This early wall was evidently destroyed before the Palace of Nestor was built.

No trace whatever of fortifications in that late period has been observed. Extensive probing and digging in numerous places around the border of the entire acropolis have failed to discover any signs of such a structure. Why was Pylos left unprotected by a Cyclopean wall in the period when in other parts of Greece, the strongholds, great and small, were raising mighty imposing monumental defenses? That is a question which cannot yet be convincingly answered. Was Messenia a land of peace and quiet, free from fears of internal or external disturbance of security? The ultimate destruction of the palace by fire at the end of the thirteenth century implies that risks and dangers existed. Were the rulers confident that they were able without fortifications to repel invaders? Or were the finances of the state inadequate for the erection of a Cyclopean fortress? New evidence may some day shed further light on these problems.

In early Mycenaean times it is likely that the settlement extended over the entire hill, since we have evidence of houses at both ends. The community presumably continued to maintain itself through Late Helladic II, as shown by the stratification in the southwestern area. In the initial phases of Late Helladic III houses may still have stood on the acropolis, but by then—this would fall in the ceramic stages of Mycenaean III A—a residence for a king had surely been erected. Whether it stood at the extreme southwestern end of the citadel as a predecessor of the later Southwestern Building, or farther northeastward as a forerunner of the Main Building has not yet been certainly determined.

A new era is clearly recognizable shortly after the beginning of the pottery stage of Mycenaean III B, perhaps around 1300 B.C. This was marked by the construction of the new large palace in its several principal units; and, in preparation for this work, the whole top of the site was apparently cleared of all the houses, large and small, that were still standing on the hill. Observations of the stratification led us to conclude that grading on a large scale removed the remains that lay on or above the surface as well as a considerable amount of the underlying deposit in order to provide an adequately broad level area. The debris was evidently for the most part pushed over the northern, northeastern, and southeastern scarps of the citadel. When the new palace was finished no private houses appear to have remained on the hilltop: henceforth the acropolis was obviously reserved for the king and his family, no doubt with some provision for the necessary retainers and slaves. The southwestern wing was probably the first element to be built, perhaps on the foundations of an earlier palace. The Main Building was surely the next in order, followed by the Wine Magazine and the Palace Workshop. The whole northeastern area of the hillock must have stood open without buildings of any size or consequence. A roadway presumably led up to the palace from the east, approximately where the modern entrance to the site has been made. No signs of an actual road have been noted.

A lower town at the foot of the acropolis existed from the Middle Helladic Period. Remains of three building phases were seen below the northern end of the hill (Fig. 260), all accompanied by Middle Helladic pottery wares, without admixture of Mycenaean. In trenches dug at the other end of the elevation, below the southwestern slope (Figs. 258, 411), the bottom layer yielded house-walls and pottery comprising wares of Middle Helladic types as well as of Late Helladic I and II. The next higher layer contained habitation deposits and many pots of Mycenaean III A; and the uppermost layer produced ruins of houses along with pottery of Mycenaean III B. A vineyard to the northwest of the hill could not—without causing much damage—be tested by digging, but the surface of the ground was seen to be strewn with sherds, fragments of plaster, stones, and other indications that the lower town extended well down the slope on this side. The same kind of evidence was observed on the opposite southeastern declivity of Epano Englianos: much broken pottery and many stones lay scattered far down the precipitous slope beyond the highway.

In the near neighborhood many Mycenaean tombs have been found. Two tholoi (royal sepulchers, we think), one less than 100 m. to the northeast of the hill (Fig. 7), the other slightly more than that distance to the south, and a third, situated close to the highway about one kilometer southwest of the site, have been excavated (Fig. 400). Despite having been plundered in ancient times, they yielded a relatively rich harvest of gold, other jewelry, bronze, ivory, and pottery, all attributable to early Mycenaean periods before the Palace of Nestor was built. They must therefore be the resting places of kings who reigned over Englianos in earlier days. No nearby tholos has yet been found which can be dated as late as the thirteenth century. But in the general region there are still tholoi which have not been excavated.

A cemetery of chamber tombs, some earlier and some contemporary with the Palace of Nestor, has been found on a ridge two or three hundred meters to the west of the acropolis, descending toward a deep ravine through which a stream runs down to empty into the Ionian Sea. These are the burial places of the private citizens, presumably those who lived in the lower town. They too have provided us with many interesting objects of gold, bronze, and pottery.

BUILDINGS AND BUILDING MATERIALS

BRIEF preliminary survey of the building materials used and the methods of construction applied might perhaps to some extent facilitate an understanding of the description of the palace. Before proceeding to details, however, a few general remarks about the character and the component parts of the Palace of Nestor may not be out of place. The palace is not one single structure, but comprises—apart from several smaller appendages—four separate buildings, two of residential and ceremonial use, one a workshop, and one a wine magazine.

The plan of the Main Building (Key Plan, Rooms 1 to 57) is simple and straightforward. As at Mycenae and Tiryns, one enters from an outer paved area by way of a pillared gateway into an inner court (Fig. 9); crossing the latter, flanked to right and left by a colonnade and waiting rooms, one continues along the same general axis through a two-columned portico and a vestibule to a great ceremonial hall with four columns, a huge central hearth (Frontispiece) and a place where once a royal throne stood against the middle of the lateral wall on the right. A balcony, supported by the columns, ran around the four sides of the room, and a lofty clerestory or lantern towered above the hearth; it was no doubt provided near its top with openings for air and light. This main "nave" of the building was bordered on each flank by a long corridor (Fig. 88) from which doorways led into numerous chambers and storerooms, while a stairway on each side ascended to the floor above (Fig. 87); for the structure clearly consisted of two stories, in the upper of which the royal family had its sleeping, dressing, and living quarters. The central core above the Throne Room presumably rose considerably higher than the lateral "aisles." Not a single tile was found to indicate the possibility of a sloping gabled roof. The building must have been roofed by flattish terraces, tilted sufficiently to shed water from rain, and obviously laid out in successive steplike levels.

The systematic planning, the orderly division into apartments and chambers, the evidence of careful attention to detail, and the apparent endeavor to provide elegance and luxury demonstrate that the whole construction was designed and its erection supervised by a master architect.

The Southwestern Building (Rooms 60 to 81; Fig. 12), probably the earliest element to be built (p. 423) of the palace complex of the thirteenth century B.C., suffered great damage from the fire that destroyed the entire establishment, and even more from subsequent erosion and widespread looting by seekers of building material in later times. A large entrance hall with two columns in its façade, facing southeastward on an open court, gave access to a hall of greater size running southwestward—with a change of 90 degrees in orientation. This was probably the first throne room of the royal establishment in the thirteenth century. It too had four columns, if not six (Fig. 193); presumably also a hearth; but most of the floor together with the underlying deposit has been washed away and details can only be conjectured. Toward the northwest, beyond the two stately halls with their frescoed decoration, were many smaller chambers for storage and other purposes. Remnants of a stairway mounting to an upper story justify the assumption that the family's domestic quarters, bedrooms, etc., were situated on the floor above. This unit continued to exist and to be used after the Main Building had been erected; but whether it was assigned to a dowager or a crown prince, or to other occupants or purposes is a matter for speculation and hypothesis. The building had a compact, well-organized plan, and was no doubt worked out by a competent architect.

The Northeastern Building (Rooms 92 to 100; Fig. 222), which lacked paved floors, good plaster and wall paintings, and which was constructed mainly of crude brick resting on a stone socle, was clearly the workshop of the palace, where repairs of various kinds could be made and supplies of needed materials could be kept. Its place in the chronological sequence of construction is not certain, but it was probably third or fourth in the series.

The fourth unit is the Wine Magazine (Rooms 104, 105; Fig. 253), consisting of a vestibule and a spacious storeroom, large enough to hold some 60 or more wine jars of considerable capacity, though remnants of little more than half that number had survived. The Wine Magazine, like the Workshop, had only earth or clay floors and no paintings to embellish the roughly plastered face of its crude brick walls.

The less important adjuncts mentioned above comprise a group of small rooms clustered about the western corner of the Main Building (83, 84, 85, 86, 87 on Key Plan), and on the northeastern side a barracks-like structure between the Palace Workshop and the Wine Magazine (103 on Key Plan). Room 82, along with its connections to the northwest, might also have been a subsidiary to the Southwestern Building, possibly a Wine Magazine, in the early stages of the palace.

After this conspectus of the four separate buildings and the several small houses and huts which made up the whole royal establishment on the hill of Englianos, we turn now to the more specific subject of the building materials and how they were used. The principal basic items are stone, crude brick and clay, wood, metal, lime plaster, sand, and pebbles.

Stone of various kinds was of course one of the most essential elements. Flattish pieces or natural slabs were often used to form an even bedding for foundations (Fig. 19). The foundations as well as the interior walls were normally built of unworked quarry stone or rubble, though squared blocks sometimes appear in the lowest or the lower courses, especially at corners and junctions with transverse walls. Fine well-cut blocks of a sandy limestone, familiar to archaeologists in Greece as "poros," were, in the Main and Southwestern Buildings, regularly laid in ashlar style as a revetment in the outer face of exterior walls, the inner core and backing of which were constructed of rubble (Fig. 18). The blocks of poros were smoothly dressed and finished—tempting booty in medieval and later times to seekers of building material. Each block was carefully placed to make neat contact—at the face of the wall— with its neighbors; but the ends of the blocks were cut back obliquely, and the joints consequently display a spreading V-shaped form (Fig. 120), quite different from the type used in classical Greek times where contiguous stones were fitted together with the greatest care, provided with *anathyroses* making perfect, tight contact along the top and both sides of the joint.

In the Palace of Nestor the hollow V-shaped joints were generally filled with yellow clay and small stones. Since in many instances, however, the hollow cavity is found to be aligned with a vertical chase, which held an upright timber in the rubble backing, it may perhaps have received the transverse wooden strut that ran through from the inner part of the wall.

Blocks of poros, which could be worked with relative ease, provided the material for steps in the stairways leading to the upper story (Fig. 127). The lower section of the flight was supported on a solid filling of earth and clay backed by a retaining wall; the upper section was probably held up by transverse wooden beams which rested on the lateral walls.

Large blocks of limestone, occasionally also of poros, were used in most of the doorways for thresholds as well as for supports for the door jambs (e.g., Fig. 92). Anta bases, flanking doorways or at the ends of walls, were frequently made of very large squared blocks of poros or limestone (e.g., Fig. 9).

Little conglomerate, indeed, almost none, seems to have been employed in the construction of the palace, though in rare instances it may have served for sills in doorways. It had long been regularly utilized for the lintels of tholos tombs.

Crude brick was the almost invariably preferred material for the small houses mentioned above (Rooms 83-87, 103), storerooms such as the Wine Magazine (Rooms 104, 105) and the Northeastern Building (92-100) with its shrine, colonnade and workshops, as well as for the walls of the upper story in the large units, such as the Main and the Southwestern Buildings. The brickwork was usually laid on a supporting stone socle, thus rising high enough above the floor or the ground to be protected from being washed out by heavy rain or from wetting by water poured or spilled on the floor. Crude bricks also found their place in the palace for repairs and patches in the filling of gaps in the stone walls. A few examples of actual crude bricks have been recovered intact or nearly so; they are somewhat heavy and clumsy and of considerable size. One complete specimen (which had been used with several others in Room 32 to wedge firmly into place a large storage jar) is 0.52 m. long, 0.38 m. wide, and 0.09 m. thick. When laid in a wall with similar clay serving as a kind of mortar these bricks coalesced into a solid structure which, if coated with waterproof plaster, acquired an enduring quality. Throughout the whole palace abundant accumulations of clay from disintegrated bricks were encountered almost everywhere, testifying to the universal use of this material in all parts of the establishment. The clay was no doubt taken from natural beds which lay conveniently near. As we observed, it was often mixed with bits of crushed stone, potsherds, bones, plaster, and other matter, evidently added to promote cohesion. Perhaps in some instances the clay came from deposits which had previously been used and already possessed these extraneous elements. Straw may also have played a role in the making of bricks for the palace.

Clay was sometimes molded, with an admixture of small stones, into thick massive slabs of large dimensions which were set up on end to narrow or block doorways, as observed in three instances (e.g., Fig. 123).

Clay was employed in many other ways throughout the palace. It was tamped down hard to make a firm reasonably level floor in storerooms and pantries, and even in the Archives Rooms beside the principal entrance to the Main Building (Fig. 76). It was used with stones in constructing raised stands in which wine-jars and oil-jars could be set in fixed position at a height convenient for those who ladled out oil and wine; in most if not all instances these stands were coated with stucco (Fig. 22) so that liquids spilled could be wiped up without making the floor muddy. In the bathroom (43) a terracotta larnax or tub was sunk into a close-fitting container of clay, likewise waterproofed with a stuccoed surface (Fig. 139). Benches too were erected in some rooms (8, 10), coated with plaster or stucco and in one instance decorated with painted patterns (Fig. 85). A clay bench in Room 8 was apparently used as a place for filing inscribed tablets (Fig. 78). The great hearth in the Throne Room (Fig. 66) and the smaller one in the Queen's Hall (Fig. 149) were made mainly of clay, with a reinforcement of stones, the outer edge and the border around the central space for the fire being finished with a stucco surface bearing colorful painted decoration.

To the Mycenaean builders of houses and palaces wood was no less important than stone and clay. In the Palace of Nestor almost every wall, exterior as well as interior, was constructed in short sections fitted into a substantial framework of heavy upright, horizontal and transverse timbers and beams.[1] In many respects this system of building has a striking resemblance to the later, independently invented Tudor style of architecture in England—a half-timbered construction of stone and

[1] For a comparable use of a wooden framework in wall construction at Knossos: cf. *PM* I, 301ff., figs. 223-226; II, 349, fig. 251; at Troy: *TI*, 99ff., figs. 26-29; 164, fig. 62; *Troy* III, 221; on the Greek mainland: at Tiryns: Schliemann, *Tiryns*, 211f., 255ff., 262; *Tiryns* II, 166f.; III, 180f., fig. 81; 182, fig. 83; at Mycenae: Tsountas, *Mykenai*, 37; *BSA* xxv (1921-1923), 87 and fig. 20, 189f. and fig. 37, 240; at Thebes: *Praktika* 1927, 37ff., fig. 5.

wood. This technique, once common and widespread, still survives to some extent in the Greek countryside, where it is called *xylodesiá,* and it may be seen in many old houses of one or two stories which were built of crude brick. Whether this *xylodesiá* is a heritage handed down through millennia from the Mycenaean Age or was rediscovered in more recent times must remain uncertain; but it is likely that the use of a wooden framework for stone walls in Mycenaean architecture was an adaptation or borrowing from the technique of building walls with crude brick. Its transference to stonework may possibly have been an antiseismic precaution devised in a region where earthquakes frequently occur.

Informants of our own day, who are familiar with the technique of *xylodesiá,* state that the timber framework is first erected and the stone- or brickwork is then fitted into place, section by section. This was no doubt the sequence followed by the Mycenaean builders too.

The walls of the palace retain abundant evidence of the horizontal grooves which were left in the face of the wall from end to end and the vertical chases which ran through the wall from face to face and extended from top to bottom (Fig. 142). Many of the slots were found filled with black earth, charred matter and remnants of carbonized wood, giving vivid testimony to the intensity of the fire that brought the palace to its end. The timbers were of varying sizes, some apparently square in section, others logs split longitudinally in half, and some untrimmed natural tree trunks. Many seem to have been as much as 0.25 m. to 0.30 m. broad and thick.

It is possible that in the early phases of the palace some of the beams were left exposed and visible, in that event almost surely decorated in bright colors with appropriate patterns. In the late stages, however, before the final catastrophe, plaster was applied across the timbers in the chases and grooves, and the woodwork could not be seen.

Wood was freely used also for the door jambs or casings (Fig. 158), probably likewise for window frames and shutters. Occasionally too in some of the corridors, sills in doorways were made of wooden timbers, taking the place of stone thresholds (Fig. 169). The doors themselves were surely fashioned of wood, those inside the building probably brightened with painted patterns, while those in the outer walls were no doubt studded with bronze nails or sheathed with bronze plating. A good many doorways inside the palace offered no surviving indications of pivots or fastening bars, and it may be that such openings were closed—when desired—by hangings of skins or heavy fabrics, no traces of which have been found.

The balcony running around the four sides of the Throne Room was presumably in its entirety a wooden construction, supported by four substantial columns of the same material (Frontispiece). The clerestory or lantern too was surely built mainly of wood. The great timbers or joists that held up the weight of the earthen or clay roof were evidently stout tree trunks, resting on the walls and the upper tier of columns (Fig. 418), and carrying smaller transverse logs, laid contiguously, side by side, the chinks filled with clay.

The porch flanking the Court of the Megaron on the northeast was no doubt built in the same manner as the balcony in the Throne Room, its floor supported by beams extending from the wall at the rear to the architrave borne by the two wooden columns.

The columns, which were wholly destroyed in the burning of the establishment, seem to have been a distinctive feature of the palace. They were of somewhat varying sizes, the diameter ranging from ca. 0.40 m. to 0.52 m., so far as it can be measured and calculated, from the evidence of the raised ring on the top of the stone base and from the impressions of the flutings preserved in the stucco floor or the decorative stucco molding that ran around the bottom of the shaft. In any event, the standing place for the column, as marked in low relief on the base, can indicate only a maximum, and not a precise diameter for the wooden shaft. But in the Portico and probably also in the Throne Room the columns must have been made from trees of great size with a bole of half a meter or more.

The palace at Englianos is notable for its evidence of fluted columns and for the decorative ring of stucco that was modeled around the bottom of the shaft (Fig. 47). Remains of the ring have survived in many instances, but invariably in a much damaged state; it seems to have had a simple profile, flat on top and slightly convex on its outer sloping face. Traces of red paint on the top are all that is left us of the decoration. At the outset the ring rose only one or two centimeters above the floor, but in the course of time it grew much higher, as layer after layer of stucco was added, presumably to cover or repair damages, no doubt frequently suffered in this exposed place. So far as could be seen, each of the successive coats was painted red. The flutings are well-preserved in the impressions on the inner face of the stucco ring which had been laid directly against the column. No complete ring was found, but arcs ranging from a quarter to more than half of the circle permitted a fairly close calculation of the number of flutings: the columns in the Propylon had 64, those in the Throne Room 32 (Fig. 67); 44 were counted on those in the Entrance Hall of the Southwestern Building (Fig. 200). The relatively delicate columns that held up the porch on the northeastern side of the Court of the Megaron seem to have had 60.

The engaged half columns of gypsum in the façade of the "Tomb of Clytemnestra" at Mycenae, probably of the thirteenth century B.C., had 13 flutings.[2] Columns rep-

---

2 *BSA* xxv, 359f.; Perrot & Chipiez, *Art in Primitive Greece* (London, 1894), II, 83, fig. 284.

resented on carved ivories found at Mycenae are also of the fluted type.[3] Similarly fluted columns appear somewhat rarely in Minoan Crete.[4] In the north entrance to the domestic quarters from the great court in the palace at Phaistos columns with flutings have been recognized.[5] In the Little Palace at Knossos a blocking wall of clay, which had apparently been erected to shut off communication through a colonnade, was found still retaining clear impressions of the convex flutings of two wooden columns that perished by fire in the second millennium B.C.[6] The prevailing view about origins is that the custom of cutting flutings on columns, both of the concave and the convex types, was somehow derived from Egypt. The many wooden pillars which stood in the Palace of Nestor were all burned to ashes, and no evidence now exists to reveal their provenience—if they were imported—nor to shed fresh light on another vexing problem, namely whether they tapered downward or upward or had approximately the same diameter from top to bottom.

Some slight evidence observed on the walls points to the probability that decorative wooden wainscoting was used in several of the principal apartments in the palace, such as the Portico and the Vestibule of the Throne Room, and perhaps also in the Propylon. This may have been of oak or other material with fine graining, and the surface polished, or of plainer wood bearing painted patterns.

However that may be, it is clear that a vast amount of wood was required and used in the construction of this building complex, and it ultimately contributed abundant fuel to the inevitable fire that in the end razed the palace, consumed everything that was inflammable within it, and even melted gold ornaments into lumps and drops of metal.

The fixed as well as the movable furniture and the fittings in the palace no doubt had an appreciable effect in adding to the intensity of the final conflagration. The royal throne itself was almost certainly made of wood, probably carved and also ornamented with inlays in other material. Wooden benches may perhaps have been set up against the walls in some rooms. Inventories recorded on the Linear B tablets make mention of tables and stools; and other items may easily be imagined.

Lime and sand must likewise be recognized as important components used in Mycenaean architecture at Pylos as well as elsewhere. Interior walls were regularly plastered, coated with clay or mud in storerooms or chambers of little consequence, and with fine lime plaster in the better rooms and the apartments of state. It was often applied in two or three coats, a rough backing containing straw or other cohesive material, and one or two finer coatings, the outermost with a smoothly finished surface that could bear wall paintings.

---

[3] *EphArch* 1888, cols. 146, 164f., pl. 8 no. 8 (24 flutings); *BSA* 49 (1952), 241, pl. 40 (c); 50 (1953), 187ff., pl. 30 (a).

[4] *PM* I, 344.

[5] *MonAnt* XII, 56; XIV, 363, fig. 19.

[6] *PM* II, 520ff., fig. 323; Evans, *Tomb of the Double Axes*, 62ff., figs. 76, 77.

Floors too were made of sand or gravel and lime mixed with bits of broken pottery, plaster, and other serviceable matter, occasionally also with small pebbles; the pavement was usually composed of a thickish underlayer and a thin smoothly polished top. In the great halls and the principal apartments the floors were decorated in bright colors, the design usually laid out in relatively large checkerboard squares which were marked out by paired incised lines enclosing between them a band of red paint. Each square contained multiple linear patterns of considerable variety (Fig. 73), and sometimes marine motives, such as the octopus and fish (Figs. 166, 167).[7] Some squares enclosed smaller rectangles or squares executed in incised technique in addition to painted designs (Fig. 69).

A coat of very fine cement-like plaster, appearing to be waterproof, was found lining the walls and forming the floor of a small compartment (102) which we ventured to identify as a reservoir for water, outside the northeastern façade of the Main Building. It probably belonged to an early phase of the palace.

Metal may likewise have played an appreciable role in the Mycenaean building technique, although little obvious evidence for details of its use has survived at Pylos and elsewhere. One may assume with some confidence that pivots and sockets for swinging doors were made of bronze, perhaps soldered in place with lead, of which shapeless, melted chunks were recovered here and there. Bolts and bars of the same metal were no doubt likewise needed and installed. Small nondescript bits of bronze were found in profusion scattered throughout in almost all the rooms. Many were twisted, warped and even melted into lumps by the heat of the fire; and altogether they gave little or no clear indication of their original form and purpose; but they must have belonged to fixtures and accessories of various kinds that were attached to doors, thresholds, and walls. Hundreds of such fragments were collected, and with imagination one can reconstruct a faint image of the Throne Room with its polished bronze adornment in addition to the frescoes and the floor paintings and the brightly colored decoration of the woodwork in columns, balcony, and doorways (see Frontispiece).

Despite the disorder and damage caused by the destructive fire that wrecked the palace, an observer cannot fail to note in the ruins some little evidence, at least, suggesting that respectable or even high quality was present in the original construction of the Main and Southwestern Buildings. The straightforward architectural design of each must have been carefully worked out in advance. In the later phases traces of decline in artistic standards are perhaps to be seen in the repairs and renewals which were evidently needed from time to time. This change shows itself especially in the succession of stucco floors, particularly in the Throne Room (p. 82); and in the superposed coats of plaster with painted decoration on the hearths,

---

[7] For some comparable decoration at other sites cf. p. 84.

where the upper layers seem to be inferior in quality as compared with some of those below. A development of this kind no doubt reflects a normal law of human nature.

In the early stages, however, the exterior walls with their outer facing of well-fitted squared blocks laid in ashlar style, the methodical use throughout both units of a heavy timber framework—*xylodesiá*—to reinforce the interior and outer stone walls, the neatly planned staircases with steps of poros, the doorways with antae and threshold blocks, the corridors giving access to many rooms, and the underground system of drainage, all these and other details point to competent and painstaking supervision and workmanship.

Only the empty shell—and that merely in part—is left to us now; but the simple directness and clarity of the plan preserved by the surviving stumps and foundations of the walls, and the hearths, and the bath make it relatively easy to form some idea of the modest splendor, now gone, which once reigned in these halls; and visitors who have struggled to understand other monuments less fortunate in their conservation, are helped to envisage to some extent how Mycenaean palaces may have looked.

MAIN BUILDING

THE EXTERIOR WALL

THE Main Building of the palace (Key Plan), exclusive of Courts 42 and 47 which were open to the sky, has a maximum width of ca. 30 m. across its south-eastern front; its greatest length from southeast to northwest, including Magazine 27, is ca. 54.30 m.[1] On the southeastern, southwestern, and northwestern sides, the exterior wall is almost wholly missing except for some parts of its foundation, or the bedding stones of the latter, and except for a few remnants along the southwestern flank, where the inner backing of rubble stands to a maximum height of 0.50 m. above the floor.[2] Along the northeastern side, however, a considerable extent of this wall survives to a height of 0.80 m. above ground on the outside and 1.05 m. above the floor on the inside in Room 31 (Fig. 18). It is in this section of the wall that we obtain our best illustration of the methods used in the construction of the outside wall of the palace.

On all flanks the wall was built in the familiar Mycenaean manner in two parts: an outer facing of large squared blocks of poros laid in ashlar style and an inner backing, usually of unworked stone or rubble, coated with lime or mud plaster. The two faces were more or less welded together by variations in the thickness of each element permitting an overlapping of squared blocks by rubble and of rubble by squared blocks. On the exterior the poros blocks were neatly fitted together in close vertical joints, but the ends of the blocks were almost always cut back obliquely so that the joint broadened toward the core of the wall, forming a V-shaped cavity. This space was usually filled with small stones and clay but in a good many instances a horizontal strut from a beam on the inner face of the wall seems to have projected into the V-shaped opening. On its inner side the stone wall was constructed within a massive framework of vertical and horizontal timbers, as explained above (pp. 37f.). In the same manner the exterior face in ashlar work also had great horizontal wooden beams, fastened by dowels into the poros structure at two if not more levels, marking off horizontal panels. There were probably likewise upright timbers.

After this preliminary survey each of the four parts of the wall will be described briefly, beginning with the southeastern front and proceeding clockwise around the southwestern, northwestern, and northeastern sides.

The southeastern wall has been stripped of all its poros blocks and the pillagers penetrated deep into the foundations, pulling out whatever material they thought

---

[1] Over-all measurements based on the foundations are naturally only approximate. The bedding stones and the foundations were normally somewhat broader than the walls they supported and the exact lines of the latter cannot be surely fixed. Many minor irregu-larities in the alignment and thickness of the walls imply that differences of a few centimeters here and there were not regarded as of great importance.

[2] In Rooms 12: 0.10 m.; 15: 0.50 m.; 17: 0.40 m.; 19: 0.43 m.; and 20: 0.42 m.

useful. In one section, outside Room 50, Corridor 49, Room 53 and Corridor 52, they reached a level 0.65 m. below the floor of those rooms (Fig. 19). Here a good many blocks of considerable size remain *in situ*. Farther to the southwestward only small stones are left at the bottom of the bedding trench (Fig. 13). The outer face of the foundations shows no trace of a setback and it looks as if the wall of the final phase ran straight from the east corner until it intersected the prolongation of the northeast line of the Propylon. At any rate the Division of Reconstruction of the Greek Archaeological Service has followed this indication in rebuilding with small stones the stretch of the southeastern wall to a height of 0.40 m. to 0.50 m. above the floors of the palace in this quarter (Fig. 11).[3] Across the space between the end of the wall and the northeast anta of the Propylon a bedding of small stones continued northwestward. It may have supported a wall or a doorway that led into Room 57.

Approximately parallel with the outer wall (Fig. 424z) and only 0.30 m. to 0.40 m. northwest of it, is a foundation composed of large poros blocks laid transversely (Figs. 13, 424y). No inner face of this foundation has been recognized, but small bedding stones continue to the northwestward to end in a line 2.10 m. to 2.20 m. from the outer face of the large blocks. Whatever its thickness, the wall that was supported on this substructure was surely an older exterior wall of the Main Building, belonging to an earlier phase. Exactly how this outside wall was connected with the anta of the Propylon has not been ascertained. A third and probably yet older wall (Fig. 424m), also parallel (p. 227), apparently goes back to a still more ancient phase.

From 1 m. to 3 m. outside the demolished southeastern wall were found several blocks of poros (Fig. 13), accompanied by rubble and clay, which had obviously fallen from that wall. An even more regular row of poros blocks lay outside the Propylon (Fig. 14), no doubt wreckage fallen from the façade that was supported by the antae and the column.

Beyond the gateway to the southern corner of the building similar debris, including some poros blocks, was scattered about here and there on the pavement of the outer court. These too must have come from the southeast wall, but the wall itself has disappeared and only the small stones forming the bedding of the foundations remain (Fig. 17). The original thickness of the wall cannot now be determined; in the restoration made by the Service of Reconstruction it has been given a width of 0.85 m. (Fig. 12). Directly behind it, and only ca. 0.10 m. distant, is an earlier wall represented by three blocks of poros with a backing of rubble. Incised on the face of the middle block is the sign of the double axe (Fig. 16). The older structure might well be of the same building period as the wall to the northeast of the

---

[3] The southeastern, southwestern, and northwestern walls were first rebuilt to a height of ca. 1 m., but were later lowered to the dimensions given above.

Propylon, just mentioned, which had a foundation of poros blocks laid transversely.

The southwestern wall of the Main Building is also for the most part preserved chiefly in its foundations (Fig. 20). The latter, in the southeastern section, generally lie ca. 0.60 m. below the floors of the bordering rooms. Here the substructure was laid in a bedding trench cut down into *stereo*. The material used consists mainly of fairly large flat blocks and slabs laid transversely, but toward the southeastern end beside Room 7, almost everywhere only the small bedding stones are preserved (Fig. 21).

Farther to the northwest, alongside Rooms 17, 19, 20 and 21, the foundations, composed mainly of small stones, rise a good deal higher and in some places remnants of the rubble inner backing of the wall itself have survived (Fig. 63). This northwesternmost section in its style of building differs appreciably from that of the section toward the southeast and probably represents a reconstruction in a late phase after the west corner of the building had suffered damage.

Nowhere in the entire length of this wall (45.92 m.) from end to end, has a single block of poros belonging to the visible part of the structure remained *in situ*. Most of this good building material has been carried away by looters. Here and there, alongside the wall, however, somewhat rarely in Court 88 and more numerously in Court 63 and in Ramp 59, were exposed, along with many fragments and splinters, squared blocks of poros which had certainly fallen out from the face of the wall (Figs. 20, 21). They had presumably become deeply enough covered by debris to escape the attention of the stone robbers.

Throughout its entire length the southwest wall has been rebuilt by the Greek Service of Reconstruction to a height of 0.40 m. to 0.70 m. above the pavement, that is to say, high enough to indicate the limit of the Main Building on this side (Figs. 9, 12).[4] This modern work has been constructed mainly of rubble and cement, but with the reuse of some of the original poros blocks that were found alongside it. The evidence from surviving foundations was insufficient to fix precisely the exact lines or thickness of the wall and the positions and depths of the several offsets it contained. For the most part the edges of the stucco floor, on the one side or the other of the gap left when the building material was torn out, gave the clue that was followed by the restorers. In the actual rebuilding the wall does not run straight throughout its course: in the stretch alongside Rooms 9 and 10 it diverges appreciably from the orientation of the sectors to the southeast and the northwest. Whether this divergence existed in the original wall is uncertain. The doorway in the rebuilt wall alongside Room 12 is conjectural, but some circumstantial evidence (pp. 108f.) persuaded us that there must have been an opening here leading from the palace into Court 63.

4 See note on p. 44.

The enormous breadth (ca. 1.50 m.) of the southeasternmost sector of the wall in its course beside Rooms 7 and 8 was definitely indicated by the break in the pavement of the ramp on the southwestern side, and by the back of the bench in the Archives Room on the northeast (Fig. 21). Why so massive a support was required at this corner of the building is not clear. Perhaps reinforcement was thought necessary since the angle is placed on a descending slope. Another possibility is that a lofty tower stood in this place beside the Propylon, which may have had a corresponding bastion on the northeast.

The northwestern wall of the Main Building, like the southeastern and southwestern, had been despoiled of its original facing of poros blocks (Fig. 22). A few of the latter together with many chips and fragments were found where they had fallen spreading out behind the building (Fig. 24), one block leaning against the wall of the circular structure (87 on Key Plan). Except for a small stump of the actual wall in Rooms 21 and 22, only the foundations below floor level are now preserved. The stump built of small stones stands to a maximum height of ca. 0.35 m. in Room 21, and is 0.30 m. to 0.40 m. high in Room 22. Laid on the earlier foundation, it is evidently an element of the repair that was carried out after some accident necessitated the rebuilding of the western corner (p. 130). The repair was carelessly executed, diverging somewhat from the line of the foundation. The modern restoration of the wall, rising only to a height of 0.40 m. to 0.50 m. above the floor, follows the line of the anciently reconstructed patchwork.

The foundation itself is a solidly built structure (1.20 m. thick), firmly founded on *stereo* along Rooms 21 and 22. Farther northeastward, beside Rooms 23 and 24 and Corridor 25, it is very deeply bedded though not actually reaching *stereo*. The wall had an offset, ca. 0.85 m. deep, in line with the exterior face of the southwestern wall of the Throne Room, though the foundation, as is frequently seen in similar situations, projected well beyond the face of the wall. The rear edge of the stucco-coated stand in which oil-jars were set in Magazines 23 and 24, here clearly gives us the line of the inner face of the wall. The exact thickness of the superstructure with its outer veneer of ashlar masonry and its backing of rubble cannot be determined; as rebuilt by the Service of Reconstruction (Fig. 10)[5] it has a width of 0.90 m. and a maximum height of 0.65 m. above the floor.

Just as was noted along the southeastern front of the palace, so also at the northwestern end traces of earlier building periods present themselves. It is likely that the outer northwest wall turned southeastward along Corridor 25 for a distance of ca. 4.30 m., and then swung again northeastward as the northwesterly side of Magazine 32. Here it is a normal exterior wall, made with an outer facing of poros blocks

[5] See note on p. 44.

(Fig. 23) and a backing of smallish unworked stones, finished inside with a coating of lime plaster.

Magazine 27, along with Corridor 26 leading to it, must then be an addition to the original building (Fig. 25). It juts out northwestward 5.18 m. from the outer face of the northwest wall of the palace and has an over-all width of 9.05 m. The southwest, northwest, and northeast walls of this addition must thus be reckoned as outside walls of the Main Building and require brief mention here. All three are represented mainly by their foundations, almost the whole of the superstructure above the floor having disappeared. All are substantially built, the southwestern and northeastern being 1.05 m. thick, and the northwestern, which supported the building in the steep slope of the hillside, having a thickness of 1.20 m. Despite the damage they have suffered, the three walls enclosing Magazine 27 retain enough evidence to show that they were built in the canonical Mycenaean manner with vertical chases and horizontal grooves for the heavy timbers of the wooden framework. Outside the northwestern wall lay two or three poros blocks, and outside the northeastern many more, accompanied by chips and fragments of others, indicating that the walls on those sides had a revetment in ashlar masonry. Whether the southwestern wall was also finished in this style is uncertain, but it probably was.

The northeastern exterior wall extending from the north corner to the east corner of the Main Building has a total length of 54.46 m.[6] It is of varying thickness in different parts of its course, ranging from 0.85 m. to 1.28 m.[7]

The first section, 9.60 m. long, flanking the extension that was added on to the northwest of Magazine 32, is sufficiently dealt with above and on pages 145, 147f. At the junction an offset juts out ca. 0.04 m. From this point on, some remains of the superstructure, both on the inner and outer face, are still preserved to a continuous length of 39.79 m., all of which must have been constructed in one and the same building period (Fig. 18). This includes one gateway (41), certainly part of the original design, and one doorway (in Room 46), which was obviously an afterthought, inserted later. The stretch of nearly 40 m. also displays five additional projecting offsets at irregular intervals, a niche sunk into the face of the wall bordering Room 33, and a broad recess between two antae beside Room 40. Toward the southeastern end to a length of 5.07 m. the wall is represented only by foundations of poros blocks, not intended to be visible (Fig. 39).

The first course meant to be seen above ground extends, except in the door opening, in an unbroken sequence of 39 blocks (see table of measurements, p. 49). They

---

6 The discrepancy of 0.16 m. between the length on the northeast and that along the axis of the building, 54.30 m. (p. 43), is caused by the fact that the northwest wall of Magazine 27 is not exactly parallel to the transverse axis, and when its line is projected southwestward to intersect the longitudinal axis it deviates 0.16 m. from a parallel to the transverse axis.

7 Thickness of wall along: Corridor 26 1.05 m., Room 32 1.10 m., Room 31 1.20 m. to 1.25 m., Room 33 1.28 m., Room 34 1.20 m., Room 40 1 m., Room 43 0.85 m., Room 46 0.85 m.

vary considerably in length, ranging from 0.37 m. to 1.52 m.; 14 may be grouped between 0.80 m. and 1.05 m., 25 between 0.70 m. and 1.10 m. In height they are more nearly uniform: in the section to the northwest of Court 42, where in some instances their full height could be measured, they show variations from 0.435 m. to 0.515 m., but they were set on bedding stones laid in *stereo* and adjusted so that the upper surface of the course was approximately level. Farther to the southeast-ward a similar adjustment was made so that in each section the top of the course was reasonably even, although the height above the pavement is not uniform because the pavements are irregular. In the northwestern part of Court 42 the blocks stand to a height of 0.34 m. above the pavement; in the southeastern part 0.38 m. to 0.40 m.; in Court 47 0.40 m. to 0.43 m.

The second course is preserved northwest of Court 42 in 18 blocks (Figs. 18, 413) extending to a length of 15.87 m. (see Nos. 40 to 57 in table of measurements, p. 49). They vary from 0.47 m. to 1.25 m. in length with an average of 0.91 m. They have a height of 0.44 m., but differ considerably in thickness, ranging from 0.35 m. to 0.54 m. In many instances thick blocks are laid in alternation with less broad ones, presumably in an attempt to bond together the outer ashlar part of the wall with the rubble backing. Along the top of this whole section the upper surface of the blocks was worked smooth to a width varying from 0.25 m. to 0.35 m. or more, obviously as the bedding for large rectangular timbers laid horizontally. These beams were fastened by means of dowels, cuttings for which appear at irregular intervals.

From northwest to southeast the intervals, measured from center to center, are the following: 1.29 m., 0.82 m., 0.76 m., 1.66 m., 1.62 m., 1.78 m., 1.17 m., 0.90 m., 1.32 m., 1.38 m., 0.90 m., 0.89 m. It has not yet been determined whether these spacings are merely accidental, depending on whim or chance, or were planned to suit the lengths of the wooden timbers, and, when analyzed, might shed some light on the basic units of measurements employed in the construction of the palace.

Southeastward from the northwest end of Court 42 to the termination of the wall as preserved, only a single course is left *in situ*. It differs from the plain bottom course in the northwestern section just described, but resembles the second course in that section, since it carried the horizontal timbers. In this stretch the timbers lay at a level 0.32 m. lower than in the northwestward continuation. Perhaps it was the descending slope of the ground that determined the change. The three dowel holes in the wall beside Room 40 are spaced 1.13 m. and 1.22 m. apart. In the three facing blocks alongside Room 43 are three dowel holes, spaced 0.93 m. apart (Figs. 37, 414). In the transverse block at the end of the partition wall between Rooms 43 and 46 there are two dowel holes in line with those farther southeastward. In the next three blocks alongside Room 46 three dowel holes appear 0.72 m. apart (Figs. 40, 415). Beside the middle of the room, in two deep slots apparently cut for upright timbers,

Dimensions of blocks, beginning at corner of Corridor 26 and Room 32: Nos. 1-39 in lowest course meant to be visible, Nos. 40-57 in upper course.

block number	length	height	level (top) above datum	maximum thickness	block number	length	height	level (top) above datum	maximum thickness
1.	0.98	0.49		0.415	31.	0.72	0.43		0.49
2.	0.98	0.515	13.36	0.425	32.	0.70	0.43	13.52	0.54
3.	1.03	0.51		0.455	33.	0.78	0.43		0.43
4.	0.96	0.51			34.	0.99	0.43	13.35	0.42
5.	0.84	0.465			35.	0.81	0.43	13.35	0.55
6.	1.05	0.465							
7.	1.12	0.485			36.	0.81	0.43		0.38
8.	0.91	0.495			37.	0.37	0.43		0.42
9.	0.72	0.50			38.	0.82		13.50	1.03
10.	0.83	0.47			39.	0.92		13.51	0.54
11.	0.92	0.465							
12.	0.98	0.465			40.	0.54	0.44	13.79	0.98
13.	0.96	0.49			41.	1.08	0.44	13.80	0.43
14.	1.11	0.48			42.	0.59	0.44		0.445
15.	0.83	0.475	13.51		43.	0.86	0.44		0.51
16.	0.87	0.47		0.38	44.	0.83	0.44		0.46
17.	0.47	0.46		0.60	45.	0.47	0.44	13.85	1.15
18.	1.52	0.435							
19.	0.64	0.435			46.	1.20	0.44		0.40
20.	0.87	0.60	14.01	1.05	47.	0.77	0.44		0.54
21.	0.84			0.49	48.	0.68	0.44		0.50
22.	0.89		13.69	0.66	49.	1.03	0.44	13.89	0.42
23.	0.49			0.55	50.	0.75	0.44		0.53
24.	0.97			0.75	51.	0.97	0.44		0.47
25.	0.95		13.65	1.00	52.	1.16	0.44		0.40
26.	0.70	0.40	13.60	1.00	53.	1.07	0.44		0.35
27.	1.00			0.55	54.	1.05	0.44	13.83	0.51
28.	0.70		13.59	0.45	55.	1.25	0.44		0.45
29.	0.84			0.31	56.	1.02	0.44		0.44
30.	0.70		13.54	0.90	57.	1.03	0.44	13.99	0.51

are dowel holes spaced 1.09 m. apart. Between, on the upper surface of the block, is a dowel hole for a horizontal beam. Beyond the southeastern slot is a further single dowel hole. Alongside Corridor 48 are two dowel holes, 0.385 m. apart, in the large block beyond the anta base (Figs. 39, 415).

The backing of rubble in the northwestern sector of the wall still stands, though in a much dilapidated and calcined state, to a maximum height of 0.35 m. to 0.40 m. above the poros blocks of the outer face. The intensity of the fire along this wall, no doubt produced by the burning of the vertical and horizontal timbers, melted much of the stone into lime; the latter flowed over the slots in which the beams were laid, covering the ashlar blocks below with a fused mass of *migma*. Beside Rooms 40 and 43 very little of the rubble has survived, but along most of the northeast side of Room 46 the central core of the wall (ca. 0.35 m. thick) still stands to a maximum height of 0.45 m., partly melted and fused together (Fig. 40). Here horizontal timbers on both sides of the wall contributed to the destructive fury of the fire.

The original height of the wall can be approximately, if not precisely, conjectured.

Outside the northwesterly part of the building, beside Rooms 27, 31 and 32, a large section of the wall seems at the time of the fire to have fallen outward more or less in a single unit. It was perhaps an explosion of the olive oil stored in Magazines 27 and 32 that, with tremendous force, blew the wall out as a whole, both the outer veneer of poros blocks and the inner backing of rubble, along with abundant remains of dissolved crude brick and other burned matter. This mass of stone, though buried just below the plowed surface of the ground, somehow escaped the attention of the plunderers. When the area was excavated in 1954 we first came upon a vast spread of small stones that stretched out in a continuous layer nearly 4.50 m. wide and more than 22 m. long (Fig. 26). When the rubble was removed the squared blocks from the face of the wall came to light lying in fairly regular rows, six of which could be distinguished (Figs. 27, 413). Each row evidently represents a course: counting the two still *in situ*, we may thus conclude that there were originally at a minimum eight courses of stone blocks in addition to at least two horizontal timbers, as indicated by dowel holes along the second course of the wall and in some of the fallen stones. Blocks ranging from 0.37 m. to 0.44 m. in height are present in the material on the ground and it is evident that the courses diminished somewhat in height toward the top of the wall—a common practice in classical Greek architecture. Allowing an average of 0.40 m. to a course, eight courses would account for a wall 3.20 m. high, and two beams would raise it to 3.70 m. or more. It is likely in any event that the stone wall continued up to the floor of the second story and perhaps formed a socle above it. From this point on, the upper story clearly had walls of crude brick continuing up to the roof and undoubtedly constructed with a heavy framework of timbers. The evidence of the southwestern and northeastern stairways (pp. 113, 168) agrees reasonably well with the conclusion drawn from the rows of blocks, for here too the 21 or 22 steps that must be postulated would indicate that the floor of the upper story lay between 3.25 m. and 3.50 m. above the ground floor.

The exterior face of the northeastern wall is interrupted by six projecting offsets in the Mycenaean manner. The first, between the original construction and the addition at the northwest, juts out only ca. 0.04 m. (Fig. 18). Exactly 6 m. beyond it, in line with the northwest face of the partition wall between Rooms 31 and 32, is a second offset, projecting ca. 0.12 m. (Fig. 18). The third offset comes 12.53 m. farther southeastward, where a great anta block projects almost in line with the northwestern face of the wall between Rooms 34 and 40 (Figs. 34, 414). The anta block juts out 0.965 m. from the wall on its northwestern face and is 0.92 m. broad. On its southeastern side it returns 0.855 m. to the face of the northeast wall. The latter then continues southeastward with its face 0.11 m. northeast of the line of the preceding section. At 3.16 m. it meets another anta block which, extending 0.80 m. out from the wall, flanks Gateway 41 (p. 180). The northeast face of this anta determines the line of the gateway and the wall beyond it to the southeast (Fig. 35), a distance of 8.38 m. from the north corner of the block. The next offset (Fig. 36) of ca. 0.17 m. is aligned with the northwestern face of the partition between Bathroom 43 and the Queen's Hall (46). From this angle the wall runs 7.10 m. to the southeastern edge of the doorway that opens from Room 46 into Court 47. Here the final offset juts out 0.14 m. For the remainder of its length, 6.78 m. to the east corner of the building, the wall, so far as one can judge from the foundations, ran straight (Figs. 39, 41, 415).

The purpose of these offsets was presumably in part aesthetic, to break up vertically a long blank expanse of wall. It is worth noting, however, that all six of the offsets in this wall line up more or less nearly exactly with intersecting interior walls. Consequently we may conclude that structural considerations too had something to do with the offsets. It may be observed, moreover, that in all the surviving junctions of partitions with the exterior wall, the latter shows a regular alternation from course to course of stretchers running lengthwise and headers running crosswise aligned with the interior wall (Fig. 18). This arrangement thus bonds the two walls firmly together.[8]

The northeast wall was provided at intervals with what we take to be small drainholes or "weepers," four in number (Fig. 18). The first one, outside Room 32, 2.99 m. from the offset marking the corner of Corridor 26 and Room 32, is a slot 0.17 m. wide (Fig. 29). It is framed by the neatly cut vertical ends of two poros blocks in the lowest course meant to be visible. The slot has the full height of that course (0.51 m.), going down to the bedding stones laid in *stereo*. It was cleared inward to a distance of 0.50 m. from the face of the wall and was found to stop against small stones in the middle of the wall. No opening that could connect with it was to be seen in Room 32. In the core of the wall above the end of the slot a small gap between stones may have served as a channel to lead moisture from the wall into the "weeper."

The second slot (Fig. 30), outside the north corner of Room 31, 4.87 m. to the southeast of the first, is made in exactly the same manner as the latter. It is 0.155 m. wide and occupies the full height (0.50 m.) of the lowest course of the wall. At its outer face the top edge has been damaged slightly, perhaps by someone trying to break into the opening. The latter was cleared to a depth of 0.25 m. into the wall where it apparently ended against a stone. How it could have served any useful purpose as a "weeper" is not clear.

The third slot, 6.38 m. farther southeastward, is opposite the middle of Room 33, below the niche (Fig. 33). It is 0.22 m. wide and runs back 0.42 m. to the full thickness of the blocks (Fig. 31). In the face of the recess the upper edge of the slot has

---

8 Even when there is a doorway in the partition close to the exterior wall, a short stub of the transverse wall projects to form a doorjamb, and the wall is carried across the door-opening.

been carelessly gouged out in roughly arched form. Toward the interior this cutting slopes downward to the level of the top of the slot. Whether this was caused by accident, or intentionally hacked out by some intruder seeking to explore the "weeper," remains an open question. The bottom of the slot reaches the bedding stones of the wall. In Room 33 there is no sign of any connection whatever with the drain hole. The slot was found packed tight with sandy brown earth containing a stone, many sherds and some fragments of painted plaster, all similar to the deposit found everywhere outside the palace.

Barely 0.89 m. to the southeast of this slot is another, 0.18 m. wide, also bordered by the vertical ends of the adjacent poros blocks (Figs. 32, 34). The latter are 0.48 m. high, but the "weeper" continues somewhat below the blocks, apparently reaching the bedding stones. We were able to clear the slot only to a distance of 0.60 m. inward from the outer face, and it may have continued farther. This opening too is alongside Room 33 near its eastern corner. At floor level inside the room in line with this slot was a shallow channel-like hole (0.18 m. wide, 0.11 m. high), running through a peculiar inner reinforcement of the wall (p. 162). It seems not to penetrate into the core of the wall itself and no proper connection with the "weeper" could be recognized.

Since all four thus appear to have no relation to drainage from the floors of the palace, we can only conclude that they must have been designed to carry out moisture or water that somehow seeped into the wall from above.

In the outer face of the exterior wall, alongside Room 33 but not exactly centered on its axis, is one of the notable features of the northeast wall, a broad niche, 0.18 m. deep and 2.49 m. wide (Figs. 18, 33). Its bottom is formed by the top of the lowest visible wall course which has the appearance of a ledge cut back into the face of the wall. At the northwest the niche is bordered by the straight finished end of a regular wall block. The southeastern edge, however, was cut back into the face of a block to a length of 0.33 m. Between this and the northwest end two wall blocks were set back to the required depth of 0.18 m. from the outer face. In the top of the second course of the wall two dowel holes, 1.32 m. apart, show that a horizontal wooden timber ran across the niche at this height. How high the recess was cannot be certainly determined. It is obviously an architectural refinement of some kind, possibly an embrasure for a window. The wooden beam lying on the second course of wall blocks could have served well as the sill of a window opening or as a support for a wooden sill and jambs; and three or four courses higher there was presumably another band of wooden beams which might have formed the lintel of such an opening. The recess must almost surely have been carried up to the upper story and it is not unlikely that the important window was there. An opening to give light and air close to the landing at the top of Stairway 36 would certainly have been highly useful.

Next beyond the niche, only some 3.02 m. farther to the southeast, we come to the two large anta bases, 3.16 m. apart, which jut out from the wall just to the northwest of Gateway 41 (Figs. 28, 34, 35). The two bases are not set at the same level: the north-western one has its top at 14.01 m. above datum, 0.36 m. higher than the anta base beside the gateway. But the two seem to belong together in framing a much larger and deeper niche than the one beside Room 33. Both anta bases are generously pro-vided with dowel holes, seven on the higher northwestern one and at least six on the other as shown in Figure 414.[9] The dowels probably fastened massive upright wooden timbers, perhaps in a paneled arrangement framing the recess. Little or nothing was found in Room 40 behind this bay, certainly nothing to identify its use. May it possibly have been a shrine, perhaps with a broad window or series of window openings, looking out toward the northeast, and conceivably constructed largely of wood? Or, failing that, was it perhaps one of the administrative offices of the palace? Only one large poros block and a few fragments were found in the court directly out-side this recess (Fig. 35).

Farther southeastward, and some 2.20 m. distant from the façade of Gateway 41, a good many blocks were found. They had evidently fallen from the superstructure of the gateway. This gateway too, like the Propylon (1), had a single column between antae in its façade (Fig. 36). The anta bases have numerous dowel holes, the one on the northwest six, as already mentioned, that on the southeast four (Fig. 414);[10] and it is likely that both were sheathed on their visible sides with wooden uprights. The single column as well as the architrave it supported must have been made of wood.

Beyond the gateway toward the southeast one may plausibly conjecture that the bathroom (43) also had a window opening of some kind (Figs. 35, 36). Here too relatively few fallen blocks were found in the court (Fig. 28) and this section of the wall, a little more than 2.50 m. long, might well have been largely built of wood, with one or more window frames.

[9] Block No. 20, anta base in the west corner of Court 42: dimensions of the seven dowel holes:
a. 0.045 m. by 0.04 m. by 0.075 m. deep.
b. 0.06 m. by 0.03 m. by 0.085 m. deep.
c. 0.03 m. by 0.04 m. by 0.045 m. deep.
d. 0.035 m. by 0.025 m. by 0.065 m. deep.
e. 0.035 m. by 0.065 m. by 0.065 m. deep.
f. 0.035 m. by 0.045 m. by 0.095 m. deep.
g. 0.03 m. by 0.04 m. by 0.06 m. deep.
Block No. 25, anta base on northwestern side of Gateway 41 (accurate measurements of dowel holes impossible because top of stone is badly worn):
a. ca. 0.05 m. square.
b. 0.055 m. long from northeast to southwest by 0.04 m.
c. ca. 0.05 m. square.
d. 0.055 m. long from southeast to northwest by 0.04 m.
e. ca. 0.045 m. long south-west to northeast by 0.04 m.
f. 0.055 m. long by 0.045 m.

[10] Block No. 26, anta base southeast side of Gateway 41. Beginning on the northeast side and continuing to the northwest and the southwest, the dowel holes indicated by a, b, c, d:
a. 0.06 m. by 0.035 m. by 0.07 m. deep.
b. 0.05 m. by 0.04 m. by 0.05 m. deep.
c. 0.05 m. by 0.07 m. by 0.06 m. deep.
d. 0.03 m. by 0.06 m. by 0.05 m. deep.

Finally, outside the middle of Room 46, the two slots (0.88 m. apart) in the poros blocks, each with its hole for a dowel to fasten an upright beam (Figs. 41, 42) must presumably be interpreted as evidence that there was a window in this position too, ventilating and lighting the Queen's Hall.

The generous measure of detailed information about Mycenaean architecture that has been preserved for us in the ruins of the northeastern wall, with only parts of two courses *in situ*, leads us to regret that so relatively little had survived unscathed. Had the wall been standing somewhere in part at least to its full height we should have a much broader knowledge of Mycenaean building technique. On the other hand, however, we can be grateful that in a palace so utterly devastated by fire some not inconsiderable bits of evidence have come down to us.

P R O P Y L O N

A broad open court (58 on Key Plan and pp. 227ff.) stretched along the entire southeastern front of the central unit of the palace. Crossing this paved area, visitors reached the principal entrance, which was laid out in the form of a simple classical Greek propylon; it has in plan the shape of a capital letter H with a single axial column set between antae in both the inner and outer façade and a transverse wall in the middle, through which the actual doorway opens (Fig. 9). This Propylon was not symmetrically placed along the median axis of the building nor did it follow that of the Megaron, but it lies considerably to the southwest of both these axes. The two columns of the gateway are approximately in line with the southwestern column of the main Portico and the two southwestern columns in the Throne Room; and the northeastern wall of the Propylon is nearly aligned with the northeastern column bases in the Portico and the Throne Room. This asymmetry, which is obvious in the plan but could hardly have been recognized by a casual visitor, is probably of no special significance. The architect of the building undoubtedly designed it as he wished and did not feel bound to make it symmetrical.

A further irregularity is to be seen in the southeastern wall of the central unit, since it does not form a straight line all the way across the front of the structure. The section to the northeast of the Propylon projects some 2 m. southeastward beyond the alignment of the gateway itself and the wall to the southwest of it (Fig. 43).

P R O P Y L O N ,   O U T E R   P O R C H   (1)

The outer portico of the Propylon (1 on Key Plan) is ca. 4 m. deep and 6.50 m. wide. The southwestern wall was removed almost to the bottom of the foundations, possibly in Venetian times or later, but its line could be approximately determined from the bedding blocks of its substructure and from the edge of the pavement along the southwestern side of the gateway (Fig. 45). The thickness of the wall was probably ca. 1 m., as may be conjectured on the analogy of the corresponding northeastern wall. The latter, rising to a maximum height of 0.80 m. from the floor with a thickness of 1.05 m., is preserved to a length of 3.35 m. from the crossbar of the H. The anta, which must have formed the outer end of the wall, is missing, having been carried away by seekers of building material.

The crosswall is approximately 0.80 m. thick, ending in an anta on each side of the doorway (Fig. 9). The anta base is ca. 0.10 m. thicker than the wall and therefore projects from the line of the latter in a slight offset on each face. The opening between the two antae is 2.40 m. wide (Fig. 429). In the middle, slightly below the floor level, lies a block 1.21 m. long, 0.72 m. wide, which formed the threshold. The last stucco floor was probably laid over this block. The threshold itself at its northeastern end rests on a projecting tongue of the jamb base (0.50 m. by 0.72 m.) which has its surface some 0.04 m. higher than the threshold. The wooden door jamb probably extended to within a few (ca. 0.05 m.) centimeters of the threshold. The latter was supplemented by a small separate block, 0.21 m. wide and 0.02 m. higher. Beyond it is a block 0.48 m. by 0.72 m., which provided support for the southwestern jamb of the doorway. It rises 0.04 m. above the level of the large threshold block. The jambs were presumably made of heavy wooden timbers forming a pi-shaped projection from the anta and either hollow or filled in with clay or earth. The face of the anta base toward the opening is countersunk to a depth of 0.06 m. to 0.07 m., framed by a raised edge on each side of the block. This countersinking presumably facilitated the attachment of the wooden door jamb.

In the outer portico of the Propylon a deep slot or groove for a great horizontal beam resting on the dado course, which corresponds in height to the anta base, is well preserved on both sides of the doorway as well as in the northeast wall. The beam extended on each side across the anta base to which it was attached by two dowels, set in rectangular holes, 0.03 m. to 0.055 m. deep. The groove for the beam is 0.24 m. deep or more from front to back, and in several places in the clay facing of the core of the wall, impressions of the graining of the wood are well-preserved. The timbers therefore must have been in some instances at least 0.24 m. thick and perhaps even higher than that. At intervals of 0.80 m. or more, comparable upright chases for vertical beams occur and it is clear that transverse struts went through the wall connecting the framework of one face to that of the other. The core of the wall is built of smallish stones mortared with clay, which made a smooth backing for the horizontal and vertical beams. In the northeastern part of the crosswall the core is 0.30 m. to 0.45 m. thick, and it is preserved to a height of 0.38 m. above the dado course, a total maximum height of 0.85 m. above the floor. The face of the crosswall and its antae—as well as that of the northeast wall—was coated with a good lime plaster; at least three or four successive applications of plaster can be recognized in some places, especially on the antae, and each bore painted decoration. No surface is preserved above the dado.

The lower part of the walls to the height of the dado course still retains its plaster *in situ,* bearing remains of a typical dado design: red vertical bands marking off panels which repeat with variations a constant pattern of wide blue, pink, and red arcs. Two or more layers are represented, painted in similar colors. On the anta southwest of the door a second layer is preserved in red, white, and black. Many fragments of fallen plaster lay on the floor, spreading out toward the middle of the portico. Much of it consists of heavy pieces in blue from an upper floor; some in plain red may be from a ceiling.

Numerous fragments of fresco were also recovered. Miss Lang's analysis records that several compositions are represented. One group has large areas of pink with graining lines associated with broad alternating bands of red and white. Other pieces show the same deep red adjacent to areas of blue and yellow. A large group has blue areas on which red shapes appear, bands, waves, elements of circles or rectangles. A part of a life-size red head on blue ground occurs in one complex. It seems likely that the outer Propylon was decorated with a tribute-bearing procession.

The floor of the outer portico of the Propylon is made of stucco. The uppermost and latest coat is blue-gray at the surface and it flakes off in thin layers. Underneath is a coating somewhat thicker, white on the surface and throughout. No trace of painted decoration was observable. The pavement has suffered considerable damage in several places not only through the action of the fire but also from the roots of olive trees which forced their way and grew underneath it, causing it to crack and buckle rather badly (Fig. 43). The floor extends almost horizontally some 2 m. southeastward from the doorway, then after a gradual slope descends more sharply as it emerges from the portico into the outer court.

Centered in the outer façade of the Propylon in the axis of the doorway is a rounded stone base with a flat roughly circular raised standing place for a column (Fig. 47). The diameter of this circle varies from 0.425 m. to 0.47 m. The shape of the stone itself and its over-all dimensions are not determinable without destroying the floor. The wooden column was evidently set directly on the stone and a ring of stucco, perhaps for protection as well as for decoration, was laid around its bottom. The ring was made of many successive layers, some six or seven of which can be distinguished. The layers vary considerably in thickness, ranging from 0.005 m. to 0.025 m. They look as if they had been laid successively at different times and, so far as can be seen, each one bears a coat of red paint. The ring was perhaps easily damaged and had to be repaired or replaced from time to time. The final coat which is very thin made a flat band, ca. 0.09 m. broad, around the column and was then carried down to the floor in a smooth slope. The ring, as finally formed of many layers, had a total height of 0.095 m. It has suffered a good deal of injury especially on the northerly side, where the successive layers of plaster have been broken and displaced, and accurate measurements are no longer possible. The final coat had a diameter of ca. 0.66 m. at the top, and at floor level 0.715 m. The stucco of each layer which was laid directly against the column has preserved the impressions of the fluted shaft. The flutings are all small, shallow, and of irregular size and, because of considerable damage, are difficult to count but there seem to have been 64.

To the left of the doorway and directly in front of the anta block on the southwest side of the opening is a roughly rectangular sunken area paved with stucco (Figs. 9, 45). It seems to have belonged to an earlier phase before the final pavement of the outer portico of the Propylon was laid around it, raising the floor 0.015 m. to 0.02 m. higher. The sunken area extends approximately 1 m. outward from the anta and has a width of 0.85 m. to 0.90 m. On the analogy of similar areas marked off beside other doorways in the palace we think it may be explained as the stand for a sentry or an attendant.

The deposit covering the outer Propylon was 1.06 m. deep at the crosswall but diminished with the slope of the hillside toward the southeast to 0.56 m. The top stratum consisted of earth thrown out from the excavations of the preceding year. Beneath that was a layer of black cultivated earth, 0.10 m. to 0.15 m. thick, then a much deeper deposit of disintegrated crude brick of varying thickness covering a heap of blackish debris and fallen stones just outside the crosswall. This heap and the dissolved brick farther to the southeast rested on a thin stratum of dark gray ashy burned matter which covered the floor. In the debris of brick, from ca. 0.40 m. to 0.55 m. above the floor, were many fragments of plaster flooring or ceiling fallen from above. Throughout the whole deposit scattered potsherds occurred in abundance at all levels. Small objects and pieces of metal and stone lay well down in the layer of dissolved brick or directly on the floor. At a considerably higher level, however, mainly in the surface soil, were recovered numerous fragments of a silver cup which was decorated with gold inlays of bearded heads in a zone bordered by foliate sprays. A large nest of fragments of pottery, representing perhaps ten or a dozen stirrup-vases, was found in the southern quarter. Six have been restored.

O B J E C T S   F O U N D

G O L D

Heavy lump of melted gold, found near northeast wall.

Three small pieces, one with a hole in it, possibly a button; one attached to a chunk of bronze.

G O L D   A N D   S I L V E R

Fragmentary remains of a silver cup with inlaid decoration of gold and niello: several fragments of base, rim and handle (Fig. 263); nine pieces of gold inlay representing foliate bands (Fig. 262); five representations of bearded human heads in gold and niello, to which may be added, as belonging to the same cup, a fragment of the latter and five further heads found in surface soil above the floor of the inner porch of the Propylon (p. 62), another head, the eleventh, with a countersunk setting-place for a twelfth, which came from plowed earth above Ramp 59, and some additional pieces probably from the same vessel, which were recovered in Stoa 44 (p. 194), nearly all of which are illustrated in Fig. 261.[11]

The cup, which it has not yet been possible to reconstruct from its scanty fragments, was of relatively shallow rounded form; it was evidently similar to an example found by Tsountas in Chamber Tomb 24 at Mycenae.[12] Like the latter, it seems to have had, just below the rim, a decorated zone slightly more than 0.02 m. wide, which was presumably bordered above and below by a horizontal, delicately made, foliate band (Figs. 262, 267), the lower one broader than the upper.[13]

The heads, perhaps originally some 22 in number, were fitted into suitably shaped setting-places countersunk into a plain band; the latter was made of an alloy of metal, evidently not ordinary bronze. This band was fastened—perhaps by hammering—into a shallow horizontal chase or sinking which ran around the cup. The heads in their turn were fixed into the setting-places, no doubt by the same method of hammering, though carefully and neatly executed with a jeweler's tools and skill. The details of the heads were inlaid in gold and niello: gold rendering the skin of the face, ear and neck, niello outlining the head and delineating eyes, brows, hair and beard.

The heads vary considerably in their state of preservation and in their appearance. Four or five bear a fairly strong resemblance to one another, but there are no exact duplicates. The face, shown in profile, is regularly that of a youngish man with thick black hair hanging in waves down to the back of the neck and, in some instances, curling out at the bottom. Heavy eyebrows, almond-shaped eye, straight nose with the classic Greek profile, slightly parted lips (the upper lip shaved), heavy beard extending down the cheek from hair to chin and terminating in an elegant projecting point.

One would be rash to assert that these little heads present actual portraits of one or more specific individuals, although several of the face masks and a gem from the Shaft Graves at Mycenae give good ground for believing that some Mycenaean artists may have had real persons in mind, and even in their presence, when they worked. Surely these masks and the heads on the silver cup were not pure creations of fancy; they must have been drawn in part at least from life. It is likely that the artist who fashioned this cup has given us in these heads an authentic representation of the physiognomy of a wellborn young man of the Mycenaean *haut monde*—perhaps even a royal prince.

S I L V E R

Ribbed fragment, l. 0.025 m., w. 0.016 m., possibly belonging to cup with gold heads, and small curved piece (Fig. 265 Nos. 1, 2).

B R O N Z E

Rivet-head and many other fragments, for the most part badly twisted and corroded (e.g., Fig. 267).

---

[11] Heads (NM. 7842) vary from 0.018 m. to 0.02 m. in height, and from 0.013 m. to 0.014 m. in width. Strips decorated with foliate spray: nine pieces (NM. 7843, Fig. 262) range from 0.008 m. to 0.0115 m. in width and from 0.015 m. to 0.048 m. in length.

[12] NM. 2489, *EphArch* 1888, col. 143, pl. 7, 2; Mar-

inatos-Hirmer, *Krete kai Mykenaïke Hellas*, fig. 196 (at top).

[13] For the motive cf. *MP*, 396, fig. 69, Motive 64:23 and 24, although the cup is probably considerably later than the period to which Furumark attributes those motives.

STONE

Pendant or amulet of polished black stone with white striations—banded agate— (NM. 7798, Fig. 266 No. 4). Shaped like a flattened or broadened V, 0.039 m. long, 0.016 m. wide; small hole for attachment in upper edge near each end.

Fragment of ornament in banded agate (NM. 7799, Fig. 266 No. 3), 0.025 m. long, 0.022 m. wide.

Fragments of rock crystal (e.g., Fig. 267).

Small rectangular bead or button of dark gray stone (Fig. 267), 0.015 m. long, 0.014 m. wide, 0.003 m. thick; d. of hole 0.003 m.

Small leaf-shaped arrowhead of light gray flint (?) neatly worked (Fig. 267), l. 0.023 m., max. w. 0.016 m., max. th. 0.002 m.

Two joining fragments of a stone lamp (NM. 7809, Fig. 269 No. 12), 0.175 m. long, 0.06 m. wide. Edge of bowl, ca. 0.04 m. high, decorated with irregular horizontal flutings or grooves—seven grooves, eight ridges.

PASTE

Fragment of *kyanos* or blue paste, very finely and delicately decorated with wings of a griffin (?) (Fig. 266 No. 5). Rounded in shape with part of the edge preserved, ca. 0.022 m. by 0.02 m.; max. th. ca. 0.003 m.

CLAY

Sealing: NM. 8527 = *CMMS* 310, lion from left and above attacking woolly sheep or goat to right with head turned back.

Tablets: Nos. 1176, 1177, 1180-1182.[14] In addition fragments which joined pieces previously found in neighboring areas and already numbered (e.g., Nos. 695, 937).

POTTERY

Krater (Shape 59, p. 396)
No. 828 (Fig. 383).

Stirrup-vase (Shape 65b 3, p. 406)
Nos. 1164 (Fig. 389), 1165-1169 and four other unrestorable examples; all decorated.

Stirrup-vase (Shape 65d, p. 408)
Incomplete example; no decoration in shoulder zone.

Among the miscellaneous potsherds were counted 80 kylix stems and bases and 90 flat bases of cups or bowls. Other shapes represented: basin with pinched-out handles, jug, tankard; and in coarse ware, cooking pot, tripod-vessel, pithos. Almost all of the pottery was of plain undecorated types but a few fragments bore painted patterns.

PROPYLON, INNER PORCH (2)

As shown by the threshold the doorway leading from the outer to the inner portico of the Propylon was approximately 1.40 m. wide (Fig. 429). On the outer side no evidence was found to indicate the character of the door and how it opened. On the other side, however, in the inner portico of the gateway (2 on Key Plan) is a rectangular hole lined with stones at the northeastern end of the threshold block overlapping the latter and the block supporting the door jamb. This hole, measuring roughly 0.20 m. by 0.24 m. and 0.315 m. deep, might well have held the lower end of a substantial post on which a door could have swung or it might possibly have been the setting-place for the socket of a pivot. The stones lining the hole are blackened and some carbon was found in the earth filling. At the southwestern side of the doorway nothing indicated that there ever was a door post or pivot.

The inner portico of the Propylon presumably had the same width as the outer (since the southwestern wall is missing, exact measurements are not possible) but it is slightly deeper (Fig. 46), having a depth of 4.05 m. The crosswall on the inner

---

14 Tablets are published in *PT II* unless otherwise specified.

side shows a groove for a horizontal beam like that on the southeast but its level is 0.05 m. to 0.07 m. lower and the two anta blocks have been cut down on top and adjusted to that level. Here also two dowel holes appear in the southwestern block (Fig. 429); but in the northeastern there are four which look as if they may represent two phases. The horizontal groove extends to the northeastern lateral wall and then continues northwestward in that wall. Here it is almost exactly like the corresponding groove in the section to the southeast of the crosswall with a height of a little more than 0.30 m. and, in some places, the graining of the wood[15] is visible, impressed in the clay at the back of the groove. Four vertical chases may be counted between the crosswall and the anta block at the northwest end of the wall. Scanty traces of plaster are preserved here and there up to a height of 0.95 m. The highest point of the wall still surviving is 1.10 m. above the floor.

The anta block at the end of the northeast wall is ca. 0.40 m. high determining the height of the dado (Fig. 44). It is 0.93 m. wide from southeast to northwest and 1.05 m. long from northeast to southwest. Including two or three coats of plaster it measures 0.94 m. by 1.10 m. Of the four dowel holes one or two perhaps served for the fastening of the beam coming from the southeast, the others held the timber running northeastward. It is possible that the two beams met in a dovetailed joint.

The southwestern part of the crosswall has a length of 1.91 m. beyond which it was destroyed at the time the southwest wall of the Propylon was removed (Fig. 44). On the northwestern face of the crosswall remains of three or four successive coats of plaster can be recognized. Each bears traces of painted decoration in multiple arcs, in colors varying from phase to phase, similar to those used on the other side of the wall and elsewhere in the palace in the corresponding dado course (p. 249). The horizontal groove for a large beam directly above the dado is like that on the northeastern side of the doorway.

The stucco floor of the inner portico has suffered considerably more damage from fire than that of the outer porch. The original surface is preserved only in a few patches, one on the northeasterly side and two on the southwesterly, all exhibiting a dark blue shiny finish, which may have been produced by paint or by smoke. The greater part of the rest of the area has been burned and worn down into the rough pebbly core of the pavement.

On and above the floor were found quantities of fallen plaster; much of it, white or plain blue with red splashes, came from a floor or floors, some pieces composed of several layers. Another variety, plain and finer, either blue or black, may be from ceiling. Plaster with painted decoration came for the most part from the northeast

---

[15] A sample of charcoal (P 329), found in the groove above the dado at the eastern corner, was submitted to the C14 Laboratory at the University of Pennsylvania. The results of the examination yielded datings of 1306± 55 B.C. and 1437± 57 B.C. For details of method see *AJA* 65 (1961), 366.

wall. The composition, as reconstituted by Miss Lang and Mr. de Jong, is laid out in zones: above a lower border formed by four horizontal stripes of white, brown, and blue and brown, was a frieze of alternating purple and yellow argonauts with tentacles of the alternate color. Above this, the border stripes are repeated and in the next zone appears a variety of motives: horses' hoofs, architectural façades, feeding deer, and seated ladies. The nautilus frieze was repeated still higher together with the border stripes so that the total height was ca. 0.65 m. The composition as a whole thus somewhat resembled the repeating scenic wallpapers of the eighteenth or nineteenth century. It is likely that the missing southwest wall and the southeast wall on each side of the doorway bore decoration of the same general kind.

A few small bits of frescoes, which appear to be of earlier date, had probably been incorporated in the crude bricks of the superstructure that had disintegrated and filled the Propylon or in the floor or ceiling fallen from above. One piece has a procession of small red men in blue and another has a rosette apparently from a running spiral like that from the drain under Room 60.

Centered along the axis of the doorway and no doubt once equidistant between the two antae, is the stone base of the column that faced the inner Court of the Megaron (Figs. 43, 48). The stone has been considerably damaged by the effects of the fire but like the one in the outer portico it had a raised circular standing place, 0.47 m. in diameter, for the wooden column. The base itself cannot be measured without destroying the floor covering it. Powdery, carbonized remains of the actual column, roughly cylindrical in shape, with a diameter of ca. 0.25 m., were found still rising to a height of 0.72 m. directly above the base (Fig. 46). It is evident that in the burning the shaft must have shrunk considerably. This column too was fitted with a decorative painted stucco ring, the southeastern half of which has suffered great damage. The northwestern half is much better preserved: some seven successive coats of stucco can be counted, each, so far as discernible, still showing some traces of color, probably once red. In the northwestern part of the ring the impressions of the flutings of the column have survived in a remarkably good state. Count of a quarter circle indicated 16 flutings and the column must therefore have had 64. The diameter of the column was calculated to be ca. 0.47 m. The thickness of the successive stucco layers in the many rings varies considerably from less than one centimeter to 0.03 m. The total height of the ring in the latest phase can only be estimated but it was probably at least 0.10 m.

Approximately 0.25 m. to the northwest of the stucco ring, 4.11 m. distant from, and parallel to the threshold block of the doorway, a distinct strip of weathering is visible in the floor stretching across the whole width of the Propylon (Fig. 44). This obviously marks the line of the edge of the roof and was presumably made by the drip of rain water from the overhang.

The inner stoa of the Propylon was filled with deposit, 1.04 m. deep, similar to that in the outer stoa: cultivated earth, ca. 0.20 m. thick, on top; under it debris containing a good many stones, then yellowish dissolved crude brick and below black carbonized matter going down to the floor. In the southern quarter, near the line of the missing southwest wall, the dissolved brick was red and hard baked, overlying a thin gray ashy stratum that covered the floor. Here was exposed a large group of more than 50 fragments of tablets, some of them almost fused to the floor with the inscribed face down. On the floor near the doorway were the shattered remains of a large pedestaled krater, some pieces of which had been badly warped, twisted, and partly vitrified by the fire (Fig. 387 No. 1151). Scattered about, but mainly concentrated just inside the doorway, relatively high above the floor, were many fragments of gold inlay and silver, further remnants of the shallow cup found in the outer stoa.

The columns of the Propylon both in the outer and the inner portico supported a relatively heavy entablature which evidently was made of large squared blocks of poros. On the pavement outside both façades many blocks of this kind were found extending in an irregular row across each end of the building as they had fallen at the time of the fire (Figs. 14, 49). They must have been carried by extremely heavy wooden beams that served as architraves spanning the space from the lateral walls to the column. So far as we could observe no evidence remained to give details regarding the exact form of the entablature. The considerable number of fragments of stucco floor which had fallen from above suggests that there may have been an upper story or a flat terrace.

OBJECTS FOUND

GOLD
Bead.
Fragment of narrow band with holes in it.
Five heads belonging to silver cup (p. 58 and Fig. 261).

SILVER
Piece of handle of cup with the gold heads (Fig. 263).

BRONZE
Strip with one edge rolled, the other also apparently finished (Fig. 265 No. 5), l. 0.062 m., w. 0.015 m., th. 0.001 m. to 0.002 m.
Many thin twisted pieces and shapeless bits (e.g., Figs. 267, 265 No. 4).

LEAD
Shapeless lump.

STONE
Crystal: two pieces from narrow strip, perhaps an inlay; a thicker piece with two smooth faces, smoked and much damaged by fire (e.g., Fig. 267).
Flint: tip of small, light red arrowhead (Fig. 267), l. pres. 0.021 m., w. 0.012 m., max. th. 0.003 m.

CLAY
Tablets: Nos. 853-886, 954-975, 1174, 1175, 1178, 1179. Two fragments were found to join tablets which came from nearby areas and had already been numbered (Nos. 502, 851).

POTTERY
Pedestaled krater (Shape 63, p. 400) No. 1151 (Fig. 387), decorated.

Potsherds collected in considerable quantities from top to bottom of the deposit include 26 kylix stems, 44 flat bases of bowls and cups, fragments of jugs, basins and bowls with pinched-out handles and, in coarse ware, pieces of tripod cooking vessels and a jar. A few bits bear traces of painted decoration including one stray sherd of LH I.

COURT OF THE MEGARON (3)

From the Propylon one enters the Court of the Megaron (3 on Key Plan), which is some 12.90 m. long from northeast to southwest and 7.30 m. wide. The whole court was open to the sky and was paved with stucco (Part 2, Frontispiece and Fig. 9). In order to carry off the rain water the entire area was given a general slope toward the south corner, near which three holes open through a stone slab into an underground channel (Fig. 44). The latter ran southwestward and, joining another branch, turned more to the southward to empty into what seems to have been the main drain of this section of the palace (p. 233 note 78).

The southeastern wall of the Court to the northeast of the Propylon juts out 0.40 m. beyond the anta of the latter (Fig. 44). The superstructure of the wall has been destroyed except in the last 1.45 m. of its course, where the core and rear face still stand to a height of 0.80 m. above the dado course. The latter, rising 0.38 m. above the floor, is formed by four large squared blocks of poros of varying lengths but aggregating 3.60 m., each one bearing on its face toward the Court remnants of plaster lacking its finishing coat. The blocks are level on top and each has a dowel hole for the fastening of a horizontal wooden beam. Impressed on the clay of the rubble backing above the dado course appears the graining of wood in two horizontal strips, the lower 0.20 m. high, the upper 0.10 m., with an intervening space 0.15 m. wide that shows no imprint of wood. Consequently it looks as if horizontal beams alternating with bands of other material, presumably stone, decorated the face of the wall. This type of wainscoting, if it may be so called, seems to be represented elsewhere in the palace.

At its northeastern end the dado course meets a large anta block projecting 0.80 m. into the Court. It has a width of 0.90 m. and properly belongs to the Stoa which faces the Court on the northeast (pp. 190ff.).

In the corner to the southwest of the Propylon nothing has survived of the southeastern boundary of the Court which was presumably removed by seekers after building material. The wall was, in any event, hardly more than 1.80 m. long to its junction with the southwestern wall of the Court. Whether it had a projecting angle to balance that on the northeastern side could not be ascertained.

The southwestern wall (0.80 m. high, 0.85 m. thick, and 5.94 m. long) is built in the manner that prevails throughout the palace with horizontal grooves and vertical slots for the wooden framework. There were apparently seven uprights in the total length. The wall has suffered considerable damage at its southeastern end where the stones of the face toward the Court are missing. What is left at this end consists largely of chunks of *migma*, fused together by the fire.

The pavement of the Court has almost everywhere lost its upper finishing coat, except in the easterly corner where some traces of it have survived. Near the southern corner, where a break in the pavement allowed probing, it was found that the stucco varies from 0.065 m. to 0.12 m. in thickness, and four successive coats could be distinguished. Whether they belonged to as many different phases or indicate that the floor was laid at one time in multiple coatings could not be determined, but the former alternative seemed more likely. A court without a roof, exposed to the elements, must surely have suffered damage from time to time that required repairs if not the relaying of the whole pavement. In the western angle, too, where the pavement of the Court joined that of the Portico, it was possible to examine the method of paving the Court and the thickness of the stucco. Here only a single coat 0.07 m. thick could be recognized, but the upper surface was lacking. In its present state the Court showed no sign that the pavement once bore painted decoration.

When excavated in 1952 and 1953 the Court was found covered to a depth of ca. 1.20 m., diminishing in a slope from northeast to southwest: at the top, plowed earth 0.15 m. deep; below that, stretching across most of the Court as if filling a hollow, a deep deposit of small stones and very black earth containing some scattered fragments of late Geometric ware of the seventh century, from which part of an oenochoe with trefoil mouth was put together. To northeast and southwest of this hollow the accumulation consisted of ash and rubble. Under this and under the black layer resting on the floor was a stratum of firm brown or yellow clay, dissolved crude brick. Throughout the debris scattered fragments of pottery occurred in profusion.

On the stucco pavement alongside the four dado blocks of the southeast wall some pieces of plaster were recovered showing traces of decoration.

O B J E C T S   F O U N D

From deposit of black earth and small stones

STONE

Fragment of the foot of a table or lampstand of veined purplish-red stone (Fig. 271 No. 5) calcined. Has simple molding at bottom; pres. h. 0.17 m., pres. w. 0.10 m., pres. th. 0.05 m.

POTTERY

Oenochoe (Fig. 347 No. 827). Most of rim, scattered parts of body and all of base missing. H. pres. 0.268 m., d. neck 0.064 m., d. body 0.187 m., w. handle 0.024 m. Mottled light and dark greenish-gray clay. Geometric, probably of seventh century.

Numerous small fragments of Geometric ware coated with blackish glaze.

From deposit of yellow clay above floor

GOLD

Earring or pendant (NM. 7778, Fig. 273 No. 1), l. 0.016 m., w. 0.0065 m.: broken at upper end; hollow, made of thin plate in two pieces soldered together.

SILVER

Two pieces.

BRONZE

Fragment of knife in two pieces (e.g., Fig. 268 c); one thick heavy chunk, three flat pieces.

STONE

Obsidian: arrowhead (point missing), tip of another and a blade (Fig. 268 c).

Fragment of lamp or vase of dark gray with flecks of white (Fig. 268 c), two joining pieces of which (Fig. 269 No. 11) were found nearby in the Portico.

Fragment of vase? (Fig. 269 No. 4).

CLAY

Tablet: No. 637, fragment from the end of what appears to be a long narrow tablet with two incised lines but no signs; found in brown earth below black intrusion.

POTTERY

Amphora (Fig. 345 No. 3): fragment comprising complete rim, narrow neck with upper half of one flattened handle, part of shoulder and lower half of the other handle. Damaged by fire. Surface mottled; possibly had painted decoration.

Hydria (Fig. 345 No. 4): one third of shoulder and neck preserved (no rim) along with one flat vertical handle from zone above shoulder almost to top of neck and one of the two horizontal round loop-handles in middle zone. Body divided into three zones by broad triple parallel bands. Wavy line descends handle and continues down across triple bands and middle zone. Similar spiraliform pattern in upper zone on each side.

The casual sherds include: 92 kylix stems, 21 flat bases of bowls and cups, fragments of conical cups, a good many pinched-out handles of bowls and basins, a krater and, in coarse ware, scoops, tripod vessels, and pithoi. The pieces with painted decoration represent a kylix, a jug or jar, an amphora, stirrup-vases, a krater-bowl. Among the patterns noted are spirals, rosettes, tennis racquet, etc. One piece probably of LH II, two fragments of Mycenaean III A, most pieces of III B.

PORTICO OF THE MEGARON (4)

Facing the Court on the northwest is the Portico that leads to the Vestibule and the Throne Room (Part 2, Frontispiece). The Portico (4 on Key Plan) is 11.27 m. broad and has a depth of 4.34 m. from front to back (Fig. 9). The northeast wall, ca. 1.20 m. thick and preserved to a maximum height of approximately 1 m., ends at the southeast in an anta that rests on one great block (Fig. 45). The anta base, which has the same height as the baseboard (0.26 m. to 0.27 m.) and projects in an offset ca. 0.05 m. from the line of the latter, is 1.37 m. long and 1.27 m. wide. The baseboard serving as a dado is faced with a veneer of limestone almost like marble, 0.045 m. thick, with smoothly finished surface. When originally set, the stone was probably intended to be visible but in a later phase it was covered with plaster, nearly all of which is rough; but in one place, where the smooth surface is preserved, traces of painted arcs and vertical lines follow the customary pattern. On the dado course rested the usual large horizontal beam. It may have been part of a wooden panel or wainscoting nearly 0.45 m. high, which was crowned by another band of stone and then in turn by another wooden beam. In this wall, as shown by the chases, were five vertical timbers on each face connected by transverse struts. The wall suffered great damage from the fire and much of the stone was burned into lime. Some pieces of charred wood and carbon from the lowest horizontal beam were submitted for analysis under the Carbon 14 method to Miss Elizabeth K. Ralph, scientist of the University Museum, Philadelphia. The result for this sample (P 328) when the calculation was made on the basis of the Libby half-life value gave a date of 1265±57 B.C.; using a new measurement of the half-life of 5800 years, the calculation worked out the date of the sample to 1394±59 B.C.[16]

The section of the rear wall of the Portico to the northeast of the doorway, ca. 1 m. thick, 3.90 m. long, and standing to a maximum height of 1.05 m., seems in its details to have been almost exactly like the northeast wall just described, having the same limestone baseboard and evidence of the same wooden wainscoting surmounted by a course of stone. In the total length there were at least three vertical beams on each face of the wall. This section, too, was largely converted into lime by the fire. Toward the southwest it ends in an anta (Fig. 50), projecting from the baseboard in an offset of ca. 0.05 m. The block that forms the base of the anta, including its plaster, is 0.98 m. long on the side toward the Portico and 1.04 m. wide.

At its junction with the baseboard the beveled end of the latter was fitted into a diagonal V-shaped slot cut into the end of the block. On the top along the outer edge of the block is a line of weathering, corresponding in width to the offset. The end toward the doorway was cut back to a depth of 0.055 m. to 0.09 m. in an area 0.265 m. high, leaving only a projecting edge along the southeast side and the bottom of the block. The edge along the outer face is ca. 0.10 m. broad but there is no corresponding projection of the stone on the inside face of the block, where, however, a thin projection in plaster seems to have been substituted.

On the top of the block are five rectangular dowel holes, ca. 0.095 m. deep, two on the southeast, three on the northwest (Fig. 430); and traces of charred wood indicate that wooden beams rested along the outer[17] and inner side and the end toward the doorway. These timbers were probably square in section, measuring 0.25 m. or more on a side. The weather line mentioned above might be taken to show that the beam on the side toward the Portico was set back 0.05 m. from the face of the block, leaving exposed a strip as wide as the offset.

The section of the same wall to the southwest of the doorway, 3.91 m. long and

16 *AJA* 65 (1961), 366f.

17 A sample of charcoal (P 330) from a horizontal beam above the dado, behind the sentry stand on the northeast side of the doorway, was examined at the University of Pennsylvania; the results gave alternative datings of 1405±40 B.C. and 1540±42 B.C. Cf. *AJA* 65 (1961), 366.

ca. 1 m. thick, stands to a maximum height of 1.05 m. above the floor. The anta block flanking the doorway is almost square, measuring approximately 1 m. on a side not including plaster. The end of the block toward the opening (Fig. 52) shows the same treatment as that of the corresponding block on the other side of the doorway, save that the cutting is more regular (0.07 m. deep). Here too a projection of the stone along the inner face was lacking but was supplied by a narrow application of plaster. Only two of the dowel holes for the wooden timbers have been seen; the other two no doubt exist under the fused ruins of the wall.

In the form of the joint between the anta and the limestone baseboard (now largely missing) and in its apparent alternation of wooden wainscoting and stone bands this section of the wall was like the part to the northeast of the doorway. Here too there seem to have been three vertical slots for timbers. In both sections of the wall the paneling toward the Vestibule differed from that toward the Portico.

Only a short piece of the southwest wall (Fig. 53), ca. 1.20 m. thick, is preserved, the limestone baseboard extending 1.29 m. from the corner.[18] The foundations, resting on *stereo*, continued only 1.46 m. farther; beyond that point no further trace has survived (Fig. 51). It is likely that the end of the wall was removed long ago for the planting of an olive tree, though the massive anta block, if it was like the one on the opposite side of the Portico, might well have aroused the cupidity of seekers of building material. The preserved part of the wall with its foundation retains evidence for two upright beams with cross struts.[19]

In the façade of the Portico stood two columns almost symmetrically spaced between the antae of the lateral walls and nearly opposite the antae of the doorway.[20] The columns were, of course, made of wood and only the stone bases are left (Fig. 50). The northeast base was very badly cracked by the effects of the fire. It is a roughly circular block of stone with a diameter of approximately 0.68 m. On the upper surface in low relief is a smaller circle some 0.48 m. in diameter which was the standing place of the column and presumably indicates the diameter of the shaft. A decorative stucco ring was evidently laid around the foot of the column as in the Propylon but almost no remains of it have survived. Only the slightest traces of impressions of flutings—if they are real—can now be seen.

The southwest base is also a circular block of stone 0.70 m. in diameter, and it is still unbroken. On its upper surface are slight traces of an inner circle in low relief

[18] This part ends in a finished edge and thus indicates that the slab of the baseboard was 1.29 m. long. The adjoining section in the northwest wall is only 1.20 m. long.

[19] On the northeast face of the wall at 1.47 m. to 1.67 m. from the west corner, the chase filled with soft black carbonized deposit continued down 0.13 m. below the floor where it rested on a packing of small stones. The shape of the chase suggests that the beam was half of a tree trunk with the flat side toward the face of the wall.

[20] All measurements to center of column bases: anta of northeast wall to northeast column base 3.54 m.; column base to column base 4.04 m.; southwest column base to line of southwest wall 3.62 m.; anta northeast of doorway to northeast column base 3.57 m.; anta southwest of doorway to southwest column base 3.54 m.

with a diameter of ca. 0.49 m. Some remains of the decorative stucco ring are preserved on the northerly side of the base. The ring seems to have been built up of plaster over a core of smallish stones, the latter resting on the stone base and the plaster overlapping the painted floor of the Portico. Several applications of plaster apparently formed the ring, but the surfaces exposed are not sufficiently well preserved to retain any certain traces of color.

Against the northeast anta of the doorway is a raised platform projecting into the Portico 0.90 m. from the plastered face of the anta (Fig. 50). It rises ca. 0.08 m. or 0.09 m. above the floor of the Portico. At the outer end it is somewhat damaged and exact measurements are not possible but it may have been 0.92 m. wide. At its inner end it is only 0.85 m. wide and here it extends 0.21 m. southwestward beyond the anta block. Belonging obviously to the last phase of occupation, this platform was carelessly made, jutting out from the wall at an awkward angle. In the damaged outer part of the stand the stucco pavement of an earlier underlying stand still retaining traces of paint can be seen rising no more than 0.01 m. above the floor of the Portico. Like the one in the Propylon this was presumably the post of a sentry beside the doorway.

In the southwestern part of the area it was possible, as already mentioned above, to determine that the thickness of the pavement in the Court is 0.07 m. and that of the Portico 0.055 m. where they meet. In each instance we seem to have a single thick underlayer; in the Portico as well as in the Court it was laid on a sterile bedding, 0.16 m. deep, apparently made of the same material as that of the *stereo* on which it rested. On the thick stucco base relatively thin smooth finishing coats were successively applied to bear the painted decoration of the floor.

Just outside the column bases and approximately in line with the ends of the antae, a strip of pavement, varying from 0.15 m. to 0.30 m. in width and relatively well preserved, runs all the way across the front of the Portico (Fig. 50). This clearly follows the line of the drip from the edge of the roof above. Whether it represents a patchy repair in the final phase of the palace or owes its preservation to dampness from the drip or to some other kind of protection is not now determinable. Behind the strip across the middle part of the Portico, the floor is very badly damaged, rough and uneven except in one section in the southwestern area. Along the northeastern, northwestern, and southwestern walls the state of preservation is much better and remains of the floor decoration in some places have survived remarkably well (Fig. 56). Several layers are certainly represented and it is very difficult to recognize the continuity of any one coating. The final coat is missing or has suffered serious injury almost everywhere; but near the southwestern wall some traces of red color indicated that the finished surface was once decorated.

In the next earlier phase the decoration of the floor was laid out in three rows of almost square rectangles running from northeast to southwest; they were separated one from the other by paired incised lines, 0.05 m. to 0.06 m. apart, which enclosed between them a band of darkish red paint. The middle row was slightly wider than the one along the rear wall of the Portico; the outer (southeastern) row has suffered almost total destruction, and neither its width nor its relation to the columns in the façade of the porch can now be determined. The general design was not carefully worked out to fit symmetrically the space between the lateral walls of the Portico. Eight rectangles, with an average length of 1.35 m., plus the total width of the eight bordering stripes, would have filled the available area very tidily; but the eight rectangles that were actually marked out were only ca. 1.28 m. long, and in consequence a space of some 0.425 m. (about one third of a normal rectangle) was left over at the southwestern end of the row. It was decorated in the same manner as the ordinary quadrangles. Similar irregularities occur even in the Throne Room (p. 83) and it is clear that in the late phases of the palace aesthetic sensibilities were not easily offended.

The badly damaged state of the floor made it extremely difficult to see and identify minor details of the decorative elements; but from faint traces here and there Mr. de Jong was able to make out and record many of the patterns represented. In the row alongside the back wall of the porch, beginning from the northeast, we see in the first rectangle a favorite motive made up of four groups of concentric arcs, radiating from each corner, with a central unit formed by two concentric diamond-shaped figures. The second rectangle was filled with closely spaced parallel zigzags; No. 3 was occupied by numerous small single dotted circles scattered about fairly thickly, but without perceptible order. No. 4 bears remains of a net- or scale-pattern. The fifth rectangle is blank, owing to injury by the fire. No. 6 displays vestiges of parallel zigzags, and No. 7 repeats freely the dotted single circles, while No. 8 reverts once again to the motive of the four groups of concentric arcs. The little extra panel at the end of the row seems to have had a different decoration of transverse parallel bands.

In the second or middle row, following the same order from the northeast, we see in rectangle No. 1 remnants of parallel zigzags. No. 2 is undecipherable; No. 3 bears a net-pattern; Nos. 4 and 5 are damaged beyond recognition. Four groups of concentric arcs appear again in No. 6; No. 7 bears a repetition of the net-motive; parallel zigzags, like those in No. 1, appear in the eighth rectangle; and the narrow panel forming the end of the row has a similar zigzag, but it is turned around to run at right angles to the same motive in the neighboring No. 8.

In the third row the only preserved remnants of decoration which may be seen in Rectangle 7, probably belong to another repetition of the four groups of concentric arcs.

In general it may be said that the patterns which are repeated are never exact duplications: each was made freely, with variations in details, in color, in orientation as well as in the whim of the painter of the moment.

At the northeast end of the third row, near the face of the anta, a remnant of floor painting in a different style has survived. Two odd-looking fish, each represented with a broad head and a body tapering to a spreading tail, resemble some fish uncovered in Room 50 (p. 214 and Fig. 163). They seem to be painted in a space, 0.16 m. to 0.20 m. wide, alongside the wall, and bordered on the southwest by a pair of incised lines which frame a rectangle to the southwest. This marine scene appears thus not to belong to the system described above, and it is equally difficult to recognize any connection with the ruined upper coat of the stucco pavement. The fish probably belong to a phase antedating the two already mentioned. The stucco floors in the palace, which were evidently accustomed to rough treatment, were no doubt frequently damaged to an extent requiring repair or replacement, and there is no occasion to assume that there was any great lapse of time between such accidents.

The Portico was buried under an accumulation, ca. 1.25 m. deep: plowed earth at the top; beneath it, in the center, a continuation of the depression filled with black earth and stones seen in the Court (p. 64), here 0.50 m. deep. Under the black stony deposit and at each end of the depression, fine brown earth, dry, ashy, and sandy but fairly hard with many patches of dissolved red crude brick. At bottom, resting on the floor, a firm light brown stratum.

From the Portico came a considerable amount of fallen plaster decorated with the wavy arcs customary in dados. The biggest pieces, one of which is an outside corner, are painted in black, red, white, and yellow. Some fragments are painted red with black lines representing wood-graining. A few small fragments, possibly from compositions representing animals, may have come from crude bricks or the clay filling of the wall.

The deposit filling the Portico contained in addition to a good many miscellaneous objects made of various materials, badly damaged by fire and for the most part of unrecognizable use (e.g., Fig. 268 b), a fairly large quantity of scattered potsherds and a coarse pot which lay on the floor.

OBJECTS FOUND

SILVER
Five thin fragments.

BRONZE
Knife (NM. 7796, Fig. 274 No. 5), l. 0.218 m., l. tang 0.043 m., max. w. 0.027 m., w. tang 0.018 m., broken into two pieces but well preserved; slightly curved tapering blade, blunt end; one rivet hole centered at junction of blade and tang, another about midway up tang and two more side by side near end of tang; the latter terminated in

two prongs or projections which have crumbled away.

38 pieces: mostly shapeless, some large, twisted and bent, some thin and flat; one bit of thin bronze wire; one piece from rim, flat on top and 0.0035 m. wide, of a very small vessel; two from a knife, one piece with rivet hole, the other with end of rivet.

IVORY

Seven bits.

STONE

Two joining fragments of vase or lamp of dark gray with flecks of white (NM. 7795, Fig. 269 No. 11), l. 0.06 m., w. 0.045 m., th. of wall 0.015 m. Hole or opening has a diameter of 0.022 m. Another piece of the same found in Court 3 (Fig. 268 c).

Two fragments of lamps (Fig. 269 Nos. 8, 9).

PASTE

Fragment of *kyanos*.

POTTERY

Krater (probably Shape 59, p. 396)

Fragments fused to the floor and partly vitrified.

Scattered sherds

Shapes represented: in coarse ware, pithos, cooking pot; in fine ware, kylix (more than 20 stems), conical cup, bowl with pinched-out handles, alabastron. Some pieces bear traces of painted decoration.

VESTIBULE OF THE MEGARON (5)

The doorway leading from the Portico to the Vestibule (Figs. 54, 430) and approximately centered in the axis of the latter, has a maximum width of 3.48 m. between the ends of the flanking antae. At about the level of the floor this space was filled with three large squared blocks; the central one, 1.95 m. long and 0.93 m. wide, formed the threshold and a lateral block on each side, 1 m. deep and 0.75 m. wide, must have supported the wooden door casing and jambs. The actual opening was thus narrowed to approximately the length of the threshold. It is not clear precisely how far the wooden casings framing the doorway extended. Abundant remains of charred wood and ashes were found on the southwestern block, but they did not indicate the exact size and limits of the casing. The blocks that supported the jambs rise up 0.01 m. to 0.02 m. above the level of the threshold and the one to the northeast was cut back on its northwestern face (Fig. 55) 0.05 m. for a distance of 0.28 m. perhaps to adjust its width to that of the contiguous threshold block. The latter was covered on top with a thin coat of stucco, possibly in connection with one of the later renovations of the adjacent floors.

At each end of the threshold block, on the outer face at its junction with the jamb base, is a roughly rounded cavity apparently cut partly in the threshold block but extending out into the stucco floor. Both are in a bad state of preservation; the one on the southwest has a diameter of 0.065 m. The other is somewhat larger but the edge is broken away. They look as if they could have held a socket for a pivot on which the door swung or perhaps for a bar to hold the door open. The workmanship is clumsy and careless and must presumably be assigned to one of the late phases of the palace.

Alongside the inner face of the northeasterly jamb block and overlapping the end of the threshold by some 0.12 m. is a curious irregular slot 0.70 m. long and 0.15 m. to 0.20 m. wide and with a maximum depth of 0.23 m. (Fig. 55). Its purpose is problematical. It does not look like a hole for the socket of a pivot on which a door could swing. It might possibly have been made to support a stand of some kind for spears and other weapons kept in this place against the ·door jamb. Was it perhaps the bottom of a spear-rack like that in which Telemachos placed the spear of which he relieved Athena when she came to the palace of Odysseus in the guise of Mentes, leader of the Taphians (*Odyssey* I, 127ff.)?

At the other end of the threshold there is no corresponding slot nor is there any trace of a pivot on the inner side. If there were no pivots in the earlier phases, it is imaginable that hinges of some kind could have been attached to the wooden jambs. One may, however, regard it as perhaps more likely that the opening was closed by heavy hangings rather than by a real door.

The Vestibule itself (5 on Key Plan) has a depth from front to back of 4.54 m. and a width from northeast to southwest of 11.62 m. (Fig. 57). Opposite the entrance from the Portico is an equally broad doorway that led into the Throne Room (Fig. 54). Centered in the northeasterly end of the Vestibule a narrower door opening gave access to a long lateral corridor and beyond it to a stairway ascending to an upper floor (Fig. 58). It is likely that a similar doorway at the southwestern end of the Vestibule opened into another lateral corridor on the far side of which was also a stairway. But the evidence for this southwestern doorway is lacking since the greater part of the wall and its foundations have been destroyed (Fig. 60), perhaps having been removed to allow the planting of an olive tree some 7 m. distant from the conjectural olive tree mentioned above (p. 67). That is the standard interval between trees in laying out olive groves in this part of Messenia today.

The walls of the Vestibule except on the southwest are preserved to a height of ca. 1 m. to 1.20 m. (Fig. 59). The construction in general is like that of the walls already described. The vertical chases indicate that the upright beams were of the usual generous size.[21] The horizontal beams on the inner face of the outer wall of the Vestibule, on the contrary, seem to have been much smaller both in width and thickness.[22] On the outer wall both northeast and southwest of the doorway a good deal of rough plaster still remains in its place. In the late phases of the palace at least, this coating was laid over the wooden beams in their grooves and chases, hiding them

---

[21] The middle one of the three upright beams in the outer wall to the northeast of the doorway seems to have rested on a stone at a level ca. 0.10 m. below the floor.

[22] One apparently was laid at the level of the top of the anta base, another some 0.33 m. higher. These seem to have been only 0.09 m. or 0.10 m. thick. A third, so far as surviving evidence in the wall indicates, lay 0.50 m. still higher.

from view. Nowhere is the smoothly finished final coat preserved but a good many fallen pieces of painted plaster lay on the floor.

The northeastern wall, ca. 1 m. thick, conforms in almost every respect with the one just described. The doorway seems not to have been flanked by well marked antae and the exact form of the door jambs is not clear. The threshold consists of a massive block 1 m. wide on the Vestibule side, 1.05 m. on the corridor side, and 1.12 m. long from front to back (Figs. 58, 448). It is set 0.025 m. deeper than the floor in the Vestibule and 0.03 m. higher than the floor in the corridor. On each flank is a smaller block of approximately the same length as the threshold, the north-western 0.50 m. wide, the southeastern 0.52 m. Each was laid with its top 0.03 m. higher than the level of the threshold block. Each one on the side toward the open-ing, and 0.16 m. from the inner edge of the threshold, has a rectangular cutting 0.07 m. square and from 0.055 m. to 0.07 m. deep, obviously intended to hold the socket for a pivot. From this socket to the face of the block in the corridor a rabbet has been cut 0.01 m. deep, splaying slightly toward the corridor. It is clear that a door with two leaves swung outward from the Vestibule. The face of the wooden door jamb may have coincided with the line of the rabbet.

The surviving stump of the southwestern wall, ca. 1 m. thick and only 0.95 m. long, requires no detailed description (Fig. 60). Its foundations rest on *stereo* some 0.40 m. below the floor. Its inner face retains considerable remnants of rough plaster in a thick coat.

The rear wall of the Vestibule consists of two sections: the one to the northeast of the doorway is 4.08 m. long, the one to the southwest 4.02 m. Each terminates toward the door opening in an anta which projected in a slight offset from the face of the wall. The base of the anta was formed on each side by a large block with plastered face, the one on the northeast 0.96 m. long and 1.03 m. thick through the wall, that on the southwest 0.94 m. long and 1.04 m. thick rising ca. 0.26 m. above the latest floor. Each block was prepared on top to receive a thick wooden timber on its three exposed sides. These timbers were no doubt fastened by dowels on all three sides but the actual dowel holes have been seen only on the southeast near the edge of each block. The face of each anta toward the Vestibule may have been dec-orated with wooden wainscoting. The rest of the wall beyond the anta on the north-east side shows three vertical chases with corresponding transverse slots through the wall and two horizontal grooves, one approximately at floor level and the other at a height of 0.74 m. A good deal of backing plaster has survived on this wall.

In the southwest section of the wall beyond the anta are four vertical chases, with corresponding transverse slots running through the wall. Evidence of a horizontal groove appears at 0.80 m. above the floor, and another probably exists at a lower level; but, since the entire southeastern face of this section of the wall is still covered with a thick coating of plaster, which formed the backing for the finished surface, it is not possible without destroying the plaster to determine the exact position of the lower groove.

The floor of the Vestibule (Fig. 56), which suffered a great deal of damage from the fire that destroyed the building, has lost most of its original smoothness and is now rough and uneven over a large part of the area. Several earlier layers of stucco are represented here and there, but nothing can be said about them, since they are covered by the final coating. This latter has retained relatively little of its decoration. Two workmen spent considerable effort and time in cleaning away the superficial incrustation of lime, and ultimately some modest vestiges of the floor paintings were exposed. From the scanty evidence brought to light Mr. de Jong was able to identify some of the patterns and to draw a reconstruction which gives a good idea of the general arrangement. His investigation ascertained that there were four rows running from northeast to southwest, each comprising ten approximate squares. The two middle rows in the central part of the floor yielded nothing. It was only in a narrow strip close beside the northwest and southeast walls that some patches had withstood adverse circumstances sufficiently to give a clue to the decorative patterns employed.

Our survey, as in the Portico, begins at the northern corner and proceeds southwestward along the northwest wall. Square 1 contained some seven or eight irregular rows of single circles in red against a lighter ground. No. 2 was filled with four groups of concentric arcs, radiating from the corners of the square. Nos. 3, 4, 5, 6, and 7 were hopelessly ruined. In No. 8 the four groups of concentric arcs are repeated. No. 9 is a blank but No. 10 has a net- or scale-pattern. In row 2 nothing can be made out with certainty. Row 3 has likewise lost all its painted decoration, but squares 1 and 6 retain traces of incised lines which apparently divided each into small squares or bands. In row 4 square 1 is blank. Square 2 seems to have had seven or eight careless rows of small circles, each enclosing a central dot. Whatever there once was in squares 3, 4, and 5 had been completely obliterated. In square 6 single dotted circles are repeated. Nos. 7 and 8 have been ruined beyond interpretation. Square 9 appears to have borne a net-pattern like that on No. 10 in row 1. The last square, No. 10 in the southeastern row, apparently contained two groups of concentric arcs radiating from opposite corners.

At the right of the doorway leading into the Throne Room is another stand for a sentry (Fig. 61). It projects into the Vestibule 1.20 m. from the face of the anta and is 1.10 m. wide. It has a raised edge of stucco 0.09 m. wide, rising some 0.03 m. or 0.04 m. above the floor along the southwest and southeast sides. On the northeast was probably a similar edge which at some time was for the most part covered by the stucco floor. A stucco border also runs along at the rear, 0.095 m. thick and 0.08

m. high, where the stand was backed mainly against the wooden door jamb though it also overlapped the anta some 0.40 m. The stand is paved with stucco of a good quality, cracked, but fairly well preserved, which now has a uniformly blue color.

The walls of the Vestibule were decorated with frescoes many fragments of which were found lying on the floor, almost all in the northern corner. As interpreted by Miss Lang, some of these pieces suggest that a procession of men, ca. 0.30 m. high, was represented. Six or more figures, all moving toward the left, wear long straight robes with short sleeves elaborately decorated with dots, dotted rosettes, or other motives; one figure appears to be carrying a large tray. A taller man with a necklace or an embroidered collar above a plain white robe may possibly represent a king or a deity. Another group apparently consists of men wearing shorts, one carrying on his shoulders a frame resting on a pillow. One female figure, with flounced skirt, seems to be similar in size and may belong to the procession. Other fragments, with brown and white border, bear a rosette frieze and still others wood-graining. A bull's head, depicted at a larger scale, was found in the same area and possibly gives a clue to the subject of the composition as a sacrificial procession. Some pieces, especially those showing men wearing shorts, are very dark and difficult to see, perhaps blackened by smoke and fire. Others escaped with relatively little discoloration; whether they all actually came from the walls of the relatively dark Vestibule or, in the course of the destructive fire, spilled over from the Throne Room or fell from an upper story, remains uncertain.

The deepest part of the accumulation covering the palace stretched across the Vestibule, ranging from 1.20 m. to 1.30 m. in depth, sloping gently downward toward the southwest. At the top, plowed soil accounted for 0.25 m.; next below, reddish debris from the destruction containing a great mass of large stones extended to the floor. On the latter, vitrified remains of a pot were noted near the north corner of the room. The fallen wreckage contained the usual quota of potsherds.

O B J E C T S   F O U N D

G O L D

East Quarter

Brooch in form of a ewer with traces of blue inlay (NM. 7776, Fig. 273 No. 20). Found 0.30 m. above floor close to southeast wall. H. 0.048 m., max. w. 0.023 m., w. of neck 0.011 m. Ovoid body, high neck with concave profile, horizontal ridge at junction of body and neck. Long upward slanting beak 0.019 m. long. Vertical flutings on body and neck, each terminating at top in an arch; flutings were filled with blue paste.

Beak has two longitudinal flutings and inverted arches between them; all were filled with inlay.

South Quarter

Three tiny splinters just above floor; fragment of thin plate, 0.35 m. above floor.

S I L V E R

North Quarter

One thin bent piece (e.g., Fig. 268 a), 0.10 m. above floor.

BRONZE (e.g., Fig. 268 a)

East Quarter

Nine small thin flat pieces from surface soil; large thin curved piece, possibly from a blade, 0.75 m. above floor; one thin flat bent piece, near lower part of southeast wall.

North Quarter

Three thin flat pieces, 0.25 m. above floor; three thin flat fragments and two tiny bits, 0.10 m. to 0.15 m. above floor; six thin flat bits, near floor.

Arrow or javelin point (NM. 7793, Fig. 274 No. 7), found 0.15 m. above floor, near doorway to Throne Room. L. 0.052 m., max. w. of blade 0.015 m., l. of blade 0.024 m. Shank rounded, thickish to length of 0.012 m. from blade, then somewhat reduced to a length of 0.015 m.

Fragment of rim of large vessel (NM. 7753, Fig. 274 No. 2) with traces of beading and other decoration. Badly damaged; 0.055 m. long, 0.05 m. wide.

West Quarter

Eight nondescript fragments, in surface soil.

South Quarter

Seven thin flat tiny pieces, 0.40 m. above floor; large shapeless lump, apparently a round thin flat object that had been folded over, ca. 0.25 m. above floor.

STONE (Fig. 268 a)

Three pieces of quartz, near bottom of southeast wall, east quarter.

IVORY (Fig. 268 a)

One fragment burned black and a piece of ivory or bone, east quarter.

Two flat pieces of ivory or bone, 0.10 m. above floor, north quarter.

Small burned fragment, 0.30 m. above floor, south quarter.

PASTE (Fig. 268 a)

Bits of *kyanos*, ca. 0.20 m. above floor, south quarter.

CLAY

Tablet: No. 636, found 0.45 m. below grass level, almost directly above east corner of sentry stand.

POTTERY

Small gray bowl, vitrified and fused to the floor in northeast corner. Exact type unrecognizable. Apparently had three handles (Fig. 346 Nos. 2, 3).

Shapes recognized: in coarse ware, pithos (many fragments), tripod-vessel, lid; in fine ware, kylix (a great many stems), shallow bowl with pinched-out handles, conical cup. A few sherds with painted decoration including a tankard with a spiraliform design: one fragment in LH II Palace Style.

THRONE ROOM (6)

The doorway from the Vestibule to the Throne Room was set in an opening 3.48 m. wide measured across the threshold and the lateral blocks that supported the casings and jambs of the door (Figs. 54, 431). The threshold block is 1.90 m. long and 0.87 m. to 0.90 m. wide from front to back. It was found almost entirely covered with a coat of stucco and the exact dimensions of the stone are therefore difficult to determine. This stucco must presumably represent the floor in use at the time of the disaster. Underneath it are remains of an earlier and smoother floor that seems also to have been laid over the stone. It bears traces of painted decoration or was blackened by the fire. The bases that supported the door frame[23] are a few centimeters wider from front to back than the threshold block but they were adjusted approx-

[23] The northeastern block extends out 0.78 m. from the end of the anta, the southwestern 0.79 m.

imately to the width of the latter by a rabbet cut on the inner side of the doorway.[24] A similar cutting in the northeastern block on the side toward the Vestibule may be concealed by the stucco rim behind the stand.

The reconstruction of the door frame on each side of the opening must be largely conjectural. Abundant remains of carbonized wood, which were found on and above the base blocks, suggest that the casings were built of very heavy timbers (Fig. 62). Considerable charred matter spread out over the blocks extending from front to back formed a layer 0.05 m. thick. This may perhaps indicate that the space was floored with thick planks. On the side toward the door opening alongside the threshold were seen carbonized remains of two substantial posts probably 0.20 m. or 0.25 m. by 0.25 m. in section and set 0.40 m. or more apart. The black charred matter was preserved to a height of some 0.35 m. but the posts themselves must have continued on to the top of the doorway. It is likely that a casing made of heavy wooden boards was attached beside the opening to the posts, and was somehow fitted at the other end into the countersinking in the anta. Each of the six anta blocks that have been examined (pp. 55, 66) has a projecting edge only at the outer side of the doorway but apparently in all instances at the inner side a corresponding raised edge was applied in stucco. The back of the casing could well enough have been fastened by nails or wooden pins to the heavy transverse struts that ran through the wall at the end of the anta. It is difficult to understand why a casing so massive was necessary on each side of the door. Did it perhaps enclose a hollow recess that might serve as a sort of cupboard with a decorated wooden panel that could be opened? It might well have been in such a place that the weapons were stored in the palace of Odysseus in Ithaca.[25]

Above the stone bases of the door frame the whole space was found filled with disintegrated stone and brick. It must have been fused into a molten mass by the tremendous heat of the fire and have flowed down from above into the casing. When it cooled it hardened into something very much like concrete and extremely difficult to .excavate.

The Throne Room of the palace (6 on Key Plan), or the Megaron proper as it has often been called, is a spacious hall 12.90 m. long and 11.20 m. wide, only slightly smaller than its counterpart at Mycenae.[26] A central rectangular area was marked off by four wooden columns resting on stone bases (Fig. 22); they supported not

---

24 The rabbet was 0.26 m. long in the southwestern block, 0.20 m. in the northeastern. The opening between the door jambs was approximately 2.42 m. broad.

25 *Odyssey* I, 127-129.

26 A.J.B. Wace gives the dimensions of the megaron at Mycenae as approximately 13 m. long by 12 m. wide (*BSA* xxv [1921-1923], 239f.) Tsountas had measured it as 12.92 m. long and 11.50 m. wide (*Mykenai*, 36). In Tsountas and Manatt, *The Mycenaean Age*, 56, those metric figures were erroneously calculated as equivalent to 42 ft. 5 in. by 27 ft. 9 in. instead of the correct 43 ft. 8 in. by 37 ft. 4 in. The great megaron at Tiryns, as measured by Dörpfeld, is 11.81 m. long, 9.75 m. - 9.86 m. wide (Schliemann, *Tiryns*, London 1886, 216).

only a balcony running around all four sides of the hall but also a lofty clerestory or lantern (Frontispiece) which no doubt provided air and light. Enclosed in the rectangle is a great circular ceremonial hearth which no doubt served also for heating the apartment in the winter; it could well have been used even for roasting a whole ox for a banquet. Beneath the balcony against the middle of the northeastern wall on the right as one entered the room and facing the middle of the hearth, stood the royal throne. In its original state the Throne Room must have been a bright and cheerful apartment, especially in the light of a great fire blazing on the hearth. The stucco floor was divided by red borders into squares adorned with linear patterns in many colors. The edges and border of the hearth were likewise painted with various designs. The walls were coated with plaster bearing wall paintings, surviving fragments of which indicate in lively colors compositions of several different kinds. The woodwork too in the door jambs, columns, ceiling, and the balcony was almost surely gaily decorated. The smoke from the fire that often doubtless burned on the hearth rising up to the clerestory was carried through the roof in a cylindrical chimney made of two terracotta pipes.

The front wall of the Throne Room varying slightly in thickness from 0.97 m. to 1.05 m. (depending on the thickness of the plaster) still stands to a height ranging from 0.85 m. to 1.05 m. (Fig. 59). The section to the southwest of the doorway had five vertical chases, the one on the northeast only four. The latter may have had a horizontal beam at floor level or thereabouts, and a horizontal groove, perhaps for a relatively thin beam, seems to have run at 0.70 m. above the floor. The spaces between the upright chases in this section are 0.80 m. wide. The southwestern section of the front wall probably had roughly corresponding horizontal beams, one near the floor, the next at a height of 0.80 m. above. The uprights were spaced at intervals varying from 0.55 m. to 0.70 m.

The lateral walls (Fig. 22) have a thickness of 1.25 m. to 1.30 m.; the northeastern one is preserved to a height of 1.05 m. at its southeastern end, diminishing gradually to 0.65 m. at its northwestern end, corresponding to the descending slope of the hill. The southwestern wall, standing to a height of 1.10 m. at its corner with the front wall, shows a similar state of preservation, sinking to a height of 0.50 m. at its northwestern end. On each side there are 13 chases for vertical timbers. One appears at each corner and the spacing averages 0.80 m. Clear evidence for horizontal grooves is recognizable at 0.70 m. above the floor on the northeastern side and at 0.75 m. on the southwestern. On the latter side a horizontal timber lay at approximately floor level or just below. In the northeastern wall the surviving plaster has restricted probing but so far as could be ascertained it seems probable that a similar beam was placed at the same low level.[27]

---

[27] The evidence was observed in the transverse chase 1.10 m. from the northwestern end of the wall.

The rear wall of the room, ranging in height from 0.45 m. at the western corner to 0.60 m. at the northern corner, and with a low point of 0.31 m. near the middle, has a thickness of 1.05 m. In the wall ten vertical chases are recognizable beginning at each end 0.65 m. to 0.70 m. from the corner. Spacing of the chases is somewhat irregular, ranging from 0.70 m. to 0.90 m. A horizontal timber seems to have been set at or slightly below the floor. The next one must have been more than 0.60 m. above the floor since no trace of it remains in the surviving part of the wall.

Except for some insignificant remnants still in place on the northeastern wall, and on the front wall a small patch on the anta base to the northeast of the doorway, which retains traces of a linear pattern, and a somewhat longer stretch to the south-west of the doorway, the smooth finishing coat of plaster no longer survives *in situ* in the Throne Room. The relatively rough backing coat, however, is fairly well preserved on the southwestern wall and in the lower part of the northeastern. Some considerable patches remain at the southwestern end of the southeastern wall and also on the lower existing part of the northwestern wall.

Around all four sides of the Throne Room, however, fragments of plaster were found lying on the floor, to which they had fallen presumably at the time of the disaster. The accumulation was especially abundant along the northeastern and south-eastern walls; painted pieces provided evidence to show that a heraldic composition of griffins and lions decorated the space behind the throne (Fig. 74). From the scanty material surviving it is impossible to reconstruct all the details: nonetheless there can be no doubt that a pair of griffins confronted each other somewhat in the manner of the composition at Knossos, though here the king was not only protected by these strange hybrids combining the head and the wings of an eagle and the body of a lion but, to make assurance doubly sure, a reinforcing lion, the most powerful of all beasts, was added on each side. The griffin may well have been the symbol and "totem" of the royal family that ruled here for they are generously represented in other parts of the palace on frescoes, seals, and sealings. Lions are lacking in the throne room at Knossos and the griffins are wingless but surely a close relationship in spirit unites these two Mycenaean compositions.

Toward the eastern corner were recovered remains of a different scene showing a male figure seated on a rock and playing a lyre, apparently charming a strange flying creature before him (Fig. 75). It may be Apollo playing the lyre or Orpheus or alternatively it might be Thamyris whose ill-fated end in Messenia is recorded in the *Iliad* (II, 595ff.). It probably came from the northeastern wall, though it is not impossible that it fell from the balcony above.

Too little is left from the other sides of the room to allow certain identification of the scenes represented but Miss Lang discusses the material fully in the volume on the frescoes.

The rectangle formed by the four columns is roughly 5.80 m. long by 4.80 m. wide (measured to the outside of the bases). The northern (Fig. 67), eastern, and southern stone bases were badly cracked by the heat of the fire and only the western one is tolerably well preserved (Fig. 68). The northern one was found covered with a thick deposit of charred and carbonized wood, undoubtedly remains of the column it supported. So far as they can be measured, the bases have a diameter of somewhat more than 0.50 m. The full size and shape of the stones could not be determined without damaging the floor. All the bases lie with their tops considerably below (0.07 m. to 0.12 m.) the level of the latest floor; presumably they were more or less nearly level with the earliest floor when they were originally placed.[28] But the floor itself is now rough and uneven, rising in some places, sinking in others. The columns must have been set on the bases before the floor was made: when the stucco was laid, just as we have seen in the Propylon, it took the imprint of the lower ends of the columns, and the flutings of the latter are clearly indicated as 32 in number. No ring retains the impression of all 32 flutings in sequence but the western and southern circles, which are relatively well preserved, have 16 flutings in half the circuit and the northern and eastern, which have at least a quarter segment of the circle preserved, seem to have been made with the same number. The floor as we have it consists of several layers, one above the other; at least four are recognizable around the northern and western bases and two or three in the others. They probably represent successive phases of renovation. In all four instances the floor rises appreciably around the bottom of the column. No clearly marked decorative ring such as those seen in the Propylon is now preserved, but it is possible that in some earlier phase there were rings of that kind, which, in the final stage of the palace, were very carelessly replaced by a sloping rise in the floor toward the foot of the column.

The wooden columns at their lower ends, as indicated by the flutings, had a diameter of 0.51 m. or 0.52 m. How high they were can only be conjectured, and there is no evidence to show whether or not they increased in diameter toward the top as represented at some Minoan and Mycenaean sites.[29] The form of the capital is unknown and nothing has survived to indicate the type of the entablature above it. We are equally uninformed regarding details of the balcony that extended around the four sides of the hall. The restoration by Mr. de Jong illustrated in the Frontispiece is a free rendering of the appearance the Throne Room might have had; the details of the ceiling and the balcony are based on constructive imagination but most

[28] The north and south bases, which are badly cracked and broken, are now slightly lower than the east and west which are in a better state of preservation.

[29] *PM* I, 342f.; III, pl. XVI, facing p. 47, 321f.; Dinsmoor, *Architecture of Ancient Greece*, 33; Lawrence, *Greek Architecture*, 59, 79; Pendlebury, *Archaeology of Crete*, 153; Perrot and Chipiez, *Art in Primitive Greece* II, 83, fig. 284; *BSA* XXI, 359f.; *EphArch* 1888, 146, 164f., pl. 8 no. 8; *BSA* 49 (1952), 241, pl. 40 c; ibid. 50 (1953), 187ff., pl. 30 a; *Transact. APS*, new series, 48 (1958), 12, fig. 73; G. E. Mylonas, *Ancient Mycenae*, fig. 30.

of them, we believe, are not of altogether inappropriate character for the time and place.

The evidence for the existence of a balcony is derived mainly from the distribution of the various objects which were recovered in the Throne Room well above the floor and which, therefore, had certainly fallen from above. These included 14 fragments of tablets, a number of bits of gold, silver, and bronze, and a good many fragments of pottery. All these lay outside the central rectangle in the area covered by the surrounding balcony.

The only objects found above the hearth were numerous small pieces of two coarse large cylindrical pipes of terracotta which ultimately turned out to be the remnants of the chimney already mentioned. The two pipes (Figs. 271 Nos. 2, 3; 272 Nos. 6, 7) are incomplete, their height not known.[30] They seem to taper somewhat from one end to the other. Each had its interior surface blackened with soot. The identification of these cylinders as chimney pipes was fully confirmed by the discovery in 1956 of a similar pair, much better preserved, found in a similar position above the hearth in what we have called the Queen's Hall (p. 200).

It is possible that the two pipes were fitted together end to end, one slightly overlapping the other, to form a single chimney which carried the smoke through the roof. Alternatively, as envisaged by Mr. de Jong and as shown in his drawing (Fig. 418), there may have been two separate flues, each in its own smokestack, side by side. The plan and section present a suggestion of how the balcony, the roof, and the lantern could have been constructed with the generous use of heavy timbers for the main support. The reconstruction is necessarily based on a study of the ground plan, since no actual remains of the superstructure have survived.

The contemporary palaces at Tiryns and Mycenae, as well as elsewhere on the Greek mainland, were no doubt similarly equipped with chimneys in their apartments of state, which contained hearths and consequently raised the problem of smoke disposal. The examples from Pylos, the first which favorable circumstances for discovery permitted to be recognized, owe their survival to the abandonment of the site after the great fire and its escape from later re-occupation.

The balcony was probably built entirely of wood with a wooden floor and no doubt had a railing along its open edge. It may be conjectured that a second tier of columns supported a lantern built of timbers and crude brick. The lantern might have had openings which could presumably be shuttered in times of storm or rain. It may have risen still higher, tapering to a narrow peak in which the chimney pipes were fixed. They could have been sheathed with small stones and clay, considerable

---

[30] No. 1145: many pieces missing, almost all of one end preserved; height ranges from 0.28 to 0.53 m., outside diameter of preserved end 0.652 m., average thickness of wall 0.021 m. No. 1146: many pieces miss-ing, one end restorable; height ranges from 0.29 to 0.49 m., outside diameter 0.665 m., average thickness of wall 0.021 m., greatest thickness at end varies from 0.03 to 0.035 m.

remains of which were found high above the hearth overlying the fragments of the chimney.

The columns and the four walls of the room could easily enough have supported a superstructure of this kind (Fig. 418). The spans from the lateral walls to the columns (measured to the center) are: northeast wall to north column 3.54 m., to east column 3.53 m.; southwest wall to south column 3.39 m., to west column 3.315 m. Those from the end walls to the columns are somewhat longer: northwest wall to west column 3.84 m., to north column 3.89 m.; southeast wall to east column 3.79 m., to south column 3.70 m. Transverse spans from column to column are west column to north column 4.355 m. and south column to east column 4.26 m., a span which could fairly easily be managed with stout timbers, and the longest of all, from the east to the north column, 5.22 m., and from the south to the west column 5.36 m., which offer no insuperable problem. The thick walls themselves would have supported the upper structure of crude brick which in turn, along with the upper tier of columns, held up the flat roof; the latter was probably made of horizontal timbers laid close together and covered with earth or clay.[31]

The stucco floor of the Throne Room was evidently often repaired or remade as shown at the edges of the northern (Fig. 67) and western column bases (p. 80) and in breaks here and there. How many times it was renovated is not now determinable. It is likely that these floors all bore painted decoration but only the last one of the series is open to view and can be studied. It is fairly well preserved immediately around the hearth, in front of the throne and the doorway, and in general along the walls. But even in the best-preserved places the whole surface is badly smoked and blackened from the effects of the fire and it is almost everywhere extremely difficult to determine with certainty the colors and details of the painted ornament. In a strip ca. 2.75 m. wide across the northwestern part of the room, beginning some 0.65 m. from the walls, the floor has suffered its greatest damage, and the surface is almost entirely gone (Fig. 65). The section nearby, toward the hearth, is also badly cracked and buckled, possibly from the effects of olive roots that had worked their way along under the pavement, as well as from the fire that wrecked the building and the debris that fell from above. Elsewhere relatively few areas in the room retain a smooth and level flooring. Nevertheless, in spite of the damage it has suffered from various causes, the floor still preserves considerable remains of the painted decoration that existed on the day the palace was burned.

The whole floor of the room, except the circle occupied by the hearth, was laid

[31] Professor W. B. Dinsmoor and a good many others believe that the Mycenaean megaron had a pitched, or gabled, roof (*Architecture of Ancient Greece*, 19). No traces of tiles of Mycenaean times have been found on the hill of Englianos, and we are still convinced that the roof was flat, built in a series of terraces at different levels, inclined enough to shed rain water.

out in squares, normally measuring approximately 1.08 m. on a side. They were separated by bordering bands consisting of two parallel incised lines, varying from 0.056 m. to 0.065 m. apart. When the floor was first exposed we saw some traces of red paint in these dividing bands. Along the sides of the room twelve squares were laid out, and there were ten along the ends. The grid was apparently designed without specific reference to the hearth and to the columns, as may be seen in Figure 404. In the final phase of redecoration—before the fire—a curious irregularity somehow crept into the renewal of the chessboard design. In the normal course of events it was presumably laid out by fixing a series of measured points at roughly equal intervals along the opposite walls from which strings could be stretched across the room. Nine points along the end walls would simply provide for a series of ten equal divisions, and eleven points along the lateral walls would similarly serve for the twelve squares in the longitudinal direction. In the actual execution, which apparently started from the northwest and progressed toward the southeast, the tenth and eleventh points on the southwestern side, probably because of a slight miscalculation, had to be fixed at shorter intervals than the nine others, thus reducing the sizes of the last two rows of squares. A considerably more awkward result was obtained, however, when the transverse line drawn from the seventh point on the southwestern wall was carried only to the southerly edge of the hearth and not to the northeastern wall, while, to make matters worse, the next transverse line was laid out from the eighth point on the southwest to the seventh point on the northeast; and all the succeeding lines followed approximately the same parallel divergence from the perpendicular. The last four rows of the grid were thus transformed into trapezoidal figures instead of squares. Mr. Hill, who was much interested in this little lapse in accuracy and care, suggested that the floor-painters may have made the change on their own initiative when they found that they could not stretch a string straight across the room to connect the eighth points on the two sides, since it would have encountered the two solid southeastern columns which supported the balcony and the clerestory. It is obvious from other scattered bits of evidence that the quality of workmanship in various fields of activities had fallen off appreciably at the end of Mycenaean III B.

Had the points along the northeastern wall corresponded with those on the southwest the whole floor of the great hall would have been divided into 120 squares. Four were actually lost in the seventh row from the northwest, through the omission of the one point on the northeast. Four whole squares were eliminated and parts of 11 others were covered by the hearth. One was occupied by the royal throne, thus leaving for decoration precisely 100 complete squares or trapezoids and parts of the 11.

Sixty-four of the squares in addition to the 11 partial squares around the hearth still retained sufficient traces of their decoration to allow the pattern in some measure to be recognized and reconstructed in the water color (Fig. 73) by Mr. de Jong.[32] Only a single square presents a somewhat naturalistic, pictorial composition, delineating a huge octopus with large eyes and symmetrical curving tentacles; this is the second square directly in front of the throne. In all the other squares, so far as could be determined, abstract linear motives prevail: parallel lines in diagonal or transverse arrangement; parallel wavy lines or bands running transversely or diagonally; multiple parallel chevrons; single circles scattered about close together in no recognizable order; crosshatching; concentric arcs, sometimes in two groups, touching back to back, extending directly or diagonally across the square, but more often in four groups radiating from the four corners with a diamond-shaped central lozenge; parallel zigzags; large or small scale-pattern; and wavy net-motive. All these elements are used in red, yellow, blue, black, and white in numerous variations, combinations, and colors, sometimes supplemented with superposed white dots, thus giving a variety of decoration with almost no exact repetition. In general, however, the chief patterns recur in diverse minor modifications helter-skelter, displaying little or no systematic composition, although in five or six instances near repetition appears to follow the knight's move in chess.

The decoration of the floor in the Throne Room at Englianos is strikingly similar to that exposed in the excavations by the British School along the northerly side of the court of the palace in front of the megaron at Mycenae.[33] In the decorative motives, the colors employed, and the workmanship, in almost all the details, there is an unmistakable close resemblance: and, as noted by Miss W. Lamb, even the knight's move plays a role in the arrangement of some of the patterns which are repeated. A comparison with the floor paintings in the throne room at Tiryns discloses clearly a near kinship, although the Tirynthian artists seem to have been much more orderly in their general design and not afraid of exact repetition.[34]

Incision in the form of small squares and rectangles was also occasionally used to supplement the painted decoration. This may be seen in Squares F1 and G1 against the southwest wall, in J5, K4, K6, K7, K8, and in L9 and L10 in the eastern corner (Fig. 69). The incised lines separating the squares and those within them have been omitted in the water color. Whether these incised squares were thus differentiated from the others for some particular purpose has not surely been ascertained: Squares F1 and G1 are directly opposite the throne on the other side of the hearth; those in Rows J and K are grouped in front of the entrance from the Vestibule, and those

[32] In some instances the patterns have been almost completely obliterated by fire and other calamities, and their identification is consequently to a great extent a matter of individual interpretation and conjecture. The difficulty of removing the adhesive accretion of lime coating the floor has also gravely obstructed the observation and recognition of many details. Thus in a photograph (Fig. 72) the eye of the camera seems to have seen minor elements which do not exactly agree with the reconstruction in the water color.

[33] *BSA* xxv (1921-1923), 193-195, pl. xxxv b.

[34] *Tiryns* ii, 223f., pls. xix, xxi.

in Row L are in the extreme eastern corner: were these places possibly indicated for some of the officials of the court on occasions of state?

The great hearth was approximately but not quite accurately centered in the room.[35] In its present state it does not form an absolutely perfect circle, but it has an average diameter, measured on the floor, of 4.02 m. The outer edge, rising from 0.10 m. to 0.17 m. above the floor, has an inward slope and at the outer edge of a narrow step or ledge the diameter is reduced to 3.94 m. This ledge, also sloping upward slightly, has a width varying from 0.10 m. to 0.12 m. The side then rises ca. 0.035 m. to 0.045 m. to the edge of a broad flat border, ranging from 0.32 m. to 0.36 m. in width, that runs around the entire hearth. Within this wide bordering band the interior of the hearth, sinking 0.02 m. to 0.03 m. in level, has a diameter of ca. 3 m. The inner circle, which was the actual fireplace, seems to have had a floor of rough stucco. Over it was found a deposit, ca. 0.05 m. deep, of ashes and charred matter. The floor, which is blackened over all and is somewhat broken, cracked, and buckled, displays a good many dents, probably made by wreckage that fell from the clerestory.

The surrounding border, the narrow ledge, and outer riser were all coated with fine smooth stucco and decorated with painted patterns (Fig. 66). The outer edge of the border has suffered a good deal of damage in its western quarter and here a succession of five coats of stucco can be distinguished. The upper coating carries a running pattern of large connected spirals. They are of the double or "in and out" type and there were 39 or 40 all told in the whole circuit (Fig. 73). The spirals seem to have been done in red, or some of them possibly in yellow, outlined in black. The central core was probably red and the triangles, above and below the connecting lines of the spirals, outlined in black, were divided into an outer V-shaped figure filled with orange and an inner triangle of red. Along the inner and outer edges of the flat border, framing the spirals, is a band of red between the usual black lines; it has a disconcerting habit of changing to orange without notice. Blackened and lightened patches here and there, left by charred wood and by intense heat, have made it difficult to determine exactly what the original colors were.

Some parts of the second layer, belonging to an earlier phase, are visible along the northwestern perimeter of the hearth. It was decorated with an almost identical pattern of spirals and had, above and below the connecting lines between the spirals, the same kind of orange and red triangles.

The third coat, surviving from a still earlier phase, is represented on the northwestern side of the hearth by one of the angle ornaments in which the same combination of orange and red with black outline occurs, but here the outside band seems

[35] Distance from northwest wall to edge of hearth at floor 4.57 m., from southeast wall to edge of hearth 4.34 m., from southwest wall 3.55 m., from northeast wall 3.67 m.

to be filled with orange instead of red. On the southeastern side a whole spiral is visible; it seems to have been done in yellow, outlined in black with a red core. Here the flat border itself appears to be some three centimeters narrower than that of the top coat.

The fourth and still deeper layer is recognizable peeping out from a break with a tantalizing remnant in yellow, bordered by a black line. Underneath it is another layer, the fifth from the top, but only the edge of it is visible and nothing can be said regarding its surface and decoration. There is no evidence to indicate the length of time represented by these five successive layers and decorative phases. The outer edge of the fifth coat from the top lies ca. 0.05 m. inside the perimeter of the final coat.

The narrow ledge outside and below the upper flat border of the hearth was likewise decorated; the topmost coat of stucco, belonging to the final phase, bore a sawtooth or notched pattern. The notches, pointing inward, now appear black against a lighter ground; but what the original colors were is not certain. A section of the next underlying coat on the southeastern side of the hearth reveals a similar pattern, but here the surviving notches, applied in what now appears black, but may have been red on a lighter ground, point outward. In the intervening spaces between the notches are irregular black dots which seem to surround a central blob or ring. Mr. de Jong in 1953 regarded them as crudely made dot rosettes, following a Minoan tradition, and believed he could see a small white dot applied on each black one and a white ring on the central blob or ring. In 1961 no trace of superposed white could be distinguished. On the southeastern side of the hearth some scanty glimpses of the third coating from the top are visible through cracks in the overlying layer. Here parts of three black notches pointing inward are recognizable against a white ground. What patterns were painted on the fourth and fifth layers from the top could not be determined, since they are completely covered by the later coatings.

The upright edge of the hearth below the ledge is well preserved around the northwestern half of the circle. It was decorated in the last phase of the palace with what might be called a flame pattern which now stands out in black against a lighter ground (Fig. 66). The flames, as we take them to be, bend regularly toward the left. Some preserve traces of what seems to have been outlining, which Mr. Vanderpool in 1952 saw as red. No evidence survives to indicate that the spaces between the flames were decorated. On the southeastern side of the hearth a section of the riser of the next to the last coat shows what we have called the flames bending toward the left in light against a dark ground. Here too there seems to be an outline which in some places still has a reddish tinge. A small broken area on the northwestern side of the hearth, where the two outer coats of stucco are missing, exhibits the decoration of the third from the last phase. Here we have neatly drawn flames, now black, against an almost white background, which appears not to have been damaged at all by fire or smoke. The white here is very different from the light ground mentioned in connection with the later coats, but corresponds with the white seen in the third from the last coating on the ledge. In this phase the flames bend to the right instead of to the left. No ornaments appear in the spaces between them. Although relatively little of the decoration applied in the third from the last stage can now be seen, it gives the impression both on the flat spiral border and on the outer riser, and even on the small bit of the ledge that is visible, of much greater care and precision in drawing than is apparent in the subsequent phases.

The hearth at Englianos closely resembles its counterpart in the great hall of the palace at Mycenae, though the latter was found only partly preserved. Its original diameter is calculated to have been ca. 3.70 m. Miss Lamb[36] observed that it was "built on a ring of poros, enclosing a clay centre, all being overlaid with plaster." It was not possible without doing damage to ascertain if the construction at Englianos was similar. At Mycenae ten successive coats of stucco had in the course of time been applied to the hearth, each bearing traces of painted decoration. The notched plume and wave patterns on the riser are essentially the same as what we have called a "flame" motive; on the narrow step a comparable wave appears instead of the tooth pattern at Englianos. In one instance at Mycenae there is a second riser of undetermined height also decorated with waves. The upper flat border surrounding the place for the fire (preserved in one instance only) bore a running spiral design, as on the Messenian hearth. Dot rosettes in the interspaces between the waves or flames were recognized in most of the successive coats of plaster, but not in all.

The hearth in the megaron at Tiryns[37] was presumably also much like the one at Englianos. Except that its diameter was ca. 3.50 m., little is known about its form and decoration. The outer edge is missing, the profile undeterminable, no succession of stucco coatings has survived; and nothing remains of the broad border around the central area for the fire. There was apparently no stone core such as that at Mycenae.

The royal throne stood against the northeastern wall, not quite accurately centered in the transverse axis of the room. From his seat the king could look across the middle of the hearth. The throne itself is missing (Fig. 70); no remains of it were found, and one can only conjecture that it was made of perishable material. It was most probably built of valuable kinds of wood, perhaps inlaid with ivory or *kyanos* or some other delicate material. If there had been any appreciable use of stone or metal, some traces of them would surely have survived, unless the entire throne was carried off as booty by the conquerors. In any event the throne must have been set on a bedding of pebbles, clay, and perhaps broken and dissolved brick tamped down hard

[36] W. Lamb, *BSA* XXV (1921-1923), 241-243, pls. XXXIX, XL, XLI; Rodenwaldt, *Jhb.* (1919), 88f.

[37] Müller, *Tiryns* XXX, 144-145.

in an area extending out 1.07 m. from the wall and 0.90 m. to 0.91 m. wide. This space was surrounded on all four sides by a rim of stucco, 0.04 m. to 0.06 m. wide, rising above the floor on the northwest and southwest and merging with the floor on the southeast. At the back it has a maximum width of 0.08 m. The somewhat rough and ready adjustment of the rim to the floor must have been made in the last phase of the palace, which seems to have been a relatively careless age. The throne that stood here was apparently somewhat larger than the well-known throne in the Palace of Minos at Knossos,[38] which no doubt was set up by a Mycenaean conqueror from the mainland; but it might be imagined as having a generally similar form.

During the excavations of 1952 the central part of the space enclosed within the rim was found filled with burned red earth extending down to virgin soil at a depth of ca. 0.40 m. In the upper part of this filling were recovered two small groups of ornamental jewelry (Fig. 273 Nos. 2-11). One comprised a fragment of a pendant of banded agate, beautifully worked, a piece of burned and decomposed blue paste or *kyanos* and a partly melted gold bead; the other group yielded a ring of silver, or bronze covered with silver and its bezel of lead, a twisted wire loop of silver (perhaps from a bracelet), a twisted wire loop of gold, a large cylindrical bead of carnelian, an amygdaloid bead of banded agate, an amygdaloid bead of bronze, possibly decorated, a fragment of bronze, a small spherical bead of amethyst, and half of a whorl. How and when and why these objects came to be placed here must remain a minor mystery.

Directly beside the throne and sunk into the stucco floor on the king's right, is a roughly circular basin-like hollow with a diameter of 0.32 m. and a depth of 0.06 m. From it a narrow channel, 0.04 m. wide at the top and 0.04 m. deep, leads 2.01 m. northwestward in a slightly curving line, not far from the wall, to a similar shallow hollow (0.34 m. in diameter, with a depth of 0.06 m.) at a somewhat lower level. The hollows and the V-shaped channel are rather clumsily made (Fig. 70), but at the northwestern end evidence shows that they had been much more carefully executed in an earlier phase, which is represented by an underlying pavement. In the latest period of use the hollows and channel became uniformly coated with some dark matter which has not been identified.

No comparable installation has been recorded in any other Mycenaean palace. What its purpose was is problematical. We suggest that it was made to provide a place for the king to pour out libations on ceremonial occasions without having to rise from his throne. Other possible uses can no doubt be imagined. Dr. Valmin, who saw it, said it reminded him of a custom observed in palaces of the old Iron Age in Sweden, where each king had his own spittoon or cuspidor beside the throne.

[38] The throne made of gypsum which was discovered in the Throne Room at Knossos by Sir Arthur Evans is described in *PM* IV, 917-919, figs. 889-892, 895. He points out several details which clearly indicate that the stone seat was a descendant of originals in wood.

On the floor to the southeast of, and close to, the western column stood a fairly large table of offerings made of clay, coated with fine stucco (Fig. 65); it was found in a badly cracked and damaged condition. On it lay two miniature two-handled kylikes, probably votive offerings (Fig. 68). Mainly in the southern quarter, but spreading into the eastern, were recovered remnants of a large pithos, including pieces of the rim. Several fragments lay 0.70 m. above the floor, others much deeper, reaching the floor itself. The vessel must surely have fallen from the balcony above. Some pieces were found coated thickly both inside and out with a heavy deposit of lime, white as plaster (Fig. 71). What other furniture, if any, formed the equipment of the hall is unknown. There may perhaps have been stools or benches of wood which have, however, left no recognizable traces. More elaborate seats and chairs are also possible, but they belong only to the realm of conjecture.

As it appears today with its walls preserved continuously on all sides, its painted stucco floor, though somewhat battered here and there, still extending from wall to wall, its four column bases in their original position, the great central hearth surviving throughout its entire circuit, and the place of the royal throne clearly marked against the wall on the right hand as one enters, and with its clear evidence of the catastrophic destruction by fire, the Throne Room is an impressive monument of Mycenaean architecture and it somehow conjures up a lively vision of vanished pomp and majesty.

The deposit covering the Throne Room had a maximum depth in its southeastern section of 1.25 m. but it grew much shallower, following the descending slope of the hill toward its northwestern end where the depth was only 0.70 m. At the top was a plowed layer, 0.15 m. to 0.25 m. deep. Beneath it was a stratum of black earth and small stones occupying somewhat more than the whole central square of the hall reaching a depth of 0.40 m. to 0.48 m. Beneath the black stratum and spread out over the area of the hearth, from −0.42 m. to −0.50 m., were numerous small fragments of coarse terracotta which eventually were recognized to be remains of the two chimney pipes mentioned above (p. 81). Underneath these pieces the hearth was covered with yellowish disintegrated brick, hard and filled with burned matter, charcoal, and ashes. The area outside the central square, from plowed earth to the floor, was filled with debris of burned and dissolved crude brick, generally red but with a sloping yellow patch toward the western corner. In the northwestern quarter the deposit of red burned brick with an admixture of black was very loose in contrast to the southwestern section where it was extraordinarily hard. Masses of relatively large stones fallen from the walls appeared in all quarters, in many places going down to the floor, and a particularly large heap of stones was observed just inside the doorway all the way across the width of the opening and more. Near the northeast wall were the crumbling remains of poros blocks. Extending ca. 4 m.

from the eastern corner alongside the northeast wall, lying face down or sloping, was a considerable concentration of fragments of fallen plaster. They continued northwestward to the end of the wall in diminishing quantity perhaps corresponding to the diminishing depth of the deposit. A fair amount of fallen plaster was recovered beside the southeastern wall but very little along the southwestern and the northwestern.

Very few objects of any kind were found on the floor. Almost all of the objects were recovered in the debris of disintegrated brick, plaster, and stones that fell outside the central square of the room.

OBJECTS FOUND

GOLD

20 mostly nondescript fragments.

From floor or just above

Six very small shapeless pieces, one a melted drop: found in doorway, just inside doorway, near edge of hearth, above place of throne, near south column base.

From layer of fallen debris

Northwest section

Four small fragments: one of gold leaf attached to flat piece of silver, one with *repoussé* net-pattern, one melted and one shapeless.

Southwest section

Six small fragments including two with traces of decoration (e.g., NM. 7759, Fig. 273 Nos. 13-15), one rolled over silver, and one bead.

Southeast section

Three small bits and one thickish leaf-shaped piece.

SILVER

17 fragments (e.g., Fig. 270)

From layer of fallen debris

Northwest section

Three small pieces, one with scrap of gold attached.

Southwest section

Three thin, bent and fused fragments.

Southeast section

Eleven thin pieces, eight of them probably from rim and handle of a cup, one possibly a rivet-head.

BRONZE

162 fragments (e.g., Fig. 270)

From fallen debris

Northwest section

26 pieces, mostly nondescript, damaged by fire and fused: heavy nail, l. 0.052 m., max. w. 0.005 m., d. head 0.012 m., square in section; four joining pieces of horizontally grooved neck, 0.025 m. high, of small vessel with thin splaying rim and place of handle attachment or stumps of rivets; fragment of sturdy round loop-handle; two joining pieces of a circular object (semicircular in section in its present state).

Southwest section

76 fragments: nearly all nondescript, some thin and some thick flat pieces, some twisted and fused; three possibly from blade with rivet-holes.

Southeast section

53 chunks, scraps, and thin pieces, fused, nondescript: one large fairly thick fragment probably of weapon or knife with remnants of rivets, fused and bent, l. pres. 0.09 m., w. 0.04 m. to 0.07 m., th. 0.003 m.

Northeast section

7 pieces: one large thick flat bent piece; six thin bent pieces.

STONE

(e.g., Fig. 270)

Northwest section

Quartz: eleven pieces, some probably worked.

Southwest section

Flint: small light tan blade with serrated edge, l. 0.023 m., w. 0.014 m.

Steatite: shanked button, d. estimated 0.015 m., h. 0.009 m., d. shank 0.007 m., d. hole 0.003 m.

Northeast section

From fallen debris

Quartz: chunk.

On floor near the east column base

Steatite: shanked button, d. 0.018 m., h. 0.012 m., d. shank 0.005 m.

BONE

Southeast section

Small boar's tusk (Fig. 270).

CLAY

Tablets: 16 fragments found in debris outside the central square, all fallen from above.

Northwest section: No. 628, just below plowed earth at 0.32 m. below the surface.

Southwest section: Nos. 622-625, 627, 634-635, 638, from 0.40 m. to 0.52 m. below the surface in dissolved red brick.

Southeast section: Nos. 626, 630, 631, 633, from 0.27 m. to 0.63 m. below the surface at the top of and in dissolved red brick.

Northeast section: Nos. 629, 632, 635, on top of red brick at −0.25 m., and in it at −0.40 m. and −0.47 m.

Table of offerings (Figs. 271 No. 11, 272 No. 5). Found just to southeast of western column base (Fig. 65) in crumbling state. Coated with stucco, made in the usual manner with three legs. Most of the table is missing, and a good many of the preserved pieces do not join; but much of the legs and a fair section of the rim fit together; d. at top restored 0.58 m.; h. restored 0.20 m., h. raised rim 0.02 m., w. of raised rim 0.06 m.

POTTERY

Basin (Shape 1, p. 355)

No. 1152, found on floor in southeastern quarter.

Diminutive kylix (Shape 26, p. 366)

Nos. 332, 333, found on table of offerings; No. 1171 found against northeast wall near northwest end.

Pedestaled krater (Shape 63, p. 400). Fragments found in Section C of Trench 1 in 1939 (Fig. 346 No. 1), comprising pedestal base and part of side rising to rim. Decorated in blackish paint with running spirals in shoulder zone, bordered below by three horizontal bands; lower part of body and pedestal coated solidly in same paint. Section C crossed the Vestibule and the eastern corner of the Throne Room.

Very small stirrup-vase (decorated): No. 334. Found over hearth in the layer of black earth with stones. Incomplete; faint traces of paint, pattern not recognizable.

Sherds from all sections numerous; shapes recognized: in coarse ware, pithos with flattened rim, tripod-vessel, brazier, scoop, griddle, large pedestaled pot of some kind; in fine ware, kylix, diminutive kylix, angular bowl and basin with pinched-out handles, conical cup, small dipper, small tankard, squat alabastron, feeding bottle with tubular spout. A few pieces are coated over-all in solid color and some bear painted decoration: horizontal bands, spiraliform and linear motives, parallel chevrons, net- or scale-pattern, nothing of any distinction. Most of these pieces are of Mycenaean III B; a few may be attributed to III A, and three small sherds may go back to LH II or I. They may come from dissolved crude brick along with four or five bits of Middle Helladic types, Mattpainted and coarse incised wares. A few Geometric fragments came from surface soil.

Small treasure found under the place of the throne

Group A

Fragment of pendant of banded agate (NM. 7762, Fig. 273 No. 9) broken through suspension hole; scalloped edge. H. 0.041 m., w. 0.043 m.

Piece of blue paste or *kyanos* (not photographed or given number in Inventory of National Museum).

Gold bead (NM. 7763, Fig. 273 No. 8), partially melted and misshapen from heat, l. 0.01 m.

Group B

Ring of silver or bronze covered with silver (NM. 7764, Fig. 273 No. 5) and its bezel of lead (NM. 7770, Fig. 273 No. 4), l. 0.025 m.; w. 0.016 m.

Loop of twisted silver wire (NM. 7765, Fig. 273 No. 6), l. 0.044 m., w. 0.003 m.

Loop of twisted gold wire (NM. 7766, Fig. 273 No. 7), l. 0.031 m., w. 0.003 m.

Large cylindrical bead of carnelian (NM. 7767, Fig. 273 No. 3), h. 0.012 m., d. 0.019 m.

Amygdaloid bead of banded agate (NM. 7768, Fig. 273 No. 11), l. 0.022 m., w. 0.011 m.

Amygdaloid bead of bronze that may have been decorated (NM. 7769, Fig. 273 No. 2), l. 0.017 m., w. 0.01 m.

Small spherical bead of amethyst (?) (NM. 7771, Fig. 273 No. 10), d. 0.005 m.

Fragment of bronze and half of a terracotta whorl (not photographed or entered in Inventory of National Museum).

ARCHIVES ROOM (7)

To the southwest of the Propylon, on the left as one enters the Main Building of the palace, are two relatively small chambers connected by a doorway which we have called the Archives Rooms (Fig. 9). The outer one (7 on Key Plan) is directly alongside the outer portico of the Propylon. The exterior walls on the southwest and southeast and the party wall toward the gateway have been despoiled of their stones (Fig. 45) down to the deepest course of their foundations but the latter define the approximate limits of the room. The exact thicknesses of the walls are not known. The only piece of original wall surviving above ground is the lower part of the partition between the outer room and the adjoining room (8); to the southwest of the doorway connecting the two, it is 2.35 m. long, 0.80 m. thick, and it stands to a height of 0.30 m. above the floor. No evidence of horizontal grooves or vertical chases is preserved. On the southeastern face some remnants of mud plaster are still in place.

Room 7, which was probably the office of the tax collector, was approximately 4 m. square. It had a floor of tamped clay, thick and uneven, and was thus not one of the elegant apartments in the palace which were regularly floored with stucco. On the floor in the south corner of the room on the day of the fire an enormous ribbed pithos evidently stood, covered with its lid (Fig. 381). It apparently contained a large quantity of olive oil, perhaps having been filled by numerous tithes paid in kind by those subject to internal revenue tax. It was a fortunate accident from the archaeological point of view that in the course of the fire the jar fell over and collapsed into the room spreading its fragments and inflammable contents over the floor (Fig. 77). For it thus probably helped to bake the many clay tablets which happened to be in this outer office as well as those in the adjoining filing room.

It is not possible to determine certainly where entrance to the room was gained. In the plan and in the reconstruction of the wall we have restored a doorway opening from the outer portico of the Propylon (Figs. 9, 417). This seemed to be a suitable ingress for transactors of business rather than to enter first the inner room (8), which must have served principally to store the records. One piece of evidence offers corroboration of this conjecture about the position of the doorway, namely that the stand for a sentry was placed on the left-hand side of the doorway of the Propylon instead of the right. In all the other three instances in the palace in which sentry stands were found they lay at the right. From this stand the sentry could control those entering what may have been a treasury office as well as those going straight on into the palace. One further bit of supporting evidence may be noted in the state of the edge of the pavement of the Propylon adjacent to the hypothetical position of the doorway. For here, when the wall was torn out by the pillagers, the stucco floor of the outer portico of the Propylon was broken away with a ragged edge ca. 0.30 m. to 0.40 m. beyond the line of the wall (Fig. 45). This suggests to us the possibility that the extra damage was caused by the removal of a large threshold block at this point.

With reference to the furniture of the room, not much can be said. The presence of the pithos in the south corner has already been mentioned. A considerable heap of burned animal bones lay in the western corner, and close beside them near the northwest wall were found 11 diminutive kylikes, probably votive offerings. What these apparent remains of sacrifices and dedicatory vessels had to do in the tax collector's office raises an unsolved problem.

In the northeasterly half of the room some 300 inscribed tablets and fragments of tablets were recovered. They lay for the most part in six or seven or more irregular groups spread out over the floor presumably as they had fallen from shelves or other storage space. Nearly all were cracked and badly broken, but the fragments, including bits and scraps, were meticulously collected; the earth removed was sifted and a few additional remnants, which had escaped the eye of the diggers, were salvaged in this way. Some further pieces were found in the loose earth which was thrown back by the looters into the trench that marked the line of the wall they had despoiled of its stones. In the catalogue following the description of the room the tablets it yielded are listed simply by the final numbers given them in other publications,[39] since it is our hope that full details of their distribution, as revealed by the excavation, will be presented in a later volume accompanied by photographs and sketches.

Lying on the floor among the tablets, not far from the doorway leading into Room 8, were uncovered a spearhead and a badly damaged sword of bronze (Fig. 77).

Room 7 was found to be buried beneath a deposit, not more than 0.60 m. deep,

39 E. L. Bennett, Jr., *The Pylos Tablets: Texts of the Inscriptions Found, 1939-1954* (Princeton, 1955); Bennett, *The Olive Oil Tablets of Pylos, Texts of Inscriptions Found, 1955* (*Minos* Supplement No. 2, 1958); M. Lang, *AJA* 62 (1958), 181-191; 63 (1959), 128-137; 64 (1960), 160-164; 65 (1961), 158-163; 66 (1962), 149-152; 67 (1963), 160-162; 69 (1965), 98-101.

consisting of only two layers. At the top was the usual plowed earth ranging in depth from 0.15 m. to 0.20 m. Underneath lay red debris containing a good many stones which had fallen when the fire wrecked the building. This extended down to the floor of earth or clay on which the tablets and other objects lay. A good many scattered potsherds and a few fragments of plaster with traces of painted decoration were found in the disintegrated crude brick which had evidently come from the upper story.

Along the southeastern side of Room 7 the clay floor was laid over an earlier exterior wall (Fig. 15). Only a short stretch of it, truncated at each end, 0.52 m. high and 2.73 m. long, is left. Resting on a slightly projecting foundation of worked stones, it was built with an outer facing of large blocks of poros, one of which is inscribed with the sign of the double axe (Fig. 16).

Two full blocks are preserved and a short remnant of a third where the wall was broken off at the southwest. Of the two complete stones the northeastern is 1.13 m. long, 0.26 m. to 0.375 m. thick. On its top is a dowel hole and a shallower cutting, perhaps a pry hole. The second, which bears the double axe, is 1.20 m. long and slightly thicker (0.42 m.) than the other. It also has in its top a pry hole. The backing, which formed the greater part of the wall, was made of rubble and the total thickness was at least 1.20 m. The earth floor of Room 7 passed directly over this wall some 0.18 m. to 0.30 m. above it. The wall must belong to a forerunner of the palace of Mycenaean III B; and another part of the same building may be recognized in a wall of the same general thickness, remains of which have been found underneath Room 57 (pp. 226f.) on the northeastern side of the Propylon. The new exterior wall of the palace erected in Mycenaean III B lay alongside to the southeast of its forerunner; the only surviving remains are the flat bedding stones (Fig. 17) on which the Archaeological Service based the modern rebuilt wall. No decisive evidence has been found to fix the date of the earlier wall.

OBJECTS FOUND

SILVER

One fragment (NM. 7787, Fig. 266 No. 2), ca. 0.02 m. long, 0.012 m. wide; longitudinal groove down middle.

BRONZE

Spearhead (NM. 7791, Fig. 274 No. 3) with separate tubular socket for shaft: thick and well preserved, l. blade 0.258 m., w. across barbs, which have disintegrated, 0.065 m., tapering toward sharp point; tip broken off but preserved. Instead of midrib two longitudinal incised lines ca. 0.016 m. apart narrowing to ca. 0.008 m. One large rivet-hole near butt end of blade enclosed within the incised lines. Traces of two other rivet-holes have disappeared with barbs. Socket for handle or shaft, 0.092 m. long, d. 0.024 m., made of rolled plate with rivet-hole near upper end.

Sword (NM. 7792, Fig. 274 No. 4) in very bad state of preservation, broken into 18 fragments. As found 0.46 m. long, blade 0.40 m., tang 0.06 m. Blade 0.06 m. wide at shoulder, latter apparently rounded; no midrib. Two rivets preserved in place near butt end of blade; one rivet-hole and traces of another in tang. End of the latter has two projecting horns.

Slightly curved fragment of a rather solid and substantial blade (Fig. 265 No. 3), l. pres. 0.034 m., w. 0.019 m., th. 0.002 m.

Fragment of heavy implement (NM. 7788, Fig. 266 No. 1), possibly also part of a blade. L. 0.047 m., w. 0.032 m. at one end, 0.017 m. at other end; part of rivet-hole preserved at broad end.

CLAY

Sealing: NM. 8477 = *CMMS* 307 (Fig. 275 No. 10), found with Tablet No. 650. Scene represented: two men back to back, each fighting a lion.

Tablets: Nos. 641-839, 917-940, 944-953, 976-977, 988-993, 998. There were also some fragments which were found to join other pieces that had previously been recovered and numbered.

POTTERY

Diminutive kylix (Shape 26, p. 366)
Nos. 1153, 1154, 1155-1156 (Fig. 359), 1157-1160, 1161-1163 (Fig. 359).
Large pithos (Shape 55b, p. 394)
No. 1147 (Fig. 381).
Lid (Shape 77, p. 417)
No. 1144 (Figs. 381, 397).

The scattered sherds found in the room represent the following shapes: plain kylix, diminutive votive kylix, bowl and cup, small stirrup-vase (at least two), three-handled jar, krater-bowl, basin (Shape 2), ribbed pithos made of clay containing mica and decorated with raised bands bearing thumb impressions.

ARCHIVES ROOM (8)

A doorway at the northeastern end of the partition wall connected the two Archives Rooms. Most of it was destroyed by the looters who carried off so much stone from the palace, but one large block on the southwestern side of the opening is still left *in situ* (Figs. 12, 76, 432). It is 1 m. long projecting ca. 0.10 m. beyond each face of the wall and 0.50 m. to 0.52 m. wide. The upper surface is not very smoothly finished; a shallow roughly circular cutting, 0.08 m. to 0.09 m. in diameter, and set 0.14 m. inside the northwest line of the wall, may have been or have held the socket for a pivot. The casing or jamb of the door must have rested on the southwestern part of the block, where it was apparently attached to a slotted end of the wall in the same manner exemplified in the doorways described above (pp. 55, 66, 77). On the northeastern side of the opening there was probably a similar block and the space between the two may have been floored with stones or earth. Some slight evidence suggests that the foundations of the partition wall continued across beneath the doorway. Soundings here revealed that the floors of the two Archives Rooms were laid over a fairly thick deposit of burned brick and calcined stones, evidently the debris from an earlier phase or building.

The Archives Storeroom (8 on Key Plan) has the same length from northeast to southwest as its neighbor, but it is much narrower, having a width of 2.90 m. (Fig. 45). The partition wall on the southeast has been described and the only thing to add is that its northwestern face bears some remains of thick coarse plaster. A similar stump of a wall exists on the northwest, 2.80 m. long, 0.85 m. thick, and varying from 0.35 to 0.80 m. in height. Both ends have been destroyed, no doubt by the quarrying activities so often mentioned. The southwest and northeast walls are represented only by the bedding slabs of their foundations. The trench marking the line of the northeastern wall, separating the Archives Storeroom from the inner portico of the Propylon, was refilled by the looters with loose earth and small stones after the useful material had been extracted. In this debris were recovered many tablets and fragments which the marauders must have thrown back as of no value or interest, if indeed they noticed them. Along with these Mycenaean records, and almost equally exciting, was the discovery in the same fill of a coin which might give some evidence for the date, or at least the date *post quem* of the removal of the stones from the wall. It is a gold ducat (Fig. 273 No. 19), minted by Lodovico Manin, the last Doge of Venice, who abdicated in 1797 before the advancing forces of Napoleon. Two Venetian copper coins of Morosini's expeditionary force of the late seventeenth century were also recovered in the debris on the southwest slope of the hill which may already have been exploited as a source of squared blocks in the time of the great expansion of Venice.

The inner Archives Room has a clay floor, ca. 0.10 m. thick, with a rough and irregular surface. No trace of movable furniture was found in the room but around the southeastern, southwestern and northwestern sides it was provided with a fixed bench or stand varying from 0.30 m. to 0.40 m. in height. The outer edge is rounded and the front generally slants outward toward the floor. The top is not level but slopes irregularly away from the front edge toward the walls. The southeastern section, which begins some 0.22 m. southwest of the base of the door jamb (measured at floor level), has an average width of 0.75 m. on top. It extended southwestward to the exterior wall. At 1.50 m. it meets the southwest bench, which is 0.55 m. wide at the top and which was backed against the outside southwestern wall. Some 1.60 m. from the corner mentioned the southwest section in turn joins, in an approximate right angle, the northwestern bench, which has a length of 2.50 m. and a width on top of 0.45 m. The northwestern section ends in a rounded corner about 1 m. short of the missing northeastern wall which divided the room from the inner stoa of the Propylon. The bench seems to have been made of clay or crude brick, the outer surface being coated with rough clay plaster similar to that noted on the southeastern wall.

Much more interesting than the bench itself are the many inscribed tablets which were discovered lying on it (Fig. 78). They lay in several groups which could be fairly well differentiated, one on the southeastern, two on the southwestern and a larger lot on the northwestern sections of the bench. The total number of the tablets which had found a resting place on the stand was about 150, in addition to fragments that could be joined to others. A great many more, however, were spread out, likewise in groups, on the earth floor between the stands (Fig. 79) and farther to the northeastward as far as the line of the northeastern wall, as well as also in the doorway leading to Room 7. One further heap lay directly above the disturbed earth marking the line of the partition wall that separated Room 8 from the inner stoa of the Propylon. Yet another group, which had evidently been shifted to an even greater distance away from its original place of storage, was brought to light lying on the stucco floor beyond the vanished dividing wall, just inside the interior portico.

How and when these tablets made their way to that area can only be conjectured: was it perhaps in the disruption at the time of the fire, or could it have been effected when the marauders pulled out the stones of the wall? Or alternatively, as believed by Professor Bennett, may there have been a door leading out from the Archives Storeroom into the inner porch of the Propylon through which the clay documents could have been precipitated? The somewhat ragged outline of the trench dug by the pillagers could possibly be interpreted as indicating that a substantial threshold and jamb bases had been extracted along with the stones of the wall, but the evidence is not indisputable. In any event it might have been useful to the keeper of the economic records to have a doorway to the inner stoa just as well as the one we have likewise conjectured to have given access to the outer portico of the Propylon.

The catalogue following the description of Room 8 presents a summary list by numbers of the components of the various groups. A detailed analysis of the heaps and the relationship of one to another will be provided in the separate volume dealing with the tablets. As mentioned, many fragments of tablets were also found in the loose earth that had been thrown back into the gap between Room 8 and the inner stoa of the gateway when the wall was torn out; these too and a few others, which came from the disturbed earth in the similar gap or chasm along the southwestern side of the Archives Rooms, will be listed by number in the catalogue.

All the tablets found in the Archives Storeroom must surely have fallen to the bench and the floor from some filing place higher up in the room. Some may have been stacked in bundles or packages on the benches or kept on shelves which were somehow attached to the walls, or suspended in baskets from pegs. No traces of post holes to support systematic shelving were seen, nor were any remains of carbonized timbers or boards observed or recognized.

The records stored in this room, presumably representing the accounts of the current year (or month) in which the palace was destroyed, were evidently arranged in some kind of proper classified order and duly labeled. Some were clearly tied up in bundles with string or ribbon (obviously, if one may judge from the bureaucratic texts of the documents, a forerunner of red tape); others seem to have been packed in wicker baskets, provided with labels which were pressed against the wicker-work. Several fragments of bronze (Fig. 274 No. 1), resembling hinges, indicate that in some instances wooden boxes with hinged covers were used for storing some tablets in the manner noted also at Knossos by Sir Arthur Evans.[40]

Room 8 was filled with the same kind of debris as that in Room 7 consisting of two layers, the upper of plowed earth, the lower mainly of burned matter and dissolved crude brick. A good many miscellaneous fragments of pottery were found in this deposit as in all other parts of the palace..

O B J E C T S   F O U N D

BRONZE

Fragments of seven hinges or handles (NM. 7755, Fig. 274 No. 1). The best preserved have the form of a narrow strip bent to make a loop with a straight extension through which runs a short sturdy bolt or rivet for attaching hinge to box or lid. Found on floor at southwestern end of room associated with Tablets Nos. 590ff. and Sealing No. 593.2.[41]

STONE

Fragment of quartz. Found with Tablets 345 ff.

Steatite shanked button. Found with Tablet 642.

CLAY

Sealings

NM. 8472 = CMMS 302, with Tablet 467 (Fig. 275 No. 1): in center horselike animal to left with head turned back; in front of it man to left warding off attack by lion (?).

NM. 8473 = CMMS 303, with Tablet 99 (Fig. 275 No. 2): above, head and forequarters of wild goat facing left; below, hindquarters and long tail of a lion (?).

NM. 8474 = CMMS 304, with Tablet 169 (Fig. 275 No. 3): two winged griffins facing, heads turned back; miniature griffins in field above at left and right. Another impression of same seal (Fig. 275 No. 7).

NM. 8475 = CMMS 305, with Tablet 154b (Fig. 275 No. 4), one half preserved: bull-leaping scene; forequarters and head of bull facing left; in front, man with arms

raised toward bull. Spiral border below. Two additional impressions (Fig. 275 Nos. 5, 6).

NM. 8476 = CMMS 306, with Tablet 154a (Fig. 275 No. 15): in center large man moving to right attacking small man facing left; leg of another man at right.

NM. 8528 = CMMS 311 under stone in doorway, fragment: rear part of animal (wild goat ?) to left.

NM. 8553 = CMMS 308 = No. 01 with inscribed obverse and reverse (PT II, 112, 196): animal, wild goat, galloping to right; hound underneath, pursuing (Fig. 275 Nos. 8, 9).

Two fragmentary sealings (Tablet Inventory Nos. 430c and 593.2: Fig. 275 Nos. 11-12, 13-14), with impressions made by the same seal as NM. 8477 (Fig. 275 No. 10) found in Room 7. In each case the small piece of clay had apparently been laid over a broad string and pressed against the flat surface of the object around which the string was tied.

Fragment: about half of sealing with impression of a fish or dolphin preserved (Fig. 275 No. 18).

Fragment, slightly more than half preserved: impression almost obliterated, apparently an animal going right (Fig. 275 No. 16).

Pieces Used to Seal Containers

Many small pieces of clay (e.g., Fig. 275 Nos. 17, 19-23) showing impressions of the string or cloth presumably used to tie up bundles or baskets of tablets. Some pieces

---

[40] PM IV, 668; J. Boardman, The Date of the Knossos Tablets, 23, fig. 5.

[41] The numbers are those of the Tablet Inventory.

bear traces of the impression of a seal on which there was no scene or none is now preserved. On many there are clear finger marks.

Tablets

On southeast wall behind bench: Nos. 1-5.

On southeast clay bench: Nos. 6-43, 129-137, 1003-1004, 1006.

On southwest bench, south corner: Nos. 44-49, 1007.

On southwest bench, west corner: Nos. 50-59, 138-146.

On northwest bench: Nos. 60-128, 165, 1008, 1009.

Above floor, east area, near surface: Nos. 147-149 (150-152), 153-164, 166-183, 185, 1010, 1012.

Southeast side below top of bench and around corner: Nos. 186-203, 210, 1013, 1014.

Central area between northwest and southeast benches below top of shelf: Nos. 204-209, 211-340, 1015-1018, 1021-1044.

Easterly area of room, but not down to floor: Nos. 346-407, 471, 852, 1047-1051.

West central area: Nos. 408-464, 1053-1072, 1074.

In or near doorway to Room 7: Nos. 465-468, 603-613-620, 1117-1139, 1148-1156.

Southwest area on floor: Nos. 472-493, 1075-1079.

Easterly area on floor: Nos. 494-511, 1082, 1083, 1248.

Easterly area on floor near doorway to Room 7: Nos. 512-566, 1084-1107, 1160.

Under preceding: Nos. 570-588, 1108-1115.

Western end of room: Nos. 590-602, 1116.

Tablet Material: No. 538[42] (Fig. 276 No. 9): squeezed up piece of clay probably once a tablet or tablet blank and intended to be used again.

No. 619[43] (Fig. 276 No. 8): surplus piece cut off from Tablet 704.

POTTERY

No pots were found on the floor. The sherds from the debris covering it represent many kylikes, cups and bowls with flat bases,

basins and bowls with pinched-out handles, a dipper, a stirrup-vase, a jug or jar, and a ribbed pithos. A few pieces bear traces of painted decoration, bands, dots, etc.

In loose earth between Archives Rooms and Propylon filling the chasm where stones of wall had been removed

GOLD

Narrow strips of thin leaf cut to form a rectangle with two crossbars making a very small object resembling a buckle in shape (NM. 7779, Fig. 273 No. 16). From chasm between Rooms 2 and 8.

Two fragments of narrow curving strips, possibly from inlay (NM. 7785, Fig. 273 Nos. 17, 18). From chasm between Rooms 2 and 8.

Tiny fragment and one small disk, d. 0.015 m., of thin leaf.

Ducat or sequin of Venice (NM. 7841, Fig. 273 No. 19). From chasm between Rooms 2 and 8; d. ca. 0.02 m., weight 3.51 grams.

SILVER

Three very small bits; fragment of little pin or rivet, l. pres. 0.018 m., slightly bent, d. of head 0.005 m., d. of pin 0.003 m.

BRONZE

Small flat piece.

STONE

Banded agate: finely worked and polished piece, with perforation, probably fragment of bead or pendant (Fig. 265 No. 7); surface slightly curved, w. 0.011 m., one straight edge, l. 0.018 m., th. 0.002 m.; end with perforation, d. 0.002 m., rounded.

Flint: tan chip.

Quartz: three small bits.

Schist?: fragments (three joining pieces) of a disk, d. ca. 0.04 m., with central perforation; poorly preserved, edges uneven, thickness irregular the surface having flaked off in places. Traces of very finely cut decoration possibly representing wings.

---

[42] Tablet Inventory number.

[43] Tablet Inventory number.

Unidentified stone: fragment of whetstone (?), l. 0.065 m., w. 0.02 m., th. 0.005 m.

CLAY

Tablets from chasm between outer Propylon (1) and Room (7): Nos. 840-851, 891, 941, 1186-1188, 1263-1271; from chasm between inner Propylon (2) and Room 8: Nos. 852, 891-916, 979-987.

POTTERY

Relatively few nondescript sherds, for the most part heavily coated with lime accretion.

In loose earth filling the chasm where the southeast and southwest walls of Room 7 and the southwest wall of Room 8 had been removed

SILVER

Three joining fragments of thin piece bent double to form what may be the lip of a jug (Fig. 264 No. 1), h. 0.028 m., w. across 0.022 m.

Another piece may be silver to which bronze has adhered (Fig. 264 No. 2).

BRONZE

Four nondescript fused and bent pieces (Fig. 264 Nos. 3-5, 7).

Arrow point, barbed type, thick point and one barb broken off (Fig. 264 No. 6), l. pres. 0.028 m., th. 0.003 m.

LEAD

Large shapeless chunk fused with clay, disintegrated brick, carbonized wood (Fig. 264 No. 12), l. 0.08 m., w. 0.04 m., th. 0.022 m.

STONE

Obsidian: three blades (Fig. 264 Nos. 8-10), several chips.

Flint: blade (Fig. 264 No. 11), l. 0.035 m., w. 0.022 m., th. 0.01 m.

Arrowhead (Fig. 264 No. 13): short, barely noticeable barbs (one broken) and a short tang; gray, l. over-all 0.024 m., tang 0.006 m., w. pres. 0.017 m., th. 0.004 m.

Many chips and flakes.

CLAY

Sealing: NM. 8526 = *CMMS* 309, fragment with both ends missing: winged griffin to right framed by two uprights resembling human legs, on each side. Trace to left possibly of another griffin.

Tablets from chasm southwest of Archives Rooms: Nos. 887-890, 1184-1185, 1189, 1191-1193, 1195-1197.

POTTERY

Considerable quantity, many nondescript sherds, mostly coated with lime: 60 kylix stems, 5 or 6 votive kylikes, more than 70 flat bases counted; other shapes noted: stirrup-vase, tankard, jug or jar, spouted vessel. Relatively few decorated pieces: bands, dots, spirals, etc. Pottery for the most part Mycenaean III B, some III A, a few Middle Helladic.

ROOM 9

To the northwestward beyond the Archives Rooms is another suite of two chambers, one evidently a waiting room and the other a pantry (Fig. 21). The latter (9 on Key Plan) is almost square, measuring ca. 3.70 m. from southeast to northwest and ca. 3.80 m. from northeast to southwest. The southeastern wall (Fig. 20), which separates the pantry from the Archives Room, has already been mentioned. On this side it extends from the eastern corner to a length of 2.75 m., the further course of it toward the southwest having been torn out down to the bottom of its foundation. In the preserved stretch three transverse grooves for beams, no doubt corresponding to vertical chases, are indicated spaced at intervals of 1 m. and 0.90 m. They seem to be relatively narrow, designed to receive small timbers. No incontrovertible evidence for the position of the horizontal beams was found but the wall as preserved has for most of its length a more or less nearly level top at ca. 0.30 m. above the floor, which probably marks the setting place of the timber. Some remains of plaster are still preserved attached to the wall, both of the backing coat and the smoothly finished surface, the latter possibly bearing vestiges of bluish paint unless it is—more probably—merely discolored by smoke or carbon.

The northeastern wall, 0.80 m. thick and 0.82 m. high, forming the partition between the pantry and the Court, extends along the whole side of the room (Fig. 21). Its eastern corner has suffered considerable damage, many stones having been removed from its northeastern face. There are four vertical chases for upright beams and the transverse connections that run through the wall. The slots average 0.25 m. in width and the spaces between them range from 0.45 m. to 0.60 m. On the side toward the pantry a horizontal groove runs along at 0.30 m. to 0.35 m. above the floor. This wall still bears considerable remains of its plaster, for the most part representing the backing; what is left of the finished surface is blackened.

The southwestern wall, which was the exterior wall of the building, is missing except for the lowest course of its foundation, but a small remnant of its plaster face (varying from 0.05 m. to 0.10 m. in height) has survived, extending 1.60 m. from the western corner of the room and also blackened.

The northwestern wall (Fig. 80) is pierced by a doorway that connects Rooms 9 and 10. The section to the northeast of the opening, 1 m. long and ca. 0.70 m. thick, still stands to a height of ca. 0.80 m. On the southwestern side of the doorway, which is not centered in the axis of the room, the wall continues ca. 1.40 m. to the west corner, descending from a maximum height of 0.43 m. to 0.10 m. The northeasterly section seems to have been provided with two vertical chases and there were probably at least two in the southwest section. A good deal of rough plaster is preserved on the northeastern part of the wall, concealing the position of the horizontal groove. In the southwestern piece some of the rough backing plaster is preserved along with a relatively small patch of the smooth finished coat, here too with traces of paint or smoke.

The floor of the room was made of stucco and two or three coats of it are recognizable. At least two phases seem to be represented. The last coating is in a badly damaged condition, very rough and uneven. Two holes appear in the middle of the floor, one small, the other larger and oval in shape, which seems to have resulted from the collapse of stone slabs that covered a drain underneath (p. 233). There is a larger and more irregular depression near the west corner and a considerable part of the floor is missing in the south corner; it was probably removed when the southwest wall and the adjoining part of the southeastern wall were pulled out. Toward the southeast end of the room is a gap in the final coating beginning at ca. 0.50 m. from the wall and roughly 0.25 m. wide, which stretches all the way across from the northeastern wall as far as the pavement is preserved. We have not been able to determine what caused this damage to the floor. The most notable thing in the room is the mass of broken pottery lying on the floor and extending 1.20 m. out from the northeast wall (Fig. 81). So far as can be determined, all these vessels are drinking cups or kylikes of the tall-stemmed type. How many are represented can only be conjectured, but the number might run to five or six hundred or more. All of them were subjected to intense heat at the time of the fire and a great many are badly warped and twisted, and some have been vitrified. They lie upside down or on their sides, or right side up, in complete confusion and disorder, as they fell, probably from wooden shelves along the wall. None could be put together and restored; most of them have been left on the floor just as they were exposed, to serve as a permanent exhibit illustrating the effect of a devastating conflagration on a well-stocked pantry. For this was surely a serving room from which guests in the adjoining apartment could be offered refreshment while they waited.

Room 9 was found covered by a deposit a little more than a meter deep: at the top, plowed earth accounted for ca. 0.30 m.; beneath it lay a stratum of reddish disintegrated crude brick mixed with small bits of calcined stone; next below was a layer of scattered stones embedded in fused brick in the eastern section. The western corner was filled with fused *migma* fallen from above. Large stones were scattered close to the walls; two heavy blocks, not squared, had fallen near the doorway above a stratum of burning ca. 0.10 m. thick.

O B J E C T S   F O U N D

S I L V E R
One small piece.

B R O N Z E
Awl (Fig. 278 No. 1): rectangular in section, l. 0.055 m., max. w. 0.0035 m., tang 0.00125 m. by 0.00175 m.

Curved fragment, possibly from a tubular socket (Fig. 278 No. 5), max. l. 0.042 m., max. w. 0.02 m., th. 0.002 m.

L E A D
One piece.

I V O R Y   O R   B O N E
Two joining pieces (Fig. 278 Nos. 3, 4), max. l. 0.02 m., max. w. 0.021 m., max. th. 0.007 m., burned black, surface damaged. Incised crosshatching.

Another piece (Fig. 278 No. 2), l. 0.036 m., w. 0.017 m., th. 0.0065 m., with similar crosshatching; burned blue-gray.

P O T T E R Y
In addition to the mass of broken and fused kylikes found lying on the floor along the northeast wall, were found numerous potsherds distributed through the deposit; plain kylikes, cups and bowls with flat bottom by far the most numerous; other shapes represented: basin with pinched-out handle, jug, krater and, in coarse ware, pithos, cooking pot on legs, scoop or brazier. A few pieces bear traces of decoration; one stray sherd of Palace Style.

R O O M   1 0

The doorway leading into the waiting room is marked by a stone threshold and bases for the door jambs (Figs. 83, 433). On each side is a block 0.46 m. to 0.50 m. broad and 0.80 m. long through the doorway. The top of each base is rabbeted beside the opening (0.025 m. to 0.03 m. deep) and, some 0.16 m. from the northwestern edge of the doorway where the rabbet broadens, is a rounded socket for a pivot (from 0.015 m. to 0.02 m. deep and ca. 0.07 m. in diameter). The width of the actual opening, as indicated by the distance from the edge of the rabbet on one side to that of the rabbet on the other, is almost exactly 1 m. These lateral bases, in addition to supporting the double doors swinging on their pivots, also carried the wooden casing of the door frame on the raised part of the stones beyond the rabbet. Abundant remains of carbonized wood were found lying on the top of each block. It is clear that the double doors swung back against the casing within the depth of the doorway. The leaves could have been no more than 0.45 m. wide. Between the lateral bases the threshold itself is made of two blocks of no great size, a small one on the southeast, 0.59 m. wide and 0.29 m. deep, and a larger one, 0.67 m. wide and 0.51 m. deep, on the northwestern side. The bases of the jambs were notched back on each side to receive this larger block. The rabbets on the two lateral blocks are not absolutely symmetrical, the one on the southwest being 0.23 m. wide, the one on the northeast only 0.165 m. The main block of the threshold is at about the same level as the rabbeted part of the lateral blocks, the smaller stone in the southeast face of the doorway is set slightly (0.02 m.) lower.

The waiting room as we have called it (10 on Key Plan) is an L-shaped apartment (Fig. 80), 3.95 m. long from southeast to northwest and 4.18 m. wide along the base of the L next to the pantry. The width is reduced to 2.98 m. in what forms the upright bar of the L. This reduction in the area of the northwestern part of the room was effected in order to provide a suitable entrance into Room 10 for those who came from the Court around the southwestern anta of the Portico.

The southeastern wall has already been described in the account of the pantry. The only information to be added is the evidence for a horizontal beam at a height of 0.35 m. above the floor. The northeastern wall (Fig. 82) between the lower bar of the L which ends in an alcove and the Court is 1.18 m. long, 0.83 m. thick, and stands to a height of 0.90 m. Built in the customary style, it has two chases for uprights and struts extending through the wall. The northwestern chase is actually just beyond the corner with the northwestern wall of the alcove. This latter wall, running southwestward along the side of the alcove, is only 0.60 m. thick and is preserved to a height of 0.85 m. Its southern corner seems to have been formed by a large vertical timber fitting into a chase which measures approximately 0.30 m. by

0.20 m. The distance, including the doorway, from the corner of the alcove to the northwest wall of the room is 2.80 m. The section between the alcove and the door opening is 1.30 m. long, with a thickness of only 0.40 m. and a height of 0.82 m. Beyond the doorway the wall projects barely 0.13 m. from the north corner.

The northwest wall is 0.85 m. thick and stands to a height of 0.90 m. On its northwesterly side it is preserved to a length of 3.17 m. On the southeastern face the wall can be seen only to ca. 1.70 m. from the northern corner; beyond this point it disappears behind the bench (Fig. 80) which will be described below. On this side there is a horizontal groove at 0.37 m. above the floor and two vertical chases run through the wall, ca. 0.60 m. apart. The southwestern wall has been wholly destroyed almost to the bottom of the foundations and nothing is left above ground to describe (Fig. 80). The other walls all bear considerable remains of plaster, in some places showing two or more coats; but for the most part it is only the undercoating and not the finished surface that survives. No traces of painted patterns can be recognized.

The floor of the room was made of stucco. It is now rough and uneven, evidently much damaged by the fire. It has a general slope toward the south and near the southeastern wall is a large stone slab in which a circular hole (Fig. 20), ca. 0.08 m. in diameter, leads downward to an underground drain (p. 233 note 79).

The furniture in the room comprises a fixed bench in the western corner and a stand in the south corner (Fig. 83). The bench on the northwestern side is 1.40 m. long to its junction with the southwestern bench which has a length of 1.32 m. Its height from the floor varies from 0.36 m. at its northeastern end to 0.31 m. at the southeastern. The width averages 0.45 m. The bench was made largely of clay coated with layers of stucco on its upper surface and all its visible vertical faces. The final coating, where preserved, is white and smooth and bears some remains of painted decoration (Fig. 85). The patterns on the northeast end, so far as they can be recognized, seem to be similar to those that recur in other places in the palace on dadoes, here comprising curved yellow bands outlined in black. On the southeast parallel curving and vertical yellow bands outlined in black suggest a decorated leg from which horizontal rungs, yellow bordered in black, extend across the front of the bench. Traces of a comparable decoration appear on the outer corner of the southwestern bench.

The stand in the south corner, 1.60 m. long against the southwestern wall and 0.75 m. wide, is preserved to a height of from 0.36 m. to 0.50 m. It was built of stones of no great size and clay, mainly the latter, and its faces toward the room were coated with excellent plaster, which bears black-outlined designs difficult to interpret. The purpose of the stand was to hold two capacious jars or pithoi. Considerable remains of the bottom of one were found in place in the northwestern end of the stand, but only a fragment of the second had survived along with the impression of its setting. The upper part of the stand was destroyed, probably when the stones of the southwest wall were pillaged, and its original height is uncertain. The size of the jars too can only be conjectured. It is to be noted that both the stand and the bench, in their present form at least, were built after the floor had been laid and after the walls had been plastered; but they may well have been replacements of forerunners that had suffered damage.

The purpose of this room with a fairly comfortable bench on which visitors could sit and rest and the stand in the corner containing two large wine jars can safely be interpreted in connection with the adjoining pantry, which was provided with an abundance of drinking cups. Surely this was a waiting room where guests could be entertained with refreshment while they awaited their turn to be introduced into the presence of the king on his throne.

Many fallen pieces of plaster were recovered in the room, which, Miss Lang believes, was decorated in a symphony of brown, orange, black, and white. Dado fragments are numerous and striped pieces and upper borders indicate that the wall paintings extended well above the dado.

The accumulation filling Room 10 was ca. 1 m. deep. Under the surface soil, 0.30 m. to 0.35 m. thick, was a confused mass of calcined stone and disintegrated crude brick, which covered the bench and, with many stones, continued down almost to the floor. Just above the latter the earth had a green color, no doubt somehow produced by the fire.

O B J E C T S   F O U N D

BRONZE

Small fragment of weapon—dagger, rapier, or spearhead—with strong midrib on both sides (Fig. 278 No. 7), l. pres. 0.027 m., w. pres. 0.015 m.

Piece of plate with rivet, possibly from a knife (Fig. 278 No. 6), max. l. pres. 0.03 m., max. w. 0.015 m.

Several other small nondescript fragments.

LEAD (?)

Lump with bit of bronze adhering to it.

STONE

Fragment of obsidian, possibly an arrowhead (Fig. 278 No. 8), l. pres. 0.019 m., w. 0.018 m., max. th. 0.003 m. From fused brick deposit in alcove.

Fragment of rim of small basin or bowl of schist-like stone (Fig. 269 No. 10), much damaged by fire, h. pres. 0.046 m., max. w. 0.042 m., th. 0.0285 m.: carving in low relief of running spirals on upper surface and vertical outer edge of rim; possibly from a lamp. Found near bench under fallen plaster.

IVORY

Small burned piece.

POTTERY

Casual nondescript sherds not from floor deposit: 43 kylix stems, 28 flat bases of cups and bowls counted; other shapes recognized: basin with pinched-out handles, spouted vessel, krater, pithos, cooking pot on legs. A few pieces with painted decoration: bands, loop, stippling.

LOBBY 11

Close to the northern corner of Room 10 a doorway opened into a small lobby (11 on Key Plan) through which one had to pass to enter the room from the Court. The doorway is marked by three small slabs of poros (Figs. 84, 434) almost of equal size (0.46 m. by 0.50, 0.52, 0.53 m.). The central stone is sunk ca. 0.01 m. below the other two. These blocks served as threshold and supports for the door jambs on each side of the opening. How wide the actual doorway was cannot be exactly determined, but it probably overlapped to some extent the lateral blocks; as indicated by relatively smooth wear of their surface at their inner ends the opening must have been ca. 0.90 m. No cutting for a socket of a pivot exists and it is likely that hangings took the place of a swinging door. The northwestern block was cut back 0.20 m. in its northern corner to receive the angle of the southwestern base of the jamb of a doorway opening northwestward into a large chamber (12 on Key Plan).

The lobby itself is ca. 1.55 m. wide from northeast to southwest and 2.17 m. long (Fig. 84). On its southeast side it is bordered by the lateral wall of the alcove already described. At its northeast end this wall has a slot, ca. 0.17 m. by 0.25 m., probably indicating that an upright wooden beam, resting on a stone ca. 0.15 m. below the floor, formed the actual corner. At 0.25 m. above the floor is a horizontal groove for a beam. The wall itself still retains some remains of plaster representing at least two coats. Most of it is only the rough backing, but there are some patches of the finished surface coat of both layers, each with remnants of painted decoration. Parallel curving lines in black and red on a pink ground can be seen and the patterns seem to be of the types common on dadoes.

On the southwestern side the lobby was bordered by the doorway and the adjoining wall of the waiting room. The wall apparently had a horizontal beam ca. 0.10 m. above the floor, and vestiges of rough plaster on its face. The northeastern side of the lobby must have opened from the western corner of the Court. A narrow gap in the floor, 0.25 m. to 0.35 m. wide, extends more than 1 m. to the northwestward from the corner (Fig. 84). How much farther it continued is uncertain, since the whole floor has been torn out along with the great anta block. The gap showed traces of a finished edge and the deposit filling it contained black carbonized matter. This evidence suggests that the space had been occupied by something of perishable material. There is no indication that it was made of stone; it may have been a wooden sill jutting out from the corner post. Sills of that kind appear in a corridor on the northeastern side of the central building (pp. 216, 217f.). The sill does not necessarily indicate that there was a real door, but it could mark the transition from the Court into the lobby. The latter is bounded finally on its northwestern side by a proper doorway which led into Room 12.

Below the plowed earth the room was filled with the wreckage of the fire: dissolved crude brick and calcined stones. Extending over part of the threshold of the doorway into Room 12 was a thin stratum of black, presumably the carbonized remains of wood. On the northeast the deposit had been cut away and loose earth and stones filled a broad chasm left by those who removed the large poros base of the southwest anta of the Portico and also carried off half of the threshold and the jamb base from the doorway leading into Room 12.

A good many fragments of painted plaster were collected from the debris. Above the dado, as analyzed by Miss Lang, there seems to have been an architectural composition using wood-graining, knots, and rounded beams and beam-ends.

O B J E C T S   F O U N D

BRONZE
Rivet-head, found in plowed earth.

STONE
Flake of obsidian (Fig. 278 No. 11).

TERRACOTTA
Small conical whorl (Fig. 278 No. 10), h. 0.021 m., d. 0.025 m.; found on floor in doorway into Room 12.
Weight ? (Fig. 278 No. 9), h. 0.017 m., d. 0.038 m., d. of perforation 0.008 m.; apparently made from the raised base of small pot.

POTTERY
Small jar, No. 1173 (Fig. 348 No. 5): flat bottom, rounded body, oval collar-neck, two horizontal handles and four vertical lugs pierced horizontally set on shoulder; misshapen, vitrified, and fused; h. ca. 0.095 m., d. ca. 0.08 m., rim 0.042 m. by 0.052 m. Found on floor.

ROOM 12

The doorway into Room 12 (Fig. 435) was considerably damaged probably at the time the anta was removed: the northeastern base of the door casing is missing and the threshold block was partly hacked away on that side. What is left of it, 0.53 m. wide at the southeast and 0.43 m. at the northwest, extends through the doorway with a length of 1.03 m. The block is 0.13 m. thick. The top of the stone, now somewhat pitted, was at one time covered with stucco; the original surface, which appears here and there, had previously been worn smooth. The base of the southwestern door jamb, 1.15 m. long, projects southeastward 0.13 m. beyond the threshold. It is ca. 0.50 m. wide at its southeastern end (where a little notch has been cut into it to fit a corresponding notch in the base of the door jamb of the waiting room) and 0.52 m. at its northwestern end. On the side toward the threshold a rabbet has been cut in the top of the block, 0.02 m. deep, and 0.17 m. to 0.18 m. wide. Some 0.18 m. in from the northwestern edge of the stone is a shallow depression at the inner limit of the rabbet (0.075 m. in diameter and 0.025 m. deep), which either served as the pivot itself or held a socket in which a single door or one wing of a double door swung, folding back against the casing. The latter was of course made of wood which was no doubt firmly fastened to the upright beams and horizontal struts that occupied the chase directly behind it.

Room 12 (Key Plan) is a fairly spacious apartment, ca. 5 m. long from northeast to southwest and 4.25 m. wide (Fig. 86). On the southeast it was bounded by the wall that separated it from the waiting room. This has already been described as seen from the southeast. Its northwestern face, which is not preserved to its full length, has four vertical chases set at intervals of from 0.60 m. to 0.65 m. There was also a horizontal groove for a beam at 0.25 m. above the floor. Some remains of plaster still cling to the wall; but no traces of the final smooth coat survive.

The northeastern wall which divides the room from the Portico and the Vestibule consists largely of a mass of calcined stone and dissolved brick solidly fused together. It is preserved to a maximum height of 0.95 m. and on its lower part just above the floor some plaster is still visible. There seems to have been a horizontal beam at floor level and at least three vertical chases, roughly 0.70 m. apart, have been noted.

Only a low stump of the northwestern wall has survived, ranging from 0.08 m. to 0.35 m. in height, with a thickness of 0.68 m. It extends some 3.35 m. southwestward from the doorway that leads from Room 12 into Corridor 13. No evidence for the position of horizontal beams is preserved and the bottom of only one chase can now be recognized; but the wall was no doubt built in the normal manner. On its southeastern face where the plaster is fairly well-preserved traces of red and white paint can be seen.

The southwestern wall has vanished entirely except for the bedding stones of the foundations (Fig. 80); but near the western corner a small strip of plaster is still in place, ca. 0.10 m. high, giving us the line of the inside face of the wall for a distance of some 0.90 m. Beyond this point toward the southeast, the floor of the room and the stucco of the pavement of the court outside have been hacked away. Ragged edges were left on each side and between them the gap, through which the stones of the foundation were extracted, ranges from 0.90 m. to 1.20 m. in width. The shape and width of this gap give no evidence for or against our conjecture that there was an opening through the southwestern wall from Room 12 to the court in front of the Southwestern Building. The foundations themselves, preserved only in their lowest course, shed no real light on this problem (Fig. 20). But it seems almost sure that the exterior wall, in its extent across the southwestern side of Room 12, was narrower than the rest of the wall to the northwest and southeast. This suggested to us that there might have been on this side of the central building a doorway, or perhaps rather a portal, with a single column in its façade. If it were like that on the northeastern flank of the building (41 on Key Plan, and p. 179), it would require only a very narrow threshold block, which might account for the reduction in width of the foundation mentioned above. It would surely be altogether suitable to have a proper way of communication between the two residential establishments.

Room 12, in any event, seems to have been an elegantly decorated apartment, with wall paintings on all sides and a fine hard polished stucco floor, now a dark blue. As one came in from Court 63—if our interpretation is correct—one would find a pleasant entrance hall, with a doorway on each side at the inner end, giving access to different quarters of the palace. The evidence for the wall paintings is very clear. Many fragments of fallen plaster and flooring were found beginning to appear just below plowed earth but with the greatest concentration lying face down on the floor. Many had piled up in heaps from the western corner, where they lay five deep, and continued in front of the northwestern, the northeastern, and the southeastern walls. Few if any pieces are recorded from the extreme southwestern side of the room. Nearly all of these fragments were in a very bad state of preservation, broken and crumbly, but it has been possible to recognize some of the motives: large semicircular or trefoil blobs, sometimes on orange background, perhaps representing hairy or bristly animals with mottled coats, bulls or lions or possibly bull-hide shields. Jagged rocklike forms also occur.

As excavated, Room 12 was found covered with a top layer of plowed earth 0.25 m. deep; beneath it lay gray calcined debris including many stones, in the northeasterly part ranging from 0.10 m. to 0.30 m. deep. This deposit rested on dark red disintegrated crude brick which, farther southwestward, rose up much higher to the cultivated earth with a total depth of 0.70 m. A thin stratum of ashy calcined matter was spread over the floor. Here and there throughout the debris were black patches which probably represent the carbonized remains of timbers or boards.

O B J E C T S   F O U N D

GOLD
Small shapeless fragment, on floor.

SILVER
Small flat piece, l. 0.02 m., w. 0.007 m., below carbonized beam; twisted melted chunk.

BRONZE
Nail, rectangular in section (Fig. 278 No. 14), l. 0.034 m., d. head 0.07 m., d. shaft 0.0035 to 0.0045 m. Found on floor.

Thick twisted fragment, possibly from a vessel (Fig. 278 No. 17), l. pres. 0.06 m., h. pres. 0.035 m.: heavy, much battered and melted; traces of spiraliform decoration in relief. Found 0.30 m. above floor.

Fragment apparently from blade of a knife or cleaver (Fig. 278 No. 15), l. pres. 0.029 m., w. 0.015 m. Found on floor.

Fragment from tang of thin knife with one rivet and two further rivet-holes (Fig. 278 No. 12), l. pres. 0.036 m., max. w. 0.013 m. Found ca. 0.35 m. above floor.

Several nondescript pieces on floor and just above (e.g., Fig. 278 Nos. 13, 16).

STONE

A few scraps of quartz and obsidian.

IVORY

Several small pieces.

POTTERY

Krater-bowl (Shape 60, p. 397)
  No. 1172 (Fig. 385), decorated.

Much broken pottery was found on the floor under the fallen plaster. The material represents some 25 or more high-stemmed kylikes and several cups or bowls with flat bottoms. In the superincumbent deposit were recovered the usual miscellaneous fragments of kylikes, flat-bottomed cups and bowls, pithoi and cooking pots with legs. A few pieces bear traces of painted decoration.

CORRIDOR 13

Along the southwestern side of the Megaron Suite there seems to have been originally a long corridor corresponding more or less to that on the northeastern flank. Each of these passages had regular doorways at intervals shutting off different sections. Corridor 13 (Key Plan) is a section of this kind (ca. 4 m. long) between two such doorways alongside the greater part of the Vestibule. The doorway from Room 12 has been partially destroyed, presumably at the same time that the southwest wall of the Vestibule itself was demolished (p. 72). The base block for the southwest jamb is preserved and the greater part of the threshold, but a considerable part of its northern corner has been hacked away and the base of the northeast jamb is missing (Fig. 89). The threshold block (0.20 m. thick) was almost square, extending 0.82 m. through the doorway with a width of 0.78 m. between the lateral bases. In its northwestern part it has a relatively smooth surface probably worn by many feet, but the southeastern part of it has suffered a good deal of superficial damage, perhaps as a result of fire, and is pitted and rough. The base of the jamb, which is 0.83 m. long through the doorway and 0.38 m. wide, so far as can be measured, was cut on its upper surface with a rabbet almost exactly like that we have seen in the doorways between Rooms 9 and 10 and 11 and 12. Here the rabbet ranged from 0.10 m. to 0.12 m. wide and was cut to a depth of 0.015 m. Ca. 0.13 m. from the northwest edge is a circular hollow, 0.03 m. deep with a diameter of 0.065 m. to 0.07 m., which must be the socket, or the setting-place for the socket, in which the door or one leaf of it swung. It looks as if a second and very crudely cut hole for a socket of about the same size, but shallower, was at sometime made just to the southwest of the first.

The northeastern wall and presumed doorway separating this part of the corridor from the Vestibule had been demolished except for the northwestern part of it (Figs. 60, 86), ca. 1.65 m. long (p. 72). On its face toward the passage the wall bears evidence for a horizontal beam at floor level and for another at a height of 0.75 m. above the floor.

On its southwestern side Corridor 13 was bordered by a stairway, fragments of two steps of which have survived (Fig. 89). The width of the stairway can only be conjectured; it was estimated by Mr. de Jong to have been 1.75 m. Exactly how the corridor was flanked on this side farther northwestward beyond the stairway is not certain because of extensive destruction, apparently carried out by those who searched the ruins for building material. There must have been a wall which came from the southwest up to the corridor, dividing Rooms 14 and 15 (Key Plan) and supporting the stairway. No trace of it has survived except the empty trench from which its material was taken (Fig. 87). To the northwest, beyond the end of this vanished wall, is a curious structure of brick and stone, faced with plaster. It was set somewhat obliquely instead of paralleling the wall on the opposite side of the corridor. This slab looks as if it constituted the filling of an earlier doorway leading into Room 15, but no actual remains of a proper threshold were found under it. A comparable filling with a slab of clay and stone is to be seen between Lobby 29 and Room 30 (p. 152) and Rooms 31 and 33 (p. 161). The filling between Corridor 13 and Room 15 is 0.42 m. thick, 1.43 m. long, the southeastern part being 0.58 m. high. It rests on bedding stones which lie on *stereo,* 0.30 m. below the floor. The northwestern part, separated from the southeastern by a vertical chase 0.07 m. wide, is only 0.35 m. high. The northeastern face of this slab is coated with fine plaster, which passed directly over the chase mentioned. It bears remains of a fresco (Fig. 90) apparently representing a processional scene: what is preserved is the lower part of a spreading black robe beneath which appear two bare feet in red. The figure is therefore that of a man, in natural size, perhaps a priest, moving to the left. Behind him is a tall slender lamp stand, or column, with spreading base. The bottom of the fresco extends down at least 0.04 m. below the last floor of the corridor and must therefore be associated with an earlier phase.

The stucco floor of Corridor 13 is 0.04 m. to 0.06 m. thick. In a small area near the threshold it is well preserved, dark blue, smoothly worn, possibly from use; beyond that it is very rough and irregular from the effects of the fire. Along the northeastern side, toward the conjectured door to the Vestibule, the floor is missing and a broad gap extends northwestward, opposite the trench left by the removal of the wall mentioned above. Beyond the gap the floor continues, for the most part in damaged condition, as far as the northwestern doorway. It was laid on a deposit of red dissolved burned brick and rubble resting on yellowish hardpan-like earth above true *stereo.*

Some 0.07 m. to 0.08 m. below the floor in the southeastern part of Corridor 13 is an earlier pavement, also in damaged state. It is 0.04 m. to 0.05 m. thick and lies on *stereo.* Beyond the gap toward the northwest no trace of the earlier floor was observed.

The deposit that was found filling Corridor 13 had suffered much from intrusions, one probably connected with the planting of an olive tree, another with the removal of the wall between Rooms 14 and 15. Where it remained undisturbed, however, it showed at the top the usual cultivated soil; next below, calcined earth and small stones which continued down to 0.85 m. to 0.90 m. below the surface; there reddish disintegrated crude brick appeared extending to the floor. Toward the southeast, in front of the steps, greenish-yellow clay lay on a thin stratum of black earth and carbonized matter covering the floor.

Very few fragments of plaster were recovered in the debris or on the floor. Some much damaged pieces may be from the pink background of the scene representing the processional figure. Odd bits of blue and red may have fallen from above.

O B J E C T S   F O U N D

B R O N Z E

Two flattish pieces: one thick (Fig. 278 No. 18), l. 0.035 m., w. 0.025 m., th. 0.022 m., decorated with impressed diamond or lattice pattern and one thin, 0.038 m. by 0.023 m., from burned debris.

One slightly curved fragment, possibly from a socket, l. 0.043 m., w. 0.018 m. Found in plowed earth.

Small scraps from calcined mass against northeast wall.

O B S I D I A N

Flake (Fig. 278 No. 19), l. 0.03 m., w. 0.016 m., from against northeast wall.

I V O R Y

Blackened fragment, 0.019 m. by 0.008 m.

P O T T E R Y

Relatively few nondescript calcined sherds, including five kylix stems, three flat bases of cups or bowls, and a hydria. Scanty remains of painted decoration.

S O U T H W E S T   S T A I R W A Y   1 4 - 1 5

The stairway seems to have occupied the space previously taken up by two small rooms (14 and 15 on Key Plan) that were separated by a wall no stone of which now survives in place (Fig. 87). The whole area measures ca. 4 m. from northeast to southwest by 4.10 m. from southeast to northwest. The stairway thus must have comprised three flights, the first ascending toward the southwest to a landing, the second rising to the northwest to another landing, and the third turning back to the northeast. Only the battered remnants of the two lowest steps of the stairs are now preserved (Fig. 89) at the left side. The bottom one is a complete block finished at each end, 0.59 m. long and 0.22 m. high; the second, with a maximum length of 0.48 m., now ends in a jagged break. It must originally have been much longer, and it is likely that there was an alternation of joints similar to that which appears in the northeastern stairway (36 on Key Plan). The first step, worn and damaged on top, now rises 0.12 m. to 0.14 m. above the last stucco floor of Corridor 13, which is also far from level, and stands 0.17 m. and more above the earlier floor of the corridor. The tread so far as it can be measured is 0.30 m. deep. The second step, which is tilted backward now, rises 0.16 m. to 0.17 m. above the first and has a tread 0.32 m. broad. The injured state of the two steps makes precise measurements impossible. In the northeastern stairway (pp. 167f.) the bottom step is 0.18 m. high, but the average rise of those preserved is 0.155 m. and the average depth of the tread is 0.31 m. The reconstruction of the southwestern stairway is, in the light of the scanty evidence available, somewhat hazardous.

Mr. de Jong has studied the problem and suggests that there were eight steps ascending southwestward to a landing in nine risers (Fig. 436), then a turn northwestward to another landing with one riser and finally a further turn to the northeastward with eight treads and nine risers to the floor above. He allows an average height of 0.171 m. for each riser and of 0.312 m. for the width of each tread. In this way he reaches the upper story, with his 19 steps, at 3.25 m. above the ground floor. This scheme provides landings, 1.50 m. deep and 2.05 m. long, at the double turn of the staircase and exactly fills the space available. It lays out the lower flight 2 m. wide resting in part on a shelf of the supporting wall while the upper flight, 1.50 m. wide, is borne on the rest of the wall.

Mr. Buck, who supervised the excavation of this area, also studied the problem and evolved a slightly different solution: he provides eight steps and a landing, that is, nine risers in the first flight, three risers including another landing in the second flight and eight steps, nine risers, in the third. This plan, too, fills the space adequately, accounts for an aggregate height of 3.30 m. with an average height for riser of 0.157 m. and an average width of 0.312 m. for the tread; it also makes the landings 1.50 m. wide, which is the width of the stairway itself in all three flights.

The first flight, in any event, was founded on a solid fill of yellow-brown earth and greenish-yellow clay, the whole packed down hard above the earlier floor and held up on the northwest by the wall now missing, which may have had a thickness of ca. 1 m. This latter must have provided the main support for the steps of the second flight. The second landing and the third flight must have been held up by wooden timbers stretching from the missing wall to the northwestern wall of Room 15. Three squared blocks, 0.63 m. apart in the lowest course of that wall, might perhaps indicate the position of the principal supporting beams (Fig. 91). However that may be, the steps in this last flight, too, were made of stone, as demonstrated by many fragments found in the burned debris that filled Room 15, most of them in calcined crumbling condition. If Mr. de Jong's reconstruction is approximately correct, the landings were somewhat longer from southeast to northwest than in their depth from northeast to southwest. The vanished wall is not exactly in the middle of the space occupied by the stairway and this fact leads to some discrepancies in the width of the staircase so far as the lower and the upper flights are concerned. It may be that the steps in the lower flight, which was supported on a solid earth fill, were longer than those in the upper flight which had to be held up by wooden timbers. The space on the southeast side is 1.70 m. wide, that on the northwest is 1.40 m. This difference might likewise suggest that the middle flight had three steps instead of two. But this would mean that the floor of the upper story on the southwest side of the building was somewhat higher than that on the northeast side. A difference so small, however, might well have been adjusted in the slightly varying height of the steps themselves.

Room 14 (Key Plan), under the first flight of the stairs, was in an earlier phase 3.35 m. long by 1.70 m. wide (Fig. 87). The southeast wall alongside Room 12 has already been described. The walls on the southwest and northwest no longer exist. On the northeast there must have been an opening of some kind through which the room could be entered; but the stairway which was later installed here has displaced these earlier constructions altogether and nothing can now be seen where the steps have in their turn been pulled out except a gap 0.65 m. wide between the room and the corridor. The stucco floor of Room 14, which is ca. 0.09 m. thick, is in relatively good condition. A straight edge on the northeast gives the line of its front wall and a similar edge on the northwest rises toward the vanished wall.

Ca. 0.15 m. beneath this floor is another stucco pavement which must be assigned to a still earlier phase. It is 0.04 m. thick and has a smooth shiny black surface under an incrustation of lime. At the point examined it appears to rest directly on *stereo*. Only a small part of it was seen but it shows a straight edge (ca. 0.80 m. long) toward the vanished wall, which must already have existed in that earlier phase, and there is also a short bit of straight edge on the northeastern side aligned with the edge of the upper pavement. Perhaps this lower floor was contemporary with the similar underlying one already mentioned in Corridor 13 (p. 111).

Under the usual plowed ground lay the solid deposit which supported the first flight of the stairway. It consisted of mixed yellow-brown earth with greenish-yellow clay lying directly on the floor, and contained no burned debris.

O B J E C T S   F O U N D

Scattered about in the deposit on which the first flight rested

GOLD

Three very small fragments of foil (NM. 7801).

SILVER

Nondescript thin flat piece.

BRONZE

Many thin crumbling fragments.

IVORY

Numerous scraps, some white, some burned black, or blue-gray. A few bearing diagonal crosshatching in delicately incised lines (e.g., Fig. 278 Nos. 20-23).

Two very small fragments of an edge preserving part of carved spiral pattern.

FLINT

Blade of brown flint, l. 0.036 m., w. 0.017 m., th. 0.006 m., with serrated edges.

On the earlier floor

Nondescript sherds like those found in the debris almost everywhere throughout the palace.

A few fragments of bronze, a flake of obsidian, and some pieces of ivory.

ROOM 15

Room 15 (Key Plan) under the third flight of the stairway is 3.20 m. long and ca. 1.40 m. wide. It was bordered on the southeast by the vanished wall, on the northeast by the stone and clay slab described above (p. 111). Its northwestern wall still stands to a maximum height of 0.95 m. above the floor (Fig. 87) and is preserved to a point 0.80 m. short of the exterior southwest wall. Here there is a gap down to floor level where the line of its plaster, however, continues on its northwestern face to its junction with the outer wall. Three large squared blocks (Fig. 91), resting at floor level, are more or less evenly spaced, ca. 0.65 m. apart, as mentioned above (p. 113). No remains of plaster have survived on the southeast face of the wall but that there once was plaster is clearly shown by the upturning edge of the stucco on the floor. The inner face of the southwestern wall still stands to a maximum height of 0.50 m. across the end of the room. This remnant, constructed of rubble, somehow escaped when the ashlar blocks of the outer face were removed by the marauders. The inner face was sheared off in a straight vertical cut aligned with the northwest face of the vanished wall. Here too the wall plaster is gone.

The floor is made of good stucco, but is cracked and damaged in many places. It ends in a fairly straight line along the vanished wall. On the northeast it stops in a somewhat ragged edge against the clay and stone slab. If there ever was a doorway here giving access to the room, all traces were destroyed by the installation of the clay slab. After the latter was set up, at any rate, there could be no entrance into the space beneath the upper flight of the stairway. It does not seem to have been filled up solidly with earth; for, when excavated, it was found to contain a great deal of burned material, calcined stone, fragments of stone steps, burned brick, and other debris that fell in the final conflagration.

In the mixed deposit filling Room 15 no objects of any consequence were recovered except the fragments of steps of poros and some nondescript stray potsherds.

These two rooms, 14 and 15, which were made over into a stairway and which must represent at least three phases, offer many puzzling problems.

ROOM 16

We turn now to the doorway that leads northwestward from Corridor 13 to the next section of the former corridor (16 on Key Plan). It has a stone threshold ca. 0.80 m. wide and 0.53 m. deep from front to back (Figs. 92, 437). Since the stone,

0.11 m. thick and damaged by fire, is in part coated with floor stucco, exact measurements are difficult. On each side is the base of the door frame, the southwestern 0.95 m. long by 0.52 m. wide, the northeastern 0.90 m. long by 0.50 m. wide by 0.35 m. thick. The bases of the jambs at the southeast side of the opening extend out ca. 0.22 m. to 0.24 m. beyond the southeastern face of the threshold. The bases for the door casing have been badly damaged by fire. Each block has a rabbet cut in its upper surface, apparently rather roughly executed, but in the same general manner as in the corresponding blocks in the doors between Rooms 9 and 10, 11 and 12, and 12 and 13 (pp. 103, 107, 110).[44] The rabbets are not symmetrical on the two sides, the one on the northeast being ca. 0.225 m. broad, the one on the southwest only 0.12 m. A shallow pivot-hole, 0.06 m. in diameter and 0.15 m. from the northwest face of the doorway, has been cut in the northeastern block. There is a very rough smaller cutting in the southwestern block, but whether it served for a pivot or for a locking bar or was accidentally made is uncertain. The door opening had a width of ca. 1 m. The wooden door jambs on each side had left abundant powdered ash and carbonized remains on each lateral base. The fire had raged with particular intensity in this region and the walls on each side are now thoroughly calcined on the northeast and fused into hard *migma* on the southwest.

Room 16 is merely a short section of the southwestern corridor, 1.64 m. wide by ca. 3.25 m. long (Fig. 88). On the northeast, separating it from the Throne Room, is the enormously thick wall that has already been described (p. 78). The wall stands to a maximum height of 1.20 m. In it are four vertical chases that ran through the wall from top to bottom, spaced with intervals of ca. 0.80 m. There is some evidence for a horizontal beam at or just above floor level and a groove for another appears at a height of ca. 0.75 m. above the floor. Considerable remains of plaster adhere to this wall; most of it is the rough undercoating, but at the northwestern end some of the thin fine surface layer is still preserved.

The northwestern wall, if our interpretation of the corridor is correct, is a later insertion. In any event, it is only 0.60 m. thick and it is not bonded with the lateral walls. It stands to a maximum height of 0.83 m. and was apparently erected without a framework of horizontal and vertical beams. The southeastern face retains a large part of its plaster, but it is all merely the rough backing coat.

On its southwestern side the room is bordered by a wall which at its southeastern end contains a doorway leading into Room 17 (Fig. 92). The wall proper is ca. 1.60 m. long, 0.83 m. thick, and stands to a maximum height of 1 m. Traces of a horizontal groove show that a beam lay about 0.60 m. above the floor. Rough plaster is also preserved on this wall to a height of ca. 0.60 m. but there are no remains of the finishing coat.

[44] The base on the southwest was notched at its western angle to receive the corner of the jamb base in the doorway that led into Room 17.

When excavated the room was found to contain a mass of burned debris, calcined stones, dissolved crude brick, unmistakable evidence of the great intensity of the fire on this side. Above the floor were recovered many fragments of plaster which had once been painted, some lying face down, partly covered with stones that had fallen after them. Many fragments of stucco flooring must have fallen from the upper story, probably along with the plaster. From the debris were collected some 120 miscellaneous potsherds, mainly fragments of kylikes and flat-bottomed bowls and cups and a few of coarse ware. Several pieces bear remains of painted decoration. The floor is in extremely bad condition, cracked, rough and blistered, obviously from the effects of the fire.

ROOM 17

The doorway opening into Room 17 is 1.73 m. broad, measured across the threshold and bases of the jambs (Figs. 92, 438). The threshold block, 0.80 m. wide and 0.69 m. deep through the doorway, is still coated with stucco flooring. The northwestern base of the door casing, set at the same level as the threshold, is 0.46 m. wide and 0.83 m. long, projecting 0.15 m. into Room 17 beyond the edge of the threshold. The corresponding base on the other side of the doorway is 0.47 m. wide and 0.84 m. long and juts out 0.20 m. beyond the threshold slab. At its eastern corner it was fitted into a small notch cut into the western angle of the base for the jamb in the adjoining doorway between Corridor 13 and Room 16. The two bases for the door frame leading into Room 17 bear in the top traces of a barely perceptible rabbet of the kind seen in so many of the doorways already described. On the northwestern side it is 0.11 m. to 0.14 m. wide and on the southeastern only 0.10 m. The cutting is very shallow and shows the same signs of wear as the threshold. The rest of the base in each instance is only roughly finished where the door jambs stood. On the southeastern side, some 0.17 m. from the line of Room 16, is a sinking 0.05 m. or 0.06 m. deep and nearly 0.15 m. in diameter, very roughly cut. It must have held the socket for the pivot in which the door swung. Both bases were found covered with a deposit, 0.26 m. deep, of carbonized matter which stretched out to the very edge of the shallow rabbet. This must represent what was left of the door frame after the fire. Above this deposit lay masses of dissolved crude brick.

Room 17 (Key Plan) is nearly square, measuring ca. 3.20 m. from northeast to southwest and 3.05 m. from southeast to northwest (Fig. 87). The wall on the northeast side beyond the doorway has already been described as it appeared in the corridor; on its southwest face rough plaster, preserved to a height of ca. 0.70 m., covers virtually the whole of the wall. Almost nothing is left of the final coat bearing decoration. At 0.65 m. above the floor there seems to have been a horizontal groove for a beam. The northwestern wall, 0.85 m. to 0.90 m. thick, is preserved to a maximum height of 0.70 m. Throughout its length it still bears thick rough plaster like that on the northeast wall, but of the finished coat only a trifling patch survives. A horizontal beam is marked at approximately 0.60 m. above the floor. On the southwest the inner rubble backing of the exterior wall is preserved to a maximum height of 0.40 m., though the outer face has been stripped down to the bedding course by looters of its large squared blocks (Fig. 63). On this low remnant the plaster, which still remains in place, is mainly of the rough variety, but enough of the fine coat is retained to show traces of painted curving bands and stripes. The southeastern wall of the room, which has been described as seen from Room 15, stands to a maximum height of nearly 1 m. Between its southwestern end and the outside wall a gap, 1 m. to 1.20 m. long, from which the stones have been removed, displays the work of seekers of building material, so often mentioned. What remains of the wall is still covered to a height of ca. 0.70 m. from the floor with plaster, 0.05 to 0.06 m. thick. Two coats are distinguishable: the outermost ca. 0.02 m. thick, without its final smooth surface; the earlier layer, 0.03 m. to 0.04 m. thick, with a good deal of its fine painted face surviving. It shows in red, blue, and thin white various large indistinct shapes that cannot be interpreted. The groove for a horizontal beam is visible at ca. 0.70 m. above the floor. The squared blocks which were seen in Room 15 presumably extended through the wall but are hidden by the plaster. The northeasternmost of these blocks certainly did run through the wall and shows itself behind the base of the door casing.

The floor of the room was made of stucco. In a few places it has a fairly smooth surface with signs of wear, but in general it is rough and badly damaged by the effects of the fire. It is likely that Room 17 was a storeroom of some kind but we have no evidence to indicate what was kept here. When excavated the whole area was found filled with the usual burned debris—hard red burned brick and chunks of soft white crumbly, disintegrated or calcined stone. Intermixed with the remains of crude brick were numerous large fragments of flooring, both blue and white; also a good many pieces of plaster with red dots painted on a blue ground, belonging to a scene representing a dappled deer, only the rump of which is preserved, against a background of papyrus leaves. Much if not all of this material found in Room 17 seems to be drawn at too large a scale to fit into so small a chamber, and it must presumably have fallen from the upper story. Since some fragments probably of the same composition fell into Room 16, it may be conjectured that a large chamber extended across the whole area in the upper story.

A chunk and several bits of bronze and a few nondescript sherds were the only other objects found in Room 17.

ROOM 18

Room 18 (Key Plan) is a further section of the original southwestern corridor, 8.35 m. long by 1.65 m. wide (Fig. 88). At the southeast end the wall separating it from Room 16 seems to have been inserted over what was once a doorway. Under it on each side are remains of the two lateral bases of the door frame. The threshold block is missing, if it ever existed; and it probably did, for a bedding of tamped down clay-like earth resembling hardpan had been prepared for it. No plaster remains on the northwest face of this wall.

On the northeast, Room 18 is bounded by the wall of the Throne Room (Fig. 64) which has been described above (p. 78) with its numerous vertical chases running through from side to side. On the face toward the room traces of a horizontal groove are clear 0.60 m. above the floor of the last phase, and another runs just below the level of the floor. Remains of coarse mud plaster appear here and there on the wall, which was solidly constructed founded on hardpan.

The northwest wall is 0.75 m. thick (Fig. 93). It is built of small unworked stones without a deep foundation, and now stands to a height of 0.50 m. to 0.60 m. above the floor of the final phase, with which it must be associated.

The southwest wall of Room 18, 0.85 m. thick, rises to an average height of 0.50 m. above the clay floor of the final phase. At 1.80 m. from its northwestern end the wall is pierced by a doorway, 1.10 m. wide, opening southwestward into Room 20 (Fig. 96). Beyond the doorway the southwest wall shows signs of rebuilding in the course of which it was thickened 0.05 m. to 0.10 m. Perhaps the door jamb was damaged and the contiguous wall had to be reconstructed. The work was somewhat carelessly done and a relatively large block, inserted alongside the door opening, projects awkwardly into the room. Some scanty patches of mud plaster were seen on the southwest wall.

Room 18 had a rough floor of clay and earth. It was not easily recognizable as a floor but its position was marked by the many pots lying on it. They totaled 474 representing 30 different shapes. The majority were broken, though some were taken out intact; altogether 130 have been inventoried (Fig. 323). Most of the pots were found in the northwestern half of the room in several groups, many to the north of the doorway, many in it and stretching across the room in front of it, and many to the southeast of it (Fig. 94). Big and little pots were found together, but some groups also contained pots mainly of one shape. For instance, a collection of small pedestaled amphoras lay with handles side by side as if they had been strung together on a string. Numerous little one-handled jugs decorated with painted bands were heaped in front of the doorway. Pots were jammed up against the walls on both sides of the room. Along the southwest wall many lay in a badly damaged and disintegrated state in a strip of black earth, which probably represented carbonized remains of a wooden shelf.

At the southeastern end of the room lay part of a table of offerings surrounded by small pots (Fig. 95) at some 0.30 m. above the floor in the reddish earth from dissolved crude brick. Also collected around the table were 36 disks from the bases of kylikes, ranging from two very small and flat (possibly from the little votives) to several very large. In a few instances the stem or part of the stem is preserved, but for the most part they were only the disks. From its position one might conclude that the table of offerings stood in Room 18 on a raised stand or bench of clay, but it is equally possible that it and the pots around it fell from a household shrine in the upper story.

Under the surface soil Room 18 was found filled with hard burned red disintegrated crude brick mixed with carbonized material and fallen plaster. No pots were found until the floor was reached at 0.45 m. below the preserved top of the walls. At this level the great accumulation of pottery was spread out lying partly in the dissolved brick and partly in a grayish-black stratum.

Among the pots and over them were found numerous fragments of flooring amounting to more than five square meters, for the most part with hard fairly smooth surface and a pebbly texture visible, resembling terrazzo. There were also a few pieces of plaster with painted decoration and a small number of casual extraneous sherds which had no connection with the pottery stored in the room. All these had certainly fallen into Room 18 from above, the floor and plaster from the apartment in the second story and the nondescript sherds embedded in the dissolved clay and earth from the upper floor and roof.

Before turning to the catalogue of objects found, mention should be made of a stucco floor which was uncovered 0.20 m. to 0.30 m. beneath the level of the earthen floor on which the pots lay (Fig. 88). The largest part preserved is a strip, 0.45 m. to 0.77 m. wide and 3.65 m. long, beginning opposite the middle of the doorway and running southeastward along the southwest wall. At the northwest it turns up against a wall, 0.85 m. wide, that ran from northeast to southwest, the foundations of which are still in place. Beyond the wall a stucco floor at the same level continues toward the northwest. Farther in that direction, in Rooms 21 and 22, remains of a parallel wall were found. In Room 20 part of what was evidently a connecting wall appears. Against it a pavement, which is probably a continuation of that just mentioned in Room 18, turns upward. In one or two places in Room 18 there seem to be vestiges of a still earlier floor. In any event all of these remains are those of buildings of earlier periods antedating the palace as we have it; for the walls and floors were cut through when the bedding trench for the southwest wall of the Throne Room was dug. In the burned deposit between the floor on which the pots rested and the underlying stucco pavement were recovered many fragments of bronze and ivory. But the information available is still insufficient for the exact determination of the date and character of the earlier structures.

OBJECTS FOUND

SILVER
Small, curved fragment.

BRONZE
Tip of arrowhead with medial rib (Fig. 279 No. 1), l. pres. 0.018 m., w. at bottom 0.009 m. From hard red earth at 0.60 m. below the surface.

Rivet-head and part of shank (Fig. 279 No. 2), h. pres. 0.005 m., d. 0.018 m., th. 0.003 m. With pots in northwest end of room.

Nondescript pieces (Fig. 279 Nos. 3-6).

BONE
A few burned bits.

CLAY
Table of offerings (Fig. 271 No. 10): fragment comprising part of flat floor, d. 0.34 m., with raised rim, 0.065 m. to 0.072 m. wide, separated from central bowl by narrow molded strip that is slightly higher. Rim is ca. 0.08 m. thick measured on outside. No trace of legs was found; table lay flat in horizontal position. Painted decoration not preserved.

POTTERY [45]

	Examples Counted	Examples Numbered
Basin (Shape 1, p. 355)	14	11
Nos. 211 (Fig. 349), 212, 216, 217, 224 (Fig. 350), 225 (Fig. 350), 226-229, 277.		

	Examples Counted	Examples Numbered
Bowl (Shape 3, p. 356)	7	7
Nos. 87, 88 (Fig. 349), 89 (Fig. 349), 90, 91 (Fig. 349), 92 (Fig. 350), 93.		
Bowl (Shape 4, p. 356)	2	—
Bowl (Shape 9, p. 358)	3	3
Nos. 230 (Fig. 351), 231, 232 (Fig. 352); all decorated.		
Cup (Shape 13, p. 360)	4	3
Nos. 220, 241 (Figs. 355, 356), 242 (Fig. 355).		
Cup (Shape 18, p. 362)	5	5
Nos. 243 (Figs. 355, 356), 244, 283, 305, 329.		
Cup (Shape 19, p. 363)	4	1
No. 246 (Figs. 355, 356); decorated.		
Dipper (Shape 20, p. 363)	16	11
decorated: Nos. 85, 106, 249 (Fig. 358), 250, 252, 253, 254 (Fig. 357), 255-256, 285 (Fig. 357). plain: No. 286.		
Dipper (Shape 21, p. 364)	35	12
decorated: Nos. 86 (Figs. 357, 358), 247 (Fig. 357), 248, 258-259, 260 (Fig. 357). plain: Nos. 261, 262, 271-273, 287.		
Dipper (Shape 23, p. 365)	13	1
No. 274.		
Kylix [46]	308	

[45] As the pots were being removed in 1953, the different shapes and variations were counted where possible and estimated. This material was worked over and partly mended especially in 1953 and 1954 but also later and was studied in 1961. The results of this work, extending over a long period, have been used in the preparation of the accompanying catalogue, which shows that some 474 pots all told were recovered representing 30 different shapes and variations. As of July 1961, 130 intact or restored pots had been inventoried

from Room 18 (Fig. 323).

[46] When found, though the general shape was recognizable, the kylikes were all shattered; until they were worked over, there was no possibility of differentiating the variations. In the catalogue, therefore, under the general heading "kylix" the total number counted is given and in the next column the actual number of each variant of the shape, put together and accessioned, is recorded.

	Examples Counted	Examples Numbered		Examples Counted	Examples Numbered
Kylix (Shape 29b, p. 368) Nos. 201, 202, 203 (Figs. 361, 362), 268 (Fig. 361), 280.		5	Jug (Shape 35, p. 375) Nos. 121-131, 290; all decorated.	12	12
Kylix (Shape 29c, p. 369) Nos. 278, 281.		2	Jug (Shape 36, p. 376) No. 77 (Fig. 367).	3	1
Kylix (Shape 29f, p. 370) Nos. 239 (Fig. 361), 265.		2	Jug (Shape 42, p. 380) No. 245 (Figs. 369, 370), decorated.	1	1
Kylix (Shape 29g, p. 371) Nos. 213, 214, 215 (Fig. 363), 284 (Figs. 363, 364).		4	Amphora (Shape 46b, p. 383) No. 270 (Figs. 371, 372).	1	1
Kylix (Shape 29i, p. 371) No. 218 (Figs. 363, 364).		1	Amphora (Shape 47, p. 383) Nos. 108, 109 (Fig. 372), 110-113, 114 (Fig. 372), 115 (Fig. 371), 116, 117-118 (Fig. 371), 119, 120, 263, 296-304.	23	23
Kylix (Shape 30a, p. 372) Nos. 237 (Figs. 365, 366), 240 (Fig. 365), 279.		3	Fragmentary pots, types of shapes not specifically identifiable		
Kylix (Shape 30b, p. 373) Nos. 235 (Fig. 365), 236 (Figs. 365, 366), 266.		3	Bowl: handleless (?), small, with slightly outturned rim	1	
Kylix (Shape 30c, p. 373) Nos. 219, 264 (Fig. 365).		2	Bowl: handleless, small, with flat bottom, straight flaring sides	1	
Kylix (Shape 31, p. 374) No. 238.		1	Jug: large, one-handled	1	
Jug (Shape 34, p. 375) Nos. 78, 79 (Fig. 368), 80-84, 107, 134, 289, 291-295; all decorated.	15	15	Jug: two handles Jar: small, three horizontal handles	4 1	
				474	130

DOORWAY BETWEEN ROOMS 18 AND 20

The doorway leading out to the southwest from Room 18 is 1 m. wide on the inside, broadening to 1.10 m. on the outside (Fig. 96). No stone threshold was found nor any trace of bases for the door jambs. It looks as if there never was a proper door. The opening was filled with debris of dissolved red burned brick, fragments of floor, a few fallen stones, and the large root of an olive tree. Below, on the trodden earth in the doorway, were heaped up many pots at the same level as those found in Room 18 (Fig. 97). In the northwest part of the opening were bowls, a large tankard, little painted jugs, and against the southeast side was a group of 43 diminutive votive kylikes. Of the 71 pots counted 29 were restored (Fig. 324).

OBJECTS FOUND

		Examples Counted	Examples Numbered		Examples Counted	Examples Numbered
POTTERY				Bowl (Shape 4, p. 356)	2	—
Basin (Shape 1, p. 355) No. 288.		1	1	Dipper (Shape 20, p. 363) No. 257 (Fig. 357), decorated.	1	1

	Examples Counted	Examples Numbered		Examples Counted	Examples Numbered
Dipper (Shape 21, p. 364)	1	1	Jug (Shape 34, p. 375)		1
No. 105 (Fig. 357), decorated.			No. 133, decorated.		
Kylix (Shape 26, p. 366)	43	20	Jug (Shape 35, p. 375)		1
Nos. 308-313, 315, 316 (Fig. 359),			No. 132, decorated.		
317-318, 319 (Figs. 359, 360), 320,			Amphora (Shape 46, p. 383)	1	1
321 (Fig. 360), 322-325, 326 and			No. 180.		
327 (Fig. 359), 328.			Fragmentary pots, types of shapes		
Kylix (Shape 31, p. 374)	1	1	not specifically identifiable		
No. 269 (Figs. 365, 366).			Bowl	6	
Tankard (Shape 33, p. 374)	2	2	Bowl or dipper	1	
Nos. 233 (Fig. 365), 234 (Figs.			Kylix	1	
365, 366), decorated.			Tripod-pot	1	
Jug (Shapes 34 and 35)	10	—		71	29

ROOM 19

The "kylix pantry" (19 on Key Plan) is a rectangular room 3.87 m. long from southeast to northwest and 3.03 m. wide (Fig. 64). On the southeast it shares a wall with Room 17, which has already been described (p. 118). This wall, rising to a maximum height of 0.55 m. above the floor,[47] has been considerably damaged and its upper part has slipped outward toward the northwest, overhanging the bottom course some 0.15 m. to 0.20 m. The northeast wall, separating the Kylix Pantry from Room 18, has likewise been shaken out of alignment, its upper courses spreading out beyond the lower. At the top, 0.60 m. above the floor, it now has a maximum thickness of 0.95 m.; at the bottom it is not much more than 0.80 m.

The northwest wall is 1 m. long on the northeast side of the doorway that leads into Room 20. The opening is not axially placed, since the wall on the southwestern side is only 0.70 m. long.

The southwestern wall, which has been deprived of its outer facing of squared blocks (Fig. 63), stands on its inner side to a height of 0.43 m. above the floor. All these walls lack evidence for beam-grooves and -chases and only scanty traces of mud plaster can be seen, although the stucco floor turns up against the northeast and southeast walls. The northwest and southwest walls surely had a similar coating, but it is now missing.

The floor is made of stucco 0.03 m. thick. The surface is badly damaged by fire, cracked and uneven, and partly broken away in the middle of the room. In some spots the surface looks blue, in others white. Beginning 0.33 m. from the northwest

47 The floor of Room 19 is ca. 0.15 m. higher than that of Room 17.

[123]

end, along the northeastern side of the room are three roughly circular holes[48] at intervals of 0.54 m. and 0.66 m., set out 0.20 m. to 0.29 m. from the wall (Fig. 63). They were evidently made to receive posts which held up wooden shelves that probably stretched all the way to the southeastern end of the room. For there, a fourth hole in the form of an approximate half circle or a little less, continues the line. Similar shelves must have run around the other sides of the room, as one may safely deduce from the multitude of pots found inside. Perhaps they were supported by posts standing on the floor itself. In the west corner a shallow aperture (0.56 m. by 0.44 m.) in the floor, ca. 0.07 m. deep, still contains a large flat stone. This no doubt provided support for the northwestern end of the southwest shelving. At the time of the great catastrophe the shelves must have burned and the kylikes were precipitated to the floor in heaps, accompanied by much debris, not only from the walls of the room itself but from the floor above. When excavated the room was found completely filled to a height of 0.60 m. to 0.70 m., that is, to a point just below the grass, with a solid mass of crushed, cracked, and broken kylikes, though in many instances retaining their shape (Fig. 98). Mixed with them and obviously fallen from above, were chunks and slabs of flooring, some fragments of plaster with painted decoration, red burned disintegrated crude brick, stone calcined until soft and crumbly, almost like powder, and very soft pulverized gray matter. It was difficult to extract the pottery both from the hard and the soft mass of wreckage. A systematic and laborious count of stems revealed an impressive total of 2,853 kylikes which were actually stored in Pantry 19 on the fatal day. This number must be taken as an absolute minimum, since considerable parts of the accumulation may have been carried away by plowing and erosion. The room seems to have been used exclusively for kylikes. At any rate only a handful of sherds of pots of other shapes were recognized and they may well have come down with the clay and brick from the upper floor. One may wonder why so great a number of drinking cups was needed. When one reflects, however, on the predilection of the heroes in the *Iliad* and the *Odyssey* for pouring libations and drinking wine, one can easily imagine the need for abundant cups. It might well have been the custom, which has survived in many countries until our own day, when the wine had been drunk to shatter the goblets on the floor, the debris to be swept up and disposed of by servants. Habits of this kind might explain the fact that fragments of kylikes have been found in uncountable numbers everywhere outside the palace and even in some of the rooms of the building itself.

[48] First from northwest: diameter 0.26 m., depth below floor 0.15 m.

Second from northwest: diameter 0.22 m., depth 0.12 m.

Third: diameter 0.20 m., depth 0.19 m.

OBJECTS FOUND

BRONZE

Several insignificant, shapeless bits and chunks found in the debris.

POTTERY

The kylikes seem to be mostly of one type with slight variations in size and proportions. Since the number is so enormous, we take this to be the standard size of the most commonly used drinking cup (Shape 29c, p. 369). Only a dozen examples have yet been put together and accessioned (Fig. 325). Hundreds more could no doubt be reconstructed by a technician with abundant time and patience, but it seems to us unlikely that any commensurate advance in our knowledge of Mycenaean kylikes would be promoted.

	Examples Counted	Examples Numbered
Kylix (Shape 29b, p. 368) No. 282.		1
Kylix (Shape 29c, p. 369) Nos. 184, 185 (Fig. 362), 186 (Fig. 361), 187 (Fig. 362), 188, 189, 190 (Figs. 361, 362), 191, 1133-1135.	2,853	11

Only seven sherds were recognized as coming from pots of other shapes. They were fragments of: the base of a bowl, the flat bottom and pinched-out handle of a bowl, bottoms of two cups, the flat raised base of a large jug or jar, the handle of a coarse storage jar, and a pithos. It is probable that these stray pieces fell along with the debris from above.

ROOM 20

The doorway leading to Pantry 20 is 1.33 m. wide (Fig. 96). The stucco floor of Room 19 is carried more than halfway through the opening and between it and the floor of Room 20 there is a gap 0.315 m. wide in which a wooden door sill may have been set. This gap was filled with very black earth which extended 0.10 m. to 0.15 m. below the floor to a bedding of small stones. The blackness of the deposit might perhaps have come from a carbonized wooden sill. Higher up was one fairly long piece of carbonized wood surrounded by a *migma* of fused stone and disintegrated brick, no doubt representing the remains of the southwest jamb of the door. Some kylikes had spread out from Room 19 into the doorway.

Room 20 (Figs. 64, 96) has an average length of 3.49 m. from southeast to northwest and a width of 3.02 m. The northeast and southeast walls, each containing a doorway, have already been described (pp. 119, 123). The northwestern wall has a maximum height of 0.48 m. and is 0.87 m. thick. On the southwest, only the inner backing of the exterior wall is preserved, standing to a maximum height of 0.42 m. A doorway leads out into Court 88 (Key Plan) that separates the Main Building from the Southwestern Building. The opening is almost but not exactly centered in the wall. No remains of plaster of any kind were found still adhering to the walls of the room.

The floor is made of stucco which, in breaks and holes, is seen to have a thickness of 0.03 m. It is not level, has been much damaged by fire or wear, especially in the middle of the area, and is badly cracked almost everywhere. Along the northwestern side, somewhat irregularly spaced and varying from 0.24 m. to 0.32 m. distant from the wall, are four holes roughly circular in shape (Fig. 96) ranging from 0.18 m. to 0.25 m. in diameter. They vary from 0.10 m. to 0.20 m. in depth and have stones at the bottom. They must have been for posts supporting shelving such as we have postulated in Room 19. At the north corner the shelving probably turned to the southeast and was supported on a smaller post, set only 0.15 m. from the wall. Near the east corner, 0.32 m. from the northeast wall, 0.42 m. from the southeast wall, is a fairly large hole which alone must have supported a shelf occupying the angle. Near the south corner and only 0.28 m. apart, are two similar slightly smaller holes, 0.40 m. from the southwest wall and 0.27 m. apart, for timbers that supported a shelf on this side also. We may thus conclude that there was shelving on all four sides of the room. No actual remains of carbonized wood were recognized, but a thin stratum of black earth that lay beneath some of the pots may have been the residue of wooden boards that were burned up.

In any event this was a pantry, for it contained more than 500 pots of at least 25 different shapes (e.g., Fig. 328). In the general confusion caused by the disaster one could nonetheless observe the appearance of what must originally have been a more or less orderly arrangement of the many different kinds of pots. In the south corner was a mass of large stemmed kraters and large kylikes, to the exclusion of almost every other shape. Some of the kraters were found upside down, stacked one inside the other. Slightly to the southeast of the center of the room were small pedestaled amphoras and kylikes. Against the southeast wall near the east corner were shallow angular bowls with pinched-out handles and a variety of small and medium-sized kylikes. The northwestern section of the room contained a great jumble of shapes, but even here there was a semblance of order: kylikes were in groups, dippers with high handles were in clusters, shallow bowls in stacks that had toppled over, teacups in heaps, little votive cups in piles, and even the rare jugs came in pairs. Little kylikes were wedged tightly together with stems lying across each other. Directly in the north corner of the room, pressed together by the root of an olive tree, was a collection of very large kylikes, some low-stemmed, some high. The pots for the most part lay beneath great slabs and chunks of flooring fallen from above, which became visible almost immediately below the surface of the ground. Many of them lay face up, others stood on edge. Numerous fragments of wall plaster bearing remains of painted decoration were likewise recovered. Miss Lang's survey of the material reports that "with blue background and much use of red and black are pieces representing architectural façades, a deer at an altar, the rear ends of two boars, horses on rocks. All of these, especially since they are accompanied by . . . the typical nautilus frieze, . . . are reminiscent of the inner Propylon in a different color scheme." Probably belonging to the same group are fragments of a heavy border with painted black, blue, white, and red, as well as incised lines; also many other unidentifiable red and blue pieces. All this debris must have fallen into Room 20; some of the smaller fragments may have drifted over from the balcony of the Throne Room but the large and heavy pieces and the flooring are more likely to have fallen from an important room or hall directly above in the upper story.

Almost all of the pots were cracked or badly broken by the wreckage that had fallen on them, but when first uncovered they usually retained their form long enough for their shape to be identified. As they were taken up, however, the fragments fell apart. Some of the pots had become misshapen and badly warped from the heat of the fire, and a good many can therefore never be put together again; but they had not become vitrified and twisted as had the kylikes in Room 9 (p. 102). In removing the pots we counted stems or bases in order to obtain some idea of the numbers of each shape represented.

Worthy of special note is an inscribed tablet (No. 996) which was found in badly damaged condition in many small fragments. It lay near the north corner of the room in the upper part of the deposit amidst many pieces of flooring, and it had evidently fallen from the upper story.

Near the western corner of the room an accidental break in the stucco floor, extending southward from the second post hole, gave an opportunity for probing into the underlying deposit (Fig. 96). At a depth of only 0.13 m. the edge of an earlier stucco floor of good quality, turning up alongside a wall, runs northwestward; it seems to be aligned with a similar floor-edge and wall, some remains of which were uncovered beneath the last floor in Room 21, and it is probably part of the building seen beneath Room 18 (p. 120).

O B J E C T S   F O U N D

B R O N Z E
Shapeless bits (e.g., Fig. 279 Nos. 8, 9).

L E A D
Melted piece (Fig. 279 No. 7).

O B S I D I A N
Blade with one serrated edge (Fig. 279 No. 10), l. 0.03 m., w. 0.009 m., th. 0.002 m., and two flakes.

C L A Y
Tablet: No. 996 (*PT II*, 108, 188 and *AJA* 58 [1954], pl. 7 fig. 8)

P O T T E R Y[49]

	Ex- amples Count- ed	Ex- amples Num- bered
Basin (Shape 1, p. 355)	1	—
Bowl (Shape 4, p. 356)	75	7
Nos. 380, 398, 632-635, 637.		

[49] The pots from Room 20, as well as those in Room 18, were counted when possible or estimated and the shapes identified while the vessels were being lifted. Several different menders worked over parts of the material through many seasons of excavation and, as tabulated in 1961, the total number reconstructed and inventoried reached 117 (Fig. 328). What is left unmended still offers an opportunity for putting together many more pots, but we think that what has been done gives us adequate examples of all the different types represented.

	Ex-amples Count-ed	Ex-amples Num-bered		Ex-amples Count-ed	Ex-amples Num-bered
Bowl (Shape 5, p. 356)	1	1	Kylix (Shape 29h, p. 371)		6
No. 636 (Figs. 349, 350).			Nos. 267 (Fig. 363), 367 (Figs. 363, 364), 368, 381, 387, 620.		
Cup (Shape 12, p. 360)	72	13	Kylix (Shape 29i, p. 371)		5
Nos. 172-175, 357-361, 362 (Fig. 353), 363, 371, 638.			Nos. 337 (Fig. 363), 338 (Figs. 363, 364), 366, 621, 629 (Fig. 363).		
Dipper (Shape 20, p. 363)	7	2			
Nos. 364 (Fig. 357), 365; both decorated.			Tankard (Shape 33, p. 374)	1	1
			No. 336 (Fig. 365), decorated.		
Dipper (Shape 23, p. 365)	7	2	Jug (Shape 34, p. 375)	—	2
Nos. 192, 223 (Fig. 358).			Nos. 135, 168 (Fig. 367); both decorated.		
Dipper (Shape 24, p. 365)	—	1			
No. 639 (Figs. 357, 358).			Jug (Shape 35, p. 375)	—	4
Dipper (Shape 25, p. 365)	8	5	Nos. 136 (Fig. 367), 169 (Fig. 367), 170, 171; all decorated.		
Nos. 194 (Fig. 358), 306, 623, 624 (Fig. 357), 625.			Jug (Shape 36, p. 376)	5	5
Kylix (Shape 26, p. 366)	19	1	Nos. 182 (Figs. 367, 368), 183 (Fig. 368), 374 (Fig. 367), 375, 671.		
No. 314.					
Kylix (Shape 27, p. 366)	174	8	Amphora (Shape 46a, p. 383)	2	2
Nos. 176 (Fig. 360), 177, 178, 179, 392, 393, 626, 627.			Nos. 181 (Fig. 372), 376 (Fig. 371).		
Kylix (Shapes 29c and 29d)	54[50]		Amphora (Shape 47, p. 383)	6	—
Kylix (Shape 29c, p. 369)		2	Jar (Shape 51, p. 386)	—	3
Nos. 384, 389.			Nos. 377 (Fig. 375), 378 (Figs. 375, 376), 379.		
Kylix (Shape 29d, p. 369)		12	Stemmed krater (Shape 62, p. 399)	24	8
Nos. 195 (Figs. 361, 362), 350, 355, 385, 386, 388 (Fig. 361), 390, 391, 392a, 622, 628, 631.			Nos. 197, 198, 208 (Fig. 388), 209 (Figs. 387, 388), 210, 222 (Fig. 387), 369, 370.		
Kylix (Shape 29e, f, g, h, i)	51[51]		Fragmentary pots, types of shapes not specifically identifiable		
Kylix (Shape 29e, p. 370)		18	Bowl	8	—
Nos. 339 (Figs. 361, 362), 340 (Fig. 361), 341-348, 354, 372, 373, 383, 396, 397, 399, 630.			Bowl: rounded, outturned rim	1	—
Kylix (Shape 29f, p. 370)		6	Cup: a little larger and heavier than "teacup"	3	—
Nos. 349, 351, 354, 356 (Figs. 361, 362), 382, 673.			Jug	2	—
Kylix (Shape 29g, p. 371)		3		522	117
Nos. 352, 394, 395.					

DOORWAY FROM ROOM 20 INTO COURT 88

The doorway leading out from Room 20 into the adjacent court is marked by two thresholds of poros (Figs. 64, 439), laid transversely across the opening, with a gap of 0.28 m. between, which was filled with earth. Both are cracked; the inner is made

[50] Counted together as of medium size.   [51] Counted together as of large and very large size.

of two blocks, 0.60 m. by 0.40 m. and 0.40 m. by 0.38 m.; the outer is a single block, 1.08 m. long and 0.40 m. to 0.44 m. wide. No lateral bases were provided for jambs. This door is therefore different from all those we have yet seen in this building. Although the edges of the actual opening cannot now be determined, it is likely that the wooden door casing was substantial. The outer threshold block has a roughly rectangular cutting in its southeastern end which might conceivably have had something to do with the fixing of a socket to hold a pivot. The outer threshold is slightly higher than the inner and slightly lower than the pavement of the court outside. The doorway was found filled with badly smashed pots which had spilled over from the room.

ROOM 21

The doorway leading from Court 88 into Room 21 (Fig. 440) is 0.95 m. wide; in it are laid transversely two blocks of poros that formed the threshold. Both are somewhat rough on top and damaged. The inner, which projects 0.12 m. into the room, is 0.90 m. long and 0.52 m. wide. Near its northwestern end a rough hole has been gouged out, possibly for a socket of a pivot, 0.10 m. from the edge of the doorway and 0.25 m. to 0.30 m. from the northeastern face of the block. The outer stone of the threshold, 0.56 m. wide, had probably about the same length as the inner, but it has suffered much injury along its southwest edge and its southeast end. The exterior edge does not now reach the stucco pavement of the court, nor is it adjusted to the latter, which is ca. 0.10 m. higher in level. These two blocks may have been reused in a battered state after the accident that made the reconstruction of the western corner of the building necessary.

Pantry 21 (Key Plan) in the western corner of the central building (Fig. 99) has an average length of 3.37 m. from southeast to northwest and a width of 3.08 m. The southeast wall, which separates it from Pantry 20, 0.87 m. thick, is preserved to a height of 0.58 m. The wall leans over somewhat toward the northwest. No traces of grooves or chases for beams are visible in what remains. The foundations go down to an earlier pavement 0.18 m. below the floor.

The northeast wall, which is 0.80 m. thick, is preserved to a height of 0.55 m. Approximately but not exactly centered in it is a doorway, 1.27 m. wide, leading into Pantry 22 (Figs. 64, 99). On each side of the opening the wall seems to have ended with a projecting core of stone, 0.59 m. thick; into each angle beside it was presumably fitted a substantial wooden post. These posts must have taken the place of door casings or jambs, or permitted a rather thin door frame to be fastened against them. On the northwestern side the projecting core is plastered on its face toward the opening and also on each side against which the door posts were set. On the southeastern side of the opening only scant traces of the plaster are now in place. The posts were consumed by the fire, leaving a soft gray ashy deposit and also pieces of carbonized wood, particularly on the southeast side in Pantry 21. Many cups, all damaged by fire, were pressed against the ashy material and were heaped up in the doorway.

All that is preserved of the northwest wall is a stump, 0.35 m. high (Fig. 99). This section of the exterior wall of the building, along the northwestern side of Rooms 21 and 22, seems to belong to a reconstruction of the western corner in one of the late phases of the palace, and it diverges somewhat from the original line (p. 46).

The southwestern wall of Room 21, through which a doorway opened onto the court, as already mentioned above, is in an even worse state of preservation than the northwestern (Figs. 64, 99); for the part to the northwest of the doorway has been demolished down to the floor level and below, though the section to the southeast of the doorway still stands to a height of 0.40 m.

The floor of Room 21 was made of trodden earth. In it were set two fairly flat stone slabs, ca. 0.80 m. apart, not far from the northwest wall. They are almost symmetrically spaced with reference to the lateral walls and they were obviously intended to support heavy wooden posts that held up shelving along this side of the room. No similar bases appear along the other walls of Room 21, but posts may well have been set on the floor itself. A good deal of shelving space was needed for this too was a storeroom for pottery.

Pantry 21 was found filled with the usual mass of red burned brick, extending out a meter or more from the walls, and was chock-full of pots. Near the northwest wall were fragments of bricks still retaining their shape. In the center of the room, where there were fewer pots, the deposit consisted of disintegrated stone, sandy gray material, and hard fused chunks of burned debris. Scattered everywhere throughout the room were stones, slabs of fallen flooring, and pieces of plaster, some with painted patterns.

The latter were found by Miss Lang to be much like those from Room 20. Some are coated with red wash on which blue was applied except in reserved areas. Two horse's legs standing on rocky ground must be from the same composition as the similar legs in Room 20. Other pieces belong to red and blue borders; a large fragment of a lion's mane may have come from the Throne Room.

Remains of fallen flooring in general lay above the pots. The red burned earth, and with it the pots, stopped at the level of the threshold block, which corresponds with the level of the pots in Pantry 18. The lowest pots lay in yellowish earth on a floor of hard-packed earth.

Pantry 21 was evidently the "bowl and cup department" of the palace. The pots must have been neatly arranged in stacks on shelves or stands ranged against the walls, two-handled shallow bowls on the southeast (Fig. 101), cups on the northwest (Fig. 100). They began to appear immediately below the preserved top of the walls and made great heaps, which extended 0.60 m. out from the southeast wall and at least 1 m. from the northwest wall, and sloped down toward the middle of the room. The cups were smashed into tiny pieces, and the fill consisted more of pottery fragments than of earth. Some were even pressed into the crevices between the stones of the wall. Along with 1,024 "teacups" in the cup section, were found four dippers with one high flat handle, three shallow angular bowls with two pinched-out horizontal handles, and, in the north corner, eight small kylikes and one somewhat larger. A two-handled jug was pressed up against the northwest wall lying in yellowish earth that showed no signs of burning. The bowl section contained 1,099 shallow angular bowls with pinched-out handles, three teacups, three dippers, three kylikes, and two large storage jars (Fig. 101). It was often possible to remove whole stacks of as many as ten bowls, but we were unable to determine what was the usual number in a stack. The two pithoi, both badly crushed, stood in the southeast part of the room (Fig. 101), one on the right inside the doorway from the court, the other in front of the doorway into Pantry 22. Each was found in an upright position with its bottom resting on the floor, not sunk into a hole. The first was in poor condition and is unrestorable. It was filled with debris—earth, stones, and plaster—which give no clue as to its original contents. The walls of the pot were thin in comparison with the relatively thick outturned rim and large handles. The second pithos was preserved standing to 0.43 m., which apparently was almost its full height. It was filled to the bottom with stones, brick, and chunks of flooring with no indication of what it originally held.

Fragments of a large vessel were found flattened out on the threshold of the southwest door and on the floor close to the pithos inside the door. When it was put together it proved to be a large two-handled basin-like lid, which must have been used as a cover for the pithos. Similar lids were found in considerable numbers in Magazines 23 and 24, where they had obviously been used to cover the storage jars.

Of the 2,146 pots counted, representing only seven different shapes, 126 have been inventoried (Fig. 324, two lower shelves at right with the exception of three votive kylikes).

O B J E C T S   F O U N D

GOLD
Tiny bit of foil.

SILVER
Flattened amygdaloid piece, l. 0.018 m., w. 0.009 m., th. 0.002 m., possibly head of pin.

BRONZE
Two rivets, bent and broken; flat thin fragment.

IVORY
Small broken fragments, burned black.

POTTERY

	Ex- amples Count- ed	Ex- amples Num- bered
Bowl (Shape 4, p. 356)	1,099	58
Nos. 67-74, 75 (Fig. 350), 76, 94-99, 100 (Fig. 349), 101-104, 137-141, 142 (Fig. 349), 143-167, 199 (Fig. 350), 200, 204-207.		
Cup (Shape 12, p. 360)	1,024	62
Nos. 1 (Fig. 354), 2 (Fig. 354), 3 (Fig. 354), 4 (Fig. 353), 5-15, 16 (Fig. 354), 17-26, 27 (Fig. 353), 28-31, 32 (Figs. 353, 354), 33 (Fig. 354), 34-42, 43 (Fig. 353), 44-48, 49 (Fig. 353), 50-62.		
Dipper (Shape 23, p. 365)	7	1
No. 193 (Fig. 357).		
Kylix (Shape 27, p. 366)	12	4
No. 63 (Fig. 359), 64-66.		
Lid (Shape 77, p. 417)	1	1
No. 307 (Fig. 397).		
Fragmentary pots, types of shapes not specifically identifiable		
Jug: two handles	1	—
Pithos: small	2	—
	2,146	126

ROOM 22

The doorway leading into Room 22 had no threshold block and no bases for jambs. It was floored merely with trodden earth, continuing on through the opening from one room to the other.

Room 22 (Key Plan), 3.40 m. long from southeast to northwest and 1.60 m. wide, is the northwestern end of what we take to be the original southwestern corridor (Fig. 93). This end was shut off in one of the late phases of the palace by the construction of a wall built largely of pieces of poros blocks. The material was probably re-used in the reconstruction that we believe followed the collapse of the western corner of the building. The wall has no deep foundations but rests on earth at the level of the floors of Rooms 18 and 22. On the northwest side it rises to a maximum height of 0.62 m.

The southwestern wall, separating Room 22 from Room 21, consists of two sections already described, the one to the southeast of the doorway, 1.10 m. long, and that to the northwest, 1.14 m. (Fig. 102). The doorway was somewhat carelessly made, not quite at right angles to the wall. On the northeastern face the slots for the posts are not so deep as those on the southwest. Some traces of mud plaster are still preserved both to the southeast and the northwest of the door opening.

The northwest wall of Room 22 is a continuation of the reconstruction we have already mentioned along the northwestern side of Room 21. Its face toward Room 22 is still preserved to a height of 0.30 m. to 0.40 m. Its foundations go down only some 0.30 m. to rest on the wall of an earlier period. No plaster remains in place on this wall.

The northeastern wall, through which a doorway leads into Oil Magazine 23, is of much better construction than those on the other sides (Fig. 102). It is 1.02 m.

thick and is preserved to a maximum height of 0.40 m. to the northwest of the door-way, and 0.46 m. to the southeast of the opening. The northwestern section of this wall offers evidence of two vertical chases running through from one face to the other, and there was a horizontal wooden beam at a level below the floor of Room 22. The foundations of the wall are carried down to *stereo*, and since they are 0.04 m. to 0.05 m. thicker than the wall they support, a narrow ledge projects at the bottom of the groove for the horizontal beam. To the northwest of the doorway on the face of the wall above the floor of Room 22 a thick coating of mud plaster is fairly well preserved.

The floor, like that of Room 21, was made of earth. In this room, too, there must have been shelves around all four sides. Lying in place against the southeastern wall is a flat stone that might have supported a wooden post. Elsewhere the uprights for the shelving no doubt stood on the floor itself, unless the shelves were somehow fastened to the walls. When the final catastrophe came, the shelves were burned and the pots stored on them were thrown to the floor, those at the southeastern end being covered by a fall of stones which protected them from later damage by the plow.

The mass at the southeast end comprised some 353 pots of which 141 were shallow bowls with pinched-out handles, 33 or more teacups, and 178 dippers (Fig. 103). The pots in the northwest part of the room were badly disturbed by the roots of an olive tree and very likely also by plowing. Many fragments, which were found dispersed beyond the limits of the room, thus probably came from the same deposit. Remaining in the room itself, however, 249 vessels were counted, comprising six shallow bowls with pinched-out handles, 22 teacups, and 221 additional dippers. Perhaps it was not by mere chance that so many dippers were kept in this pantry adjoining the magazines in which olive oil was stored in numerous large pithoi. From the total of 601 pots counted, representing only three shapes, 70 have been inventoried (Fig. 324, left).

At this point brief mention may conveniently be made of an earlier floor beneath Room 22. From 0.10 m. to 0.20 m. below the earth floor of the room an earlier stucco pavement has been found here and there (Fig. 104). It appears in the south-east end of the room, evidently a continuation of the same stucco floor found in Room 18 (p. 120). Farther toward the northwest it has been exposed at the same level beneath the earth floor, continuing as far as a contemporary wall which runs from northeast to southwest. Another section of this wall has been seen under the northwestern part of Room 21, and here it makes a right-angled turn toward the southeast. Several patches of the stucco pavement still survive in the corner formed by these two walls. The wall running southeastward is evidently the same as the wall seen under the floor of Room 20. All of these elements seem to belong together in a building antedating this part of the palace. When the southwest wall of the

Throne Room was erected a bedding trench was cut through the wall and pavement in Room 22 and in Room 18. In the deposit between the floor and the underlying pavement were found a few nondescript bits of bronze, ivory, and pieces of pottery.

O B J E C T S   F O U N D

GOLD

Two fragments of gold plating on bronze perhaps from rivet of sword or dagger (Fig. 279 Nos. 14, 15).

SILVER

Piece apparently from lip and rounded side of cup (Fig. 279 No. 11), h. 0.015 m.: found on stones of wall under floor.

Fragment with ribbed decoration (Fig. 279 No. 12).

Thick piece possibly fragment of handle (Fig. 279 No. 13), l. 0.025 m., w. 0.013 m.

Nondescript scraps.

BRONZE

Small piece with part of rivet-hole (Fig. 279 No. 17).

Part of a rivet (Fig. 279 No. 16).

Some 21 shapeless pieces.

STONE

Bits of flint, obsidian, and quartz.

IVORY

Eight fragments burned black.

POTTERY

	Ex- amples Count- ed	Ex- amples Num- bered
Bowl (Shape 4, p. 356) Nos. 221, 569, 570 (Fig. 349), 571-572, 1060-1084.	147	30
Cup (Shape 12, p. 360) Nos. 515, 516 (Fig. 353), 517, 518, 575 (Fig. 353).	55	5
Dipper (Shape 23, p. 365) Nos. 509 (Figs. 357, 358), 510-512, 513 (Fig. 358), 514, 568 (Fig. 357), 1032-1059.	399	35
	——	—
	601	70

R O O M 23

In the doorway from Room 22 to Room 23 are set two substantial stone bases for the door jambs, 0.58 m. apart (Fig. 441). The space between them was filled with a pavement of stucco, 0.04 m. thick, instead of an actual threshold block (Fig. 102). The base of the jamb on the southeast is a large block of poros, 1.17 m. long through the doorway, 0.49 m. wide, and 0.35 m. thick. It projects 0.12 m. into Room 22. A rabbet, of the kind seen in other doorways (pp. 103, 107, 116), has been roughly cut in its upper surface, 0.17 m. wide, narrowing slightly toward the northeast. At the southwest end of the rabbet, some 0.21 m. from the outer edge of the block, is a squarish cutting, 0.105 m. on a side, 0.04 m. deep below the rabbet, and 0.08 m. lower than the surface of the block. This was clearly the pivot itself, or the setting place for the socket of a pivot. The base of the jamb on the northwestern side is 1.24 m. long, 0.52 m. wide, and has a thickness exceeding 0.28 m. It projects 0.17 m. into Room 22. On the side toward the opening, in the edge of the block, opposite the setting for the pivot, an irregular cavity has been gouged out; it looks as if caused by accident rather than an intentional cutting for a locking bar. The door itself must then have been some 0.90 m. wide, and it would have swung back against the casing within the depth of the doorway. The top of the block shows some slight traces of a shallow rabbet, 0.17 m. broad, extending to the northeast. Its edge must mark the face of the wooden door frame that rested on the base. On the southeast the jamb may have been fitted into a countersinking with plaster edges in the end of the wall. But the latter is here formed by a mass of fused brick and stone, what we call *migma*, which, melted together, may have flowed down into the hollow of the door casing. In any event, with this doorway and the contiguous wall we return to the original solid construction of the palace beyond the relatively shoddy repair of the damaged western corner.

The earth floor of Room 22 is higher than the stucco in the doorway and the latter slopes down appreciably to merge with the floor of Room 23.

Room 23 is 5.56 m. long and 3.93 m. wide (Fig. 102 and Key Plan). On the south-west it is bounded by the doorway and wall separating it from Room 22. On the southeast it shares the rear wall of the Throne Room (p. 79). On the northeast it is divided from Magazine 24 by a wall, 0.87 m. wide, with a doorway at its north-western end. This wall stands to a height ranging from 0.40 m. to 0.60 m. The northwest side of the room was formed by the outer rear wall of the Main Build-ing; only its foundations, 1.20 m. thick, are preserved. No remains above the floor level have survived.

The floor of the room was paved with stucco, from 0.015 m. to 0.025 m. thick, which is now in a badly damaged state, cracked, buckled, and dented as a result of the action of fire, falling debris, roots of an olive tree, and the underlying thrust of an earlier wall. The surface of the pavement, moreover, when first uncovered had an oily, fire-blackened appearance.

Along all four walls were ranged pithoi, or large jars, set with their bottoms well below the level of the floor (Fig. 22). A stand, ca. 0.80 m. broad, made of clay, was built around the jars to hold them firmly in place. It was constructed directly against the walls after the latter had been coated with rough plaster. The stand rose vertically 0.30 m. to 0.35 m. above the floor to a rounded edge and then sloped upward toward the wall behind. It was coated with good stucco, 0.01 m. to 0.02 m. thick. The stucco of the floor in some places turns up and continues on the face of the stand, indicating that it was applied on floor and stand at the same time. Beginning 0.20 m. inside the doorway from Room 22, the stand on the right juts out from the wall with a rounded end; between it and a corresponding curved end of the bench on the left, the passage into the room was limited to a width of ca. 0.60 m. (Figs. 102, 420). The southeast stand, running straight to the far end of the room, encloses seven pithoi (Nos. 1 to 7) and there are two more (Nos. 8, 9) in the right-angled continuation against the north-east wall. The jars vary considerably in size and shape. The shoulder and the neck rose high above the top of the stand and, since they reached the plowed ground, every pithos has lost its rim and most of its neck. Between the northeastern and the northwestern stands with their rounded ends the approach to the doorway into Room 24 was narrowed to 0.83 m. Along the northwestern wall the stand has suffered much damage. Practically all the stucco coating is missing, but the clay structure, with an admixture of small stones, still stands to a height of 0.30 m. Counted from the end near the north doorway, four pithoi (Nos. 10 to 13) are in large part preserved, though the neck and shoulders are gone. Diameters that can be measured here range from 0.65 m. to more than 0.80 m. Farther to the southwest this stand has for the most part disappeared, but the fragments of another pithos (No. 14) remain in place. Between the northwest and the southwest stands is a rounded construction, built of earth and stones, coated on its outer perimeter with stucco (Fig. 22). It breaks the continuity of the stand, which presumably once turned the corner in the same manner that we have seen in the eastern angle of the room. Behind this platform, at any rate, in the western corner, are fragments of yet another pithos (No. 15). Against the southwestern wall finally, and overlapping by some 0.15 m. or more the jamb of the southwest doorway, the bench continues, retaining its stucco coating, though in badly cracked condition. It holds two more pithoi (Nos. 16 and 17), the latter possessing part of its neck. The rounded platform (Fig. 102), which interrupted the sequence of the jars in the western corner, may have been built to serve as a standing place on which could be set the portable containers that were used to bring in or to take out olive oil from the magazine.

There can in any event be no doubt that this was a storeroom for olive oil, an identification demonstrated by the discovery of 56 inscribed tablets and fragments of tablets. Some were found on the stand among the jars, others lay scattered about on the floor below (Fig. 105). All deal with various kinds of olive oil, and in five instances the word used for oil, as transliterated by Ventris, is e-ra₃-wo, which may be interpreted as ELAWON. This in turn must be an early antecedent of *elaion*, which in our own day continues to be the Greek name for olive oil.

Scattered about mainly on the floor, but in one or two instances on the stand, were recovered a dozen or more small twists of clay. They had evidently been somewhat molded by fingers which had left their prints on a few pieces. Mr. Hubbe has ingeniously suggested that these were pinches of clay, carried about by the scribes who kept the records in this magazine and who could shape them into tablets of the size and form that might be required. Their survival is owed to their baking by the fire that destroyed the palace (Fig. 276 Nos. 1-7).

The stucco floor and the stucco coating on the stand greatly facilitated the use of the storeroom, especially in the filling and emptying of the jars, for the oil that was spilled could be easily wiped up. Standing on the floor in the angle between Pithoi

Nos. 6 and 8, was a large pithoid jar, perhaps one of the vessels in which oil was transported. A similar jar stood on the northwestern side of the room in front of Pithos No. 11, and a fairly large krater lay beside Pithos No. 12. Two small jugs, perhaps used as dippers, were found on the stand next to Pithos No. 2. Fragments of heavy lids were recovered scattered about on the benches and on the floor. Two types are represented: one, usually rounded on top, with one central arched handle; the other type, flat on top, has two lateral oblique handles set horizontally.

All the pithoi were emptied to their bottoms; they yielded only earth, charcoal, and a few small items, similar to those found elsewhere in the room.

O B J E C T S   F O U N D

SILVER

Two nondescript fragments. One piece with end of bronze rivet attached (Fig. 280 No. 12), l. 0.016 m., max. w. 0.013 m.

BRONZE

Fragment of a heavy curved piece, broken on all sides (Fig. 280 No. 13), l. 0.034 m., w. 0.015 m., th. 0.005 m.

Fragment of round handle (Fig. 280 No. 9), l. pres. 0.025 m., d. 0.01 m.

Fragments of rivet-head (Fig. 280 No. 11), d. 0.012 m.

252 nondescript pieces.

BONE

Fragment, cut, 0.018 m. by 0.02 m., 0.005 m. thick; has incised lines which may be characters or perhaps slips of the knife in cutting.

STONE

Flint: 26 pieces.
Obsidian: 10 pieces.
Quartz: 16 pieces.

IVORY

Many fragments: three pieces with incised lines, one bit with carved spiraliform pattern (Fig. 280 No. 7).

PASTE

Fragment of greenish bead.

TERRACOTTA

Whorl (Fig. 280 No. 6), h. 0.03 m., d. 0.025 m., found on floor.

CLAY

12 pinches or twists, probably raw material for tablets, and fragments of others (e.g., Fig. 276 Nos. 1-7).

Tablets: Nos. 1215-1246, 1249 (*OOT*, 47-65, 68, pls. VIII-XVII).

POTTERY

Jug (Shape 34, p. 375)
No. 574 (Fig. 367), decorated.
Jug (Shape 35, p. 375)
No. 573 (Figs. 367, 368), decorated.
Jar (Shape 54b, p. 392)
No. 542 (Fig. 379).
Krater (Shape 59, p. 396)
No. 1085.
Lid (Shape 75, p. 416)
Nos. 586 (Fig. 398), 1137.
Lid (Shape 76, p. 416)
No. 1136.
Lid (Shape 77, p. 417)
Nos. 519 (Fig. 398), 825, 1086.
Other shapes represented by sherds: basins and bowls with pinched-out handles, kylikes of various sizes, high-handled dippers. Among the fragments with painted decoration are three large kylix bases and a stem, fragment of a Vapheio cup, a piece decorated in Palace Style: spiraliform pattern also noted.

Pithoi[52]

No. 1: depth 1.05 m.; d. 0.72 m., d. neck 0.35 m. to 0.42 m., most of neck and all of rim missing. Contents: red burned earth near top changing to black toward bottom; six bits of bronze; small fragment of tablet (?), no letters; a few fragments of pithos itself; scattered sherds, mainly of kylikes; three bits with painted decoration.

No. 2: depth 1.10 m., d. 0.64 m., d. neck 0.36 m. to 0.44 m., rim missing. Contents: red burned earth at top, many large stones, blackish earth at bottom; two fragments of lid deep down; seven scraps of bronze, tiny bit of obsidian, small bit of bone; a few nondescript sherds, and part of a conical cup.

No. 3: depth 1.08 m., d. 0.68 m., d. neck 0.37 m. to 0.44 m., most of neck and all of rim missing. Contents: reddish-brown burned earth on top, blackish toward bottom; 8 pieces of bronze, including a curving strip (Fig. 280 No. 5), l. pres. 0.052 m., w. 0.019 m., with raised decoration: amygdaloid alternating with round shapes in three alternating rows; 2 chips of flint, one bone, 12 coarse, 20 fine sherds.

No. 4: depth 1.12 m., d. 0.78 m., d. neck 0.38 m. to 0.45 m., most of neck and all of rim missing. Contents: reddish-brown earth in upper part, grayish toward bottom; 14 bits of bronze, 4 scraps of ivory, good many small stones, fragments of stucco or plaster; a few miscellaneous sherds, 5 coarse, 27 of finer ware.

No. 5: depth 0.50 m. below top of stand but rises 0.20 m. above stand, d. 0.52 m., d. neck 0.28 m. to 0.31 m.; most of neck and all of rim missing; raised band with transverse impressions just below junction of neck and body. Contents: red burned earth on top, gray below; 3 coarse, 9 finer sherds of the common types.

No. 6: depth 1.02 m., d. 0.74 m., neck and rim missing. Contents: reddish-brown earth on top, dark below; 5 thin, twisted pieces of bronze; a scrap of ivory; 7 coarse, 28 fine sherds.

No. 7: depth 0.98 m., d. 0.74 m. Two joining fragments of rim found inside indicate total height of between 1.15 m. and 1.21 m. Contents: brown earth on top, changing to black below; some fragments of mud plaster; fossil with leaf impression; bronze rivet (Fig. 280 No. 10) with its two flat heads, d. 0.014 m. and 0.01 m., and 15 nondescript pieces of bronze; 47 fragments of burned ivory. A few sherds of kylikes, etc.

No. 8: depth 1.08 m., d. 0.79 m., neck and rim missing. Contents: reddish earth at top, very black at bottom; 26 bits of bronze and one flat piece with running spiral decoration bordered on one side by band with diagonal incisions (Fig. 280 No. 4), l. 0.036 m., w. 0.022 m.; 7 coarse, 43 finer sherds.

No. 9: depth 1.08 m., d. 0.76 m., neck oval but missing. Contents: brownish earth at top, grayish at bottom; 14 small pieces (e.g., Fig. 280 No. 2) and one large fragment of bronze with two rows of running spirals preserved (Fig. 280 No. 3), l. 0.045 m., w. 0.04 m., th. 0.01 m.; one obsidian blade (Fig. 280 No. 1); 9 scraps of burned ivory; 10 coarse, 45 finer sherds, some from conical cups and kylikes.

Nos. 10, 11, 12, 13, 14, 15 not well enough preserved to give useful measurements.

No. 16: depth 1.03 m., d. 0.76 m., most of neck and all of rim missing. Contents: reddish-brown earth at top, dark at bottom; 11 pieces of bronze; one bit of ivory; a few small stones; 15 coarse, 45 finer sherds, one fragment of Vapheio cup with painted stripes; one piece of a brown kylix like those found in Room 60.

No. 17: small pithos but relatively well preserved, depth 0.80 m., d. 0.60 m., d. neck 0.30 m. to 0.36 m., h. neck above stand 0.17 m., raised band around junction of neck and body, decorated with broad thumb impressions. Contents: reddish-brown earth at

---

[52] Many of the pithoi seem to have had oval necks; in most instances they were set with the longer diameter running approximately from back to front of the stand. Measurements of depth were made from the top of the stand to the bottom of the inside of the jar; diameters of body and neck are inside dimensions.

top, grayish-black at bottom; fragments of neck and of lid found inside; eight nondescript pieces of bronze; two small bits of ivory; an obsidian blade; some 80 sherds, including five kylix stems, two flat bases, one bit with remains of painted decoration.

ROOM 24

The doorway leading from Room 23 to Room 24 (Fig. 442) is of the same type as that from Room 22 to Room 23 (Fig. 102). On each side is a fairly large stone base for the jamb, and the space between, ranging from 0.56 m. to 0.63 m. in width, was paved with stucco, a continuation of the floor from the connecting rooms. Most of it has been broken away and is now missing. The base of the jamb on the southeastern side was 0.95 m. long, 0.35 m. wide at its southwestern end, and 0.405 m. toward the northeast. In its top is a rabbet beginning 0.15 m. from the southwestern end, where it is most deeply cut, 0.05 m. to 0.06 m., probably for the reception of a socket for a pivot. The rabbet, running through the doorway, diminishing from 0.17 m. to 0.10 m. in width, was very roughly executed, or has been damaged by fire.

The base on the northwestern side is 1.02 m. long, 0.44 m. wide at its southwestern end, and 0.38 m. at the northeastern. It too is carelessly finished, and it is cracked in many places. There must have been a wooden door frame, but no trace of it now remains. On the southeastern side of the doorway, however, a mass of fused stone and brick, what we have called *migma*, projects from the middle of the wall into what may have been the hollow of the door jamb. At this end of the wall each face is seen to bear a thick coat of rough plaster behind the stands holding the oil jars.

Room 24 is 5.28 m. long from southwest to northeast and 3.94 m. wide. On the southwest it is bounded by the party wall with Room 23 already described (Fig. 22); on the southeast by the rear wall of the Throne Room (p. 79); and on the northeast by a wall 0.93 m. thick which separates it from the Northeastern Corridor. This wall, preserved to an average height of 0.50 m. and continuing the northeastern line of the Throne Room, has a doorway opening through its northern end into the Northeastern Corridor 25. On the northwest was the exterior wall of the Main Building, no part of which is now preserved above floor level.

In almost all respects this room is like its companion magazine, with a stuccoed stand running around all four sides and enclosing jars for olive oil (Fig. 420). There are some differences in details. For instance, the stand on the right as one enters, instead of having a rounded end, runs out to an almost angular corner (Fig. 22). Its northwestern face, however, slants obliquely toward the east, in order to leave a passageway of adequate width, 0.80 m. In another respect a difference may be noted: this stand is considerably higher, rising vertically to a height of 0.45 m. at both ends of the room, and across the southeast side averaging 0.40 m. high. At the northeastern end too it is only 0.70 m. wide. It might also be added that Magazine 24 contains only 16 jars, as compared with 17 in Room 23 (Fig. 420).

Beginning at the right, as one enters, along the southwest wall are Pithoi Nos. 1 and 2; in the southeastern stand are seven (Nos. 3 to 9) and against the northeast wall are two somewhat smaller jars (Nos. 10 and 11). The stand here has a well-rounded end, and the passage between it and the rounded end of the northwest stand is nearly 0.90 m. wide. The latter, which has lost most of its stucco facing and all its stucco top, contains the lower parts of five additional pithoi (Nos. 12 to 16). On the opposite side of the room too the stand has suffered some damage, especially Pithoi 5 and 6, and in many places the stucco coating is badly cracked and broken.

The floor of Room 24 is somewhat better preserved than that of Room 23, though it too has suffered much damage from the same causes that operated in the neighboring room. Two terracotta lids for the oil-jars were found on the floor, one at the south corner and the other at the east corner of the stand (Fig. 106). Likewise on the floor, beside Pithos No. 11, was recovered a diminutive tablet or label which has the distinction of being the smallest one in the entire collection from the palace. In the middle of the room are three or four dents in the floor, where the stucco has suffered more damage than elsewhere. Perhaps they were caused by the fall of heavy stones from above. Among them were two worked pieces, cut to form sections of a pi-shaped water-channel or gutter.

Many fragments of stucco pavement had fallen from above into Rooms 23 and 24, probably coming from a terrace or an upper story. There were also a few pieces of wall plaster with remains of frescoes, some perhaps contemporary with the palace, some, possibly of earlier style, which may have been used in the bedding for the upper flooring.

O B J E C T S   F O U N D

GOLD

Fragment of thin foil, possibly representing petals of a flower (Fig. 281 No. 1), l. 0.052 m., max. w. 0.017 m.

SILVER

Two pieces.

BRONZE

One fairly large flat piece, one side engraved or stamped with ivy leaf pattern (Fig. 281 No. 5), l. pres. 0.044 m., w. pres. 0.039 m., th. 0.004 m.

Bar with two rivets and hole for a third (Fig. 281 No. 3), l. pres. 0.053 m., w. pres. 0.013 m., th. 0.014 m.; slightly curved; very heavy and solid.

Rivet-head, flattened conical (Fig. 281 No. 2), d. 0.015 m.

Tiny ball, d. 0.002 m., no perforation.

102 nondescript pieces.

LEAD

Fragment, red inside, possibly lead (Fig. 281 No. 4).

STONE

Flint: 21 pieces.

Obsidian: 6 pieces.

Quartz: 2 pieces.

BONE

Small bits; 1 cut piece.

IVORY

729 pieces counted; probably there were twice that many. One fragment, 0.025 m. by 0.018 m., burned blue-gray, possibly with incised character. Other pieces with incised lines (e.g., Fig. 281 Nos. 9, 10). One small bit burned black, ca. 0.01 m. square, with spiral carved in relief (Fig. 281 No. 8).

TERRACOTTA

Hind part of animal figurine, comprising one leg and rump with tail (Fig. 281 No. 12), l. pres. 0.032 m., h. pres. 0.03 m.

Fore part of animal figurine, with head and feet missing (Fig. 281 No. 11), l. pres. ca. 0.049 m., h. pres. 0.04 m.

CLAY

Label: No. 1247 (*OOT*, 67, pls. XVI-XVII).

Sealing: NM. 9050 = *CMMS* 382 = No. 1437 (*AJA* 66 [1962], 149, 151, 152, pls. 38, 39). Goat, or perhaps two, one going left, one going right. Greater part of impression missing.

POTTERY

Lid (Shape 75, p. 416)
 No. 543 (Fig. 397).
Lid (Shape 76, p. 416)
 No. 1132 (Figs. 397, 398).
Fragments of many other lids some of which may be of the two-handled variety.

Other shapes represented by sherds: diminutive votive kylix (2), bowl and possibly basin with pinched-out handles, kylikes of various sizes, dipper with heavy high handle.

Pithoi

No. 1: depth 0.90 m., d. 0.73 m., neck missing. Contents: reddish-brown earth at top; some small stones; blackish earth near bottom; four thin bent pieces of bronze; 22 sherds including kylix stems, conical cups, and handle of a scoop.

No. 2: depth 0.92 m., d. 0.71 m., neck missing. Contents: black earth near top, toward bottom earth is dark gray; four coarse, 27 finer sherds.

No. 3: depth 1.14 m., d. 0.79 m., d. neck 0.39 m. to 0.45 m., most of neck and all of rim missing. Contents: reddish-brown earth at top; blackish at bottom; a few small stones; a handful of sherds, including fragments of kylikes.

No. 4: depth 0.97 m., d. 0.69 m., neck missing. Contents: reddish burned earth at top; far down very black carbonized earth; many large stones had fallen into pithos, which was badly cracked and broken. A few sherds, mostly fragments of kylikes.

No. 5: depth 0.88 m., d. 0.72 m., neck missing. First seen in a trial trench in 1952. Contents: reddish-brown burned earth at top, small deposit of black earth at bottom; 28 sherds, some representing kylix and basin with pinched-out handles.

No. 6: depth 1.05 m., d. 0.81 m., neck missing. Contents: reddish-brown earth at top; a huge block of stone had fallen into the pithos and smashed most of the neck and upper part; many other large stones; earth turns dark at bottom; some fragments of stucco; 18 scattered sherds including 3 of coarse fabric.

No. 7: depth 1.04 m., d. 0.69 m., d. neck 0.37 m. to 0.44 m.; neck rises 0.14 m. above stand. Contents: reddish-brown earth in upper part; many small stones; some fragments of plaster or stucco flooring; in middle part, blackish earth, two fragments of lid and many stones; at bottom, reddish-brown earth again; scattered sherds, mostly fine, of the usual kinds.

No. 8: depth 0.98 m., d. 0.65 m., d. neck 0.32 m. to 0.35 m.; raised band decorated with thumb impressions at junction of neck and body. Contents: reddish-brown earth in upper part; some bits of bronze and one large fused chunk (Fig. 281 No. 6), l. 0.04 m., w. 0.025 m., th. 0.008 m.; at very bottom, black earth; one very small fragment of bone; piece of lid; small lot of fine sherds including rims of kylikes and one flat base.

No. 9: depth 1.13 m., d. 0.79 m., d. neck 0.36 m. to 0.45 m.; neck rises 0.10 m. above stand. Contents: reddish-brown earth at top changing to dark toward bottom; many fragments of the pithos and of a lid in coarse ware; a few bits of burned bone; one flat fragment of bronze (Fig. 281 No. 7), l. 0.032 m., w. 0.024 m.; one terracotta spindle whorl (Fig. 281 No. 13); a large lot of sherds, including pieces of kylikes, one flat base.

No. 10: depth 0.98 m., d. 0.73 m., d. neck 0.33 m., most of neck and all of rim missing. Contents: reddish burned earth at top, brown below, black at bottom; several stones; many bits of stucco floor or plaster; many sherds, chiefly of plain kylikes; conical cups, angular bowls with pinched-out handles also represented.

No. 11: depth 0.87 m., d. 0.64 m., most of neck and rim missing, d. neck 0.29 m. to 0.31 m.; at junction of neck and body raised band with deep impressions, carelessly made and of varying sizes. Contents: many fragments of stucco flooring near top; a few sherds, mostly of bowls and kylikes; four pieces of bronze, one of flint, two of quartz, 69 of ivory, one of which is decorated. This fragment measures roughly 0.02 m. by 0.015 m. and the pattern resembles a feathered wing (Figs. 266 No. 6, 280 No. 8).

N O R T H E A S T C O R R I D O R , S E C T I O N 25

The doorway opening into the Northeast Corridor is of the same type as that leading in from Room 23 (Figs. 22, 443). There is no central threshold block, but on each side of the opening is a rectangular base of poros which supported the door frame as well as the pivot in which the door swung. The space between, 0.45 m. wide, was paved with stucco. The base on the southeastern side is 0.50 m. wide and 0.96 m. long. It has some slight traces of a shallow rabbet and it shows signs of wearing, 0.25 m. wide, along its northwestern half. The northwestern base is 1.01 m. long and 0.50 m. wide. This too exhibits weathering to a width of 0.30 m. from its southeast edge. A transverse cutting, 0.04 m. deep, 0.08 m. wide, and 0.28 m. long, beginning 0.18 m. from the northeast end, was probably made for the setting of the pivot of the door. From this transverse cut, instead of the usual rabbet another more or less rectangular cutting, 0.10 m. wide and 0.03 m. deep, extends southwestward some 0.45 m. The actual door was evidently a single leaf, which swung against the northwest jamb within the depth of the door opening. How the jamb was fitted to the wall on this side is not certain. On the southeastern flank of the doorway, however, a corner post was apparently set in the angle toward the corridor, in the manner seen in the doorway between Rooms 21 and 22. The inner corner shows no corresponding arrangement, but the plaster on the wall ends in a straight vertical edge against which the door frame must have been set.

Passing through the doorway one enters the northwest end of the Northeast Corridor (Fig. 23). The latter is one of the outstanding features of the palace, extending through a total length of 28.63 m. along the northeast side of the Megaron Suite and giving access at intervals to the various storerooms, chambers, stairway, and passages in the northeasterly side of the building (Fig. 107). The main corridor, however, was not an open unobstructed passage. It was interrupted by two doorways which divided it into three sections of varying length, each of which could be shut off when desired. The northwestern section (25 on Key Plan), varying in width from 1.48

m. to 1.55 m., depending on the thickness of the plaster, is 13.575 m. long, measured from the inside face of the plaster on the northwest wall to the northwestern face of the first doorway.

Only the foundations of the northwest wall have survived. The superstructure is missing to a point below the level of the floor in the corridor, but the plaster is preserved to a height 0.10 m. above the floor. The corridor is bordered on the southwest by the wall separating it from Magazine 24 and by the northeast lateral wall of the Throne Room (Fig. 107 and p. 78). Throughout the greater part of its length the wall on this side has retained a thick layer of mud plaster which was finished with a coat of whitewash. The plaster was regularly laid across the horizontal grooves and vertical chases for beams. Two horizontal grooves are visible, one at 0.32 m., the other at 0.83 m. above the floor. At the southeastern end of the section the wall stands to a maximum height of 1.18 m.

The corridor is bounded on the northeast for 1.60 m. by the remnant of a wall, the plaster face of which still rises to a height of 0.35 m.; then for 1.63 m. by Corridor 26; finally for the rest of its length, 10.34 m., by a wall separating it from Magazine 32 and Room 30 (Fig. 23). This wall, 1.20 m. thick, including its plaster, rises from a minimum of 0.40 m. above the floor at the northwest to a maximum of 1.15 m. toward the southeastern end of the section, generally conforming to the modern slope of the plowed ground. The wall has the normal horizontal grooves and 11 vertical chases before it reaches the doorway ending this section of the corridor. The spacing of the vertical chases is irregular, varying from 0.45 m. to 0.90 m. A thick coat of mud plaster covers the greater part of the wall, except at its northwestern end, and for the most part conceals the position of the horizontal beams. Signs of a groove appear at 0.45 m. above the floor and of another at about 1 m., but exact measurements are not possible. As on the other side of the corridor, this wall had a finishing coat of whitewash.

The corridor is paved with good stucco (Fig. 107). It has been seen in section in three places, where holes were cut for the concrete foundations for the Dexion pillars that support the new roof. The thickness varies from place to place, ranging from 0.025 m. to 0.095 m. Where thickest, it seems to have been applied in two separate layers which might represent phases, since red earth from crude brick lies between. The stucco on the floor turns up at the sides to meet the plaster on the wall. In some parts of the corridor the flooring is not in good condition, especially opposite Corridor 26, where many stones, including a squared block, had fallen on it, cracking and breaking it.

This section of the corridor when excavated was found filled with relatively large fallen stones, red earth from disintegrated crude brick, quantities of fragments of stucco pavement of two or three different kinds, and not a few pieces of wall plaster with painted decoration. Very few potsherds were recovered here, but a number of fragments of ivory with carved decoration were found. All these things had evidently fallen from the floor above. Deeper, near the stucco pavement itself, was the usual black stratum, probably the remains of burned wood.

O B J E C T S   F O U N D

BRONZE

Fragment possibly from outturned rim of small vessel (Fig. 283 No. 1), h. 0.025 m., w. 0.023 m., th. 0.002 m.

A few shapeless pieces (e.g., Fig. 283 Nos. 2, 3).

FLINT

Several flakes and chips.

OBSIDIAN

Blade (Fig. 283 No. 4), l. 0.025 m., w. 0.01 m., th. 0.003 m., and several flakes (e.g., Fig. 283 No. 5).

IVORY

Fragments including several with carved decoration: one ribbed barrel-like, one piece with running spiral, two with feather-pattern or foliate spray.

NM. 7835 (Fig. 284 No. 3), l. 0.044 m., h. 0.034 m., th. 0.008 m.: fragment of ornament or open receptacle with finished rim-like top; outer face decorated with carved spiraliform design perhaps in panels separated by upright ridges and horizontal beading; spiral has dotted circle at its center; fine lines scratched on back. Found outside

northwest wall of Corridor 25, presumably fallen from the upper floor.

WOOD

Two carbonized pieces that seem to have a carved pattern, l. 0.011 m., w. 0.013 m.

POTTERY

No whole pots; relatively few sherds, which somehow found their way into the debris at the time of the destruction or later. They include the usual fragments of kylikes (20 stems), cups, bowls with pinched-out handles, conical cups, tripod-vessels, and pithoi, some with painted patterns. Four joining pieces of oatmeal ware decorated in brown paint on a creamy white background in a flamboyant imitation of the Palace Style with bands, triangles, spirals or concentric circles bordered with dots, and a plantlike filling ornament. Other motives seen in fragments of oatmeal ware are overlapping vertical arcs, wide and narrow bands, and curving lines. Patterns noted on pieces of finer ware: scale, dotted net, concentric circles or spiral, curving bands enclosing a curving row of dots, multiple chevrons, etc.

CORRIDOR 26

The doorway leading from Corridor 25 northeastward into Corridor 26 (Figs. 23, 445) is of the same general type as the one from Magazine 24 to Corridor 25, with a substantial base for the door jamb on each side, no threshold block between them, but a continuation of the floor through the opening. The floor overlapped and covered an underlying projection, or rabbet, of each jamb base. The stucco continued from the southwest some 0.10 m. into the doorway, and beyond that point was an earth floor like that in Corridor 26 (Fig. 108). The base of the jamb on the northwest is 0.60 m. long from southwest to northeast, varying from 0.40 m. to 0.48 m. in width, and 0.32 m. thick. What we have called the rabbet is cut in its top along the side toward the opening, ranging from 0.04 m. to 0.10 m. in width, with a depth of 0.03 m., the inner edge of the cutting being parallel to the side of the doorway. The southeastern base is 0.57 m. long, 0.48 m. wide, and 0.35 m. thick. A rabbet, like that on the other block, 0.10 m. wide and 0.04 m. deep, is cut along the northwestern edge; from it a cutting extends almost at right angles 0.22 m. toward the southeast. Exactly how the door casing resting on these blocks was fitted against the walls on each side was not clear, since neither is preserved to a sufficient height to provide evidence.

Corridor 26 (Key Plan) is 7.44 m. long and 1.63 m. wide (Fig. 23). On the southeast side it is bordered by a section of what was evidently once the exterior wall of the building. This wall is 1.10 m. thick and stands to a height of 0.84 m. On the northwest face two courses of ashlar blocks are preserved to a point 1.07 m. from the southwestern end of the wall. The lower course, rising 0.37 m. above the floor, forms a dado and the second course is set back 0.06 m., leaving a narrow ledge. This second course seems to have been built of nine large blocks, two of which are now missing, one at the western corner and the other, the fourth from the northeastern end. This course shows the usual V-shaped joints. On the inside of the wall, opposite each of these joints, is a chase for vertical beams. Eight such chases are spaced along the wall at intervals of ca. 0.80 m. The evidence of two dowel holes suggests that a horizontal beam was laid along the top of this second course which corresponds with the level of the horizontal beam in the exterior northeast wall. Just 5.71 m. from the west corner is a gap in the second course, 0.21 m. wide, between two of the ashlar blocks. This gap is directly opposite a chase, well marked on the inner face of the wall, and may have been filled with an upright timber. The top of the wall, which lay only a few centimeters below the surface of the ground, is scarred with marks of the plow; it was also much damaged by the fire that destroyed the palace.

In a pit near the southwestern end of the wall its foundations were exposed: one course of poros blocks here lies below the floor level, founded on unworked stones that continue down to a depth of 1.10 m. They rest in part on the wall of an earlier building, running from southeast to northwest, which was bedded on *stereo* at a depth of 2.34 m. below the southwest jamb base of the doorway into Corridor 25.

At its northeastern end Corridor 26 terminates against what appears to be a later extension, added on without bonding, to the northeast exterior wall (Fig. 23). This extension is 1.05 m. thick and is preserved to a height of only 0.40 m. above the floor of the corridor. On the exterior face is one large ashlar block, 0.48 m. high, 1.20 m. long, and 0.60 m. wide (Fig. 109). Beyond to the northwest the wall continues, constructed of rubble. The inner face too at the end of the corridor is built of that material. A gap, 0.30 m. wide, in the inner face, ca. 0.80 m. distant from the southeast wall, might perhaps be evidence for a chase. No remains of plaster are recognizable.

The northwest wall also was built of rubble. Almost exactly centered in it is a doorway leading into Room 27, another oil magazine (Fig. 111). The northeastern section of the wall, which is 0.85 m. thick, stands to a height of 0.50 m. to 0.55 m. In the southeastern face three chases are visible at intervals of 1 m. and 0.90 m. One of the chases is at the end of this section, directly beside the doorway into Room 27 (Fig. 112). There may have been a groove for a horizontal beam ca. 0.25 m. above the floor. Some remains of mud plaster still cling to the face of the wall.

The section southwest of the doorway is missing almost down to floor level and below, and little remains except large chunks of mud plaster still standing upright in and next to the doorway into Corridor 25. The foundations go down to 0.40 m. below the floor, where they rest, in part at least, on an earlier wall running in the same direction (Fig. 108). Evidence for a vertical chase appears beside the doorway, matching the one just mentioned on the northeastern side of the opening (Fig. 112).

The floor of the corridor was made of earth or clay packed down. It was covered with the usual wreckage of fire, including several poros blocks that had presumably fallen from the wall on the southeast (Fig. 111). No separate catalogue of the potsherds, etc., found in Corridor 26 will be given: this material at the time of the excavations was included with that from Room 27.

Explorations under the floor revealed considerable remains of earlier phases and periods (Fig. 108). The bottoms of several pithoi, set 0.35 m. to 0.40 m. below the level of the floor, must belong to an antecedent phase, for they would have seriously impeded circulation if they stood in the corridor. A wall, built of unworked stones in many courses, was founded on *stereo* at a depth of 1.90 m. This wall, mentioned above (p. 145), runs from southeast to northwest; it has been exposed to a thickness of 1.35 m. but its northeasterly face was not reached. Alongside the wall on the southwest was a deep deposit, beginning a little more than a meter below the floor, continuing to *stereo* at −2.34 m., and containing Middle Helladic pottery.

About 1 m. northeast of the inner edge of the doorway from Corridor 25, remains of an underground drain were encountered. It was 0.24 m. wide and 0.24 m. high, its top lying 0.35 m. below the floor. Coming from the direction of Room 32, it passes through the foundations of the wall between that room and Corridor 26 and continues downward toward the northwest.

ROOM 27

As defined by the two lateral bases for the jambs, the doorway leading from Corridor 26 into the "North Oil Magazine" has a maximum width of 1.66 m. (Figs. 112, 447). It has no central threshold, but the space between the blocks, ca. 0.70 m. wide, was merely paved with trodden earth. The base on the northeast is 0.53 m. wide, 1.03 m. long, and 0.42 m. thick. The upper part of the block was trimmed 0.04 m., on the side toward the door opening and somewhat less on the northwest to a depth of 0.12 m. About 0.19 m. from its southeastern end a slot, 0.14 m. long, 0.06 m. wide, and 0.04 m. deep, has been cut into the top of it from its southwestern edge. Whether this cutting had anything to do with a pivot for the door is doubtful. It is probably evidence rather for the reuse of the block. The surface of the block is rough and gives little understandable information on wear or weathering.

The block on the other side of the doorway has a maximum length of 1.13 m., a thickness of 0.38 m., and an average width of 0.45 m., measured on its surface. But, like its mate, this block had been trimmed 0.05 m. to 0.06 m. along its northeast edge and 0.03 m. along its northwest edge to an irregular depth of 0.13 m. to 0.15 m. below the top. We have not been able to determine whether the cutting was made for the adjustment of the block into this particular doorway or is merely a sign of earlier use elsewhere. Both blocks project a few centimeters beyond the door opening into the corridor and into Room 27. A wooden door frame stood on these two bases, but how far out it extended is not clear. On each side toward the wall, however, it was no doubt firmly fastened to the upright timbers that occupied the chases mentioned above (p. 146).

The North Magazine (27 on Key Plan) is 6.90 m. long from southwest to northeast and 5.85 m. wide. The southeast wall in both its sections has just been described from the side of Corridor 26 and little need be added. The section to the northeast of the doorway, standing to a height of ca. 0.50 m., retains a good deal of mud plaster; the section to the southwest is preserved only to a height of 0.25 m. above the jamb base. Almost no mud plaster remains in place on the wall.

The southwestern wall, 1.05 m. thick, was at some time demolished down to floor level and nothing can be said about its superstructure (Fig. 25), except that visible evidence demonstrates at least three vertical chases, spaced ca. 0.80 m. apart. A horizontal beam lay at or just below floor level. What can be seen of the foundations is built of rubble with an occasional large stone inserted. The northwestern wall, 1.20 m. thick, is likewise represented almost exclusively by its foundations in which one large squared block and several big stones appear among the rubble. Indications of at least two vertical chases show that this wall too was built in the regular Mycenaean style. About 1.25 m. from the western corner a small opening through the wall, 0.30 m. wide, approximately at floor level, evidently served for drainage (Fig. 421).

The northeast wall, 1.05 m. thick, is in a similar state of dilapidation, having been removed down to the level of the floor and deeper. Nevertheless signs of four or five chases have been recongized. The outer face of this wall, as well as that of the northwestern wall, was built of squared blocks laid in ashlar style, for fragments of such blocks were found lying outside along the northeastern and northwestern sides of the room (Fig. 111).

The floor of the magazine was not made of stucco but of trodden earth and clay. It seems to have had a considerable slope downward toward the northwest. Since the room was large it was apparently judged necessary to have interior supports to hold up the ceiling and roof. A row of bases for posts was laid almost, but not exactly, along the longitudinal axis (Figs. 25, 421); they were made of bluish-reddish stone, perhaps some kind of quartzite. The northeasternmost block has been somewhat displaced and shifted 0.25 m. or 0.30 m. to the southeast. The other three seem to be in their original positions. They are of two different shapes, oblong and square blocks in alternation. The first on the southwest, 1.12 m. from the face of the wall to the center of the block, is 0.56 m. long from northwest to southeast, 0.37 m. wide, and 0.08 m. thick. The next, 1.62 m. distant, center to center, is 0.50 m. long from southwest to northeast, 0.40 m. wide, 0.10 m. thick. The third, of the oblong type, running from southeast to northwest, is 1.62 m. distant center to center. It is 0.60 m. long, 0.33 m. wide and 0.11 m. thick. The fourth, which is no longer *in situ*, now lies somewhat askew about halfway between the third base and the northeast wall, and close to a large pithos. It is 0.58 m. long by 0.52 m. wide, and 0.13 m. thick; its upper surface has been hollowed out to a depth of 0.04 m. perhaps by wear. It has been suggested that it might have been used as a standing place for jars that were brought into the magazine to be emptied into the pithoi or to be filled from them. It seems likely, however, that the stone may first have been used for a time as a base for a post.

Large pithoi, but not of uniform sizes and types, were ranged around all four sides of the room (Figs. 25, 421). To the left of the door, to the southwest on entering, are two; along the southwestern wall, counting the corner one twice, stand five jars; there are five, again counting the one in the corner twice, against the northwest wall. No jar occupies the north corner, though four stand fairly close against the northeastern wall. Beyond the eastern corner which was also left empty, only one jar was set beside the southeast wall between the angle and the door to the corridor. We thus have a total of 16 jars in the magazine. In the northwestern part of the room, not far from the jars against the wall, is an irregular row of smallish flat stones, five in number (Fig. 25). They may have served as stepping stones at times when the floor was muddy or alternatively may have been used as convenient stands for containers brought into the magazine. It was not possible to determine whether or not Magazine 27 had an upper story.

The first trial trench in 1939 passing through the room revealed plowed earth to a depth of 0.25 m.; below, a layer 0.80 m. deep composed mainly of yellowish-green clay, dissolved crude brick.

O B J E C T S   F O U N D

GOLD

Fragment of gold-plated bead (NM. 7802), l. pres. 0.011 m., d. ca. 0.006 m.

BRONZE

Curved piece probably of a socket (Fig. 283 No. 11). Found in pithos.

10 pieces, mostly very small, shapeless, some thin, flat (e.g., Fig. 283 No. 10).

STONE

Obsidian: piece of a core (Fig. 283 No. 6), a flake (Fig. 283 No. 7) and another bit.

Flint: three fragments, red or pink (e.g., Fig. 283 Nos. 8, 9); greenish: large conical button or whorl, h. 0.014 m., d. 0.025.

PASTE

One white piece (burnt?), fluted, hollow, tapering, possibly fragment of a bead (Fig. 283 No. 12), l. 0.019 m., d. 0.005 m.

BONE

Two burnt pieces; two small boar's tusks.

IVORY (OR BONE)

Flat bit with one scratched line.

TERRACOTTA

Half a whorl, gray clay; flattened spherical (Fig. 283 No. 13), h. 0.016 m., d. 0.031 m.

Small head, broken off below neck, probably from disk- or crescent-shaped figurine (Fig. 283 No. 14): protruding nose damaged by pick, eyes indicated by applied blobs; no trace of paint; h. pres. 0.032 m., max. w. 0.022 m., d. neck 0.012 m.

POTTERY

Apart from the remnants of the 16 pithoi only a single pot, found in Pithos 14, was recovered.

Krater-bowl (Shape 60, p. 397) No. 862 (Figs. 385, 386), decorated. Found in pithos.

Shapes represented by sherds: large basin-like lid, kylix of various types and sizes (199 stems), bowl and cup (10 bases), cup with straddle handle, dipper, tripod-vessel.

NORTHEAST CORRIDOR, SECTION 28

Section 25 of the Northeast Corridor ends at a doorway which leads into Section 28 (Figs. 107, 444). The lateral bases of the jambs indicate the position of the doorway (Fig. 113). The base on the northeast side is of poros stone, 0.70 m. long, 0.40 m. wide. In the top of the block, a rabbet, 0.14 m. broad, cut along the northwest end of the block, intersects a similar rabbet, 0.15 m. wide, running through the doorway on the southwestern side of the stone. The rabbet is 0.05 m. to 0.06 m. deep. The remaining uncut part of the top, 0.25 m. wide and 0.56 m. long through the opening, was presumably the setting place for the wooden door frame. The rough plaster on the wall behind it ends in a fairly regular vertical line where it evidently bordered the casing. On the opposite side of the corridor is a somewhat similar block, 0.75 m. long, 0.44 m. wide and 0.20 m. thick,[53] with a comparable rabbet on the north-

[53] It was possible to measure the thickness of the stone and of the floor in the side of the hole dug for the foundations of one of the metal columns supporting the modern roof.

east and northwest. The former is 0.27 m. broad, the latter 0.14 m. The rabbet is also carried around the southeastern side to a width of 0.05 m. The remaining uncut surface on the top of the block, 0.56 m. long, which bore the casing, has the same length as that on the other side, but is only 0.16 m. wide. On the southwest wall too the plaster terminates in a straight vertical line indicating the edge of the door jamb.

The stucco floor of the corridor, 0.025 m. thick, extends through the opening in the space, 0.72 m. wide, between the two bases. It was probably intended to have the floor at the same level as that of the rabbet on each side, but the pavement seems to have been carelessly made. On the northeast it reaches approximately the level mentioned, but on the southwest it is 0.04 m. to 0.05 m. below the cutting in the stone. Perhaps it has suffered a good deal of wear.

Section 28 of the corridor (Key Plan), 5.10 m. long and 1.48 m. wide, is like Section 25. The southwest wall, which it shares with the Throne Room, has a maximum height of 1.20 m. Almost its whole face is still coated with rough plaster (Fig. 113). Its vertical chases have already been mentioned (p. 78). A horizontal groove for a beam is visible at 0.80 m. and what seems to be another at 0.15 m. above the floor. The northeastern side of the passage is bordered by a broad doorway (Fig. 114) leading to a lobby that opens into a suite of five rooms (29 to 34 on Key Plan). Beyond the doorway the southwest wall of Room 33 (1.12 m. thick) stands to a maximum height of 1.35 m. Its coat of rough plaster is almost intact, but four vertical chases running through the wall are recognizable as well as a horizontal groove 0.60 m. above the floor.

This section of the passage was found filled here and there with a mass of disintegrated crude brick, burned red and very hard. Many fragments of flooring and remnants of frescoes had fallen into it from above. Beneath this deposit were quantities of stones almost wedged together, lying on the black stratum that covered the floor. The floor itself of stucco is fairly well preserved in some places, damaged in others. Near the southeastern doorway were found fragments of a stirrup-vase retaining traces of painted decoration.

O B J E C T S   F O U N D

B R O N Z E
Tiny piece.

F L I N T
Blade, purplish, l. 0.039 m., w. 0.014 m., th. 0.006 m.

O B S I D I A N
Irregular chip and four flakes (e.g., Fig. 283 Nos. 15, 16).

I V O R Y
Bits: one, a rectangular piece, l. 0.018 m., w. 0.008 m., th. 0.006 m., with vestiges of incised chevrons (Fig. 283 No. 17).

P O T T E R Y
Small decorated stirrup-vase, fragments (similar to or possibly part of pot found south-

east of doorway into the Vestibule from Corridor 35).

Shapes represented by sherds: kylix (6 stems), cup and bowl (many bases), conical cup, basin with pinched-out handles, large stirrup-vase, coarse tripod cooking pot, coarse pithoid jar with flat bottom, large coarse brazier with pierced handle, pithos (fragment of offset rim, flat on top).

Sherds with painted decoration: disk and one handle of a large stirrup-vase with circle on disk, bands around base of neck and base of handle, which bears diagonal stripes; flat bottom and lower part coated all over with brown paint. Motives include: bands, panels, crosshatched triangle, spiral or concentric circles, opposing triangles in mat paint on light brown surface.

LOBBY 29

At the northwest end of Section 28 of the corridor a doorway opens northeastward into a small lobby (29 on Key Plan). On each side of the opening is a large stone base for the door frame (Figs. 113, 449). The one on the southeast is 1.14 m. long, running through the opening, 0.49 m. wide, and rises 0.17 m. above the floor. That on the northwest is 1.19 m. long and 0.53 m. wide (Fig. 114). At its southwestern end this stone has been notched to fit it around the base of the jamb in the doorway between Sections 25 and 28 of the corridor. No cuttings are visible in the top of either base, but it is likely that there was a great vertical post at each corner to which the wooden casing was fastened. On the southeastern base lay a thick deposit of carbonized matter and the end of the wall above it was noticeably blackened. Between the posts at the angles on both sides the core of the wall seems to have projected slightly into the hollow.

The opening (1.38 m. wide) between the bases has no threshold block but is paved continuously from the corridor. No evidence was observed to indicate that an actual door was fitted into the opening. Perhaps it was closed only by a hanging of some kind.

Lobby 29 is roughly 1.50 m. square, bordered on all four sides by doorways (Figs. 113, 117, 118). It has a stucco floor.

O B J E C T S   F O U N D

IVORY

Thick fragment, burned black, l. 0.035 m., w. 0.025 m., th. 0.011 m.; found in the doorway into Room 33, 0.25 m. above floor. Rectilinear pattern quite different from that on pieces found elsewhere in the palace: a diagonal multiple stepped meander incised on a curved surface.

ROOM 30

To the northwest of the lobby is a narrow room (30 on Key Plan) 3.45 m. long and approximately of the same width as the lobby (Fig. 117). On the southwest it is bordered by the thick wall already described that runs along Section 25 of the corridor (Fig. 107). On the northeast it is separated from Room 31 by a wall 0.60 m. thick, preserved to a maximum height of 1.05 m. This wall is well constructed in the normal manner: three chases run through the wall for upright beams and transverse struts, and a horizontal beam lay in a slot 0.33 m. above the floor. The foundation was a bit thicker than the wall leaving a slight shelf, 0.10 m. wide.

On the northwest the room is divided from Room 32 by a continuation of the wall that runs between the latter and Room 31 (Fig. 117). It is a substantial wall, 1.10 m. thick. In Room 30 it retains that thickness only to a height of 0.45 m.; above that point it was narrowed to 0.90 m. The projecting lower part makes an irregular shelf, 0.17 m. wide, along the end of the room. No plaster was seen on this lower part. In the northwest wall are two vertical chases, 0.70 m. apart. All three walls enclosing Room 30 retain almost everywhere a thick coating of coarse plaster.

At its southeast end the room seems to have had no door, but the opening was narrowed by the insertion of a large slab of crude brick at least 1.16 m. high (Fig. 117). At the top it is 0.59 m. wide, at the bottom 0.52 m.; the irregular state of the edge suggests that part of it has been cut away, and its original width, as well as that of the opening into the room, cannot be determined. The southeast face is coated with plaster. On the latter is a rather deeply scratched upright stroke which may have been crossed by a short horizontal line—or possibly two— (Fig. 115); the whole somewhat resembles a carelessly made sign similar to the second or third in the standard table of characters in the Linear B syllabary, transcribed as "ro" or "pa." It is more likely, however, that the scratch was of accidental origin. The slab is now only 0.14 m. to 0.17 m. thick and has no finished face toward the northwest. It was evidently once considerably thicker, but the exact dimension is not measurable. This panel of crude brick is somewhat similar to the one blocking the entrance to the area below the upper flight of the southwest staircase (p. 111) and it finds another analogy in the slab closing the doorway between Rooms 31 and 33 (p. 161).

The floor of the room, made of earth, could hardly be certainly recognized as a floor. The purpose of the room, which must have been dark and airless, has not been determined, though it may have been used for storage. When excavated the area was found filled, below the plowed earth, with red disintegrated brick continuing to 0.60 m. below the tops of the walls and resting on an unusually thick black stratum above the floor. The latter contained many fragments of burned ivory, certainly fallen from above.

O B J E C T S   F O U N D

BRONZE

Fragment.

FLINT

Several flakes.

OBSIDIAN

Several tiny bits.

BONE

Fragment of a pin.

<table>
<tr><td>

IVORY

Many fragments, some decorated in carved relief and others undecorated, nearly all damaged by fire and in bad condition. Several bear a row of beading or reeding, alone or in combination with a curvilinear motive (e.g., NM. 7818, Fig. 285 No. 4) or large disks bordered by beading (e.g., NM. 7818, (Fig. 284 No. 8); others show remnants of spirals (e.g., NM. 7818, Fig. 285 No. 5), a foliate spray, a groove (NM. 7818, Fig. 285 No. 22) and, on three pieces, fine scratched lines, one looking like a sign.

</td><td>

POTTERY

Shapes represented by sherds: kylix, large low-stemmed krater, bowl or basin with pinched-out handles.

Fragments with painted decoration include: flat handle of pedestaled krater with brown stripes on creamy white; broad, thin offset rim with row of dots between bands; spout of stirrup-vase; handle of dipper with transverse stripes. The rim and side of a small cup has three lines below broad band.

</td></tr>
</table>

ROOM 31

The doorway from the lobby into Room 31 has a threshold block and a base for a jamb on each side (Figs. 118, 450). The threshold block is 1.02 m. long, 0.54 m. to 0.57 m. wide; its upper surface, bearing traces of stucco which is considerably worn, rises 0.06 m. above the floor in the room and the lobby. The southeast base of the jamb is 0.55 m. long through the opening and 0.35 m. wide. It rises 0.025 m. to 0.03 m. above the threshold. The northwest base is 0.57 m. long and ca. 0.30 m. wide; its top lies from 0.03 m. to 0.06 m. above the level of the threshold. No cuttings are visible in any of these blocks and there probably never was an actual door. The opening may have been closed by hangings.

On the southeast side of the doorway the rough plaster is still preserved, showing a slot, 0.13 m. wide, on the face toward the lobby, probably marking the return of the wooden casing. A much shallower sinking, only 0.02 m. deep and 0.16 m. wide, facing the opening along the inner edge of the backing of the jamb, probably marks the setting place of a post or timber which may have rested on a horizontal wooden support. No comparable indications appear on the opposite northwestern side of the opening, but it had presumably a casing of some kind.

Room 31 (Key Plan) is almost square with a width of 4.76 m. from southwest to northeast and a length of 4.93 m. to 5 m. (Fig. 116). The southwest wall, which divides the room from Storeroom 30, has been described from the other side (p. 152). It stands to a height of 1.05 m. The presence of three vertical chases was noted and evidence of a horizontal groove may be seen at 0.50 m. above the floor. The wall is heavily coated with mud plaster with a finish of whitewash (Fig. 119).

The southeast wall, 0.95 m. thick, is preserved to a height of 1.10 m. Near its northeastern end it once had a doorway, which was later blocked up with a great slab of clay (Fig. 120). In the southwestern part of the wall are three chases for vertical and transverse beams, 0.90 m. apart. A horizontal beam rested at 0.50 m.

[153]

above the floor. High up on the wall, 0.82 m. to 1.05 m. above the stucco floor, between the doorway and the first chase, patches of finished plaster *in situ*, bearing remnants of curvilinear patterns in dark paint, are preserved. Elsewhere a good deal of coarse plaster has survived in place, and the blocked door is also coated with mud plaster.

The northeast wall, which is at the same time the exterior wall of the Main Building, is 1.20 m. to 1.25 m. thick (Fig. 120). Its outer face, 0.40 m. to 0.55 m. thick, was made of squared blocks laid more or less in ashlar style, the inner part, 0.80 m. thick and 0.95 m. high, is built of rubble. On the inner face, partly concealed by plaster, are indications of five vertical chases. Their exact relation to the ashlar blocks on the outer face of the wall is not clearly determinable, but in some instances chases are aligned with V-shaped joints in the outer veneer. A suggestion of a horizontal groove is recognizable in the northwesterly part of the wall at a height of 0.50 m. above the floor. A good deal of coarse plaster still adheres to this wall, though in a badly cracked condition; at the northern corner a patch of the finished coat, smoked dark gray, remains *in situ*, and continues around the angle onto the stub of the northwest wall which forms the side of the doorway into Room 32.

The northwest wall, 1.10 m. thick, stands to a height of 0.95 m. (Fig. 116). Near its northeast end it is interrupted by a doorway 1.51 m. wide. In the southwestern part of the wall are three chases for vertical beams and cross struts, at intervals of 0.70 m. The southeast face of the wall is almost entirely covered with rough plaster (Fig. 119) which was apparently applied over a groove for a horizontal beam at 0.55 m. above the floor. Below this, remains of a thin finished white coat have survived in a patch just beside the door, 0.95 m. long and 0.42 m. high.

The floor of the room was made of good stucco, which is well preserved generally along the sides and much damaged in the middle of the room except for a small rectangular area evidently covered by something that fell on it and protected the surface (Fig. 119). The damage may have been caused in part by the big stones that fell from above making large dents in the flooring, but most of it resulted from the fire itself.

The room was found filled with the usual debris of disintegrated red burned crude brick and fallen stones. Underneath was an unusually thick stratum (0.25 m. deep) of black matter, perhaps the burned remains of the wooden ceiling and floor joists which fell first from the upper story. From this black stratum came numerous fragments of ivory and a few bits of metal and stone. All the objects had obviously fallen from above.

O B J E C T S   F O U N D

GOLD	SILVER
Eight bits of foil (NM. 7806).	A few pieces.

BRONZE

Fragment, l. pres. 0.02 m., w. 0.018 m.

Rivet-head (Fig. 283 No. 18).

Thin slightly bent strip, possibly a rim (Fig. 283 No. 19), l. 0.032 m., w. 0.018 m.

Three shapeless bits (e.g., Fig. 286 Nos. 1, 2).

STONE

Steatite: fragment of tiny conoid button of shanked type (Fig. 283 No. 21), h. pres. 0.007 m., d. estimated 0.015 m.

Obsidian: blade (Fig. 286 No. 3), l. 0.017 m., w. 0.009 m., th. 0.004 m., and five flakes (e.g., Fig. 283 Nos. 22, 23, Fig. 286 No. 4).

Flint: small arrowhead, brownish-mauve (Fig. 283 No. 20), l. 0.023 m., w. 0.013 m.; a few chips and flakes.

Quartz: one piece.

Other stone: three fragments of a bowl, finely cut; stripes of variegated color (Fig. 269 Nos. 1, 3, 7).

IVORY

Of the great many fragments collected at least 52 bear traces of carved or incised decoration. In the order of their frequency the patterns are: spirals and spiraliform figures, 14 examples, e.g.:

NM. 7831a, Fig. 284 No. 6
NM. 7831b, Fig. 285 No. 1
NM. 7831c, Fig. 285 No. 8
NM. 7834, Fig. 284 No. 2

grooved or reeded, 11 examples, e.g.:

NM. 7790, Fig. 285 No. 9
NM. 7810, Fig. 285 No. 14
NM. 7825, Fig. 285 No. 16
NM. 7828, Fig. 285 No. 11

curvilinear, 6 examples, e.g.:

NM. 7790, Fig. 285 No. 6

foliate spray, 5 examples:

NM. 7834, Fig. 284 No. 2
NM. 7823b, Fig. 284 No. 5
NM. 7826, Fig. 285 No. 13
NM. 7815, Fig. 285 No. 15
NM. 7831d, Fig. 285 No. 17

meander-like, 3 examples:

NM. 7832, Fig. 284 No. 9
NM. 7839, Fig. 284 No. 11
NM. 7828, Fig. 285 No. 20

fine incised or scratched lines on the back, 3 examples

raised disks, 3 examples, e.g.:

NM. 7828, Fig. 285 No. 11

streamers, 2 examples:

NM. 7823a, Fig. 284 No. 7
NM. 7790, Fig. 285 No. 19

spiraliform and beaded, 1 example:

NM. 7810, Fig. 284 No. 1

multiple chevrons, 1 example:

NM. 7790b, Fig. 284 No. 10

petals, 1 example

unclassified, 2 examples

In some instances paneled arrangements seem to be represented. The fragments of ivory are all small, the largest measuring 0.06 m. by 0.025 m. with a thickness of 0.011 m. The patterns show considerable differences in scale because the pieces are apparently from objects of various sizes. A very few pieces have a finished edge (e.g., NM. 7790, Fig. 285 No. 18) but even these do not give any clue as to the original shape or use of the object. One fragment (NM. 7838, Fig. 285 No. 23) seems to have had inlay of some other material. Not only have trefoil-shaped hollows been cut in the surface to receive the inlay but many smaller holes in the hollows must, in some way, have served to hold the inlay in place. Some of the fragments have turned jet black in the fire and the ivory is hard and firm. Other pieces are gray although still hard, but most of the gray pieces are rather soft and in poor condition.

Handle (NM. 7828, Fig. 285 No. 21): straight, circular in section, tapering.

POTTERY

Stirrup-vase: part of a very small, very fine example, too badly damaged by fire to be restorable. On lower part of body, just above foot, two broad bands enclosing four thin lines, repeated higher on body with three lines enclosed; on curve of shoulder between bands vertical parallel wavy lines; on shoulder Mycenaean III Flower with double row of dots. Found in stratum with fragments of ivory.

Considerable number of sherds; casual, no joins. Shapes represented: kylix (at least 38 stems of various sizes and types), stemmed krater (2 bases), cup or bowl (many flat bases), basin with pinched-out handles (several), scoop with pierced grip-handle (2), shallow spouted bowl (bottoms of two), cooking pot on three short flat legs, pithos.

Fragments with painted decoration: disks of two large stirrup-vases, one bearing concentric circles or spirals, the other band and central dot, and pieces of another stirrup-vase. Other shapes represented: alabastron with unusual irregular design in red outlined in smeary black; Vapheio cup, one with lozenges, another with vertical stripes or rippling below rim; krater-bowl, small dipper, cup with row of dots below band on rim and spiral below dots. In addition to allover coating of paint, decoration consists of bands, scattered dots and diagonal band, curving lines and spirals, and a stalk-like figure with buds.

ROOM 32

In the doorway leading from Room 31 to Room 32, set slightly above floor level, are three fairly large blocks of limestone, laid side by side with a total width of 1.51 m. (Figs. 120, 452). They form together the threshold and the bases for the door jambs. Beginning from the northeast they measure 0.50 m. by 1.20 m., 0.53 m. by 1.21 m., and 0.47 m. by 1.21 m. respectively. On the side toward Room 31 the southwestern block projects 0.06 m. into the room. On the side toward Room 32 all three stones project 0.06 m. to 0.07 m. beyond the face of the wall. A short piece of wall, 0.15 m. to 0.20 m. long, juts out from the exterior wall to form the northeastern edge of the door opening. Against it was built the framing, which rested on the northeasternmost base. How far out the casing extended is not certain but a line of weathering suggests that it was about 0.30 m. deep. On the other side of the doorway in the southwestern base, 0.15 m. from its northwestern edge, a square hole, ca. 0.08 m. on a side and 0.035 m. deep, evidently held the socket for the pivot of the door. A rabbet, very roughly cut, in the top of the block and 0.25 m. wide, extends southeastward from the southwestern edge of the socket hole. This presumably indicates the line to which the door could swing back. The space for the casing on the southwest of this rabbet is 0.25 m. deep. The actual door, which seems to have consisted of a single leaf, must accordingly have been approximately 1 m. wide. The central one of the three blocks is set with its surface 0.01 m. to 0.03 m. below that of the lateral bases. On the northwestern side of the opening the cutting and weathering in line with the socket-hole indicate the face of the doorway. When excavated the doorway was found filled with a mass of fused calcined stone and dissolved crude brick and, below, a stratum of black earth, containing pieces of carbonized wood, extending through and across the opening.

Room 32 (Fig. 116 and Key Plan) is 6.72 m. long from northeast to southwest and 4.94 m. wide. The northeast wall, which is a continuation of the exterior wall of the building, is here 1.10 m. thick; the thickness has been reduced because of an offset,

0.11 m. deep, in the outer face of the wall, approximately in line with the partition wall between Rooms 31 and 32. For most of the length two courses of squared blocks survive in place on the outside, but toward the northwest end only a single course is left. The inner part of the wall, built of rubble, stands to a height of 0.75 m., except at the northwest, where that too is missing; here next to the corner is a large squared block on the inside of the wall, 1.10 m. long and 0.30 m. high above the floor. The part of the wall built of rubble, which is coated with plaster on its face toward the room, reveals indications of three chases for vertical beams. No evidence for the position of horizontal grooves is now clearly marked. The finished coat of plaster is preserved, though not in good condition, to a height of 0.30 m. above the floor; it continues along the face of the ashlar block. The surface of the smooth coat, both on the wall and on the squared block, is dark blue, probably from the effect of fire and smoke rather than from paint.

The northwest wall, which separates Room 32 from Corridor 26, has already been described (p. 145) from the side facing that passage. In Room 32 it is built largely of rubble and it stands to a height of 0.67 m. (Fig. 116). Seven vertical chases running through the wall are visible spaced at intervals of 0.85 m., 0.85 m., 0.72 m., 0.67 m., 0.72 m., and 0.67 m. They are regularly aligned with the V-shaped joints between the ashlar blocks in the outer face. The wall is coated with plaster, badly cracked and thrust out of line in some places. It is a well-finished white coat, which was smoked dark blue-gray toward both ends of the room.

The southwest wall which separates Room 32 from Section 25 of the Northeast Corridor has been described (p. 143). On its face toward the room it varies in height from 0.45 m. at the northwest end to 0.90 m. near the south corner (Fig. 116). Five vertical chases run through the wall at intervals of 0.80 m., 0.85 m., 0.85 m., and 1.50 m. There may have been a sixth chase in that long interval. Some patches of smoothly finished white plaster, clinging to the lower part of the wall, have turned smoked-blue-gray just above the floor.

On its southeastern side (Fig. 18) the room shared a wall with Rooms 30 and 31 (pp. 152, 154). On the face toward Room 32 the wall stands to a height of 0.87 m. Between the doorway and the south corner at least five vertical chases can be seen spaced at intervals of 0.70 m.; there probably was a horizontal groove at 0.40 m. to 0.45 m. above the floor. On this side some smooth white plaster, in badly cracked condition, remains near the bottom of the wall, and here too smoke has discolored it dark bluish-gray. The ravages of the fire are particularly notable in this room, especially in the southern corner, near which parts of the southeastern wall have been calcined and eaten away. Except for one large and a few small dents and several cracks, the floor of good white stucco, 0.02 m. to 0.03 m. thick, is in a relatively good state of preservation.

Room 32 contained at least a dozen pithoi of moderate size some of which stood in an orderly arrangement against the southeastern, southwestern, and northwestern walls. A special concentration in the south corner comprised many jars that had been wedged into place with large crude bricks and were found standing upright. Others had fallen over on their sides, and one or two had been displaced; perhaps they had fallen from a higher position. Several pithoi and one large krater were ranged beside or near the northwestern wall. Farther along toward the north corner are setting places for two more big pots. Round about the pithoi and other capacious containers were found many smaller pots of various kinds, some plain, but most of them with painted decoration. The most notable are three-handled pithoid jars, stirrup-vases, small, medium, and big, and double-spouted jugs. Almost all the pots in this room were badly cracked and broken, though many still retained their form sufficiently for recognition and 19 could be restored (Fig. 329). The fire had been particularly intense: many of the pots were blackened and the paint had in some instances turned gray. Certainly the pithoi must have contained olive oil of some kind. It may have been a specially refined type, since the storage jars are distinctly smaller than those in the other oil magazines, but it certainly fed the flames. Moreover, the accompanying smaller pots with their painted decoration add a touch of elegance that is wanting in most of the other storerooms.

Three fragments of inscribed tablets were recovered in the room, one near Pithos No. 11, one between Pithoi No. 1 and No. 2, and one in the western corner. A label was found in sifting.

The debris filling Room 32 was of various kinds in the different parts of the room: soft and sandy in the west quarter, greenish claylike in the north quarter, disintegrated red burned brick along the northeastern and half the southeastern wall, white calcined stone in the south corner. In the center of the room were two fallen ashlar blocks accompanied by a good deal of decomposed crude brick, black burned matter, carbonized wood, small stones, and many chunks of flooring, evidently fallen from above. How the squared blocks came to be in this position is difficult to explain.

Numerous fragments of plaster—from flooring, ceiling and walls—were collected in the room, below, intermingled with, and above the pots. A study of this material gave ground to conclude that the walls of the room had been decorated with a bluish dado (some of it still in place, possibly smoked) surmounted by alternating red and white bands, the red carrying darker red lines perhaps representing wood-graining. Many pieces showing red on blue are probably from the ceiling or the floor above.

O B J E C T S   F O U N D

GOLD

BRONZE

Bit of foil.

Rivet-heads (Figs. 283 No. 25, 286 No. 5).

19 shapeless bits (e.g., Figs. 283 Nos. 24, 26-29, 286 No. 6).

STONE

Carnelian: tiny melon-shaped bead divided into five segments (NM. 7806, Fig. 282 No. 1), h. 0.005 m., d. ca. 0.006 m.

Obsidian: 3 small chips (e.g., Fig. 283 No. 32).

Flint: 13 flakes (e.g., Figs. 283 No. 33, 286 No. 7).

Quartz: 3 small chips (e.g., Fig. 283 No. 31).

Other stone: fragment of a vessel of gray stone with brownish and tannish stripes and polished surface, wall ca. 0.011 m. thick (Fig. 269 No. 2); possibly from a rhyton.

IVORY

Many small fragments (e.g., Fig. 283 No. 30), one with traces of carved decoration.

PASTE

Blue piece possibly from a bead.

CLAY

Tablets: Nos. 1194 (found with pithos No. 11 in the west corner), 1198 (between and in front of pithoi No. 1 and No. 2), 1200 (with sherds from west corner); for all three see *OOT*, 41, pls. II-III.

Label: No. 1199, found in sifting (*OOT*, 66, pls. II-III).

POTTERY

Thirty-seven pots or groups of sherds were numbered as they were removed. At the time it was possible to identify the shapes of many of them and to take approximate measurements. The material has now been studied and 19 of the counted pots were found to be restorable and were inventoried (Fig. 329). Three others (Nos. 405, 412, 414) were put together from sherds not previously recognized as pots.

The pots were found more or less in groups: in the south corner, in the west corner, near the center of the northwest wall, in the center of the room northeast of the fallen ashlar blocks, in the northeastern part of the room, and against the southeast wall. Following the list of inventoried pots are notes on the pots found with them in the various groups.

Jug (Shape 43, p. 380)
Nos. 404 (Fig. 369), 405 (Figs. 369, 370), both decorated.

Jar (Shape 49, p. 385)
No. 467 (Fig. 374).

Jar (Shape 51, p. 386)
No. 415 (Figs. 375, 376), possibly decorated.

Jar (Shape 52, p. 386)
Nos. 413 and 471 (Fig. 375), both decorated.

Jar (Shape 53, p. 388)
Nos. 403, 406, 408, 409 (all on Figs. 377 and 378); 407 (Fig. 377); all decorated.

Jar (Shape 54a, p. 390)
No. 418 (Figs. 379, 380), decorated.

Pithos (Shape 55a, p. 393)
No. 416 (Fig. 329 at left).

Krater (Shape 58, p. 396)
No. 417 (Figs. 329 at left, 382 rim).

Squat jar or alabastron (Shape 64, p. 402)
No. 410 (Figs. 385, 386), decorated.

Stirrup-vase (Shape 65a, p. 403)
No. 402 (Figs. 389, 390).

Stirrup-vase (Shape 65b 3, p. 406)
No. 414, decorated.

Stirrup-vase (Shape 65c, p. 407)
No. 411 (Figs. 391, 392), decorated.

Stirrup-vase (Shape 65d, p. 408)
No. 412 (Figs. 391, 392), decorated.

Stirrup-vase (Shape 65e, p. 410)
No. 401 (Figs. 329 at right, first in second row; 392), decorated.

Lid (Shape 73, p. 415)
Nos. 469 (Fig. 397), 470 (Figs. 397, 398).

In the south corner along with Nos. 406, 408, 409, 410, 411, 415, 418, 467, 469, 470 and 471 were found the following unrestorable pithoi:

1. h. pres. above floor 0.75 m., d. 0.59 m. Upper part missing. Found standing on its bottom wedged around with fragments of brick. Filled with soft decomposed stone, stones, chunks of plaster.

2. h. pres. above floor 0.55 m., d. 0.65 m. Upper part missing. Base found in place with bricks wedged around it.

3. h. 1.30 m., d. rim 0.50 m., d. neck 0.40 m., d. 0.75 m., d. base 0.17 m. Found fallen on its side with its bottom parallel to and pressed tight against the south-

east wall of the room, 0.45 m. above the floor. Under base, two pieces of brick. Full of hard red brick and stone. In front of its mouth and under it, a group of sherds with painted decoration, including at least one jar (No. 406).

4. h. 0.95 m., d. rim estimated 0.35 m., d. 0.68 m., d. base 0.115 m. In bad condition. Same type as No. 12 in west corner. Smaller than No. 3. Covered with thick lime incrustation. Burnt stone inside. Plaster found under it and small stirrup-vase (No. 411).

5. high-necked variety. Neck and rim only preserved. Coarse and in very bad condition; splintered and soft. Large brick under it; Nos. 410, 467, 471 in front of it.

Other shapes:

6. stirrup-vase: slightly more than one-third of side, false neck with part of its disk, one handle and base of spout; h. pres. 0.21 m., d. 0.30 m., d. false neck 0.03 m. Decoration: curving diagonal stripes like Nos. 401 and 595 (Shape 65e, p. 410).

7. large tankard (Shape 33, p. 374): h. pres. 0.14 m., d. waist 0.15 m., d. base 0.165 m.; traces of band decoration.

In west corner with No. 413 were other unrestorable jars:

8. h. from floor to rim 0.70 m., d. 0.48 m. Broken and cracked. Wedged around with pieces of brick. Filled with powdery gray earth. Fine lime plaster from wall found between bricks and bottom of jar.

9. h. 0.85 m., d. rim estimated 0.45 m., d. 0.65 m. Filled with red and black burned clay. In many fragments: wide mouth, flattened offset rim (w. 0.045 m.), bulging body, thick walls, very thick round loop-handles set horizontally (one pres., d. 0.04 m.). Fabric soft and friable, containing pebbles and bits of stone; surface rather rough.

10. d. rim 0.34 m., d. base 0.125 m. Very much broken, shape uncertain, probably like Nos. 4, 11, 12. Base lay next to No. 8 and was held in place by two half bricks. Rim flattened on top (w. 0.05 m.) with rounded edges. Walls relatively thin. No handles or traces of handles.

11. h. 0.95 m., d. rim 0.50 m., d. 0.75 m., d. base 0.26 m. Badly broken into small pieces but much preserved. Large, grooved, round loop-handles set horizontally (two preserved). Neck lower than that of No. 3. Rim offset, very flat on top. Base larger than most, with round edge. Fabric solid, not friable.

12. h. 0.84 m., d. rim 0.42 m., d. 0.64 m. Filled with black earth. Like No. 3, but neck is shorter (h. 0.13 m.) and practically straight, splaying only slightly. Plain rim, flattened and grooved on top. Fabric very coarse and soft. One vertical loop-handle (h. 0.145 m., d. 0.035 m.) and part of a second preserved. Fragment of bottom too small to permit an estimate of the diameter.

In center of room were found No. 407 and fragments of at least three jars with pedestal bases and band decoration.

Against middle of southeast wall: Nos. 403, 416.

In northeast part of room along with No. 402: top, handles and spout of stirrup-vase; h. pres. 0.20 m., d. ca. 0.28 m. Thick walls. No trace of decoration.

Put together from scattered sherds: Nos. 405, 412, 414; also recognized were four stirrup-vases, a shallow cup and a large kylix, all with painted decoration.

Sherds collected from the deposit filling the room above the level of the pots lying on the floor show a relative scarcity of kylix fragments: only 31 stems were counted, their types for the most part indeterminable.

Other shapes identified: conical cup, shallow bowl and large basin with pinched-out handles, large dipper, scoop, coarse tripod-vessel.

Approximately 150 nondescript sherds in very bad condition with only faint traces of painted decoration. Patterns include: spirals, triple chevrons, stippling, waves, concentric circles, and reversed Z. A few pieces may be earlier than Mycenaean III B. Some are of coarse fabric resembling "oatmeal ware."

ROOM 33

From Lobby 29 a doorway opens southeastward into Room 33 (Figs. 113, 122, 451). This doorway seems to have been made in connection with a remodeling, probably in one of the later phases of the palace. In any event the original wall alongside the lobby was certainly thinner than the section to the northeast. An opening must have been cut in this thinner structure to make the new doorway. A remnant of the thin wall built of small stones was apparently left to serve as a substitute for a threshold, 0.53 m. deep from front to back. Some of the stones exhibit marks of wear on top. No evidence exists to indicate that an actual door was ever installed in the opening; it could have been closed only by hangings. The level of the floor in Room 33 is more than 0.30 m. higher than that in the lobby. This height is greater than one normal step in Mycenaean architecture and a low outer step of small stones and crude brick, 0.13 m. high and 0.48 m. wide, was built in the lobby outside the stone threshold. The clay step extends ca. 1 m. southwestward from the inner end of the lobby and stops in a straight though oblique edge. The threshold of small stones also ends at approximately the same line. Beyond it is a sinking that looks as if it was the setting place for a projection of the wall from the southwest that formed a rounded southwestern limit of the doorway. The actual opening would then be ca. 1 m. At best it was an awkward and clumsy piece of work. The fire was particularly severe in the region of this doorway and much damage was done. It is therefore impossible to reconstruct the original arrangement in detail.

Room 33 (Key Plan) is 6.85 m. long from southwest to northeast and varies in width from 2.75 m. at the southwest to 2.98 m. at the northeastern end (Fig. 28). Beyond the lobby toward the northeast Room 33 is separated from Room 31 by a wall 0.95 m. thick which stands to a height of 0.98 m. above the floor of Room 33 (Fig. 117). Three vertical chases running through the wall are spaced ca. 0.85 m. apart. Some slight indications suggest that there was a horizontal groove for a beam at 0.35 m. or 0.40 m. above the floor, though the wall is coated with coarse plaster which is preserved to a height of 0.78 m. throughout most of its length. It probably never had a fine finishing coat. The wall stops 1.65 m. short of the northeast wall and this was the place of the original door between Rooms 31 and 33 (Fig. 454). Presumably at the time of the remodeling mentioned above this doorway was closed by a huge slab of clay, 0.45 m. thick and 1.17 m. to 1.15 m. wide. It is preserved to a height of 1.10 m. above the stone threshold on which it mainly rests, overlapping the bases of the jambs on each side (Fig. 123). The slab was set with its northwestern face almost aligned with the northwestern face of the wall. On the side toward Room 33 a recess 0.60 m. deep remains where the door had been. The threshold of the earlier doorway is 0.90 m. long between the lateral blocks. Its depth through the opening cannot be measured, as its northwestern edge is covered by the blocking slab. On each side, rising 0.01 m. to 0.02 m. above the threshold, is the base of the original door frame. Neither block can be accurately measured, since both are still to a great extent hidden by the clay slab and the ends of the wall. The northeastern base is 0.50 m. wide, however, and the southwestern base, 1.06 m. long; 0.16 m. from its northwestern end is a rectangular cutting presumably for the pivot of the door. In its general style this doorway is similar to the one between Rooms 31 and 32 and it occupies a corresponding position.

On the northeast is the exterior wall of the building. It is 1.28 m. thick but alongside Room 33, above the bottom course of ashlar blocks, a recess, 0.18 m. deep and 2.48 m. wide, was left in the exterior face (Figs. 33, 110). The recess was presumably carried on into the upper part of the wall, reducing its thickness alongside this room to 1.10 m. The inner two thirds of the wall was constructed of rubble in the usual manner and vertical chases appear to be aligned with the V-shaped joints between the outer ashlar blocks. The inside of the wall in its lower part is coated with plaster, two successive layers of which can be distinguished, to a height of 0.53 m. A single row of small stones from one to four courses high is laid on the floor against the plastered face of the wall projecting 0.15 m. to 0.20 m. in front of it, and rising from 0.15 m. to 0.45 m. At the east corner this clumsy addition reaches a height of 1 m. or more and fills up the northeastern part of the doorway that opens into Room 34 (Fig. 121). This whole intrusive construction must belong to the late phase to which has been attributed the shift of the entrance to Room 33 from its original place in Room 31 to the Lobby 29. No satisfactory explanation for the change at the northeastern end of Room 33 has yet been found.

The southeast wall, which is pierced by a doorway near its northeasterly end, is 0.78 m. thick and stands to a height of 0.95 m. above the floor (Fig. 113). It separates Room 33 from Room 34 and Stairway 36. Six vertical chases extending through the wall are spaced at intervals of 0.53 m., 0.80 m., 0.80 m., 0.85 m., and 0.73 m. Rough plaster covers most of the face of the wall toward the room but there is evidence for a horizontal beam-groove 0.17 m. above the floor.

The southwest wall, standing between Room 33 and Section 28 of the Northeast Corridor, is 1.12 m. thick and rises to a height of 0.95 m. above the floor (Fig. 28). In its top is evidence for four vertical chases running through the wall, 0.80 m. apart. The northeast face of the wall though coated with thick rough plaster offers some indications of a groove for a horizontal beam 0.15 m. to 0.20 m. above the floor.

The latter is paved with stucco which has a blue-gray finished surface, perhaps discolored by smoke and carbon. Though cracked in many places it is remarkably well preserved. It slopes downward from southwest to northeast. The stucco is 0.07 m. to 0.08 m. thick and seems to consist of one single layer. At the northeast end of the room the floor is 0.13 m. or 0.14 m. higher than the threshold of the original doorway into Room 31 (Fig. 123). It was beveled down sharply in a distance of 0.25 m. to reach that level. On the opposite side of the room a comparable arrangement was made in the approach to the threshold of the southeastern doorway where the difference in level is 0.09 m. (Fig. 121). Here the floor was beveled off in an arc.

The burnt debris filling the room was of the usual variegated kind: in the northwestern part a thick deposit of disintegrated brick burned red with many tightly wedged stones, in the north corner a particularly solid mass of stones, and on the southeastern side, much calcined matter. An extraordinarily hard and very black stratum covered the entire floor to which roots of an olive tree had penetrated. Quantities of fallen flooring and wall plaster were recovered fairly high up in the debris more than 0.50 m. above the floor. It must have come from the upper story. In the deposit, 0.35 m. above the floor, lay a good many fragments of ivory, at least 22 of which show traces of carved decoration. These too must have fallen from above. In the same context were found some pieces of bronze, miscellaneous bits of bone, shell, flint, and obsidian, but only a very few nondescript sherds. In all this material there is nothing that sheds any light on the purpose and use of Room 33.

O B J E C T S   F O U N D

GOLD

Tiny perforated disk (NM. 7808, Fig. 273 No. 12), d. 0.008 m.

SILVER

Plating on piece of bronze (Fig. 286 No. 8).

BRONZE

Fragment of rivet, l. 0.014 m., d. 0.005 m., and seven shapeless thin pieces.

STONE

Flint: 8 chips and flakes (e.g., Fig. 286 No. 10).

Obsidian: blade and four flakes (e.g., Fig. 286 No. 9).

IVORY

A great many burned and damaged fragments; most are small, longest 0.035 m.; 22 show traces of carved decoration (e.g., NM. 7811, 7830, 7822; Fig. 285 Nos. 2 and 7, 3 and 10, 12). Patterns include about equally spirali-form—concentric circles or spirals of some kind—and bead or reed. One bit resembles a single strand of twisted rope. Impossible to determine what they once adorned. One piece may be from a bead, broken through the perforation, where it is nicely smoothed and polished.

POTTERY

Relatively few sherds. No fragments that join. Shapes represented: kylix (39 stems), shallow bowl and basin with pinched-out handles, conical cup, tripod-vessel, pithos.

Shapes identified among fragments with painted decoration: alabastron, one example with dot-rosette on shoulder; tankard, one with stemmed spiral below thick and thin band on rim, another with lily-pattern (?) outlined in dots; Vapheio cup, kylix, cup, narrow-necked jug or jar. In addition to solid coating and bands patterns are spiraliform, multiple wavy vertical parallel lines above bands.

ROOM 34

The doorway leading into Room 34, which seems to have had a width of 0.77 m., is 0.74 m. deep from front to back (Figs. 121, 453). It was floored with three blocks of poros: a large one on the northeast, 0.86 m. long from southwest to northeast and more than 0.75 m. wide, and two smaller blocks on the southwest, 0.55 m. long from southwest to northeast; their other dimensions are not measurable, since they are covered by the floor on each side. The actual width of the opening between the jambs is given by the arc-shaped bevel mentioned above. On each side was evidently a wooden door frame against which the floor was laid in a straight line both in Room 33 and Room 34. This sharp edge of the stucco suggests that the door frame projected 0.33 m. from the wall on each side toward the opening in the original doorway. After the reconstruction, however, no room for a door frame was left on the northeasterly side of the opening.

Room 34 (Key Plan) is a small compartment under the upper end of Stairway 36, 3.26 m. long from southwest to northeast and 1.52 m. wide (Figs. 28, 34). The northwest wall, which, with its doorway, divides Rooms 33 and 34, has already been described as seen from the northwest. It stands to a height of 0.98 m. Two vertical chases, 0.58 m. apart, appear in the top of the wall. Its southeast face is coated to a height of 0.80 m. with thick mud plaster.

The wall on the southwestern side, which rises to a height of 1.19 m., is 0.70 m. thick. Its northeast face, in the southeasterly part at least, also bears a coating of mud plaster. This is a retaining wall, which helped support Stairway 36 and held in the earth filling on which the southwestern half of the stairway was laid. The face of the wall would be approximately aligned with the back of the fifteenth step. According to this calculation the head room at the inner end of the compartment would have been somewhat more than 2 m. high.

The southeastern wall of the room, 1.10 m. thick and badly dilapidated, is preserved to a height of 0.85 m. at the southwest, descending to 0.30 m. at the other end (Figs. 34, 36). On its face toward the room, however, thick mud plaster still stands to a height ranging from 0.89 m. at the southern corner to 0.40 m. at the eastern corner. One vertical chase running through the wall, 0.90 m. from the corner, can be recognized. If there is a horizontal groove it is concealed by the plaster.

The northeast wall too is considerably damaged. This is a section of the exterior wall, 1.20 m. thick, with an outer facing of ashlar blocks (0.40 m. to 0.60 m. thick) and an inner backing of rubble, which stands to a height of 0.80 m. A suggestion of a horizontal groove appears at a height of 0.55 m. above the floor and of a vertical chase aligned with a V-shaped joint between ashlar blocks. Some remnants of mud plaster survive on the inside of the wall.

The stucco floor of Room 34, well preserved, though cracked here and there, at least 0.05 m. thick in some places, is much like that in Room 33 but not so blackened by fire. It turns up against the walls on all sides and ends in a straight line along the face of the doorway in the north corner.

Standing on the floor in the south corner and crushed against the southwest wall by stones and steps fallen from above, were fragments of a large krater. What its purpose was here and what it once contained could not be determined. It may have been oil, it may have been water. The room itself was filled with the usual burned debris fallen from above, but it included also many fragments of stone steps which had belonged to the upper part of Stairway 36. They extended out into the room 1.40 m. to the northeast of the retaining wall. Nothing else of any consequence was found in this room.

O B J E C T S   F O U N D

GOLD
Tiny piece of foil embedded in a hard bit of clay (0.70 m. above floor).

BRONZE
Three nondescript fragments (Fig. 286 Nos. 11-13).

FLINT
Flake of red flint, l. 0.034 m., w. 0.021 m., th. 0.005 m., from doorway; three chips.

POTTERY
Krater (Shape 58, p. 396)
  No. 400 (Figs. 382 rim, 383, 384).

A good many sherds, evidently fallen from the upper story, almost all fragments of large pithoi, some bubbly and fused. Rim pieces of at least six different jars. One fragment decorated with horizontal and curving rope bands and thumb impressions, another with similar coarser bands.

Other shapes represented by a few sherds: kylix (8 stems), handleless cup, bowl with pinched-out handles, basin, jug.

The few pieces showing remnants of painted decoration were in poor condition and no patterns were recognizable.

N O R T H E A S T   C O R R I D O R ,   S E C T I O N   3 5

Returning now to the Northeastern Corridor, one proceeds southeastward to the doorway that opens into Section 35 (Fig. 446). Its position is given by the two lateral bases of the door frame (Figs. 107, 113). The southwestern base is 0.70 m. long running through the doorway and 0.45 m. wide. On the side toward the opening the top of the block has been cut down 0.055 m. to a width of 0.30 m. Across the corridor is a similar block, 0.72 m. long and 0.365 m. wide. Its top has been treated in the same manner as that of its companion across the passage, though the cutting is only 0.19 m. wide. Between these lateral blocks the stucco pavement of the corridor continues without interruption. On the southwestern wall the edges of the plaster that abutted against the wooden door casing show that the latter had a width of 0.58 m. Corresponding evidence on the other side of the corridor gives the same result, although here the casing at the southeast was set into a rabbet cut into the base block beside Stairway 36. Each of the lateral blocks near its northwestern end has a squarish cutting, 0.10 m. by 0.10 m. on the northeast and 0.08 m. by 0.09 m. on the southwest, obviously to hold the sockets for the pivots. Accordingly, we may assume a closeable door with two leaves, each 0.63 m. wide, and the door frame would have had a projection of 0.16 m.

Section 35 of the Northeast Corridor (Key Plan) is 1.40 m. wide and 8.21 m. long, ending beside the anta of the Portico in a doorway that opens into the Northeast Stoa (Fig. 124). On the southwest it is separated from the Vestibule and the Portico by a continuing wall (Fig. 113). The part alongside the Vestibule, which has a doorway opening into the corridor, is 1 m. thick, not including the plaster. Along the side of the Portico it is 1.20 m. thick, the added breadth having been applied on the southwest side. To the southeast of the doorway from the Vestibule, the southwestern wall stands to a height of nearly 1.30 m. above the floor (Fig. 125). In this stretch seven vertical chases are clearly marked, spaced at intervals of 0.98 m., 0.53 m., 0.75 m., 0.70 m., 0.75 m., and 0.75 m. A groove for a horizontal beam, at least 0.20 m. thick, is distinguishable at 0.34 m. above the floor. A good deal of rough, badly damaged plaster surviving on the face of the wall makes it difficult to determine the position of the next higher groove but it may have been 0.30 m. above the first. The plaster apparently had a finishing coat of whitewash.

The northeastern side of Section 35 of the corridor is bounded by a stairway leading to an upper floor, farther to the southeast by a partition wall shared with Room 39 and a branch passage running northeastward (Fig. 113). This wall, 0.85 m. thick, has suffered great damage from the fire and is much dilapidated, but parts of it stand to a height of 1.40 m. above the floor. In this section five vertical chases running through the wall are conspicuous, spaced at intervals of 0.65 m., 0.55 m., 0.60 m., and 0.65 m. A horizontal groove appears at 0.40 m. above the floor and it may possibly have been 0.45 m. high. Perhaps the corridor was lined here with a wooden wainscoting of that height. What we interpreted as two horizontal grooves on the other side of the corridor might conceivably have been a single groove matching the one on the northeast. On the northeast wall the coarse plaster is preserved almost all the way along this section up to the horizontal groove, and above the latter are some further remains.

The floor is in a relatively good state of preservation, especially near the walls. In the middle of the corridor, however, it is bulged, buckled, and fused with material fallen from above. A thin black stratum extended over the floor and in it, close to the base of the southeast jamb of the doorway from the Vestibule, lay the fragments of a small decorated stirrup-vase, together with two tiny bits of gold leaf and some pieces of bronze.

The corridor was found filled with burnt debris, vividly illustrating the intensity of the fire: much calcined stone, a great deal of *migma*. It is likely that the abundant wooden beams and woodwork along the passage had turned the flames into a holocaust.

OBJECTS FOUND

GOLD

Two tiny pieces of foil (NM. 7806).

SILVER

Strip of something bluish in color, probably silver, l. 0.048 m., w. 0.012 m., th. 0.005 m.

BRONZE

Fragment of small barbed arrowhead, l. pres. 0.013 m., w. 0.013 m.
Eight nondescript fragments.
Thin flat piece, slightly curved, from doorway.

STONE

Obsidian: four chips.
Flint: four pieces.
Other stone: fragment of vase (Fig. 269 No. 6) probably belonging to same vessel as piece found in Room 32 (p. 159).

POTTERY

Small stirrup-vase from floor, badly shattered, not restorable: decorated with horizontal stripes and on shoulder zone a band of paired concentric arcs or U-figures, alternating up and down.
Relatively few sherds. Shapes represented: kylix (5 stems), conical cup, basin with pinched-out handles, tripod-vessel, brazier, pithos (many pieces fused and vitrified: handle, three flat bottoms, piece of rim). Fragments bearing decoration come from two large stirrup-vases and from an alabastron of earlier style than Mycenaean III B.

NORTHEAST STAIRWAY 36

On the far side of the corridor, almost directly opposite the doorway from the Vestibule, a flight of steps ascends northeastward (Fig. 126). The stairway (36 on Key Plan) is 1.50 m. broad and eight steps remain *in situ* (Figs. 58, 455). Each is made of two blocks of stone of varying length, but with consistent attention to the breaking of joints from one step to the next. The risers have an average height of 0.155 m. and the treads have an average depth of 0.32 m. The three lowest steps are bordered on each side by an anta-like block of poros (Fig. 127).

The base on the southeast side, set flush with the bottom step, is 0.45 m. high, 0.78 m. wide along the corridor, and 0.94 m. long, extending as far back as the riser of the fourth step. The face of the stone toward the corridor was plastered continuously with that of the wall. The block was found covered to a depth of 0.90 m. by a solid mass of fused melted stone and brick which had evidently flowed down from above. Four dowel holes in the top of the block (Fig. 455) indicate that a horizontal wooden beam, continuing that along the corridor, was laid here up to the edge of the stairway and beside the latter. A bedding for the timber was provided by a rabbet, 0.025 m. deep, cut in the top of the block to a width of 0.35 m. and running around the corner. It is likely that some kind of decorative paneling, perhaps in an alternation of stone and wood, framed the lower end of the staircase. This suggestion is supported by the evidence on the northwestern side of the stairs, where a corresponding anta block, 0.465 m. high, 0.56 m. wide, 1.15 m. long, extends 0.27 m. beyond the face of the fourth step. In the top of this block are six dowel holes, presumably for the fastening of a wooden beam and paneling. On this side too a high mass of *migma* was found resting on the stone. Behind it appears a finished surface which seems originally to have been in contact with a wooden beam or a panel of wood to a height of some 0.50 m. above the stone. The graining of the wood that lay against it is imprinted on the clay backing.

The northwestern anta block was set back ca. 0.05 m. behind the front of the lowest step. Only a narrow strip of its face, 0.17 m. wide, is now left on the side toward the corridor. The rest was cut back 0.05 m. to receive part of the wooden casing of the doorway between Sections 28 and 35 of the corridor.

The total space available from the southwestern end of the staircase to the inside face of the exterior northeast wall of the building is 8 m. long and 1.50 m. wide. In the reconstruction by Mr. de Jong (Fig. 455) 20 treads, 21 risers, and an upper landing about 1.60 m. deep serve admirably to fill the whole disposable area. The lower part of the stairway, comprising steps one to fifteen, was evidently supported on a solid filling of clay and earth which was held in place by a transverse retaining wall, the latter also forming the southwestern end of Room 34 (p. 164). The distance from the corridor to the northeastern face of that wall is as near as may be to 4.80 m., exactly enough to provide for 15 treads having an average depth from front to back of 0.32 m. With risers averaging 0.155 m. high, we calculate that the top of the fifteenth step would reach a height of 2.325 m. above the pavement of the corridor and approximately the same above the floor of Room 34. Allowing for the substantial thickness of the stone step-blocks as well as the heavy underpinning that held them up, we estimate that Room 34 would have had headroom of more than 2 m. at the lowest point.

In any event the continuation of the staircase to the landing on the upper floor was, like the lower flight, built of poros slabs. Remnants of some of them, in a much damaged state, were found in the debris filling Room 34 (p. 165) and in the neighboring Room 40 (p. 177). The stone blocks were undoubtedly supported by stout wooden beams running from wall to wall across Room 34, in the same manner that we have seen in the construction of the southwest staircase (p. 113). So far as concerns the details of the upper end of the stairway we are left almost entirely to conjecture. The landing itself was small, presumably only 1.50 m. wide and 1.60 m. long. It is likely that doorways opened on one side or on both into a lobby or a passage from which larger apartments could be reached. This northeastern wing of the Main Building was surely the domain belonging to the women of the palace, as demonstrated by the many remains of artistic objects made of valuable materials, such as gold, ivory, etc., which had fallen from the upper story into Rooms 30, 31, 32 and others nearby. In addition to bedchambers there were no doubt dressing rooms, storerooms, and perhaps halls for social purposes.

O B J E C T S   F O U N D

GOLD

Small rivet with flattened head (NM. 7807, Fig. 282 No. 3), l. 0.009 m., d. 0.003 m.

PASTE

Two shaped pieces, bluish, iridescent, rounded on top and flat on back, probably inlays or possibly pendants (NM. 7807, Fig. 282 Nos. 2, 4): one piece is like a figure 8 (h. 0.05 m., max. w. of upper part 0.03 m., min. w. 0.019 m., max. w. of lower part 0.035 m., th. 0.004 m.); the other, almost pear-shaped (h. 0.036 m., max. w. 0.033 m., th. 0.004 m.), was found with the gold rivet in a hole at the narrow end.

POTTERY

A few sherds. Shapes represented: kylix (only one stem), conical cup, bowl with pinched-out handles, pithos.

CORRIDOR 37

Approximately 1.35 m. short of the southeastern end of Corridor 35 another passage (37 on Key Plan) branches off to the northeast (Figs. 124, 125). No doorway marks the intersection. On the northwest Passage 37 is bordered by the southeast wall of Room 39 (Fig. 36). It is 0.80 m. thick and stands to a height of 1.40 m. The topmost stone appeared at the surface of the ground when excavation began. This wall consists largely of fused debris which makes it difficult to distinguish grooves and chases, but at least one of the latter is clear, as is also a horizontal groove at 0.50 m. above the floor. The groove may itself have been 0.45 m. high, perhaps for wooden wainscoting. No certain remains of the original plaster can be recognized on the southeastern face of the wall.

The opposite side of the corridor is flanked by a wall 0.60 m. thick. This too has suffered greatly from the effects of fire and now consists largely of fused *migma*. It stands to a maximum height of 1.25 m. above the floor. In its face toward the corridor signs of two horizontal grooves for wooden beams are visible 0.35 m. and 0.85 m. above the floor. Two vertical chases also run through the wall, 0.55 m. apart. Some scanty remains of plaster can be seen near the bottom of the wall.

The stucco floor is fairly well preserved, especially against the walls. The whole corridor was filled from top to bottom with a solid mass of fused debris, beneath which lay fragments of two pithoi. The pieces were scattered along the floor all the way from the outer end (Fig. 124) to the doorway into Room 38. All of them had been turned by the heat of the fire into a molten vitrified layer which ran over the whole floor. Two bases and some rim fragments were recognizable. On the day of the disaster these vessels must have been standing at the junction of the two corridors (Fig. 125).

POTTERY

Very little, all heavily encrusted with lime accretion. Shapes represented: kylix, basin, conical cup, pithos (large torus base and other fragments of the jars that were found melted on the floor).

ROOM 38

The doorway leading from Corridor 37 into Room 38 is clearly marked by the three stone blocks that formed the threshold and bases for the jambs (Figs. 128, 456). Laid side by side through the opening, they have a length of 0.89 m. The central stone is 0.69 m. wide. The lateral blocks have a width of 0.49 m. and were overlapped by the actual opening of the doorway, ca. 1 m. broad. On the top of each block was cut a shallow rabbet, 0.02 m. deep, at the northeast end of which is a rectangular cutting, the one on the southeast ca. 0.10 m. square and 0.03 m. deep, the one on the northwest somewhat smaller. The rabbet on the northwestern side of the opening is 0.15 m. wide; the one on the southeast splays from 0.15 m. to 0.20 m. in width. The edge of the rabbet on each side presumably gives the line of the wooden door casing. How the latter was fastened in its place is difficult now to determine in the fused and ruined state of the wall. The two rectangular cuttings for pivot-sockets suggest that the door originally consisted of two leaves that swung southwestward within the depth of the doorway. In a later phase the cutting for the socket on the northwestern side seems to have been filled with stucco; henceforth the door could have had only a single leaf, if there was one at all. It may be noted that the door opening is not accurately centered along the axis of the corridor.

Room 38 (Key Plan) has an average length of 4.20 m. from southeast to northwest and is 3.33 m. wide. It is thus a fairly large room, but its character as a lobby (that is, a room through which one passes to other rooms) is clearly demonstrated by the fact that it has a doorway on each of its four sides (Figs. 35, 36). Beyond the doorway from the corridor it is bounded on the southwest by a wall 0.90 m. thick, which still stands to a height of 1.06 m. above the floor. It is built in the regular Mycenaean style, exhibiting three vertical chases that run through the wall, spaced 0.60 m. apart, and two grooves for horizontal beams at 0.20 m. and 0.60 m. above the floor. Plaster is preserved all along below the lower groove, but only patches remain in place at the higher level. A piece in the southern corner has been applied straight across the horizontal groove.

The southeastern wall (Fig. 35), pierced by a doorway not far from the southerly corner, is 0.85 m. thick and stands to a height of 1.10 m. The small stump to the southwest of the doorway has been largely converted by fire into fused debris. To the northeast beyond the doorway three vertical chases can be recognized at intervals of 0.50 m. and 0.45 m., as well as a horizontal groove for a beam at 0.45 m. above the floor. The plaster is preserved up to this level near the doorway and in the easterly corner it rises much higher, passing over the horizontal groove.

The northeast wall, 0.75 m. thick, is in a badly damaged condition. The core stands to a height of 0.85 m. in the east corner from which it descends to 0.65 m. near the doorway. Plaster survives *in situ* on the wall to a height varying from 0.10 m. to 0.40 m. above the floor. A broad doorway (Fig. 36), continues the line of this wall to its intersection with the northwest wall.

The latter, nearly 0.85 m. thick, is preserved to a height ranging from 0.50 m. at the doorway to 0.89 m. at the southwest end, beyond which another doorway leads northwestward into Room 39 (Fig. 35). Plaster is preserved from 0.43 m. to 0.70 m. above the floor, extending from door to door. One vertical chase is indicated, but the horizontal grooves are concealed by plaster.

The stucco floor is still in relatively good condition around the four sides of the room, especially near the walls. Two coats can be distinguished and the final one has a smooth bluish-gray finish. In the center of the area it is broken and damaged.

When excavated the room was found jammed to the very surface of the ground with fallen stones, burned and fused debris, fragments of brick, and crushed pots, for the most part jars or pithoi of large and moderate sizes (19 pots, representing 11 different shapes, were restored, Fig. 330). Except for a few that seemed to be standing on the floor, these pots lay in a great jumbled and confused mass, one on top of another, many warped and twisted, some burnt out to the consistency of pumice, others bubbly and vitrified and shiny; and along with them were wedged many crude bricks and fragments which had accompanied the pots in their fall.

In the disorderly wreckage it was difficult to determine exactly how this great accumulation had taken on the form that it had when exposed. Some of the jars may have been standing in a row along the southwest wall of the room, where a supply of oil and ointments might have been kept ready at hand for use in the adjoining bathroom. One large pithos was found standing upright wedged in by others on their sides which must have come from above. The great mass certainly was precipitated during the fire from the upper story, where there surely was an oil magazine; and a large quantity of inflammable oil poured into the flames must account for the extreme intensity of the fire in this place. The heap of debris descended toward the northeast and filled the doorway leading out into the Northeast Gateway (Fig. 129). In the doorway were found some of the smaller jars with a strange kind of decoration resembling that of Middle Helladic Mattpainted Ware. Here and there in the upper parts of the debris were recovered 19 fragments of inscribed tablets all dealing with olive oil.

O B J E C T S   F O U N D

GOLD

Small bit of foil, found 0.15 m. above floor.

BRONZE

Rectangular fragment in fairly solid condition (Fig. 286 No. 14), l. 0.023 m., w. 0.006 m., th. 0.003 m.

FLINT

Flake (Fig. 286 No. 16).

TERRACOTTA

Biconical whorl (Fig. 286 No. 15), h. 0.019 m., d. 0.024 m., found just below surface.

CLAY

Tablets: Nos. 1201-1212 and probably the fragment found in 1956, No. 1260, which with No. 1210 was joined to No. 1206 (*OOT*, 41-46, pls. II-IX); No. 1214, fragmentary (*ibid.*, 11 note 4).

Sealings: pieces of clay that had apparently been used to seal containers of various kinds and had been baked hard in the conflagration (Fig. 277 Nos. 1-12).

POTTERY

Some 31 pots were counted as they were uncovered, cleaned, and removed. The mass of fragments must have represented many more vases (mostly storage jars), however, since there are extra bases for which we could not find rims and vice versa. The material has been worked over and it was possible to restore 19 pots which have been inventoried (Fig. 330).

Amphora (Shape 45, p. 381)
  No. 619 (Fig. 371).
Jar (Shape 50, p. 385)
  Nos. 597 and 598 (Figs. 373, 374), decorated.
Jar (Shape 54a, p. 390)
  No. 610 (Figs. 379, 380 rim), decorated.
Jar (Shape 54b, p. 392)
  Nos. 600 (Figs. 379, 380), decorated; 603 (Fig. 380); 604 (Figs. 379, 380 rim), decorated; 605 (Fig. 380); 606 (Figs. 379, 380 rim), decorated.
Pithos (Shape 55a, p. 393)
  No. 602 (Fig. 382).

Storage jar (Shape 56, p. 395)
  Nos. 601 (Fig. 384); 607 (Figs. 382 rim, 383), decorated; 611 (Fig. 384).
Storage jar (Shape 57, p. 395)
  No. 599 (Figs. 382 rim, 383).
Krater (Shape 58, p. 396)
  No. 609 (Fig. 382 rim).
Pedestaled krater (Shape 63, p. 400)
  No. 596 (Figs. 387, 388), decorated.
Stirrup-vase (Shape 65d, p. 408)
  Nos. 613 and 614 (Figs. 391, 394), decorated.
Stirrup-vase (Shape 65e, p. 410)
  No. 595 (Fig. 391), decorated.

A decorated pithoid jar of Shape 54a too bubbly and fused to be restorable. Same fabric as the other Palace Style jars and probably the finest of the lot. Pattern reconstructed from pieces of rim and neck and side near base: six petal-shaped motives above base, with octopus, palm trees and flowers on side (Fig. 344).

Base of large Palace Style jar (Fig. 346 No. 4).

Large stirrup-vase (Shape 65b 1), decorated with painted bands; partially vitrified and bubbly; unrestorable (Fig. 345 No. 1). Wheel-pattern (*MP*, 403, fig. 70, 68:2) on disk.

Fragments of another large stirrup-vase (Fig. 345 No. 5).

Two small stirrup-vases (Shapes 65d), found with Nos. 613 and 614, are not restorable. They have similar decoration of painted bands and fine lines on body and shoulder but between handles patterns differ. On one (h. pres. 0.11 m., d. 0.14 m., d. base ca. 0.075 m.), concentric semicircles alternately pointing up and down; on the other (h. pres. 0.105 m., d. ca. 0.15 m., d. base 0.067 m.), groups of short diagonal lines alternately pointing to right and left. The fragments are much warped and discolored by fire— gray with brownish paint.

Many fragments of a fine jar badly burned and now bubbly and fused and with surface flaked off. Torus base, spreading body that rises from pedestal-like bottom (h.

pres. 0.23 m., d. base 0.16 m.); traces of bands painted in red on buff. High, slightly concave neck with rounded offset rim (h. neck 0.105 m., d. neck 0.145 m.) coated all over with streaky reddish-brown paint.

The sherds, collected from all parts of the room, that remained after the pots were put together are mostly small and nondescript. No joins; probably not from pots found in the room: may have been in the clay that was used to make the bricks that fell into the room. The 100 or more small sherds with decoration almost certainly came out of the bricks, for when chunks of *migma* were broken up many fragments popped out. Some look early (LH I, LH II, and LH III A). Many fragments bear spirals, several have double axes, others bands with dots.

Shapes noted in the usual plain fabric, buff, tan, greenish, or pinkish in color: kylix (bases of 6 fairly large, 3 small), stemmed krater, bowl with pinched-out handles, large dipper, conical cup.

A number of sherds of reddish-brown and red fabric with roughly polished surface like the pottery found in Room 60 (p. 240). No shapes recognized.

Coarse ware includes sherds with painted bands from large pots fused and damaged by fire. Some are made of "oatmeal ware," others have smoother almost polished surface. No shapes identifiable except possibly a basin and a jug or jar with low neck and outturned rim.

In especially coarse ware: enormously thick rim (squarish in section and painted on top) of a pithos, which had relatively thin walls; rims of jars and basins and the straight rim of a huge lid with flaring sides.

ROOM 39

The doorway giving northwestward from the lobby into Room 39 has the usual threshold block and lateral jamb bases (Figs. 130, 457) almost exactly as in the contiguous doorway leading from Corridor 37 into the lobby (Fig. 128). The threshold block, 0.83 m. long through the opening and 0.68 m. to 0.71 m. wide, has been worn smooth on top, but is cracked across the middle and is damaged somewhat, especially towards its northeast edge. The base of the jamb on the northeast, which has the same length as the threshold, is 0.58 m. wide. In its top has been cut a rabbet nearly 0.02 m. deep and varying from 0.19 m. to 0.22 m. in width. Some 0.17 m. from the southeastern edge of the stone is a square cutting (0.08 m. on a side and 0.03 m. deep) for the socket of the pivot. The jamb base on the southwestern side has approximately the same length as the others and is 0.48 m. wide. In its top beside the threshold block is a shallow rabbet corresponding to the one on the opposite side, but ranging from 0.10 m. to 0.12 m. in width. This rabbet was at some time filled with plaster. The outer edge of the rabbet on each side presumably marks the line of the wooden door casing which framed an opening ca. 1 m. broad. How the door frame was attached to the wall is not clear. On both sides of the doorway abundant remains of the wooden jamb were represented by black earth and carbonized wood. The black deposit on the southwestern side of the opening was continuous practically from ground level to the base at the inner face of the opening. Above the middle of the northeastern base the deposit was 0.30 m. deep and at the inner edge of the doorway were remains of carbonized wood. So far as the evidence goes, the door must have been single-leaved, unless another pivot hole lies hidden beneath the plaster on the southwestern base.

Room 39 (Key Plan) is almost square with an average length of 3.57 m. from southwest to northeast and ca. 3.50 m. from southeast to northwest (Fig. 35). The southeastern wall beyond the doorway is 0.80 m. thick and stands to a height of 1.40 m. (Fig. 36). Built in the usual manner, it displays two vertical chases, 0.55 m. apart, and two horizontal grooves for beams at 0.40 m. and 0.78 m. above the floor. Along the wall plaster is preserved up to the lower horizontal groove and in the south corner it rises to 0.91 m.

The southwest wall, which separates Room 39 from the Northeast Corridor, is 0.85 m. thick and has a height of 1.30 m. (Fig. 35). Five vertical chases are visible in the top of the wall, as mentioned on page 166, and are clearly marked on its northeastern face. At least one groove for a horizontal beam is indicated 0.72 m. above the floor. Whether there is one below this cannot be determined, since a thick coat of plaster on the lower part of the wall conceals the evidence.

The northwest wall, which divides Room 39 from Stairway 36, is 0.90 m. thick and rises to a height of 1.30 m. (Fig. 35). The southeastern face has retained much of its coating of coarse plaster, but four vertical chases seem to be indicated at intervals of 0.75 m. to 0.80 m., and at least one horizontal groove 0.80 m. above the floor. The plaster is cracked and somewhat damaged but a good deal of it has survived.

The northeast wall, in which there is a doorway leading to Room 40, is 0.78 m. thick, standing to a height of 1.10 m. To the southeast of the doorway it has one vertical chase and a horizontal groove at 0.47 m. above the floor. On both the northwestern and southeastern parts of this wall the plaster is well preserved; in the latter section it ends in a straight line which evidently abutted against the frame of the door leading in from the lobby. At the other end it also shows a straight edge where it was laid against the casing of the doorway to Room 40. Although the plaster on all four walls was properly made of lime with a good blue-gray surface, it seems not to have borne painted decoration.

The stucco floor is generally well preserved around the four sides of the room near the walls, but toward the center in an irregular area some 2 m. long and 1 m. wide the top coating has been broken away and an under layer exposed. Spread out in the black deposit over the floor inside the doorway from the lobby, were recovered the fragments of a large narrow-necked, three-handled jar with painted decoration. In the same stratum, farther along in front of the door leading into Room 40, lay another group of sherds from which was reconstructed an urnlike vessel standing on three legs: it has four lugs and two horizontal handles and was decorated with painted patterns in a near approach to the Close Style. A third pot was put together from fragments found in the western corner of the room also in the black layer: it is a brazier of a familiar Mycenaean type with a straight projecting handle. All these pots have turned gray from the effects of fire (Fig. 326).

Room 39 was found filled with burned debris. In the western corner lay a mass of disintegrated crude brick sloping down toward the center of the room and covered by quantities of fragments of stucco flooring. Many of these with their backing of clay were as much as 0.10 m. thick. Embedded in the clay were sherds, bits of painted plaster, bones, pebbles, and lime. Some pieces of decorated plaster retained bright colors that had not been dulled by fire and many of them showed traces of recognizable patterns. Several chunks of mud plaster had a thin coating of white, resembling whitewash. Under the plowed earth over the southeasterly part of the room was a very black layer containing small stones; it formed the northwestern limit of an intrusive deposit of late Geometric times that extended many meters northeastward into Court 42. Underneath was dissolved material of crude brick burned red. This in turn, especially along the walls, rested on a very hard sterile gray stratum, perhaps the powdered remains of fallen plaster.

O B J E C T S   F O U N D

SILVER

Small piece of what may be silver, found above floor.

BRONZE

Small piece with edge of rivet-hole (Fig. 286 No. 17), found above floor.

STONE

Obsidian: blade (Fig. 286 No. 19), l. 0.029 m., w. 0.012 m., th. 0.003 m., found near southwest wall.

Pointed chip, l. 0.017 m., w. 0.01 m., th. 0.005 m., from above fallen plaster.

Blade, l. 0.019 m., w. 0.01 m., th. 0.004 m., found 0.30 m. above floor.

Chip from floor.

Flint: blade (Fig. 286 No. 20), l. 0.033 m., w. 0.018 m., th. 0.004 m.

A few chips found with fallen flooring.

IVORY

Several small annular beads (NM. 7837, Fig. 285 Nos. 24-27), three intact, one broken and mended, and fragments of another, d. 0.011 m., th. 0.002 m.: burned black; perforation small and off center; found on top of fallen plaster.

HORN

A large piece of carbonized horn found under fallen flooring.

TERRACOTTA

Undecorated bead or button, h. 0.009 m., d. 0.018 m., went to pieces in washing; found in black stratum above pavement.

Small undecorated whorl (Fig. 286 No. 18), h. 0.015 m., d. 0.022 m., found with pot in front of southeast doorway.

POTTERY

Jug (Shape 44, p. 381)
No. 544 (Figs. 369, 370), decorated.
Brazier (Shape 67, p. 412)
No. 458 (Figs. 395, 396).
Tripod-jar (Shape 68, p. 412)
No. 457 (Figs. 395, 396), decorated.
Aside from these three pots not much pottery was collected; the sherds are mostly nondescript and coated with lime accretion. Shapes noted: pithos (several pieces of high sloping neck with offset rim flat on top), cooking pots, jar with splaying rim, kylix (9 stems), dipper, basin. Several fragments

with red polished surface, like the pots from Room 60. Some 50 pieces with painted decoration include fragments of Vapheio cups of early Mycenaean date which prob-ably came in with the crude brick or clay. Most of the pieces are of the palace period with bands, spirals, and panel arrange-ment.

ROOM 40

The doorway into Room 40 is spaced 0.58 m. distant from the north corner of Room 39 (Figs. 34, 36). It was built in the usual manner with a threshold block and lateral bases for the jambs (Fig. 458), all three having approximately the same length, 0.87 m. (Fig. 132). The threshold block, 0.465 m. wide, was set with its upper surface 0.01 m. to 0.03 m. lower than that of the contiguous jamb bases. It is cracked across the middle. The southeastern block, 0.52 m. wide, has the customary rabbet in its top, averaging 0.30 m. in width. Some 0.16 m. from its southwestern end is a rectangular cutting, 0.08 m. by 0.085 m. and 0.05 m. deep, for the socket of the pivot. The northwestern jamb, 0.52 m. wide, has a corresponding rabbet, ranging from 0.195 m. to 0.23 m. in width, and a similar cutting for the pivot-socket. The edges of the rabbet on the two sides show that the actual opening inside the door frame was ca. 1 m. broad. The door must have had two leaves swinging northeast-ward within the depth of the opening. In the present state of the wall it is not pos-sible to determine how the door frame was fixed in its place, but on the southeastern side its limit is given by the straight edge of the plaster that came up against it.

Room 40 (Key Plan) has an average length of 3.455 m. from southeast to north-west and a width varying from 3.09 m. to 3.14 m. (Fig. 35). The southwest wall, pierced by the doorway just mentioned (Fig. 34), has been described as seen from Room 39. On the side toward Room 40 it gives evidence of a horizontal groove at 0.44 m. above the floor, and the plaster is well preserved to that level. On the north-west it is bordered by a continuation of the wall beside the stairway and Room 34 (Fig. 36). In the west corner it stands to a height of 0.97 m., but it has suffered much damage and has been reduced at the north corner to no more than 0.10 m. At least three, perhaps four, vertical chases have left their marks through the wall, varying somewhat in their spacing. Traces of a horizontal groove for a beam are visible at 0.43 m. above the floor. Here too the plaster is preserved along the lower part of the wall, discolored near the floor in an irregular streak of smoky blue-gray.

On the northeast the room is bordered by the exterior wall of the building (Fig. 28). This section, lying between two antae that project into the court (p. 50), is only ca. 1 m. thick. Four squared blocks, forming the lowest course, make up what survives of the outer face of the wall (Fig. 414). They were laid in alternation, first a large block extending through three fourths of the thickness of the wall, then a smaller and much shorter one, then again a large block, followed by another of small size. The much dilapidated inner face, only 0.40 m. high, was built of rubble coated with plaster, which still survives to a maximum height of 0.18 m. above the floor. Not enough of the wall remains to make certain the exact position of chases and horizontal grooves.

The southeastern wall, which separates Room 40 from the Northeast Gateway (41), is 0.85 m. thick; it is preserved to a height of 0.86 m. at its southwestern end, diminishing to 0.25 m. at its northeastern (Fig. 131). On its northwestern face the plaster still survives in some places to a height ranging from 0.13 m. to 0.45 m. above the floor. Traces of a horizontal groove for a beam may be recognized at 0.44 m. above the floor and scanty marks indicate at least one vertical chase.

As in so many other apartments, the stucco floor is best preserved along the walls; toward the middle of the room, however, it has suffered a good deal of damage, cracked and broken here and there, and perhaps in part disrupted by the roots of an olive tree. A large dent may have been made by a squared block that presumably fell from the outside wall. Several other blocks from the same source lay above and to the east.

The northwestern part of the room contained a good deal of disintegrated crude brick and also many fragments of steps of poros, obviously fallen from Stairway 36.

The southeast side of the room was covered by a continuation of the stratum of black oily earth and stones already mentioned as appearing in Room 39 (Fig. 133). Toward the northeast the oily matter had penetrated more and more deeply into the ground, reaching the lowest course of squared blocks of the exterior wall. Some kind of acid in this matter burned into the surface of the blocks, which are now badly pitted and eaten away. Here and there in this widespread black layer were found scattered sherds which point to a date in the late Geometric Period, toward the end of the seventh century. The stones that were blackened presumably came from the wreckage of the palace, but the substance that discolored them may have been the waste that seeped through into the underlying deposit from an olive press of about 600 B.C.

The two connecting rooms, 39 and 40, well laid out (Fig. 35) and well built, with proper doorways, good stucco floors, and plastered walls, yielded nothing to explain for what purpose they were used. In this position beside an entrance they may have formed the headquarters of palace officials who, before Court 42 was enclosed, controlled the approach to the building from the northeast. If they had been less well finished they might have been explained as storerooms, in the latest phases, equipped with wooden cupboards and chests for linens, towels, raiment, and unguents that might be needed for the bath on the opposite side of the lobby. Or they could have been repositories for perishable furniture or equipment that occasions might require in Court 42. But we cannot escape the impression that originally some hall or room of state looked out on this side, perhaps in the upper story, if not below.

O B J E C T S   F O U N D

S I L V E R

Nondescript fragment (Fig. 286 No. 21).

B R O N Z E

Small bits, including what may be barb of arrow point.

S T O N E

Flint: pointed implement (broken), possibly arrowhead (Fig. 286 No. 25), l. 0.046 m., w. 0.016 m., th. 0.005 m.; small flake.

Obsidian: three small pieces (e.g., Fig. 286 Nos. 22, 24).

T E R R A C O T T A

Biconical·whorl or button of light buff clay (Fig. 286 No. 23), h. 0.02 m., d. 0.022 m.

P O T T E R Y

The scattered sherds from the deposit represent, in coarse ware, tripod-vessels, pithoi, brazier, and in finer ware, kylikes (32 stems), flat bases (7 counted) of cups and bowls, stirrup-vase, and alabastron. Decorated pieces show broad and narrow bands, curving lines, net, dots, and vertical stripes. A good deal of Geometric ware for the most part coated with black or brownish glaze.

N O R T H E A S T   G A T E W A Y   4 1

The doorway leading from Room 38 into the portal (41 on Key Plan) is of the regular type common in the palace, fitted with a central threshold block, flanked on each side by a base for the door casing (Figs. 134, 459). The three lie side by side, running through the door opening, which has a depth of ca. 0.85 m. The central block forming the threshold is 0.91 m. wide. It has sunk down in its middle, where it is cracked, and there is also a transverse crack. It is badly worn and still partly covered by remains of stucco. The southeast jamb base is 0.46 m. wide, rising nearly 0.05 m. higher than the threshold. It has a rabbet along its inner edge 0.06 m. wide. About 0.15 m. from the outer edge of the block is a rectangular cutting, 0.14 m. long and 0.07 m. wide, which must have held the pivot-socket.

The northwestern base is 0.45 m. wide. In its top toward the door-opening it has a rabbet, 0.07 m. to 0.08 m. wide, corresponding to that on the southeast side. A rectangular cutting, 0.07 m. by 0.09 m., 0.15 m. from the northeast edge of the stone, is now filled with stucco. It may originally have held a pivot-socket, but in the late phase it was no longer used. The edges of the rabbets on the two sides, 1.175 m. apart, presumably mark the limits of the wooden door casing, which undoubtedly returned around the corners alongside the core of wall; but nothing is left to show details. Perhaps, like the southwest and northwest door of the lobby, this too was converted from a two-leaved to a single-leaf door.

The doorway from the lobby leads into a small gateway, porch, or portal (41 on Key Plan). It is 2.95 m. deep from southwest to northeast and 4.14 m. wide (Figs.

35, 414). It was open on the northeast, the walls on each side ending in a large anta. Between the latter, approximately but not exactly centered,[54] is a stone column base, roughly rectangular with rounded corners (Fig. 135). It is 0.62 m. long from northeast to southwest and 0.51 m. wide. The block is aligned with the inner ends of the antae, but is set back 0.35 m. from their outer line (Fig. 36). On the top of the block are faint traces of a slightly prepared standing place, not circular in shape as was usual for normal columns, but 0.46 m. long (from northwest to southeast) and 0.35 m. wide; perhaps it indicates that a rectangular wooden pillar stood here. Between the northwest anta and the stone base is a long narrow threshold block: it was slightly cut to overlap the column base, but stops 0.06 m. short of the anta. It is 1.93 m. long and ca. 0.35 m. wide with a thickness of 0.115 m. Its top is scored with shallow longitudinal grooves, perhaps to hold the stucco pavement that was at some time laid over it. No corresponding block has survived to the southeast of the column base, but a gap with broken edges between the pavement of the gateway and that of the court, 0.24 m. wide and ca. 1.25 m. long, implies that a continuation of the threshold, probably of stone, possibly of wood, has been removed. The gap was filled with soft black earth resting on small bedding stones at the bottom of it. Beyond the gap a poros block, 0.43 m. long, lies in the same line to within 0.43 m. of the southeast anta. Here too bedding stones continue. The poros block was, in the later phases at least, covered over by the pavement.

The northwest wall of the gateway, separating it from Room 40, and the southwestern partition between it and the lobby have been sufficiently described from the other sides. The southeastern wall, between the gateway and the bathroom (43), is 0.85 m. thick (Figs. 34, 36). At the south corner it stands to a height of 0.75 m.; but it slopes downward toward the northeast to a low of 0.50 m., where it reaches the inner end of the anta block. Three vertical chases are clearly marked 0.60 m. and 0.70 m. apart. Suggestions of a horizontal groove are visible at ca. 0.32 m. above the floor.

Some remains of the plaster are preserved along the bottom of the northwest wall in a strip from 0.08 m. to 0.28 m. high. Very little is left on the southwest wall, but on the southeast some patches survive to a height of 0.50 m.

The stucco pavement of the gateway is in a bad state of preservation except in the south corner and along the southwest wall and in a few spots here and there (Fig. 36). It consists of two coats, the uppermost of which, 0.02 m. thick, is almost entirely lacking. They seem not to belong to two phases: the bottom one was probably the foundation for the finished surface. On the floor against the northwest wall were found the remains of a pithos including the base and fragments of the rim. It was

[54] 2.10 m. from center of base to northwest anta, 2.045 m. to southeast anta. The stone is 0.12 m. to 0.13 m. thick and rests on small stones.

not well enough preserved to be reconstructed. No other pots and very few sherds were found on the floor.

Gateway 41 was filled with the usual burned debris from the destruction of the palace. In the northwestern half of the room this fill was covered and its upper part was discolored by the oily black matter that has already been encountered in Rooms 39 and 40 (Fig. 133). In the southeastern quarter of the gateway the Mycenaean deposit was not affected by this Geometric intrusion. Near the southeast wall, at the bottom of the plowed earth, was found a fragment of an inscribed tablet (No. 1211).

The lateral walls of the gateway end toward the court in antae (Fig. 36). The anta on the southeast formed the actual corner, where the southeast wall of the gateway met the exterior wall of the building. Only the base of it is now preserved, ca. 1 m. long on its northwestern face, 0.70 m. wide toward the court, and rising to 0.40 m. above the pavement. It has been badly damaged by fire and the upper edge has almost everywhere been broken away. Although the upper surface is badly pitted, four dowel holes are recognizable,[55] one near the northeastern end, one in the middle of the northwestern side, and a pair toward the southwest.

The northwestern anta, though aligned with the southeastern, projected into the court since the exterior wall of the building beyond it was set back 0.80 m. to the southwest (Fig. 28). The base of the anta is a large block, 1 m. long from southwest to northeast, 0.95 m. wide along its face toward the court, and at least 0.49 m. high above the pavement. This block too is much damaged along its edges and the surface is badly pitted. In the top of the block are six dowel holes, 0.10 m. to 0.12 m. from the outer edge: three set along the southeastern edge at intervals of 0.30 m., three along the northeastern, ca. 0.35 m. apart, and two, ca. 0.35 m. apart, on the northwestern side, the corner dowels being counted twice. These dowel holes are roughly 0.06 m. to 0.07 m. deep and vary slightly in size.[56]

The dowels in both antae must have fastened thick horizontal beams at this level. At the back of the block the beams were presumably attached to heavy timbers in a vertical chase; they also continued along the outer face of the wall both to the southeast and the northwest of the gateway. The anta itself, on each side, may have been built in alternating courses of wood and stone. What kind of a capital it had, if any, is not known, but the antae and the wooden column between them certainly supported an entablature that stretched across the opening. It was made in part at least of squared blocks of poros many of which were found lying in the court outside the entrance (Fig. 28). These blocks were not long enough to span the inter-columniations of somewhat more than 2 m.; consequently it must be assumed that an architrave made of sturdy timbers carried the weight of the entablature.

[55] See plan Fig. 414 block No. 26 and footnote 10, p. 53.   [56] See footnote 9, p. 53.

OBJECTS FOUND

From stratum of black earth with stones

BRONZE

Three thin flat pieces (e.g., Fig. 286 No. 26).

STONE

Obsidian: flake.
Flint: two pieces (Fig. 286 Nos. 27, 28).

IVORY

Four very small bits.

CLAY

Tablet: No. 343 + No. 1213 (*OOT*, 11, 39, pls. II-III).

POTTERY

Largely pithos fragments possibly belonging to the decorated storage jars found in Room 38, including fragments of base with ridge just above, ridged handles, neck with ridge at its base, small torus base.

Finer ware nondescript in very small pieces: kylix only shape recognized (14 stems).

Sherds with painted decoration include much Geometric ware.

COURT 42

The gateway leads into an open court (42 on Key Plan) enclosed on all sides (Fig. 28). The walls surrounding it obviously belong to one of the last phases of occupation, but in earlier stages a roadway or street ran northeastward to the end of the hill. This was probably a heritage from early Mycenaean times before the palace of Mycenaean III B was built. We have traced the course of an aqueduct, which for a long distance bordered this roadway and which brought water to the palace probably from the spring called Rouvelli 1,360 m. to the northeast of Epano Englianos. The architectural embellishments of the northeastern exterior wall of the Main Building with its recess opposite Room 33, two great antae framing a deep recess just to the northwest of the gate, and yet another offset in the wall some 3.30 m. to the southeast, must be taken to indicate that this was an important façade of the palace suitably designed by the architect to fit its significance.

Originally the gateway probably led out into a broad open court on the northeastern side of the palace. In one of the closing phases part of it was enclosed within a stone wall which offered no exit to the outside world. Accessible only from the palace, it might have been a private patio reserved for the use of the last king himself, but it must have impaired the aesthetic effect of the somewhat elaborate architectural treatment bestowed on this side of the building.

The court has a maximum length of 13.54 m. from southeast to northwest and a width (measured from the southeast anta of the gateway) of 5.55 m. (Fig. 28). On the southwest the court is bordered by the gateway and the exterior wall of the building itself (Fig. 35). The wall to the northwest with its alternation of large and small squared blocks outside Room 40 (Fig. 34) has already been described (p. 176). It ends at a corner with a huge anta base which projects 0.87 m. from the wall into the

west corner of the court (Fig. 110). The block has a length of 1.05 m. from southwest to northeast, a width of 0.92 m. across the front, and a height of 0.60 m. It is
set back into the wall on the southwest, where a notch was cut into its south corner
to receive either a stone block or, more probably, the end of a wooden beam coming
from the southeast. The base rests on a foundation of smaller poros blocks, which
rise a few centimeters above the pavement and project from 0.12 m. to 0.14 m. on
the southeast and from 0.10 m. to 0.13 m. on the northeast. Seven irregular dowel
holes appear in the top of the block, three not very carefully aligned along the southeastern side, three others along the northeastern side, and still another on the northwestern side. The dowels must have fastened horizontal wooden beams which either
covered the whole top of the block or were set around three sides of it, and perhaps
supported upright timbers. Horizontal beams at the same level as the top of the anta
base continued along the face of the wall to the northwest. At the south corner of
the large anta base the level of the beam running southeastward along the wall
steps down 0.31 m., and it was presumably the end of this beam that fitted into the
notch in the anta block mentioned above (Fig. 35).

To the southeast of the gateway, beyond the anta block, the wall extends 2.70 m.
along the end of Bathroom 43, then turning outward in an offset 0.17 m. deep, continues southeastward (Fig. 36). The angle block that forms the offset is aligned with
the northwestern face of the partition wall between the bathroom and the Queen's
Hall. In the space between the anta base and the offset three large squared blocks
form the dado course of the same height as the anta base. They were loosely fitted
together with the usual V-shaped joints. Dowel holes in the top of each indicate that
a horizontal beam lay at this level. No part of the wall above these blocks is preserved.

Some 0.25 m. southeastward beyond the offset the southeast wall of Court 42
abuts against the exterior wall of the building (Fig. 28). The wall of the court,
0.80 m. thick, and standing to an average height of 0.60 m., is built mainly of unworked stones. It shows no sign of horizontal grooves or vertical chases for beams.
Its northwestern face was originally coated with lime plaster, some scanty remains
of which survive on the wall. Much more had fallen to the pavement alongside the
wall, and it is clear that there were several successive coats.

The northeast wall of the court is made up of three sections: the first, forming an
approximate right angle with the southeast wall and running almost exactly northwestward, is 7.20 m. long (Fig. 28); the second, turning slightly more westward,
has a length of 3.49 m.; the third, veering more sharply westward, continues 3.27 m.
farther to the northern corner of the court. Section 1 (Fig. 136) is ca. 1 m. thick
and stands to a height of 0.70 m. to 0.80 m. through most of its length. It is built
mainly of rough unworked stones, but near its southeastern end two large blocks of

poros were laid in the bottom course of the wall. At its northwesterly end this section meets, but is not bonded with, a wall that comes from the northeast and turns to the northwest. Some 0.20 m. short of the junction and 0.40 m. above the pavement, is a small opening in the wall, almost square, measuring 0.23 m. on a side. A thin, flat stone forms a cover slab. Some 0.10 m. inside the face of the wall appears the broken end of a terracotta pipe (Fig. 137). Although cracked and therefore slightly compressed, the pipe still retains its cylindrical shape.[57] It must have brought running water to this place, probably from the aqueduct mentioned above (p. 181) or from a reservoir supplied by the aqueduct. It is likely that the pipe originally projected from the face of the wall and that a vessel of some kind stood below to receive the water. The floor showed no traces of a built catch-basin. This first section, like the southeast wall, had once been coated with plaster, remains of which are preserved along the very bottom of the wall. It varies from 0.05 m. to 0.08 m. in thickness and several coats are distinguishable.

The second section is actually the southwestern end of a small earlier building which happened to be aligned more or less nearly with the border of the court and was therefore incorporated as part of its wall (Fig. 28). It is constructed, for the most part, of small flat unworked slabs of limestone (Fig. 136) and not of rubble such as appears in all the other sections of the wall that surrounded the court. Two small blocks of poros were used in the south corner of the little building. The wall varies from 1.05 m. to 1.10 m. in thickness and stands to a height of 0.85 m. As shown by remains along the base of the wall, this section too had once been coated with thick plaster.

Section 3, which follows, is built of rubble and a few fragments of poros. It is 3.27 m. long, ca. 1.10 m. thick, and stands to a height of 0.75 m. Only scanty remnants of its original coat of plaster have survived at the bottom of the wall.

The northwest wall (Fig. 28), which completes the enclosure of the court, is 3.56 m. long, 0.70 m. thick, reaching a height of 0.80 m. The lower part is built mainly of rubble, but in the upper part are many pieces of poros, and one large block of the latter juts outward from the lowest course of the wall. The inside of the wall abuts against the north corner of the large anta base that projects from the outside wall of the central building. Little or no plaster is preserved on the inner face of the wall, but the edge of the pavement, turning up, indicates that this section too once bore a very thick coating.

The entire court was paved with heavy white stucco, much of which survives in two layers in reasonably good condition although it is buckled and cracked in some

[57] Outside diameter 0.17 m., inside diameter 0.14 m., thickness of walls 0.015 m. Probing into the wall revealed a finished end of the pipe at 0.68 m. from the broken end. The pipe must therefore have had a total length of considerably more than 0.80 m. if it was a single piece. It was not possible to ascertain whether the line through the wall was composed of two units fitted together.

places. The later coat was apparently 0.02 m. thick on the southwest, and elsewhere ranges from 0.03 m. to 0.07 m. On all sides the pavement turns up to join the plaster on the walls and it slopes downward from northwest to southeast. Near the south corner is a drain hole (Fig. 138), ca. 0.15 m. in diameter, cut through a flat stone and leading to an underground drain which apparently ran southeastward. The pavement also shows a slight slope downward into the gateway, where it overlaps the threshold block.

The northwestern part of the court contained few blocks dislodged from the outside wall of the Main Building (Fig. 28). Opposite the gateway, however, and farther southeastward, a good many had fallen some 2.20 m. distant from the façade, and were spread out to the northeast wall of the court. Some of these had presumably come from the entablature that was supported by the antae and the column.

The whole court had become filled with wreckage from the time of the fire. All along the outer walls was heaped up a mass of whitish earth, perhaps representing the backing of the plaster. In the northwestern part lay much brownish and yellowish earth above and around the worked blocks; there also were found numerous fragments of pottery, mainly pieces of kylikes, which had evidently been broken and thrown out as fragments. In all the rest of the court, beginning opposite the middle of Room 40, a similar deposit had in part been permeated and discolored by the black oily waste which has already been encountered in Rooms 40 and 41. The acid in this liquid had seared and pitted the poros blocks which it touched and in some places it had permeated even to the stucco pavement.

Many sherds were recovered from the black stratum, most of them in bad condition, coated with a blackened lime incrustation. The great majority clearly represent Mycenaean types, but a not inconsiderable number stood out as of a different character: from this material it was possible to reconstruct in whole or in part four pots which may be assigned to a late Geometric phase, perhaps to the turn from the seventh to the sixth century. From near the top of the black stratum came four nails or spikes of iron. Whether they too may be attributed to Geometric times or belong to some subsequent period was not determined.

O B J E C T S   F O U N D

From stratum of black earth

IRON

Fragments of four spikes rectangular in section (Fig. 287 Nos. 1-4), l. 0.165 m., w. 0.01 m.; l. 0.135 m., w. 0.008 m.; l. 0.22 m., w. 0.005 m.; l. 0.08 m., w. 0.012 m. One spike found near fairly large chunk of carbon.

Ring with hook attached (Fig. 287 No. 5), l. 0.07 m., d. of ring 0.025 m., th. ca. 0.005 m.

Flat piece with one concave edge (Fig. 287 No. 8), max. l. 0.10 m., w. 0.055 m., th. 0.01 m.

OBSIDIAN

Two flakes (Fig. 287 Nos. 6, 7).

Geometric

One-handled cup (Fig. 347 No. 615). H. 0.10 m., d. rim restored 0.087 m., d. body 0.108 m., d. base restored 0.055 m. About half preserved comprising bit of base, part of body and one third of rim—enough to give complete profile. Flat bottom, globular body, straight collar-neck; flattened handle coming out straight from rim and curving down to widest part of body. Light brick-red clay, dark brown-red glaze inside and out, now much worn. Walls very thin.

One-handled cup (Fig. 347 No. 616). H. 0.095 m., d. rim 0.095 m., d. body 0.12 m., d. base restored 0.05 m. Slightly more than half preserved comprising bit of base and a good deal of body—giving complete profile; handle restored but ends preserved; bottom slightly hollowed, squat globular body, slightly concave neck with plain thin rim. Yellowish-tan clay with streaky brownish-black glaze inside and out, now much worn. Walls very thin.

Two-handled jar (Fig. 347 No. 617). H. 0.142 m. as restored, d. rim 0.09 m., d. body 0.143 m., d. base 0.062 m. Base, side, neck, and rim give complete profile. One handle preserved but does not join; setting places and stumps provide evidence for two handles. High splaying raised base, hollow underneath, depressed ovoid body, straight collar-neck, thin plain rim. Rather large arched handles set obliquely and horizontally, rounded but flattened on sides. Light tannish-gray clay, coated with streaky blackish glaze inside and out, now much worn.

Pedestal-base, fragment (Fig. 347 No. 618). H. pres. ca. 0.10 m., d. edge base 0.21 m., d. at top 0.153 m. Almost one half pre-served. Rounded edge at bottom, flaring sides contracting to almost straight cylinder where body of vessel was attached. Bottom concave inside but practically flat underneath. Gray, well-levigated clay with black streaky glaze on exterior.

Mycenaean

Much coarse ware: fragments of small pithoi and large jars, a torus base, a large lug and various handles, legs of tripod-vessels.

Shapes in fine ware: kylix (183 stems counted), bowl with pinched-out handles or cup (52 bases counted), tankard (1 base), stirrup-vase (2).

From below black stratum

BRONZE

Small shapeless pieces.

STONE

Flint: blade (Fig. 287 No. 11), l. 0.036 m., w. 0.019 m., th. 0.006 m.; chips and flakes.
Obsidian: two flakes (e.g., Fig. 287 No. 9).
Quartz: two pieces (Fig. 287 Nos. 10, 12).

IVORY

Some very small fragments, possibly ivory.

POTTERY

Mycenaean sherds from light earth

Very little coarse ware; shapes noted: small pithos, large flat pan, cooking pot on three legs, basin. Great quantities of fine plain ware in shattered condition representing kylix (348 stems counted), bowl or cup (154 bases counted), tankard (1 base), spouted bowl, stirrup-vase, dipper, bowl and basin with pinched-out handles, jug or jar with narrow neck. Some 45 sherds bearing traces of painted decoration.

ROOM 43

The doorway from Room 38 into Room 43 was fitted with the usual central threshold and lateral jamb bases (Figs. 35, 460). The threshold block is 0.80 m. wide and extends 0.90 m. through the doorway. It is cracked down the middle and shows signs of wear and pitting on top. Its northwest end is almost entirely concealed by stucco that carries over from the floor of Room 38. The base on the northeast, which is also cracked, is 0.52 m. wide and 0.84 m. long to the point where it disappears under the floor of Room 38. The southwestern base is 0.48 m. wide and was at least 0.79 m. long, both ends being concealed under the pavement. In this block, 0.12 m. from the northwestern face of the door opening, is a rectangular cutting measuring 0.10 m. on a side, undoubtedly for the socket of a pivot.

At some time both jamb bases were partially covered and replaced by a thick coat of stucco. The socket for the pivot on the southwestern side seems still to have been used in the later period; and traces in the stucco on the northeastern side suggest that a pivot-socket existed here too, though only approximately opposite that on the southwest. Perhaps more than two phases are represented. The stucco conceals the rabbets, if there were any, in the jamb bases. The straight edges of the stucco replacements toward the wall mark the face of the door frame on each side, and indicate that the actual door-opening was 1.13 m. wide.

The room with the bath (43 on Key Plan), 6.34 m. long and 2.56 m. wide, is separated from Room 38 by a wall 0.85 m. thick, standing to a height of 1.20 m. (Fig. 36). It is badly damaged, but shows remains of six vertical chases, spaced 0.45 m., 0.40 m., 0.65 m., 0.65 m., and 0.75 m. apart. There is evidence for a horizontal beam at ca. 0.60 m. above the floor, possibly also for one near the level of the floor. Some plaster is preserved to a maximum height of 0.65 m. near the door, diminishing to a narrow strip, then rising again toward the north corner. Some parts of the smoothly finished surface are preserved showing a wavy band in blue-gray just above the floor but whether it was painted or caused by smoke and carbon is not certainly determinable.

The northeast wall, 0.85 m. thick, part of the exterior wall of the building, with its outer face of squared blocks (Figs. 37, 414), has been described as it appears from Court 42 (p. 182). The inner part of it, built of rubble, has a plaster face rising to a height of 0.40 m. A considerable extent of the finished surface is still in place, but damage by fire has made it impossible to see more than blue smears. A horizontal beam was almost surely laid at ca. 0.40 m. above the floor, corresponding to the one on the exterior, and two vertical chases were probably aligned with the V-shaped joints between the ashlar blocks.

The southeastern wall which separates the room from the Queen's Hall is 0.80 m. thick, including the plaster, and it stands to a height ranging from 1.05 m. near its southwestern end to 0.75 m. at the northeast (Fig. 37). Traces of at least seven vertical chases can be seen 0.74 m., 0.72 m., 0.67 m., 0.71 m., 0.65 m., and 0.68 m. apart. A horizontal groove for a beam at floor level or slightly above, and another at 0.76 m. above the floor are indicated. Some plaster is still in place here and there on the wall to a height of 0.70 m. The finished surface is preserved near the floor (Fig. 37), where it shows a bluish-gray wavy band like that on the opposite wall.

The southwest wall, 0.90 m. thick, stands to a height of 1.05 m. (Fig. 36). In its top evidence may be seen for five vertical chases, approximately 0.60 m. apart. The lower part of the wall is covered with plaster which conceals the position of the grooves for horizontal beams. The finished coat just above the floor shows traces of the irregular wavy blue-gray band noted on the northwest and southeast walls.

The stucco floor is very uneven, perhaps pushed up by olive roots below, and broken and pitted by fire on top. The surface is largely missing in the middle of the room, but along the walls it is better preserved, except for a curious sinking toward the northwest wall to the northeast of the doorway. The floor has a general slope downward toward the northeast, where, near the eastern corner, one if not two drain holes led out under the wall (Fig. 138) probably to the drain we have already seen in Court 42 (p. 184).

Against the southeast wall of the room a larnax was set in a large base made of clay (Fig. 37). The vertical end of the latter is 1.15 m. distant from the east corner of the room. The clay container is 1.78 m. long against the wall. It extends into the room to a width of 0.78 m.; the sides taper inward somewhat and the outer face, therefore, is only 1.47 m. long, the corners being neatly rounded. It is 0.43 m. to 0.45 m. high and is coated with smooth white stucco. In it was fitted the terracotta larnax of the "narrow-waisted" type with broad flat rim (Fig. 422).[58] The side toward the room has been bent over the top of the base in a broad curve (Fig. 139). This seems to have been done intentionally from the beginning, for the measurement on this side from the floor of the larnax to the rim is 0.515 m. as against 0.445 m. on the side toward the wall. The purpose of rolling the upper part of the side outward was presumably to make it easy for users to step in and out of the larnax and perhaps to sit on the rounded edge. Another measure with the same object was the placing of a step, 0.54 m. long, 0.40 m. wide, and 0.165 m. high, on the floor of the room against the northwest side of the clay base. The step too was coated with stucco on its top and sides.

The larnax, though made with its two sides of different heights, is in other respects of the ordinary type. It had handles at each end, and also one in the middle of the outer long side, which probably has a mate on the side toward the wall. This latter item could not be certainly ascertained without causing irreparable damage. When uncovered, the larnax, though almost complete, was found cracked and broken at the ends and along the outer edge. The loose pieces, which were removed for safe-keeping, revealed not only the handles but the painted decoration of the exterior. The interior of the larnax also bears painted decoration in two broad zones, bordered and separated by horizontal lines (Fig. 140). Each zone encloses a band of simple

[58] Total length, including rim, from end to end 1.78 m.; width from front to back, near end 0.75 m., at middle 0.69 m.; width of flat rim 0.045 m.; length of bottom inside 0.94 m.; minimum width of bottom inside 0.44 m.; depth of larnax from its floor to rim: 0.445 m. at middle, near ends ca. 0.50 m.

spirals connected by tangents. The spaces above and below the latter were filled with somewhat irregular chevron-like rows of dots. In the lower zone at the back only faint traces of the pattern are now recognizable, but elsewhere it is well preserved. At each end below the lower zone, are many parallel horizontal lines. All this decoration is done in white paint on a darker ground, and the rim too bears transverse dashes close together in the same medium.

The inside of the larnax shows some discoloration, caused by fire. Originally the vessel was dark red; at the time of the catastrophe it was more than half filled with debris which somehow protected what it covered from excessive heat; but the upper part, not so shielded, must have been in contact with burning wood and carbonized matter and was blackened. The outer part of the side and the rim were also darkened.

In the deposit found in the larnax were crushed remains of a shallow bowl with pinched-out handles, a ladle, two kylikes, and in fragments on the floor itself, a complete kylix (Fig. 139). The latter may have served to pour water over the last person to take a bath. A small dipper was recovered lying on the floor against the western corner of the stucco step.

The larnax is too short to allow a person of any size to stretch out at length; it was rather a *sitz-bad* in which the bather sat while water was poured over him by an attendant. Such was no doubt the bath in which Telemachos was scrubbed and rubbed down by Polykaste as recounted in the *Odyssey*.

Farther to the southwestward, 1.86 m. from the base of the larnax, is a much higher stand, also built of clay and coated with stucco on its sides and top (Fig. 37). It was fitted into the south corner of the room, 1.505 m. long from northeast to southwest and 0.73 m. wide. The stand rises to a height ranging from 0.85 m. to 0.87 m. above the floor. In it were set, packed around with stones, two large jars, only the massive rims of which projected above the top of the stand (Fig. 36). The rims were very badly damaged in the fire; both are fused and bubbly from the effects of the heat. Little more than a quarter of the northeastern one is preserved, about three fourths of that on the southwest. They were exposed immediately under the surface soil and it is likely that the plow carried off the missing parts. The jars had a diameter of ca. 0.60 m., a depth of ca. 0.75 m., and flattish bottoms, 0.21 m. and 0.24 m. wide respectively, all measurements taken on the inside.

The southwestern jar was decorated with painted patterns which were visible through a break in the stuccoed top of the stand. Not enough was seen to disclose the whole design, but it seemed to be a combination of chevrons and spirals or circles. On the handle are transverse parallel lines. All this decoration was executed in creamy white against the red background of the jar.

The stuccoed exterior faces of the stand itself were likewise painted in at least one of its phases of use. Horizontal red bands can be recognized, but what, if anything, was between them has not survived. The last coat of stucco shows near the floor a wavy gray-blue band similar to that seen on the walls, and on the clay base of the larnax, whether made by paint or by smoke and carbon is uncertain.

Both the larnax in its base and the stand were installed after the wall behind them had been coated with plaster.

The two jars were found filled with debris. The southwestern jar contained many fragments of plaster obviously fallen from above. At the bottom lay seven small, low-stemmed, one-handled kylikes, almost all intact. At its bottom, the other pithos likewise contained seven small kylikes of the same type, two intact, the others broken but complete, and also two somewhat larger kylikes and three teacups. These pots were all badly burned, warped, and incrusted with lime. Whether the jars were used to hold water or oil cannot be certainly determined; perhaps one was for oil and the other for water.

Near the southwestern corner of the room was found the greater part of a large pithoid jar with painted decoration, the rim and neck of which lay nearby in the doorway. Here and there on the floor were also noted heaps of sherds from which it was possible to put together two krater-bowls, one with painted decoration, and a large plain jug. In all it was possible to restore 28 pots from Room 43 (Fig. 331).

The room was filled with burned debris much of which was loose and soft, not fused and hard. It included quantities of fragments of flooring and of plaster of diverse kinds. Many of the latter bore painted decoration belonging to at least two different scenes. Some pieces represent lions and griffins at life size; others, at a small scale, belong to a hunting scene with men and dogs; still other fragments cannot be certainly associated with either of the foregoing compositions. Most of this painted plaster lay fairly high above the floor, appearing even in the surface earth and just below. Nothing now left on the walls in the bathroom suggests that wall paintings of this kind adorned that room. It is likely therefore that the plaster fell both from Room 46 (lions and griffins) and from an apartment in the upper story (hunting scene), but specific evidence is wanting to fix its original position.

O B J E C T S   F O U N D

SILVER
Small fragment.

BRONZE
A few shapeless bits.

STONE
Flint: three flakes (e.g., Fig. 288 No. 2).
Quartz: opaque fragment, incised line on each side (Fig. 288 No. 1).

POTTERY
From Pithos 1
Kylix (Shape 27, p. 366)
  Nos. 524-530.

From Pithos 2
Cup (Shape 12, p. 360)
  Nos. 566, 567.
Kylix (Shape 27, p. 366)
  Nos. 531, 532, 536-539, 564.

Kylix (Shape 29c, p. 369)
  Nos. 562, 563.

From bath
Bowl (Shape 4, p. 356)
  No. 587.
Kylix (Shape 29c, p. 369)
  No. 588 (Fig. 361).
Ladle or scoop (Shape 66, p. 411)
  No. 589 (Fig. 395).

From floor or near floor of room
Dipper (Shape 22, p. 364)
  No. 590 (Figs. 357, 358), found next to step
  of bath.
Kylix (Shape 29c, p. 369)
  Nos. 591, 592.
Jug (Shape 37, p. 377)
  No. 608 (Figs. 367, 368).

Jar (Shape 54a, p. 390)
  No. 612) Figs. 379, 380 rim), decorated.
Krater-bowl (Shape 60, p. 397)
  Nos. 593 and 594 (Figs. 385, 386), both
  decorated.

Shattered material that could not be put together comprises: in coarse ware, fragments of pithoi, neck of jar or jug. Shapes recognized in fine ware: kylix (4 stems), cup and bowl (9 flat bases), conical cup, bowl with pinched-out handles, scoop with round grip-handle. The usual complement of sherds bearing decoration; patterns distinguished in addition to allover coating: horizontal bands, spiraliform and ripple motives, and zigzags.

NORTHEAST STOA 44

The Northeast Corridor comes to its end at the southeast in a doorway that opened into the Northeast Stoa (Figs. 124, 461). It seems to have had no closeable door, though the doorway has the usual threshold block and lateral bases for the door casing (Fig. 125). The central block is 0.96 m. long and 0.62 m. broad from one face of the opening to the other. No cutting of any kind could be observed in the threshold block nor in the bases on either side. The northeastern base is 0.62 m. long through the doorway and 0.54 m. wide. A setting line, 0.11 m. to 0.12 m. from the joint with the threshold block, probably marks the edge of the wooden casing on the northeastern side. The block on the southwest has the same length through the opening and is 0.36 m. wide to its joint with the base of the anta of the Portico. The lateral block may have been merely an extension of the threshold rather than a base supporting the jamb; for the latter was apparently recessed in a countersinking, 0.155 m. deep, into the northeastern face of the anta, evidence for which is preserved in the anta base. Whether the jamb fitted wholly into the slot or extended out over the lateral base is not quite certain. In any event the doorway must have been closed by a hanging if it was closed at all.

The Northeast Stoa (44 on Key Plan), with its facade of two columns opening southwestward on the Court in front of the Portico (Part 2, Frontispiece and Fig. 44), is 6.29 m. long beside the northeastern wall. It has an average width or depth of 3.325 m. from that wall to the outer edge of the stucco ring surrounding the foot of the columns.[59]

[59] Northeast wall to outer edge of northwest ring 3.29 m.; northeast wall to outer edge of southeast ring 3.36 m.

On the northwest it is bounded by the doorway from Corridor 35 and a partition wall between it and Corridor 37 (Fig. 9). The wall, badly damaged by fire and consisting in part of *migma*, has been described with its two vertical chases on page 169. On the side toward the Stoa grooves for horizontal beams are indicated at 0.30 m. and 0.90 m. above the floor (Fig. 124). Some remains of plaster survive along the bottom of the wall and in the north corner. The outer surface is lacking and no traces of painted decoration have been recognized.

The northeastern wall, forming the back of the Stoa and separating it from Rooms 38 and 43 (pp. 170, 187), is 0.90 m. thick and stands to an almost uniform height of 1 m. (Fig. 142). Eight vertical chases running through the wall may be recognized, spaced at an average distance apart of just under 0.60 m. The southeasternmost chase, which it was possible to examine, continues down to a depth of 0.15 m. below the floor, where a flat stone was laid to support the beam. Grooves for horizontal timbers appear at 0.10 m. and 0.60 m. above the floor. Remnants of plaster are preserved along the foot of the wall with a few patches rising to ca. 0.45 m. Much of it is rough, but near the floor the smooth finished coat *in situ* bears some scanty traces of a painted blue-gray wavy band, unless it is merely discoloration from fire. The plaster was applied in several successive layers: first a coating of mud, then a second application of the same mixed with straw, then a plaster of lime and sand, and finally a fine finish that bore the painted decoration.

On the southeast the Stoa was flanked by two doorways, side by side, one opening into Corridor 45 that gave access to the Queen's Hall, the other leading to a stairway that ascended southeastward perhaps to an upper story of the tower-like structure alongside the Propylon (Fig. 141).

In the southwestern façade of the Stoa the stone bases of two wooden columns still remain in place in what seems to be a rather awkward position. Approximately 2.28 m. apart, center to center, they are aligned to the northwest and to the southeast not with the usual antae but with door openings which would seem to offer dubious means of lateral support. The columns were set on flat stone bases the size and shape of which cannot be measured because of the surviving stucco ring, but on each stone there was a slightly raised circular standing place for the column. The decorative stucco ring laid around the foot of each column is fairly well preserved on both bases. The one on the southeast still retains its ring, 0.06 m. to 0.07 m. high, 0.07 m. to 0.08 m. broad on top, and sloping outward toward the floor (Fig. 141). It is made of at least four or five successive layers of stucco, one above the other. The inner face of the ring, which was laid up against the foot of the wooden column, bears clear impressions of the fluting of the latter. The impressions are preserved more than three fourths of the way around the circle and calculations indicate that the total number of flutes was 60. The diameter of this column, as indicated by the circle on the stone and by the flutings, was 0.41 m. to 0.42 m. Traces of red color appear on two of the earlier coats, where the ring is broken away, but the uppermost layer has lost its finished surface and no trace of color now survives.

The northwestern base is similar to the other in most respects, but the stucco ring has suffered greater damage, having been in part dislodged by the root of an olive tree, as a result of which it has to some extent lost its circular shape. Precise measurements are not now possible, but the diameter seems to have been 0.40 m. to 0.41 m. Here too at least four layers of stucco can be counted, and several of them bear remains of paint. The greater part of the ring now stands to a height of 0.06 m. above the base. The ring is 0.07 m. to 0.08 m. wide on top, and on the outside its face slopes outward toward the floor. Impressions of the flutings are still to be seen through perhaps half of a circle, and the original number of flutes was calculated to be 60, as in the other column.

Large pieces of wood and carbonized wood, probably remains of beams, were found lying 0.20 m. to 0.60 m. above the floor in the burned debris above and near the southeastern column base. One piece, no longer continuously preserved, but estimated to have been at least 0.75 m. long, lay from northeast to southwest between the base and the southeast anta. Beyond and almost at right angles to the first timber, another, calculated to have been ca. 1.90 m. long, extended roughly from southeast to northwest. Remains of several other beams were represented by chunks of carbonized matter, one crossing over the top of the second piece mentioned above and two others farther to the northeast. All of these pieces seem to have been squared, one measuring some 0.13 m. or 0.14 m. on a side, another chunk 0.27 m. by 0.35 m. Lying across the northwest column base was another chunk of wood and carbonized matter, 0.13 m. thick, 0.26 m. wide, running from southeast to northwest; though not continuous, the wood and ash together were at least 0.70 m. long.

Most of these pieces must be remnants of the beams that supported the balcony above the Stoa. An exact reconstruction is of course impossible, but it may be conjectured that two heavy timbers resting on the rear wall of the Stoa, extended out to and perhaps nearly a meter beyond the columns; at their outer extremity they could have supported transverse beams laid from southeast to northwest, terminating at each end on an anta. Between the outer beams and the rear wall, parallel intermediate beams might have rested above the northeast door jamb on the northwest and on the wall between the stairway and the corridor on the southeast. On this framework, we may suppose, were laid, side by side and close together, smaller timbers not squared but left in the round, on which the floor itself was based. Evidence for the use of such unshaped logs was discovered in some fragments of fallen plaster: several pieces, more or less triangular in shape, concave on two sides, must have fitted between two contiguous timbers of this kind. What the floor was made of is not certain. It may have been of wood or it may have been of clay and stucco. Along the front of it, to prevent accidents, there was, no doubt, a substantial balustrade or railing. Those who sat on the balcony doubtless enjoyed a fine view of the interesting scenes that must have taken place from time to time in the Court.

The floor of the Stoa was paved with the usual stucco, but it had become calcined in the intense heat of the fire and had turned soft and was difficult to recognize. In some places, where protected by fallen stones and debris, it is still hard and well preserved. Near the back wall it is in good condition and it looks as if it once bore painted decoration. In front of the anta of the Portico remains of red and blue paint were seen.

A distinct line of division between the floor of the Stoa and that of the Court defines the outer edge of the porch and its roof—ca. 1 m. to the southwest of the axis of the two columns (Fig. 141). The junction of the two pavements is aligned with the southwestern face of the southeast anta; it ends at the northwest against the base of the great anta of the Portico. The floor of the Court seems to be much better preserved than that of the Stoa, where the many beams, timbers, and the woodwork provided much fuel for the destructive fire.

In three or four places on the floor remains of pots, which had been converted by the heat of the fire into shapeless, glassy, bluish, twisted lumps, have been left as they were found (Fig. 141).

The whole area of the Stoa was filled with burned debris appearing directly beneath the plowed earth and continuing to the floor. Calcined stones and disintegrated brick had become fused into a hard mass in the southeastern part of the Stoa. In the northwestern quarter disintegrated red brick and soft, loose, powdery calcined matter in a deep accumulation overlay many stones that had fallen first to the floor. High up in the deposit filling the doorway that leads to Corridor 35 were recovered several fragments of poros blocks, 0.15 m. high. They must surely be parts of steps which had fallen from above; their original position is not known. The steps may possibly have provided access to the balcony above the Stoa from the living quarters in the upper story.

At the other end of the Stoa between the southeastern anta and the column base, just under the modern surface were uncovered two fairly large squared blocks; one of poros still retained plaster on two faces, one of which showed traces of decoration executed in diagonal lines in brownish-black paint. These stones may have come from the upper part of the anta.

In the rear part of the Stoa, beginning 1.50 m. out from the wall in a strip 1.10 m. wide, a large accumulation of pieces of stucco flooring was encountered. The fragments, many of which stood on edge, extended down to a depth of 0.60 m. below the surface of the ground. The pieces, varying in thickness from 0.02 m. to 0.06 m., were made of hard stucco containing bits of stone. The surface, where preserved, blue-gray in color, is firm and smooth with a waxy feeling. These pieces are surely from the pavement of the balcony. Somewhat nearer the wall were chunks of painted plaster: among the motives recognized by Miss Lang are wood-graining, beam-ends, net- and ripple-patterns, diagonal waves, band of argonauts, two kinds of drapery, lion's mane. The survey suggests that figured scenes may have filled in the space between the dado and frieze of beam-ends on the back of the Stoa.

OBJECTS FOUND

GOLD

Small piece of foil (Fig. 288 No. 3), found in east corner ca. 0.30 m. above floor.

SILVER

Nine fragments (e.g., Fig. 288 No. 4); two, retaining setting-place for gold head (Fig. 288 Nos. 5, 6), must belong to the inlaid cup, remnants of which were found scattered across the Propylon and into Ramp 59.

BRONZE

Thin twisted fragment with outturned edge, l. 0.038 m., w. 0.02 m., may have come from a small vessel.

Many shapeless bits, chunks, fragments, and pieces, scattered from surface to floor throughout the deposit (e.g., Fig. 288 Nos. 7-13).

STONE

Obsidian: small blade (Fig. 288 No. 14), l. 0.026 m., w. 0.009 m., th. 0.002 m.; two flakes (e.g., Fig. 288 Nos. 15, 16).

Flint: many chips.

Steatite: small flat button (Fig. 288 No. 17), h. 0.003 m., d. 0.015 m., found 0.70 m. above floor.

Quartz: piece of rock crystal pointed at one end, broken at other. Discolored and damaged by fire (Fig. 282 No. 5), l. 0.065 m., th. 0.04 m., w. of facets varying from 0.017 m. to 0.021 m. Found against northeast wall.

IVORY

Burned bits.

PASTE

Fragments of beads and miscellaneous pieces (e.g., Fig. 288 Nos. 18-21).

CLAY

Tablet: No. 1213, fragment from plowed earth above northwestern wall of the Stoa. Probably belongs with tablets from Room 38. Joins No. 343 found in 1939 in Trench VI in what later proved to be just inside Gateway 41 near its southeast wall, i.e., next to Room 38 (*OOT*, 11, 39, pls. II-III).

POTTERY

At the time of the fire several pots stood on the floor and were partially melted and vitrified. Some of them bore painted decoration and one at least was a small stirrup-vase. Many sherds found in the lower part of the deposit near the floor had suffered similar damage and may have come from pots kept in the Stoa or on the balcony above it. Among the sherds of coarse ware, shapes identified were: small pithoi, cooking pots of various sizes and kinds mostly of good hard fabric, tripod-vessels with squarish flattened legs (6 legs). In finer plain ware shapes include: kylix (18 stems), bowl with pinched-out handles, small conical cup, dipper with high loop-handle, possibly small jar with raised base. Two sherds have incised and many have painted decoration.

DOUBLE DOORWAY

At the southeastern end of the Stoa is the double doorway mentioned above (p. 191 and Figs. 125, 462, 468). It was certainly constructed all at the same time and it occupies the space between what we have called the southeast anta and the rear wall of the Stoa (Fig. 141). The two doorways are separated by a wall, 0.80 m. thick, which extends southeastward. A wooden door frame was set against its northwestern end, overlapping the core of the wall. This served as the left jamb of the doorway on the southwest and the right jamb of the one on the northeast. A single block, 1.045 m. long and 0.64 m. deep, served as the base for this double casing. In the southwestern edge of the block, 0.19 m. from its northwestern face, in a very shallow rabbet, is a rectangular hole, 0.11 m. by 0.09 m. and 0.05 m. deep.

Across the middle of the southwestern opening runs the threshold block, 0.89 m. long and 0.64 m. wide, considerably pitted on top, presumably by fire. Its surface is 0.01 m. to 0.02 m. higher than that of the floor of the Stoa. Between it and the anta toward the southwest is a narrow base for the right-hand jamb of the doorway, 0.21 m. to 0.23 m. wide. On the side toward the threshold this too has a rectangular cutting 0.07 m. wide, 0.135 m. long, and 0.06 m. deep. The two cuttings were probably the setting places for pivots, and the actual door-opening was 1.05 m. wide. The frame on the southwest side was fitted into a shallow countersinking, 0.56 m. wide, in the northeastern face of the anta.

The doorway on the northeast (Fig. 462) is almost an exact twin of the one just described. The threshold block is 0.91 m. long and 0.64 m. wide. The northeast edge of the jamb base, which this doorway shares with its neighbor, has been badly damaged by fire, but it looks as if it once had a pivot cutting to match that on the southwestern side. A corresponding cutting, 0.08 m. wide by 0.11 m. long, and 0.06 m. deep, overlaps the threshold block and the lateral base of the doorcasing on the northeast of the door-opening. The base itself varies from 0.21 m. to 0.23 m. in width and is 0.61 m. long. The threshold block is set with its surface 0.04 m. to 0.08 m. below the tops of the jamb bases, and it is slightly lower than the floor of the Stoa. The width of the door-opening, as calculated from the pivot holes, is 1.05 m. Each of the twin doors seems to have consisted of two leaves, unless the cutting on one side served for a locking bar instead of a pivot.

SOUTHEAST CORRIDOR, SECTION 45

Passing through the northeast doorway one enters another longish corridor (11.45 m.) extending southeastward (Fig. 141), which was divided by two doorways into three sections (Fig. 148). The first (45 on Key Plan), 4.67 m. long and 1.31 m. wide, is bordered on the southwest by the wall which separated the two doorways described above. This wall, 0.80 m. thick, stands to a height ranging from 0.90 m. to 1.25 m. near its northwest end. In this stretch five chases mark the position of vertical timbers, spaced at intervals of 0.70 m., 0.79 m., 0.74 m., and 0.80 m. Indications of a groove for a horizontal beam are recognizable at ca. 0.50 m. above the floor, and another at 1.10 m. The surface of the wall is largely covered with coarse plaster, but no remains of the finished coat have survived in place.

On its northeastern side Corridor 45 is bordered by a wall, 1.95 m. long, and by a broad doorway that led into Room 46 (Fig. 143). The wall, 0.88 m. thick and preserved to a height of 1.28 m., shows evidence of three chases for vertical timbers at intervals of ca. 0.70 m. There are also clear indications of horizontal grooves at 0.16 m. and 0.76 m. above the floor. The wall is coated with rough backing plaster but no remains of the surface coat are now to be seen.

The floor of the corridor, made of stucco, was badly damaged by fire and its surface had become soft and powdery. Where it was least injured, along the walls, it was 0.055 m. thick. The original thickness may have been considerably more. No trace of an earlier floor was seen.

On the floor opposite the doorway into the Queen's Hall lay the remains of a small stirrup-vase. Much of it, melted in the heat of the fire, had run over the stucco pavement, but part of it managed to retain its shape along with some traces of its decoration of painted bands.

Corridor 45 was found filled with the usual debris. Near the surface was a great mass of stones including large fragments of blocks of poros, two just inside the door from the Stoa, three others farther along the passage, and one on top of the wall toward the northeast. Under the poros blocks was a stratum of dissolved crude brick, then gray earth, and finally lying directly on the floor a thick deposit of lime.

The main root of a large olive tree had penetrated deep into the hard fill and, dividing into two branches, had made its way into the next section of the corridor as well as through the doorway into Room 46 to the northeast.

The debris contained many fragments of plaster bearing painted decoration. Miss Lang suggests that they come from a frieze imitating beam-ends and other associated pieces show wood-graining and knotholes.

O B J E C T S   F O U N D

GOLD

Three very small bits of foil (Fig. 291 Nos. 1-3).

BRONZE

A few shapeless pieces (e.g., Fig. 291 Nos. 4-6).

PETRIFIED BONE

Small astragal and fragment of a second.

POTTERY

Stirrup-vase, heavily incrusted with lime, warped and fused beyond restoration;

traces of horizontal bands. Found on floor opposite doorway into Room 46.

Sherds scarce and for the most part nondescript, also covered with lime, several light in weight, bubbly and fused. Shapes represented: kylix, bowl with pinched-out handles, small handleless cup, dipper with high loop-handle. Shapes in coarse ware, except for a few fragments of pithoi, unrecognizable. A few small pieces bear painted decoration; motives noted, curving lines and rippling.

HALL 46

The doorway leading into the Queen's Hall is 2.70 m. wide (Figs. 143, 463). The threshold is formed by one great block, 1.16 m. long and 0.90 m. wide, corresponding to the depth of the opening (Fig. 144). It is cracked across the middle, worn on top and damaged by fire, and partly covered with stucco overlapping it from the corridor and from the room. On the northwest it is flanked by a block, 0.80 m. wide, also running through the opening. On the southwest is a similar lateral block of approximately the same length and 0.83 m. wide. A small notch, ca. 0.14 m. deep, was cut into the south corner of the block; perhaps for the fitting of a threshold at right angles across the corridor. Apart from this, none of the three blocks forming the floor of the doorway shows signs of a cutting for a pivot or any other fixture. It therefore seems certain that there was no actual swinging door, but perhaps the opening could be closed by hangings. How much space was taken up by the door frame is largely a subject for conjecture, but evidence of charred and burned matter lying on the lateral bases suggests that the casing projected some 0.50 m. from the outer edge of the blocks, leaving a strip on each side to supplement the central threshold. This conclusion is supported to some extent by the line of the flooring on the inside of the doorway.

The Queen's Hall (46 on Key Plan) is 6.50 m. long from southwest to northeast and 6.23 m. wide (Fig. 144). It is one of the larger apartments in the central building. The southwestern wall, through an opening in which one enters from the corridor, is 0.88 m. thick. The doorway is not centered in this side of the room, but lies considerably to the southeast of the axis (Fig. 145). The section of the wall to the northwest of the doorway, 2.45 m. long, stands to a height of 1.28 m. In it three vertical chases are recognizable at intervals of ca. 0.60 m. A groove for a horizontal beam is indicated at 0.20 m. above the floor, with traces of another at ca. 0.50 m. Up to the lower groove the plaster cn the wall is fairly well preserved and somewhat higher a piece of the finished surface coat, 0.50 m. long, retains vestiges of its painted decoration (Fig. 146). It might represent part of the body of an irregularly spotted animal with shaggy hair or, more probably as Miss Lang thinks, a dado pattern of blobs, perhaps imitating hide. This piece, if it is *in situ*, as it seems to be, may belong to a coating of plaster earlier than that of the final phase.

The southeastern section of the same wall is badly swollen and tilted outward on both faces. Standing to a height of 1.22 m., it is only 1.10 m. long from the jamb base to the corner of the room. One vertical chase is recognizable as well as a horizontal groove, 0.20 m. above the floor. The position of the beam next above is concealed by the backing plaster, which is preserved almost to the top of the wall. Below the horizontal groove a finished coat is still *in situ*.

The southeast wall, 0.94 m. thick, separates the Queen's Room from Corridor 48 (Fig. 144). It rises at the south corner to a height of 1.10 m. above the floor and slopes down to 0.60 m. at the northeasterly end where it is interrupted by a doorway. The wall has suffered great damage from the fire, its stones being for the most part badly calcined, while its face toward the room has crumbled away. Five vertical chases for upright beams are distinguishable, spaced at intervals averaging nearly 0.70 m. A groove for a horizontal beam is marked 0.20 m. above the floor, with probable traces of another at slightly more than 0.40 m. All the plaster remaining on the wall is near the bottom, below the groove at 0.40 m.

On the northeastern side the room is bounded by a section of the exterior wall of the building. The wall is 0.88 m. thick, with an outer facing of squared blocks and an inner core and backing of rubble (Figs. 40, 415). A doorway was cut through its southeastern end at the time Court 47 was enclosed. The core of the wall, 0.33 m. thick, reduced largely to lime and calcined stone by the fire, stands to a height of nearly 0.85 m. but the inner face is nowhere preserved higher than 0.35 m. Indications of five vertical chases are spaced ca. 0.75 m. apart. The horizontal beam ran along the wall at 0.30 m. above the floor. It may have formed a continuous wainscoting to a height of 0.45 m. or more. Below the groove some plaster is preserved through the greater part of the length of the wall, though in a badly damaged and cracked condition. At least three layers can be differentiated. The two outermost still bear some remains of their painted decoration (Fig. 147); the patterns appear to be diagonal, straight or wavy lines or bands, recalling the treatment of the dado in other parts of the palace.

To the northwest the Queen's Hall is separated from the bathroom by a wall, 0.80 m. thick, which has a maximum height of 1.10 m. at the southwest end and diminishes to 0.60 m. at the other end (Fig. 148). This wall too is in a bad state of disrepair and has lost much of its southeastern face. Seven vertical chases have left their marks in the wall, the spacing averaging not far from 0.70 m. A horizontal groove is visible at 0.25 m. above the floor, and this wall too looks as if it had borne wainscoting or paneling to a height of at least 0.50 m. On the lower part of the wall, below the horizontal beam, remains of at least two coats of plaster appear. A very small piece of the outer coat shows a linear pattern of fine black curving lines and some patches of red. The painted decoration of the earlier coat, which is also represented only by scanty bits, seems to consist of horizontal bands in black and red. Higher on the wall are other remains of plaster, but the surface is missing with all traces of decoration.

When the room was excavated it was found filled almost to the surface of the ground with masses of burned debris. On the northeast side lay the wreckage of the inner rubble part of the exterior wall along with fragments of squared blocks, all covered by a slope of dissolved red burned crude brick. The southwest area was banked up with quantities of fallen plaster and pavement mixed with disintegrated brick. Along the walls were heaps of calcined stones. Patches of blackened earth throughout the deposit probably came from burned wood. The room was a large one and the numerous substantial joists required to hold up the ceiling and the roof certainly provided material for a devastating fire. Even the floor was covered with more than the usual black accumulation which had discolored everything it touched. It is not impossible that olive oil from the magazine in the upper story that fell for the most part into the lobby and the bathroom had somehow flowed down over the floor of the Queen's Hall too.

Almost exactly centered in the middle of the hall is a raised circular hearth, presumably made of clay coated with stucco (Fig. 144). Though smaller, it is very much like the hearth in the Throne Room both in its form and in its decoration. It has an over-all diameter of 1.88 m., rising 0.07 m. to a narrow step, 0.06 m. wide, then rising 0.025 m. higher to a flat border, 0.16 m. wide. Within the border, slightly sunk and 1.38 m. in diameter, is the place for the actual fire and this too was paved with stucco. About 0.03 m. from its outer perimeter it is surrounded by a red band (0.015 m. wide). Four successive coats of stucco can be recognized on the border and outer step, and each one bore painted decoration (Fig. 149). The earliest is visible only on the southwestern side in two small areas of the border, where the second and subsequent coats are broken. The paint is well preserved in one of these holes, disclosing a tiny bit of red spiral and blue filling ornament. Here too the edge of the rim is preserved, indicating that the diameter of the hearth was some 0.04 m. smaller than in the second period. No part of the earliest vertical face can now be seen.

In the succeeding second phase the border, which is exposed to view for more than a third of the circuit, was decorated with running spirals in red outline, the central dots and the filling ornament red in some places, blue in others. This difference in color may have been caused by the effects of the fire. The spiral pattern, which is of the "in and out" type, is framed within two red bands. On the narrow step and its riser is repeated a flame-like motive, bending toward the right, similar to that on the third coat of the hearth in the Throne Room but broader and more

[199]

squat. A narrow border in red runs along the top of the riser and the flames are likewise done in red.

The third coat in the sequence, which is partly exposed for a third of the circuit, is almost identical with the second in its decoration, both on the border and the riser (nothing is visible on the narrow step), except that the flame motives seem to have been more distinctly outlined.

The fourth and final coat, though preserved around almost half the circumference, is in a wretched state, its surface having been worn or eaten away in the fire. No trace of its decoration is now to be seen except for the red stripe around the depressed area mentioned above.

Concentrated mainly over the hearth and extending beyond it to the northeast with scattered pieces spread even more widely, were found the fragments of two cylindrical chimney pipes of terracotta (Figs. 271 Nos. 7, 8; 272 Nos. 8, 9). One (No. 725) is almost completely preserved, 0.77 m. to 0.79 m. high, with a lower diameter of 0.507 m., and, as restored, 0.48 m. at the top. Its wall ranges from 0.015 m. to 0.02 m. in thickness, and its lower edge is 0.028 m. thick. The second pipe (No. 726), though not so well preserved, retains its full height of 0.713 m., with a lower diameter of 0.5725 m.; and enough of the upper end survives to indicate a diameter of 0.4532 m. The larger pipe could have been fitted over one end of the other, as was verified by an actual test when one pipe was found to fit neatly into the end of the other, and the chimney going through the roof may thus have consisted of two sections. Exactly how the pipes were held in place is not clear, but it is likely that they were supported through the thick roof in a packing of clay.

A good many remains of shaped stucco were found scattered about in the debris that filled the room. They had unquestionably fallen from an upper story. These pieces, with profiled edge resembling that of the hearth, are not curved, but straight, and several joining fragments make up an incomplete section 0.97 m. long. There is at least one right-angled corner. What we have is apparently part of a low raised coping, or border, which framed a rectangular opening in the floor above Room 46. The coping had a vertical riser, a flat horizontal step or top, and a small molding in relief on the side toward the opening. The riser, 0.105 m. high, in some phases was decorated with a flame pattern in red against a blue ground and blue dot-rosettes in the spaces between the flames. The top, or step, 0.16 m. to 0.17 m. wide, bore—in the same phases—a running spiral in red and black on a bluish ground. Some of these pieces retain three successive coats of plaster, each clearly bearing the same or similar decorative patterns. Several fragments which seem to be plain may belong to an undecorated section or phase.

The reconstruction worked out by Miss Lang and Mr. de Jong (Fig. 423) presents a good idea of how the border may have looked. The size of the open area or shaft has not been determined; it may have been relatively small, or a broad light-well, surrounded on its four sides by a narrow walk, or a balcony, of unknown width, somewhat like that of the Throne Room. Whether the decorated stucco border supported a railing of some kind is uncertain: no evidence has been recognized. The drawing illustrating the second phase, as concluded by Mr. de Jong, gives two views of the border, the lower one as seen from the balcony side, the upper one as it looked from the shaft.

It seems clear, in any event, that there was a light well or a shaft directly over the hearth, and presumably a clerestory rising still higher and probably tapering toward the apex at which was no doubt fixed the chimney pipe that carried off the smoke from the hearth.

Along with the fragments of the chimney and of the stucco base were found many pieces of a very large, thick-walled, flat-bottomed basin, with flaring sides and two handles (Fig. 333). When they were put together it was seen that roughly opposite each other were two large gaps in the rim and side of the vessel. This pot had evidently been used as a cover, somehow fixed in position over the top of the chimney protecting it from rain, while still allowing smoke to escape through the lateral openings. Since remains of only a single cover were brought to light, it is fair to conclude that there was only a single chimney made up of the two terracotta pipes, one fitted into the other.

The floor of the hall was made of stucco. The surface has been destroyed almost everywhere by fire and only small patches are left to give an idea of the original smooth finish, the largest just inside and to the left of the doorway opening into the court (Fig. 144). Even these remnants are black, badly discolored by fire, and no decoration can be seen.

Seven groups of potsherds were found on the floor along the southeastern, southwestern, and northwestern walls and to the northeast of the hearth. All were crushed and badly burned. From this material were put together (Fig. 332) two amphoras, one decorated, the other not; two jugs, one plain, the other decorated with bands; a two-handled jar with horizontal bands; a krater-bowl; a plain krater, and a stirrup-vase. The style of the krater-bowl suggests that it is one of the latest pots found in the palace.

Some 0.30 m. from the southeast wall and nearly 2 m. from the southwestern wall an impression in the floor forms a quadrant of a circle, with a radius of ca. 0.45 m. (Fig. 144). The purpose of this cutting is uncertain; perhaps it indicates the position of a piece of furniture. A small slab of bluish stone lay nearby to the northwest. To the northeastward, almost parallel with and 0.35 m. to 0.38 m. distant from the southeast wall, are traces of another line scratched in the floor. It seems to have had a length of ca. 1.70 m. Whether it is accidental or had a meaning is not clear, but it might mark the edge of a bench along the wall.

In general it may be said that the painted decoration on the hearth, though in a sadly injured state, gives a suggestion of delicacy in execution which has had some influence on our conjecture that this was the Queen's Hall.

The character of the frescoes that decorated the walls, however, appears to reflect a bold masculine spirit and one might wonder if this were not the room assigned to a huntsman son. At any rate numerous fragments found scattered about along the southeastern, southwestern, northwestern and northeastern walls, through the middle of the room, and also in layers on the floor, seem to come from representations, on a fairly large scale, of griffins and lions. Exactly where these compositions were placed is problematical, but they were presumably high up on the wall, above the dado course.

The combination of griffins and lions is a much favored motive in this palace and indeed it may have been the special badge or coat of arms associated with the royal family established here. As such it would not be out of place even in the Queen's Hall and, as we shall see, there are other reasons for thinking that this corner of the palace was the especial apartment of the queen.

O B J E C T S   F O U N D

GOLD LEAF

Small fragment (Fig. 291 No. 7), found near floor.
Two little pieces (Fig. 291 Nos. 8, 9), pressed up against bottom of southwest wall.

SILVER

One nondescript fragment.

BRONZE

Shapeless bits and several large pieces (e.g., Fig. 291 Nos. 13-15).

STONE

Amethyst: three small, well-cut spherical beads (Fig. 291 Nos. 10-12), d. 0.007 m., 0.008 m. and 0.0085 m.; found 0.85 m. above floor.
Obsidian: small blade, l. 0.023 m., w. 0.01 m., th. 0.003 m., and several flakes.
Flint: small barbed arrowhead, l. 0.018 m., w. across barbs 0.012 m.
Quartz: one piece.

IVORY

Genius: small figure in gray polished, finely carved ivory (NM. 7840, Fig. 284 No. 4), h. 0.024 m., w. 0.0095 m., th. 0.003 m. Perhaps it served as an inlay, since the back is flat, or it may have been fastened onto a background. It represents a lion-headed genius standing upright on his hind legs, holding something now missing, probably a ewer. Strikingly similar to the genii represented on the huge gold ring from the Tiryns hoard and discussed fully by Sir Arthur Evans (*PM* IV, 452ff., particularly figs. 385, 387). Found in plowed earth over north corner of Hall 46.

POTTERY

Jug (Shape 37, p. 377)
Nos. 676 (Fig. 367), decorated; 1139.
Amphora (Shape 45, p. 381)
Nos. 675 (Fig. 371); 1138 (Fig. 371), decorated.
Jar (Shape 49, p. 385)
No. 1141 (Fig. 373), decorated.

Krater-bowl (Shape 60, p. 397)
  No. 677 (Figs. 385, 386), decorated.
Krater (Shape 61, p. 399)
  No. 1131 (Figs. 387, 388).
Stirrup-vase (Shape 65b 2, p. 405)
  No. 1140.
Lid (Shape 77, p. 417)
  No. 1143 (Fig. 333).
A tall stirrup-vase too badly warped and damaged to be put together or restored. Found in group with two-handled jar, No. 1141. Much like stirrup-vase No. 1140 except that it has a cross on the disk.
From the floor came also sherds of conical cups, kylikes, bowls and basins with pinched-out handles, and a cup of thin fabric with outturned rim.

Many sherds from the debris filling the room. Shapes recognized: pithos, tripod-vessel, pot with spout; in finer ware, kylix (31 stems counted), bowls and cups (39 flat bases), bowls and basins with pinched-out handles, conical cups, jug, scoop with grip-handle, feeding bottle. Some pieces bear traces of painted decoration; motives noted: horizontal bands, spirals, white dots on dark patterns. Some sherds show no signs of burning, probably having been used in crude bricks or clay packing. Stray fragments of a Vapheio cup and of Minyan Ware. Most of the sherds belong to Mycenaean III B, a few Geometric.

COURT 47

Near the east corner of Room 46 a doorway opened northeastward (Figs. 144, 464) into an unroofed court (47) enclosed within a stone wall. The doorway was not an original feature of the hall but was contrived later by breaking through the existing exterior wall of the building and inserting bases for jambs and a threshold block adjusted to the level of the floor inside (Fig. 145). The opening in the wall was 1.30 m. wide. The squared block in the lowest course of the wall to the north-west of the opening still retains its obliquely cut end which, in the regular manner all along this outside wall, had formed one side of a V-shaped joint shared with its neighbor (Fig. 155). The oblique end here was hidden behind the wooden casing which rested on the jamb base and projected 0.18 m. from the wall. The rest of the jamb base must have been visible in the doorway supplementing the threshold block. In it, 0.13 m. from the outer face of the doorway, is a rectangular cutting which presumably served as the socket for the pivot. At its bottom it has a circular sinking which may have been the actual socket. The threshold block is approximately rectangular, measuring 0.90 m. from front to back by 0.75 m. in width, but its edges are largely covered by a coat of stucco. At the southeast near its outer face it makes a notched joint with the jamb base on that side. The latter is 0.25 m. wide toward the court, toward the other end beyond the notch only 0.18 m. The whole floor of the doorway was covered generously with stucco and near its outer edge the stucco rises 0.01 m. above the level of the threshold to form a regular sill, 0.15 m. to 0.16 m. broad, against which the door could close. When open, the door swung back to the northwest for the most part within the depth of the opening. This doorway was very badly damaged in the fire. The walls near it on each side show abundant evidence of the intensity of the heat, with calcined stone and melted plaster along the door casing.

Just above the floor, partly in the doorway, was found a rectangular mass of crude brick and small stones enclosing a large stone, 0.62 m. long, 0.33 m. high and 0.28 m. thick, coated with plaster and bearing traces of contact with wooden beams on three sides (Fig. 154). It was not possible to determine whether it came from the lintel, from the wall, or from some other place.

Outside the doorway, more or less like a door mat, 0.06 m. below the sill, lies a large block, 0.91 m. long and varying from 0.40 m. to 0.47 m. in width, which was heavily coated with stucco.

Court 47 (Key Plan) was laid out with some care and is almost exactly rectangular (Fig. 11); it has a length of 11.58 m. and is 5.47 m. wide at its northwestern end and 5.56 m. on the southeast. The doorway, which was the only entrance, is not exactly centered in the southwestern wall but lies 0.50 m. northwest of the transverse axis of the court (Fig. 150).

The court is bounded on the southwest by the exterior wall of the building (Figs. 151, 415). To the southeast of the doorway it is preserved to a length of no more than two blocks of poros, beyond which only the foundation survives (Fig. 39). This also was made of poros blocks set with their tops 0.13 m. below the floor of the court. The anta base, if it may be so called, beside the doorway is peculiar, as it does not extend through the full thickness of the wall but is supplemented by a thin slab of poros[60] set on edge along the outer face of the wall. On the side toward the door opening it projected 0.05 m. beyond the northwest face of the block (Fig. 39); this offset, which corresponds to the treatment of anta bases beside doorways in the Propylon, Portico, and Vestibule, probably facilitated the attachment of the wooden jamb. The poros slab juts out into the courtyard, forming a projecting offset in the line of the wall that continues southeastward to the corner of the building. The block forming the main part of the anta base[61] had in its top toward the inner and the outer faces a broad rabbet, ranging from 0.25 m. to 0.29 m. in width, while the middle of the block rose 0.02 m. to 0.03 m. higher. These cuttings were made to receive wooden timbers: one dowel hole is preserved in the middle of the southwestern rabbet, two on the northeastern side.[62] The two latter still retain calcined remains of rectangular stones which may have been the actual dowels (Fig. 155). Two additional dowel holes appear in the top of the supplementary block along

[60] Supplementary slab (Fig. 464): 0.82 m. long from southeast to northwest, 0.15 m. thick, 0.42 m. high above the pavement of the court. Two dowel holes: northwestern 0.03 m. square, southeastern 0.04 m. square.

[61] Anta base: 0.88 m. long from southwest to north-east, 0.80 m. wide, 0.47 m. high above the base of the jamb. Two dowel holes on northeastern side, ca. 0.04 m. by 0.06 m., one on southwestern ca. 0.04 m. by 0.05 m.

[62] See note 61.

the outer face of the wall. The top of this anta base has suffered much damage from the fire, the two rabbets having been worn and calcined away.

The succeeding block[63] to the southeastward also has a peculiarity since it was notched to fit around the eastern corner of the main anta base described above (Fig. 155). At the other end it has the usual oblique cutting for a V-shaped joint. A rabbet, 0.23 m. broad, was cut along the northeastern part of the top for a horizontal timber, and two square dowel holes are preserved. This block too was badly damaged by fire.

The rest of the wall continuing to the eastern corner of the building was rebuilt in 1957 by the Greek Service of Reconstruction with the use of ancient material laid on the original foundations (Fig. 151), so far as they extend. They too were made of poros blocks in the outer face with rubble behind. The actual corner is missing along with the southeastern wall of the building, which was removed for its material by intruders. No dowel holes appear in this foundation course.

The section of the wall beyond the doorway to the northwest (4.70 m. long) retains on the exterior its lowest course built of seven blocks of poros (Figs. 40, 415), varying in length and thickness, but all standing to a uniform height of 0.43 m. above the pavement of the court.[64] The central core of rubble rises to a maximum of 0.45 m. higher. Along the top of the poros blocks five rectangular dowel holes occur at irregular intervals, presumably for the fastening of horizontal timbers. At 1.18 m. to the northwest of the doorway in the third block a transverse slot, 0.24 m. wide at the outer face and 0.16 m. deep, runs through the block and the wall (Fig. 38); 0.88 m. farther northwestward in the next block is a second transverse slot of the same kind and approximately the same dimensions. In the bottom of each slot is a rectangular dowel hole, evidently intended to hold an upright timber. Two such timbers, 0.88 m. apart, might conceivably at a higher level frame a window opening. All the poros blocks with their dowel holes were covered by a fused mass of calcined stone, melted plaster, and other debris, burned gray and white.

The seventh facing block fits into a notch cut in a much larger poros block which forms the end of, or continues the line of, the wall separating Rooms 43 and 46 (Fig. 40). The northern corner of this block juts out into the south corner of Court 42, where it marks another offset in the exterior wall (p. 182 and Fig. 153).

Abutting in part against this large block and in part against the seventh block in the wall we have been describing, is the northwestern wall of Court 47 which separates the latter from Court 42 (Fig. 42). This partition ranges in thickness from 0.80 m. at its northeastern end to 0.90 m. at the southwestern. Except for a few fragments of poros, it is built of rough unworked stones laid in irregular courses

[63] Dimensions of block: length 0.92 m., thickness 0.54 m., height above pavement of court 0.46 m. Dowel holes: ca. 0.05 m. square.

[64] See table, p. 49.

and reaching a height of 0.85 m. above the pavement of the court. No plaster remains in place on the southeastern face of the wall, but it is clear from the upward turn of the stucco pavement that it once met a thick coating of some kind. How high the wall originally was and how it was finished at its top can only be conjectured.

At the northern corner the wall ends against the northeastern exterior wall of the court, which continues the line of the outside wall of Court 42 (Fig. 11). The wall is 0.95 m. to 1.15 m. thick and stands above the pavement of the court to a maximum height of 0.85 m. but diminishes to 0.25 m. at the southeastern end. A northwestern section is marked off by the use of somewhat irregular orthostates of poros of different sizes and shapes. The upper part is made of unworked stones laid more or less in courses. The last of the orthostates, 4.67 m. from the corner and directly opposite the doorway from Room 46, in a re-entrant angle forms an offset ca. 0.10 m. deep on the inner face but with a corresponding outward jut of 0.20 m. on the outside (Fig. 152). The angle on the outside is made of three worked blocks placed one above the other, the lowest one of poros. On its inside face the wall, which continues to the east corner, reveals the use of rubble along with a block of poros (0.75 m. long and visible to a height of only 0.11 m. above the pavement), occasional fragments of worked stones, and one large boulder of conglomerate. It is built in the same style of masonry as the upper part of the first section.

The southeastern wall, 0.85 m. thick, is less well preserved than those on the northeast and northwest (Fig. 150), surviving to a height of only 0.35 m. above the floor of the court on its inner face, though reaching 0.45 m. above the pavement of the outer court (58 on Key Plan). The exterior face of the wall was built of poros blocks of varying sizes (one of them 1.20 m. long), not carefully fitted together in their present state, but with the usual V-shaped joints. The outer face of each is much less smoothly finished than those in the exterior wall of the palace (Fig. 156). The angle stone forming the outside eastern corner is missing and a large hole, bordered by broken edges of the pavement of Court 58 and Ramp 91, indicates that a block of considerable size (possibly as much as 1.10 m. long from southwest to northeast and 0.55 m. wide) has been extracted. At the southwestern end a similar gap, no doubt caused by the same marauders, has destroyed the connection between the wall of Court 47 and the eastern corner of the Main Building. Since the southeastern wall of the palace is also missing, except for the deepest bedding of the foundation, the exact adjustment here is not recoverable.

The whole of Court 47 was filled with wreckage mainly from the fire (Fig. 153). Immediately under the surface soil over most of the area were small stones in black earth, evidently an extension of a similar deposit in Court 42, which we have suggested was discolored by the activities of an olive press (p. 177). Deeper, though in some places reaching almost to the surface, lay row after row of squared blocks

(Fig. 152)[65] and fragments in red disintegrated crude brick. While weathered and worn, they were not eaten away so badly as many of the similar blocks in Court 42. It was possible to count at least seven rows, each surely representing a course of the exterior wall of the Main Building from which they had fallen. Those that lay nearest the ashlar wall were wedged in tight against it in a deposit of red dissolved crude brick. Against the northwest wall, however, the deposit in which they lay consisted of greenish-white *stereo*-like clay. The blocks were almost all broken, cracked, worn, and eaten away, and those that lay nearest the wall of the building had suffered the greatest damage from the fire, being more badly cracked and burned red. Several blocks had cuttings, apparently intended to receive beams. Only one block with a dowel hole was seen. The best preserved blocks had a height of 0.38 m. and a maximum length of 0.72 m., but there was considerable variation in their sizes. The area immediately outside the door to a distance of 2 m. contained no blocks and this gives some indication of the height of the door opening. From the almost regular arrangement of the rows it looks as if one whole section of the wall had fallen outward as a unit in one great crash, with the worked blocks underneath and the rubble from the inner part of the wall on top.

On the pavement in an area directly outside the doorway (Fig. 154) extending almost 1 m. into the court and as much to each side, with an accompaniment of carbonized matter, were found many nests of shattered pottery. Another group lay 4 m. to the northeast of the doorway under a squared block. From this material twelve stirrup-vases have been reassembled, two of large, six of medium, and four of small size (Fig. 327). The fragments remaining represent at least 23 additional pots of the same kind. A red two-handled basin has also been put together.

The deposit in Court 47, like that in Court 42, was filled with an amazing amount of broken pottery, including kylix stems by the score, many flat bases of cups and bowls, and fragments of miscellaneous cooking pots and other vessels. How all this material came to be concentrated in this area is still unexplained.

In plowed earth over the southeastern end of the court was found a small fragment of a tablet, and a piece of another came to light when sherds from the same area were being cleaned.

The pavement of the court is of stucco and, though it is cracked and broken by the weight of the heavy stones that fell on it, it is relatively well preserved. The pavement ends with a definite rising edge several centimeters short of the stone walls on the northwest, northeast, and southeast. This indicates that the walls must have been coated with plaster as in Court 42, though none of it has here survived in place. At least two successive pavements have been recognized and, wherever it has

---

[65] The large blocks first uncovered in 1956 were left in the court until the season of 1960 when all were removed.

been possible to investigate, the total thickness seems to be about 0.10 m. At 1.50 m. to 2.50 m. distant from the southwest side of the court, a ridge bordering a slightly depressed area extends from Court 42 to Court 58. This strip of pavement, which has suffered greater damage than any other part of the floor, seems to mark the line of an underlying drain.

Two not very neatly made holes, approximately along the line of the drain, led down into it (Fig. 42).[66] In the northwesterly part of the court only a little more than a meter distant from the boundary wall on that side are two small holes ca. 3.50 m. apart (Fig. 426).[67] Farther southeastward a row of four such holes stretches almost across the court: two (Nos. 3 and 4) are 1 m. apart, and another group of two (Nos. 5 and 6), also 1 m. apart, is separated by 1.50 m. from the first group.[68] In the southeasterly half of the court six other holes of the same general kind are scattered about in no recognizable system. All must have had some purpose, but what it was is not clear. The row of four might have supported a fence or a barrier, shutting off the northwestern half of the court, or some kind of shelter providing shade from the sun. It has also been suggested that some of these holes might have held a loom or looms, and many other uses can be imagined.

It has not been possible to determine how high the walls of the court originally stood, but it is likely that they rose sufficiently to insure privacy and freedom from disturbance. We have called it the Queen's Court, since it could be approached only through Hall 46, which in its connecting apartments, with their delicate style of painted decoration, seems to us to characterize the special quarters of the lady of the household. The large collection of 34 or more stirrup-vases found in the court might be thought to offer some clue to the activities that were carried on here. They evidently required an abundance of water, or it may be of olive oil, but here too we can fall back only on conjecture.

O B J E C T S   F O U N D

B R O N Z E

One small piece.

S T O N E

Nondescript chips and flakes of obsidian, flint, and quartz.

[66] Northwestern hole (b on the plan, Fig. 426): diameter 0.15 m.; at 0.32 m. below the pavement is a stone. Southeastern hole (c on the plan): diameter ca. 0.15 m.; stones 0.415 m. below pavement. Thickness of latter ca. 0.10 m.

[67] No. 1 (southwestern of the two): diameter 0.12 m.; depth to small stones below 0.13 m. Upper pavement broken around edges, pavement ca. 0.10 m. thick.

No. 2 (northeastern): diameter 0.15 m.; measurable depth 0.18 m. below pavement; seems to be lined with stucco or possibly cut through a big stone.

[68] No. 3 (southwesternmost of the four): diameter 0.15 m., narrowing to ca. 0.10 m.; bottom of hole not reached; thickness of pavement 0.09 m.

No. 4: diameter 0.15 m., narrowing to 0.10 m.; small stones at bottom 0.15 m. below pavement; pavement ca. 0.10 m. thick.

No. 5: diameter 0.15 m., narrowing to 0.10 m., fairly regularly cut; pavement 0.105 m. thick; small stones at bottom 0.15 m. to 0.16 m. below pavement.

No. 6: diameter diminishes from 0.15 m. to 0.10 m.; small stones at bottom, 0.16 m. below pavement; pavement 0.10 m. thick.

IVORY

Small fragment.

CLAY

Tablets: No. 1259 (*AJA* 62 [1958], 182, 189, pl. 43). Found in black plowed earth above the worked blocks of the southeast wall ca. 2.50 m. from east corner of the court.

No. 1258 (*AJA* 62 [1958], 182, 188, pl. 43). Found in washing sherds from the same general area.

POTTERY

Basin (Shape 2, p. 355)
    No. 700.
Stirrup-vase (Shape 65b 2, p. 405)
    Nos. 689 and 690 (Fig. 389), decorated.
Stirrup-vase (Shape 65b 3, p. 406)
    Nos. 691 (Fig. 389), 692-694, 695 (Fig. 389), 696 (Figs. 390, 393); all decorated.
Stirrup-vase (Shape 65d, p. 408)
    Nos. 674, 697 (Fig. 391), 698, 699 (Figs. 391, 392); all decorated (Fig. 394).

Of the 23 other stirrup-vases which have not been restored 3 could be assigned to Shape 65b 3 and 15 to 65d. Shoulder patterns represented: parallel zigzags, line of U-shaped figures, parallel chevrons, concentric arcs. On disks 9 examples bear spirals, 5 concentric circles.

Shapes identified among the sherds found in debris filling the court: in coarse ware, pithos (many fragments), tripod-vessel, brazier, scoop, lid, deep spouted bowl; in fine ware, kylix (255 stems counted), votive kylix, cup and bowl (126 flat bases), bowl and basin with pinched-out handles, conical cup, dipper.

Noted on fragments bearing traces of decoration: solid coating over-all, horizontal bands, spirals (one of curve-stem type).

Geometric ware (almost all from upper black earth): numerous fragments, for the most part coated over-all with black or brownish-black glaze; a few bands.

CORRIDOR 48

In the east corner of Hall 46, contiguous with the doorway that opened into Court 47 (Fig. 144), is another doorway leading southeastward into Corridor 48 (Figs. 143, 465). In the opening, with a maximum breadth of 2.13 m., were fitted three poros blocks, a central threshold and a jamb base on each side (Fig. 157).[69] The threshold itself is a large rectangular block, badly damaged on top by the action of the fire. On each side, just beyond the notches mentioned, a roughly rectangular cutting has been gouged out in the threshold at the southwest, and partly in the threshold, partly in the jamb block at the northeast. These were presumably the setting-places for the pivots of a two-leaved door, ca. 1 m. wide. The northeastern jamb base, which abuts against the anta block beside the doorway into Court 47, was entirely covered with soft powdery black earth to a depth of 0.20 m. The southwestern jamb showed equally good evidence of the fire: it lay under a similar deposit, which was deeper, 0.40 m., toward the inner and outer face, and retained in the central part remnants of actual wood, not carbonized (Fig. 158). The doorway must therefore have been provided with substantial wooden jambs.

[69] Threshold block: 0.90 m. deep from northwest to southeast, 1.08 m. wide on the southeast, 0.94 m. on the northwest, where a notch, 0.06 m. wide and 0.18 m. long, has been cut into each corner to receive the corresponding projection of the jamb base. Northeast jamb base: 0.94 m. deep from northwest to southeast; 0.56 m. wide at southeast end, 0.60 m. at northwest. Southwest base: 0.58 m. wide at northwest end, 0.50 m. at southeast. Cutting for pivots ca. 0.09 m. by 0.10 m.

A sample of charcoal from the southwestern door jamb was sent for examination to the Carbon 14 Laboratory of the University of Pennsylvania and the University Museum. The result of the investigation, calculated on the basis of the Libby Half-life value of 5,568 years, gave a dating of 1500 ± 58 B.C.; calculated on a new measurement of the Half-life value at 5,800 years, the resulting date was 1638 ± 60 B.C.

Corridor 48 (Key Plan) is 6.70 m. long from northeast to southwest and 1.56 m. to 1.62 m. wide (Fig. 143). On the northeast it ends against a remnant of the exterior wall of the building which is preserved to a length of 0.67 m. from the north corner (Fig. 145). This is the inner rubble part of the outside wall behind the large poros block described above (p. 205). On the face toward the corridor plaster of good quality, but badly cracked and damaged, is preserved to a height of 0.43 m., curving around on the anta block beside the doorway.

On the southeast the corridor is bordered by a wall, 0.75 m. thick, interrupted by a doorway that opens into a little passage, 49 (Fig. 143). This section, 2.65 m. long, contains traces of four chases for beams at intervals of 0.50 m., 0.50 m., and 0.40 m. The wall stands to a height of 0.53 m. above the floor of the corridor. Carbonized matter indicates that there was a slot for a horizontal beam at 0.24 m. above the floor. Remains of plaster are preserved in some places to the height of this groove.

Beyond the doorway mentioned the wall continues 2.45 m. It has indications of four chases at intervals of 0.40 m., 0.60 m., and 0.50 m., and a horizontal groove ca. 0.20 m. above the floor of the passage. This section of the wall too has suffered much from fire, but it is preserved to a height of 0.75 m. and some remains of plaster survive to a height of 0.68 m. The southwestern end of the corridor is occupied by a doorway leading to Corridor 51 (Fig. 143). On the northwestern side Corridor 48 is flanked by the partition wall separating it from Hall 46. At the northeast it stands to 0.70 m. above the floor, rising gradually to 1.30 m. at the southwestern end. On this side six chases appear at intervals of 0.70 m., 0.60 m., 0.60 m., 0.60 m., and 0.80 m. A horizontal groove runs along the wall at 0.20 m. above the floor. Below it are preserved some remains of wall plaster.

Corridor 48 had once possessed a floor of good stucco, but the northeastern part of it has been badly damaged by fire, the whole surface having been eaten away, leaving rough pebbles exposed. Toward the southwest, however, especially in a strip along the northwestern side, it is relatively well preserved with its finished coat still black and shiny in some places. No decoration has survived on the floor or on the walls; but great sections of plaster, some of it painted, had fallen on the floor throughout the length of the corridor. They presumably came from the lateral walls.

The corridor was filled for the most part with stones, calcined remains of stones, chunks of crude brick as well as disintegrated material of the same, and loose sandy earth. Near its southwestern end, however, it was blocked by a solid mass of fused melted stone and brick, as hard as rock, which had spread across the doorway and into the passage beyond. It had to be chiseled and chopped out by sheer force in order to open the corridor. Here and there in the fused mass were fragments of plaster bearing painted decoration, many of which were laboriously carved out of the *migma*. Among the pieces thus salvaged one bears the representation of a warrior wearing a tunic, another, a man's head and the forelegs of a dog. Additional fragments of the same composition, which were found in Room 43 and Corridor 51 indicate that the wall paintings came from a room in the upper story. There are also many fragments of flooring of two different kinds, blue, sometimes with red bands, and white. All the material that had coalesced into an almost unbreakable mass had evidently fallen from above.

O B J E C T S   F O U N D

BRONZE

More than 50 shapeless pieces fused with chunks of disintegrated crude brick (e.g., Fig. 289 Nos. 1-8).

FLINT

Thin flat tan piece (Fig. 289 No. 9), l. 0.019 m., w. 0.015 m.

PASTE

Fragment, possibly of a bead, melted by heat and flattened out (Fig. 291 No. 16), l. 0.045 m., w. 0.024 m., th. 0.004 m.

POTTERY

Fragments of gray stirrup-vase, found on the floor, too badly damaged and fused by fire to be reconstructed.

Relatively few other sherds. Shapes recognized: in coarse ware, pithos, lid; in finer ware, kylix (3 stems), bowl and cup (5 flat bases), conical cup, bowl with pinched out handles, krater-bowl.

CORRIDOR 49

The doorway leading from Corridor 48 into the smaller passage (49) is 1.60 m. wide (Figs. 148, 466). It was marked at floor level with the usual three blocks of poros,[70] a jamb base on each side and a threshold in the middle, but here the latter is smaller than the bases of the jambs (Fig. 159). On each side of the doorway had stood an upright wooden beam which had been fitted into a slot (0.20 m. wide) close against the outer edge of each jamb base. This chase was found filled with carbonized wood and black earth. The door casing was presumably attached to the beam and extended out some 0.33 m. before it turned through the door opening to return again on the other side of the wall. A stump of the wall may have projected to fill the hollow of the casing. Two rectangular cuttings in the jamb bases on the side toward Corridor 48 probably served to hold the sockets for the pivots of a two-

---

[70] Threshold block: 0.50 m. wide, 0.78 m. long through the doorway. Northeast jamb base: 0.55 m. wide by 0.78 m.; cutting for socket: 0.16 m. long by 0.07 m. wide, 0.05 m. deep; southwest jamb base: 0.55 m. wide by 0.78 m. long; cutting for socket: 0.14 m. long, 0.09 m. wide, 0.055 m. deep.

leaved door or for a socket on one side and a bar for fastening on the other, since the space between is only 0.84 m., measured center to center. The surface of the stones is cracked and damaged by fire and much carbonized matter from the wooden casings still remains on the base of the jambs on each side.

Corridor 49 (Key Plan) is 1 m. wide and 2.67 m. long from the doorway to the southeast exterior wall of the building (Fig. 148). The latter is missing down to the bedding of the foundations, 0.65 m. below the floor, and a modern wall has been built to show its line (Fig. 11). The northeast and southwest walls are thin partitions (0.25 m. and 0.30 m. thick respectively). Each was built with a core only a single stone wide, coated on both faces with plaster, 0.02 m. to 0.03 m. thick. The two walls stand in their northwestern part to a height of 0.45 m. above the floor, but sink to floor level at the southeast end where the northeastern wall was interrupted by a doorway (Fig. 160). Though some remains of the finished coat of plaster survive in place on both sides of the passage, only a faint red line is preserved to suggest that the walls were once decorated.

The doorway leading into the passage from Corridor 48 was filled with soft burned matter; farther southeastward the deposit was a hard fused mass, containing part of a squared block badly damaged by fire, fragments of flooring fallen from above, stones, disintegrated brick, and pieces of plaster.

Near the doorway enough of the floor is preserved to give an idea of the arrangement of the painted patterns with which it was decorated (Fig. 161). As observed by Mr. de Jong, the area had been laid out into rectangles approximately 0.30 m. by 0.35 m. (Fig. 163). Across the passage they measure 0.30 m. in width separated by pairs of incised lines, 0.02 m. apart, and bordered by a strip 0.03 m. wide along each wall. Lengthwise the rectangles are 0.35 m. long, 0.035 m. distant from the doorway and the line of the southeastern wall and 0.025 m. apart. Although the floor was very much damaged by fire Mr. de Jong was able to identify the patterns in 10 of the 21 rectangles. In the first row of three inside the doorway the central panel contains a red octopus with eyes set at its waist and white suckers on the tentacles (Fig. 167). In the panel to the left of the octopus is a double scale pattern in black and to the right double concentric circles enclosing a white dot. The central rectangle of the second row may have contained three dolphins. The panel on the right has a group of triple concentric arcs in one corner in antithetic position to a similar group in the opposite corner. These three or comparable linear designs seem to be repeated in five other rectangles along one side or the other of the passage. No further patterns in the central rectangles could be recognized and we were unable to determine whether they too were reserved for marine motives. A few pieces of fallen plaster seem also to have been decorated with comparable subjects.

OBJECTS FOUND

OBSIDIAN

Core (Fig. 282 No. 6).

POTTERY

A few nondescript sherds were collected from red brickish earth filling the corridor. Shapes recognized: kylix, handleless cup, and bowl with pinched-out handles. Several sherds with traces of painted decoration.

ROOM 50

The doorway leading into the corner room (50) is marked by a slot in the floor, 0.25 m. wide, 0.20 m. deep below the floor level and 1.17 m. long to the outer edge of the floor (Fig. 160). Whether the doorway originally extended all the way to the exterior wall or stopped short of it could not be ascertained, since the latter is now missing. The slot was filled with ashes, carbonized remains of wood, many pieces of stucco, with some stones at the bottom. The latter probably supported a wooden sill that extended across the opening and the doorway must have had a wooden casing. Some of the fragments of stucco mentioned were strips (0.022 m. to 0.032 m. wide) which may have been fitted along the edges of the sill or the door casing or the lintel. Pieces of similar character were found in the debris filling Corridor 49. Another problem concerns the actual door. No evidence has survived to show if there really was one that turned on a pivot or swung on hinges fastened to the casing.

Room 50 (Key Plan) is approximately square, ca. 2.67 m. on a side (Fig. 143). The southwestern partition separating it from Corridor 49 and the northwestern wall, which it shares with Corridor 48, have already been described. On the northeast some remains of plaster in a strip ranging from 0.07 m. to 0.27 m. in height still give the line of the inner face of the wall (Fig. 160), though the outer facing of big blocks and most of the rubble backing are missing. The southeast exterior wall has likewise vanished, but the floor of the room has survived with a finished edge to a length of 0.70 m. that marks the inner face of the wall against which it once abutted (Fig. 145).

The plaster on the southwestern and northwestern walls is *in situ* in a continuous strip reaching a maximum height of 0.50 m., but the finished surface has been worn off everywhere and no vestiges of painted decoration can now be seen.

The room was found covered with a deposit of red burned clay, ca. 0.25 m. deep, resting on the floor and containing stones, chunks of pavement, and plaster showing impressions of beams, and a few fragments of frescoes, a granule of gold attached to a shapeless piece of silver, fragments of silver, bronze and crystal, a small flat piece of glass paste, and a scattering of potsherds. Remnants of wall painting seem to represent a flounced skirt, apparently belonging to a figure of life size.

The floor of the room was decorated with painted designs, the best preserved remains of which are in the eastern corner. The rest of the floor, with only minor exceptions, had been too severely damaged by fire for any decoration to be visible after the thick lime accretion was removed. The whole area of the room was apparently divided into seven rows of seven squares, each measuring 0.35 m. on a side, marked off by pairs of incised lines, 0.025 m. apart. Patterns were distinguished in 16 of the 49 squares by Mr. de Jong who made a reconstruction in water color of what has survived (Fig. 163). Many of the motives are the same as those used in Corridor 49. We have numbered the rows from northwest to southeast and we begin at the northeastern end of each row. In the north corner of the room the first square in row 1 is decorated with double concentric circles in grayish-black paint around a white dot. Nothing else could be recognized in that row. The first square in row 2 has traces of two short parallel diagonal lines in black. In the rest of this row and the whole of row 3 the surface is gone and no decoration can be discerned. The first square in row 4 has groups of triple concentric arcs of wavy or scallopy black lines backing up to each other. In the fifth row square one is decorated with a scale pattern in double lines, red and black (Fig. 166); square two contains a pair of leaping dolphins facing left, between two sharks or other fish heading in the opposite direction, all painted in blackish outline and the dolphin with touches of yellow on the side; square three contained a red octopus. In the sixth row square one has double red concentric circles around white dots; square two has a red octopus with head toward the northwest and white dots on its tentacles (Fig. 164); in square three are three dolphins heading left in black outline with black snouts and yellow stripes on the sides (Figs. 162, 165); square four had another red octopus; square five two fish in black outline headed southeast. In the seventh row square one has blackish triple concentric arcs backed up on the north-south axis of the square; square two, an irregular amoeba-like motive done in double lines, red outside of black; square three, a scale pattern in double lines, red and black; square four, double black concentric circles enclosing white dots; square five, a few scattered curving black squiggles which defied interpretation; square six is now blank; square seven with a pinkish background has a small patch of decoration consisting of three black circles each enclosing a white dot, a southwest-northeast line met by two others coming from the northwest and several indeterminate curving lines.

The general scheme of decoration may have been a border of squares containing geometric patterns running around the outer edge of the room against all four walls while the central five rows of five bore marine motives—octopuses alternating with dolphins and other fish. Enough of the octopus is preserved in three squares and of the fish in three others to confirm an arrangement of this kind, and it must have been highly effective.

The delicate style of the floor decoration, the good quality of the plaster and the measures, represented by the many doorways, taken to insure privacy have led us to conclude that this corner of the Main Building contained the reception room and private apartments of the queen.

O B J E C T S   F O U N D

GOLD

Tiny droplet attached to thin piece of silver (Fig. 291 No. 17).

SILVER

Two fragments: one small thin (Fig. 291 No. 17), one heavy, badly fused piece (Fig. 291 No. 18).

BRONZE

Three fragments: two thin (Fig. 291 Nos. 19, 20) and one twisted.

STONE

Obsidian: part of a core and two chips.
Flint: one scrap.
Quartz: three small pieces.
Fragment of veined marble-like stone possibly from a decorative ring large enough for a bracelet or part of the ornamental handle of a large stone vessel. Ring with outer rounded part and an inner flanged section, smooth on the inside, finished edges above and below, broken only at ends of segment; somewhat unsymmetrical in section (Fig. 269 No. 5), 0.025 m. high.

PASTE

Oval, flattened piece, badly vitrified, possibly from bead or inlay (Fig. 291 No. 21), l. 0.025 m., w. 0.02 m., th. 0.004 m.

POTTERY

Shapes represented: pithos, kylix (2 stems), cup and bowl (7 flat bases), basin with pinched-out handles, dipper. Traces of decoration: horizontal bands, spiral, dots. One stray piece with incised crisscross lines probably Middle Helladic.

SOUTHEAST CORRIDOR, SECTION 51

At the southwest end of Corridor 48 a doorway (Figs. 143, 467) opens into another corridor (51 on Key Plan). The lateral jamb bases and the central threshold block are equally substantial with those we have seen in the doorways opening southeastward and northwestward toward the other end of Corridor 48. This doorway, however, was covered so generously with stucco and so much damaged by the heat of the fire that it is difficult to give accurate measurements.[71] The whole width of the corridor was occupied by the doorway with jambs projecting ca. 0.30 m. from each side. A fairly large rectangular cutting near the southwestern end of each jamb base presumably held the sockets for the pivots of a two-leaved door. The over-all width measured between the outer edges of the two cuttings is 1.05 m. The stucco floor of the corridor from each side was carried over the threshold in the latest phase.

[71] Width of opening 1.68 m.; depth 0.80 m. Width: northwest base 0.52 m., threshold block 0.62 m., southeast base 0.54 m.; thickness of southeast base more than 0.22 m. Cuttings for sockets: northwest base 0.08 m. to 0.085 m. by 0.15 m. and 0.04 m. deep; southeast base 0.08 m. by 0.155 m. and 0.05 m. deep. Blackened marks on northwest base extend inward 0.35 m. from southwest face of the stone and 0.18 m. from the northeast face leaving a rectangular area on the stone white, presumably where it was covered by a stone core within the wooden casing.

Markings on the northwestern jamb base indicate that a core of the wall projected into the hollow casing. The graining of the lower end of the upright timber that formed the corner of the wooden jamb has been indelibly imprinted in the stone base (Fig. 168). The state of the doorway when excavated has already been mentioned (p. 211).

Corridor 51 is the middle part of the relatively long passage that extends from the Northeast Stoa (44) to the southeastern exterior wall of the building (p. 195 and Fig. 148). This section, 3.24 m. long, has a doorway at each end. The one at the northwest is now represented by a transverse slot in the floor, ca. 0.40 m. wide, 0.15 m. to 0.17 m. deep, and also by a break in the plaster on the face of the wall on each side which marks the place where wooden door jambs had once been set (Fig. 170). At the bottom of the slot are stones laid in disintegrated crude brick which apparently supported a wooden sill. The jamb probably stood on that threshold and was of the regular hollow type, partly or wholly filled by a projection from the lateral walls. Gray ash was found in what looked like the chase for a timber forming the north corner of the jamb, where it may have stood in contact with the jamb of the door leading into Room 46.

A similar slot, ca. 0.50 m. wide and 0.15 m. deep, fixes the position of the southeastern doorway (Fig. 148) contiguous to the jamb of the doorway coming in from Corridor 48. This slot was found filled with soft black earth, reddish clay from dissolved brick, a few loose stones, fragments of pavement, bits of carbonized wood, and a good many potsherds. The bottom of the slot was formed by a foundation of flattish stones (Fig. 171), not very large but fairly well fitted into one another; it is likely that they supported a wooden threshold. A break in the plaster on the southwestern side of the corridor gives some grounds for believing that wooden jambs rose on each side of this doorway too.

This section of the corridor is bordered on the northeast by the wall of Hall 46 which rises here to the highest point preserved anywhere in the building (Fig. 148). The corner between Corridors 48 and 51 still stands to a height of 1.40 m. above the floor, 14.30 m. above datum. It is composed largely of the fused hard mass of stones and crude brick that we call *migma*.

The wall on the southwestern side of the corridor is a continuation of the one that bordered Corridor 45 (p. 196), though here its thickness increases to 0.90 m. It is preserved to a height of 0.93 m. above the floor but sinks considerably toward the southeast. At the end of this section two massive poros blocks form the dado course of the wall. Scanty indications of at least three chases are recognizable. Throughout the section a thick coat of backing plaster adheres to the wall to its full preserved height, probably hiding a horizontal groove. A patch of the same kind of plaster survives also on the northeastern wall, but nowhere in this section is a finishing coat with painted patterns left *in situ.*

The fused wreckage that flowed over the northeastern wall also spread into the corridor, filling it with a cement-like solid mass. It was extremely difficult to excavate and a further complication was offered by the presence of many small and large pieces of frescoes embedded in the *migma.* Beneath this was a stratum of loosely packed pebbles and other small material, then calcined stones lying in dissolved crude brick. Much melted lime had also run over the floor which was made of stucco. This too offered great resistance to cleaning; it proved to be badly cracked and broken with its finished surface worn and burned away. Only a few nondescript sherds were recovered from the debris.

One cannot help wondering why there should be so many doorways in this passage. If they were closed, it must have been exceedingly stuffy in this part of the palace. If they could not be closed what was the point in having them? Apart from ventilation, light too must have been a problem; without some illumination the corridor was surely dark as night when the doors were closed. Certainly the whole arrangement supports the view expressed above that privacy was desired in these apartments. Another puzzling question raises itself: why was the fire so remarkably intense in this particular quarter that it heaped up so great a mass of smelted wreckage?

SOUTHEAST CORRIDOR, SECTION 52

The final section of the long corridor (52 on Key Plan) extends from the last-mentioned doorway with the wooden threshold (p. 216) to the line of the southeastern exterior wall of the building (Fig. 148), with a length of 2.85 m. and a width of 1.34 m. The bordering wall on the southwest, built in part of large blocks or fragments of poros, is preserved only to a length of 0.50 m. in the part visible above the floor; beyond, the foundations, also built of big blocks, continue 1.10 m. farther. The remnant of the wall retains a patch of thick backing plaster.

On the opposite side the corridor is bordered by a partition wall, 0.28 m. thick, built for the most part of a single row of stones faced with rough backing plaster on the side toward the passage (Fig. 171). It is preserved to a height of 0.45 m., ending after a length of 1.40 m. at a slot, 0.33 m. wide and 0.10 m. to 0.15 m. deep, the latter sunk beneath the floor (Fig. 169). It is preserved to a length of 1.05 m. beyond which the floor on both sides is broken away; whether the slot once extended all the way to the outside wall of the building or stopped short of it against a projecting spur cannot now be determined. In any event, with stones laid along its bottom, the groove must have held a wooden threshold like those we have seen at each end of the middle section of the corridor. The sill seems to have been broader at the bottom than at the top as indicated by the sloping sides of the slot. The cavity was filled with burned reddish clay from dissolved crude brick and along the sides were strips of stucco, 0.06 m. wide, which may have served to fit the edges of the sill to the floor. The doorway that opens northeastward presumably had wooden jambs and a wooden lintel, but no evidence has survived to give the details, though one may probably assume that the door swung northeastward into the room.

Corridor 52 was floored with stucco like that in the preceding Section 51. Its surface is badly damaged by fire. It is preserved, in a length of 2.46 m., to a jagged break which shows the activity of the stone robbers who dismantled the southeastern wall along with most of its foundations.

The northwestern part of the corridor was filled with *migma* continuing from Corridors 51 and 48, and the southeastern part had been disturbed by looters of building material from the outside wall. So far as could be determined two pots, badly shattered, warped and fused by fire, lay on the floor. A few nondescript sherds came from the overlying burned debris.

O B J E C T S   F O U N D

S I L V E R
Two small pieces (e.g., Fig. 290 No. 1).

B R O N Z E
Javelin point, barbless (Fig. 291 No. 22): slightly raised midrib, rectangular butt, 0.006 m. square in section, rectangular tang, 0.003 m. square in section; total l. 0.05 m., l. blade 0.022 m., l. butt 0.009 m., l. tang 0.019 m., max. w. across shoulders 0.013 m. Found in cleaning southwest wall.

Handle: heavy, very solid, rounded in section, becoming rectangular where fastened to the pot (Fig. 290 No. 13), d. 0.009 m., span 0.045 m. and h. above rim measured inside 0.036 m.

Chisel (?): flat tapering piece, slightly bowed end (Fig. 290 No. 4), l. pres. 0.016 m., w. 0.016 m. to 0.02 m., probably tip of a chisel-like implement.

Many fused chunks and thin flat pieces, some with rivets and rivet-holes (e.g., Figs. 265 No. 6, 290 Nos. 2, 3, 5-12).

F L I N T
Blade (Fig. 265 No. 8).

O B S I D I A N
Arrowhead: long barbed type, tips of barbs missing (Fig. 290 No. 14), l. pres. 0.029 m., w. 0.011 m.

P O T T E R Y
Stirrup-vases: fragments of two (Fig. 346 No. 5). Burned gray; decorated with horizontal bands.

R O O M   5 3

Room 53 (Key Plan and Fig. 148) is 2.95 m. long from southwest to northeast and 2.65 m. wide. The southwestern partition wall which has already been described stands to a height of 0.40 m. above the floor, the greater part of it coated with plaster of good quality. The northwestern wall, which separates the room from Corridor 48 and stands to 0.75 m. above the floor, also retains a considerable extent of plaster. The northeastern partition between Room 53 and Corridor 49 rises to a height of 0.35 m. above the floor, with plaster *in situ* in patches ranging from 0.09 m. to 0.30 m. in height. The southeastern wall was removed by pillagers to its foundations.

This room too suffered much from the fire-fused debris that spread over it from the northwest and covered the greater part of the floor. The latter, except for some patches along the northwestern and northeastern sides, is in miserable condition. It had been subjected to great heat and the surface was melted or consumed, leaving only the rough under part of the layer. Where the original finished coat had escaped, no trace of painted decoration could be seen.

In the southwestern part of the room in front of the door and along the north-western wall many pots were revealed, partly embedded in as well as under the *migma* and spread out over the floor. Through the heat of the fire many of the vases had become cemented to the stucco flooring and their removal required much toil and trouble. After cleaning and mending they were found to represent at least 17 stirrup-vases, 13 of large size, 10 of which have been restored, and four small, one of which could be reconstructed (Fig. 335). All the jars are decorated with simple horizontal bands. No other shape was recognized in the material recovered on the floor.

A good many fragments of plaster were found in the debris filling the room. Some of these pieces are from flooring, no doubt fallen from the upper story, some having been attached to wood, others to brick. A few are pieces of wall plaster with traces of color, but all were too severely injured by fire to show the nature of the pattern.

A small sinking was noted in the north corner of the room where the floor was broken. Soft earth was found beneath and possible traces of a small drain leading southwestward, perhaps to turn southeastward to join the channel mentioned in the next paragraph.

Some 0.92 m. from the east corner of Room 53 a stone covered an opening into a proper underground drain (Fig. 148). Beneath some small fallen stones under the cover lay a broken slab of poros in which part of a neatly cut circular hole (ca. 0.10 m. in diameter) going through the block is preserved. This led into a channel running southeastward and bordered on each side by a well-cut block of poros,[72] extending somewhat obliquely through the foundations of the southeast wall of the building (Fig. 426). At the bottom of the drain are smallish stones, carelessly fitted together, not an ideal floor for a drain. The channel was packed with broken pot-tery—fragments of kylikes, bowls with pinched-out handles, and handleless cups being recognizable. From these, five pots could be restored (Fig. 334). The deposit in the drain was loose, rather soft and greenish, and the sherds were stained. Along with the sherds were several small painted bits of plaster, including four joining fragments with red and white daisies on a yellow ground.

---

[72] Southwestern block: 0.84 m. long, 0.48 m. high,   m. high, 0.32 m. thick.
0.52 m. thick. Northeastern block: 0.78 m. long, 0.30

The presence of a carefully built drain under the floor and a properly made hole leading to it, not to mention a supplementary connection in the northern corner, and the concentration of many capacious vessels presumably for water, lead us to suggest that Room 53 was a washroom or perhaps a water closet. That might explain the effort to achieve so much privacy in this corner of the building. Stirrup-vases were certainly used in many places as containers for olive oil, but they were also employed for water. As we have observed in various parts of the palace, it seems to have been customary to keep a stirrup-vase beside a doorway. It could conceivably have held olive oil to reduce the squeaking of pivots when doors were opened and closed; but water might also have served for that purpose. One cannot exclude the possibility that rare oils and perfumes may have been stored here, but the good quality of the stucco floor and the plaster on the walls are not usually found in storerooms.

O B J E C T S   F O U N D

B R O N Z E

Nondescript fragment.

P O T T E R Y

From the room

Stirrup-vase (Shape 65b 2, p. 405)
  Nos. 678 (Figs. 390, 393), 679-681, 682-685 (Fig. 393), 686, 687 (Fig. 393); all decorated.
Stirrup-vase (Shape 65b 3, p. 406)
  No. 688, decorated.
Two more large stirrup-vases were partially restored and the top and base of another are preserved. Three small incomplete examples not numbered.
No other shapes represented among the sherds from this room.

From the drain

The drain was packed with sherds. Recognizable shapes; kylix, bowl with pinched-out handles and conical cup. Several were restored:
Bowl (Shape 4, p. 356)
  No. 722.
Cup (Shape 11, p. 359)
  Nos. 723 and 724 (Fig. 353).
Kylix (Shape 27, p. 366)
  No. 720.
Kylix (Shape 29a, p. 368)
  No. 721 (Figs. 359, 360).

S O U T H E A S T   S T A I R W A Y   5 4

A stairway (54 on Key Plan), 1.18 m. wide, led to the upper floor of the tower-like structure flanking the Propylon on its northeastern side. It was accessible through a doorway that opened from the southeastern end of Stoa 44 (pp. 191, 195 and Figs. 141, 468). Three steps, a landing, and a fragment of a fourth step were found in place. The bottom step is set back 0.64 m. from the inner edge of the threshold block in the doorway, the intervening space being floored with stucco. The step, 0.14 m. high with a tread 0.34 m. deep, consists of two blocks, 0.28 m. and 0.90 m. long, the shorter one on the northeast. The second step, a single block filling the width of the stairway, is 0.14 m. high and 0.34 m. deep. The treads tilt inward noticeably.

The third step is made up of three parallel blocks laid lengthwise from northwest to southeast so that they not only serve as a step, 0.13 m. high, but also as a landing (Fig. 172). The block at the left along the wall is cracked in the middle of its length, the center one is somewhat shorter and the southwestern is another long block.[73] The inner ends of the three were, of course, covered by the fourth step. A fragment of it found *in situ* against the northeast wall shows the landing to have been 0.70 m. deep.

That is all that has actually survived of the stairway and its reconstruction offers difficult problems. Remains of a transverse wall (e on the plan, Fig. 424) 1.10 m. thick, running from northeast to southwest 1.50 m. beyond the landing, may possibly have had some connection with the stairway. Just beyond it two relatively short foundations (f and g), extending from northwest to southeast, could also conceivably have provided support for the upper part of the stairway. Less than 1 m. still farther southeastward is another transverse wall (c) 0.80 m. thick, standing to a height of two or more courses and made largely of smallish pieces of poros on its southeast face. Beyond this latter wall is a further space, 2.90 m. wide, before the outer wall of the building is reached. All of these elements, together with the lateral walls (b and d) of this tower-like unit beside the Propylon, must be considered in any attempt to reconstruct the stairway. Because of the dilapidated condition of almost all these structural elements, little more than conjectures are possible. Walls f and g and c were judged to have been in use at the time of the final destruction. Wall e was apparently built earlier, perhaps even before the northeast wall (b) of the Propylon. Whether it still existed in the latest phases of the palace cannot be determined. The greater part of it was at sometime removed either by the builders of the Propylon and the adjoining "tower" or by later stone robbers, more probably the latter.

Stairway 54 may have continued southeastward without change of direction, passing through wall c to the floor of the upper story. Another possibility, as shown in the plan (Fig. 468) by Mr. de Jong, might provide a right-angled turn either to right or left or both along the northwestern face of wall c. Yet another scheme might have a turn to the northwest with additional steps supported by wall g. All of these plans could lead comfortably to an upper story. Still another conceivable solution, though not likely, might be to turn the corner along the line of wall e, if that had been torn out or cut down to fit the purpose at the time of the building of the Propylon. In the present ruined state of the walls it is not possible to determine which of these schemes, or others, was followed. In any event it is clear that the stairway somehow ascended to an upper floor of the tower.

[73] Dimensions of blocks: at left, 1.03 m. long, 0.32 m. wide; in center 0.77 m. long, 0.40 m. to 0.43 m. wide; at right 1.04 m. long, 0.47 m. wide, south corner broken off. Fourth step, length preserved 0.20 m., depth preserved 0.14 m., height 0.18 m.

The deposit over the steps and landing consisted of a gray and white mixture of calcined stone and pebbles, loosely packed, crumbly, and disturbed by intrusive roots of an olive tree. It contained many large pieces of fallen frescoes heavily coated with lime. The back of one piece showed striations from the grain of the wood against which it had been pressed. Three pieces each have a straight edge. One group of fragments from above the landing, some of which join together, comes from a frieze of rosettes with streamers. The rosettes are done in black and brown, the streamers in black, orange and tan. Other pieces found above the steps bear streaky orange-red paint, possibly a free imitation of wood-graining. Many fragments of blue flooring were also found. Under the fallen plaster was a layer of soft red clay from disintegrated crude bricks.

The northeastern side of the stairway is bounded by the wall which we have already seen from the side of Corridor 45. Toward the stairway it is coated with good finished plaster. No recognizable remains of wall paintings are preserved. On the other side of the entrance and stairway a patch of rough plaster still clings to the wall.

The steps themselves, like those in the northeast stairway, were damaged considerably by the fire. In fact this whole area of the palace seems to have suffered more intensely than almost any quarter. What the particular circumstances were to rouse the flames to so great a violence here has eluded our investigation.

OBJECTS FOUND

SILVER

Fragment (Fig. 291 No. 23), l. 0.02 m., w. 0.0125 m.: extremely thin, ridged, with fluting at one end possibly representing drapery.

IVORY

Petal- or leaf-shaped piece with central incised line; burned a light blue (Fig. 291 No. 24), l. 0.03 m., max. w. 0.011 m.

POTTERY

Sherds for the most part embedded in *migma* and coated with lime incrustation. Shapes identified: pithos, large jar, tripod-vessel; in finer ware, kylix, bowl and cup, dipper, basin. Some fragments retain traces of decoration; motives identified: horizontal bands, stripes, spirals. Stray fragments of LH I and Middle Helladic Mattpainted Ware.

ROOM 55

To the southwest, beside the landing at the top of the third step in the staircase, a threshold block of poros marks the doorway that opened into Room 55 (p. 221 and Figs. 172, 469). The block is 0.81 m. long from northwest to southeast, 0.44 m. wide and 0.18 m. high. The doorway seems to have had wooden jambs which were consumed by fire and have left gray ash to a depth of 0.16 m. on each side. Neither appears to have stood on a stone base, the jamb on the northwest projecting 0.27 m. from the lateral wall; the other on the southeast jutted out 0.38 m. from the end of the wall which must have helped to support the southwestern side of the staircase that continued beyond. The foundations of this wall are preserved, 1.47 m. long, to the line of wall e (Fig. 424), the course of which runs transversely from northeast to southwest. Wall e may have formed the boundary of Room 55, if it survived into the late phases of the palace. On the northwest the room is bordered by wall a, the southeast wall of Court 3 (p. 63). This wall originally was 1.31 m. thick with ashlar blocks on its northwestern face and a backing of rubble (Fig. 174). In a later phase, to which Room 55 must belong, the inner part of the wall seems to have been shaved away, reducing its thickness to 0.75 m. Above the level of the floor in Room 55 the wall is preserved to a length of 2.50 m., and its coating of whitewashed mud plaster survives to a height of 0.90 m. above the floor (Fig. 143). On the southwest no boundary now appears until the northeast wall (b) of the inner portico of the Propylon is reached, and this presumably is the limit of Room 55 (Fig. 11). No plaster is now to be seen on this wall, which is very badly calcined; it retains clear evidence of four vertical chases at intervals of 0.48 m., 0.51 m., and 0.70 m. Along the northeastern side of the wall a bedding trench was recognized. The builders had cut directly through wall e which therefore must have been built in an earlier phase, but could have survived into the later.

The floor of Room 55, laid at a level 0.17 m. below the threshold, was made of hard-packed earth with a crust of clay. It had a width of 2.70 m. from the north-west wall (a) to the line of wall e. From northeast to southwest it has survived only to a length of 2 m., although it almost certainly extended to the northeast wall of the Propylon (b) to a total length of ca. 4 m. Earlier digging and disturbance before our time had here reached a level below the floor, but traces of burning on the northeastern face of wall b were observed to stop at the floor level. Under the floor was found a large jar which contained five (or more) conical cups (Fig. 337), apparently belonging to a stage before the palace was built.

When the undisturbed section was excavated a white deposit, 0.90 m. deep, made up of calcined stone and pebbles (Fig. 173) and very hard, was found to extend to a distance of 1.40 m. from the northwest wall (a). It was a solid mass resting directly on the floor. Beyond, to the line of wall e, 1.20 m. farther, the floor was covered by reddish clay, disintegrated material of crude brick, to a depth of 0.33 m. to 0.40 m. Above this red earth was a fall of pebbly white matter and stones, 0.30 m. to 0.50 m. thick; upon this rested in turn disturbed earth which continued southeastward and filled the trench marking the course of the missing wall e.

Scattered about on the floor were found eight smallish pieces of worked and partially worked poros, badly damaged by fire, of various shapes, cubical, cylindrical, campaniform, rectangular blocks, etc. (Fig. 271 No. 6). One is an unfinished lamp stand, a concave column on a square base. Also on the floor were many nests of potsherds which, when cleaned and mended, allowed the restoration of ten vases (Fig. 336), including four kylikes of several types, a small bowl with pinched-out handles, three shallow cups, one cup with high handle and one squat, round vessel with hole-mouth, and much additional fragmentary material that could not be put together. Other objects recovered include a bit of bronze, a neatly worked piece of ivory, perhaps an inlay.

The objects found in this room provide the only available source of information regarding its use. The collection of unfinished articles in poros suggests that this was the modest workshop of a stone cutter who made lampstands and bases for ornaments, votives, or articles, such as the double axe, to be set up in a shrine.

O B J E C T S   F O U N D

B R O N Z E
Nondescript bit.

S T O N E
Eight objects made of poros (Fig. 271 No. 6) partially worked or finished and worn or damaged by fire:

1. Small block roughly rectangular in section, 0.16 m. by 0.16 m. by 0.09 m.; edges worn at ends and on one side.

2. Small piece, 0.11 m. high, roughly cylindrical, but with somewhat concave sides, tapering from a diameter of 0.14 m. at bottom to 0.115 m. at top; edges broken. From top near edge a small perforation slanting, 0.03 m. long, runs down to a hole in upper part of side, visible at right in Fig. 271 No. 6 (second from left).

3. Small block, 0.16 m. long, roughly rectangular in section, 0.13 m. by 0.08 m. Edges broken.

4. Roughly cylindrical piece, 0.09 m. high; diameter at base 0.13 m.; sides slightly concave; upper edge worn away on one side.

5. Unfinished lamp stand. Base: 0.19 m. square, h. at corners 0.04 m., h. in center of side 0.05 m.; concave column: h. 0.18 m., d. 0.14 m.-0.15 m.; flat top: 0.19 m. square, h. 0.04 m. Hole, 0.015 m. deep, in center of one side where concave curve begins and a larger hole, 0.027 m. deep,

in top near edge. Purpose of these cuttings not obvious.

6. Small block rectangular in section, almost a cube, measuring 0.14 m. by 0.14 m. by 0.12 m.

7. Similar block rectangular in section, measuring 0.17 m. by 0.15 m. by 0.14 m. About half the surface is badly worn and broken.

8. Similar block rectangular in section, 0.18 m. by 0.13 m. by 0.10 m. Rectangular cutting, 0.12 m. by 0.05 m. and 0.01 m. deep, in one short side or end, and a similar cutting, 0.12 m. by 0.07 m. and 0.02 m. deep, on one long side. Purpose of these slots uncertain; possibly a mold (?), but more probably preliminary cutting for shaping some object.

I V O R Y
Fragment, flat, rectangular, burned black (Fig. 291 No. 26), l. pres. 0.028 m., w. 0.021 m., th. 0.007 m.: three finished polished surfaces, one flat with intersecting raised edges, two narrow; other two narrow sides broken; back has fine diagonal crisscrossed lines and well-cut hole, d. 0.0055 m., depth 0.004 m., with smaller hole in its center.

P A S T E
Blue bead: fragment, broken at larger end through perforation (Fig. 291 No. 25), l. 0.012 m., max. w. 0.01 m., th. 0.005 m.

POTTERY

Bowl (Shape 4, p. 356)
    No. 702.
Cup (Shape 12, p. 360)
    Nos. 703-705.
Cup (Shape 14, p. 361)
    No. 717 (Figs. 355, 356).
Kylix (Shape 27, p. 366)
    Nos. 716, 718.
Kylix (Shape 29a, p. 368)
    No. 701 (Figs. 359, 360).
Kylix (Shape 30c, p. 373)
    No. 715.
Disk-shaped pot (Shape 80, p. 418)
    No. 706 (Figs. 397, 398).

Sherds from accumulation filling room. Shapes noted: coarse ware, pithos, basin or lid; finer ware, kylix (Shape 27, 5 counted; others 13), conical cup, bowl or cup (56 flat bases), dipper. Fragments bearing remnants of decoration: very small angular alabastron (dots, quirks on rim and sides, wheel-pattern on bottom), one piece of Mattpainted Ware; piece of neck of wide-mouthed vessel with incised vertical lines between horizontals.

Found in jar under floor

Cup (Shape 11, p. 359)
    Nos. 1103-1107 (all in Fig. 337).

ROOM 56

The space between walls e and c (Figs. 9, 424) has been numbered 56 on the Key Plan. It was probably limited on the northeast by wall f, though there may have been a cupboard under the stairway. Room 56 thus appears to have been 3.86 m. long from northeast to southwest and 3.12 m. wide from northwest to southeast. These measurements depend on the assumption that wall e was still standing and that the short piece of foundation g offered no hindrance in the latest phases of the palace. This area too had been much disturbed before the time of our excavations and our conclusions regarding Room 56 can only be conjectural. If it was a room, it must presumably have been entered from Room 55 on the northwest, since there is no sign of any opening on the other three sides. No remains of the floor are left, though the discoloration of the southwestern wall (b) by fire gives some slight indication that it lay approximately at the same level as that of Room 55. What we have called foundation g, 0.80 m. wide and 1.55 m. long, is built of a single course of stone, for the most part broken pieces of poros. It may never have been any longer and could have served, if not for the stairway, merely as the support for a table, a platform, a bench or a couch. It belongs in any event to one of the late phases. Since no traces of the floor survive nor any objects that lay upon it, we have no means of determining for what purpose the room was used.

Deep beneath the conjectural floor of Room 56 remains of earlier periods have been brought to light. They include two remnants of walls founded on *stereo* and running from southeast to northwest (l and n, Fig. 424), connecting with another running from northeast to southwest (m). The latter, which is in part under wall c, is parallel to wall e and it may be that these four walls all formed part of an older building but it is not certain that wall e is of the same date. Adding to the complications are remnants of three floors, two of stucco (q) and one a pebble pavement (s) laid over wall l. Fragments of two pithoi sunk into hollows cut in *stereo*, and a third hollow, from which a pithos must have been removed, should also be mentioned. In the present disturbed state of these remains it is not possible to determine the exact sequence.

ROOM 57

Room 57 (Key Plan) comprises the area between wall c and the southeastern exterior wall of the building (Figs. 13, 424). On the northeast it is bounded by a prolongation of wall d, a section of the foundations of which is preserved; and on the southwest in part by the northeastern anta of the Propylon, which is missing except for the bedding stones of its foundations. The area thus enclosed is 5.25 m. long from southwest to northeast and 2.89 m. wide. The best preserved of these structures is wall c, 0.80 m. thick, which stands to a height of two courses, built chiefly of fragments of poros. On the northeast the continuation of wall d, also constructed to a considerable extent of fragments of poros, juts out 0.70 m.; its foundations, in which are two large blocks (Fig. 148), extend 1.20 m. farther.

On the southeast nothing is left of the wall that was in use in the last phases of the palace, except a layer of small stones which apparently supported the bedding slabs of the foundation (Fig. 13). The exact dimensions of the wall cannot be certainly fixed, but it is likely that from its corner with wall d it was broadened by an offset, 0.15 m. to 0.20 m. deep on its inner face, to a total thickness of 1.10 m. But in Court 58 the straight edge of the pavement which is preserved outside the building does give the approximate exterior line of the front wall. The end of the wall is almost equally well defined by the sharp turn of the pavement's edge toward the northwest. But what relation or connection this wall had with the northeast anta of the Propylon still presents an unsolved problem; for the anta itself was long ago despoiled of its squared blocks and large stones and is now represented only by its bedding stones. But there surely must have been an opening between the anta and the end of the southeastern wall. How it was adjusted, whether it had a door that could be closed and opened, or how otherwise it was arranged, we have no means of telling.

No trace of a floor has survived in Room 57 and its level is unknown, though it was presumably not far from that of the pavement in the Propylon.

At a much deeper level two, if not three, earlier walls have been exposed, all approximately parallel with the exterior wall of the last phase (Fig. 13). The southeasternmost has a good face of worked blocks, some 0.30 m. to 0.40 m. northwest of the inner face of the exterior wall of the last phase, as rebuilt by the Greek Service of Reconstruction in 1957 (Fig. 176). How thick this earlier wall was is not clear:

the first finished inner face that can now be recognized to the northwest is 2.10 m. to 2.20 m. distant from the outer edge of the worked blocks. If the two belong together, the wall would have a formidable thickness. Whether this inner face is actually part of the same wall or belonged to yet another is not clear. About 0.80 m. still farther northwestward, and directly underneath wall c, another wall (m) faced with poros blocks runs from northeast to southwest (p. 44). It has a thickness of 1.20 m. and a backing behind the poros blocks of unworked stones. Thus we have at least three, if not more, successive exterior southeast walls of the Main Building. They must be successive and the natural sequence would seem to be from northwest to southeast, though we have no conclusive ceramic evidence to fix the date of any of these walls specifically. The outer reconstructed one, however, is surely the latest in the series.

To the southwest of the Propylon a somewhat similar situation exists, for there we have two, if not more, successive exterior southeastern walls (p. 44), the earlier one, which bears a double axe sign on one of its poros blocks, having been buried under the floor of Archives Room 7 (Fig. 16). In both areas great damage and disturbance had been caused not only by those who removed building stones on a large scale but long before that by the ancient workmen who carried out the repairs and reconstructions of this unit of the palace. A kindly fate preserved the Archives Rooms of the final period reasonably well, but on the other side of the Propylon the remains of the last phase have been almost obliterated along with those of the earlier stages.

Since floor and floor deposits were altogether lacking, Room 57 yielded no evidence to shed light on its specific purpose. It was, in any event, surely utilitarian: for, however it was arranged, it could not—in its position just beside the principal gate—have contributed to the aesthetic effect of the façade of the palace. It must have had something to do with the guarding of the entrance. Was it perhaps the headquarters of the security forces who protected the residents of the palace? There was surely a palace guard, which could also show the proper honors to distinguished visitors, and a headquarters room in this strategic place would have been advantageous and almost necessary.

COURT 58

The southeast front of the Main Building faced a broad open court (58 on Key Plan) which was paved with stucco. The latter stretched continuously to a total distance of 44.90 m. from the northeastern side of Ramp 91 (Fig. 150) to a point beyond Ramp 59, where a stub of a wall projects from the southeast wall of Room 60 (Fig. 12). Whether the pavement continued still farther to the southwestward cannot now be determined, since the descending slope of the hill in that direction has cut away almost all the evidence. The original breadth of the court toward the southeast, owing to the same cause, is likewise unascertainable. All that can be said is that the broken ragged edge of the pavement has been exposed to a maximum distance of 7.10 m. from the southeastern wall opposite the lower end of Ramp 91 (Fig. 150). How it terminated on this side is uncertain. No indication of a boundary or a terrace wall has been seen in any of the numerous exploratory trenches that were dug down the slope.

It is not impossible that the principal entrance to the citadel in the time of the palace followed approximately the line of the modern driveway, which was laid out at the beginning of the systematic excavations in 1952. This took advantage of the most favorable route for an ascending roadway for wheeled traffic. If this conjecture is correct, visitors who came in chariots could probably drive up a gradual slope, passing below the southeastern end of the palace workshop, to gain approximately the level of the outer court, where at some suitable place they could dismount and walk across the pavement to the Propylon. Whether the court was enclosed on the southeastern side we do not know. A huge mass of fallen stones and some scanty traces of construction below and to the east of the Northeastern Building might conceivably be regarded as the remains of a lower gateway admitting to the ascent to the acropolis.

At its southwestern end, however, Court 58 was evidently bordered by a building of some kind. For here, 5.40 m. distant from the east corner of Room 60 (at 12.05 m. above datum), was found a lone column base of limestone, 0.64 m. in diameter, rising just above the stucco pavement of the final phases (Fig. 175). It has no recognizable architectural relation or meaning in connection with the Main Building or the southwestern unit of the palace. Consequently one may conjecture that it belonged to a colonnade extending southeastward, facing the court with a porch and possibly rooms behind it. It must be mentioned, however, that erosion on the southeastern and southwestern sides of the hill has carried away all traces of any walls that may have been associated with the column.

The only other structure which seems to have extended into the court jutted out from the southeastern wall of the Main Building outside Corridor 52 and Room 53 (Fig. 150). Seven poros blocks (Fig. 19), despite several missing elements, clearly indicate the roughly rectangular ground plan, 4.52 m. long from northeast to southwest, 2.24 m. wide at the northeast end and 2.07 m. at the southwest. The surviving blocks rise to ca. 0.20 m. above the pavement and the latter turns up where it meets the blocks. Of varying sizes and heights[74] they were set on small stones resting

---

[74] Dimensions of blocks beginning on the southwest at the southeast wall of the palace: block a (Fig. 425) 1.06 m. by 0.31 m. to 0.35 m.; b 0.62 m. by 0.28 m., the two separated by vacant space 0.18 m. long presumably

on *stereo*-like earth and adjusted so that their tops reached an approximate level. Within the enclosure was a fill of the same greenish-white *stereo*-like earth. The structure looks as if it was not expected to support any great weight. What was actually built on this poros foundation and how high can only be imagined as nothing has survived. Perhaps what we have is a rostrum (kings in the Nestorian tradition were eloquent speakers) or a reviewing stand, where royalty could sit to observe ceremonies on gala occasions, or maybe it was just a shady porch.

In and about this projecting structure clear evidence appeared to show two periods, represented by successive pavements, 0.07 m. to 0.13 m. apart. The earlier pavement (h), preserved inside the rectangular foundation (Fig. 177), turns up at its southwestern end as if to meet a wall which is now missing. This probably indicates that there was a similar platform in the earlier period though not in exactly the same place. On the earlier floor were found a small conical cup (Fig. 353 No. 719) and bases and stems of several kylikes.

On the pavement of Court 58 not far from the southeast wall of the Main Building outside Room 50 and Corridor 49 lay several large poros blocks and many fragments (Fig. 143). They must have fallen from the wall and had obviously escaped the attention of the stone robbers. The blocks lay just under the surface of the ground, surrounded by small stones and black earth and some sherds of the late Geometric Period.

In the black stratum as well as in the underlying whitish limey layer were recovered in abundance fragments of Mycenaean pottery mainly belonging to the later phases during which the palace was occupied.

Toward the southwest end of the court, outside the Propylon, several large blocks of poros and other debris lay more or less in a line as if fallen from the entablature of the gateway (Fig. 14 and p. 44). Some 8 m. to 10 m. farther southwestward the pavement sinks to a fairly deep hollow where the water from rain was concentrated to run into an underground drain. Round about this hollow, on the pavement that was in use at the time of the destruction, were found numerous fragments of a circular marble table. Many pieces had been fused together with the stucco floor from which they could be separated only with great difficulty. Almost all the pieces could be fitted together to make more than half of the table top. Its upper surface bore inlaid decoration.

Yet farther southwestward, in the neighborhood of the column base mentioned above, two stucco pavements were seen, the earlier one only some 0.10 m. to 0.12 m. below the later. Still deeper, toward the west, part of a rather fine stucco and

---

for a wooden upright. Southeast side: space 1.73 m. long, where one or more blocks are missing; c 1.16 m. by 0.37 m.; space 0.17 m. wide; d 0.85 m. by 0.35 m., this block abutting against a block (e) forming the corner and running from southeast to northwest. Northeast side: e 0.39 m. by 0.34 m.; f 0.40 m. by 0.39 m.; g 0.62 m. by 0.38 m.

pebble pavement has been uncovered; this must no doubt be assigned to an earlier period, perhaps contemporary with a similar mosaic floor noted under Rooms 55-56-57 (p. 226).

OBJECTS FOUND

Stratum of black earth and small stones

IRON

Spike, square in section, slightly bent (Fig. 293 No. 9), l. bent 0.119 m., w. head 0.015 m.

Fragment of another spike (Fig. 293 No. 8).

Below black stratum

BRONZE

Nondescript chunks and pieces (e.g., Fig. 293 No. 7).

STONE

Obsidian: flakes.

Flint: chips.

Quartz: pieces.

Variegated marble: 37 or more fragments of various sizes which have been fitted together to make up slightly more than half of a circular table top (Figs. 271 No. 4, 272 Nos. 3, 4); d. 0.518 m., thickness at edge 0.026 m., increasing toward center to 0.035 m. or more. It was probably supported on three sturdy legs, now missing. Under side thickly coated with plaster to hold the heavy mended pieces together. The fragments lay some face up, others face down; many badly damaged, partly calcined and fused to stucco pavement. Upper surface was once smooth and polished, decorated with inlays of small white or reddish circular stone disks, set in neatly drilled shallow cuttings. A scanty few remained in place; some others were found along with the marble fragments. The disks were inserted into the sockets singly or in double, triple and quintuple clusters. No quadruple group was noted. When three were used they were arranged in a straight line or in a triangle; when five, in a T-shaped formation, with three in the upright and three in the crossbar on top. Sometimes longer pieces instead of disks may have been fitted into the cuttings, but the latter regularly show marks of the circular drills. These figures seem to have been distributed over the table in a hit or miss fashion with no recognizable design or order.

Worked fragment (Fig. 293 No. 10), 0.01 m. thick, of black and reddish "bastard marble."

POTTERY

Much shattered material collected from all parts of the court. Shapes recorded: in coarse ware, pithos (some with linear painted decoration), tripod-vessel, lid, baking pan (Shape 78), scoop, cooking pot; in finer ware, kylix (76 stems), cup and bowl, etc. (41 flat bases), bowl with pinched-out handles, conical cup, dipper. A good many pieces bear traces of painted decoration: krater-bowl with red bands; stirrup-vase (many examples) with horizontal bands and dotted rosettes; neck of jug solidly coated. Other motives seen: stripes and rippling, spirals, net-pattern, curving parallel lines. A few stray sherds of earlier date: one Mattpainted, one fragment of Vapheio cup, and piece with punctated dots.

DRAINS

Beneath the northeastern end of the rostrum mentioned above, 0.30 m. to 0.40 m. below the pavement of Court 58, was uncovered the drain emerging from Room 53 (p. 219 and Figs. 148, 425). It was built with lateral walls of stone enclosing a channel, 0.26 m. wide at the top and 0.30 m. to 0.34 m. at the bottom. Upon the walls transverse cover slabs of considerable size were laid. At a distance of 1.50 m. from the exterior wall this drain joined another larger channel running from northeast to southwest, roughly parallel to the southeast wall of the Main Building (Fig. 177).

From the short section that emerged from Room 53 were recovered a heaping handful of animal bones and many sherds, mostly of kylikes and handleless cups along with some fragments of bowls with pinched-out handles, and dippers. Noted also were splaying rims of cooking pots and the ring-base of a flat plate.

The more important drain too was lined with a wall on each side, built of smallish stones laid fairly regularly in three or four courses, rising to a height of 0.47 m. *Stereo* served as the bottom of the channel which was 0.30 m. to 0.34 m. wide. Large and very large blocks of poros were placed across the top as cover slabs, lying 0.20 m. to 0.55 m. below the pavement of the court. The drain was traced 1.40 m. toward the northeast of the junction and 6.60 m. toward the southwest (Fig. 426), where in a gradual turn it approached nearer (0.70 m.) the outside wall of the palace (Fig. 179). In this latter part only about 50 very small sherds were collected from deep down, just above the floor of the channel. Four were pithos fragments, while other recognizable bits were rims, handles, and bases of kylikes and rims of handleless cups.

The drain was explored to a total length of 8 m.; it continued in both directions but could not be exposed farther without destroying the pavement of the court, which is still well preserved. Some 20 m. to the southwest, however, just below Ramp 59, a further section of it has been examined. It had been found by illicit diggers before our time, who had opened a large hole (Fig. 178) and broken into the drain in a search for treasure. We entered through this break and cleared the drain 5.50 m. to the eastward and 2.75 m. to the westward (Fig. 426).

This section evidently forms one of the main drains of the palace. In the part to the east of the opening cut by the intruders it is built with stone walls on each side, containing many blocks of poros and flat slabs of considerable size laid in fairly regular courses (Fig. 181). It varies from 0.45 m. to 0.60 m. in width and from 0.60 m. to 0.80 m. in height. It is covered by large blocks of poros laid transversely and resting on the walls. About 3 m. to the northeast of the break two of the cover slabs were set 0.33 m. to 0.43 m. apart (Fig. 182). Over this gap was placed a poros block 0.14 m. thick, in which were cut three neatly made circular holes, 0.105 m. to 0.11 m. in diameter, symmetrically arranged in an equilateral triangle, 0.235 m. apart, center to center. The top of the stone with the holes (11.84 m. above datum), was fixed opposite Ramp 59 in a hollow of the pavement of Court 58 to which the floor on all sides sloped downward (Fig. 12). The holes conducted into the drain below rainwater that fell in this area from the roof of the building. The channel was cleared ca. 2 m. northeastward under the preserved pavement beyond the stone with the openings. Still farther northeastward it was possible, by means of a flashlight, despite some obstructions and a slight bend, to see the continuation of the channel for an additional distance of 3 m. or 4 m. In the section to the northeast of the drain holes the floor seems to have been cut in *stereo*, but under the pierced block and toward the southwest the channel had a floor of stone slabs.[75] In the part between the pierced stone and the intrusive break, ca. 0.75 m. from the east edge of the latter, a tributary drain, No. 4,[76] comes in from the north (Fig. 183).

From the break made by the intruders the drain was followed mainly westward with a slight bend to the southwest 2.75 m. to an interruption caused by the collapse of a cover slab and the consequent subsidence of the floor in the southern corner of Room 60. This break is 1.10 m. long. At the end of it, in a sharper turn, the channel swung to the southwest in a steep descent down the slope of the hill through a maze of ruins to a length of 8.36 m. Here is another angle, as the drain veers again westward to a length of 4.97 m., where it bends once more to the southwest continuing 4.60 m. to the outer edge of the excavation.

In the first of the foregoing four sections the channel, with a width of 0.38 m. and a height of 0.82 m. above a stone floor, shows no change in the style of construction from what we have seen on the northeastern side of the break. The second section has been recognized only from above, where most of the cover slabs are still in place. In two gaps between covering blocks the width of the channel varies from 0.32 m. to 0.37 m. The cover slabs are made of heterogeneous material, several poros blocks, obviously reused, half of a shaped column base and a few unworked stones. This section, passing underneath the southwest foundation wall of Room 62, was clearly built before the latter. But higher up on the slope, below the floor of Room 62, a broad gash was cut through an earlier wall to make way for the drain.

The third section, turning westward, has its northern wall standing to a height of 1.40 m. (Fig. 180). The three lowest courses are made of substantial poros slabs, rising to 0.92 m. with several courses of rubble above. On the south side only a single course of large poros blocks (0.46 m. high) remains in place. The floor is paved with flat stones.

The fourth section at a considerably deeper level (ca. 0.44 m. wide) is paved with large flat slabs and lined on each side by a wall built of big blocks of poros and standing to a height of 0.45 m. to 0.50 m. Its southwestern end is still full of earth and covered with long unworked slabs of limestone.

---

[75] Stone of floor 0.90 m. below the top of the pierced block, i.e. 10.94 m. above datum.

[76] Drain 4 is 0.55 m. broad. Its cover is made of two partially worked stones forming a sort of vault. It may have been older than the Main Drain, as the cover slabs of the latter rest on masonry above the vault of Drain 4.

The various sections of the drain we have studied are far from uniform. There are many differences in dimensions, in the materials used in the construction of the walls and the cover slabs, and in the arrangement of the floor. One cannot fail to wonder if several periods of building are not represented. In any event it is likely that various parts of the drain came occasionally to be blocked up and had to be cleared and perhaps rebuilt.

We have called it one of the main drains of the palace and considerable evidence is available to support that view. In a good many places along its course this channel was joined by branches coming into it from various parts of the building. It is likely that one such affluent entered from the northwest, coming from Court 42 and also from Court 47, if it did not actually constitute the beginning of the drain itself. Another branch certainly flowed into it from Room 53. Between that and the break caused by illicit diggers beneath Ramp 59 some other small channels may have opened into it. Toward the west several further tributary channels appear: about 1.50 m. from the break coming from the north, is Drain 6[77] which had already absorbed Drain 2 (Fig. 184);[78] the latter, emerging originally from Court 3 and passing beneath the floor of Room 9 was joined there by Drain 5[79] which came from Room 10. Farther in its course, after turning southeastward under Ramp 59, Drain 2 apparently received Drain 7[80] from the southwest and continued southeastward to join Drain 6 just before entering the Main Drain. Two other drains on this side of the building, Drains 1 and 3,[81] almost parallel and only 1 m. apart, seem to have

[77] Drain 6 is very narrow (0.26 m.) and could be cleaned for a distance of only 0.50 m. Through it Drain 2 appears to have emptied into the Main Drain. Though the earth between was not cleared, two workmen, one in Drain 2 and the other in Drain 6, were able to see each other by using a flashlight. Drain 6 produced a number of fragments of kylikes.

[78] Drain 2 begins near the south corner of Court 3, where in a hollow of the pavement three perforations through a poros block conducted rainwater from the court into the drain (p. 63). The first section runs 8.80 m. southwestward. Nearly all of this stretch was cleared, except a short piece under the floor of the court, though the pierced block was reached by probing. The lateral walls are built of large and smaller flattish blocks and slabs. The channel, 0.34 m. wide, was exposed to *stereo*, 1.10 m. below floor level. Immediately beneath the floor were the cover slabs made of big blocks. About 0.35 m. after passing under the exterior wall of the Main Building Drain 2 (Figs. 80, 186) turns southeastward for a further course of 7.80 m. (Fig. 185). At this point it is 0.50 m. wide and 0.70 m. high. At a distance of 2 m. from the angle a rectangular hole from above in Ramp 59 opened into it (p. 236, Fig. 21). Almost immediately under the hole, a little to the northwest, were found a small angular

kylix and two votive kylikes. Nearby in more fragmentary condition lay an angular kylix, an unusually large votive kylix, a dipper, and a cup. At its lower end Drain 2 seems to have joined Drain 6 before entering the Main Drain.

[79] Drain 5 apparently begins beneath a drain hole near the south corner of Room 10 (p. 104). It runs southeastward 3.40 m. and empties into Drain 2. A relatively narrow channel, only 0.27 m. wide, it could not be cleared without destroying the floor of Room 9.

[80] Drain 7, indicated by scanty evidence, came from the southwest, joining Drain 2 under the square drain hole in Ramp 59. It is only 0.22 m. wide and could not be explored for any distance. It may have come from Drain 8 which starts in Court 63.

[81] Drain 1 is known only by a short section, 1.20 m. long, running from north to south just outside the western corner of the Archives Room (8). A circular hole, 0.16 m. in diameter, drilled through a large rectangular block, 0.58 m. by 0.53 m. by 0.12 m. thick, of poros apparently led down into the drain (Fig. 21). The lateral walls were made of smallish stones and the cover consisted of overlapping slabs, three of which remained in place. The exact relation of this drain to some of the others in the same general area is not now clear. Drain 1 may perhaps belong to an earlier build-

run diagonally from north to south through the foundations of the southwest wall of the Main Building and under Ramp 59; they too may have emptied into Drain 2 or Drain 6 before reaching the Main Drain if they did not join the latter independently.

Yet another line, Drain 8,[82] came southeastward from Court 63 and presumably delivered its contents somewhere into the Main Drain. Still another, Drain 9,[83] if it is not an older drain, may have debouched into the lowest section which was called the fourth in the preceding paragraph.

O B J E C T S   F O U N D

Main Drain

GOLD
Tiny fragment of foil.

BRONZE
Eleven tiny barbed arrowheads, average l. 0.017 m., w. across barbs 0.007 m., and fragments of many others (e.g., Fig. 295).
Many nondescript pieces (e.g., Fig. 294 Nos. 1, 2).

LEAD
Six twists of lead melted in the fire (Fig. 294 Nos. 3-8).

STONE
Steatite: two conoid whorls, or large buttons (Fig. 294 Nos. 14, 15), h. 0.017 m., 0.02 m.; d. 0.025 m., 0.031 m.; d. perforation 0.006 m., 0.005 m.
Two buttons: conoid (Fig. 294 No. 13), h. 0.01 m., d. 0.021 m., d. perforation 0.003 m.; shanked (Fig. 294 No. 12), h. 0.011 m., d. 0.02 m., d. perforation 0.002 m.
Fragment, about half, of lentoid seal, NM. 7804 = *CMMS* 296 (Fig. 311 No. 25): hind quarters of an animal moving to right; two branches of foliage above.

Flint: fragment of small tan arrowhead (Fig. 294 No. 9), l. pres. 0.013 m., w. pres. 0.01 m. Several chips.
Obsidian: flakes.
Quartz: several very small bits.
Other: egg-shaped pellet, apparently polished and used (Fig. 294 No. 10).

BONE
Small knuckle bone (Fig. 294 No. 11).

TERRACOTTA
Fragment of crescent-shaped figurine with modeled breasts, hollow stem (Fig. 294 No. 21): head, tips of crescent and bottom missing; h. pres. 0.07 m., w. across crescent pres. 0.042 m., d. stem 0.03 m. to 0.02 m. Fine pinkish-buff clay, buff surface. Decoration painted in red: bordering bands around bottom of neck and bottom of arms, joined by curving vertical stripes on back and front; the two stripes in middle of front connected by horizontal lines; two vertical bands on back and front of skirt and one on back and front of neck.
Fragments of two animal figurines (Fig. 294 Nos. 16, 17).

---

ing period. To the northwest of the pierced stone were found at 0.42 m. below the pavement of the ramp four handleless cups, three of them intact, and one small broken kylix (Fig. 187).

Drain 3 was discovered ca. 1 m. to the southeast of Drain 1 and approximately parallel to it, running from north to south across the line of the southwest exterior wall of the building. Only a short piece was exposed. It was in a ruinous state and nothing much can be said about its construction, but it is probable that this drain formed an upper section of the one that has

been numbered 6 on page 233.

[82] Drain 8 apparently begins under the triple drain-holes in the southeastern part of Court 63 (p. 245 and Fig. 188). It can be traced ca. 4 m. southeastward to the boundary wall of the court. Thence its course is uncertain. It may have continued in the same direction and joined the Main Drain, or it may have turned northeastward along the line of what we have called Drain 7.

[83] Drain 9 is largely hypothetical and may not be a drain at all.

Whorl (Fig. 294 No. 20).

Pestles (?): two cylindrical objects, rounded tops, flattened bottoms (Fig. 294 Nos. 18, 19).

POTTERY

From sections extending southwestward from outside Room 7 to near southwest wall of Room 60

Krater-bowl (Shape 60, p. 397)
No. 1150 (Fig. 385), decorated.

Sherds: a great quantity. Shapes recognized: in coarse ware, pithos, tripod-vessel, scoop, pan (Shape 78); in finer ware, kylix (329 stems counted), votive kylix (18 stems), bowl and cup (181 flat bases), cup with straddle handle (10), conical cup, bowl and basin with pinched-out handles, red basin with horizontal handles (Shape 2), spouted bowl, cup with two high handles, jug with rim cut away above handle, tea-pot, rhyton, stirrup-vase, tankard. Decorative motives: bands, stripes (horizontal and vertical), wavy lines, Mycenaean III Flower, net-pattern, parallel chevrons, murex, panel decoration, spirals, dots and spirals, flower design on oatmeal ware, festoon, concentric arcs. Almost all these patterns are typical of the late Mycenaean III B Period.

Drain 1

Cup (Shape 11, p. 359)
Nos. 550 and 551 (Fig. 353), 552, 553 (Fig. 354).

33 miscellaneous sherds: chiefly fragments of kylikes and flat-bottomed cups; one coarse bit.

Drain 2

Diminutive kylix (Shape 26, p. 366)
Nos. 555, 556.

Kylix (Shape 27, p. 366)
No. 554

Kylix (Shape 29b, p. 368)
No. 557.

34 miscellaneous sherds: 5 coarse, 29 finer. Kylix and flat-bottomed cup well represented. Other shapes: krater-bowl.

SOUTHWESTERN BUILDING

RAMP 59

FROM the open court outside the southeastern façade of the palace a ramp (59 on Key Plan) leads upward, forming the principal approach to the Southwestern Building (Fig. 12). It ascends between the southwestern wall of the Main Building outside the Archives Rooms (7 and 8) and Pantry 9 and the northeastern wall of Room 60, which probably constituted part of the Southwestern Building. This open passage must have been like a somewhat imposing deep canyon, for on the right rose a high wall built of large blocks of poros laid in ashlar style and on the left the wall of Room 60 coated with mud plaster.

The line of the wall on the northeast cannot be precisely fixed for this whole section was demolished and removed down to the bedding of the foundations (Fig. 178). In any event, the bordering walls are not parallel and the ramp broadens as it ascends from a width of 2.90 m. at its lower end to 3.90 m. at a point 7 m. to the northwestward. Here a deep projecting offset in the wall of the Main Building, opposite the partition between Rooms 8 and 9, reduces the breadth of the ramp from 3.90 m. to 3.09 m. Beyond this angle the passage continues almost level 4.85 m. farther to end against a transverse wall. This terminal wall once abutted against the outside wall of the Main Building, but when the latter was despoiled of its material the connection was broken away. At its upper end the ramp is 3.41 m. wide. It turns southwestward and ca. 1 m. from the corner reaches a doorway marked by large jamb bases of poros (Fig. 191). Here the passage, now 2.68 m. wide, flanks the northwest end of Room 60 and is bordered on the opposite side by an extension, after a projecting offset 0.70 m. deep, of the terminal wall.

The ramp was provided with a good stucco pavement, 0.02 m. to 0.03 m. thick, throughout its whole length. Along the southwestern side it is reasonably well preserved except for wear and the usual cracks. In the middle and toward the northeast, however, it has suffered considerable damage. Almost opposite the offset in the exterior wall of the Main Building and 0.75 m. from the projecting corner an opening led into an underground drain. How the water was conveyed through the floor is not now clear, but underneath the stucco is a rectangular shaft, 0.15 m. by 0.17 m., neatly built of small stones, which leads down into the underlying drain some 0.80 m. below the floor (p. 233 note 78).

The whole ramp was filled with a deposit of burned debris of the usual kind, fused and calcined stone, disintegrated crude brick, ashes and carbonized matter. In it were more than a dozen large blocks of poros which had fallen from the ashlar wall and eluded the attention of the plunderers (Fig. 21).

At a depth of 0.10 m. near the line of the missing wall was found a fragment of a silver cup. It retains one bearded head in gold and niello inlaid in the silver and the countersunk setting for a second, similar to some ten other examples recovered farther eastward in the Propylon (p. 58). The topsoil in the upper part of the ramp also yielded a fragment of an almost illegible tablet.

On the floor of the ramp were found remains of at least a dozen pots, many of which lay crushed under a mass of fused and calcined stone not far from the southwestern side of the passage. They include (Fig. 338) a one-handled jug; a three-handled jar, a small stirrup-vase and fragments of a krater-bowl, all three with painted decoration. Farther northwestward on the pavement were found an amphora and two decorated three-handled jars. Fragments of several other vessels were insufficient to allow the pots to be put together and the exact shapes to be recognized.

O B J E C T S   F O U N D

GOLD AND SILVER

Three fragments of the silver cup with part of handle and remains of one bearded head in gold and niello and countersinking for reception of inlay of a second (NM. 7842, Fig. 261 No. 1 and p. 58). Found in surface soil.

BRONZE

Nondescript fragments (e.g., Fig. 293 Nos. 5, 6).

LEAD

Weight, disk-shaped (Fig. 293 No. 3), d. 0.032 m., th. 0.007 m.

STONE

Steatite button: conoid (Fig. 293 No. 4), h. 0.021 m., d. 0.021 m.; discolored by heat.
Fragment of obsidian, two of flint.

CLAY

Tablet: No. 1250 (*OOT*, 12, 66, pls. XVIII-XIX), found in topsoil.

POTTERY

Jug (Shape 37, p. 377)
No. 520.
Amphora (Shape 45, p. 381)
No. 435 (Fig. 372).
Jar (Shape 52, p. 386)
Nos. 419 and 460 (Fig. 375), 521 (Figs. 375, 376); all decorated.
Krater-bowl (Shape 60, p. 397)
No. 576 (Figs. 385, 386), decorated.
Stirrup-vase (Shape 65f, p. 410)
No. 545 (Figs. 391, 392), decorated.

R O O M   6 0

Just before the ramp reaches the above-mentioned turn, a doorway opens southwestward into Room 60 (Fig. 12 and Key Plan). The exact width of the opening is no longer determinable, as each side is filled with a *migma* of melted and fused stone and crude brick; but some slight evidence showing where wooden jambs were attached gives ground for estimating that the full breadth was 1.77 m. The actual door opening was considerably narrower than that, possibly no more than 1 m. Carbonized matter observed on each side implies that the casing projected into the opening nearly 0.45 m. from the northwest and 0.30 m. from the southeast. No threshold block and no bases for jambs were found *in situ* but the broken edge of the stucco floor of the ramp indicates that a threshold block may have been removed by marauders. In any event something of the sort was required at this place, for the clay floor inside the room (12.62 m. above datum) lay 0.20 m. below that of the ramp and a step must have been necessary.

Room 60 is not rectangular in plan, since the opposite walls are not parallel. The interior has a length from southeast to northwest ranging from 6.77 m. against the northeast wall to 7.34 m. along the southwestern. The width on the southeast is 3.14 m., on the northwest 3.01 m. The northeastern wall, 1.02 m. thick, stands to a height of 0.65 m. above the floor of the room. At least four chases at intervals of 0.80 m., 1.20 m., and 1.10 m., mark the position of the upright beams. The southeastern wall is 1 m. thick until, at 2.20 m. from the east corner, it reaches a projection, 0.60 m. thick, jutting out toward the southeast (Fig. 189). Beyond this projection the thickness of the wall, which rises 0.77 m. above the floor, is 0.90 m. Indications of at least four chases appear in the wall. Whether the projection toward the southeast marks the beginning of a wall extending in that direction could not be ascertained, for illicit diggers had here excavated a deep hole into the Main Drain (p. 227) and no trace of a continuation of a wall now exists (Fig. 178). If there was a wall—and the variation in the level of the floors to the northeast (12.19 m. above datum) and southwest (12.08 m.) of the existing stub might point to that conclusion—it could only have been a thin partition. Perhaps it was part of an engaged pier for decorative purposes.

The southwestern wall of Room 60 (Fig. 189), which is 0.90 m. thick, has lost most of its outer face in the erosion and demolition that marked the edge of the hill on this side. On its interior face, however, it is preserved to a height of 0.70 m. Four chases are visible in the top at intervals of 0.80 m., 0.80 m., and 0.70 m., and traces of several more are barely recognizable in the southeastern part of the wall.

The northwestern wall is 0.90 m. thick and stands to 0.63 m. above the floor. Signs of at least four chases are visible with average intervals of 0.70 m.

All these walls were coated with mud plaster, which survives in some places to the height of the wall it covers. On every side is displayed abundant testimony of the great heat of the fire that destroyed the building. Calcined remains of stones and fused *migma* of stone and crude brick are conspicuous in all parts of the walls. The framework of heavy timbers indicated by the many chases undoubtedly provided much of the combustible material. But Room 60 was clearly used as a pantry and wooden shelves were built around all four sides of the storeroom.

The floor of earth or clay which has already been mentioned is somewhat rough and irregular with a general slope to the southeast (12.62 m. above datum inside the doorway and 12.37 m. at the southeast end). On the northwestern side are four small post holes (perhaps there were originally five) unevenly spaced (Fig. 189). They undoubtedly serve as the setting places for wooden posts that held up shelving. Similar holes of like dimensions were found on the other three sides of the room;[1] seven appear in an irregular row along the southwestern wall though not exactly parallel to the latter. There was probably an eighth hole originally, the south-easternmost having disappeared in the collapse of the floor into the drain. Along the southeastern side only two holes are now visible; a third may be hidden under a mass of *migma*. On the northeast eight post holes are well preserved in an irregular line; the southeastern one, only 0.29 m. distant from the southeastern wall, and 0.35 m. from its neighbor to the northwest, perhaps having been inserted as a reinforcement of the corner. Some of the holes have a flat stone at the bottom; in others smallish stones appear along the side, perhaps wedged in to hold the uprights in position. All this wooden shelving was of course consumed by the fire and what-ever it held fell to the floor.

The pottery had clearly been arranged in order, vessels of each kind placed together, and even after they fell and were shattered the semblance of orderly arrangement persisted. A great heap of broken pottery was piled up along the walls on all sides. In the eastern corner some 30 or 40 large bowls with two horizontal handles and bridged spouts were stacked on the floor in rows one inside the other upside down. The total number of pots stored in the room exceeded 730 and at least 24 shapes and varieties were represented, ranging from miniature votives to capacious bowls. The kylix is by far the commonest shape, occurring in many variations, followed in order of frequency by bowls, basins, cups, scoops, kraters, jugs, incense burners, and lids (Fig. 340).

The entire deposit of pottery in the room was buried under a mass of burned debris consisting mainly of calcined stones and crude brick, broken up and dis-integrated, containing likewise in considerable abundance the usual flotsam and jetsam of scattered sherds. Many streaks of carbonized matter also appeared, some below the pots, some above in the wreckage, perhaps representing the wooden shelves or their supports or the timbers in the walls or the beams in the ceiling. A good many fragments of painted plaster and also of stucco flooring with smooth blue surface were found throughout the deposit and also deeper in an area near the southeast end of the room, where the floor had partially collapsed into the underground drain. Much of this material had obviously fallen from above, but the collection of sherds and plaster found in the drain itself must be in part of earlier date.

[1] The holes range from 0.10 m. to 0.12 m. in diameter and from 0.10 m. to 0.20 m. in depth. Position of holes: along northwestern wall: set out 0.36 m. to 0.40 m. from the wall measured to center, at intervals ranging from 0.44 m. to 0.64 m.; along southwest wall: set out 0.48 m. to 0.77 m., at intervals ranging from 0.52 m. to 0.80 m.; along southeast wall: set out 0.42 m. to 0.52 m., 0.67 m. apart; along northeast wall: set out 0.43 m. to 0.52 m. from wall, at intervals ranging from 0.35 m. to 0.83 m.

In view of the thick substantial walls and the generous use of wooden timbers in their construction, it seems likely that this part of the Southwestern Building had an upper story, and that would account for much of the fallen debris. No remains of a stairway have been recognized, but it might have been installed farther to the southwestward where the devastation has left no surviving evidence.

The large collection of pottery found in this pantry raises some problems that ought to be mentioned. In the first place, what was it doing in this location at the very entrance to the southwestern residential unit of the palace? On the analogy of the Main Building one might have expected here a guard room or the quarters of some official of standing. Were the pots assembled here for sale or for distribution and why at the front door? The comparable stores of pottery in Rooms 18, 19, 20, 21, 22 were decently segregated in a remote corner of the Main Building where they would not intrude on the sensitivities of fastidious guests. These are questions which we have not been able to answer satisfactorily. The character of the pottery itself moreover deserves some study and it might shed light on the purpose of this storeroom. Although the tall-stemmed drinking cup is the commonest shape here as well as in Pantries 19 and 20, and some of the other pots too are similar to types found in the five storerooms of the Main Building, the wares themselves differ conspicuously and each group contains pots of a good many shapes that are not represented in the other. It seems logical therefore to conclude that the selections of the types of vessels themselves and the wares were intended for different purposes and users.

OBJECTS FOUND

SILVER

Fragment, possibly of rim (Fig. 293 No. 2).

BRONZE

Tiny arrowhead, tips of point and barbs missing (Fig. 293 No. 1).

Arrowhead with socket for shaft to fit into (Fig. 292), l. 0.036 m., w. across barbs 0.019 m., d. of shaft 0.006 m.

Crumbling bits.

FLINT

Two flakes.

BONE

Knucklebone.

POTTERY

	Examples Counted	Examples Numbered
Basin (Shape 2, p. 355)	75	3
Nos. 441 (Figs. 349, 350), 466, 508 (Fig. 350).		
Bowl (Shape 4, p. 356)	51	2
Nos. 455 and 456 (Fig. 349).		
Bowl (Shape 6, p. 357)	9	6
Nos. 448 (Figs. 351, 352), 449-451, 666, 667.		
Bowl (Shape 7, p. 357)	46	12
Nos. 500 (Fig. 352), 502, 503, 549, 558-561, 642 (Fig. 351), 643, 644, 645 (Fig. 351).		
Bowl (Shape 8, p. 358)		1
No. 668 (Figs. 351, 352).		
Bowl (Shape 10, p. 359)	33	6
Nos. 506, 507 (Fig. 352), 533-535, 548, (Fig. 351).		
Cup (Shape 12, p. 360)		1
No. 452.		
Cup (Shape 15, p. 361)	83	12
Nos. 423 (Fig. 356), 424 (Figs. 355, 356), 477-480, 522 (Fig. 355), 523, 540, 661-663.		

	Examples Counted	Examples Numbered
Cup (Shape 16, p. 362)		2

Cup (Shape 16, p. 362)   2
Nos. 664 (Figs. 355, 356), 665
(Fig. 355).

Cup (Shape 17, p. 362)   4
Nos. 438 (Figs. 355, 356), 462
(Fig. 355), 463, 660.

Cup (Shape 19, p. 363)   3
Nos. 439 (Fig. 356), 655 and
656 (Fig. 355).

Kylix (Shape 26, p. 366)   82   1
No. 641 (Fig. 359).

Kylix (Shape 27, p. 366)   3
Nos. 425 and 426 (Fig. 359),
465.

Kylix (Shape 28, p. 367)   5
Nos. 442 (Figs. 359, 360), 483,
501 (Fig. 359), 640, 648.

Kylix (Shape 30c, p. 373)   253   23
Nos. 433 (Fig. 365), 434 (Fig.
366), 436 (Fig. 366), 454 (Fig.
365), 472, 474, 475 (Fig. 366),
484, 485, 488-499, 646, 647.

Kylix (Shape 32, p. 374)   6
Nos. 473 (Fig. 365), 476 (Fig.
365), 651, 652 (Fig. 366), 653
(Fig. 366), 654.

Jug (Shape 41, p. 379)   20   4
Nos. 420, 421 (Figs. 369, 370),
422, 486.

Jar (Shape 52, p. 386)   1
No. 461 (Fig. 375), decorated.

Krater (Shape 59, p. 396)   31   3
Nos. 437 (Figs. 383, 384), 453
(Fig. 383), 672 (Fig. 383).

Squat jar (Shape 64, p. 402)   1
No. 464 (Fig. 385), decorated.

Stirrup-vase (Shape 65b 3, p. 406)   1
No. 459.

Ladle or scoop (Shape 66, p.
411)   39   18
Nos. 427 (Fig. 396), 428-432,
440, 443 (Fig. 395), 444-447,
481, 482, 487, 657-659.

Tripod "incense-burner"
(Shape 71, p. 414)   5   5
Nos. 504 (Fig. 395), 577, 578,
579, 580 (Figs. 395, 396).

Lid for "incense-burner"
(Shape 72, p. 415)   6   6
Nos. 505 (Fig. 395), 581, 582
(Figs. 395, 396), 583, 584, 585.

CORRIDOR 61

The doorway opening southwestward at the upper end of Ramp 59 has been mentioned (Fig. 191). It is marked by a poros block on each side forming the bases for the jambs.[2] Neither has a cutting for a pivot-socket and it is likely that the opening could be closed by a gate rather than by a door. It was in any event framed by a substantial wooden casing the carbonized remains of which had survived on the northwestern stone block. The width of the opening between the jamb bases decreases from 1.61 m. on the northeast to 1.50 m. on the southwest. The stucco pavement of the ramp continues through this space between the poros blocks and, though worn, is fairly well preserved.

Beyond the gateway the passage (61 on Key Plan) continues with its stucco pavement bounded by a wall on each side (Fig. 12). The pavement has been traced 5.50 m. southwestward to the edge of the hill beyond which all remains of the floor have disappeared, though the foundations of the lateral walls continue at a much

2 Northwest base: length 0.72 m., width 0.54 m. to 0.58 m.; southeast base: length 0.68 m., width 0.59 m. to 0.61 m.

deeper level. At its northeastern end Corridor 61 is bordered on the southeast by the northwestern wall of Room 60, which is preserved to a height of 0.42 m. The wall opposite is 0.80 m. to 0.85 m. thick, standing 0.28 m. high. It is not parallel to the wall of Room 60 but is oriented slightly farther to the south. At 2.51 m. from the doorway it terminates in a jamb base which flanked an opening leading north-westward into Court 63 (Fig. 188). In its course to this point the corridor diminishes in width from 2.65 m. to 2.31 m. Farther southwestward beyond the opening no accurate measurements of the width can be made since both lateral walls have been destroyed to a level well below the pavement. Some small pieces of worked blocks in the northwestern wall may perhaps be taken to mark the position of the south-western jamb base. If this deduction is correct, the over-all width of the entranceway, including the jamb bases, leading into Court 63, would be 3.56 m., and the actual opening ca. 2.80 m.

Corridor 61 was found filled with the usual burned debris, which had presumably fallen from above. The fire in this area had been equally destructive with that in Room 60. On the right-hand side of the passage, just inside the doorway from Ramp 59 and close to the northwestern wall, stood a stone lamp made of marble-like limestone (Fig. 190). It is of a type familiar in Crete and known also on the main-land with carved spiraliform decoration. It has a shallow bowl on top with two channels for wicks. One side has suffered some damage from fire but the other is relatively well preserved. Apart from a small fragment of ivory and a considerable assortment of potsherds, nothing else of any significance was found.

As mentioned, the corridor continued southwestward, how far it is not now possible to determine. The foundation walls on both sides have been followed nearly 7 m. beyond the southwest side of the entrance into Court 63. It is not im-possible that the corridor became a broad stairway that descended to a lower level on this side of the building or even to an exit into the lower town. No actual evidence can be adduced to confirm this conjecture.

OBJECTS FOUND

STONE

White marble: lamp on low cylindrical pedes-tal with torus molding (now almost worn away) at bottom (Figs. 271 Nos. 1a, 1b; 272 Nos. 1, 2). H. 0.145 m., d. lamp 0.25 m., d. of pedestal, including torus 0.115 m., d. of bowl 0.127 m., depth of bowl 0.046 m. From central bowl, which has flat rim, 0.007 m. wide, two splaying wick-channels (one directly opposite the other) edged by ex-tension of rim of bowl. Shoulder on each side between wick-channels bears a row of five snail-like spirals in relief. Between lat-ter and rim of bowl on one side four wavy parallel lines somewhat carelessly carved; on the opposite side only two similar lines. Exterior vertical side of lamp decorated by alternating convex and concave bands, sep-arated by incised lines. The three upper bands are interrupted by the snails; the lower concave band continues beneath them. In middle of each side (between wick-channels) a broad, lug-like projection hangs down; on it is carved another convex horizontal band.

Lamp considerably damaged by fire, especially at bottom; snails also badly calcined and worn. Original smooth polish lacking over greater part of surface. Wick-channel on one side much blackened.

Comparable, though not identical, decoration appears on an amphora of alabaster from Knossos (*PM* IV, 897ff., fig. 875 a and b). Cf. also a marble lamp from Mallia, *Études crétoises,* Tome XI (1959), pl. XLIX, 3.

I V O R Y

Small fragment of inlay with carved spiral resembling volute of a capital, probably from a toilet box or chest (NM. 7800, Fig. 285 No. 28), 0.019 m. by 0.022 m. Cf. *ChT,* 84, fig. 30 from Tomb 518, no. 54.

P O T T E R Y

Remnants of several large coarse vessels of undeterminable shape. Many fragments of pithoi, tripod cooking pots. In finer ware, kylix, angular kylix, bowl or basin with pinched-out handles, conical cup, jug, stirrup-vase. A few sherds with painted decoration, chiefly horizontal bands.

R O O M   6 2

Somewhere, perhaps opposite the entrance to Court 63 or not far to the southwestward, a doorway must have opened into Room 62 (Key Plan), situated directly alongside Pantry 60. Little is left of this room except for a narrow strip along its northeastern side but the foundations of the other three sides are recognizable and they indicate that this apartment had a length from northwest to southeast of ca. 7 m..and a width ranging from 2.65 m. to 2.80 m. The northeastern wall, which separates it from Room 60 and which has lost most of its southwestern face, has been described above (p. 238). Where the face is preserved, it retains some of its mud plaster. A remnant of the northwest wall alongside Corridor 61 survives to a length of 0.90 m. to 0.95 m., rising 0.35 m. above the floor of the room. It ends in a straight line toward the southwest and we take this to mark the edge of the doorway through which one could enter Room 62. A fill of *migma* occupies the space beyond the end of the wall and under it are carbonized remains, probably of the door casing. How wide the opening was is unknown, since the wall has been demolished on the other side. Room 62 had a stucco floor some remnants of which are preserved at the northwestern end and in a strip along the northeastern wall.

The narrow strip of fused debris found along the northeastern side of the room yielded a bronze chisel, a fragment of a clay sealing, and a small lot of scattered sherds. There was, however, no specific evidence to reveal for what purpose this room was used. The presence of a stucco floor implies that it was more than a storeroom. Perhaps it provided the quarters for the palace guard directly opposite the gateway leading to the Southwestern Building. No clear indication has come to light, but it is likely that Room 62 shared with its neighbor, Room 60, an upper floor.

O B J E C T S   F O U N D

BRONZE

Chisel: solid, well made, and in remarkably good condition (Fig. 300 No. 11), l. 0.135 m., max. w. 0.018 m., min. w. 0.01 m., max. th. 0.008 m., min. th. ca. 0.001 m.

CLAY

Sealing: small fragment (about one third preserved) showing lower part of impression (Fig. 300 No. 9). Of excellent workmanship but scene represented unintelligible.

POTTERY

Shapes recognized: kylix (4 stems), conical cup, basin with pinched-out handles, krater-bowl, tankard with raised ridge and decorated with vertical stripes or rippling.

COURT 63

The entrance to Court 63 retains on its northeastern side the base that supported the wooden jamb (Fig. 470). It is a block of poros and in its upper surface are two dowel holes,[3] no doubt for fastening the upright timbers of the casing (Fig. 188). The top of the stone rises 0.10 m. to 0.12 m. above the stucco pavement that extends across the actual opening. The latter, as already mentioned, appears to have been 2.80 m. wide. The base of the southwestern jamb is missing but its position is approximately indicated. The space is very wide for swinging doors and we have no evidence of cuttings for pivots. If the entrance was closeable at all, it might have been managed by wooden gates or bars.

When one passed through this entrance one saw directly before him the façade of Hall 64 with its two columns between antae, dominating a court (63 on Key Plan) which had a depth ranging from 11.90 m. to 14 m. from southeast to northwest and a length of 17.40 m. from southwest to northeast (Fig. 192). On the northeast it was bounded by the exterior wall of the Main Building, which may possibly have had a doorway opening from Room 12 (p. 108). On the northwest it merged into Court 88 (p. 293), separating the Main Building from the Southwestern, and extended across the front of Hall 64 (Fig. 12). On the southwest Court 63 was flanked by a structure of several rooms (now missing), running southeastward and probably connecting the main part of the Southwestern Building with the extension that included Rooms 62 and 60.

The whole court was covered with a stucco pavement of good quality, which is relatively well preserved through a large part of the area. The pavement turns up against the southeastern boundary wall shared with Ramp 59 and Passage 61 (Fig. 188) and also against the now missing southwest wall of the Main Building. On the northwest it continues on through Court 88, passing under the superposed walls of Areas 89 and 90 (pp. 295ff.), rises against the northeast anta of Hall 64, and extends without a break into the portico of that hall. On the southwest the pavement

[3] Northeast block: length through opening 1.02 m., width 0.38 m.

ends now in a somewhat ragged line approximately opposite the southwestern column base in the façade of Hall 64. In this direction the flooring must originally have been carried southwestward as far as the bordering wall of the conjectural connecting building mentioned above.

In the court along the side toward the Main Building were found many large poros blocks that obviously had fallen from the exterior wall (Fig. 178). They lay on the pavement more or less aligned in rows, presumably representing courses in the wall, five of which could plausibly be counted.

In front of Hall 64 some dents and cracks in the pavement and fragments of poros blocks were recorded; the large stones from the entablature over the columns had presumably fallen in this direction. Here and there about the court, especially near Areas 89-90, and for the most part immediately under the plowed soil, were patches of black earth and blackened stones similar to the accumulation in Court 88 (p. 294). Elsewhere at deeper levels, particularly in the eastern corner above the fallen blocks, were many small unworked stones; these probably came from the inner backing of the exterior wall behind the veneer of squared blocks. The pavement in general was covered by a gray ashy deposit sometimes under a layer of dissolved crude brick.

Relatively few objects of any consequence were recovered in the court. From the topsoil came a fragment of an inscribed tablet. (No. 1252), and another piece (No. 1251) was found not far from the entrance gate. Other items that may be mentioned include two fragments of terracotta figurines of the crescent type, some bits of ivory, a section of a pi-shaped gutter in poros stone, a bead, and a button of steatite.

Set into a hollow in the stucco pavement of the court, 4.40 m. from the entrance gate, is a circular block of poros through which are pierced three round holes.[4] They served to convey rainwater to an underground drain (Figs. 192, 426). The latter, covered by stone slabs, one of which has been seen, runs southeastward under Corridor 61 and presumably joins the main drain probably under Room 62 (p. 234). The line of the drain is clearly indicated by a depression in the stucco pavement of the court.

Court 63 was a spacious open area flanked on the northeast by the ashlar wall of the Main Building and on the northwest by the two-columned façade of Hall 64 with their monumental aspects. How it was bordered on the other two sides must be left to the imagination, but the building on the southwest that we have postulated may well have been two stories high. The wall on the southeast, only a remnant of which is left, separating the court from Passage 61, gives no evidence as to its original height. It is not possible to determine with certainty whether or not the passage was roofed, though Rooms 60 and 62 may have risen to an upper story. In any event,

---

[4] Diameter of block 0.42 m.; diameter of holes roughly 0.14 m. to 0.16 m.

the court surely provided shade on one side in the morning and on the other in the afternoon and was no doubt a comfortable place for the occupants of the Southwestern Building, especially in the summer; and in the winter warm sunny areas could certainly be found. The court apparently offered no vantage point from which the surrounding countryside could be viewed. But in all the Mycenaean palaces known those who wished to gaze on the scenery, which the site dominated, could no doubt ascend to the flat terraces which probably formed the roof. Visitors who were conducted up the broad ramp and passage and through the wide entrance into the open court were left in no doubt that they were entering a royal residence.

OBJECTS FOUND

BRONZE

Flat piece (Fig. 296 No. 15), l. pres. 0.019 m., w. pres. 0.017 m., average th. 0.004 m., ribbed or grooved surface. From plowed soil.

Rivet (Fig. 296 No. 14), more than half of thin flat head preserved, d. estimated 0.02 m., l. of shaft 0.008 m. From plowed soil.

Nail (Fig. 296 No. 18), end bent, point broken; l. pres. 0.042 m., d. shaft 0.004 m., d. head 0.013 m.; head slightly convex on top. Very solid.

Piece of bent wire (Fig. 296 No. 17), l. 0.0235 m. plus 0.0235 m., d. 0.003 m.

Thin flat strip (Fig. 296 No. 16), l. 0.027 m., w. 0.009 m., th. 0.0005 m.

Fragment, possibly head of a pin, l. pres. 0.025 m., d. 0.006 m. Found embedded in pavement.

STONE

Obsidian: three blades (Fig. 296 Nos. 10-12), l. 0.0255 m., 0.0235 m., 0.021 m.; w. 0.0115 m., 0.009 m., 0.014 m.; th. 0.0025 m., 0.0025 m., 0.004 m.; several flakes (e.g., Fig. 296 No. 13).

Steatite: cone, deep purplish-red in color (Fig. 296 No. 1), h. 0.022 m., d. 0.03 m., no perforation, possibly an unfinished button; fragment of dark blue spherical bead (Fig. 296 No. 5), d. estimated 0.0135 m., h. 0.008 m., d. hole 0.002 m., incised decoration—groups of striations going in different directions.

Whetstone (Fig. 296 No. 4), l. 0.06 m., w. 0.025 m., th. 0.008 m. tapering to 0.001 m. at narrow end.

Pounder, almost spherical, with one flattened surface (Fig. 269 No. 14), h. 0.0475 m., d. 0.056 m., white marble-like stone, coated with lime accretion.

Stopper or plug (?), almost cylindrical (Fig. 269 No. 13), h. 0.06 m., d. 0.095 m. tapering to 0.085 m.

IVORY

Fragment, white, in relatively good condition; very finely cut spiraliform design with row of beading above (Figs. 266 No. 7, 296 No. 8), l. pres. 0.018 m., w. 0.01 m., th. 0.005 m.; on flat back very fine crossing lines.

Two small pieces, burned bluish-black: finely incised diaper or lattice design (Fig. 296 Nos. 6, 7).

Small fragment burned blue-gray, traces of carved spiraliform pattern (Fig. 296 No. 9).

Other burned scraps.

TERRACOTTA

Female figurine, crescent type, upper half (Fig. 297 No. 2). H. pres. 0.052 m., w. across arms pres. 0.038 m., w. waist 0.012 m., d. head 0.015 m., d. headdress 0.02 m. to 0.024 m. Brick-colored clay; black paint with metallic luster, very worn. Saucer headdress, very shallow. Head tilted back slightly. Pellet eyes and breasts. Outstretched arms, one broken. Decoration: circular band on inside of saucer near rim; another thicker band just above forehead; band at back of neck, paint around eyes; three vertical strokes down back, from apex of which a loop perhaps goes out to tip of each arm; front decorated with two, possibly three vertical strokes. Found in surface soil.

Female figurine, crescent type with modeled breasts and plastic braid hanging down back almost to waist (Fig. 297 No. 1). H. pres. 0.055 m., w. pres. 0.051 m., th. 0.013 m. Head, stem with base missing; tips of arms damaged. Buff clay, worn black paint. Decoration of vertical lines, front and back; thick band around neck; arms outlined.

Animal figurine (Fig. 297 No. 3), fragment of front part, head and feet missing; no painted decoration preserved.

Whorl (Fig. 296 No. 2), h. 0.025 m., d. 0.03 m., d. hole 0.005 m., biconical; coarse reddish clay, surface partially burned black.

Whorl (Fig. 296 No. 3), h. 0.021 m., d. 0.04 m., d. hole 0.006 m., flattened spherical; coarse reddish clay showing black and brown grits.

CLAY

Tablets: Nos. 1251 and 1252 (*OOT*, 12, 14, 65, 67, pls. XVIII-XIX)

POTTERY

Innumerable scattered sherds. Shapes recognized: in coarse ware, pithos, tripod-vessel; in fine ware, kylix (275 stems), cup and bowl, etc. (144 flat bases), bowl and basin with pinched-out handles, conical cup, jar with torus base and horizontal handles, large spouted bowl, jug, krater; in ware with painted decoration, kylix, bowl, krater, feeding bottle, stirrup-vase, three-handled jar, tankard. Many pieces bear remains of painted decoration for the most part coated solidly or with horizontal bands, net, spirals and spiraliform motives. A few stray sherds of earlier Mycenaean style (LH II), and two or three with incised decoration or in mat paint.

HALL 64

On the northwestern side of Court 63 is the entrance hall to the state apartments of the Southwestern Building (64 on Key Plan). Its façade was formed by two columns set between antae (Figs. 192, 193). The columns, made of wood, presumably perished in the disaster that brought an end to the palace but the stone bases on which they stood remain *in situ*, the one on the northeast retaining some remnants of the ring of stucco that had been laid around the bottom of the shaft (Fig. 200). The southwestern column was no doubt similarly protected; though the actual ring is now missing, there are indications that it once existed.

The base of the anta on the northeast, though considerably damaged by fire, has to a great extent survived, while the corresponding base on the southwest has vanished altogether (Fig. 194). The existing base, 1.11 m. long from southeast to northwest and 1.06 m. wide, set so as to project 0.05 m. from the face of the wall behind it, rises to a height of 0.58 m. above the floor of the hall. On the southwest, southeast, and northeast sides a broad rabbet has been cut in the top of the block, reducing the height on those sides to 0.50 m. The rabbet, 0.30 m. wide on the southwest, 0.71 m. on the southeast, and 0.35 m. on the northeast, and somewhat roughly finished, was made to receive thick wooden blocks and horizontal beams. Five dowel holes show how the timbers were fastened in place: one cut on the southwest, two on the southeast, a double one on the northeast, and one near the middle of the block, close to the inner end of the broad rabbet.

The entrance hall (64) is a spacious room ca. 10 m. long from southeast to northwest and 7.29 m. wide measured to the plastered faces of the walls.[5] The northeast wall, which terminates in the anta described above, extends northwestward 8.68 m. to another massive anta base which forms the northern corner of the hall (Fig. 195). This exterior wall of the Southwestern Building, 1.02 m. thick including the plaster on the inner face and 0.98 m. thick without it, was constructed in the same manner as the outside walls of the central unit of the palace, namely with an outer face made of large dressed blocks of poros and an inner backing of rubble. The dado course on the exterior consists of nine substantial blocks, ranging from 0.66 m. to 1.30 m. in length and from 0.43 m. to 0.61 m. in thickness. The blocks rise 0.30 m. to 0.32 m. above the pavement of Court 88 while the rubble work on the inside is preserved to a height of 0.42 m. above the floor of the hall. This latter is uneven, varying from 12.99 m. to 13.14 m. above datum and it lies 0.27 m. below the level of the pavement in Court 88. The poros stones were set in the same manner as we have seen in the Main Building making fairly close contact on the exterior face but with splaying joints that open widely toward the core of the wall. These V-shaped spaces were packed with small stones and yellow clay. Directly on the dado course had lain the usual horizontal timber probably in several sections. Many of the stone blocks had a dressed bearing surface for these beams ranging from 0.32 m. to 0.40 m. in breadth. The timbers were fastened in place with dowels. The spacing of the dowel holes is somewhat irregular[6] but it suggests that there may have been five relatively short timbers, ca. 2.10 m. long at each end, where they overlap the anta base, and varying from 1.80 m. to 1.92 m. in the middle. It is likely that the wooden beams were nearly square in section, as we have concluded in several places in the Main Building of the palace.

The inner part of the wall, made of rubble, reveals traces of the vertical slots for the customary wooden uprights, perhaps eight all told, but the evidence in some places is scanty and the spacing cannot be accurately fixed. The inner face of the wall was coated with plaster, a thick underlayer and a fine finishing coat. The latter, which was aligned with the projecting face of the anta base, was well preserved *in situ* on the wall throughout the greater part of its length; but the surviving strip, ranging in height from 0.30 m. to 0.47 m., formed only the dado. It was decorated

---

[5] Measured to the stone itself the length is 10.07 m. and the width is 7.47 m.

[6] The dowel holes average 0.08 m. by 0.06 m. by 0.08 m. deep. The spacing between holes was roughly: hole in anta at southeast end of wall to hole in second block, 2.10 m.; block 2 to block 4, 1.92 m.; block 4 to block 6, 1.90 m.; block 6 to block 8, 1.80 m.; block 8 to block 9, 0.92 m.; block 9 to second hole in block 9, 0.14 m.; second hole in block 9 to hole in anta block at the end of the wall, 2.12 m.

with a typical dado design: red vertical bands marking off panels which repeat with variations a constant pattern of different colored arcs (Fig. 199).

No part of the wall and its plaster survives above the dado, but on the floor of the hall lay innumerable fragments, heaped up one above the other and extending throughout the length and breadth of the room; some face down, some face up, others tightly fused to the floor, they were all very difficult to remove and to salvage.[7] All these pieces had suffered great damage from fire. Much of the material could be arranged to show a frieze of hunting dogs in natural size (Fig. 198), both red and spotted black and white (height ca. 0.60 m.). Above this frieze, presumably at eye level, was a zone with a battle scene (Fig. 197).

At its northwestern end the wall meets an enormous anta base (Fig. 195), made from a single block of poros, ca. 1.20 m. square and 0.67 m. high. It was set below the level of the floor so that the top rises only 0.44 m. above the paving inside the room. A notch cut in the south corner of the block fitted it both to the width of the wall we have been describing and to that of the northwestern wall of Hall 64. The exterior wall of the building continued farther northwestward and a rough cutting in the western corner of the block adjusted it to the wall beyond. The latter was removed to the foundation slabs by seekers of building material and only through some fortunate circumstance had the section alongside Hall 64 escaped the rapacity of those marauders. In the top of the base, near its northeastern edge, are two dowel holes,[8] one close beside the other, only 0.012 m. apart. They must have been made for dowels to fasten a horizontal beam which evidently continued northwestward along-side Rooms 67, 68, and beyond. Why there were two cuttings is uncertain: if it was not the result of a miscalculation, it might mark a repair or reconstruction.

The northwestern wall of Hall 64 consists of two sections separated by a doorway that leads into the domestic quarters of the building (Fig. 194). The northeastern section, 3.20 m. long and ca. 1 m. thick, is preserved to a height of 0.55 m. Three slots for vertical and transverse timbers are recognizable at intervals of 0.65 m. On the interior face of the wall its original plaster was preserved to a height of 0.52 m. above the floor and a length of 2.32 m. This strip, bearing the same kind of decoration as the corresponding dado on the northeastern wall, was removed from its position for conservation by Mr. Kanakis.

The southwestern section of the wall, which has a length of 2.82 m., stands to a height of 0.21 m. above the floor. In its present condition the positions and spacings of the chases for the wooden framework are not determinable, but the presence of a considerable amount of carbonized matter allows the deduction that a horizontal

---

[7] Much of this work was done by Zacharias Kanakis, chief technician in the Museum at Herakleion.

[8] Northeastern hole: 0.09 m. long, 0.05 m. wide, 0.075 m. deep; southwestern hole: 0.055 m. long, 0.03 m. wide, 0.075 m. deep.

timber lay at about floor level along the southeastern face of the wall. Some remnants of plaster are preserved just above the floor all along the wall from the door jamb to the corner. Traces of color may be seen but the patterns could not be recognized; they were presumably the same as those on the northeastern section of the wall.

The southwestern wall has suffered even greater damage than the northwestern (Fig. 194). This wall too was divided into two sections by a great doorway that led southwestward into the principal hall of state in this building, Hall 65. The northwestern section is 2.85 m. long to the end of the anta base beside the doorway. It is 0.95 m. thick, including the plaster, and varies in height from 0.09 m. to 0.24 m. above the floor of Hall 64. The anta base, however, stands 0.42 m. above the same floor. No traces of horizontal grooves or vertical chases are preserved in the surviving remnant of the wall and no dowel holes are now visible in the top of the anta base. The latter, which has been badly worn away, apparently by plowing, is made from a block of poros 0.94 m. square. It has been largely cut away at its northwestern end, except where it juts out into Hall 64, projecting some 0.07 m. or 0.08 m. from the face of the wall. At the southeastern end, along the same edge of the block another projection, 0.08 m. thick, extends 0.07 m. toward the door opening from the end of the block (Fig. 196): this formed the lateral frame of a countersinking like those we have seen in the anta bases in the more important doorways of the central building (pp. 55, 77). No corresponding frame appears along the southwestern edge of the block, though it may have been replaced by an applied strip of stucco. Parallels for this too may be found in the doorways from the Portico to the Vestibule (p. 67) and from the Vestibule to the Throne Room in the Main Building (pp. 76f.).

The doorway leading from Entrance Hall 64 into Hall 65 is described below (pp. 253f.). Beyond the base of the southeastern jamb is a gap where the anta block must have stood. It was no doubt removed by the looters of building material so often mentioned. On the evidence of the surviving line of the stucco floor in Hall 64, the base seems to have had a width of ca. 0.80 m., corresponding closely to the size of its opposite number on the northwestern side of the doorway. Farther southeastward the foundations of the wall continue 3.07 m. to end approximately opposite the outer face of the northeastern anta of the façade of Entrance Hall 64. The southwestern anta base is, however, missing.

The two column bases in the façade were set with remarkable accuracy 2.61 m. apart, center to center, and each 2.37 m. (again measured from the center), from the lateral face of the northeast anta and from the prolongation of the line of the southwestern wall respectively. The size and exact shape of the northeasterly column base (Fig. 200) cannot be determined without destroying the stucco floor around it, though it has a diameter of more than 0.64 m. A crack runs across the southerly part of the stone. The surface lies 0.13 m. below the last floor of the hall, which seems to be the sixth in a succession of such floors. Above this final paving, on the northeasterly side, are remains of a raised ring of stucco, 0.04 m. high and 0.10 m. wide and flat on top, which had been laid around the bottom of the shaft. The successive floors as well as the ring have taken the impression of the flutings of the column. The impressions are not preserved around the whole circle, but enough remain to show that the column had 44 flutings and a diameter of ca. 0.50 m. Some of the layers bear traces of red paint as in corresponding places in other parts of the palace.

The southwestern column base, which is cracked in several places, cannot be measured without damaging the floor; its diameter, however, is more than 0.64 m. Some slight suggestions of a raised standing place appear on it, though not enough to give the diameter of the shaft. The top of the base lies 0.12 m. below the final floor of the hall. Here too six successive floors can be counted, none retaining traces of color. The stucco ring around the bottom of the shaft is missing, but it looks as if the last flooring was laid up to a ring made in the preceding phase. The impressions of the fluting appear in a considerably damaged state; they were, in any event, surely equal in number to those of the northeast column and they indicate a diameter approximately the same.

Almost exactly centered on the longitudinal axis of the hall, 3.65 m. from the plaster on the northeast wall and 3.70 m. from the line of the southwestern wall, is the stone base of an interior column (Fig. 194). Its center is 4.18 m. distant from the face of the northwest wall and 5.02 m. from a line drawn between the centers of the two column bases in the southeastern façade.[9] The stone which is cracked in many places lies with its surface 0.12 m. below the floor of the hall (Fig. 201). Although the size and shape of the base are hidden from view by the surrounding floor, the diameter of the block must be more than 0.52 m. In the stucco that abutted against the bottom of the column some eight coats or layers can be distinguished, probably representing successive relayings of the floor. No trace of color is visible on the topmost and the others are concealed from view. The impressions of the fluting are remarkably well preserved through almost half of the ring. In this distance on the southeastern side 20 flutes in unbroken succession can be counted and the total was evidently 44. Measurements here give 0.495 m. as the lower diameter of the wooden column.[10] Some slight evidence shows that the usual stucco ring surrounded the bottom of the column, though no remains of it were found in place. Several chunks of edged plaster, which were recovered in the neighborhood in the course of excavation, probably came from such a ring.

[9] The span, center to center, from the interior column to the northeastern one is 5.22 m., to the southwestern 5.19 m.

[10] The impressions of the flutes vary in size: the majority measure 0.035 m. from arris to arris, a few as much as 0.04 m.

How high this column was is not known, nor can the height of the two exterior columns be determined. The latter evidently supported a fairly heavy entablature that extended across the façade. Some large blocks of the superstructure had fallen in a line outside the front of the building and that they fell from a considerable height is shown by the deep dents, breaks and cracks they made in the paving. The roof was presumably flat with a slight slope toward the southeast: the line between the area that was covered and that which was open to the sky is fairly well defined. The Southwestern Building, however, had stairways and surely was in part at least a two-storied structure; it is likely that there were rooms above this entrance hall. Substantial supports were therefore required.

But what exactly was supported by the interior column is not easy to understand. In its central position it could well bear the weight of a sturdy beam reaching across to the northeastern wall; a similar timber extending northwestward, however, would have to rest on the lintel of the doorway opening into the domestic quarters. Moreover, a beam running southwestward could at its far end find support only over the middle of the doorway leading into Hall 65. Toward the southeastward also the structural problem would be similar, for there the outer end of the beam would have to be borne by the entablature stretching from column to column in the façade.

Despite the unorthodox manner of the support provided, such an arrangement of the girders is suggested by Mr. de Jong (Fig. 419), who postulates main beams running from the southeast façade to the central column and from the latter to the northwest end of the hall, and transverse timbers similarly resting at one end on the same pillar and spanning the width of the room. This solution is surely the most likely. The floor and the roof, undoubtedly made of wood, could easily enough have been held up by such a structure, the northwestern and the lateral walls being built of crude brick in the upper story. Whether the upper floor extended across the whole of the hall or stopped in the middle above the column, forming a balcony over the rear part of the room, could not be determined.

Other possibilities in the placing of the girders to support the upper floor are not altogether excluded. One can imagine that the architect, in order to avoid imposing most of the weight on the lintels of the two doorways and the middle of the intercolumniation in the façade, might have devised a scheme of a double x-shaped framework laid out longitudinally and transversely and crossing above the central column. Such a plan might account for the unusual full-width construction of the stone wall within the door jamb which was observed (p. 260) on the northeast side of the doorway opening into the domestic quarters. But no decisive evidence has survived to settle the problem, and the actual design of the floor construction in the upper story remains in the realm of conjecture.

The floor of Hall 64 was made of stucco, 0.06 m. thick in some places, where tested; it had a fairly smooth bluish surface which is well preserved in some areas, especially in the southeastern end and along the walls. Here and there in the middle of the room the surface has suffered damage from fire and from numerous cracks and upheavals, probably caused by the action of roots of olive trees.

Traces of brownish-red paint have been noticed near the column bases and around all sides of the room. As a result of fire the floor was blackened by carbon above which lay an accretion of lime, 0.05 m. thick in the west corner, extremely hard, fused together and to the floor (Fig. 194), making the cleaning of the latter extremely difficult. It has not yet been determined whether the remains of reddish-brown paint once constituted patterns or a solid coat.

No evidence of fixed furniture of any kind has been recognized anywhere in the room. In the southwestern part of the hall, however, backed against the anta base beside the doorway that led into Room 65, is a sentry stand, 1.02 m. wide and projecting 1.12 m. into Hall 64. Its floor, which is made of good stucco, though cracked in many places, is sunk along the edges nearly 0.05 m. below the paving of the room, but it rises somewhat toward the middle of the stand. No recognizable traces of painted decoration survive.

On the floor beside the sentry stand and extending into the adjacent doorway were found many fragments of a pedestaled krater decorated with painted patterns.

Entrance Hall 64 with its fine proportions and its considerable size is one of the notable rooms in the palace complex. Distinguished by its columnar façade and central pillar, painted floor, and, extending around the three walls above the multi-colored dado, a band of crouching dogs, with battle scenes at a higher level, it must have made an impression on visitors. But it was clearly only the entrance hall to a much grander adjoining apartment that lay to the southwest.

OBJECTS FOUND

BRONZE

Nondescript burned bits.

OBSIDIAN

Small blade and a chip.

POTTERY

Pedestaled krater (Shape 63, p. 400) No. 826 (Fig. 387), decorated. Sherds generally nondescript, badly burned, encrusted with lime. No difference between material found in plowed earth and that from underlying burned deposit extending to the floor. Shapes recognized from fragments: kylikes, bowls, jars, jugs—the ordinary shapes in plain ware found elsewhere in the palace; in coarse ware, pithoi, tripod-vessels, other cooking pots, and braziers. Twenty-two battered sherds bearing painted decoration—bands or over-all coating.

HALL 65

The doorway from Hall 64 to Hall 65 is suitably broad for its purpose. It has on each side a large base for the wooden door jambs (Fig. 471). The stone on the northwestern side is a block of poros (cracked across the middle from northwest to southeast), 0.91 m. broad in the line of the wall and 1.06 m. long through the door opening (Fig. 196). It is approximately rectangular but not accurately squared. A notch has been carelessly cut into its northwest edge at the northern corner. At the southwest a long hole has been gouged out, 0.58 m. long, 0.21 m. broad at the southeastern end, narrowing in two notches to 0.10 m. at the northwestern end; it ranges in depth from 0.15 m. at the southeast to 0.10 m. at the other end. Several small flat stones have been laid to form its floor. This hole recalls a similar arrangement in the same relative position in the doorway leading from the Portico to the Vestibule in the Main Building (p. 72).

The southeastern jamb was supported by a comparable block of poros, 0.95 m. wide, in the line of the wall and 1.13 m. long through the door opening, with a thickness of 0.41 m. (Fig. 194). This too was cracked, but from southwest to northeast, almost in the preserved line of the wooden jamb. A small notch cut in the eastern corner, 0.07 m. wide by 0.16 m. long toward the northeast, is of undetermined purpose, though it may have served in some way to fasten the jamb. The similar notch, in a like position in the northwestern base, also lacks an adequate explanation.

The space between these two large bases is 1.41 m. wide. It is now covered with the stucco flooring which continues from Hall 64 through the doorway into the adjacent hall (65). The actual opening through the doorway may have been considerably wider; for on each side the surface of the jamb base has been worn smooth in a strip some 0.25 m. broad. This would imply an original width of ca. 1.90 m. No cutting for the pivots could be recognized, unless the hole on the southwestern side of the northwestern block served for that purpose.

Passing through the southwestern doorway from the Entrance Hall, if permitted by the sentry, one reached what must have been the Throne Room (65 on Key Plan) of the Southwestern Building (Fig. 193). It was a stately apartment 8.76 m. wide and 11.10 m. long from northeast to southwest (measured inside the walls or the foundations). It has been sadly treated by an unkindly fate: not only wrecked by the disastrous fire but stripped of its stone walls by many intruders and worn away by erosion. Its stucco floor has survived only in a narrow ragged remnant at the northeastern end with a maximum breadth of 1.40 m. on the northwestern side of the doorway, diminishing to nothing near the eastern corner. A single stone column base survives *in situ*, 2.63 m. from the line of the northwestern wall, 1.72 m. from the northeastern (measured from the center of the base). What little has been spared of the northeastern wall has been described above (Fig. 194): on the northwestern, southeastern, and southwestern sides the foundations alone give evidence of the lines of the walls that have lost their superstructure. It is only by a study of these incomplete and scanty remains that one can form some slight idea of the plan and original grandeur of the room.

The foundation on the northwestern side, 1.35 m. thick, was built of relatively small unshaped stones laid in a fairly regular manner along the outer and inner face, the core being less carefully filled with rubble. At its northeastern end it meets the northwestern wall of Hall 64 with the inner face of which it is aligned. It is, however, 0.60 m. thicker than that wall, perhaps because it was thought necessary to have heavier foundations for the Throne Room, which was built across the descending slope of the hill. This additional width of 0.60 m. was apparently gained by means of a normal projecting offset on the outer face of the wall. The extra thickening seems to have been demolished for a short distance from the offset, perhaps when a stairway to the upper floor was built on the northwest side of the wall. At the junction only a low foundation was required, resting on *stereo*-like earth, at 12.56 m. above datum. At the southwestern end of the room, however, an immensely deep substructure was necessary, laid on bedding slabs at ca. 10.50 m. above datum. The part of the wall preserved slopes sharply downward toward the southwest evidently following the line of erosion.

The southwestern foundation is very thick, ca. 1.85 m. (Fig. 203). Along its inner face it is preserved to a height of 11.08 m. above datum, but the outer face has been removed throughout the entire length behind the Throne Room down to the bedding of the foundation, which lies at 9.88 m. above datum. The outer face was built of squared blocks all of which were removed by marauders. The rear wall of this room is also the exterior wall of the Southwestern Building which continued both to the northwest and the southeast in a series of offsets (Fig. 204). Behind the Throne Room it juts out 0.40 m. at the west corner and at the south corner it returns ca. 0.80 m. In the section to the northwest of the room the lower part of the wall is built of relatively thick natural slabs of limestone and this material is used all the way to the western corner of the building and around it to the northeast (Fig. 202). But on the ground outside the wall a few squared blocks of poros were found along with many fragments and splinters of the same material: this fact supports the conclusion that the upper part of the wall, perhaps beginning at the level of the floor inside (13.01 m. above datum in Hall 65) was built in ashlar style of poros blocks such as we have seen in the northeastern wall of Hall 64. Evidence of the same kind has been observed farther to the southeastward and some poros blocks have there been found still in place in the lower part of the exterior wall. The core and northeastern face of the substructure directly behind the Throne Room is composed mainly of relatively small unworked stones laid in the same fashion that we have noted in the northwestern foundations.

The lower part of the southeastern lateral wall of Hall 65, built in the same manner as the northwestern but much better preserved, has neatly laid flattish stones on each face and a core of rubble (Fig. 205). Resting at its southwestern end on bedding slabs at 9.85 m. above datum, it rises toward its northeastern end almost to the level of the floor of the hall (13.01 m. above datum). The foundations at this end, however, are much less deep than those at the southwest, since they rest on the *stereo* which ascends steeply in the bank forming the southwestern slope of the hill.

Neither of the lateral walls makes a proper bonded junction with the front wall of the hall. On the northwest side, as we have seen, the deep foundation is 0.60 m. wider than its prolongation, which forms the inner end of the Entrance Hall (64). On the southeastern side too an irregularity appears: the foundation turns northwestward 0.80 m. short of the line of the southwestern face of the partition wall between Halls 64 and 65. This part of the foundation, which thus seems to have served no useful purpose, was covered over by the floor of the hall and is only visible near the east corner of the room, where the paving has been broken away. Here it has been traced to a length of 1.92 m. and seems to end not far from that point. The evidence of the foundations thus suggests that the front wall of Hall 65 represents a reconstruction or remodeling of a preceding structure.

The surviving strip of the floor of Hall 65 is in a miserable state of preservation. Immediately in front of the entrance the surface is all worn away; in some sizable patches to the southeast and to the northwest, where a very hard accretion of lime afforded some protection, the final coat is still smooth and shiny, but it has been blackened so much by fire that no trace of paint can now be distinguished. Incised lines dividing it into squares are not visible, but the floor of this room must surely have borne painted decoration. The thickness of the floor ranges from 0.03 m. to 0.06 m. In some places it seems to have been laid directly on *stereo* and the latter exhibits the discoloration effected by heat from the fire. The few scattered sherds found on and above the floor indicate that the room was being used at the time of the final destruction.

The column base was made from an unshaped natural block of limestone, 0.65 m. long, 0.62 m. wide, and 0.35 m. thick (Fig. 206). It has been flattened on top and has been dressed so that an almost regular circle with a diameter of 0.52 m. rises slightly above the rest of the surface to form the standing place of the column. The base was set with small flat stones wedged under it, probably on *stereo*, and was surrounded by a well-laid ring of rubble. The top of the base was leveled at 12.95 m. above datum or 0.06 m. below the floor of the hall. The stucco paving around the column is missing and nothing remains of a decorative collar with impressions of flutings; but we may safely conjecture that the shafts of the columns in this room too were fluted.

There were certainly four columns in the room, if not six. Apart from the single base preserved, the ringlike foundations of three others have been uncovered and they indicate the approximate positions of the columns (Fig. 193). These foundations are roughly circular, substantially built of unworked stones around flattish slabs that provided the bedding for the bases. The foundations vary from 1.23 m. to 1.45 m. in diameter and were sturdy enough to support the column bases firmly. The arrangement is not perfectly symmetrical.[11] The spans from the foundations of the south and west column bases to the rear wall of the hall are relatively long (5.25 m. to 5.29 m.) but they are by no means impossible; for in the Throne Room of the Main Building the south and west columns are 5.36 m. apart and the north and east columns 5.22 m. Nevertheless, if Hall 65 had only the four columns indicated, the southwestern end, apart from rendering the plan of the room unsymmetrical, would offer a somewhat awkward problem for the support of the ceiling and the roof. It is not altogether excluded that two further columns stood in this relatively wide space. Ample room exists for a third pair of columns to be set approximately as far from the southwestern wall as those at the other end of the hall are from the northeastern wall, namely 1.71 m. In that case the intervening span between this conjectural pair and what we have called the south and west columns would be ca. 3.55 m., which is very close to the span between the east and north and south and west columns. No traces of foundations have survived to support this theory, but erosion has cut away the sloping edge of the hill to a level lower than the bottom of such foundations. It would be tempting to restore the apartment as a hypostyle hall with two rows of three columns, but so far as known to us, no actual parallel for such an arrangement has yet been found elsewhere on the mainland. At all events, the plan of Hall 65 with four columns spaced as shown by the foundations, is not a normal one and there must be some explanation for the disproportionate size of the southwestern area. Was the throne perhaps erected at the far end of the hall facing the doorway with room for a considerable audience before it, or did it stand against the wall on the right hand side as in the main Throne Room? Where was the hearth? If there was one, it was most probably in the rectangle framed by the four columns, which could have supported a clerestory with provision to carry off the smoke rather than in the rear part of the hall. Soundings made in this rectangle revealed no traces of a hearth but the ground was badly eroded to a depth well beneath the floor and the existence of a hearth at a higher level cannot be ruled out. These soundings uncovered a fairly large underlying deposit of pottery which belongs to an earlier phase evidently Mycenaean III A.

[11] Approximate spans from center to center between column base and circular foundations: north to east 3.41 m., east to south 4.12 m., south to west 3.57 m., west to north 4.20 m. North column to northwest wall 2.71 m., to northeast wall (anta base) 1.72 m.; east foundation to northeast wall (jamb base) 1.71 m., to southeast wall 2.59 m. South foundation to southeast wall 2.59 m., to southwest wall 5.25 m. West foundation to southwest wall 5.29 m., to northwest wall 2.60 m. Diagonals: north base to south foundation 5.35 m., east foundation to west foundation 5.51 m.

One may wonder also whether there was a balcony across the northeasterly end of the hall, or the southwestern part, or running around three sides or all four sides. In the lack of authentic evidence one can only speculate and it is unlikely that these problems can ever be solved with certainty.

In an attempt to give some idea of the original appearance of the superstructure, next to nothing of which has survived, Mr. de Jong has drawn a plan and section of Halls 64 and 65 (Fig. 419). This study was based on the assumption (which we take to be the most likely conclusion) that the room possessed only four columns. The central square marked out by them provides an adequate area for a hearth of some size which almost certainly once existed, though no actual remains of it were found. Mr. de Jong's restoration of an upper story, however, rests on the valid evidence of two badly damaged steps belonging to a staircase which ascended in a stairwell along the northwestern side of the hall. The precise height is uncertain, but a doorway from the landing at the top of the stairs must surely have opened into the room or balcony directly above Hall 65 which presumably communicated with the similar upper floor over Room 64. There must have been a clerestory of some kind, supported by the columns in the main hall, and in addition to openings for air and light, which were no doubt provided near the top, we have ventured to add for good measure at the apex a conjectural flue—or flues—to carry off the smoke from the conjectural hearth.

However that may be, this was clearly the principal hall of the Southwestern Building and it was surely no less brightly decorated than the corresponding hall in the Main Building. The woodwork was no doubt painted as well as the floor, the walls were plastered and bore frescoes as shown by fragments fallen on the floor in the northern corner of the room. The destruction wrought here by fire, weather, and human beings is deeply to be deplored, but we may be grateful that enough has somehow been preserved in the main Throne Room to give us an idea of how Hall 65 looked. The strange plan, with its turn of 90 degrees from the Entrance Hall into the Throne Room, may well indicate that the Southwestern Building was still experimental, erected before the adoption of the straightforward axial design which certainly, long before the mid thirteenth century, had become the orthodox megaron of the great Mycenaean palaces on the Helladic mainland.

O B J E C T S   F O U N D

Except for a few miscellaneous potsherds all objects came from the vast amount of debris accumulated over the eroded slope under Room 65.

SILVER

Ring of thin wire (Fig. 300 No. 12), d. of ring 0.021 m., d. of wire 0.0015 m.; circle not complete, apparently held a setting of some kind.

BRONZE

Strip, slightly curved, solid and heavy (Fig. 300 No. 14, l. pres. 0.071 m., w. 0.02 to 0.022 m., th. 0.002 m.

LEAD

Pellet, almost cylindrical in shape (Fig. 300 No. 15), l. 0.018 m., d. 0.005 m.

STONE

Steatite: conoid button, purplish (Fig. 300 No. 6), h. 0.011 m., d. 0.021 m.

Obsidian: core and several flakes.

Flint: arrowhead, tan, with long barbs, one missing (Fig. 300 No. 8), l. 0.029 m., th. 0.004 m.; flakes, one large dark red-brown, another smaller red.

PASTE

One half of very thin, light blue bead or button, d. 0.011 m., th. 0.003 m.

TERRACOTTA

One third of a flat disk or button, h. 0.005 m., d. 0.04 m.; biconical whorl with beveled top, tan clay, h. 0.022 m., d. 0.026 m.; large spherical whorl, half missing, coarse dark gray fabric, h. 0.038 m., d. 0.043 m.

Horn of animal figurine decorated with broad red transverse stripes, l. 0.035 m.

CLAY

Tablet: No. 184.

POTTERY

Cup (Shape 11, p. 359)

Nos. 864, 865 and 866 (Fig. 353), 1177, 1178.

Sherds, shapes recognized: in coarse ware, tripod-vessel, pithos, storage jar, lid, cooking pot, domestic jar, brazier; in fine ware, kylix (442 stems counted), votive kylix, cup, bowl, etc. (630 flat bases), conical cup, basin and bowl with pinched-out handles, dipper, scoop, basin with horizontal handles (Shape 2), jug or jar, teapot with tubular spout; with painted decoration, kylix, krater-bowl, amphora, tankard, alabastron, Vapheio cup. In addition to solid coating, motives noted: horizontal bands and lines, stripes, stippling, spiral, net, dots. Most of the sherds belong to Mycenaean III B, a good many to III A, a few to LH II and LH I, and in lesser numbers to Middle Helladic (Mattpainted and incised). Almost all the fragments recovered came from the deep intrusive deposit of debris which, after the destruction of the building, covered the slope to a depth far below the floor level of Hall 65.

LOBBY 66

Returning to Entrance Hall 64 and going out through the northwestern doorway leading to the domestic quarters, we find ourselves in a small lobby (66 on Key Plan). The width of the opening in the doorway is 1.31 m. (Fig. 472). This is the measurement from the edge of the northeastern jamb base to the edge of the corresponding southwestern base, which apparently marked the limit in that direction. No threshold block was found in this space, which has a stucco floor that continues from Hall 64 through the doorway. The base of the northeastern jamb is 1.10 m. long through the doorway; it has a width of 0.82 m. on the southeast and 0.75 m. on the northwest. The other base has analogous dimensions of 1.08 m. in length and 0.89 m. in width on the southeast side, where a tongue, 0.17 m. wide juts out 0.11 m. into the opening; the width on the northwest cannot be measured but was presumably shorter by 0.11 m. than the southwestern face.

On each side of the doorway to right and left abundant remains of carbonized wood indicate that a wooden door jamb extended back ca. 0.80 m. along the inner face of the wall. The jambs must have turned at right angles and run through the opening. Behind the jamb on the northeasterly side the wall seems to have been built up to its full width almost to the outer edge of the base, leaving room for only a very thin door casing. In its present condition this doorway looks like a reconstruction made in one of the latest phases of the palace. In its original form it probably was like the doorways we have seen in the principal rooms in the Main Building which appear to have had little or no filling inside the door casings.

Lobby 66 (Key Plan) is 1.50 m. long from southeast to northwest and 1.40 m. wide (Fig. 207). The stucco floor, continuous with that through the doorway, is cracked and worn with rough uneven surface. On the left is part of the lowest step of a stairway that ascended southwestward to an upper floor. Straight ahead is a doorway leading to a corridor that runs southwestward. On the northeast is another doorway (Fig. 473) marked by the lateral bases of the door jambs, each made of a block of poros. In the space between the two (0.57 m. wide) the stucco pavement of the lobby continues through the opening. The block that supported the jamb on the northwest side of the doorway is 1.17 m. long and 0.40 m. wide rising about 0.04 m. to 0.05 m. above the floor. Its thickness cannot be measured. It has no visible cuttings in its upper surface but weathering marks indicate that only part of it was covered by the jamb, a strip 0.08 m. wide being exposed in the doorway. The block on the southeastern side, 1.06 m. long, 0.50 m. wide, and not measurable as to thickness, rises only a centimeter or two above the floor. About 0.17 m. from its southwestern end is a roughly cut circular cutting 0.06 m. deep and 0.09 m. in diameter, which is evidently a socket for a pivot. It is centered almost in the longitudinal axis of the stone so that somewhat less than half of the block was covered by the wooden jamb. The door, 0.85 m. wide, turning on its pivot must have swung back against the door casing.

ROOM 67

Passing through the opening one gained a diminutive anteroom (67 on Key Plan) 1.83 m. long from southwest to northeast and 1.24 m. wide. It is bordered on the southeast by the partition wall it shares with Hall 64, which has already been described. Mud plaster adheres to the northwestern face of this wall. On the northeast the room extends to the northeastern wall of the Southwestern Building, which has been denuded of all its large blocks and is represented only by small bedding slabs. On the northwest is a doorway, 1.55 m. wide, and a short stub of a wall, 0.55 m. thick, and now in a much dilapidated condition.

The stucco floor of this room is continuous with that in both doorways. It is badly cracked and sunken in the middle but is preserved across the entire room. On the southeastern side of the doorway leading from Lobby 66 to Room 67 was found a large heap of broken cooking pots which must have fallen, probably from a shelf inside the room. The whole floor of the room itself was also piled high with similar crushed pottery of the same general character, which reached the floor in three more or less superposed layers. It looks as if shelving must have been backed against the southeastern and northeastern walls of the room. The most numerous types of vessels represented (Fig. 341) are braziers with long handles pierced for hanging (22 numbered), small tripod-pots (50 numbered), and domestic jars (9 numbered). Most of the pots lay grouped separately implying that they had been neatly arranged by shape in the little storeroom.

O B J E C T S   F O U N D

POTTERY	Examples Counted	Examples Numbered		Examples Counted	Examples Numbered
Doorway between Rooms 66 and 67			841, 844, 848, 849, 867, 874, 894-898, 1002-1007, 1019, 1020, 1026, 1027.		
Jar (Shape 48a, p. 383) No. 335 (Figs. 371, 372).		1	Tripod-cup (Shape 69, p. 413) Nos. 275 (Figs. 395, 396), 276,		33
Tripod-cup (Shape 69, p. 413) No. 649.		1	832, 833, 961-969, 976-980, 984, 992, 1010, 1013, 1023,		
Tripod-cup (Shape 70, p. 414) No. 650 (Fig. 395).		1	1024.		
			Tripod-cup (Shape 70, p. 414) Nos. 970, 971 (Fig. 396), 972-		17
Room 67			975, 993-998, 1008, 1009, 1014,		
Jar (Shape 48, pp. 383f.)	10[12]		1015, 1021.		
a: Nos. 889, 999-1001, 1016- 1018, 1025 (Fig. 372).		8	Lid (Shape 74, p. 414) Nos. 899 (Figs. 397, 398),		2
b: No. 869.		1	1022.		
Jar (Shape 52, p. 386) No. 1028 (Fig. 375), decorated.		1	In addition to the pots numbered were many more of the same kinds which have not been		
Brazier (Shape 67, p. 412 Nos. 669 and 670 (Fig. 395),	51	23	put together. The ubiquitous kylix was also represented.		

R O O M   6 8

From Room 67 a doorway opens northwestward into another small chamber. The doorway is of the same type as that between Rooms 66 and 67 (Fig. 474). It has lateral bases to support the jambs, each made of a rather carelessly shaped poros block, and stucco flooring between them.[13] The block on the southwest is somewhat

---

12 See note 1, p. 384.

13 Northeastern base: 1.06 m. long, 0.54 m. wide at its southeastern end narrowing in an irregular, roughly

cut edge to less than 0.40 m.; southwestern base: 1.02 m. long, 0.50 m. wide.

higher than the pavement in Room 67 and lower than that in Room 68. The north-eastern base was laid against the inner face of the exterior wall of the building. The surface of this block is somewhat higher than that of the southwestern one. It rises some 0.06 m. above the stucco floor that fills the space between the two blocks. In the northeastern block is an irregular almost rectangular shallow cutting[14] which probably held the socket for the pivot on which the door swung inward northwest-ward within the depth of the door opening. The door was probably 0.75 m. to 0.80 m. wide. On each side the wooden casing must have covered only ca. 0.30 m. of the block, the rest remaining visible in the opening. The space between the blocks, with its floor of stucco, is 0.52 m. wide at the southeast, broadening to 0.64 m. at the northwest edge of the opening.

Room 68 (Key Plan), ca. 3 m. long from southeast to northwest measured on the floor, is 2.10 m. wide (Fig. 207). It was bordered on the northeast by the exterior wall of the building which has survived only in its bedding stones. The northwest wall, 0.80 m. thick and built of unworked stones, is preserved to a height of 0.40 m. No plaster survives in place. Two vertical chases ca. 0.75 m. apart can be recognized in the wall, one of them filled with remains of carbonized wood. The southwestern wall, standing to a height of 0.45 m., is 0.85 m. thick. This too lacks plaster on its face toward Room 68. Three chases are clearly marked at intervals of ca. 0.80 m. The stub of a wall on the southeastern side is 0.52 m. long and stands to a height of 0.43 m.

The stucco floor of the room has a somewhat roughly finished surface, now badly cracked. On all sides it turns up to meet the walls, which apparently had once been coated with mud plaster, no longer preserved.

The room was certainly a pantry, probably equipped with wooden shelves on three sides, the southwestern, northwestern, and northeastern. No holes were found in the floor like those in Rooms 19, 20, and 60 (pp. 124, 126, 239) in which wooden posts were set to support shelves, but the vertical timbers in the walls behind could have served admirably as grounds for their attachment. The whole floor, in any event, was packed with pottery, much of which had evidently fallen from the shelves. The pots (Fig. 342) are, for the most part, kraters and relatively coarse domestic vessels along with a few cups and bowls of finer ware. Two broad circular pans with ring-handles deserve mention. Some 30 two-handled deep jars or kraters were counted. Most of them had been placed on the floor, upside down, one above another, in stacks arranged in at least five regular rows. A domestic jar with one handle and relatively broad mouth represents another popular shape in this collection.

[14] Ca. 0.02 m. deep, 0.07 m. to 0.10 m. long, 0.08 m. to 0.09 m. wide.

BRONZE

Two small pieces, one possibly tip of arrowhead.

STONE

Fragment of black stone, apparently worked,
possibly obsidian (Fig. 298 No. 1).
Piece of red flint.

TERRACOTTA

Fragments of two whorls (Fig. 298 Nos. 2, 3).

POTTERY

	Examples Counted	Examples Numbered
Jar (Shape 48, pp. 383f.)	41[15]	
a: Nos. 846, 847, 868, 871, 873, 875, 877, 881, 883, 887, 891.		11
b: Nos. 842 (Fig. 371), 843, 845, 870, 872, 884, 885 (Fig. 372), 886, 888, 892, 893.		11
Krater (Shape 59, p. 396)	30	13
Nos. 541 (Fig. 384), 546, 565 (Fig. 383), 850, 876, 878-880, 882, 890, 1029-1031.		
Pan (Shape 78, p. 417)	3	2
Nos. 331 (Fig. 398), 547 (Figs. 397, 398).		

Many scattered sherds from the deposit overlying the pots on the floor; in addition to
the latter, shapes represented: kylix (12
stems counted), cup and bowl, amphora,
and, in coarse ware, tripod-vessel and brazier.

STAIRWAY 69

Southwest of Lobby 66 is a narrow space (69 on Key Plan) extending ca. 8.60 m.
southwestward between two walls (Fig. 193). The one on the left, forming the
northwest end of Hall 64 and its continuation alongside Hall 65, has already been
dealt with. The wall on the right is 0.85 m. thick, standing to a height of 0.44 m.
In the top of the wall four transverse slots for beams are clearly marked, separated
by irregular intervals of 1 m., 0.70 m., and 0.85 m. Beyond the last the wall is in-
sufficiently preserved to retain traces of further chases. No plaster of any kind seems
to have been applied to the walls inside the area, and no proper floor either of stucco
or of earth was found. It is safe to conclude that a stairway was built in this space
between the two walls, the lower part of it probably resting on a packing of earth and
clay in the manner we have seen in Stairway 36 (p. 168).

In addition to the lack of plaster on the walls and the absence of a floor more
specific evidence for this identification is provided by the badly damaged remnants
of the lowest step still *in situ* at the northeastern end. It was made of two blocks of
poros aligned with the jamb of the door from Hall 64 and on the other side with
the line of the jamb of the doorway opening northwestward. One block, 0.18 m.
high, 0.36 m. wide, is preserved to its full length of 0.59 m., though it was badly
damaged by fire and partly calcined away. A straight joint separated it from the
second block, which must have extended ca. 1 m. to the other side of the stairway.
Only a small piece of its front lower edge, 0.15 m. long, is preserved. It is probable
that this stairway, like Stairway 36, was built with two blocks to each step, one long-

---

[15] See note 1, p. 384.

ish and one short, attention being given to the alternation of joints. The blocks of the first step were set, at the front at least, on a stucco bedding that rises some 0.03 m. above the floor of the lobby. In consequence the lowest step actually has a height, including the bedding, of 0.21 m. The front edge of the block along the top is rounded by wear and further signs of the treading of feet may be seen extending some 0.30 m. back from the face. The second step apparently overlapped the first by some 0.06 m.

The space available for the stairway is more than 8.50 m. long. This would allow 21 or 22 steps with ample room at the upper end for a landing of adequate size. If the lower half of the staircase was supported by a filling of earth, the upper section could have been carried by transverse wooden beams, as in Stairway 36 (p. 168), stretching across from wall to wall, the wall on the left having been widened in a projecting offset, as mentioned above (p. 255). The timbers would have provided fuel for the fire, the ravages of which are conspicuous everywhere in the Southwestern Building.

The deposit covering the area of the stairway was not more than 0.15 m. to 0.30 m. deep, presumably having lost much of its upper part by erosion. Nothing of any consequence was found in this debris. The potsherds collected represent a good many kylikes, cups and bowls and a tankard with traces of decoration. Probing into deeper layers yielded fragments of early Mycenaean style.

CORRIDOR 70

The doorway leading northwestward from Lobby 66 had the customary lateral poros bases for the jambs (Fig. 475),[16] while the passage between them, some 0.02 m. to 0.04 m. lower, was floored with stucco.

This doorway opens into Corridor 70 (Key Plan), which runs to the southwestward 5.12 m. and has a width of 1.60 m. (Fig. 208). The northeastern wall, separating it from Pantry 68, has been described above (p. 262). A doorway, 1.76 m. wide, is almost but not exactly centered in the northwestern wall (Fig. 207). The northeasterly section of the wall, 0.65 m. thick, rises to a height of 0.47 m. and shows two transverse slots for timbers, spaced 0.62 m. apart. The southwestern section, 0.55 m. thick, standing to a height of nearly 0.50 m. above the floor, seems to have two slots for beams only 0.45 m. apart. The corridor terminates at the southwest in a doorway leading into Room 73. The southeastern wall, dividing the corridor from

---

[16] Northeast base: length 1.16 m.; width at southeast end 0.62 m., at northwest 0.52 m. Near southeast end a relatively small shallow sinking, 0.07 m. in diameter, 0.04 m. deep, probably for a pivot; from it a very roughly cut rabbet extends toward the northwest, perhaps indicating the line to which the door could be swung back against the jamb. The stucco floor of Corridor 70 overlaps the northwestern end of the jamb base ca. 0.20 m. showing the limit of the casing on this side. The door could have been 0.80 m. to 0.90 m. wide. Southwestern base: length 1.16 m.; width at southeast end 0.51 m., at northwest 0.53 m.

Stairway 69, has already been mentioned (p. 263). Some remains of relatively thick mud plaster are in place on all the walls.

The stucco floor has survived in a damaged state, badly cracked by fire and further injured by roots of olive trees. In a few small patches it exhibits a fairly smooth surface but no sign of painted decoration could be observed. Scattered about here and there throughout the length of the corridor were many fragments of a pithos. One piece from near the bottom of the vessel was found just inside the doorway from the lobby and remnants of the neck and rim lay nearby. The jar probably stood at the northern end of the corridor. It had no doubt been caught by the plow and fragments were spread over the neighborhood.

The deposit filling the corridor near the doorway from Lobby 66, ca. 0.80 m. deep, showed in its stratification plowed soil, 0.20 m. at the top, then gray ashy earth with stones, 0.25 m., covering a thicker layer, 0.35 m. deep, of disintegrated crude brick with a few stones resting on the floor. In this debris were found a good many potsherds.

O B J E C T S   F O U N D

P O T T E R Y

Jar fragment (possibly Shape 49, p. 385)

Preserved (Fig. 348 No. 10): flat bottom, almost half of ovoid body with one flattened horizontal loop-handle set below greatest diameter. H. 0.275 m., d. 0.29 m., d. bottom 0.11 m. Good rather sandy tan fabric containing mica. Surface coated with creamy white bearing decoration in light brown: three bands midway between bottom and handle zone, which is bordered below and above by single band and contains two parallel wavy bands that terminate at handle; three bands on shoulder with a fourth higher up.

Pithos: fragments not sufficient for reconstruction.

Shapes recognized among scattered potsherds: kylix (10 stems counted), bowl and cup (7 flat bases); a few pieces with painted decoration of horizontal bands.

R O O M   71

The doorway opening northwestward into Room 71 (Figs. 207, 476) is of the usual type employed in the Southwestern Building, with a central stuccoed passage flanked on each side by a stone base for the jamb, rising appreciably above the level of the floor.[17] The somewhat roughly finished surface of the jamb bases shows no cutting for a pivot or bar. A wooden door swinging on hinges, or hangings, could have closed the opening.

[17] Northeast base: length 0.90 m., width 0.50 m., height above stucco 0.08 m. to 0.11 m. Southwest base: length 0.83 m., width 0.49 m., height above stucco 0.04 m. to 0.06 m. Distance between bases: southeast end 0.78 m., northwest end 0.71 m. The stone blocks, too long for the doorway, project on each side into the connecting rooms; the stucco floor covers them in some places, elsewhere ends against the stone. Southwest block projects into Corridor 70 ca. 0.10 m., into Room 71 0.11 m. Northeast block projects into Corridor 70 0.12 m., into Room 71 0.17 m.

Room 71 (Key Plan and Figs. 207, 209) is rectangular in shape, 5.15 m. long from southwest to northeast and 4.30 m. wide. Enough has already been said about the southeastern wall, its doorway and its slots for beams. The southwestern wall, 0.87 m. thick, standing to a height of 0.25 m., has four transverse slots separated by intervals of 0.81 m., 0.78 m., and 0.77 m. The northwestern wall, 0.84 m. thick, preserved to a height of 0.35 m., has five beam slots, spaced 0.80 m. to 0.85 m. apart. The northeastern wall, 0.87 m. thick including plaster, is interrupted by a doorway. The section to the northwest of the latter stands to a height of 0.28 m., that to the southeast 0.40 m. One transverse slot for a timber is to be seen in each section. The doorway, 1.51 m. wide, including the jamb bases, is not centered in Room 71 but was shifted some centimeters nearer the eastern corner.[18] It was apparently fixed in this position so as to open into Room 72 at its south corner. All the walls bear considerable remains of mud plaster.

The room once had a floor of stucco but it is now in miserable condition, rough, worn, and partly missing in several places. Against the southeast wall near the southern corner was found a thick disk of clay (d. 0.41 m., th. 0.055 m.), showing definite traces of burning on the under side. In the northwestern part of the room, near the wall, were many pieces of a larnax with painted decoration and throughout the room numerous fragments of at least six pithoi.

Room 71 was filled, under the plowed earth, with burned debris containing many large stones evidently fallen from the northwest wall; under the stones was a hard layer of disintegrated crude brick. Around the doorways there was evidence of particularly intense fire from the burning of the wooden casings; stones were fused into a solid mass and the jamb bases were blackened. The abundance of capacious containers perhaps implies that Room 71 was used for storage of wine or oil, though the larnax might have suggested a bathroom if a drain had been found.

O B J E C T S   F O U N D

B R O N Z E
A bit of wire and several other fragments (e.g., Fig. 298 Nos. 4, 5).

S T O N E
Obsidian: small fragment.
Flint: core.
Quartz: some slivers of crystal.

B O N E
Knucklebones.

I V O R Y
Fragment (Fig. 298 No. 6).

P A S T E
Tiny granulated bead.

T E R R A C O T T A
Angular fragments, possibly from a spit-support.

P O T T E R Y
Larnax, many fragments making up large section of one end and part of bottom (Fig. 348 Nos. 6-8). Complete width of end 0.48 m., h. pres. 0.24 m., l. of bottom pres. 0.145 m. and a considerable piece of bottom and one side, 0.43 m. long, 0.23 m. wide, 0.29 m.

[18] 1.25 m. to east corner from jamb base, 1.57 m. to north corner.

high. Bottom flat, projecting angular ridge on side just above; sides flare slightly, ends considerably. Thickness of bottom varies from 0.023 m. to 0.033 m.; of side from 0.017 m. to 0.023 m. Brick-red clay containing mica mottled with gray; surface coated with light red wash on which decoration was applied in yellowish paint inside and out. On interior: on bottom, longitudinal stripes (0.008 m. to 0.012 m. wide); on sides, similar stripes running lengthwise and continuing around ends; a band of stripes (0.105 m. to 0.13 m. broad) forms lower border of a zone of connected spirals framed by an upper border of two stripes (Fig. 348 No. 7); still higher there was probably a second zone of spirals, and at the top of the vessel, just under rim, two more bordering stripes. Some triangular spaces between spirals filled with small irregular dots. On flat rim (0.04 m. wide) parallel transverse stripes in groups. On exterior, above base, five horizontal bands, then an alternation of groups of parallel wavy and horizontal bands, four of the latter forming the upper border below the offset rim. In most respects this larnax is closely similar to the complete example in Room 43 (p. 187 and Figs. 139, 140, 422).

Storage Jar (cf. Shapes 56 and 57, p. 395)

Parts of at least six examples, none restorable:

No. 1 has projecting ridge just above base like that of larnax, which it resembles in fabric. Decoration in dull yellowish, grayish-white: vertical stripes in groups alternating with wavy stripes also in groups; horizontal band under projection of rim; the latter broad (0.048 m.), bearing traces of transverse dashes.

No. 2 has narrow rim (0.043 m.) with more rounded edge, decorated with transverse stripes apparently arranged in groups. Also of fabric similar to that of larnax.

No. 3, more than half of rim with one fourth of side attached. Coarse gray fabric. H. pres. 0.54 m., d. rim calculated 0.50 m. Rim flattened on top with rounded edge. Traces of wavy band below rim. Two very large round horizontal loop-handles, high on shoulder. A flat bottom possibly belongs to this jar.

No. 4 has almost complete rim with part of shoulder and one round horizontal loop-handle. Gray clay coated with yellowish-gray wash. Shoulder bears wavy band or zigzag. Rim (0.034 m. wide) has rounded edge; top decorated with diagonal parallel stripes, possibly in groups.

No. 5, possibly a pithos. Relatively high straight slightly concave neck with offset rim (d. of rim estimated 0.40 m., w. of rim 0.05 m.). Very coarse solid fabric containing many particles; surface appears to be coated with reddish wash. Large round loop-handle probably set horizontally high on shoulder.

No. 6, fragment of rim (0.035 m. wide) slightly offset, flat on top.

Among sherds collected from debris, shapes recognized: in coarse ware, tripod-vessel, cooking pot, brazier, griddle; in finer ware, kylix (6 or more), bowl and cup, dipper, bowl with pinched-out handles. Some pieces bear painted decoration, most of them in the style of Mycenaean III B; a few stray sherds of earlier types.

ROOM 72

The doorway communicating northeastward with Room 72 (Figs. 207, 477) is of the regular plan so often seen in the Southwestern Building, with a central floor of stucco and lateral slabs of poros forming the bases that supported the wooden jambs.[19]

[19] Southeast base: length 1.11 m.; width southwest edge 0.55 m., northeast edge 0.59 m.; height above floor in Room 71 0.05 m., in doorway 0.10 m., in Room 72 0.05 m.; projects 0.20 m. into Room 71. Northwest base: length 0.95 m. to 0.97 m.; width, southwest edge 0.50 m., northeast edge 0.53 m.; height above floor in Room 71 0.05 m., in doorway 0.07 m., in Room 72 0.04 m.; projects into Room 71 0.08 m. to 0.12 m., into Room 72 0.07 m. Distance between bases: southwest end 0.46 m., northeast end 0.35 m.

No cuttings appear in these blocks and there is no evidence to show whether there was an actual door that swung open and shut or a hanging of some kind.

Beyond the northwestern base a similar smaller block of poros, 0.79 m. long, 0.54 m. wide, has been used as the foundation of the northwestern section of the wall. This block might be a re-used piece or conceivably a jamb base of an earlier doorway more nearly centered in the northeastern wall of Room 71 and still *in situ*.

Lying near the southwestern edge of the northwestern jamb base and spreading out a few centimeters into Room 71 were found remains of five narrow inscribed tablets. They had apparently been almost melted by the heat and were in wretched condition, difficult to lift and to read when cleaned. How they came to this position on the base of the door casing is hard to explain. Perhaps they should be catalogued as coming from Room 71 but it is more likely that they fell from an upper story at the time of the conflagration.

Room 72 (Key Plan and Fig. 207) is a small chamber so badly wrecked by the fire and by later disturbances that very little can be said about it with any certainty. It was 3.07 m. long from southeast to northwest and 2.24 m. wide. The southeast wall which separates it from Room 68 has already been considered. On the northeast stood the exterior wall of the Southwestern Building, only the bedding slabs now remaining in place. The northwestern wall, 0.84 m. thick, rising to a height of only a single course of small stones above the floor, is somewhat irregular. Its northeastern end, in a stretch 1.80 m. long, has been shifted slightly to the northwest of its alignment with the rest of the wall which continues southwestward alongside Room 71. The displaced part was clearly inserted as the filling of an opening in the wall in an earlier phase. A doorway undoubtedly once led from an earlier Room 72 into the long narrow area (76). The rough stucco floor of this antecedent Room 72 has been found, 0.30 m. below the later floor. On each side of the doorway a ragged-edged cutting into that flooring shows that a jamb base has been extracted.

The floor of this little chamber in its final phase is rough and irregular. Just inside the doorway from Room 71 and along the southeastern wall it is made of stucco, badly cracked and buckled. Elsewhere in the room toward the northwest only a few patches of stucco are preserved.

Room 72 was found filled with a mass of fallen blackened stones and ashes containing a few objects, scraps of plaster with traces of color, and some sherds.

O B J E C T S   F O U N D

SILVER (?)

Fragment (Fig. 298 No. 7).

BRONZE

A few nondescript pieces (e.g., Fig. 298 No. 8).

STONE

Worked piece (Fig. 298 No. 9).

IVORY

Two small fragments blackened by fire (Fig. 298 Nos. 10, 11).

CLAY

Tablets: Nos. 1253-1257 (*OOT*, 12, 65, 67, 68, pls. XVIII-XIX).

POTTERY

Sherds, shapes noted: kylix, cup and bowl, domestic jar, krater, tripod-vessel, scoop. Also fragments joining pithoi in Room 71.

Among sherds from deposit between upper and lower floors, shapes recognized: kylix (4 stems, one of a votive), cup and bowl, lid, all of Mycenaean III B.

ROOM 73

At the southwestern end of Corridor 70 is a doorway of the regular type (Figs. 208, 478) having a poros block on each side to support the door casing and between them an area continuing the stucco floor from the corridor into Room 73.[20] The door, turning on a pivot, opened southwestward and could swing back against the southeastern casing, perhaps jutting out into the room.

Room 73 (Key Plan) is 6.45 m. long from southeast to northwest and 4.12 m. wide (Fig. 210). On the northeast it is bordered by the southwest wall of Room 71 (Fig. 211) which is preserved to a height of 0.21 m. above the floor and has four chases for beams. The northwestern wall, through which a doorway leads to Lobby 75, survives only in its foundation; it has a thickness of 0.85 m. and shows no signs of chases. The southwestern wall too is represented only by foundations 1.08 m. thick and by one jamb base of a doorway at its southeastern end (Fig. 212). On the southeast the room is separated from Stairway 69 by a wall 0.80 m. thick, which stands at its northeast end to a height of 0.23 m., but for most of its length emerges only a few centimeters above floor level (Fig. 208). A good deal of fallen plaster was found on the floor, especially alongside the northeastern wall. It is of rough quality and no trace of painted decoration could be recognized, but the plaster was badly damaged by fire and perhaps the finishing coat was entirely burned away.

All the way around the room the stucco floor is fairly well preserved along the walls, where it seems to have been protected by fallen plaster. In some places a relatively smooth finished surface has survived though blackened by the effect of the fire. Remains of the stucco extended all the way across the middle of the room, although in a badly damaged state, cracked and broken, with its surface gone and with many minor or major gaps. No sign of floor painting has anywhere been observed.

Near the doorway into Room 74 was found, still in position on the floor, the flat base of a large jar of coarse fabric (Fig. 212), dark bluish-gray in color, perhaps from the result of burning. Other pieces of this jar were found scattered all over the room.

---

[20] Southeast base: length 1 m.; width 0.57 m.; height above floor, at northeast end 0.07 m., at southwest end 0.08 m.; a strip along opening, 0.13 m. to 0.15 m. wide, is more worn than the part, 0.45 m. wide, that was covered by wooden jamb; roughly rounded pivot hole, ca. 0.07 m. in diameter and 0.04 m. deep. Northwest base: length 1 m.; width 0.57 m.; height above floor, at northeast end 0.03 m., at southwest end 0.045 m.; strip 0.23 m. wide along opening worn from exposure; at northeast surface slightly higher, more or less in line with pivot hole. Space between jamb blocks 0.625 m. to 0.645 m.

Room 73 is a spacious apartment and it must have been of some importance; the scanty remnants found on the floor, however, give no clue to its specific purpose. Like its neighbor (71), it is an inside room; how light and air were provided is not clear. The possibility of a light well on the southeastern side occurred to us but that seems to be precluded by the definite evidence that a stairway ascended here. The closed lobbies on the northwest likewise rule out the provision from that direction of light and ventilation; nor could these latter be obtained from the adjoining apartment (74) on the southwest unless it was an open terrace.

The lack of decoration on the walls and floor implies that this was not a place where the household congregated or spent much of its time and we must conclude that it was a storeroom of some kind. The large jar may have contained water or wine or oil, possibly the latter, since traces of severe burning were found around it. But even if its contents were definitely known, it would probably contribute little toward the solution of the problems connected with Room 73.

Under the plowed ground the scanty layers of fire debris which covered the floor of Room 73 contained only a nondescript twisted lump of silver, a large wide bent piece of bronze (Fig. 298 No. 12), one chip of obsidian, a reddish flint flake, a black flint, a fragment of black veined stone with a worked surface, two small bits of ivory, and some broken pottery. The latter, in addition to the lower part of the large jar mentioned above, included recognizable fragments of kylikes, cups and bowls, conical cups, basins with pinched-out handles, dippers, in finer ware; legs and other parts of cooking pots and large jars in coarse ware.

ROOM 74

From the southern corner of Room 73 a doorway leads southwestward into an adjoining apartment (Fig. 479). The northwest jamb base (Fig. 208)[21] has already been mentioned. The corresponding southeastern base is missing, probably having been extracted by stone robbers or removed as a hindrance to the plow. A deep hole filled with soft earth remained to mark its place. The space between the two jamb blocks was floored with stucco: though much broken and damaged, it can still be seen to a width of 0.55 m. The exact dimensions of the doorway cannot be given, since the southeastern side is missing, but the northwestern jamb base is 1.33 m. distant from the southeast wall.

Room 74 (Key Plan), parallel to, of equal length with (6.41 m. measured between foundations), and slightly wider (4.50 m.) than Room 73, seems to have extended to the inner face of the exterior wall of the Southwestern Building. This wall is 1.85

---

[21] Length 1.32 m. from southwest to northeast, width 0.50 m.; thickness as seen at southwest end, 0.43 m.; height above floor in doorway 0.07 m. On the north-east the block projects 0.18 m. into Room 73 beyond the face of the wall.

m. thick, but little more than the deep foundation remains, ca. 1.15 m. below the floor of the room. The northeastern wall, which borders Room 73 (Fig. 210) rises only in two or three places as much as a few centimeters above the floor. The northwestern and southeastern walls barely reach floor level near the northern and eastern corners of the room. Toward the southwest they dip sharply with the eroded edge of the hill and vanish altogether before they reach the outside southwestern wall. In view of their ruined state, nothing further can be said about these walls.

In the northern angle of the room some remains of the stucco floor still survive: a strip, 2.30 m. long, runs beside the northwestern wall and, turning southeastward, continues 1.50 m. along the northeastern wall. A few broken patches appear farther out in this triangular space. Near the southwest end of the strip, the stucco floor is laid directly over a thick underlying wall of an earlier period. The stucco is white and of good quality, but has suffered badly from fire and is calcined and cracked.

Since no floor deposit had survived, it was not possible to determine for what purpose this room was used. It may have had a window or windows looking out through the exterior wall toward the sea, but no evidence for such windows has been found.

L O B B Y   7 5

In the north corner of Room 73 is a doorway leading northwestward into a small lobby (Figs. 210, 480). Two lateral bases for the door jambs and a stuccoed strip between follow the normal arrangement of doorways in the Southwestern Building.[22] A straight line of melted plaster and carbon on each base marks the face of the wooden jamb and indicates that the width of the actual opening for the door was 1.05 m. No cuttings for a pivot-hole or bar exist.

The lobby (75 on Key Plan) is 1.61 m. long from northeast to southwest and 1.22 m. wide (Fig. 211). It was bordered on the northeast by a stone wall 1 m. thick and preserved to a height of one course above the floor, with a slot for a beam in its upper surface. On the southwestern side was a narrow wall, 0.63 m. thick, only the foundations of which survive. No plaster appears on either wall. The northwestern side is taken up by a doorway that opens into a small room.

The lobby has a well-made floor of stucco, 0.10 m. thick on the southwest, ending in a straight line against the missing wall in that direction. The original surface was badly injured by fire and what is left is rough and uneven.

22 Southwest base: length 0.975 m.; width 0.60 m.; height above floor in Room 73 0.055 m., in Lobby 75 0.035 m.; deposit of carbon and fused plaster indicates line of door casing ca. 0.33 m. from edge of stone toward opening; block somewhat carelessly set, slightly askew. Northeast base: length 0.96 m.; width 0.57 m.; roughly cut rabbet (0.04 m. deep) and deposit of fused plaster and carbon fix line of door jamb ca. 0.20 m. from the edge of the block in the opening. Distance between jamb bases: at southeast end 0.52 m., northwest end 0.62 m.

Except for a few ordinary Mycenaean potsherds nothing was found on or above the floor. This lobby is extraordinarily small and it is hard to understand why two doors so close together were necessary, unless it was to safeguard something of unusual value in the rooms beyond.

AREA 76

To the northeast of the lobby but shut off from the latter by a wall, is a narrow area (76 on Key Plan) ca. 8 m. long, ranging from 1.08 m. to 1.25 m. in width (Fig. 209). On the southeastern side it is bordered by walls, with chases for beams which have already been recorded (Fig. 207). Near the northeastern end the wall is continued by the filling of an earlier doorway (p. 268). At the northeast the area ends against the foundations of the exterior wall of the building, here 1.16 m. thick (Fig. 213), where some flattish stones formed the support of the ashlar masonry which was removed by plunderers. This appears to be a corner of the outside wall which turns southwestward to a length of 5.20 m., closing the area on its northwest side. Only the foundations remain *in situ*, ranging from 1.08 m. to 1.15 m. in thickness. Beyond this point the line is continued by an interior wall, 4.79 m. long, extending to the lobby. In this southwesterly section five chases appear at intervals ranging from 0.65 m. to 0.80 m. In the northeast part, which forms the outside wall, the outer face was presumably made of ashlar blocks; in the inner backing of rubble, traces of at least two slots for beams are visible. No floor was recognized inside the area; no fragmentary plaster was found alongside the walls, nor did the latter bear any plaster *in situ*. An abundance of carbonized matter probably came from the burning of the many timbers in the framework of the walls.

In the latest phase, at least, this area was walled up on every side and inaccessible. Even the short wall separating it from the lobby, as mentioned above, has a beam slot which presumably ran all the way to the top of the wall. The area thus could have served no useful purpose for occupation or habitation. It must therefore have been a light-well somewhat in the Cretan manner, a shaft to admit light and air, especially into Room 71.

The light-wells which have been recognized in Minoan palaces, as well as in contemporary houses, are of several kinds. Some were installed in central areas of buildings, others in outer borders, even alongside exterior walls. It is this latter type which Shaft 76 at Englianos somewhat resembles, though the Cretan examples are much more elaborate. In principle, however, a comparison may in general be made with the light-wells in the domestic quarters of the Palace of Minos at the eastern end of the Hall of the Double Axes[23] and behind the "Queen's Megaron";[24] and in the

[23] *PM* III, 328ff., figs. 218, 219.　　　　[24] *Ibid.* III, 373ff., figs. 248, 249, 250.

Royal Villa at Knossos,[25] and also in the South House;[26] and even with the huge shaft at the inner end of the Great Propylon at Phaistos.[27]

In the black ashy debris filling the area were found two rivet-heads and two flat pieces of bronze (Fig. 298 Nos. 13-16), some flints, part of a boar's tusk, and a fragment of a terracotta spit-support; also a large quantity of broken pottery, shapes recognized: kylix (in abundance), conical cup, bowl and basin with pinched-out handles, dipper and, in coarse ware, griddle, jar, scoop, tripod-vessel, one fragment of connection between twin pots. A few pieces bear painted decoration, among them two or three strays of early Mycenaean and Middle Helladic types.

ROOM 77

The northwestern doorway leading out of Lobby 75 (Fig. 481) is of the familiar kind with poros bases for the jambs,[28] on both sides framing a stucco floor between them; it is 0.76 m. wide, very badly cracked and broken, extending through the doorway (Fig. 210). The actual opening, as shown by weathering marks on the bases, is 0.94 m. wide. No cutting for a pivot. The northeast jamb was notched at its northern angle in adjustment to the similarly notched base in the contiguous doorway between Rooms 77 and 78.

Room 77 (Key Plan) is 3.94 m. long from northeast to southwest and 2.93 m. wide (Fig. 211). The measurements are only approximate, since the walls on the southeast, northeast, and northwest have been destroyed to floor level or lower, and that on the southwest rises in two or three places only a few centimeters higher. On the northeast is a doorway leading to Room 78; beyond it the substructure of the wall, 0.80 m. thick, continues northwestward. On the northwest side the room is bounded by the foundations, 1.10 m. thick, of the outside wall of the building. The wall on the southwest, with a few stones rising 0.10 m. above the floor, has a thickness of 0.82 m. and shows four chases, spaced 0.65 m. to 0.70 m. apart. One or two grooves also appear in the northeast wall. The southeast side of the room is occupied by two doorways, one leading in from Lobby 75, the other communicating with Lobby 79. Between the two is the end of the narrow wall separating those two diminutive passageways.

25 *Ibid.* II, 398, fig. 228.

26 *Ibid.* II, 373, figs. 208, 375.

27 *Festos* II, 321ff., fig. 210, pl. II (69); cf. also II, 167, fig. 100; 266, fig. 166; 257, 281, 358, fig. 177.

28 Southwest base: length 0.93 m., width ca. 0.45 m., thickness 0.29 m.; height above floor in Room 75 0.035 m., in doorway 0.045 m.; a band on top, 0.06 m. wide, along southeast edge and 0.09 m. along northeast edge is lime-coated, differing from rest of the stone, and was probably covered by the wooden casing. Northeast base: length 0.91 m.; width 0.47 m.; notch in north corner, 0.115 m. by 0.18 m., cut to receive south corner of southeast jamb base of doorway from Room 77 to Room 78 which was similarly cut; height of top of stone above floor in Room 75 0.06 m., in doorway 0.045 m., in Room 77 0.05 m.; lime encrusted band, like that on southwest base, 0.09 m. to 0.10 m. wide, extends along southwest edge of block evidently marking line of door casing. Distance between jamb stones 0.76 m.

Around the four sides of the room are remnants of the fire-scarred, badly cracked stucco floor. It slopes down from the walls and has sunk rather deeply in some places. The floor shows no evidence of painted decoration and no plaster fallen from the walls was observed. The room seems to form an important unit in this little maze that occupies the western corner of the building though its exact purpose cannot be determined.

The deposit in Room 77 was mainly plowed earth with very little of the usual burned debris covering the remnants of the floor, but even here was a bronze handle (max. w. 0.039 m., l. 0.025 m., th. 0.003 m.) and the usual quota of scattered sherds. Shapes recognized: kylix (many), cup and bowl (flat bases numerous), conical cup, bowl with pinched-out handles, dipper, jug and, in coarse ware, pithos, griddle, tripod-vessel, storage jar. A few pieces with traces of painted decoration: bands, stippling, Mycenaean III Flower and over-all coating.

ROOM 78

The doorway leading northeastward into Room 78 (Fig. 482) has the usual lateral bases for the jambs[29] and a stucco-coated strip between (Fig. 209). The latter has an average width of 0.52 m., but the weathering on the stone slabs indicates that the space between the wooden jambs was 0.96 m. wide. Pivot-holes are lacking in the stones.

Room 78 (Key Plan) is almost square measuring 3.09 m. on the northeast and northwest sides, 3.29 m. on the southwest, 3 m. on the southeast (Fig. 213). In view of the ruined condition of the walls, these measurements can only be taken as roughly approximate. The southwestern wall beyond the doorway needs no further mention (p. 273). The southeastern wall separating the room from Light-well 76 (Fig. 209) is provided with five slots for transverse timbers and rises in a few places to 0.10 m. above the floor. On the northeast and northwest the room is enclosed by the exterior wall of the building, which has been destroyed to a level below the floor (Fig. 213). On the northeastern side it is 0.90 m. thick, on the northwest 1.05 m. The northeastern foundation juts out northwestward 0.85 m. beyond the corner. The foundations of the southwestern wall are also prolonged in a like extension. They might have provided the substructure for antae or buttresses at this end of the building. In the core of the northwestern wall, 0.84 m. from the north

[29] Northwestern base: length ca. 1 m., width 0.55 m. to 0.58 m.; height above floor in Room 77 0.07 m., in doorway 0.055 m.; in Room 78 floor slopes up to the block. Strip of weathering, ca. 0.12 m. wide, on top of block along side toward opening, indicating line of door casing. Southeastern base: length 1.06 m.; width 0.54 m. to 0.58 m.; south corner notched and fitted into similar cutting in jamb base of doorway from Room 75 to Room 77; height above floor in corner of Room 77 0.08 m., in doorway 0.03 m., in Room 78 0.08 m.; block projects 0.15 m. farther into Room 77 than the northwest base; weathering and remains of dissolved plaster mark strip, 0.27 m. wide, on top of block along side toward opening.

corner, is a small poros block. It is 0.185 m. wide, 0.58 m. long, but broken at one end, and in its present state ca. 0.10 m. thick. A channel, 0.135 m. broad, was cut in the top of the block but its original depth is uncertain since both sides have been broken away. Whether it lies *in situ*, or is a reused block, or has come to rest here by chance could not be determined. It looks as if it might have been a drain to carry water through the wall. About 1.40 m. to the southwest, just outside the line of the wall, is another poros block nearly 0.50 m. long, 0.24 m. wide, 0.23 m. high, but also broken at one end. This too has been made into a gutter, 0.11 m. wide and 0.10 m. deep. It is quite different in style from the other block, but the presence of these stone water channels led us to wonder if Room 78 was possibly a bathroom from which water had to be drained away.

The stucco floor of the room sinks slightly from three sides toward the northwest. It is in wretched condition, buckled, heaved up, cracked into small pieces, but the surface where preserved is good (Fig. 209). No evidence could be detected on the floor for a fixed larnax or tub or a stand for jars containing oil or water as in Room 43 in the Main Building. The identification as a bathroom, though reasonable, is therefore purely conjectural.

As in Room 77 only a thin accumulation of burned debris and surface soil covered the floor. No whole pots had survived but scattered sherds found in the disturbed layer represent the same shapes as in the neighboring room plus a gigantic loop-handle presumably from a large pithos and a very fine handle of a brazier.

In the doorway between Rooms 77 and 78 was found a bronze rivet (l. 0.033 m., d. heads 0.006 m., d. of shaft 0.004 m.).

LOBBY 79

A doorway in the south corner of Room 77 gives access toward the southeast to a tiny lobby (Figs. 211, 483). The doorway is of the standard kind with the two bases for the door casing and the stucco floor between. The blocks show no cutting for pivot or bar.[30]

Lobby 79 (Key Plan) is even smaller than its neighbor 75, 1.32 m. long from northeast to southwest and 1.17 m. wide (Fig. 211). The walls on the southeast and northeast, mere foundations not reaching floor level, have been mentioned above and the other two sides are occupied by doorways. The floor is of stucco, fairly well pre-

[30] Southwestern base: length 1.05 m. to 1.09 m.; average width 0.52 m.; height of top above floor in Lobby 79 0.10 m., in doorway 0.06 m., in Room 77 0.03 m.; at northwest end is a rabbet 0.15 m. wide, which was covered by the floor of the room leaving an exposed surface of 0.94 m.; weathering and plaster mark a strip, 0.22 m. wide, along the top of the base beside the opening.

Northeastern base: length 1.04 m.; width 0.45 m.; height of top above floor in Room 79 0.13 m., in doorway 0.10 m.; thickness of block 0.28 m.; traces of plaster and weathering, 0.12 m. wide, along top of block beside the opening. Space irregular with average width 0.72 m. Both blocks are carelessly shaped.

served but uneven and cracked. It disclosed no remains of painted decoration nor did it yield plaster fallen from the walls. This little cubicle was not a place in which to sojourn but merely a passageway leading southwestward to a larger room. Nothing was found in it.

ROOMS 80 AND 81

The doorway opening in that direction (Fig. 484) has lost its southeastern jamb base but the northwestern is preserved, as well as most of the stucco floor running through the opening.[31]

The doorway leads into an area (80 and 81 on Key Plan) some 7.20 m. long from southeast to northwest and 5 m. wide (Fig. 210). A small bit of the stucco floor is preserved not far to the northwest of the entrance and some scattered patches appear farther to the southwestward, but throughout almost the entire area erosion has worn away the slope of the hill to a level below the floor. Some slight evidence was observed suggesting that this space was divided into two rooms by a transverse wall which was aligned with an offset in the southwestern exterior wall.[32]

Nothing has survived to shed any light on the character and use of the room or rooms in this corner of the Southwestern Building. The whole complex of passages and chambers to the northwest of Rooms 73 and 74, with its many doorways, is mysterious and puzzling. It is difficult to comprehend why so devious an approach was laid out from Entrance Hall 64 to Rooms 80 and 81. One had to pass from Room 64 through Lobby 66, Corridor 70, Room 73, Lobby 75, Anteroom 77, and Lobby 79, going through seven doorways all told. The four doorways beyond Room 73, so far as shown by the remains, lack a socket for a pivot (Fig. 211) and, unless doors swinging on hinges had been invented, it looks as if these openings could not have been closed except possibly by hangings.

One might therefore conclude that this part of the building was not designed for the safekeeping of articles of great intrinsic value. The room or rooms on the southwestern side, if they had windows, looked out on a splendid panorama sweeping from the Bay of Navarino across Sphacteria and Koryphasion to the Ionian Sea. In modern times it would have been regarded as an ideal place for the master bedroom or a guest suite; but the evidence from the Main Building implies that the bedrooms and dressing rooms were on the upper floor and not at the ground level. In any

[31] Northwest base: length 1.11 m.; width 0.47 m. North corner notched 0.14 m. by 0.23 m. to receive south corner of southwest jamb block of doorway into Room 77. Stucco floor preserved to a width of 0.55 m. in space between bases.

[32] At and barely under the floor level on the right, just inside the doorway from the lobby, foundations of a wall 0.80 m. thick, extending southwestward some 2 m., are shown on the plan as an earlier wall. Its masonry, however, looks contemporary with the interior walls throughout this quarter of the palace (Fig. 210). If it is of the same date, we must conclude that one had to pass through yet another corridor running southwestward before one reached a doorway, no longer preserved, which opened northwestward into the chamber or chambers beyond.

event, lacking real evidence, one can only speculate on the use made of these quarters in the western angle of the palace and no certain conclusions are possible.

EXTERIOR WALL OF SOUTHWESTERN BUILDING

The northeastern exterior wall of the Southwestern Building and part of the northwestern have already been briefly described. It remains to examine the projecting tower-like western corner and the exterior wall on the southwest (Key Plan). Outside the northwestern wall bordering Rooms 77 and 78, almost parallel to it and only 0.75 m. distant from it, are the foundations of another wall, 0.80 m. thick (Fig. 213). At the northeast it breaks off in an irregular line and at the southwest it was apparently cut away by the bedding trench for the projecting tower to be described below. The top of this wall as now preserved is 0.57 m. below the floor of Rooms 77 and 78. The two projecting foundations of antae or buttresses mentioned above (p. 274) seem to have been built up against the southeastern face of this wall. We have been inclined to regard the wall as earlier in date of construction than its neighbor to the southeast which borders Rooms 77 and 78, but the possibility cannot be excluded that the two are contemporary. In that event we might perhaps have here another narrow light-well flanking those two rooms.

The inner wall of the two, at its junction with the southwest wall of Room 77, turns at right angles and extends ca. 1 m. toward the northwest; beyond that point it has been broken away (Fig. 214). Superposed on the projecting stub and continuing farther northwestward with a total projection of 2.35 m. to a neatly built corner, is a wall constructed in a completely different style. It is made mainly of rough slabs of limestone of varying thickness and lengths laid in fairly regular courses. At the corner mentioned it turns southwestward and extends 7.20 m. to another angle of the same kind; here it returns toward the southeast to form the southwestern face of the exterior wall of the Southwestern Building (Fig. 202). The ground level outside to the northwest in the late phase of the palace lay at ca. 11.50 m. above datum. A bedding trench for the laying of its deep foundation, 0.70 m. to 0.80 m. wider than the wall, was dug around the northeastern and northwestern sides of the tower. As mentioned above, it was hacked through the outer of the two parallel walls, and along the northwestern flank of the tower at least four walls belonging to two or more earlier periods were truncated in the same manner (Fig. 214).

The bottom courses of the tower at the western angle rested on *stereo* at 10 m. above datum. Some nine courses have been exposed on the northwestern face giving it almost a monumental aspect. On the northeasterly side the wall seems to be 1.30 m. thick, on the northwestern 1.60 m., but the inner face is not easily recognizable.

Outside the tower and sections 1, 2, and 3 of the southwestern wall a considerable deposit of debris had accumulated. It contained vast quantities of broken pottery and other objects which had evidently been thrown out from this wing of the palace. Among the most interesting items recovered is a seal impression, baked hard, bearing a cult scene of three women (Figs. 311 No. 27, 312 No. 16).

The southwestern face of the wall was built in many successive sections of varying length, each marked off by a projecting or re-entering offset or by much deeper set-backs in the exterior line of the building (Fig. 417). In some instances the offsets are aligned with interior walls of the palace.

Starting from the western corner the first section is 4 m. long and has been exposed to a height of seven courses (Fig. 202). The second section, which projects 0.20 m. beyond the line of the first, is 4.70 m. long. To a length of 1.20 m. five courses of these unworked blocks are preserved; beyond that only two, the upper part having been carried off by plunderers. Section 3, jutting out 0.70 m., stretches 9.10 m. until it reaches the junction with the northwestern wall of Hall 65. Three or four courses still stand to a length of 4 m.; beyond that point only a single course. At its southeast end, however, where it meets the northwest wall of the Throne Room, the upper part has vanished entirely. Here many of the stones have been calcined by the fire, forming a great mass of *migma*, and those that survived have been abstracted and carted away.

From its beginning on the northeastern flank of the western tower through its continuation around the northwestern side, as well as along the southwestern face, at least as far as the end of section 3 (and perhaps to the end of section 4), the entire extent of this wall—which is built of large unworked limestone blocks—looks as if it must surely be a reconstruction in a new technique and new material not used elsewhere in the southwestern unit of the palace. This whole corner of the building at some time apparently suffered damage serious enough to require widespread repairs. In their present dilapidated and plundered state the ruins yield little or no information to explain what happened and why.

The fourth section, behind the Throne Room, 12.45 m. long, jutted out 0.40 m. and at its other end has a re-entrant angle, 0.80 m. deep (Fig. 203), approximately but not exactly aligned with the southeastern wall of Hall 65. In this whole stretch, and continuing through the fifth section, no blocks of the outer face are left in place above the bedding stones of the foundations, though the inner face of the wall, which is made of small unworked stones, has not been destroyed. It is likely that sections 4 and 5 were faced with large squared poros blocks laid in ashlar style and not with the rough limestone slabs seen in the preceding sections. Some blocks and fragments of others were found lying outside and below the exterior wall. In sections 1, 2, and 3 the limestone face probably rose on the outside to a height even with the floor inside the palace, while poros blocks were used above that to the level of the upper story. The rough wall in these sections was perhaps not meant to be visible below the ground floor of the building.

The fifth section, extending southeastward from the south corner of Hall 65, is 8.40 m. long and 1.75 m. wide. The core together with the inner face of the wall is preserved to a height of ca. 10.50 m. above datum. In the rubble foundations, just southeast of Hall 65, two thick unworked slabs of limestone stand out conspicuously; they look exactly like those which appear in sections 1, 2, and 3. All the squared blocks that presumably once formed the outer face are missing; only the bedding stones, at ca. 10 m. above datum, which rested on a substructure founded on or just above *stereo*, remain in place (Fig. 204).

At the end of section 5 the wall turns at a right angle toward the northeast. The corner was laid over an underlying earlier wall with deep foundations running from west to east which were partly demolished to make room for the new structure. From this point section 6 continued in a northeasterly direction some 7 m., ascending the steep bank of the acropolis. Two squared blocks of poros, 0.33 m. high, and one of them 0.80 m. long, have survived *in situ* in the lowest course near the junction with the fifth section (Fig. 204). Farther northeastward, however, the wall must have been built on a stepped foundation rising to a much higher level. So far as it has been possible to explore the area, no dressed stones have been revealed in their original position, but many blocks were found tumbled together in a hollow to the southeastward, some 2 or 3 m. distant from the line of the wall. Badly cracked and calcined by intense heat, these blocks lead us to conjecture that this part of the building was at some time wrecked by fire and had to be reconstructed, the ruined material being thrown aside into the hollow.

The seventh section, turning again southeastward, can be traced more than 8 m. to yet another angle, where a further change in direction is recognizable. Near the southeastern end of this stretch three, or possibly four, well-shaped blocks, lying in a single course, retain their place *in situ*, forming the face of the wall—a superposed later structure concealing part of the blocks has made it impossible to differentiate their exact number. The southeast corner block is missing, though its bedding slabs have not been removed.

The angle indicated here is of ca. 30 degrees, and section 8 can be followed some 5.55 m. eastward (Fig. 215). For a distance of about 4 m. three courses of dressed poros blocks stand in their original setting in the foundations to a height of 0.90 m., fairly well preserved to a point where the wall was evidently intersected and buried by the southeastern wall of Corridor 61. Some of the blocks are 0.37 m. high, varying in length from 0.80 m. to 1.05 m. No ashlar masonry has survived in the superstructure, but the inner line of the wall is recognizable showing a thickness of ca. 1.10 m.

Section 9, beyond another corner, at which it swings again to the northeastward, retains in its outer face two courses of big blocks of poros. The angle itself lacks its superstructure, but some stones of its foundation can be recognized, although this intersection has been much dilapidated. The ninth section must have had a total length of 4.60 m., but the part surviving in two courses is only 2.97 m. long (Fig. 216). It has been damaged and leans outward. The poros blocks in the top course vary from 0.82 m. to 0.93 m. in length and are about 0.47 m. high. In the lower course they are 0.42 m. high and 0.98 m. to 1 m. long. In the top of the upper course three rectangular dowel holes appear, spaced at intervals of 0.75 m. and 0.85 m.

At its northeastern end in an angle of a little less than 90 degrees this section joins section 10 (Fig. 216), which extended some 4 m. southeastward. One course of five poros blocks is preserved, 0.34 m. to 0.35 m. high, and part of a single dressed stone represents a second course. The total length surviving is only 3.54 m. Beyond this point the wall was ruthlessly cut through transversely when the main drain of the central building of the palace was constructed or cleaned. On the southeastern side of the drain all traces of the wall are lost. Section 10 probably continued in that direction only some 2 m. farther to another angle.

The latter has left no visible traces, but some scanty vestiges of a foundation running northeastward, approximately but not exactly aligned with the southeast front of the Main Building, may possibly mark the southeastern limit of the Southwestern Building.

This exterior wall (shown in solid black on Fig. 417), in its ten sections, has been traced (by the appearance of occasional scanty blocks or fragments of poros still remaining *in situ*) through many setbacks and angles to a total length of some 70 m. We saw that the entire northwestern part—from the corner of the tower to (and probably including) the Throne Room (Hall 65)—was destroyed and was later rebuilt in a new style. It is obvious that the southeastern continuation, beyond Hall 65, suffered an even worse fate, for this part was so thoroughly demolished that its reconstruction was not attempted; instead, a new wall was erected along a different line. From Hall 65 a new broad foundation (diagonally hatched in the plan, Fig. 417) built of smallish fieldstones, was laid somewhat more than 1 m. inside the ruined wall of poros blocks. It extended ca. 12 m. southeastward, crossing section 6 of its ashlar predecessor, and then joining a new diagonal wall, also built of small stones. This ran some 11 m. eastward in a line less than 1 m. outside section 8, apparently to a junction with the southeastern wall of Corridor 61. How much farther—if at all—it continued in this direction cannot now be determined. Perhaps it swung northeastward for a stretch of 2 or 3 m. before turning eastward again to meet the descending southeast wall of Room 62. Only the inner face of this diagonal wall is preserved. How high it rose is not determinable, and its original thickness is unknown, though it was apparently greater than 1 m. This, indicated in diagonal hatching on Figure 417, was surely the exterior wall of the building in its final phase of existence.

One may safely conclude that Mycenaean palaces, in their relatively short span of existence mainly through the thirteenth century, were subject to lively changes, whether caused by accident or design. In the Main Building evidence has been noted (pp. 47, 45, 205, 115) indicating that almost constant reparations on a considerable scale were needed in many different places: a new oil magazine was added in the northern corner; the western angle appears to have collapsed and to have been rebuilt; two walled courts were enclosed along the northeastern side, where a new doorway had to be opened through a wall; and in the southwestern quarter two rooms seem to have been dismantled and converted into a stairway leading to the upper floor.

The southeast quarter of the Southwestern Building, extending from Hall 65 to the area below Rooms 60 and 62, is filled with an intricate maze of badly ruined foundation walls (Fig. 216), in many instances superposed one above another, for the most part broken away and despoiled of stones useful as building material. No floors and no floor deposits were preserved. A sequence of phases or periods is obviously represented, but in the state of the remains it is difficult to differentiate the walls of one phase from those of another. The following interpretation is based on a study of the foundations and their apparent relations one to another.

The latest walls and foundations, so far as we are able to distinguish them, are shown on the plan (Fig. 412) in diagonal hatching. Immediately to the southeast of Hall 65 three parallel walls extend southeastward, 2.08 m. and 2.60 m. apart, intersected by several transverse crosswalls, at various distances; this complex (if all the elements belong together) might have formed seven or eight small chambers or cubicles. The northeasternmost wall in the group, which seems to be traceable more than 16 m. southeastwards, probably formed the southwestern border of Court 63, to which it presumably provided access by doorways. It is possible (on the tenuous evidence of a single foundation that might have supported a column base) that a porch with a row of wooden columns lined the court on this side. Toward the southeast beyond Corridor 61 it is likely that one or two further rooms of the same shape as 60 and 62 occupied the end of the building; but a short segment of a parallel wall of the same phase, 2.70 m. distant, implies that there was still another narrow room or passage leading southwestward. No evidence was found to shed light on the character and use of the apartments in this quarter.

Foundation walls indicated in crosshatching (Fig. 412) or in solid black (Fig. 417) are those which appear to us generally to be laid at lower levels than the elements shown in single diagonal hatching, and in our judgment they must represent an earlier phase of building and occupation. Two walls of this kind likewise extend southeastward from Hall 65, one aligned more or less nearly with the northeastern wall of that hall, the other parallel to it some 1.90 m. farther southwestward. These two walls enclose what seems to be a narrow passage running from northwest to southeast, possibly a corridor or a stairway, more than 5 m. long. The walls are 0.80 m. thick and somewhat tidily built, but little is left of them. Scanty traces of crosswalls suggest that partitions may have divided this quarter too into rooms. This group, in any event, was taken by us to be contemporary with Halls 64 and 65 in the period when the exterior wall of squared blocks of poros still stood in good order.

Yet another system of walls, shown on the plans in outline with a few edging stones, came to light farther northeastward almost directly in front of the central intercolumniation of Entrance Hall 64. Here a well-constructed wall, 0.85 m. thick, containing many neatly cut small blocks of poros has been uncovered in a line more than 15 m. long from northwest to southeast. It is joined and intersected at right angles by five or more transverse walls exhibiting the same material and manner. The crosswalls continue northeastward beneath the pavement of Court 63. They must consequently be earlier than that court and also earlier than Halls 64 and 65. At the southeast the wall continues underneath the northwest wall of Corridor 61. These remains must belong to an older building that had occupied this part of the hill before the erection of the palace of Mycenaean III B. The style of the masonry is much like that of buildings of the lower town, which have been found just outside the steep edge of the acropolis at the southern corner of the site. These houses contained pottery of Mycenaean III A. The forerunner of the palace on the citadel was evidently a structure of some size, for another wall, almost surely part of it, is recognizable underneath Room 62, parallel to and ca. 3.65 m. distant from the line of the long wall with five crosswalls. This piece of wall under Room 62 is 0.90 m. broad, and it has a crosswall, 0.80 m. thick, jutting out from it to the southwest. Small squared blocks of poros were used here and there in both these structures.

Other remains of early walls appear in various places, the most notable one lying just inside the exterior wall of the Southwestern Building, 2.85 m. distant southeastward from the southeast wall of Hall 65. The ashlar-faced structure was laid up directly against this older element which must already have existed. What is left of it is ca. 5 m. long and 1.50 m. thick. At its northwest end it seems to form a corner apparently continuing northeastward underneath a wall of the last phase. It is possible that this segment is to be associated with an impressive wall, though following a somewhat different alignment, which was exposed to a length of 12 m. to the northwestward of Hall 65. It is 1 m. thick and it must belong to a major structure antedating the palace of Mycenaean III B, since it seems to have been destroyed by the bedding trench for the northwest foundation of Hall 65. It is presumably assignable to Mycenaean III A or earlier.

Although it lies toward the southeastward outside the palace, one further structure[33] deserves to be mentioned. It was a small building, only some 10.50 m. long from northwest to southeast and 6 m. wide, noteworthy because of its massive foundations, ranging from 1.75 m. to more than 2 m. in thickness (Fig. 412). The southwest wall was built in part of smallish dressed blocks of poros, but a considerable section of it appears at some time to have been reconstructed in rubble. No floor and no floor deposit have survived to throw light on the purpose of the building. On the evidence of the masonry we have conjecturally attributed it to the period of Mycenaean III A, if not considerably more ancient. A wall of the final phase (diagonal hatching) was superposed over this building.

Throughout the entire southeastern quarter of the Southwestern Building our excavations have revealed only two strata that could be clearly differentiated. At the top was plowed ground, a layer of soft darkish earth, 0.20 m. to 0.30 m. or more deep, which yielded much pottery of mixed kinds and periods, a good many fragments of inscribed tablets, some scanty fragmentary sealings of clay, and a few other miscellaneous objects. Underneath this stratum lay the red- and yellow-burned wreckage of the catastrophic fire, everywhere disturbed by erosion and the activities through several centuries of quarrying seekers of building materials. Pottery was found in great abundance comprising wares of Mycenaean III B and earlier periods in associated confusion; also a scanty few fragments of inscribed tablets, and a number of clay sealings baked hard by the fire.

All these objects had reached the places in which they were found long after the disaster; whence and just how they came cannot be determined. The broken bits of tablets, nearly all of which were recovered in the plowed earth, must have worked their way down the slope from the higher ground. The chief concentration of tablets in this area was recorded some 8 m. to 12 m. southeast of Hall 65; and another was noted some 10 m. farther toward the southeast near the bottom of the descending southern side of the hill. These latter might conceivably have been carried down by the plow and erosion from the Archives Rooms 7 and 8, though the content of the fragments offers little confirmation. The fragments from the neighborhood of Hall 65 and from the trenches dug in the olive grove below it, however, are more difficult to trace. Perhaps one of the rooms, no longer preserved beside Hall 65, was an archives room for the Southwestern Building.

The place of discovery of these tablets and all other objects of interest was in each instance duly recorded in the excavation notebooks; but since the find-spots were only

---

[33] This building lies only 1.15 m. from the southeast wall of Room 62.

the results of fortuitous circumstances, with little or no bearing on the original provenience, the material for convenience is recorded in four regional sections: northwest of the building, upper southwest, middle southwest, and south southwest in the following catalogue.

OBJECTS FOUND

Outside northwestern exterior wall

BRONZE

Fragment (Fig. 300 No. 13) possibly a piece of tubing flattened out.

TERRACOTTA

Buttons: one shanked (Fig. 300 No. 5), h. 0.013 m., d. 0.021 m., unusual shape in this material; the other flattened spherical, h. 0.012 m., d. 0.018 m.

Head of animal figurine (Fig. 301 No. 1): broken off at neck, tips of horns missing; h. pres. 0.04 m., w. across horns 0.048 m., back of neck to tip of nose 0.03 m., d. neck 0.016 m.; greenish clay, brown stripe along nose, down back of neck, across top, under bottom and around bottom of front of horns continuing down sides of neck; eyes indicated by dots.

Horns of two large animal figurines or legs of pots (Fig. 301 Nos. 4, 5), tapering and slightly curved, coated over-all with brownish paint: one, broken and mended, l. 0.065 m., max. w. 0.017 m.; the other, l. 0.053 m., max. w. 0.019 m.

POTTERY

Angular bowl with pinched-out handles (Shape 4, p. 356) No. 863.

Vast quantity of fragments evidently thrown out from palace. Shapes identified: in coarse ware, pithos, tripod-vessel, cooking pot, domestic jar, broiling-pan, scoop, large circular pan; in finer ware, kylix (650 stems counted), cup, bowl, etc. (412 flat bases), basin and bowl with pinched-out handles, conical cup, dipper, jug, krater, krater-bowl, stirrup-vase, miniature cup, spouted vessel. A good many sherds bear traces of painted decoration: most frequently solid coating in-side or outside or both and horizontal bands; spiraliform pattern; double row of U, dotted border. A few strays from pre-palace period: Ephyrean design, racquet, bits of LH I and Mattpainted Ware.

Outside southwestern wall, sections 1-5

STONE

Steatite: button (Fig. 300 No. 7), conoid, h. 0.013 m., d. 0.021 m.

Flint: large, tan flake (Fig. 300 No. 1).

Micaceous schist: fragment (Fig. 300 No. 4) of mold for spearhead (?) with midrib; l. of stone pres. 0.063 m., w. 0.04 m., l. of matrix pres. 0.055 m., w. of matrix 0.018 m., depth of matrix 0.005 m.

Other: three pieces, possibly used as whetstones (e.g., Fig. 300 Nos. 2, 3).

TERRACOTTA

Figurine, head of female (Fig. 301 No. 9), h. 0.022 m., d. 0.024 m.; birdlike face, plastic eyes, high flaring hat, hollow on top.

Fragment of female figurine (?) (Fig. 301 No. 12), h. pres. 0.056 m., max. w. pres. 0.083 m.: only neck and upper part of body with one breast and one stumplike arm preserved. Very crudely fashioned, if indeed it was a figurine, from the plain greenish clay ordinarily used for kylikes.

Quadruped or possibly two (Fig. 301 No. 13): only body preserved, legs broken off, head or heads and tail or tails missing, 0.052 m. long, d. 0.021 m. Traces of red paint.

Animal figurine (Fig. 301 No. 2): nose, tip of ears or horns, both hind legs, tail, left front leg missing; l. pres. 0.091 m., h. pres. 0.059 m., d. body 0.014 m.; elongated slender body and long neck; greenish clay with longitudinal brown band along nose, neck and back, bands around neck and down legs.

CLAY

Sealings: NM. 8493 = *CMMS* 369 (Figs. 311 No. 27, 312 No. 16). Baked red by fire. Three human figures, women (?), walking to left, central one larger than others, each has right arm bent upward from elbow and left arm bent down; in background between humans, objects resembling shields in shape of figure 8. Traces at left of border with transverse dashes which perhaps surrounded the scene.

NM. 8549 = *CMMS* 376 (Fig. 303 No. 7): cow to right standing with head turned back; underneath, calf to left nursing.

Tablets: Nos. 1419, 1420 (*AJA* 65 [1961], 159, 162, 163; pls. 58, 59).

POTTERY

Masses of fragments like deposit northwest of northwest wall. Shapes observed: pithos (one decorated with painted stripes on rim), tripod-vessel, scoop, large circular pan, domestic jar, broiling-pan; in finer ware, kylix (516 stems counted), cup, bowl, etc. (224 flat bases counted), bowl and basin with pinched-out handles, conical cup, dipper, krater-bowl, krater, jug, stirrup-vase, basin with horizontal handles, tankard, vessel with tubular spout, rhyton, diminutive kylix, stemmed krater. Decorated pieces show solid coating, horizontal bands, spirals, running zigzag.

Outside southwestern wall, sections 6-10 and beyond Building X

GOLD

Leaf-shaped strip (Fig. 302 No. 1), bent and broken, one end turned up; original form indeterminable, pres. l. 0.045 m., max. w. 0.014 m.

Piece of small cylindrical bronze bead (Fig. 302 No. 2), l. pres. 0.01 m., d. 0.005 m., bound with band of gold, 0.005 m. wide.

Two tiny scraps of thin gold leaf.

SILVER

Ring (Fig. 302 No. 3), d. 0.022 m., d. of band 0.003 m.

Coin: very thin small, d. 0.012 m., probably Turkish, illegible.

BRONZE

Chisel (?) (Fig. 302 No. 6): long pyramidal head tapering to thin flat end, l. 0.053 m., max. w. 0.005 m., min. w. 0.003 m.

Awl (Fig. 302 No. 7): rectangular in section tapering to point at each end (one point missing), l. pres. 0.063 m., max. w. 0.004 m.

Nails (e.g., Fig. 302 No. 8): 8 intact and fragments of others: rectangular in section with disk-like heads, flat on top; varying in length from 0.037 m. to 0.03 m. and in diameter of head from 0.018 m. to 0.01 m.

Miscellaneous: small piece of sword with thick midrib (Fig. 302 No. 11); fragment of thin little blade, large perforation near one end (Fig. 302 No. 5); most of a large, thick rivet (Fig. 302 No. 14); flat piece folded over (Fig. 302 No. 10); thick wedge-shaped piece (Fig. 302 No. 12) possibly the end of a large chisel; convex hexagonal object with large perforation (Fig. 302 No. 9), max. w. point to point 0.043 m., min. w. 0.039 m., d. of hole 0.017 m.; flat thick piece bent slightly at one end, in very bad condition, l. 0.078 m., w. 0.007 m., th. 0.004 m., possibly part of tweezers; two very small thin joining fragments showing traces of dot decoration; thin bent rounded fragment with numerous small perforations; small piece (Fig. 302 No. 4), 0.02 m. by 0.015 m., decorated with what appears to be a figure-8 shield; heavy bar (Fig. 302 No. 13), l. 0.05 m., w. 0.015 m., th. 0.007 m.; small section of a handle, d. 0.004 m.; various thin flat pieces, and twisted, unidentifiable chunks. One Turkish coin and little ball-shaped ornament and a large crown-shaped ring with finely chased decoration are certainly modern.

LEAD

Clamp around flint blade (Fig. 302 No. 15).
Two thin narrow strips, and one broader piece.

IRON

Many nails, rectangular in section with flat rectangular heads, and axe are probably modern.

STONE

Steatite: conoid button or whorl, purplish, chipped, h. 0.017 m., d. 0.029 m. Lentoid button or seal (Fig. 302 No. 16), d. 0.013 m., th. 0.004 m.; one surface flatter than the other (broken through at perforation) has some scratched marks, probably meaningless.

Obsidian: arrowheads: 1) small, barbed (Fig. 302 No. 20), l. 0.019 m., w. across barbs 0.012 m., th. 0.004 m.; 2) longer, possibly barbed but barbs missing (Fig. 302 No. 17), l. 0.025 m., max. w. 0.013 m., th. 0.006 m.; 3) much longer (Fig. 302 No. 18), l. 0.045 m., max. w. 0.016 m., th. 0.002 m. to 0.007 m. Blades, pieces of blades, flakes, and chunks.

Flint: arrowheads: 1) light-brown, very small, barbed (Fig. 302 No. 19), l. 0.011 m., w. across barbs 0.01 m., th. 0.0015 m.; 2) gray, larger, point and tips of barbs missing (Fig. 302 No. 22), l. pres. 0.015 m., w. 0.013 m., th. 0.004 m.; 3) dark brown, barbless (Fig. 302 No. 21), l. 0.019 m., w. 0.011 m., th. 0.002 m. Blades, flakes, chips ranging in color from light tan to dark red-brown and black.

Quartz: small crystal with five facets.

Variegated stone: two curved joining fragments, l. 0.133 m., w. ca. 0.04 m., th. 0.026 m., of a large vessel, black stone with flecks and patches of white; well cut with smooth polished surface. Another small piece found some distance away possibly from same vessel.

Sandstone (?): three pieces possibly used as whetstones.

BONE

Implement, flat, pointed, cut from a rib bone (Fig. 302 No. 23), l. 0.064 m., w. 0.012 m.

TERRACOTTA

Bead: cylindrical, fragment, l. pres. 0.012 m., d. 0.008 m.; light red clay, whitish surface.

Buttons: small, conoid with beveled top (Fig. 302 No. 26), h. 0.012 m., d. 0.017 m.; chipped; red-brown clay. Half of another, crudely shaped, flattened, h. 0.006 m., d. 0.028 m.

Whorls: spherical, red-brown fabric, h. 0.02 m., d. 0.025 m.; large biconical with beveled top, coarse brown fabric, h. 0.033 m., d. 0.04 m., decorated with irregular rows of punctated dots on top and shoulder; half of very large, shanked conoid, buff to light red fabric with traces of red paint, h. 0.03 m., d. 0.062 m.

Figurines: human head (Fig. 301 No. 8), light red fabric, too battered and worn to distinguish details, h. pres. 0.033 m., w. 0.019 m. Animal: fragments of three—one a head with long nose and ears projecting to the sides (Fig. 301 No. 3); another, horns, ears, or legs from a larger piece, both of light reddish clay with traces of reddish paint; the third, possibly a horn or leg of brick-red clay (Fig. 301 No. 6).

CLAY

Sealings

NM. 8543 = *CMMS* 370 = No. 1374 in inventory of inscriptions (Fig. 303 No. 1; cf. also *AJA* 64 [1960], 162, 164, pls. 44, 45): bull galloping to left; acrobat above vaulting across rear part of bull to right; row of dots to indicate ground.

NM. 8544 = *CMMS* 371, poor impression: two goats (?), one inverted, lying each facing right.

NM. 8545 = *CMMS* 372 (Fig. 303 No. 2): two bulls: lower to right with head turned back; upper to left, also with head turned back; horns crossed. Ground line below. Fine detail.

No. 1415 in inventory of inscriptions (*AJA* 65 [1961], 158, 161, 162; pls. 58, 59): "faint impression of seal largely obliterated by inscription: two men facing partially visible."

No. 1416 in inventory of inscriptions (*AJA* 65 [1961], 158, 161, 163; pls. 58, 59), found with No. 1415: "break in center makes both sign and seal impression uncertain; a woman appears to be holding up a goat by its horns."

NM. 8546 = *CMMS* 373, upper half preserved: horned animal to right; plant with three large leaves at left above.

NM. 8547 = *CMMS* 374: heraldic cult scene: lion rampant to right; on each side a human figure in long robe with hand raised toward lion. Two rows of dots below.

NM. 8548 = *CMMS* 375 (Fig. 303 No. 3): two impressions: three palms in center spreading out from joint stem; below on each side back of a bull with rear toward palm.

NM. 8550 = *CMMS* 377, less than half preserved: at right, dog-faced figure (monkey?) looking left with both arms or legs raised; in middle, tall human figure looking to right at dog-face. Monkey has a tail.

NM. 8551 = *CMMS* 378, fragment; scene difficult to identify: rear part of animal with long tail at left; above leg or arm of man. Or possibly woman seated on animal.

NM. 8552 = *CMMS* 379, three fragments preserving only about half of representation (e.g., Fig. 303 Nos. 4, 5): heraldic design: goddess standing in center in frontal view but with head to right; both arms raised high; on each side facing goddess a wild goat with long horns; at extreme left a dog-faced creature (demon or monkey?). Goddess has elaborate headdress with ribbons or streamers to each side. Potnia Theron.

NM. 9049 = *CMMS* 380: bull, much contorted, to right with head turned back to left; neatly curving horns; row of dots across back and turning over body; wrinkles of neck indicated by lines.

NM. 9051 = *CMMS* 381, bad impression, difficult to interpret: two animals, one to left, head in frontal view, with sheeplike horns; the other in background to right with heavy mane.

NM. 9054 (Fig. 303 No. 6) with impression similar to NM. 8549 = *CMMS* 376 but reversed: cow to left with head turned back, calf underneath to right, nursing.

Tablets: Nos. 1363-1373, 1375-1391, 1393-1414, 1417-1436, 1438, 1439, 1441 (*AJA* 64 [1960], 160-164, pls. 44-47; 65 [1961], 158-163, pls. 56-57; 66 [1962], 149-152, pls. 38-39; 67 [1963], 160-162, pl. 32).

POTTERY

Enormous accumulation of sherds, the great majority thrown out from the palace, but many apparently pushed down the slope in

grading and leveling the top of the citadel for the building of the palace. In general the discards after the palace was built lay on top but almost everywhere a confused mixture of late and early elements was noted, and uncontaminated strata could not be surely isolated.

Cup (Shape 11, p. 359)

Nos. 981 (Fig. 354), 1177, 1178.

Jug (similar to Shape 43, p. 380 but single-spouted)

No. 983.

Sherds, shapes noted: in coarse ware, pithos, tripod-vessel, brazier, broiling-pan, scoop, incense-burner, cooking pot, lid; in finer ware, kylix (1,147 stems of the palace period counted, 208 probably earlier), cup, bowl, etc. (1,038 flat bases counted), conical cup, bowl and basin with pinched-out handles, dipper, diminutive kylix, basin with round horizontal loop-handles, krater-bowl, jug, alabastron, bridge-spouted bowl, pedestaled cup or bowl. Many fragments bear painted decoration: over-all coating, horizontal bands and lines, wavy lines, chain-pattern, spirals, arcs or semicircles, net-pattern; earlier than the palace: Ephyrean style, fragments of Vapheio cups with ripple-pattern, spirals and dots, stippling, and also Matt-painted Ware. Pieces of broad spout and flanged lip of tiny jug in Gray Minyan Ware and part of a round horizontal handle of same miniature size and fabric (Fig. 302 Nos. 24, 25).

Outside southern angle of the hill

BRONZE

Small, thin, bent, and twisted shapeless pieces.

STONE

Obsidian: blade and flakes.
Flint: blade and unworked chunk.
Quartz: very small piece.

TERRACOTTA

Spherical whorl, d. 0.024 m., of soft light red fabric.

Disk, d. 0.037 m., th. 0.009 m., of brown fabric; faint scratches on one surface look like a stalk with two branches on each side rising above a straight and two wavy lines.

Stamp (?), conical with only small section of edge preserved, d. calculated 0.035 m., h. 0.015 m.; brick red fabric, gray at core. On flat surface apparently meaningless marks.

Figurines: fragment, not apparent whether human or animal (Fig. 301 No. 10); light red clay with traces of dark paint; h. or l. pres. 0.08 m., bottom (?) an oval 0.03 m. by 0.04 m., top 0.027 m. by 0.015 m.

Another very small fragment (Fig. 301 No. 7) possibly remnant of the head of a little figurine with basket-like headdress containing three little pancake-like objects, brownish; h. pres. 0.022 m., w. across 0.022 m. Fragment of torso with stumps of arms and neck (Fig. 301 No. 11); on back (?), two applied strips of clay, one long, the other short (probably broken off), purpose not clear, possibly supported the figurine.

POTTERY

This deposit except for the surface soil consists for the most part of rubbish probably pushed down from the upper levels of the acropolis to make way for the building of the palace.

Restorable pots

Basin (Shape 1, p. 355)
No. 835.

Pedestaled krater (Shape 63, p. 400)
No. 831.

Diminutive conical cup
Nos. 1108 and 1110.

Shallow cup with one high handle
Diminutive No. 1109, small No. 1111, slightly larger No. 1112.

Pedestaled cup
One-handled No. 834.
Two-handled No. 1102.

Abundant sherds, shapes recognized: in coarse ware, pithos, tripod-vessel, brazier, spit-rest, larnax (?); in finer ware, kylix (385 stems probably III B, 236 possibly III A), cup, bowl, etc. (411 flat bases possibly III B, 137 III A), conical cup, basins with pinched-out handles common in both periods, cup, dipper, tankard, stirrup-vase, jug, feeding bottle, krater, alabastron, hole-mouthed jar. A good many sherds with traces of painted decoration; motives noted: spirals, stippling, bands, fish, mainly of Mycenaean III A.

Further investigation of this ancient dump higher up on the slope yielded a rich harvest of similar lime-coated and worn sherds among which the shapes listed above appear to be represented more or less in the same proportions.

NORTHWESTERN BUILDINGS

ROOM 82

BEHIND the Southwestern Building and the Main Building near the northwest edge of the citadel is a complex of relatively small structures (82, 83, 84, 85, 86, and 87 on Key Plan) belonging to two phases in each of which they seem to have been, for a time at least, associated with the palace and to have served some useful purpose.

The earlier element is Room 82. It is 11.20 m. long from southwest to northeast and 6.70 m. wide, measured on the exterior. No trace of any partition wall has been found; the interior therefore seems to have been a single large chamber with a length of 9.20 m. and a width of 4.70 m. (Fig. 213).

When first discovered in 1956 and 1958 it was taken to be an adjunct to the Southwestern Building with much the same relationship to the latter as the Wine Magazine (104-105) appeared to bear to the Main Building; and we were inclined to believe that it may have provided storage space for wine or oil. In 1962, however, excavations farther northwestward disclosed evidence indicating that the structure originally had another room on that side of approximately the same size as Room 82 and may possibly have extended also farther northeastward. In any event, whether an oil- or wine-magazine, or whatever its function, we concluded that it must have existed and been used during the early phases of the Southwestern Building, but was ultimately demolished and replaced by a new complex (83, 84, 85, 86) superposed in part over its predecessor.

The walls of Room 82, ca. 1 m. thick on all sides, were built of relatively small unworked stones neatly fitted along the outer faces and filled in with rubble (Fig. 218). No remains of stucco flooring were revealed nor was a proper floor of trodden clay or earth recognized anywhere in the building. It is probable, however, that it lay not much above the top of a thick underlying stratum of yellowish clay mixed with earth and containing a good many potsherds. This deposit was probably spread over the area at the time of the grading operations that seem to have been carried out preceding the building of the palace when the central part of the hill was cut down, and the debris dug away was shifted towards the slopes on all sides. The walls now stand to a height of only 0.35 m. above this stratum. They are remarkably thick and substantial and it is likely that the construction in stone was only a low socle that carried a superstructure of crude brick. No evidence for an upper story came to light. Inside the room, however, two flat stone bases were discovered, the northeastern one roughly circular in shape, with a diameter of 0.67 m. and a thickness of 0.20 m. (Fig. 217). The other is an undressed block of irregular form with a length of

0.84 m. and width of 0.56 m. Both bases were wedged into position and surrounded by a ring of smaller stones. The blocks were not set in the longitudinal axis of the room but appreciably closer to the northwestern wall than to the southeastern.[1]

The bases look as if designed to support wooden columns. Neither stone, however, bears any trace of a circular standing place. The uprights may have been piers or rough timbers to help support a heavy clay roof, presumably sloping slightly toward the northwest so as to shed water in that direction. Though no actual floor could be recognized, a considerable mass of broken pottery was found along the southwestern and southeastern walls. Beside the latter, ca. 0.80 m. from the south corner, is the bottom of a pithos embedded in the clay stratum mentioned above. Farther along toward the northeast are two or three slight hollows which may have held other jars of the same kind. It is likely that the room was a magazine for oil or wine, probably containing numerous storage vessels more or less in the fashion of the Wine Magazine (104-105 on Key Plan). The flat stone bases, if they were not used to support pillars, could have served admirably as temporary resting-places for the large skins or other containers in which wine or oil may have been brought to fill the jars in the magazine.

The foundation walls, as preserved, offer little or no evidence as to the position of a doorway leading into the storeroom. An irregularity in the southeastern wall near the east corner may, however, mark the place where an entrance had been (Fig. 217). Here for a distance of some 2 m. and more the upper part of the wall is ca. 0.20 m. thinner than elsewhere and the masonry differs from that in the rest of the walls. It may perhaps represent a closing of an earlier opening.

The additional chamber which in 1962 was found to belong to the same building with Room 82 has not been fully excavated. On the southeast it shares a party foundation wall with Room 82. The northeastern and northwestern walls have also been in part exposed. They are substantially built with a deep substructure which was needed close to the steep edge of the citadel. Near its northeastern end the room has a width of 5.25 m. from southeast to northwest; and though its southwestern end has not yet been found, it probably had the same length as Room 82. No remains of a floor could be recognized, and no traces of a doorway communicating with Room 82 have been observed. A solid flat-topped block of limestone, roughly circular in shape and similar to the two bases seen in Room 82, may have supported a column or a pillar. Its position, 1.75 m. from the southeast wall and 2.65 m. from the northeast wall, displays little if any understandable relation to the two bases in the adjoining

---

[1] Northeast wall to northeast base, center, 2.92 m.; northeast base to southwest base, 3.42 m.; southwest base to southwest wall, 2.76 m.; northwest wall to northeast base (calculated), 1.35 m.; northeast base to southeast wall, 3.35 m.; northwest wall to southwest base (calculated), 1.10 m.; southwest base to southeast wall, 3.62 m. Top of northeast base, 12.64 m. above datum; top of southwest base the same. Southwest base to inner south corner, 4.57 m.; northeast base to inner east corner, 4.42 m.

room. In the absence of a floor and an accompanying deposit no conclusion can safely be drawn concerning the specific function of the room, though it was probably a supplementary storeroom.

OBJECTS FOUND

BRONZE

Small rivet-head (Fig. 299 No. 2), d. 0.009 m.

Broad thin flat piece (Fig. 299 No. 1), l. 0.041 m., w. 0.032 m., th. 0.0015 m.

Several nondescript scraps.

STONE

Pieces of obsidian, quartz, and flint including a tiny red arrowhead.

TERRACOTTA

Upper half of female figurine of crescent type; head, tips of arms, and lower half of body missing.

CLAY

Several pieces of spit-holders.

POTTERY

Many sherds of kylikes, cups, and bowls with pinched-out handles in finer ware; of pithoi, ladles, braziers, tripod cooking pots in coarse ware. The material includes mainly wares of Mycenaean III B but Mycenaean III A is also represented by several pieces with painted decoration: spirals, dots, plant- or flower-motive. A few Geometric sherds came from the upper stratum.

ROOMS 83, 84, 85, 86

Superposed over the northeasterly half of Room 82 are walls of a later house comprising three rooms or more (83, 84, 85 on Key Plan) extending ca. 15 m. to the northeastward. Its orientation, running from south-southeast to north-northwest and from west-southwest to east-northeast, diverges appreciably from that of the earlier underlying building.

The southwesternmost part of the house is approximately rectangular in plan (Fig. 218) measuring on the exterior 12.35 m. in length from southeast to northwest by ca. 8.40 m. in width. The walls on the southwest and on the northwest are substantially built, having a thickness of slightly more than 1 m. On the northeast is a partition wall, only some 0.80 m. broad, separating Rooms 83 and 84, and continuing southeastward 3.90 m. to what appears to be a finished end. In this direction the limit of the building is clearly recognizable in a stone wall, 0.55 m. thick, which extends across the area between the central and southwestern units of the palace and marks the northwestern boundary of Court 88. The moderate thickness of this wall, which was built of small stones laid on earth above the earlier pavement of Court 88, suggests that it was not designed to rise to a great height and to support a roof across a façade more than 7 m. wide. It may rather have been a low structure bordering a narrow court, ca. 3.50 m. deep, in front of the house. Near its northeastern end, 1.30 m. from the Main Building, is a slight depression ca. 1.10 m. long in the foundations, which possibly indicates that a slab of stone or wood had been laid here as a threshold for a gateway or a doorway.

The southwestern wall seems to have terminated toward the southeast in a finished face at a point opposite the similar end of the northeast wall. Although no certain remains of a crosswall have survived, many stones were found lying in this area and we conjecture that there was once an actual front wall along this line forming a room some 6.25 m. long and roughly 6.70 m. wide from southwest to northeast. All the foundation walls, which undoubtedly supported a superstructure of crude brick, were built of smallish fieldstones laid in a single course. They appeared just beneath the modern ground level; and during many years of cultivation the plow had taken and carried away a heavy toll of material wrenched loose.

No evidence could be recognized to demonstrate where the doorway or doorways were placed, although there was presumably an entrance from the southeast, and probably an opening communicating with the smaller rooms toward the northeast. The floor, which was no doubt of trodden earth or clay, had likewise vanished altogether, and no floor deposit remained.

If the lateral walls ended as we have conjectured, some 3.50 m. short of the southeastern boundary wall, it seems likely that a passage was left open on the southwestern side of the small court giving access to the area behind the northwestern rear wall of the earlier wing of the palace. A similar arrangement on the northeastern side of the little court probably offered an entrance into the area numbered 86, behind the Main Building.

Room 84 resembles a narrow magazine, 1.70 m. wide. It is preserved only to a length of 4.80 m.; but how far it originally extended beyond that point is unknown, since the northwestern ends of both lateral walls are missing (Fig. 218). These latter as well as the short southeastern wall are all ca. 0.80 m. thick. Here too no evidence now exists to indicate the position of a doorway.

Beyond this room to the northeast is another adjoining chamber (85), 3.20 m. wide from southwest to northeast (Fig. 218). This too has suffered much damage in its northwestern part and its length is unknown. With its northeast wall, also 0.80 m. thick, surviving only to a length of 2.30 m., the building comes to a truncated end.

To the southeast of Rooms 84 and 85 is an area numbered 86 which may have belonged to the house, perhaps as a court rather than a chamber, since no evidence exists for a closing wall on the other two sides.

This small complex of three or four rooms and an area has left little or no information regarding its specific purpose. It evidently consisted of a single story, rising with walls of crude brick, lacking decoration and other refinements. Perhaps it was built as a replacement for Room 82 (which seems to have suffered damages and to have been demolished) and was designed to provide storage space for various kinds of supplies and equipment belonging to the Southwestern Building. Or it may have been used as a dormitory for the accommodation of servants or slaves, corresponding to House 103 on the northeastern side of the palace. Whatever its character, all that can be said with reasonable certainty is that Rooms 82 to 86 were in existence in the last phase at the time of the destruction of the whole establishment on the site, when many blocks and fragments from the exterior walls of the central and southwestern units of the palace fell into these rooms and over the walls of this modest building.

The stratum of plowed earth yielded the usual miscellaneous nondescript sherds of Mycenaean III B but nothing that can certainly shed light on the buildings. In the lack of properly made floors and of floor deposits no catalogue of objects from Rooms 83 to 86 is of any value.

CIRCULAR STRUCTURE 87

About 0.60 m. to the northeast of Room 85 is a small circular foundation (87 on Key Plan), with an over-all diameter of 3.10 m. (Fig. 219). The wall, 0.35 m. to 0.40 m. thick, is built in two courses of small rough fieldstones laid on earth which obviously could not have supported a superstructure of any considerable height or weight. A transverse partition, made of a single line of small flattish stones set on edge in earth, runs across from southwest to northeast, dividing the space inside into two not exactly equal sections. No proper floor was found; nothing of any consequence was recovered within the circle to indicate its character or the purpose for which it was built. It is to be assigned to the final phase of the palace, since it was clearly standing at the time of the great fire; for a squared block of poros, evidently from the rear wall of the Main Building, was found lying where it fell leaning against the eastern side of the circle.

COURT 88

The Southwestern Building was separated from the Main Building by a relatively narrow court (88 on Key Plan). Since the two structures are not exactly parallel the court broadens slightly from southeast to northwest, reaching there, despite a projecting offset in the wall on the southwest, a width of 7.44 m. At the southeast beside the anta base of Entrance Hall 64 it was 7.10 m. wide. The court, measured to this point from the boundary wall described above (p. 291, Fig. 207), had a length of 19.55 m. The southeastern section of the court (89-90), in a strip ca. 5 m. wide, was walled off probably a long time after the palace was destroyed (Fig. 192).

The rest of the court to the northwest of this intrusion, 14.65 m. long on the southwestern side, 13.50 m. on the northeastern, is numbered 88 on the Key Plan. It was paved with stucco of a reasonably good quality, stretching from wall to wall and reaching an elevation of 13.27 m. above datum. In four or five places, where the pavement was damaged and it was possible to probe beneath it, an earlier stucco floor was revealed, but it could not be investigated on a large scale. The few potsherds found in the intervening deposit, 0.20 m. deep between the two floors, gave no evidence that any considerable time had elapsed between the two. From the Main Building on the northeast two doors open into the court (Fig. 209), one from Room 20 (p. 125), and the other from Room 21 (p. 129). On the opposite side no trace of an opening has been recognized, but to the northwest of the large anta base mentioned above (p. 249) the wall has vanished down to its foundations and there might have been an exit somewhere in this section.

The stratification which was noted in all parts of the court is of some interest. At the top was a stratum of plowed earth, ca. 0.15 m. deep, next came an extremely black layer, 0.15 m. to 0.25 m. deep, containing innumerable small stones (Figs. 220, 221) and some Mycenaean pottery, especially kylix stems, but also a good many fragments of brown and black glazed ware of a late Geometric type. Below the black stratum was a thin layer, 0.03 m. to 0.10 m. thick, of yellowish-white clayey deposit which rested on the stucco pavement of the court. This contained mainly Mycenaean potsherds but also some pieces of the glazed Geometric ware. The latter must somehow have penetrated from above, for the yellowish-white stratum unquestionably represents the latest phase of occupation of the palace.

The black stratum, containing a scattering of late Geometric sherds, is surely to be explained in the same way as the similar deposits in the Court of the Megaron, in a broad strip crossing the northeastern side of the Main Building of the palace and appearing again in a considerable accumulation in a hollow beyond the Northeastern Building, and comparable agglomerations of black earth and stones far down on the eastern slope near the recently erected entrance gate, and farther to the southeastward on a terrace between the acropolis and the modern highway (pp. 64, 175, 177, 180, 184, 206). It is thus evident that there was fairly widespread activity on the site in late Geometric times.

A more or less circular break (with a diameter of 0.54 m.) in the pavement in the southeasterly part of Court 88 permitted us to investigate a hollow that lay beneath. It was filled with black earth and carbonized matter, and contained some nondescript sherds including a kylix stem. Nothing was found to indicate its purpose. *Stereo* appeared at 0.55 m. below the floor.

Here and there in the court between the two buildings were uncovered squared blocks of poros which had evidently fallen from the wall on one side or the other. A good many fragments and splinters of the same stone were also noted, and it is clear that the exterior wall of both buildings rose to the level of the upper floor in ashlar masonry. The use of great horizontal beams indicated by the dowel holes in the lowest course along Entrance Hall 64 (Fig. 195) certainly suggests the possibility that the wall was provided with windows. It may be presumed that the Main Building was likewise lighted and aired. In any event the court between these two-storied structures must have offered shade in the summer through most of the day and in winter protection from cold winds. One can imagine the members of the family using this area as a pleasant promenade in the afternoon.

O B J E C T S   F O U N D

SILVER

Small piece (Fig. 299 No. 6).

BRONZE

Numerous nondescript pieces (e.g., Fig. 299 Nos. 4, 5, 7, 8).

FLINT

Blade (Fig. 299 No. 10), l. 0.035 m., w. 0.01 m.

STEATITE

Shanked button (Fig. 299 No. 9), h. 0.011 m., d. 0.02 m., d. of perforation 0.002 m.

POTTERY

A considerable quantity of sherds: chiefly of late Geometric types in the upper stratum, for the most part solidly coated with brownish-black glaze; and predominantly Mycenaean in the underlying burned layer. From the latter, shapes represented: in coarse ware, pithos, tripod-vessel, brazier, storage jar; in finer ware, kylix (more than 80 stems counted), cup and bowl (48 flat bases), conical cup, dipper, basin with pinched-out handles, tankard, spouted jug, krater-bowl (7 counted, probably Geometric). Sherds with remains of painted decoration are of Mycenaean III B: horizontal band, allover coating, transverse lines, concentric circles.

ROOMS 89, 90

In the southeast part of Court 88 two numbers, 89 and 90 (Key Plan), have been assigned to rooms or enclosed spaces. They are bordered on the northwest and southeast by roughly constructed transverse walls which extend from the Southwestern Building to the Main Building (Fig. 192). The walls were built for the most part of re-used cut blocks or fragments of blocks of poros, almost exclusively the latter, set in a double row, back to back with an occasional small stone in the middle, where filling was necessary. Both these walls rest on a thin layer of earth together with a few small stones lying on the upper of the two stucco pavements of the court (p. 244). One block, set on edge in the southeastern wall, stands to a height of 0.75 m.; otherwise the walls, which have an average thickness of 0.68 m., now rise to a height of only ca. 0.50 m. above the pavement. How much higher, if at all, they were originally cannot now be determined.

The southwestern room (89) measured on the interior is 3.50 m. long from northeast to southwest and 3.30 m. wide. This was apparently built before the northeastern room was enclosed and its northeastern wall seems to have been made of single poros blocks, 0.45 m. thick, set in a line 3.50 m. from the wall of the Main Building. Only the southeastern part of this wall is preserved, but the northwestern lateral wall ends in alignment with the outer face of the northeast wall. The room made use of the upper stucco pavement of Court 88 which, near the southeastern wall, dips sharply to the level of the pavement of Court 63. Toward the northeast the stucco apparently continued beyond the northeastern wall, probably extending through a central doorway that led into what remained of the court.

Against the northwestern wall inside was erected at some time a small boxlike contraption of flattish, unworked stones set on edge. This construction is 0.90 m. long from northeast to southwest and 0.70 m. wide. It rested on the stucco pavement which continues beneath it. One might have taken it for a sink if it had been provided with a drain; but since it was filled with very hard packed ashy earth, it may have been a firebox. Nothing was found inside the room to cast any light upon its purpose.

If our interpretation is correct, Room 90 was enclosed later, the lateral walls of Room 89 being prolonged to the Main Building. These extensions too for the most part made use of fragments of poros blocks (Fig. 192), but in a much more careless style than that represented in Room 89 and with an appreciable shift in alignment spreading on both sides and broadening the area to 4.25 m. at the northeast. Inside the room a pavement of flagstones was roughly laid (Fig. 63) apparently at the level of the stucco floor and below it and continuing to the wall of the Main Building. At the time this was done, it is likely that a doorway was left in the northwestern wall at the west corner of the room. The opening, 1 m. wide, seems later to have been partly blocked with small stones.

The poros blocks in the walls on both sides are badly worn and many of them pockmarked on top somewhat in the manner that has been observed in the northeastern quarter of the palace in Rooms 40 and 41 and Court 42 (pp. 177, 180, 184). Here on the southwestern side of the Main Building the similar black layer, noted above in Court 88, also spread over the rooms under discussion. In these rooms too some fragments of late Geometric glazed ware were recovered and we conclude that the black stratum owed its discoloration to the waste from the pressing out of olive oil.

Indeed we have wondered if this whole intrusion into the court, including both Chambers 89 and 90, are not installations dating from as late as the seventh century B.C. and perhaps built to serve in connection with the collecting and processing of olives on this hill. The walls could then have been built from the numerous poros blocks that had fallen in the space between the two Mycenaean palatial structures. To the northwest of the rooms and to the southeast an abundance of such blocks came to light lying as they had fallen at the time of the disaster. Here and beside Rooms 89 and 90 much building material of this kind must have been available in the late Geometric Period.

If our conjecture regarding the use of these walled-in areas is right, the firebox can also be reasonably explained. It might have been the "stove" where water could be boiled; and a good supply of boiling water is required in the operations concerned with the pressing out of olive oil. A storage bin paved with flagstones where the olives could be heaped without coming into contact with a dirt floor was also part of the equipment in the old-fashioned village olive presses before modern cement became available.

It remains to mention some remnants of another structure which seems to have been built in this same area before Rooms 89 and 90 were enclosed. It is represented only by foundations, ca. 0.50 m. thick, which extend southwestward from the wall of the Main Building, almost parallel to the northwest wall of Chamber 90, and some 0.50 m. northwest of it (Figs. 194, 408). At 4.10 m. the foundation turns southeastward and continues, partly underneath what we have taken to be the partition wall between Chambers 89 and 90, as far as the southeastern wall of that building. At this point it may have returned northeastward.

The foundation consists mainly of a single layer of stones, lying on earth above the earlier pavement of the court, and its top is approximately level with the later pavement on the northwest. The latter seems to have turned up against the wall, which is missing, and similar evidence appears along the southwestern line of the foundation. It looks, therefore, as if a structure of some kind once projected southwestward from the Main Building into the court. If our observations are correct, this earlier enclosure must already have existed in the last phase of the palace, to which the upper pavement belonged. Since nothing but the foundations have survived it is impossible to determine whether this was a roofed building, an open enclosure, or merely a raised platform of some kind projecting into the court, such as has been conjectured in the southeastern facade of the Main Building to the northeast of the Propylon (p. 228f.).

OBJECTS FOUND

BRONZE

Awl: pyramidal head, shaft square in section (Fig. 299 No. 3), l. 0.05 m., l. head 0.009 m., w. shaft ca. 0.003 m. Found in Room 89.

Knife (NM. 7794, Fig. 274 No. 6), l. 0.225 m., w. 0.008 m.: well preserved, tapering, flat on one side; three rivets in place in handle; may have been decorated. Found in stratum of black earth and small stones in Room 89, but surely of Mycenaean origin.

STEATITE

Fragment of conoid button, edge of top broken (Fig. 299 No. 11), h. 0.017 m., d. 0.025 m. Found in Room 89.

TERRACOTTA

Whorl (Fig. 299 No. 12), h. 0.0165 m., d. 0.028 m.: bicone, slightly hollowed around perforation. Found between northwest wall of Room 90 and northwestern foundation of the platform. Of the Mycenaean Period.

POTTERY

Few sherds, representing the usual shapes: kylikes, bowls, jugs. A number of pieces were decorated: some had painted bands, the others allover paint. Fragments (from Room 89) of a krater-bowl comprise one handle and part of rim: interior solidly coated; broad band along outside of rim; blobs on side around attachment of handle; longitudinal stripes on arched handle; blackish paint with red blushes.

From the stony black layer came a good many Geometric sherds most of them coated over-all with brownish-black glaze.

NORTHEASTERN BUILDING

THE Northeastern Building, which has been identified as the Workshop belonging to the palace, is a roughly rectangular structure ca. 32.60 m. long from southeast to northwest and from 16.01 m. to 16.23 m. wide (Fig. 150). The southeastern end of it has been demolished and carried away by erosion and looters, only the barest evidence surviving to fix its length. The southern quarter was probably in part formed by a court open to the sky facing to the southwestward and continuous with the broad court (58 on Key Plan) outside the Main Building. The northwestern part of the Workshop is well enough preserved to make the plan clearly recognizable with the walls standing to ca. 0.55 m. above the floors (Fig. 222). They no doubt constituted a stone socle that supported a superstructure of crude brick. In keeping with its purpose the Workshop was built for the most part in a relatively simple manner with few touches of elegance, without stucco floors, with only mud plaster, if any, on the walls, without wall paintings and floor decoration, without stone thresholds and jamb bases. It probably consisted of a single story, presumably with a flat roof, containing six rooms, a passage, and perhaps a colonnade. Like all the other elements in the palace, it was utterly destroyed in the great fire that brought an end to the entire complex.

RAMP 91

A broad ramp (91 on Key Plan), without a roof, separated the Workshop from the two walled courts (42 and 47) that bordered the northeastern flank of the Main Building (Figs. 151, 223). This passage has an average width of 3.45 m. and ascends from 12.90 m. above datum to 14.07 m. at its upper end, that is, rising 1.17 m. in a distance of some 20 m. It was paved with stucco, 0.05 m. thick (as measured in a break); although cracked and broken and in a few places missing altogether, the pavement is on the whole fairly well preserved. Along the southwestern side of the passage the flooring stops in an upward turn, more or less in a straight line, 0.025 m. to 0.06 m. short of the face of the stone wall. It is obvious that the floor was here adjusted to meet the thick coating of plaster that once covered the wall. This was clearly demonstrated by the remnants of plaster that lay in abundance alongside the wall. No traces of painted decoration could be discerned.

On the opposite side of the ramp no remains of plaster, whether of lime or clay, were found still adhering to the wall of the Northeastern Building (Fig. 223), but a good deal of clay had accumulated on the floor, banked up against the wall, and a coating of some kind may have been applied to the latter.

Along the foot of the wall on this side runs a gutter made of narrow blocks of

[299]

poros, varying considerably in length, in which a relatively deep channel had been cut.[1] In its present state it is somewhat irregular in alignment and pursues an undulating course, but originally the blocks were no doubt reasonably well fitted together. A heavy calcareous accretion coating the channel indicates that water had not only flowed away here but had been blocked by rubbish and given time to leave a deposit of lime. The channel has a relatively steep gradient and evidently was designed to carry off surplus water. At the upper end outside the west corner of the Workshop it is clear that running water was delivered through a pi-shaped terracotta pipe, but just how the water was received and the surplus emptied into the gutter are problems that have not yet been solved (Fig. 224). Although no fixed basin remains in place, a receptacle of some kind may well have stood on a foundation of small stones between the end of the supply pipe and the beginning of the gutter. Alongside the latter were recovered fragments of a small jug which may have been used to ladle out water from the conjectured basin. The supply channels and the distribution system will be dealt with in the description of Area 101 (p. 327).

After a course of 13.43 m. the gutter, having reached the western corner of the court (92) mentioned above, bends slightly to the eastward (Fig. 223) and continues at a more gentle slope southeastward 9.80 m. Here it now ends (Fig. 226): whether it was broken off by the plow, or when a nearby olive tree was planted, or whether it originally stopped here could not be determined. Just beside this point, however, is a hollow cut in *stereo* which may have held a vessel in which water was collected. This lower part of the channel, bordering the court, is badly worn and dilapidated, evidently because it here crosses an open paved area unprotected by a contiguous wall.

The ramp was covered by an accumulation, some 0.75 m. to 1 m. deep, consisting of black earth packed solid with small fallen stones resting on a stratum of red brick-like earth containing fewer stones. The latter stratum was banked high against the southwest wall of the Workshop and sloped down toward the center of the ramp, shading into whitish earth resembling *stereo*, then rising again toward the wall of Court 47. Everywhere directly above the pavement was a thin deposit of black matter, no doubt the fire stratum. In some places, notably toward the lower end of the ramp and beyond, in the upper black layer which was rather oily in texture, were found, along with the usual Mycenaean pottery, a few glazed sherds of late Geometric style as in so many other parts of the site, where similar deposits were encountered.

The Mycenaean layer yielded many potsherds including numerous kylix stems but no objects of any consequence.

---

[1] Length of blocks ranges from 0.75 m. to 1.10 m.; width from 0.21 m. to 0.30 m.; height above pavement from 0.03 m. at the lower end to 0.15 m. near the upper. Channel: 0.08 m. to 0.15 m. wide at the top, 0.08 m. to 0.15 m. deep.

BRONZE

Four very small bits, one rivet (Fig. 304 No. 8), l. 0.009 m., d. shaft 0.003 m., d. ends 0.005 m.; from water channel.

IRON

Nail: fragment, rectangular in section (Fig. 304 No. 9), l. pres. 0.04 m.; found in stratum of stones in black earth with Geometric sherds.

STONE

Steatite buttons: two conoid, one burned light gray (Fig. 304 Nos. 5, 6), h. 0.013 m., 0.012 m.; d. 0.02 m., 0.019 m.; one shanked (Fig. 304 No. 7), h. 0.01 m., d. 0.02 m.

Obsidian: five chips and flakes (e.g., Fig. 304 No. 3), one from water channel, one from black stratum.

Flint: six flakes (e.g., Fig. 304 No. 4).

Quartz: four pieces.

Other: worked pieces (five joining, Fig. 304 No. 1), ca. 0.008 m. thick, of variegated marble, white, black, gray, light red; another fragment, mixed green and black (Fig. 304 No. 2), 0.008 m. to 0.01 m. thick.

TERRACOTTA

Large loomweight (Fig. 305 No. 1), h. 0.08 m., w. 0.058 m., th. 0.026 m.; light brick-red clay, baked but soft; top missing, broken through perforation; rectangular, rounded at top.

POTTERY

Tankard (Shape 33, p. 374)
Fragment (Fig. 345 No. 2).

A great many chance sherds, mostly small pieces with worn edges. No difference was discernible in the many sherds collected from the various strata except for the presence of scattered pieces of Geometric ware in the black earth with small stones that lay below the surface earth. Shapes represented by fragments: coarse and semi-coarse wares: pithos, ranging from very large to small, some of fabric containing much mica, high necks, offset rims flat on top, raised bands with diagonal gashes or thumb impressions, one at least decorated with crudely painted net- or scale-pattern; tripod-vessel, brazier, lid, basin, griddle, baking pan, cooking pot. Red ware: jug, jar with horizontal handles, scoop. Finer ware: kylix (445 stems and bases counted); bowl, cup, etc. with flat base (239 counted); bowl or basin with pinched-out handles, basin with round loop-handles, high-handled dipper, tankard, conical cup, jug. Fragments of stirrup-vase with traces of painted decoration; of krater-bowl: ring-base, well-shaped rim; coated inside and out with grayish-black paint. Geometric ware, many pieces coated over-all with glaze.

COURT 92

The open court (92 on Key Plan) occupying the southern quarter of the building (Fig. 150) is ca. 5.20 m. wide; since the southeastern limit cannot be determined, its length in that direction is conjectural. It presumably extended at least as far as we were able to trace the water channel, 9.80 m. (Fig. 226), and it may well have continued to the southern end of the building. On the northeast the court seems to have been bordered by a colonnade as indicated by surviving foundations apparently of two columns (Figs. 222, 225). On the northwest the court is dominated by the façade of a small but monumental element of the building, which we venture to identify as a shrine (Fig. 223).

The most conspicuous feature of the court is a squared block of poros standing in its original position, ca. 3 m. southeast of the shrine (Fig. 227). It was set nearly, though not exactly, in the longitudinal axis of the latter, but some 0.25 m. to the northeast of it. The block is nearly square in plan, 0.64 m. long from southeast to northwest and ca. 0.60 m. wide. The southeast and southwest faces are almost wholly exposed above the pavement; the northeastern and northwestern sides are partly concealed by the rising floor of the court.[2] On each face, as well as on the top, the stone was coated with plaster which bears frescoed decoration; the design is very similar to that on the dado in Hall 64 and in a like position in the inner portico of the Propylon (2). The decoration consists of groups of three parallel wavy lines forming scallops in dark paint enclosing broad vertically rising, curving bands of cream and red (Fig. 228). Three or four underlying layers of plaster apparently had comparable decoration. Very little plaster was preserved on the flat top of the stone but enough to show that it bore the same decorative patterns as the sides and that it originally covered the entire surface. Consequently it cannot have served as a column base but it was, in all probability, an altar connected with the shrine that looked out upon it. Though it can certainly not have been used for burnt offerings, it might well have served for cult ceremonies of some kind. The tables of offerings which are familiar at Pylos and at other Mycenaean sites are analogous, since they too bear painted decoration, not only around the rim but across the top.

Court 92 had a stucco pavement of the regular kind, the greater part of it preserved, although it is cracked and broken here and there and has suffered other damage perhaps from repairs and patching. The southeastern part is approximately level at ca. 12.91 m. above datum, but the northwestern area between the altar and the shrine rises in a rather sharp slope to 13.38 m. above datum at the northern corner (Fig. 227). The adjustment between the low southeastern and this higher northwestern part has been rather awkwardly contrived. To the southwest of the altar the pavement slopes upward and covers the lower part of the decorated face (Fig. 223). On the northeast of the poros block, however, between the altar and the foundations of the column base of the portico, a row of small stones was laid to support the floor, rising in a step 0.15 m. high, which covers half or more of the northeastern face of the altar (Fig. 225). The northwestern face too is half buried beneath the level of the stucco ascending toward the northeast. This curious covering up of the decorated sides of the altar suggests that we are dealing with a makeshift remodeling in a late phase.

Throughout the lower part of the court to the southeast were found two nearly complete blocks of poros and many fragments of others, ranging widely in size from large chunks to splinters. They lay on the pavement apparently in the places to

[2] Height visible above pavement: southeast face 0.36 m., southwest face 0.38 m. to 0.30 m., northwest face 0.28 m. to 0.14 m., northeast face 0.12 m. to 0.18 m.

which they had fallen at the time of the great fire. Whether they had been thrown down from the façade of the small shrine to the northwest of the court or came from the entablature of the colonnade that stood to the northeast of the court is difficult to determine, but the latter is more likely, since the portico stood nearby while the shrine is relatively far away.

The black layer with its accompaniment of a few sherds of glazed Geometric ware which has been so often mentioned stretched over this court too. The black layer and the debris of the destruction level below contained numerous Mycenaean potsherds and a good many miscellaneous objects of various kinds together with three fragments of tablets inscribed in Linear B script.

OBJECTS FOUND

BRONZE

Many nondescript fragments, some of which had melted and adhered to stucco pavement (e.g., Fig. 306 Nos. 5-13).

Fragments of seven tiny arrowheads (e.g., Fig. 306 Nos. 1-4).

STONE

Steatite: conoid button, whitened by fire (Fig. 306 No. 17), h. 0.013 m., d. 0.022 m., d. perforation 0.003 m.

Obsidian: core and flakes (e.g., Fig. 306 Nos. 14-16).

Flint: many flakes and chips.

Quartz: three pieces.

TERRACOTTA

Large coarse whorl (Fig. 306 No. 18), h. 0.028 m., d. 0.03 m.

Loomweight, pyramidal, of light greenish-buff clay, perforation near top (Fig. 305 No. 2), h. 0.037 m., w. base 0.037 m.; possibly Greek.

CLAY

Tablets: Nos. 1285, 1322, and 1337 (*AJA* 62 [1958], 183-188, pls. 45, 49).

POTTERY

Fragments of a large stirrup-vase and of a high-necked jug in soft red fabric; surface gone except for traces of red bands. Found on upper level of court between altar and shrine.

Flat bottom and pieces of closed pot—an amphora or jug—in same red ware, found on pavement at lower level.

Many sherds collected; shapes identifiable: in coarse ware, pithos of various sizes having high necks, flat offset rims, decorative plastic bands bearing diagonal gashes or finger impressions, some with painted patterns; cooking pot on three legs; in red ware: amphora and jug with high necks, stirrup-vase, basin; in fine ware: kylix in great numbers (275 stems and bases counted), bowl or basin with pinched-out handles, dipper, bowl, cup, etc. with flat bases (67 bases counted). Pieces with decoration: Mycenaean, including a stirrup-vase, and some Geometric ware.

ROOM 93

On the northwest facing the court and the altar is the shrine (93 on Key Plan) that has already been mentioned. It consists of a single rectangular room measuring ca. 3 m. wide with an average length of 3.43 m. from southeast to northwest. It had an open façade toward the court and was enclosed by walls on the other three sides (Fig. 223). The southwestern wall which continues northwestward is the exterior wall of the Workshop, bordering the ramp described above. It is 0.85 m. thick along-side the shrine and is built of relatively small unworked stones, but with some larger ones employed here and there, laid in five or six irregular courses. It stands to a height of 0.78 m. above the pavement of the ramp. It probably never rose much higher for this was certainly the stone socle that supported a wall of crude brick.

The northwest wall, 0.85 m. thick, is built of unworked blocks, some of respectable size forming each face with a fill of rubble. One or two courses are preserved. One fairly large fragment of poros appears at the southwestern end and the northeastern termination is formed by a huge squared block of poros resembling an anta base.[3] In the top near the middle of each of the four sides is a rectangular dowel hole, pre-sumably for the fastening of wooden timbers either horizontal or upright.

The northeast wall, 0.90 m. thick, built in the same manner as the northwestern and of similar material, is preserved only to a height of one or two courses.

The lateral walls terminate on each side in a massive block of poros and it is clear that the façade of the shrine was framed by decorative antae (Fig. 223). The base on the northeast[4] has in its top three dowel holes, one each on the northeast, north-west, and southwest. The southwestern block[5] is somewhat damaged on top and though no clear evidence of dowel holes survives, there may possibly have been one on the southwest. This block has been set on some flat bedding stones and earth that lie on another block of considerable size.[6]

Between the two anta bases and projecting southeastward ca. 0.13 m. at the southwest, 0.075 m. at the northeast end beyond their front line is a row of four flat poros blocks (Fig. 223)[7] which evidently formed the bottom step of two or three that rose to the level of the floor inside the shrine. The upper steps and the floor itself have vanished altogether since they must have reached a level higher than that of the modern ground. Only the fill of clayey broken-up *stereo* that supported them was left. Evidence is lacking to indicate whether this shrine had in its façade a central pillar, like that represented on the fresco found in the Propylon, but no

[3] Length southwest to northeast 0.97 m., width 0.85 m., thickness 0.53 m., height above pavement 0.39 m. Dowel holes: on northeast side, 0.395 m. from south-east edge, 0.05 m. long by 0.045 m., 0.065 m. deep; on southeast side, 0.55 m. from southwest edge, 0.06 m. long by 0.045 m. by 0.065 m. deep; southwest side, 0.37 m. from southeast edge, 0.05 m. long by 0.04 m., 0.065 m. deep; northwest side, 0.55 m. from northeast edge, 0.05 m. long by 0.04 m. by 0.06 m. deep.

[4] Length 1.05 m. southwest to northeast, width 0.90 m., height exposed above pavement 0.39 m., total height 0.55 m. Dowel holes: southwestern, 0.37 m. from south-east edge, 0.08 m. from southwest edge, 0.08 m. long from northwest to southeast by 0.06 m. by 0.06 m. deep; northeastern side, 0.37 m. from southeast edge,

0.09 m. from northeast edge, 0.09 m. long from north-west to southeast by 0.065 m. by 0.08 m. deep; north-western side nearly centered 0.08 m. from northwestern edge, 0.09 m. long from northeast to southwest by 0.06 m. by 0.07 m. deep.

[5] Length southwest to northeast 0.98 m., width 0.86 m., height 0.48 m.; height of top above pavement in ramp 0.60 m., in front of east corner 0.55 m.

[6] Length 0.90 m., width 0.78 m., height 0.13 m., pro-jects ca. 0.08 m. to the southeast of the face of the anta base.

[7] Measurements of blocks, left to right: 0.78 m. long by 0.37 m. by 0.30 m. high above pavement; 0.78 m. by 0.38 m. by 0.16 m.; 0.80 m. by 0.38 m. by 0.14 m.; 0.56 m. by 0.37 m. by 0.13 m.

one can doubt that an effort was made to give it an appearance of elegance and distinction, looking out on the little court and painted altar with which it surely had some connection. This may well have been the palace shrine, perhaps the seat of the goddess Potnia Hippeia who is mentioned on one of the inscribed tablets found in the Workshop.

OBJECTS FOUND

BRONZE
Very small piece of wire, d. 0.002 m.

STONE
Chips and flakes of obsidian, flint, quartz.

POTTERY
Chance sherds only. Shapes represented: in coarse ware, pithos, brazier or scoop, cooking pot with thin splaying rim, small tripod-vessel; in red ware, jug or jar; in fine ware, kylix (32 stems and bases), diminutive votive kylix, bowl, cup, etc. (16 flat bases), bowl or basin with pinched-out handles, dipper.

COLONNADE 94

Along the northeastern border of the court with the altar (Fig. 222) was a roofed colonnade (94 on Key Plan). Two irregular foundations[8] made for the most part of small stones (Fig. 225), reinforced along one edge or more by some of larger size, resemble the substructures that certainly served to support the bases of columns in Hall 65. The two are approximately aligned with the northeast anta base of the shrine and the spans from the anta block to the northwestern foundation and from the latter to the next are approximately the same, measuring 3.72 m., center to center.[9] It is probable that a third base existed originally and that the colonnade extended all the way to an anta in the wall forming the southeast end of the Workshop. The descending slope of the hillside, however, cutting through the ancient ground level, has left no surviving traces of the base or the anta.

The southwestern wall of Rooms 99 and 100 constituted the rear of the colonnade, which thus had a depth of 3.76 m. from front to back. This wall, 0.94 m. thick, is sadly dilapidated and only partly preserved in a single course which rises to a height of 0.24 m. above the pavement (Fig. 222). This course seems to rest on *stereo*-like earth which contains a few potsherds and itself lies on *stereo* 0.25 m. deeper. No traces of wall plaster were found.

The colonnade has a floor of stucco, preserved only in patches and especially alongside the rear wall. The floor, apparently of the same quality as the pavement in the court, is 0.47 m. higher than the latter and the adjustment between the two levels has been clumsily effected. Between the two foundations the stucco pavement rises sharply in what looks like a careless patchwork. To the southeast of the second foun-

---

[8] Northwestern foundation: 0.95 m. from northeast to southwest, by 0.90 m.; southeastern foundation: northeast to southwest 1.35 m. by 1.20 m.

[9] This allows for a bearing of ca. 0.36 m. on the anta.

dation a conglomeration of small stones still survives, which may possibly have supported a stucco step.

In plowed earth above the stoa a fragment of a narrow tablet came to light. At the floor level were found at least six nests of potsherds, each presumably representing a shattered vessel, and scattered about here and there miscellaneous pieces of bronze, arrowheads of the same metal and others of flint.

This colonnade must have provided a sheltered place from which spectators could observe the ceremonies that we may assume were conducted at the altar before the shrine. The columns or pillars that stood on the bases supported by the stone foundations were undoubtedly made of wood and they presumably carried a roof constructed of timbers covered by clay and earth. It may be conjectured that heavy beams extended from the anta on the northwest across to the first pillar and continued from post to post along the entire façade. It is possible that they carried an entablature of stone blocks some of which, as we have seen, were precipitated into the court below. The columns and the woodwork as well as the whole façade of the shrine were almost surely decorated in bright colors as intimated by the frescoes on the altar and this might well have been one of the principal places of worship in the palace complex.

OBJECTS FOUND

BRONZE

Fragments of two tiny barbed arrowheads.

Heavy disk-like object flat on bottom, slightly convex on top (Fig. 307 No. 1), d. ca. 0.017 m., th. 0.005 m.; possibly a partially melted rivet-head.

Fragment of chisel (?), square in section (Fig. 307 No. 2), l. pres. 0.019 m., w. 0.003 m.

STONE

Obsidian: flake and point (Fig. 307 No. 3); from doorway into Room 99.

Flint: five thin, beautifully cut arrowheads (Fig. 307 Nos. 5-9), found in doorway into Room 99: reddish, l. 0.029 m., w. 0.014 m., th. 0.001 m.; blackish, l. 0.031 m., w. 0.014 m., th. 0.001 m.; grayish-tan, l. 0.036 m., w 0.013 m., th. 0.001 m.; tan, l. 0.036 m., w. 0.014 m., th. 0.001 m.; tan, l. 0.029 m., w. 0.014 m., th. 0.001 m. Numerous flakes and chips.

Steatite: button, conoid (Fig. 307 No. 4), h. 0.015 m., d. 0.025 m., d. perforation 0.005 m., edge chipped and broken.

CLAY

Tablet: No. 1283 (*AJA* 62 [1958], 183, 188, pl. 45), found in plowed earth.

POTTERY

Many pieces of two large pots in red-brown semi-coarse ware, found on floor in front of eastern anta of Shrine 93. Not enough preserved to indicate shape of vessels but they were obviously large, closed, and had flat bottoms.

Another group of sherds near northwestern column base may have come from a jug, shape uncertain and pot unrestorable.

High neck and other pieces of an amphora (Shape 45) of soft brown fabric containing particles of red lay at edge of colonnade between column bases. Nearby, much of a high-necked jar with two horizontal handles (Shape 49); very soft red fabric, originally with red-washed surface decorated with bands in darker red paint.

Farther to northeast a group of coarse, severely burned sherds that almost disintegrated when washed so no indication of the shape of the vessel was obtained.

Still farther to the northeast remains of a crude pedestaled krater (Shape 63). Soft greenish-white fabric with surface almost completely gone; traces of painted decoration—dots, a circle and bands.

Relatively few small scattered sherds, all worn. Shapes identified: in coarse ware, pithos and large storage jar, tripod-vessel, cooking pot, baking pan, the member connecting two parts of a multiple vessel. Red ware: basin, wide-mouthed jar, jug or jar with high neck. Fine ware: kylix (79 stems and bases), bowl or cup (45 bases), bowl and basin with pinched-out handles, conical cup. Decorated ware: stirrup-vase, Vapheio cup. A few Geometric sherds.

CORRIDOR 95

To the northwest of the colonnade, and entered directly from the latter without a doorway, is a broad corridor (95 on Key Plan), 7.20 m. long and 2.80 m. wide (Fig. 223). It is flanked on the southwest by the northeastern wall of the shrine already described and by its continuation as the wall and doorway of Room 96; and on the northeast by a partition wall that separates it from Room 99. This wall, 0.84 m. thick and built in the same style as its southeastern section behind the colonnade, is preserved in some three or four irregular courses rising to a height of 0.55 m. above the floor. At its northwestern end the passage gives access, again without a formal doorway, to Room 97, though the opening here is narrowed on its northeastern side by an offset in the wall, projecting ca. 0.35 m., and forming the north corner of the corridor. As elsewhere in this building, the stone walls presumably rose to little, if at all, greater height, since they carried a superstructure of crude brick. No remains of plaster were found.

The floor was made of clayey earth and could hardly be recognized except by the presence of a thin black stratum lying on it and containing groups of sherds of broken pots. A large storage jar stood in the northern angle with many fragments scattered about it. A jug lay at the southeastern end of the corridor beside the anta base, and several further pots were represented by heaps of sherds elsewhere in the passage (Fig. 339). Among the objects recovered were fragments of many tiny bronze arrowheads, a black steatite seal found in the big jar, pieces of ivory, a terracotta animal figurine, and a clay sealing. Another sealing came from the doorway into Room 96 and five more from the doorway into Room 97.

OBJECTS FOUND

GOLD
Piece of foil, doubled over several times, probably a rosette.

BRONZE
Fragments of thin little arrowheads; a bit of thick bronze wire.

SILVER
Fragments of thin flat strip, l. 0.026 m., w. 0.013 m.; coil of thin wire.

STONE
Obsidian and flint flakes, pieces of quartz, chips of colored stone.

Lentoid seal of black stone, possibly steatite, NM. 8529 = *CMMS* 297 (Figs. 311 and 312 No. 1): crudely cut, d. 0.019 m., th. 0.007 m. Impression shows two long-legged, long-necked, horned animals in heraldic composition standing opposite each other but not vis-à-vis; the one on the right looks straight ahead, the other looks back over its shoulder to the left.

IVORY

Several burned fragments including two rectangular in section, 0.07 m. and 0.05 m. long, 0.007 m. wide and 0.0035 m. thick.

TERRACOTTA

Animal figurine, probably a horse (Fig. 310), h. 0.04 m., l. over-all 0.057 m.: bottoms of three legs and tips of ears missing; grayish-tan clay, no trace of slip or of painted decoration; perforation through base of neck. Crudely modeled, long pointed nose, upright ears, rippling mane, bobbed outstretched tail.

CLAY

Sealings: NM. 8490 = *CMMS* 329a (Figs. 311 and 312 No. 2): in upper half three animals couchant, all to left, apparently a lion between two winged griffins; each of the two at left has a long tail rising in a high curving loop; griffin at right is incomplete, lacking hindquarters in all impressions. Below animals a horizontal band of large dots or spirals; underneath in lower part of sealing two squids or octopuses, each with heart-shaped body, one having four tentacles, one six. Impressions poor; finger prints at right have effaced wing of griffin and damaged squids.

NM. 8496 = *CMMS* 366, from doorway into Room 97: animal lying or running to right with head turned back; above, branch of plant.

NM. 8508 = *CMMS* 367, two impressions, from doorway into Room 97 (e.g., Fig. 311 No. 4): bull (or wild goat) to left with head turned back and horns turned down. Between the front legs a plant.

NM. 8509 = *CMMS* 368 from doorway into Room 96 (Fig. 311 No. 5): an antithetic pair of lions attacking an animal between them.

NM. 8524 = *CMMS* 323, three impressions (e.g., Fig. 311 No. 6) and seven others with similar impressions but not numbered: from doorway into Room 97: four wild goats lie, much contorted, one in each quadrant of quartered area of seal. One goat has long horns, one of which swings into two other quadrants. Three goats seem to face to right with head turned back to left; the fourth faces left with head turned back. (Cf. Room 98 for another impression also catalogued under NM. 8524, Figs. 311 No. 13, 312 No. 4).

POTTERY

Jug (Shape 37, p. 377)
No. 819.

Krater-bowl (Shape 60, p. 397)
Nos. 808 (Figs. 385, 386), 1176 (Fig. 385).

Pedestaled krater (Shape 63, p. 400)
No. 810 (Figs. 387, 388).

Large wide-mouthed storage jar. Much of rim and upper part of side with two gigantic round horizontal handles and flat bottom preserved. Unrestorable as the very coarse fabric splinters and flakes and one side of pot was damaged by fire.

Narrow-necked jug or amphora. Fragment of bottom of neck and shoulder and stump of flattened handle preserved. Fabric very soft, red, wheelmade.

Piece of flat bottom and lower part of side of large closed gray pot with painted band near bottom.

Many sherds collected from the burned debris lying above floor. Recognizable shapes: in coarse ware, pithos, storage jar, basin or bowl, tripod-vessel, bowl with open trough spout, spit-stand or pan; in red ware, jug (?) with tubular spout, tripod-vessel; in fine ware kylix (87 stems or bases), bowl, cup, etc. (40 flat bases), bowl or basin with pinched-out handles, conical cup, dipper; in decorated ware: krater-bowl, angular alabastron, filler, kylix, Vapheio cup, tankard; motives recorded: spirals, con-

centric circles, bands, vertical stripes, inverted dotted-U, solid coating.

R O O M   9 6

Room 96 (Key Plan), which could be entered through a doorway from Corridor 95, is 3.38 m. long from northeast to southwest and 2.68 m. wide. On the southeast it is bounded by the rear wall of the shrine (p. 304), on the southwest by the exterior wall of the building (Fig. 223). On the northwest it is separated from Room 97 by a wall, 0.70 m. thick and standing to a height of 0.53 m. Alongside the corridor very little remains but foundations, 0.68 m. thick, of the northeastern wall and a mass of *migma* that rises to a height of 0.44 m. just beside the doorway. Here great damage seems to have been done by the fire, no doubt fed by the wood of the door casing. On each side of the doorway, which is 1.10 m. wide, the stones have been partially reduced to melted lime, and this whole end of the room was filled with masses of fused stone and brick. The jamb on the northwest apparently projected 0.20 m. from the wall. The lack of bases for the wooden casing leaves us without evidence as to how the door turned, if there was one.

The clay floor, which rested on a fill of greenish *stereo*-like earth, was covered by a thin black stratum.

Perhaps the most curious feature of the room is the presence of two somewhat irregular niches that seem to have been gouged out, one in the northwestern wall, the other in the southwestern.[10] Neither their purpose nor the date of their making is clear. Whether they existed in the time of the occupation of the building or were caused later by casual planting or digging is indeterminable. On the floor in front of the northwestern niche was uncovered a group of potsherds but its connection, if any, with the niches could not be established. Another larger heap, representing several pots, lay farther to the northeast. What purpose this little room served remains unknown. It might have been an adjunct to the neighboring shrine on the southeast, or it could have been the office of the management of the Workshop.

O B J E C T S   F O U N D

S T O N E

Several small flakes of obsidian and flint.

C L A Y

Sealing: NM. 8481 = *CMMS* 300 (Figs. 311 and 312 No. 3): lion attacking bull from left, head of bull turned back.

P O T T E R Y

Stirrup-vase (Shape 65b 1, p. 404)
    No. 817 (Figs. 389, 390).
Stirrup-vase (Shape 65d, p. 408)
    No. 809 (Figs. 391, 392, 394).
Sherds, for the most part very small bits, prob-

---

[10] One cavity, in the face of the northwest wall, beginning 0.40 m. from the west corner of the room, is 1.03 m. long, extending to about floor level. In the southwest a semicircular place, 0.43 m. wide, has been hollowed out, beginning 0.53 m. from the west corner, where no stones were found. The sides of the niche are stepped, the depth varying from 0.20 m. at the top to 0.40 m. at the bottom, which is at floor level.

ably from the bricks. Identifiable shapes: in coarse ware, small pithos, storage jar, tripod-vessel, scoop, broiling pan with slots to hold spits, pan with ring-handle (Shape 78); in red ware, jug or jar with low neck and with high neck; in fine ware, diminutive votive kylix, kylix (145 stems and bases), bowl, cup, etc. (52 flat bases), bowl or basin with pinched-out handles, conical cup, dipper; in painted ware, krater-bowl (2), kylix (3), pedestaled krater, stand with cut-out openings; patterns noted: net, spiraliform, stippling, triple wavy lines, and Ephyrean type decoration.

ROOM 97

The western corner of the building is occupied by a large room (97 on Key Plan). It was entered from Corridor 95 through an opening 2.75 m. wide, almost the full width of the passage (Fig. 151). Above (p. 307) it was stated that there was no formal doorway; this is not strictly accurate for remains of carbonized wood on each side of the opening indicated that the ends of the walls had been sheathed in a wooden casing and large beams forming a lintel surely stretched across from one side to the other, since the corridor certainly had a roof. A foundation of stones runs across the opening; it may have supported a wooden threshold, but there is no sign of an actual door that could be opened and closed. In the debris lying on the stones were 13 clay sealings (p. 308).

The room is roughly trapezoidal in shape, its southwest and northeast walls being parallel but not of the same length.[11] The southeastern wall, forming the partition between Rooms 96 and 97, is in line with the jog on the other side of the corridor. The southwest wall, which here forms the outside of the building, is 0.75 m. thick, ca. 0.15 m. thinner than the section farther to the southeast (Fig. 223). The change in width is made on the inner face of the wall, and the outer face continues the line of the southeastern section. It stands to a height of 0.50 m. above the floor. The northwestern wall (Fig. 151) joins the southwestern in an obtuse angle. It is 0.85 m. thick, preserved to a height of 0.50 m. in three to five courses. The wall ends at a point 4.45 m. from the west corner, leaving a gap of 2.13 m. to the northern corner of Room 97. It is not possible to determine with certainty whether there was an opening here for entrance and exit or whether the wall once continued and was at some time torn out. The gap was filled with a mixture of dark and light earth and even *stereo* which had been worked over and contained small stones and pebbles together with chunks of fused brick and stone, all very soft and evidently thrown in. The gap lies almost directly in line with olive trees to the northwest and southeast and is roughly 7 m. distant from the nearest one (p. 72). It is consequently possible that the damage was done long ago in the planting of an olive tree. Why the western corner of the room was laid out in an obtuse angle can only be conjectured. It

---

[11] Approximate inside measurements of room against walls: southeast 6.79 m., southwest 6.02 m., northwest 6.62 m., northeast 6.48 m.

was probably the existence in this area of a water system, already established, that limited the length of the southwestern wall of the Workshop and thus compelled the builders to adopt their awkward solution.

The northeastern wall of Room 97, 0.65 m. thick, is a party wall between the latter and Room 98. It contains a very broad opening, 2.98 m. wide, connecting the two rooms. The opening is not centered, the wall to the southeast of it being 2.19 m. long, the section to the northwest only 1.20 m. long. It stands to a height of 0.37 m. in three or four courses of relatively small flattish stones. No plaster appeared on the walls nor fragments on the floor beside them.

The floor itself was of earth, covered with a thickish black deposit. In it were found four groups of sherds, perhaps representing an equal number of pots. Above the black deposit lay in the northeastern part of the room a great mass of broken and dissolved crude brick mixed with vast quantities of small potsherds which had apparently been left in the clay when the bricks were being shaped. Also in the debris were bits of plaster, some of it painted, pieces of pavement, and fragments of tablets. Extending in a broad strip, 1.20 m. wide, across the middle of the room was a mass of fused fire debris along with many fragments of poros blocks. They must have fallen, but whence they came is difficult to determine. In the west corner there were also carbonized remains of two wooden planks.

Room 97 is a very large apartment. Nothing was recovered to shed light on the purpose which it served. Was it perhaps a workroom where artisans could carry out repairs? Some bright yellow and red patches exposed under the burned debris might suggest the possibility that coloring matter had been kept and used here. The extent of the fire damage might imply that a good deal of inflammable material was stored here but definite conclusions are not possible.

OBJECTS FOUND

BRONZE

Fragments of two tiny arrowheads (e.g., Fig. 308 No. 1), spherical head of pin (?), thin piece folded over.

STONE

Obsidian: core, flakes, and blade (e.g., Fig. 308 Nos. 6-8).

Flint: tip of arrowhead (Fig. 308 No. 3), reddish-brown, l. pres. 0.017 m., max. w. pres. 0.009 m.; blade with serrated edge (Fig. 308 No. 2), l. 0.023 m., w. 0.017 m.

Greenish stone: end of finely worked little celt (Fig. 308 No. 4), l. pres. 0.02 m., w. 0.017 m., th. 0.005 m.

Steatite: shanked button, flat top with beveled edge (Fig. 308 No. 9), h. 0.013 m., d. 0.022 m., d. perforation 0.004 m.

Quartz: many pieces.

Sandstone: whetstone, fragment broken at both ends (Fig. 308 No. 5), l. 0.047 m., w. 0.016 m., th. 0.005 m.

TERRACOTTA

Female figurine, body bent to a sitting position (Fig. 310), h. 0.057 m., w. head 0.012 m., w. neck 0.01 m., w. across shoulders estimated 0.027 m., w. waist 0.02 m., th. body 0.008 m.; pinkish-tan clay, scattered traces of red paint on lap, neck, shoulder;

in two pieces, with one arm and bottom of other side missing. Birdlike head, eyes indicated by hollows; breasts represented by large knobs and arms by stumps.

Button, biconical; polished reddish-brown clay (Fig. 308 No. 10), h. 0.018 m., d. 0.016 m., d. perforation 0.004 m.

CLAY

Tablets: No. 1336 and probably No. 1343 (*AJA* 62 [1958], 185, 187, pl. 49).

POTTERY

Jar (Shape 49, p. 385)
  No. 818 (Figs. 373, 374).
Krater (Shape 59, p. 396)
  No. 857.
The two other groups of sherds on the floor did not produce restorable pots.

The sherds from debris filling room for the most part small and worn. Shapes identified: in coarse ware, pithos, tripod-vessel, large storage jar, brazier, scoop, griddle, baking pan of some kind, jug, and a heretofore unnoticed large, shallow, platelike dish on a raised base; in red ware, basin and jug; in fine ware, kylix (300 stems and bases) bowl, cup, etc. (122 flat bases), small and large dippers, bowl or basin with pinched-out handles, conical cup, tankard, stand; in decorated ware, Vapheio cup, stirrup-vase, krater-bowl (possibly three examples), krater. In addition to allover paint and simple lines and bands, spirals, concentric curving lines, and vertical stripes were noted.

SHAFT GRAVE UNDER ROOM 97

A conspicuous depression in the earth floor near the west corner of Room 97 invited investigation. A sounding revealed, 0.15 m. to 0.20 m. below the floor, a cistlike structure lined with neatly built stone walls on three sides and bearing the appearance of a shaft grave.[12] The walls are made of thin flat unworked stones, carefully laid in fairly regular courses, some 12 or 13 of which could be counted at the northeastern end (Fig. 229). The latter still stands to its full height of 1.05 m. The two lateral walls seem originally to have had approximately the same height, but as now preserved, each has toward its inner face a shelflike ledge (Fig. 230). On the southeast it is 0.25 m. broad and one course high. The corresponding ledge on the northwest, 0.20 m. wide, is now two courses deep, but a single surviving flat stone near its northeastern end suggests that the shelf was originally only one course deep. These slots were evidently made to receive the ends of the transverse slabs that presumably once covered the tomb or their supporting timbers. The floor is leveled in *stereo* on which the walls are founded at 12.32 m. above datum. Along the southeast side is a low platform (Fig. 229) 1.20 m. long and 0.47 m. wide, built of flat limestone slabs, which rises in one or two courses 0.18 m. above the floor and which seems to have had finished ends. At the northeast it is 0.075 m. distant from the wall at that end, on the southeast it is set out 0.10 m. to 0.125 m. from the wall. It might perhaps have been a couch on which the occupant of the tomb was laid.

The southwestern end of the shaft was not closed by a wall, but it is now partly blocked by a large irregular unworked slab of limestone standing on end.[13] Another

---

[12] It is 1.05 m. to 1.12 m. wide from southeast to northwest and 1.53 m. to 1.56 m. long.

[13] Length 1 m., width 0.72 m., thickness 0.15 m.

slab of the same rough character[14] was found lying lengthwise on the northwestern side of the pit, resting on *stereo* and on the platform mentioned above (Fig. 231). Whether these two slabs were used originally to close the end of the tomb or served as cover slabs stretching from side to side is not clear. The tomb was surely covered after the person buried was laid in it. Robbers certainly forced their way into the grave and removed almost everything of value that it contained. They may have dropped the slabs into the cavity when they refilled it. On the other hand the slab still standing upright at the southwestern end of the shaft seems to have been solidly set into position and wedged by small stones. The other piece already mentioned could have fallen from the other half of the southwestern end. A small slab set against the end of the northwestern wall, with two or three other small stones leaning against it, may perhaps have held a second upright in its place (Fig. 230). Several thin fragments of unworked limestone had fallen between the platform and the southeastern wall.

The intruders who stripped the tomb were very thorough in their work, but they left some odds and ends to cast light on the character of the monument. A few crumbling bits of bones, not identified as human, lay scattered about in the loose fill. In the space between the platform[15] and the southeastern wall were recovered two gold beads, one in the form of a helmeted head, the other lentoid; nine of amethyst, eight roughly spherical of varying sizes, one amygdaloid; two of amber and fragments of others. The earth that filled the tomb had obviously been disturbed; it yielded a piece of ivory, delicately carved with a spiraliform pattern, and a good many fragments of pottery. The earth was sifted and this operation produced two further spherical beads of amethyst, one of carnelian, several scraps of amber as well as some very small sherds. Whether the sherds had any connection with the burial offerings or merely chanced to be in the earth that was thrown in to fill the pit is not determinable. No complete pot was found. Two or three fragments belong to a conical cup. A few sherds look as if they might be attributable to the late Palace Period, but a good many appear to be earlier, including one or two bits resembling Gray Minyan, one or two of Yellow Minyan, several pieces of Mattpainted Ware, and many fragments of coarse ware.

The date of a tomb can be learned only from the objects that were surely deposited in it. The presence of amber and of amethyst beads, which finds its nearest analogy in the tholos tomb excavated to the northeast of the site in 1953, points to an era earlier than that of the palace, but how much earlier has not yet been established.

---

[14] Length 1.16 m., width 0.77 m., thickness 0.20 m.
[15] The stones of the platform were lifted so that what lay underneath them could be examined. Nothing was found and they were replaced on the *stereo* on which they had lain.

This shaft grave in the middle of the citadel at Englianos certainly antedates the surviving palace. It recalls a comparable tomb discovered by J. L. Caskey at Lerna.

O B J E C T S   F O U N D

G O L D

Bead in form of helmeted head (Fig. 309), h. 0.0195 m., max. w. 0.0165 m.; th. 0.003 m.: back flat, front neatly modeled in rather high relief, so that when viewed from side half the nose and chin are seen. Raised ridge, ca. 0.001 m. wide, marked with diagonal incisions, goes around bottom of helmet, mouth, eyes, and across top of ear. Crest on helmet is done in same manner. Flat back is folded over front modeled piece and pressed together tightly, the joint adding to the effectiveness of the crest. Perforation, ca. 0.001 m. in diameter, comes just above the ridge around the eye and at the back of the head. Eye, only slightly indicated, is very small and seems out of scale. The close fitting helmet reveals the modeling of the skull and cheek beneath it. The metal is a warm yellow, neither a red- nor a greenish-gold. Cf. the three helmeted heads, especially the lower one, on the steatite rhyton from Hagia Triada (*PM* I, 688ff., figs. 508, 511) attributed to MM III.

Bead, lentoid (Fig. 309), d. 0.016 m., th. ca. 0.005 m.: made of two pieces pressed together which have now sprung apart, and the space between has become filled with earth. Greenish-gold now stained. Technique revealed by little dents from hammering.

S T O N E

Amethyst Beads

One almost amygdaloid but diamond-shaped in section with flat sides (Fig. 309), l. 0.015 m., w. 0.01 m., th. 0.007 m. to 0.004 m., d. of perforation 0.0015 m. to 0.002 m.: incised line on each face just inside the edge; irregular short transverse lines on the ridge of both faces.

Flattened spherical (Fig. 309): 10 of varying sizes[16] all with large perforations, which were drilled from one side only, as shown by the fact that the holes are larger at one end than at the other; not perfectly shaped.

Carnelian Bead

Spherical (Fig. 309), d. 0.007 m., d. of perforation 0.001 m. to 0.002 m.: light colored with darker red patches.

Obsidian: chips and flakes.

A M B E R

Beads: one intact but in very bad condition, h. 0.005 m., d. 0.012; another complete but crumbling, h. 0.006 m., d. 0.01 m., with surface almost gone; fragments of others that have almost entirely disintegrated.

I V O R Y

Fragment with finely carved decoration (Fig. 309), h. pres. 0.018 m., w. pres. 0.02 m., th. 0.003 m.: flat on back, apparently piece of an inlay. Decoration: spiral winding right and projecting beyond two rows of beading, the one above slightly arched, the lower horizontal.

B O N E

Many pieces of boar's tusks.

ROOM 98

The doorway connecting Rooms 97 and 98 had a breadth of 2.98 m. On each side of the opening the walls terminate in a more or less finished end. No carbonized

[16] Height	Diameter	Diameter of perforation	Height	Diameter	Diameter of perforation
0.0055 m.	0.008 m.	0.0010 m. to 0.0025 m.	0.0050 m.	0.007 m.	0.0010 m. to 0.0020 m.
0.0050 m.	0.008 m.	0.0010 m. to 0.0020 m.	0.0050 m.	0.006 m.	0.0015 m. to 0.0030 m.
0.0050 m.	0.007 m.	0.0010 m. to 0.0020 m.	0.0045 m.	0.007 m.	0.0010 m. to 0.0020 m.
0.0050 m.	0.007 m.	0.0010 m. to 0.0020 m.	0.0045 m.	0.006 m.	0.0015 m. to 0.0020 m.
0.0050 m.	0.007 m.	0.0015 m. to 0.0020 m.	0.0040 m.	0.006 m.	0.0010 m. to 0.0020 m.

remains of the wooden jambs were found, but the whole area was filled with a mass of fused stone and crude brick and it was clear that the fire had burned with particular violence in the entrance as well as in the whole room.

Room 98 (Key Plan) is a very large one, roughly rectangular but not laid out with precision, and the opposite walls are not exactly parallel (Fig. 232).[17] The southwest wall with its opening has been mentioned above (p. 311). On the northwest the room is bounded by the outside wall of the building, 0.95 m. thick, which stands to a height of 0.67 m. above the floor. It is built in the same manner as the southwestern exterior wall of relatively small stones, neatly aligned on each face. Of similar construction is the northeastern exterior wall of the Workshop which encloses the room on that side. It is ca. 1 m. thick and is preserved to a height of 0.54 m. at the north corner. On the southeast Room 98 is separated from Room 99 by a partition wall 0.84 m. thick; built in the regular style of masonry employed elsewhere in the building, it rises 0.42 m. above the floor. The northwest, northeast, and southeast walls show an almost level surface (Fig. 232) and it is likely that crude brick construction rested on this socle at that level. Remains of fused brick and stone appear almost everywhere along the tops of the walls as preserved. The deposit is especially thick near the northern corner, where in some places it reached the modern ground level. No lime plaster appears to have been used in this room but the walls may have borne a rough mud coating. Some fragments of the latter, in which were embedded remnants of carbonized wood, were found along the northwestern wall and in the western corner.

Room 98 had a properly made clay floor, resembling that found in the Archives Rooms (7 and 8). Beginning high above the floor lay a fill of burned debris comprising *migma* and masses of disintegrated crude brick. The fused calcined stone lay chiefly in the southwestern part of the room, whereas the dissolved clay of the crude brick[18] predominated in the northeastern area. Almost everywhere in the room the floor was covered with a thick black carbonized deposit.

Spread out on the floor were some 30 groups of sherds representing an equal or greater number of pots. Most of them were concentrated toward the eastern corner of the room around two large wide-mouthed jars (Fig. 232). One of the latter stood upright, with its top so close to the surface of the ground that the rim had been broken by the plow. The vessels are of many different sizes and shapes (Fig. 343) including a high-handled jug of an uncommon type. The two big jars were full of an extraordinary variety of colored earths and shiny granular matter that looked like ground-up stone. The fire seems to have raged with particular intensity around

[17] The length from southwest to northeast ranges from 7.02 m. on the southeast to 7.22 m. on the northwest, and the width from 6.43 m. on the southwest to 6.07 m. on the northeast.

[18] The clay from which the bricks had been made apparently contained innumerable small potsherds.

them and this circumstance inclined us to wonder if they had not contained some highly inflammable material.

Under the black stratum on the floor, especially in the western corner, were bright yellow and red patches of color like those observed in Room 97 (p. 311). A considerable quantity of bronze came to light in all parts of Room 98, for the most part representing sheeting, strips, wire, rivets, pins, and shapeless chunks melted by the heat of the fire. Many bits and flakes of flint and obsidian, a fragment of a stone handle, a shanked conoid button of steatite, and other odd pieces were recovered here and there. Some of these had probably been in the clay from which the bricks were made.

In the dissolved brick, ca. 0.30 m. below the surface of the ground, a fragment of a tablet was brought to light. Eighteen clay sealings were found: ten lay on the floor under a group of sherds, three came from the north corner, three from the doorway and two from near the doorway. Some of the sealings had suffered damage, but many had retained clear impressions. In two instances two impressions from the same seal were recovered. The sealings must have accompanied supplies brought to the Workshop to certify their origin or quality. Five bore numbers or ideograms as well as seal impressions, but exactly what the provisions were is still problematical. One impression bore the ideogram of a he-goat.

In any event it is likely that Room 98 was used in part for storing materials that were needed for the business of the Palace Workshop. Room 97, which is only slightly smaller than Room 98 and which contained almost nothing suggesting storage, might conceivably be the apartment in which some of the actual work was carried out with easy access to the supply room.

O B J E C T S   F O U N D

BRONZE

Shapeless patch of very thin sheeting spread out on floor (Fig. 313).

Flat strip (Fig. 314 No. 2), 0.018 m. to 0.02 m. wide, doubled over and wound around itself.

Thin flat fragment (Fig. 314 No. 4), l. 0.026 m., w. 0.017 m.

Rivet (Fig. 314 No. 6), d. head 0.012 m., d. shank 0.003 m.

Piece of bent wire, probably a pin, broken at both ends (Fig. 314 No. 1), l. pres. 0.06 m., d. 0.002 m.

Many nondescript fragments (e.g., Fig. 314 Nos. 3, 5).

STONE

Obsidian (?): thick little arrowhead, barbed type (Fig. 314 No. 8), l. 0.015 m., w. 0.009 m., th. 0.003 m.; many flakes and chips.

Flint: chunks, flakes, and chips, mostly red.

Quartz: many pieces.

Other: fragment, possibly of flattened handle, of dark mottled brown and black stone, smoothly surfaced and polished (Fig. 314 No. 7), 0.025 m. wide, 0.002 m. to 0.008 m. thick.

TERRACOTTA

Whorl (Fig. 314 No. 9), half preserved, h. 0.019 m., d. 0.02 m.

CLAY

Sealings

NM. 8478 = *CMMS* 312 (Figs. 311 No. 7, 312 No. 5) = No. 1326 in inventory of inscriptions (*AJA* 62 [1958], 185, 186, pl. 49): large octopus with five dolphins swimming below it.

NM. 8479 = *CMMS* 313 (Figs. 311 No. 8, 312 No. 6), found in doorway: three women with flounced skirts before a shrine.

NM. 8480 = *CMMS* 314 (Figs. 311 No. 9, 312 No. 7), found in doorway: bull-leaping scene (?); bull moving to right with head turned back; above at left a figure not clearly recognizable; below bull, man on hands and knees.

Unnumbered fragment, also from the doorway; impression almost obliterated; half of an animal preserved.

NM. 8484 = *CMMS* 315: animal going right with head turned back.

NM. 8485 = *CMMS* 316 (Figs. 311 No. 10, 312 No. 8): winged griffin to right.

NM. 8486 = *CMMS* 317 = No. 1329 (*AJA* 62 [1958], 185, pl. 49): two goats (?), back to back, grazing; one inverted.

NM. 8487 = *CMMS* 318 = No. 1328 (*AJA* 62 [1958], 185, 187, 189, pl. 49) : two animals, probably bulls, to left; impression much damaged.

NM. 8488 = *CMMS* 319 (Figs. 311 No. 11, 312 No. 9) = No. 1325 (*AJA* 62 [1958], 185, 187, 188, pl. 49): two animals (lions or wild goats?) rampant with pillar between.

NM. 8489 = *CMMS* 320: animal running right with head turned back.

NM. 8491 = *CMMS* 321 (Figs. 311 No. 12, 312 No. 10): three women in flounced skirts; central one with forearms hanging down; the other two with one arm raised in adoration, the other hanging down.

NM. 8492 = *CMMS* 322: animal to left with head raised high; impression badly damaged.

NM. 8524 = *CMMS* 323 (Figs. 311 No. 6, 312 No. 4): four wild goats with interlaced horns (cf. three impressions of same seal found in doorway from Corridor 95 to Room 97 and described on p. 308 NM. 8524).

NM. 8525 = *CMMS* 324 (Figs. 311 No. 14, 312 No. 11) = No. 1327 (*AJA* 62 [1958], 185, 187, pl. 49). Two scenes: above, man running to right between a pair of winged griffins back to back; below, a similar scene with man running to left between two animals back to back.

NM. 8536, two impressions: a = *CMMS* 325, b = *CMMS* 326. a (Figs. 311 No. 16, 312 No. 12), man walking to right carrying under left arm an animal (deer or goat?) held upside down with head hanging down at left and legs (or another animal) at right (?). Surface of impression much worn. b (Fig. 311 No. 15), very similar but may be from a different seal.

NM. 8554 = *CMMS* 327, two impressions (Figs. 311 No. 17, 312 No. 13): animal (wild goat?) to left with head turned back, much contorted.

Tablet: No. 1313 (*AJA* 62 [1958], 184 and pl. 47).

POTTERY

Bowl (Shape 4, p. 356)
 Nos. 803, 1097.
Bowl (Shape 9, p. 358)
 Nos. 801 (Fig. 351), 804.
Cup (Shape 11, p. 359)
 No. 1099.
Cup (Shape 12, p. 360)
 No. 1098.
Dipper (Shape 21, p. 364)
 No. 1100.
Kylix (Shape 27, p. 366)
 No. 1096.
Kylix (Shape 29c, p. 369)
 Nos. 1092-1095.
Jug (Shape 39, p. 378)
 Nos. 829 (Figs. 369, 370), 830.
Jug (Shape 40, p. 378)
 No. 802 (Figs. 369, 370).
Amphora (Shape 45, p. 381)
 Nos. 805, 806.
Storage jar (Shape 57, p. 395)
 No. 820 (Fig. 384).

Krater (Shape 58, p. 396)
No. 839 (Fig. 382, rim).
Krater (Shape 59, p. 396)
Nos. 840, 1101.
Krater-bowl (Shape 60, p. 397)
No. 813 (Figs. 385, 386).
In addition to the restorable pots incomplete vessels include: in coarse ware, medium-sized, wide-mouthed jar with horizontal handles, small wide-mouthed jar with vertical handles, handmade handleless shallow bowl, scoop, deep spouted bowl; in fine ware, amphora, a large closed wheelmade pot with traces of band decoration, two large high-necked jugs or jars, a decorated pedestaled krater, two kylikes (Shape 27), two kylikes (Shape 29c).

Shapes represented among sherds: in coarse ware, pithos, cooking pot with splaying rim, tripod-vessel, large lid, brazier, and baking pan; in red ware, basin; in fine ware, diminutive votive kylix, kylix (187 stems and bases), cup and bowl (15 flat bases), bowl or basin with pinched-out handles, dipper, conical cup, jug, jar; in decorated ware, kylix, tankard, pedestaled krater. Motives noted in addition to all-over coating, horizontal bands, spiraliform figures, and vertical stripes.

ROOM 99

The largest of all the divisions in the Palace Workshop is Room 99 (Fig. 222 and Key Plan) which occupies the middle of the northeastern side of the building. A broad opening, 2.95 m. wide, leads into the hall from the northwestern end of the Colonnade 94. The opening is not centered in the transverse axis of the room, having been placed considerably to the southeast of it.[19]

Approximately, but not perfectly rectangular, Room 99 has a length from southeast to northwest ranging from 15.55 m. on the southwestern side to 15.90 m. on the northeast, and a width broadening from 6.40 m. on the southeast to 6.50 m. on the northwest. The walls, which were preserved almost to the surface of the modern ground, slope down from northwest to southeast, following the inclination of the hillside. The wall on the southwest, separating the hall from Colonnade 94 (p. 305) and Corridor 95 (p. 307), need not be described again, and the northwestern wall, shared with Room 98, has also been dealt with (p. 315). On the northeast the exterior wall of the building continues with a thickness of 1.04 m. At the northern corner of the room it rises to a height of 0.55 m. above the floor, descending toward the eastern corner to 0.30 m. or less. In its present state the wall follows a somewhat undulating course, and it also bulges out in one or two places, probably as the result of accidents at the time of the fire and destruction. The wall was founded on *stereo* which also descends irregularly toward the southeast.

The southeast wall, 0.85 m. thick, makes a good bonded corner with the northeast wall. It stands to a height of only 0.10 m. or 0.15 m. above what we take to be the level of the floor; it peters out altogether 0.50 m. before reaching, at its southerly end, the junction with the southwestern wall. The latter is also missing from a point 1.13 m. short of the place where the corner must have been.

[19] Length of wall northwest of doorway 7.57 m.; southeast of doorway 5.02 m.

No lime plaster was found adhering to the walls or fallen beside them, nor was there any mud plaster except near the eastern corner, where a strip, 0.50 m. long and ca. 0.30 m. high, was still attached to the lower part of the wall.

The entranceway into Room 99 is too broad for an actual door; it may nevertheless have had wooden casings on each side and a lintel across the top. The opening has a maximum depth of 1.15 m. from its outer to its inner face, somewhat exceeding the thickness (0.90 m.) of the contiguous walls. Each edge is lined with irregular flattish stones of moderate size and a few others lie in the middle; there were also many hollows filled with very black earth and carbonized matter which covered the stones mentioned above. One piece of carbonized wood, 0.87 m. long, lay lengthwise on the black earth. Everywhere in the opening, signs of intensive burning are conspicuous. The remains of wood and the one large piece found may have come from the paneling of the jamb or the lintel above. Alternatively it might conceivably have formed part of a wooden threshold such as exemplified in Corridors 51 and 52 (pp. 216, 217). Another possibility not to be ruled out altogether is that a stone threshold once rested on, or was bordered by, the flat stones.

In the black earth just inside the doorway, near its southeastern end, were found fragments of bronze, some in the form of strips, 0.06 to 0.08 m. long by 0.02 m. wide, apparently curved and provided with rivets and rivet-holes, and decorated with incised spirals. They may have been parts of the fixtures of chariots, although many other possibilities can be imagined. From the fill of black earth in the doorway somewhat farther to the northwest came a sturdy chisel-like implement, a clay sealing and many fragments of others. Two small shattered stirrup-vases lay just inside the opening to the northwest of the bronzes.

No continuous black deposit remained to mark the floor level. The best indication of it seemed to be a stratigraphic change from the fallen reddish disintegrated crude brick to the greenish-white stratum resembling *stereo*, though containing a few potsherds and resting on real *stereo*. In a very few places patches of smooth mud floor were found well preserved, in other places the floor was thick and cracked and was easily recognizable as in the Archives Rooms. Many tablets and much pottery that survived in the room were found at or near the bottom of the layer of dissolved red brick ca. 0.50 m. below the surface of the ground.

Further reasonably good evidence for the level of the floor is to be seen in the many flat stones that were set, some alongside the walls and close to them, and others farther out in the room. About twelve such stones, spaced at varying intervals, still remain along the northeastern wall and it seems likely that they were the standing places for strong posts that held up wooden shelving along this whole side of the room.[20] Three or four similar flat stones, which probably served the same purpose,

---

20 East corner of room to center of each stone: 0.24 m., 1.09 m., 2.55 m., 4.15 m., 5.65 m., 7.09 m., 8.78 m., 10.29 m., 10.85 m., 12.65 m., 13.55 m., 14.54 m., 15.90 m. to north corner.

were uncovered beside the southwestern wall to the northwest of the entrance.[21] Three other flat stones of considerable size are set 1.35 m. to 1.40 m. distant from the southwestern wall, one to the right and one to the left, 5.72 m. apart, as one comes through the entrance into Room 99, and the third 3.57 m. to the northwest of the latter.[22] These solid bases were evidently designed to sustain substantial weight and they must be structural elements in the building. Just what their function was in this position so close to the wall is not easily determined. They may have supported beams spanning the space between the northeastern and southwestern walls.

Two other stones of some size, one near the southeastern end of the room, the second 6.28 m. from the northwest wall, are set roughly in the longitudinal axis of the hall and they too may have had a structural purpose.[23]

Scattered about here and there in various parts of the room, at the level marking the floor, were a good many nests of broken pottery. Five such groups of sherds were spread out in an area ca. 1.50 m. long close to the southwestern wall and beginning ca. 2 m. from the western corner of the room. Around the flattened-out base of a jar 2.20 m. from the corner, were clustered 20 fragments of inscribed tablets (Fig. 233) from which 12 more or less nearly complete tablets were assembled.[24]

From 1 m. to 2.80 m. from the southwest wall and 2 m. to 3.80 m. from the northwest wall, 52 additional fragments of tablets appeared lying scattered about and in bunches, allowing 26 complete or almost complete tablets to be reconstituted.[25]

Another pot was uncovered beside the northwest wall not far from the western corner of the room. Remains of three other broken vessels lay to the west and east of the column base to the north-northeast of the doorway, together with a group of 14 pieces of tablets which combined to make eight tablets or fragments thereof.[26] Another fragment (No. 1321) lay to the north of the north corner of the base and two others (Nos. 1324 and 1284) to the east of the east corner. Two stirrup-vases had been crushed just inside the room near the middle of the entranceway and a group of small sherds was spread out on a line with the southeast side of the door, ca. 3.50 m. distant from it.

Some of the pieces of tablets were found in the reddish clay of disintegrated crude brick, others in and under very black debris of the same general character but containing considerable carbon, possibly remains of shelving on which the tablets had been filed, or of boxes in which they were kept; still others on the chunks of mud flooring. On the whole the long narrow tablets came out in better condition than those of the broad flat type.

21 Distance from northwest edge of doorway to center of each stone: 0.55 m., 2.20 m., 7.55 m.

22 Distance of southeastern base from southeastern wall 2.62 m.; northwest base to northwest wall 3.67 m.

23 Location of bases: southeast wall to southeast base 1.20 m., to northwest base 9.42 m., to northwest wall 15.70 m. Southwest wall to southeast base 3.34 m., to northeast wall 6.56 m. Southwest wall to northwest base 3.30 m., to northeast wall 6.35 m.

24 Nos. 1290-1298, 1309-1311.

25 Nos. 1281, 1282, 1286, 1288, 1299-1308, 1312, 1314-1320, 1323, 1339-1341.

26 Nos. 1273-1280.

Three fragments near the west corner were joined together to form one complete tablet (No. 1289). More widely scattered in other parts of the room were two further fragments (Nos. 1335, 1342) and one intact tablet (No. 1287) bringing the total from this one room to 53 tablets and fragments thereof.

Eleven sealings were discovered fairly close together in an area alongside the middle of the northwest wall, and six others came from more widely separated places in the northwestern half of Room 99. Some badly shattered pieces were recovered from soft earth near the southeastern end of the entranceway. Whether this distribution is of any significance or is attributable merely to chance is not yet clear; but the sealings, like those from Room 98, were no doubt attached as guarantees to some of the materials that were brought to the Workshop.

The impressions were made by several different seals. Scenes represented include: a single large octopus (six examples, but not all from the same seal, as there are variations in the arrangement of tentacles, size, and shape of body, etc.); a griffin and lion frieze with a row of octopuses below (five examples from at least two seal stones); a lion flanked by men; and an animal going right. Four of the sealings bear an inscription on one or both faces; another bore an inscription on one side but the impression of the seal was obliterated.

Vast numbers of fragments, bits, and scraps of bronze were collected from the layer of fallen dissolved brick along with the pots, the sealings, and the tablets. Many of them come from diminutive arrowheads, none intact, but one complete though broken. Other objects are for the most part not identifiable, although there is one rivet-head and a fragment that may be from a knife-blade. Pieces of lead, possibly from clamps, were found with sherds against the northwest wall.

The same deposit yielded two arrowheads of flint or chert along with many chips and flakes of flint and obsidian, a crystal bead, a button and a bead of steatite, a lentoid sealstone, the head of a figurine, and a large whorl of terracotta.

It is obvious that Room 99 was not used as a regular habitation, since nothing comparable to the ordinary household floor deposit appeared. The dozen flat stones along the northeastern wall, which probably supported posts for shelves, the similar arrangement along the southwestern wall for a bench or shelving, imply that we are dealing with a great storeroom, where materials of many different kinds could be packed away in ample storage space. The inscribed tablets and the sealings seem to indicate that the contents kept here came from many different places. Leather, bronze, and artisans are mentioned and all the evidence leads us to the conclusion we have already expressed in calling this the Palace Workshop.

BRONZE

Very small arrowheads of the barbed type: 45 nearly complete, fragments of many more (e.g., Fig. 316 No. 1).

Hemispherical rivet-head (Fig. 316 No. 4), h. 0.006 m., h. including remnant of shank 0.009 m., d. 0.016 m.

Fragment, possibly of knife-blade, with finished edge (Fig. 316 No. 3), l. 0.042 m., max. w. 0.022 m., th. 0.002 m.

Slightly curved piece with rivet-hole (Fig. 316 No. 2), l. 0.042 m., max. w. 0.03 m., th. 0.002 m.

Strip, possibly part of a chisel or tang of a knife (Fig. 316 No. 5), l. pres. 0.023 m., w. 0.01 m., th. 0.003 m.

Chisel-like implement (Fig. 316 No. 6), found in doorway. Small end rounded, sides curving gradually outward to wide rounded end, l. 0.087 m., w. 0.007 m. widening to 0.031 m., th. 0.0025 m.

Collection of broken flat strips with rivets and rivet-holes, all more or less bent (Fig. 316 Nos. 7, 8). Four pieces, average l. 0.075 m., w. 0.02 m., th. 0.005 m., slightly concave on one face, convex on the other. Longest piece, 0.21 m., doubled over, is marked off by rivet-holes into sections 0.075 m. long; some rivets still in place. Another piece, 0.135 m. long, has a straight end and forms a long curve. Some pieces are decorated with neatly incised running spirals (Fig. 316 No. 7). All these fragments presumably formed a bronze strap or band, possibly belonging to a chariot or a corselet or some fixture or attachment in the Workshop itself.

Many fused, twisted, and nondescript fragments.

LEAD

Many twisted, melted pieces (e.g., Fig. 315 Nos. 1-6), found with sherds, possibly used as clamps to mend pots.

STONE

Crystal: spherical bead (Fig. 315 No. 9), h. 0.008 m., d. 0.009 m., d. perforation 0.002 m.

Obsidian: blade, l. 0.023 m., w. 0.012 m., th. 0.004 m.; other chips and flakes (e.g., Fig. 315 No. 7).

Steatite: three buttons. 1. flattened spherical (Fig. 315 No. 10), h. 0.0065 m., d. 0.02 m., d. perforation 0.005 m.; 2. shanked (Fig. 315 No. 11), h. 0.01 m., d. 0.02 m., d. perforation 0.0015 m.; 3. conoid (Fig. 315 No. 12), h. 0.009 m., d. 0.013 m., d. perforation 0.002 m.

Flint: arrowhead (Fig. 315 No. 8), barbed type, tips missing, l. 0.028 m., w. 0.017 m., th. 0.004 m.; blade, tannish-gray (Fig. 315 No. 13); many chips, flakes.

Hematite (?): lentoid seal NM. 8530 = *CMMS* 298 (Figs. 311 No. 24, 312 No. 15), grazing animal to right, one curving horn, d. 0.015 m., th. 0.004 m.

IVORY

A few burned bits.

TERRACOTTA

Head of female figurine (Fig. 315 No. 14), bird-like face with large pellet eyes, h. pres. 0.03 m., head 0.016 m. wide by 0.019 m., d. neck 0.01 m.; greenish-buff clay, remnants of paint preserved on neck.

Large biconical whorl (Fig. 315 No. 15), h. 0.02 m., d. 0.036 m., slightly hollowed out around perforation: brick red clay, badly damaged by fire.

CLAY

Sealings

NM. 8478 = *CMMS* 312, six impressions (e.g., Fig. 311 Nos. 18, 19) including one with inscription, No. 1330 (*AJA* 62 [1958], 185, 187, 191, pl. 49): large octopus with dolphins swimming around it. Same scene on sealing from Room 98 (p. 317).

NM. 8482 = *CMMS* 331 (Figs. 311 No. 21, 312 No. 14): lion facing left attacked by two men, one in front, one behind.

NM. 8483 = *CMMS* 328: animal going right, with head turned back, plant below.

NM. 8490 = *CMMS* 329, six impressions (e.g., Fig. 311 Nos. 22, 23) including three with inscriptions, Nos. 1331, 1332, 1334 (*AJA* 62 [1958], 185, 187-189, 191, pl. 49): facing left, lion or lioness between two griffins above row of dots or running spirals; below two squids or octopuses with heart-shaped bodies. Same scene appears on sealing found in Corridor 95 (p. 308 and Figs. 311 and 312 No. 2).

Tablets: Nos. 1272-1282, 1284, 1286-1312, 1314-1321, 1323-1324, 1335, 1339-1342 (*AJA* 62 [1958], 177, 181-191, pls. 44-49), 1442 (*AJA* 67 [1963], 159, 161, 162, pl. 32).

POTTERY

One-handled coarse jug (Shape 39, p. 378)
  No. 1174
Amphora (Shape 45, p. 381)
  No. 1175 (Fig. 371), decorated.
Pedestaled krater (Shape 63, p. 400)
  No. 1090 (Fig. 387), decorated.
Stirrup-vase (Shape 65b 1, p. 404)
  No. 807 (Fig. 389), decorated.
Stirrup-vase (Shape 65d, p. 408)
  No. 1149 (Fig. 391), decorated.
Other pots too fragmentary or too badly damaged by fire to be restorable:
Krater: thickened splaying rim, parts of side and one round horizontal loop-handle preserved; oatmeal fabric, hard, wheelmade; surface mottled gray, brown, and red.

Wide-mouthed jar found surrounded by tablets (Fig. 233): complete flat bottom with adjoining section of lower part of side which has become fused and bubbly from the fire, large piece of thin splaying rim; oatmeal fabric, gray core with red and gray mottled surface.

Stirrup-vase: much preserved, burned gray and so soft that it is unrestorable; remnants of painted bands around body and groups of concentric arcs on shoulder. Part of another somewhat larger stirrup-vase also decorated with painted bands.

Another wide-mouthed jar, very coarse soft brown fabric: two fragments of splaying rim, horizontal handle and part of flat base preserved.

Sherds from deposit filling room, shapes identified: in coarse ware, pithos, lid, tripod-vessel, cooking pot, brazier, scoop, pan notched for spits; in red ware, jug or jar, basin; in fine ware, diminutive votive kylix, kylix (352 stems), cup, bowl, etc. (150 flat bases), basin and bowl with pinched-out handles (many), conical cup, dipper; in decorated ware, tankard, kylix, stirrup-vase, krater-bowl, pedestaled krater. Patterns noted in addition to solid coating: horizontal bands and parallel lines, spiraliform figures, vertical stripes, concentric curving lines, murex, tennis racquet.

ROOM 100

Room 100 (Key Plan), apparently forming the southeastern end of the Northeastern Building, balances fairly closely Room 98 at the other end of the structure. Only its northwestern and its northeastern walls have survived, but some evidence for a bedding trench marks the approximate position of the southeastern terminus of the building and the southwestern limit of Room 100 almost surely continued the line of the southwestern side of Room 99.

It is thus possible to estimate the inside dimensions of Room 100 as ca. 7 m. in length from southeast to northwest and 6.40 m. in width.

The partition wall between Rooms 99 and 100 (Fig. 222) has been mentioned above (p. 318). Only a single course appears to be preserved up to the floor level or slightly higher; the foundations, however, continue down in three further courses and stop in greenish-white earth without reaching *stereo*. Toward its southwestern end the foundations are much less deep.

The northeastern wall, continuing the exterior limit of the building on this side, runs down the relatively steep slope of the hill. It is 1.15 m. thick and is preserved to a length of ca. 7.40 m. It stops in an abrupt break beyond which it was at some time demolished. This wall too has foundations three or four courses deep, made of small stones laid on the same greenish-white earth, well above *stereo*. The east corner of the room is missing, most probably having been grubbed out when an olive tree was planted over it. The southeastern wall has disappeared entirely, but a transverse exploratory cut revealed that a trench had once run from northeast to southwest in a line just below the broken end of the northeast wall. Although no stones of the wall remained *in situ*, it is likely that this bedding trench had once been dug for the foundations at the end of the building. The southwestern wall, though it almost certainly continued the line of the partition between Colonnade 94 and Room 99, has vanished except for one block of some size, which was found standing in the line of the wall.

No proper floor was preserved inside the room; its level is indicated, however, in the same manner as in Room 99 by the bottom of the layer of fallen dissolved brick that rested on the yellowish-white stratum made up of worked *stereo*, which was no doubt prepared to support the floor. Lying on that stratum is an irregular group of flattish stones roughly circular, ca. 0.90 m. in diameter, set approximately in the axis of the room (2.33 m. from the northwest wall measured to the center of the ring); it was undoubtedly the supporting structure for the base of a column. The plowed surface earth had an average depth of 0.25 m., the dissolved reddish brick marked by burning 0.40 m., the yellowish-white stratum that rested on *stereo* itself 1.70 m.

Though nothing of consequence came from the plowed earth, the burnt stratum containing many potsherds was rich in its yield of objects. In the northern corner of the room an area, ca. 1.30 m. long from northwest to southeast and 1.15 m. wide,[27] produced a great many fragments of ivory, lying scattered and in groups. All are thin and burned, many have incised patterns, such as spirals and connected concentric circles, and some look as if they had been painted. One large assemblage could be imagined as the veneer from a piece of furniture.

Beyond the ivories toward the southwest, also in the burned stratum, were found innumerable fragments of tiny bronze arrowheads of a barbed type. A count of the points reached 501, though there were probably a great many more. Many were found in a close group under the fragments of a pot. These diminutive arrowheads had no doubt been kept in a container of some kind; the pot was too incomplete to

[27] Located 0.05 m. to 1.20 m. from the northeastern wall and 0.78 m. to 2.08 m. from the northwestern wall and at a depth of 0.15 m. to 0.35 m. below the top of the northeast wall.

serve for this purpose and the container may have been a wooden box that was destroyed in the fire.

A clay sealing was found in the same burnt layer.[28] It bears an excellent impression of a single octopus.

In the absence of two of its walls and lacking a proper floor, the room offers no evidence for its specific use, except the nature of the things found in the burnt deposit. The ivories and the arrowheads certainly point to the conclusion that this was the special section in the Workshop devoted to the making of delicate objects in bronze and ivory.

O B J E C T S   F O U N D

GOLD

Two fragments of foil (Fig. 319 Nos. 8, 9).

BRONZE

More than 501 small barbed arrowheads (e.g., Fig. 317).
Large rivet with both heads preserved (Fig. 319 No. 7).
Wide flat strip, folded over (Fig. 319 No. 3).
Nondescript pieces (e.g., Fig. 319 No. 2).

IVORY

The fragmentary material is still awaiting the attention of an expert technician for cleaning and joining.

OBSIDIAN

Core and flake (Fig. 319 Nos. 1, 4).

FLINT

Part of petal-shaped (?) arrowhead (Fig. 319 No. 5).
Blade of unusual semi-circular shape (Fig. 319 No. 6): one edge straight and coarsely serrated; the other curved.

CLAY

Sealing
Fragment (Fig. 311 No. 20; *AJA* 65 [1961], pl. 60 fig. 18a), not entered in National Museum Inventory: large octopus with dolphins swimming around it, another impression like NM. 8478 = *CMMS* 312 from Rooms 98 and 99 (pp. 317, 322 and Figs. 311 Nos. 7, 18, 19, 312 No. 5).

POTTERY

Many very small scattered sherds in miserable condition. Shapes recognized: in coarse ware, pithos and large storage jar, cooking pot, large and small tripod-vessel, baking pan; in red ware, basin, jug or jar, globular jar; in fine ware, kylix (53 stems), cup, bowl, etc. (40 flat bases), conical cup, bowl and basin with pinched-out handles, jug with rim cut out above handle; in decorated ware, tankard with horizontal bands and Vapheio cup with vertical rippling. A few stray sherds are LH I and in the whitish earth above *stereo* were Minyan and Mattpainted Wares.

---

[28] Found 0.28 m. below the surface, 1.90 m. from the northeast wall, 2.03 m. from the northwest wall.

AREA BETWEEN NORTHEASTERN BUILDING
AND WINE MAGAZINE

AREA 101

A T ITS upper northwestern end Ramp 91 reaches a corner where it joins what we
have taken to be the beginning of a street that once ran northeastward toward
the far end of the acropolis. On its southeastern side the street borders the
northwestern end of the Palace Workshop and on the opposite side it is bounded for
a short distance by a wall, flanking Area 102 and parallel to the northwest wall of
Room 97, and by the southeast wall of the long building in Area 103 (Fig. 151). The
first section of the roadway, 7.85 m. long and 4.65 m. wide, has been numbered 101
(Key Plan). It is a complicated area, because constructions of several phases seem to be
represented with little or no change in level and with encroachments on earlier
strata. It is difficult consequently to disentangle the various elements.

Masses of potsherds were found in the earth covering the roadway and the water
channels as well as the area beside them.

Attributable to the final stage, in any event, is the stucco pavement which continues that of the ramp (Fig. 234). The dividing line between ramp and street is
marked by a transverse row of narrow poros blocks, ca. 0.25 m. wide. Looking much
like a threshold at the level of the pavement it extends from the exterior wall of
Court 42 across the ramp ca. 1.40 m. to a substantial wall. Consisting of four roughly
squared poros blocks, so far as can now be seen, this wall runs northwestward 2.75
m., almost parallel with the court. The pavement of the ramp was apparently carried over the threshold in the fashion we have often seen in the palace and it also
covered the top of the wall. Only 0.47 m. to 0.58 m. farther to the northeast is evidently another nearly parallel wall across which the pavement was continued in an
abrupt rise. At its highest point it reaches an elevation of 14.25 m. above datum.
Though the stucco here lay only ca. 0.10 m. below the modern ground level,[1] it
had miraculously escaped the destruction that removed it in its extension farther
northeastward. For it surely must have continued in that direction and covered a
distributing system which channeled in different directions water that was brought
to this place by an aqueduct. The surviving part of the pavement, however, is actually
broken away at a point 4.25 m. northeast of the wall of Court 42 and short of the
channels we believe it once covered. No remains of the pavement are preserved
in situ in the street beyond this point. It is likely that the ancient ground level
lay almost as high as the modern, and cultivation in our time would account for the

[1] Scattered about in the debris covering the pavement were many fragments of a stirrup-vase decorated
on each side with a large squid (Fig. 348 Nos. 1-4).

disappearance of the surface of the road. The line of the aqueduct, presumably following the street, has been traced to the northeastern brow of the hill.

The aqueduct seems to have reached its terminus ca. 8 m. from the wall of the court near the northern corner of Area 101 (Fig. 235). Here was evidently the place from which the water was directed through three—if not more—channels, one leading westward, another southwestward, and the third to the southward. It looks, however, as if these channels were not contemporary, but represent two if not three different phases. Latest in the series appears to be the line to the south. The northerly part of this channel, ca. 0.80 m. long, where it takes off from the supply line, is built of small stones. The southeastern and longer part of it, however, ca. 4.20 m. long, is made of fairly large open pi-shaped terracotta tiles.[2] They are broader at one end than at the other, some at least overlapping, with the narrow end of one fitting into the broad end of the next. The whole channel was covered with rough irregular unworked slabs of stone laid transversely (Fig. 236). In the debris filling it near the upper end was wedged a nearly complete shallow cup. At the lower end of the channel no trace of a basin has survived, no arrangement to receive the water (Fig. 224). There must have been an installation of some kind; whatever it was, it has left no clue to its form and extent. The space between the end of the terracotta channel and the beginning of the stone gutter, 0.91 m. long and 0.43 m. to 0.37 m. wide, has a rough floor of stone at approximately the same level as the end of the channel. This space appears to have been gouged out of the northeastern part of the high wall over which the stucco pavement climbed abruptly. The difference in level between the end of the terracotta channel and the beginning of the stone gutter that slopes down sharply beside the wall of the Palace Workshop is only 0.07 m. Nothing remains to indicate that the flow of the water through the channel could be stopped or controlled, nothing to make clear how the overflow or waste was conveyed to the gutter.

On the southwestern side of this space a large poros block[3] still lies *in situ*, possibly forming the end of the wall to which we have referred. The northeastern part of the block has apparently been broken away and no proper face is here preserved (Fig. 224). On this damaged side of the stone approximately half of a roughly circular cutting can still be seen. It seems to indicate that a round hole had been bored through the stone, but in the present position of the block it is difficult to see how this cutting can have served any useful purpose in connection with the water system. The block may have been taken from an earlier installation to be reused in this wall. Several

[2] Length of individual tiles: 0.87 m., 0.43 m., 0.87 m., 0.65 m., 0.46 m. Height ca. 0.15 m., width at bottom on outside at large end 0.29 m., at top on outside at large end 0.26 m., width at bottom inside at large end 0.24 m., width at top large end inside 0.22 m.

[3] Length of block northwest to southeast 0.82 m., thickness southeast end 0.40 m., maximum thickness northwest of hole 0.53 m., full height of block 0.40 m., height above pavement 0.32 m.; hole 0.19 m. from southeast edge of stone, diameter of hole 0.15 m.

other pieces in the area had clearly been employed elsewhere before they were brought here (Fig. 237). One such is a fragment that seems to be the tip of a horn (Fig. 238) from a stone representation of horns of consecration. It was built into the threshold mentioned above, along with a stone gutter turned upside down.[4] Yet another piece lying beside the water channel described above (Fig. 224), certainly not in its original position, is apparently the lower part of one side of a large stone example of horns of consecration (Fig. 239). One of the blocks in the poros wall also seems to be a reused piece, since it bears a dowel hole in one vertical face which presumably once was the top.

We concluded that the southern channel was the latest in the series, for it brought water to the west corner of the Palace Workshop and the overflow or waste was carried away from this place by the stone gutter described above (pp. 299f.) The gutter seems to be associated with the stucco pavement of the ramp. The latter, on its southwestern side, is adjusted to the exterior wall of Courts 42 and 47, which must be among the latest elements in the palace.

The western channel, which branches off almost at right angles to the southern line that has just been described, has been traced only 4.50 m. At the point where the two branches diverge they are separated by a fairly large stone, shaped almost like a snub-nosed flat-iron. This channel, so far as seen, is made of rough unworked stones on the sides, with flattish slabs, some of considerable size, laid across the top. The wall bordering the northwestern side of the street seems to have been built directly across this channel. Whether it interrupted the flow of water and ended the usefulness of this branch or permitted the flow to continue cannot now be determined, though the first alternative is more likely. We were inclined to think that the western channel somehow led to a small reservoir (or an antecedent of the surviving one) which certainly stood, before the enclosing wall of Court 42 was built, some 4.50 m. west-southwest of the end of the aqueduct.

O B J E C T S   F O U N D

B R O N Z E

Fragment of wire, l. 0.029 m., one end bent into loop; piece of rivet-head; some 25 very small nondescript bits.

S T O N E

Two fragments of horns of consecration: tip of horn (Fig. 271 No. 9): h. 0.35 m., w. 0.27 m. at bottom, 0.25 m. at top, th. 0.185 m. It has some white plaster on three of

its faces, but two sides have been cut in order to fit the block into the space in the threshold.

Larger piece (Fig. 271 No. 9): h. pres. 0.61 m., h. to saddle 0.26 m., w. pres. below saddle 0.35 m., w. of horn tapering from 0.28 m. to 0.26 m., th. at bottom 0.26 m., th. of horn 0.20 m., th. of plaster 0.008 m. to 0.01 m. Sides have slight curvature or bulge achieved by thickening the plaster. Surface

[4] Gutter block: 0.95 m. long broken into two pieces, 0.25 m. wide and 0.16 m. high, with a channel 0.10 m. deep and 0.14 m. wide.

plastered and painted everywhere except bottom and in a break below the saddle. The small piece from the threshold may have been cut from the upper part of this larger stone. A similar fragment of horns of consecration was found at Gla (*Ergon*, 1960, 47f., fig. 58).

Obsidian: very thin arrowhead, barbs missing, l. 0.026 m., w. 0.018 m.; fragment of another; a third and thicker example with barbs and tip missing, l. 0.021 m., w. 0.015 m.; many chips and flakes.

Flint: small, gray arrowhead, barbed type, l. 0.021 m., w. 0.014 m.; blades with one serrated edge; flakes, chips.

Marble: bead, h. 0.011 m., d. 0.018 m.

Quartz: many pieces, one at least may be worked.

BONE

Fragments of boar's tusks.

TERRACOTTA

Whorls: fragments of three coarse examples: two truncated bicones, one bicone.

POTTERY

Cup (Shape 12, p. 360)

No. 811; found in terracotta water channel.

Stirrup-vase (Shape 65a, p. 403)

No. 1142 (Fig. 348 Nos. 1-4), decorated.

Krater-bowl (Shape 60, p. 397)

Fragment: part of rim, side and one horizontal handle preserved. Decoration: handle zone bordered below by two bands which in some places separate into 3 or 4 lines. Stripe on outside of handle, band around its base. Murex appears in handle zone singly in three upright examples which carry down through the lower bordering band.

Small ring-vase

No. 1148 (Fig. 348 No. 9), decorated: fragment lacking handle, which looped from top of spout to ring below, and about one third of side and bottom. H. to top of ring 0.028 m., to top of spout 0.045 m., d. 0.095 m., w. of ring 0.03 m. Gray fabric with decoration in darker gray. Whole surface bears a series of encircling bands, broad one around central hole, two narrow ones below, then two broader just below greatest diameter and above shoulder. In the uppermost reserved zone continuous parallel chevrons pointing left, in shoulder zone similar chevrons pointing right. Band around base of spout and inside rim. Outside of spout darkened, perhaps smoked if this vessel was used as a lamp. Found in a chunk of fused material above end of terracotta water channel.

Sherds almost all in miserable condition, incrusted with lime, surface worn with edges rubbed. Obviously thrown out as rubbish. Shapes represented: in coarse ware, **pithos** (abundant), tripod-vessel, brazier, scoop, lid; in red ware, basin with horizontal handles, jug and jar, deep spouted-bowl; in finer ware, kylix (243 stems counted), bowl, cup, etc. (184 flat bases), conical cup, bowl with pinched-out handles, dipper, tankard, stirrup-vase, diminutive kylix, krater-bowl, jug. Almost all of Mycenaean III B but a few of III A and some strays, LH II and perhaps earlier (Vapheio cup). Decorated ware, motives noted: over-all coating, horizontal bands and lines, vertical lines, concentric circles, spirals, parallel chevrons, murex. In surface layer a good many pieces coated with glaze of late Geometric Period.

AREA 102

The almost square reservoir or cistern (102 on Key Plan), measuring ca. 2.25 m. from southeast to northwest and 2.20 m. from southwest to northeast, was substantially constructed with walls built mainly of smallish rather flat slabs of limestone, carefully laid, with some larger blocks used at the corners (Fig. 151). The southwestern wall was incorporated in the northeastern wall of Court 42 (p. 183). Its southwestern face, bordering the court, rises 0.78 m. above the floor of the latter. The wall is 0.68 m. thick. Its northeastern face (Fig. 240) is easily distinguishable among the stones of the later wall, where it stands to a height of ca. 0.60 m. above the pavement of the reservoir.

The southeastern wall, 0.70 m. thick, is preserved to a height of 0.53 m. above the floor. Here near the bottom is preserved a strip, varying from 0.08 m. to 0.25 m. in height, of fine apparently waterproof stucco. Only a short stub, 1.05 m. long, of the northeastern wall survives (Fig. 241). Its lower part has a thickness of 1.10 m. Its southwestern side has been demolished to within 0.20 m. of the floor. This wall too retains on its inner face a thick underlayer and a fine finishing coat of the same waterproof plaster, preserved to a height of 0.15 m. The northwestern wall also survives in a short stub, 0.85 m. long, partly incorporated in the wall of the court. It projects only some 0.45 m. outside that wall and rises barely to a height of 0.35 m. The inner face here too bears fine white waterproof plaster.

The compartment was found filled on top with stones apparently fallen from the walls. Below, in the west corner, was mixed black earth containing many sherds, while elsewhere the deposit was hard and whitish with vast quantities of small sherds covered with greenish accretion. Also found were fragments of a basin retaining traces of painted decoration, part of a bead seal, pieces of bronze, flint, obsidian, and quartz, and half of a large terracotta whorl.

The floor of what we call the reservoir was paved with stucco. It is not altogether level but seems to have a slope toward the southwest and also toward the northwest. The stub of the enclosing wall on the northwestern side ends in a straight line and the stucco floor continues to the northwestward. It is therefore clear that there was an opening and that the cistern had a second chamber in this direction. A small stub of its northwestern wall has survived (Fig. 151) indicating that the annex had a width from southeast to northwest of ca. 1.30 m. Its northeastern limit is not certain, since later disturbances have destroyed all remains in that direction. The northwestern wall seems to have been 0.55 m. thick, not including plaster. No traces of a waterproof coating have survived on either wall, but the stucco floor continued across the second chamber at a level slightly lower than that of the main cistern.[5]

A stucco pavement at a somewhat higher level is preserved farther to the northwestward, extending 1.80 m. along the northern section of the wall of Court 42 (Fig. 110). That wall overlaps part of the pavement, which apparently continued farther to the southwest. Toward the northeast the pavement is broken away in an irregular line and its original extent in that direction cannot now be determined. In any event these remains suggest the possibility that the reservoir had a third chamber.

---

[5] Cistern 102, east corner floor 13.79 m. above datum, west corner 13.68 m.; second cistern floor 13.68 m.; third cistern floor 13.78 m.

In classical times cisterns and reservoirs were often made in two or more units for practical reasons. When the need for cleaning arose one chamber could be blocked off while the others remained full of water and there was no interruption in the supply. It seems likely that the same explanation is applicable here.

The suggestion that the western channel conveyed water to the multiple cistern (102) encounters one serious difficulty, for the level of the channel seems to be lower than that of the reservoir. It was this consideration that led us to wonder if there had not been somewhere in this area an earlier storage basin at a level low enough to be supplied by the channel. No remains of such a predecessor have been recognized.

What we have taken to be the southwestern channel is represented by three small remnants of terracotta pipes, lying more or less in a line. The first and most important is a cylindrical water pipe the end of which appears in a rectangular opening at 13.78 m. above datum in the inner face of the wall bordering Court 42 on the northeast (p. 183 and Figs. 136, 137). The second remnant, 4.53 m. northeastward from the inner face of that wall, is a fragment of a similar terracotta pipe of approximately the same diameter (Fig. 242). The piece is broken at both ends and only a little more than half of its circumference is preserved, but enough remains to show that it too is from a cylindrical pipe. The fragment is 0.40 m. long and, as it lies, 14.05 m. above datum, it aims directly at the pipe in the wall of the court. The third remnant was found in the same general line, ca. 8 m. farther northeastward. It is a small piece of terracotta, only 0.10 m. long, broken on all sides but curving in an arc comparable to that of the pipe.

This evidence may seem too scanty for the recognition of a third water channel; but the pipe set in the wall of the court makes it certain that water was delivered to this spot. It is true that no actual connection has been found between the pipe in the wall and the next piece; nor is there conclusive evidence pointing to the removal of a channel of any kind from this line. It is worth noting, however, that in this particular area, alongside the southeast wall of the cistern (102) and the northeast wall of Court 42, the ground under the late stucco pavement is a deep fill continuing all the way down to *stereo* at 13.44 m. above datum; it consists of earth, clay, bits of plaster, stucco, and stone, with a few sherds. This must therefore be an artificial packing probably in order to raise the level of the ground and the pavement outside the court. In the course of this work the pipes may have been removed as no longer needed, since the water must henceforth have been diverted into the southern channel.

The latter, at all events, is of later date than the pipes, although they lay at a much higher level; and the pipes in turn are later than the cisterns. The Palace Workshop, the northwestern line of which seems to have been adjusted so as not to encroach on the southern channel of the water system, must therefore be contemporary with the third phase, or somewhat later.

OBJECTS FOUND

BRONZE

Nondescript bits.

STONE

Crystal: half of lentoid seal (NM. 8533 = *CMMS* 300) carved with representation of what appears to be an animal with long tail standing toward left, probably with head turned back to right.

Flint: blade with serrated edge, chips, and flakes.

Obsidian: partially worked arrowhead.

Quartz: pieces.

TERRACOTTA

Whorl, one half, h. 0.05 m., d. 0.053 m., d. of hole 0.012 m.

POTTERY

Basin (Shape 1, p. 355)
    No. 812, decorated.

Many scattered sherds. Shapes represented: in coarse ware, pithos, tripod-vessel, griddle; in red ware, jar, deep spouted bowl; in fine ware, kylix (90 stems counted), cup, bowl, etc. (46 flat bases), conical cup, dipper, basin with pinched-out handles, alabastron, filler, krater-bowl. A few pieces bear painted decoration: over-all coating, horizontal bands and lines, stripes. Some fragments of late Geometric ware.

AQUEDUCT

The aqueduct which once brought water to this area has been traced nearly 68 m. toward the northeastern end of the acropolis (Fig. 416). Originally it appears to have been a simple ditch cut in *stereo*, varying from 0.20 m. to 0.50 m. in width at the bottom, and generally broadening somewhat toward the surface of the ground. Perhaps at first the channel was left open as in many modern irrigation ditches which may be seen not far from the site. Later it may have been thought advisable to cover the channel with stone slabs. A wall made of several courses, four or five in some places, of flattish unworked stones seems to have been built along one side of the channel (Fig. 243). Relatively short slabs could then reach from the top of the wall to the top of *stereo* on the other side of the ditch. In the course of time, and probably as the result of wear and tear along the edges, the channel here and there may have broadened so much that a wall on each side became necessary. In one section of nearly 15 m., running northeastward from the north corner of the workshop, the two lateral walls still exist with their cover slabs *in situ* (Fig. 244).

The aqueduct does not run straight but follows a meandering line, constantly weaving its way, bending slightly to the right and left again and again; toward its northeastern end it swings in two successive bends more sharply to the north. The channel was evidently cut in *stereo* by trial and error and was made deep enough by practical experiment so that the water would flow from northeast to southwest. Some 57.50 m. northeast of the distributing system in Area 101 (northwest of

Room 97), lies the highest point in the bottom of the channel (Fig. 245), which continues at almost the same level for a farther distance of 8 m. (Fig. 246). At the highest point it is 14.15 m. above datum, and at the southwestern end, where the channel divides, *stereo* was found at 13.69 m. above datum. There was thus a descent of 0.46 m. in a distance of 57.50 m., which is sufficient to keep the water actually running. The bottom of the channel near the northeastern end is 1.10 m. below the modern surface; in the middle section it is 1.25 m. deep; and toward the southwestern end, where the ground sinks, it is only 0.80 m.

The high point lies in the middle of a section of the wall, ca. 6.35 m. long, in which large blocks of poros have been used as the building material, some set on edge, some obliquely and not in any order (Fig. 245). The presence of the large squared blocks in this place seems to require some explanation, since they are nowhere else employed in the whole course of the aqueduct. In the immediate vicinity no building that might have been constructed of such blocks has been discovered. One might conclude that the stones had been brought to this place for some special purpose. This section of the conduit is close to the northeast edge of the hill. It is obvious that water could not have climbed the steep bank. As mentioned above (p. 181), the source of the water was almost surely the spring called Rouvelli, which still flows beside the highroad about 1,360 m. to the northeast of Englianos. The hollow below the northeastern edge of the acropolis must have been bridged to carry the aqueduct across the gap. The end of the structure would have to reach the high point of the channel leading across the top of the citadel toward the distributing station. A substantial foundation might then have been required to form the terminal anchor of the wooden trestle. A circular hole (0.19 m. in diameter and ca. 0.22 m. deep) was drilled vertically into a block which lay in slanting position in the wall (Fig. 245). This hole might well have been made as a socket in which to fit a sturdy wooden post to help support the bridge.

Almost directly behind the block with the hole, and ca. 0.50 m. distant, is the northeastern end of a wall, barely 1.20 m. long, and 0.50 m. thick. It was built of unworked stones laid in three or four irregular courses in a broad widening of the channel trench (Fig. 245). The wall is based on *stereo* ca. 0.20 m. above the floor of the aqueduct and rises 0.45 m. to approximately the same height as the wall made of squared blocks. Perhaps this little structure afforded some supplementary support for the end of the wooden bridge we have postulated to carry the water across the valley to the acropolis.

From the high point the channel, cut in *stereo* without an accompanying wall, and only 0.50 m. wide at the top, continued northeastward (Fig. 246), descending sharply through a gateway of a much earlier Mycenaean period by which an old roadway led out of the site. The channel, which is relatively narrow here, may have been intended to carry away water that spilled over the edges of the aqueduct or leaked from it at the junction with the section inside the acropolis.

Throughout its length the aqueduct shows many signs of reconstruction and repair. Except for the short stretch made of poros blocks, the walls are built almost exclusively of unworked stones, in some sections laid neatly in regular courses (Fig. 243), in other sections thrown in almost helter-skelter. In general the wall does not go down to the bottom of the channel but is based on *stereo* well above the floor. In the section just northeast of the Palace Workshop, where the aqueduct is bordered on each side by a wall, a terracotta larnax was inserted in its course.[6] Both ends of the tub were broken away. The wall on the southeast continued through the larnax (Fig. 247); on the northwest the cover slabs were supported by the edge of the tub. The bottom of the vessel is slightly lower than the adjacent *stereo* at each end, and the tub may have served as a settling basin. Directly beside it toward the northwest is a second tub of the same kind (Fig. 244) which is now badly cracked but originally was presumably intact. It is set at a level somewhat higher than that of the other in the line of the channel. No evidence has survived to indicate that the second tub was filled by a pipe or channel leading into it from the aqueduct. Such a channel may have existed at a higher level or the tub may have been filled by dipping water out of the channel. It served possibly as a basin from which water could be drawn, or as a drinking trough for animals.

Where the channel is bordered by a single wall the latter is always on the northwestern side. In some places the trench was narrow and little space was left between the wall and the *stereo* behind it. But in other places the bedding trench was made unnecessarily wide and had to be refilled with earth outside the wall. Towards the northeast, beyond the end of the section that is lined on both sides by a wall, no cover slabs were found. Perhaps they had lain so near the surface that all had been removed by the cultivators or by seekers of building material.

Evidence of changes of level appear here and there. About 1.30 m. to the northeast of the tub a branch, cut in *stereo*, leads out to the southeast at the level of the main channel (Fig. 244). Some 0.60 m. northeastward another channel, lined with stones, leads off in the same southeasterly direction, but 0.43 m. higher than the one cut in *stereo*.

Approximately 3.50 m. before the aqueduct reaches the distribution center remains of two channels lined with stones (Fig. 248) appear, leading off to the northwest

[6] Dimensions of first larnax: preserved length 1.20 m., length at bottom inside 0.73 m., width at top 0.70 m., width at bottom inside 0.32 m., depth 0.49 m. to 0.53 m. being higher at the southwest end. It seems to have the same width throughout its length instead of being narrower in the middle. Northwesterly larnax: length 1.56 m., length inside at bottom 0.62 m., width 0.50 m. to 0.60 m., width inside at bottom 0.32 m., depth 0.46 m.; handle at each end. The rims of the tubs are close together, separated by only 0.07 m., and the two are nearly parallel.

(p. 338), these also lying at a much higher level than the section hewn out in hardpan.

The aqueduct has been excavated throughout its entire length. Nowhere has the slightest trace of a pipe of terracotta or any other material been found. The water therefore must originally have run on the floor of the ditch. The channel was probably filled in later as the water level rose, for the branches at a high level to one side or the other, which have been mentioned, all clearly belong to a very late phase. The lack of any remnants of a closed pipe supports the conjecture that the aqueduct was carried across the hollow to the northeast of the hill by a bridge.

Although no fragments of piping were recovered, the earth filling the ditch contained vast quantities of potsherds from top to bottom of the fill. It proved to be a mixed lot representing several periods from Middle Helladic down to Late Helladic III B. The bulk of the material is assignable to the latter phase, and it was observed that countless plain kylix stems, indistinguishable from the types found in the palace, had penetrated to the very bottom of the channel. No proper stratification could be observed. The earth must presumably have washed in gradually to fill the channel after the palace had been destroyed and abandoned.

The most exciting object recovered, however, was a fragment of a tablet inscribed in the Linear B script (No. 1443). It was found beside the section of the wall that was built of large poros blocks, 0.30 m. below ground level and some 0.50 m. from the face of the wall, at a distance of 1.90 m. from the southwestern end of the section. The tablet had been turned red by the fire that hardened it. How the fragment reached this particular spot, almost 50 m. distant from the Palace Workshop, the nearest place in which a deposit of tablets came to light, is a matter of conjecture. If it was baked hard in the same fire that destroyed the palace and preserved the tablets found in the Archives Rooms and elsewhere in the building, how did it manage to wander so far afield? Was there some other collection of archives stored near the northeastern end of the acropolis? We have found no trace of it. Could this tablet, on the other hand, have been baked in some earlier fire before the final phase of the palace? These questions cannot be answered satisfactorily. Since it is a matter of only a single small fragment, no decisive conclusion is possible. One little piece might easily have been picked up by someone at any time in the many years since the fire and dropped casually elsewhere on the hill. Or it might have been carried along in successive stages of plowing. But exactly how it penetrated 0.30 m. into the ground at this point must remain a subject for speculation. The tablet, in any event, deals with *Kouroi* and belongs to a class of documents well represented in the palace.

Altogether the aqueduct with its wiggly line and its many sections of carelessly built walls is not of an architectural quality in keeping with the style of the palace itself in its best period. But very little evidence has survived in other palaces—Mycenae, Tiryns, and Thebes—to indicate that hydraulic engineering had been highly developed. In any event this aqueduct, despite some shortcomings, did somehow bring running water to the very walls of the palace.

OBJECTS FOUND

BRONZE

Nail and several nondescript bits.

STONE

Steatite buttons: one conoid (Fig. 322 No. 6), dark blue, beveled edge, h. 0.012 m., d. 0.021 m.; the other, shanked (Fig. 322 No. 7), light greenish, h. 0.009 m., d. 0.019 m.

Obsidian: arrowhead, barbed type (Fig. 322 No. 8), l. 0.017 m., w. 0.01 m.

Flint: 5 blades with serrated edge (Fig. 322 Nos. 9-13); flakes and chips.

TERRACOTTA

Figurines: fragment of female, disk-shaped (Fig. 322 No. 4); full breasts and hair down the back indicated plastically, decorated with wavy slanting lines, w. 0.045 m., h. pres. 0.029 m.

Female head and shoulders, very long neck (Fig. 322 No. 3); bird-faced with plastic dots for eyes, h. pres. 0.035 m., w. neck 0.008 m., w. head 0.016 m.

Animal: rear end of body with thick long tail hanging down (Fig. 322 No. 2), legs broken off, traces of longitudinal bands in red paint on back, l. pres. 0.045 m., d. of body 0.038 m.

Animal: rear part of body, end of tail and legs broken off (Fig. 322 No. 1), traces of red stripes around body, l. pres. 0.052 m., d. 0.017 m.

Four loomweights: red clay, flattened pear-shaped with perforation through narrow end; different sizes.

Fragment of crucible to which a bit of bronze adheres.

CLAY

Tablet: No. 1443 (*AJA* 67 [1963], 161, 162, pl. 32).

POTTERY

Cup (Shape 12, p. 360)

No. 1113: traces of painted decoration.

The sherds collected from the aqueduct were mostly small nondescript pieces from pots of the palace period, kylikes being the predominant shape. Some earlier sherds were also noted including Mattpainted and Minyan Ware and some pieces of LH II and LH III A.

AREA 103

To the northwest of the water distributing center (101) and the cisterns (102) is a relatively large area (103 on Key Plan) with a maximum length of 26 m. and a width of 24 m. extending to the Wine Magazine and to the edge of the hill northeast of it and on the southwest to the northeast exterior wall of the palace. Although no large buildings appear to have stood here, several patches of stucco pavement or floor have been exposed as well as many stone walls and foundations of separate small or connected rambling structures which clearly belong to two or more phases (Fig. 249). At the northwestern extremity of Area 103 several such walls of houses that had stucco floors were destroyed or covered over when the Wine Magazine itself was erected. Some walls of this kind to the northeast of the Wine Magazine seem to be separated by a narrow lane or passage (Fig. 250). Too little has survived of these houses antedating the Wine Magazine to give an adequate idea of the general plan and character of the prepalatial settlement in this quarter or to fix its date exactly. It is likely that these houses represent the occupation of the acropolis in Mycenaean III A, or at any rate in a stage before the palace had been built. Perhaps they were razed in the general leveling operations that were carried out in preparation for the construction of the palace in Mycenaean III B. A few of these houses were evidently of no little consequence, as shown by their good stucco floors and the presence of stone bases for columns. No proper undisturbed floor deposits were found. In the northeastern part of the area the level of the modern ground lay only 0.20 m. to 0.40 m. above the floors and recent cultivation had no doubt completed the destruction of anything that had escaped at the time of the razing.

Farther to the southeast of the Wine Magazine are remains of a building that was certainly occupied at the time of the destruction. Its walls are somewhat heterogeneous and some of them may have survived from an earlier phase, but in the final stage we seem to have a barrack-like building, 15.35 m. long from northwest to southeast and 3.10 m. to 3.87 m. wide. This building was divided into four rooms of varying sizes (Figs. 251, 427). A section of the northeast wall, 0.84 m. thick and 8 m. long, and part of a crosswall, 0.55 m. thick, running southwestward, both founded on *stereo*, are more substantially built than the other walls and are surely survivals from an earlier period. Another phase is possibly represented by the southwestern wall, 0.60 m. thick and preserved to a length of 8.37 m. In some places it stands to a height of three courses, though it is laid on a fill of burned earth and does not go down to *stereo*. The northeastern and southwestern walls in any event seem to have been combined into one building by the erection of two or three crosswalls, 0.50 m. to 0.55 m. thick, and apparently an addition toward the northwest, each represented by much dilapidated and incomplete sections, consisting of a single course, also laid on burned earth.

Almost nothing remains of the northwestern room (a on the plan, Fig. 427) except a fragment of the southwestern wall, 1.94 m. long, 0.60 m. thick, and one stone of the northwestern end, which permits an estimate of the length of the room as 3.30 m. from northwest to southeast (Fig. 252). No trace of the floor deposit or floor has survived.

In the next room (b), which has an average width of 2.60 m. from northwest to southeast, a habitation' level of black earth was encountered just below the surface soil. On it lay fragments of a "griddle" in coarse ware and some remains of a large jar. This jar and the bottom part of an amphora associated with it are made in a peculiar brick-red fabric like that well represented in the next room (c). A crude biconical whorl and several pieces of flint were also found in this deposit.

In Room c, which is 5.08 m. long from northwest to southeast, many groups of sherds were spread out on grayish-brown earth at the same general level as that noted in Room b. Numerous pots had here been badly shattered, presumably because they lay so near the surface and also had been disturbed by the roots of an olive tree. They were all made in the same brick red ware as that mentioned above. Several vessels were well enough preserved so that—though they could not be restored—their shapes could be recognized. Among them were at least four wide-mouthed jars, a jar of somewhat different shape, a large stirrup-vase, and a narrow-necked jug. All these vessels and those found in Room b are certainly Mycenaean. They lay underneath a deposit of disintegrated red brick in the destruction layer and must have been in use at the time of the burning of the palace. The same stratum yielded fragments of a female figurine of the familiar crescent type.

Chamber d with a slight change in orientation measures approximately 2.83 m. from northwest to southeast where it is bordered by the northwest wall of Area 101 (p. 326 and Fig. 251). Its southwestern and northwestern walls have the same character as the southwestern wall of Rooms b and c. Room d was 3.40 m. long from southwest to northeast, but the northeastern wall is missing except for a remnant which is preserved to a length of only 1.30 m. No proper floor was found except for a small patch of crumbling stucco (14.25 m. above datum) which might represent the final phase. Near the west corner of the room a mass of flattened spherical beads made of glass paste came to light. They were packed closely together in a heap ca. 0.13 m. deep. To the north of them was found the side of a pot in the reddish ware we have seen elsewhere in this building. The beads which had been disturbed and scattered by intrusive olive roots may have been stored in the vessel. Whether this hoard marked a floor level of an earlier phase or had been hidden in the pot beneath the floor of the last period—which is more likely—could not be certainly determined.

The character and purpose of this long building with its four chambers can only be conjectured. Perhaps we may see here the quarters of servants or slaves who worked in and about the palace. The presence of the pots in any event implies that people lived here. It is of interest to note further that two channels branching off from the aqueduct to the northeast of the distribution center in Area 101 run northwestward and one of them turns into Room c (Fig. 248). The other apparently continued on to one of the adjacent rooms. The channels are made of rough unworked flattish stones set on edge. No cover slabs were found in place; if any had existed they must have been carried away by the plow for they would have reached the level of the modern ground. The position of the water channels might imply that the barrack rooms were entered through doorways on the northeastern side of the building.

Southwest of the building with its four chambers is a group of more than a dozen poros blocks and fragments lying in disorder as if they had fallen or been thrown out

(Fig. 251). Most of them are concentrated in a length of ca. 4 m. but one or two blocks to the northwest and southeast extend the length of the fall to ca. 10 m. The blocks appeared just below the surface of the ground and they lay in a deposit of dissolved crude brick and burned debris, containing many fragments of plaster and flooring, exactly like that of the destruction level. The blocks rest on a stratum of gray earth sloping toward the southwest (Fig. 252). This layer of earth in the area opposite Room b and the adjoining end of Room c, where three of the blocks have fallen, lies on a good stucco pavement also inclined in the same direction. Toward the southeast and southwest the stucco is broken away in an irregular line but some patches found much farther to the southeast indicate that the pavement may have had a much greater extent on this side. To the northwest it also continued to the walls of one of the houses over which the Wine Magazine was superposed.

The blocks are in most respects similar, if not identical, with the squared blocks that still remain *in situ* in the northeast wall of the Main Building. Several of them have a height of 0.44 m. exactly that of the second course in the palace wall. Lengths of 0.75 m. and 0.95 m. are represented which also occur in the central building. Many of the blocks likewise have their ends cut obliquely to make V-shaped joints with their neighbors. One at least has dowel holes of the usual kind. In their present position, ca. 9 m. to 11 m. distant from the exterior wall, it is difficult to imagine how they could have fallen so far. No wall of sufficient breadth and strength to hold up so massive a superstructure has been found in the area near the blocks. They can surely not have fallen from the southwest wall of the barracks, which is much too flimsy to sustain their weight.

In the southwestern part of Area 103, some 6.50 m. from the northeast wall of the palace, a terracotta larnax or tub came to light (Fig. 110) oriented approximately from southeast to northwest, but not exactly parallel to the outside of the Main Building. It had been sunk to its rim into a deep fill of *stereo*-like greenish earth, containing many sherds, bits of plaster, small stones, pebbles, etc., and even fragments of inscribed tablets. The fill sloped sharply upward toward the northeast and probably represents the grading activities preliminary to the building of the palace and presumably formed the ground level of Mycenaean III B. The tub itself was full of red brick, some in a disintegrated state, some in hard chunks. This deposit rose in the whole area around and above the tub some 0.60 m., with its top lying only 0.10 m. to 0.20 m. below the surface of the ground. The burned debris must be part of the wreckage from the upper story of the palace the walls of which were certainly built mainly of crude brick.

The larnax, though cracked in a good many places, is remarkably well preserved, lacking only part of the rim at its northwestern end. It is 1.50 m. long, 0.625 m.

to 0.65 m. wide, narrowing slightly at the middle, and has an interior depth of 0.45 m. The flat bottom inside is 0.75 m. long and 0.42 m. wide. The rim, flattened on top, varies from 0.045 m. to 0.05 m. in width. A handle is preserved at each end; none appeared on either side. The interior is reddish in color and bears no painted decoration. The larnax is one of several such vessels which had been set out more or less in the open (e.g., p. 334). It is likely that it served as a watering trough or basin to which water was somehow brought from the main aqueduct. No trace of any conduit leading to this place now survives, but water may have come through one of the channels mentioned above on the northeastern side of the barracks. No provision for the disposal of an overflow has been found. In the present state of the remains on this side of the Main Building it is very difficult to envisage how Area 103 looked and what purpose it served in the time of the palace.

O B J E C T S F O U N D

STONE

Seal, NM. 8534 = *CMMS* 301 (Fig. 311 No. 26): blackish steatite, four-sided prism with almond-shaped, slightly convex facets, surface badly worn on all sides. Patterns: wedge-shaped dots, dashes, chevrons on all faces. Found in Room d.

Flint: many flakes and chunks.

PASTE

Flattened spherical beads (Fig. 318).

TERRACOTTA

Female figurine (Fig. 322 No. 5), crescent-type (head, ends of arms and base missing): modeled breasts, hollow cylindrical stem; h. pres. 0.052 m., w. across arms pres. 0.036 m., d. bottom 0.018 m.; remnants of painted red stripes decorating the whole figurine. Found in Room c.

Crude, slightly baked biconical whorl, h. 0.02 m., d. 0.03 m. Found in Room b.

CLAY

Tablets: No. 1338 (*AJA* 62 [1958], 185, 186, pl. 49), No. 1355 (*AJA* 63 [1959], 133, 135, 136, pls. 30, 31). Found near larnax.

POTTERY

The pottery found on the floors in these rooms was of a peculiar light brick-red fabric.

Professor Frederick Matson who examined the material noted that the pots were underfired. The edges of the fragments were soft and crumbly, and reconstruction was not possible. The pots were thrown on the wheel and the surface was coated with red wash which has been almost entirely worn away. Some examples were decorated with red bands which have also been largely obliterated. The exact shapes cannot be certainly determined but the types generally recognized are narrow-necked jugs with handles coming off the rim, narrow-necked jars with two horizontal loop-handles (Shape 49) and painted bands, kraters with two vertical handles (Shape 59), stirrup-vases (Shape 65), and griddles. Fragments of the latter have been found in several areas on the site but no complete example (Fig. 348 Nos. 11-12). Evidently circular or oval, the griddle had a thick flat bottom with a rounded slightly raised edge through part of its circumference. On some fragments the edge rises in a sharp curving slope to form a high almost vertical scalloped shield. To the outside of it is attached a thick horizontal loop-handle presumably matching a second handle and shield on the opposite side. The most striking feature of the griddle, however, is the inner surface of the bottom which bears hundreds of small shallow punched holes. These punch marks are highly irregular, some go nearly half through the thickness of the bottom, others are shallower. What the purpose of this utensil was is unknown to us though it suggests the baking of waffles or pancakes. No close parallels from other sites have come to our attention.

In addition to the foregoing a good many scattered sherds were recovered of the usual types encountered everywhere on the hill.

WINE MAGAZINE

THE northwesterly side of Area 103 was for the most part bordered by a large two-roomed building (104-105 on Key Plan) which, from the presence of many capacious pithoi (Figs. 253, 428), was conjecturally identified as a Wine Magazine. This structure (18.48 m. long from west-southwest to east-northeast and 8.45 m. wide) was laid out parallel to the steep northwestern edge of the acropolis and it consequently diverges in orientation from the other principal buildings in the palace complex. The southwestern, northwestern, and northeastern walls are all ca. 1 m. thick while the southeastern has a thickness of only ca. 0.80 m., though the actual foundations are 0.06 m. to 0.08 m. broader. All the walls are built of relatively small unworked stones with the frequent use of flattish pieces of limestone, laid for the most part in fairly regular courses in each face of the wall, the core being filled with rubble. The northwestern wall stands to a height of 0.60 m. above the floor of the magazine. Its top is fairly even and it may be that what has survived formed the stone socle for the superstructure of crude brick. The northeastern and southeastern walls are less well preserved, the northeastern standing to a height of 0.50 m. above the floor.

The southeastern wall has suffered more, especially behind the row of pithoi near the southwestern end of Room 105 (Fig. 250). As preserved, its height is far from uniform, ranging from one to three or more courses. This wall, like those on the northeast and northwest, has tilted over appreciably toward the interior of the room. The southwestern wall now rises only about 0.20 m. above the floor. In this wall three or four chases for wooden beams may be seen and in the northeastern wall at the opposite end of the building traces of at least two are visible. The northwestern lateral wall also offers similar evidence, having at least five chases; while scanty indications in the southeastern wall show that this too was built in the same manner.

These exterior walls have fairly substantial foundations extending below the floor, 0.50 m. to 0.55 m. on the northeast and southeast, 0.75 m. on the southwest, and at least 0.65 m. at the one place tested on the northwest. In the present state of the walls no sign of plaster of any kind can be recognized *in situ* either on the inside or on the outside, but it is likely that the crude brick superstructure had a coat of mud plaster.

ROOM 104

The only entrance into the building was on the northwestern side near the western corner, where a door opening is clearly indicated, ca. 1.50 m. wide (Fig. 253).[1]

[1] Position of doorway: 0.70 m. from west corner of vestibule, 1 m. from north corner.

It led into a small vestibule (104) at the southwestern end of the magazine (Fig. 428). No stone threshold and no bases for jambs remain in place, but the fairly level stone foundation that filled the whole width of the opening might well have supported substantial blocks of that kind. The top of the foundation lies 0.15 m. below the level of the stucco floor inside the vestibule and a threshold and bases for jambs could easily have been accommodated in this space, perhaps rising a few centimeters above the floor. Remains of carbonized wood and black earth, noted on the southwestern side of the doorway, indicate burning, presumably that of the door casing. On the other side of the opening in burned earth 14 seal impressions and fragments came to light, all baked hard by fire.

The vestibule (104) extending across the width of the building is 6.60 m. long from northwest to southeast and 3.17 m. wide. On its northeastern side it is bounded by a wall (0.80 m. thick) which separates it from the main storeroom of the magazine (Fig. 254). The latter could be entered through a doorway near the middle of the wall, though not accurately centered.[2] The opening is ca. 1.50 m. wide; precise measurements are not possible, since the wall on the southeastern side has been broken away.

The vestibule once had a stucco floor which has survived only in the southeastern part of the room. Toward the northwest no stucco remains, but here and there are patches of a clay floor or perhaps the bedding for the missing stucco. Apart from the sealings already mentioned nothing of any consequence was found in the vestibule.

OBJECTS FOUND

CLAY

Sealings

NM. 8500 = *CMMS* 337, less than half preserved, surface worn: animal going right, long neck turned back.

NM. 8501 = *CMMS* 338, less than one third preserved: bent hindleg and foreleg of an animal going to right.

NM. 8502 = *CMMS* 339, less than half preserved: animal going left; head not preserved.

NM. 8503 = *CMMS* 340 (Fig. 303 No. 8), less than half preserved: legs of two human figures moving to left; traces of an animal at left facing right.

NM. 8504 = *CMMS* 341 (Fig. 303 No. 9), more than half missing: head, wings, and front paw of griffin preserved.

NM. 8506 = *CMMS* 343 (Fig. 303 No. 10), almost complete: animal going left with foliage above and below.

NM. 8507 = *CMMS* 344 (Fig. 303 No. 11), almost complete: figure wearing flounced skirt and puffed sleeves (?); a dolphin on each side with head down.

NM. 8521 = *CMMS* 356, two impressions (Fig. 303 Nos. 12, 13); man moving to right with upper part of body in frontal view between two long-legged animals facing him; row of dots indicating ground.

NM. 8522 = *CMMS* 357, very poor impression: animal moving left with head turned back.

NM. 8538 = *CMMS* 360 (Fig. 303 No. 14), one half preserved, surface worn: two animals, one below to right, one above to left, upside down.

2 Distance from doorway to northwest wall 2.29 m., to southeast wall 2.64 m.

Three other fragments on which the impression is unintelligible.

Jar (possibly Shape 49, p. 385)
Fragment comprising part of side with two painted bands below horizontal handle.
The scattered sherds in the plowed earth over the Vestibule have been included with those from Room 105 (p. 349).

From the deposit beneath the surface soil, shapes identified: pithos, tripod-vessel, lid; in finer ware, kylix (118 stems), cup and bowl, etc. (77 flat bases), jug, bowl with pinched-out handles, dipper.

ROOM 105

The doorway leading into the storeroom itself is marked on each side by calcined stone and fused *migma*: the opening surely had wooden jambs and lintel which provided fuel for the fire. The stucco floor breaks off in the vestibule and does not continue through the door opening. No sign of threshold nor of jamb blocks appeared and they probably never existed.

The storeroom occupying the full width of the building (Fig. 428), 6.60 m., is 12.53 m. long from southwest to northeast. The walls have been described and need no further comment. The room was found filled under the surface soil with a deep deposit of reddish clay, clearly the remains of disintegrated crude brick. It varied from 0.30 m. to 0.50 m. in depth and contained numerous stones, some black patches, and many fragments of plaster. It was difficult in some places to differentiate between the clay fill and the floor but the latter was generally more yellowish in color. Moreover it was marked by not a few nests of pots and potsherds (Fig. 254). Considerable help toward distinguishing the floor from the fill was also provided by the presence of three rows of large pithoi set in hollows sunk into the floor.

On each side to the right and left of the doorway as one entered, stood two pithoi beside the southwestern wall (Fig. 255). Along the southeastern wall six pithoi were preserved in a fairly good condition while fragments of several others and setting holes accounted for six more. The jars in this row and the two on the same side of the doorway were propped up by thin stones set on edge (Fig. 256) both on the side toward the room and the side toward the wall, enclosing a fill of clay. Down the middle of the room, but not centered in the axis of the doorway or the room, are remains of two further rows of jars (Fig. 254). The one on the southeast contained nine jars, some fairly well preserved, others in fragments. The row to the northwest was made up of eight jars in varying states of preservation and remnants of two others. It is likely that a similar row once stood along the northwestern wall, but only a few fragments were left here and there to mark the line.

What has survived shows that altogether at least 35 pithoi stood in the magazine on the day of the fire. As preserved, they vary a good deal in dimensions and shape, ranging from 0.55 m. to 1.15 m. in height and 0.545 m. to 0.85 m. in diameter. Since they must have risen near enough to the surface of the ground to be caught by the plow in cultivation, all had lost their rims and the greater part of their necks, though some fragments were found inside and round about the jars. The heights given, therefore, represent what has actually survived in place and the original dimension can only be estimated. All the jars are badly cracked and many were broken and had collapsed. Some 18 or 19, however, still retain their shapes so far as the body is concerned. All were filled with earth and reddish clay from dissolved crude brick, containing sherds and fragments of painted plaster. Some of these fragments lay at the bottom, some higher up, some at the top as well as round about the pithoi. Each jar that was well enough preserved in its lower part to hold what was in it contained a deposit of black matter. Samples were kept for analysis.

Only two pots (neither of them restorable) were found in the pithoi: a high-handled dipper in the jar immediately to the left as one entered and a sizable unpainted stirrup-vase in the second pithos standing in the southeastern middle row. A good many other pots were recovered scattered about on or near the floor in other parts of the room. An especial concentration of vessels just inside the doorway (Fig. 256) yielded a huge lid of the basin-like type, a large jug, a "teapot," and part of an amphora. Farther toward the northwestward lay fragments of jars, a kylix, a pan for grilling meat on spits, and another lid. Beside the northwestern wall farther to the northeast were fragments of another grilling pan, and beyond it not very far from the northern corner a kylix and a third lid. Nests of sherds also appeared toward the end of the room not far from the northeastern wall, representing several jars and a kylix. Remains of yet another kylix and another jar were found wedged between the southeastern row of pithoi and the wall of the building.

Here and there about the room and in sifting the earth from it were collected two carnelian beads, two barbed arrowheads of flint or chert, two obsidian blades, two flint saws, 10 shaped and pierced bars of clay, possibly weights which had been baked in the fire.

In the south corner of the room numerous clay sealings came to light. Four lay on the northeast side of the first pithos, on the right as one entered, and one close beside the teapot mentioned above. Two were behind pithoi close to the wall that separates the magazine from the vestibule. Twenty-eight others were clustered behind the first, second, third, and fourth pithoi along the southeastern side of the room, between them and the wall, and spread out over the wall itself. These latter rested on a whitish deposit of lime.

The sealings had no doubt been used in connection with wine, either the wine brought to the magazine or the wine stored in the building. Four of the sealings, in addition to the impression of the gem, bore also on the obverse Ideogram 131 (or a modification of it) which had long ago been identified by Sundwall and generally accepted as meaning wine. In two instances the reverse is also inscribed in Linear B script, apparently guaranteeing the wine as genuine in the one case and possibly flavored with honey in the other. The sealings must, of course, have been used either in labeling the source or the kind or the quality of the wine. Sealings of this kind were no doubt applied to strings which were tied to the lids covering the jars in the magazine, and when the jars were opened for use the sealings were presumably kept and put on a shelf in the southern corner of the storeroom. Alternatively—and perhaps more plausibly—they may have come with the wine skins, which were brought to the magazine, to certify the origin, vintage, flavor, or bouquet. If this explanation is correct the sealings were presumably retained for the administrative record or checking.[3]

The presence of vertical chases in the walls puts this magazine in the same general period with the Southwestern and the Main Buildings, but whether it was actually contemporary or followed somewhat later in the sequence has not been determined. The position of the only entrance on the northwestern side of the Wine Magazine looks somewhat peculiar, since it made communication with the palace roundabout and awkward. In an age when slaves and servants were abundant that consideration might not have carried much weight. It is not impossible that a ramp or a stairway leading up from the lower town ascended the steep bank somewhere in this vicinity, but no actual evidence of it has been observed.

The walls of the magazine, though built of smallish stones, are substantial and were surely meant to support a building made of crude brick. The northwestern wall close to the edge of the hill is appreciably thicker than the southeastern and has deeper foundations, probably to insure the stability of the structure on the side toward the declivity. No signs of interior supports to help hold up the roof have been found. The transverse span of 6.60 m. is rather long, but heavy timbers would certainly be adequate to carry the weight of a flat roof made of clay and earth. No certain remains of stucco floor fallen from above appeared in the course of the excavations. The numerous fragments of painted plaster found at the top of the deposit filling the building, in the deposit, and on the floor led us in a preliminary report to suggest the possibility of an upper story that might have been decorated with wall painting. The material consists mainly, however, of smallish bits such as have been found almost everywhere scattered about the site and apparently contained in the clay from which the crude bricks were made; and they need not be taken as demonstrating that the magazine had an upper floor. Another difficulty is the absence of any trace of a stairway ascending inside the wine storeroom, although stone or wooden steps on the outside might easily have been provided.

[3] For a more detailed account of the possibilities see the discussion by Professor M. Lang, *AJA* 63 (1959), 133-135.

The vast numbers of plain wine cups recovered from the pantries and found in broken pieces strewn over the whole area of the hill have tempted us to imagine that the chief wine steward of the palace was an official of considerable importance who might very conveniently have his quarters above the wine cellar. We have no direct evidence, however, to confirm a conclusion of that kind.

It would be of great interest to know where the wine was kept in some of the other Mycenaean palaces on the Greek mainland, but no installation similar to this one in the Palace of Nestor has yet been reported.

OBJECTS FOUND

BRONZE

Large thin flat piece, slightly bent (Fig. 320 No. 1), l. 0.045 m., max. w. 0.032 m., th. 0.002 m.; two very small scraps.

STONE

Obsidian: Three blades (Fig. 320 Nos. 5-7), l. 0.021 m., w. 0.011 m., th. 0.002 m.; l. 0.032 m., w. 0.01 m., th. 0.002 m.; l. 0.033 m., w. 0.012 m., th. 0.004 m.; flakes, chips.

Flint: blade (Fig. 320 No. 12), l. 0.029 m.; w. 0.021 m., th. 0.003 m.; flakes (e.g., Fig. 320 Nos. 11, 13).

Arrowheads: small brown with inward curving barbs, tip missing (Fig. 320 No. 8), l. pres. 0.015 m., w. 0.01 m., th. 0.003 m.; brownish-gray with spreading, pointed barbs (Fig. 320 No. 9), l. 0.023 m., w. across barbs 0.017 m., th. 0.003 m.

Steatite (?): bead (Fig. 320 No. 10), irregularly oval in shape, large perforation; l. 0.011 m., w. 0.008 m., th. 0.005 m., perforation 0.0035 m. by 0.002 m.; much worn, may have been seal stone.

Carnelian (?): three very small spherical beads (Fig. 320 Nos. 2-4): dark purplish, d. 0.004 m.; light red, veined, much worn, h. 0.006 m., d. 0.007 m., d. perforation 0.001 m. to 0.0025 m.; light red, speckled and veined, about half preserved, h. 0.004 m., d. 0.007 m., d. perforation 0.001 to 0.0025 m.

CLAY

Sealings

NM. 8494 = *CMMS* 332, less than half, bad impression: animal moving to right.

NM. 8495 = *CMMS* 333, less than half: one or two animals, details not recognizable.

NM. 8497 = *CMMS* 334 (Fig. 303 No. 15): animal going left with head turned back.

NM. 8498 = *CMMS* 335, worn: two animals back to back, one inverted, one right side up.

NM. 8499 = *CMMS* 336, from rectangular seal: wild goat to right with head turned back.

NM. 8505 = *CMMS* 342 (Fig. 303 No. 17): bull going right with head turned back; man in foreground about to leap or ending leap over bull.

NM. 8510 = *CMMS* 345: animal going right.

NM. 8511 = *CMMS* 346 (Fig. 303 No. 18): obverse, bucranium above, animal below, couchant to right; reverse, same impression but fainter.

NM. 8512 = *CMMS* 347, surface worn: two animals rubbing noses.

NM. 8513 = *CMMS* 348, surface worn: animal below to left; above appears head of another animal to right.

NM. 8514 = *CMMS* 349 (Fig. 303 No. 20), worn fragment: two goats back to back, one to right, the other to left with head turned back.

NM. 8515 = *CMMS* 350 (Fig. 303 No. 19): animal going right with head down.

NM. 8516 = *CMMS* 351, fragment: unrecognizable scene.

NM. 8517 = *CMMS* 352, half missing, bad impression: two animals, one with long neck to right, the other to left.

NM. 8518 = *CMMS* 353 (Fig. 303 No. 21): long-legged animal to left.

NM. 8519 = *CMMS* 354 (Fig. 303 No. 22), one half: two rows of dots within a frame (?).

NM. 8520 = *CMMS* 355 (Fig. 303 No. 23): *agrimi* prancing right with head turned back; vegetation behind animal.

NM. 8523 = *CMMS* 358, two impressions (e.g., Fig. 303 No. 24): less than half: animal, much contorted, to right with head turned back to the ground; vertical row of dots under animal's belly, possibly trunk of tree.

NM. 8537 = *CMMS* 359 (Fig. 303 No. 25), one half: man running to left pursued by lion (?); head of latter appears above man's back, body broken away.

NM. 8539 = *CMMS* 361, two impressions (Fig. 303 Nos. 16, 26), one of them (No. 26) inscribed (No. 1361, *AJA* 63 [1959], 134, 136, pls. 30, 31): at right, knees of seated goddess in flounced skirt facing left; two women also in flounced skirts approach from left; a thin man behind and between them (?); a smaller woman approaching at extreme left.

NM. 8540 = *CMMS* 362: animal lying to left with head up; above, part of another animal.

NM. 8541 = *CMMS* 363, five impressions (e.g., Fig. 303 Nos. 27-30), three of them inscribed (Nos. 1358-1360, *AJA* 63 [1959], 133-136, pls. 30, 31): stag with branching horns galloping to left; below, a hound running in same direction; tree at extreme left.

NM. 8542 = *CMMS* 364: cow, to right, with calf, to left, nursing.

NM. 8555 = *CMMS* 365, badly damaged: animal standing to right, head turned back.

Sealings not entered in Museum Inventory:
Impression in bad condition: dog running left at bottom; perhaps dog running right (upside down) at top.
Fragment, part of an animal.
Fragment, part of an octopus (?).
Two fragments, illegible; two fragments, only back preserved.

Weights (?): seven rectangular objects and fragments thereof (e.g., Fig. 321 Nos. 1-5):

unbaked clay, with two perforations; irregularly shaped but almost square in section; apparently baked only in the fire that destroyed the palace.

POTTERY

Bowl (Shape 4, p. 356)
No. 859.

Kylix (Shape 27, p. 366)
No. 1088.

Jug (Shape 38, p. 377)
Nos. 858 (Figs. 369, 370); 1087 (Fig. 369), decorated.

Jug (Shape 41, p. 379)
No. 860.

Lid (Shape 77, p. 417)
No. 1089.

Broiling-pan (Shape 79, p. 418)
No. 861 (Figs. 397, 398).

Groups of sherds found on the floor of Room 105 provided parts of 15 additional but unrestorable pots. Shapes as far as identifiable include:

Stirrup-vase: upper part comprising spout, neck, disk, one handle, part of the other. Found in second pithos in center right row.

Amphora: at least three. Rim of one cut out over each handle; traces of painted bands preserved around base of neck, under rim, and top of rim bears dots.

Jar: fragments of at least four, apparently closed vessels, with two horizontal or two horizontal and one vertical handle.

Jug: three, one large with high neck, another small, of coarse clay burned purplish, the third a miniature.

Bowl, angular with pinched-out handles (Shape 4, p. 356)

Dipper (Shape 23, p. 365) : at least two, one from first pithos in center left row.

Kylix (Shape 27, p. 366)

Immense quantity of scattered sherds with abundant fragments of pithoi. Shapes recognized, from plowed layer, over Vestibule and Magazine: kylix (173 bases counted), cup and bowl (150 flat bases counted), bowl with pinched-out handles (common), dipper, jug, or jar; in coarse ware, pithos, tripod-vessel, cooking pot, spouted bowl;

with painted decoration, krater-bowl with panel pattern, rhyton with solid coating.

From burned debris filling Room 105, shapes recognized: in coarse ware, in addition to pithos and lid, cooking pot, tripod-vessel, scoop, broiling-pan, brazier; in finer ware, kylix (759 bases counted), cup, bowl, etc. (163 flat bases), bowl and basin with pinched-out handles, dipper, krater-bowl, rhyton, tankard, teapot, stirrup-vase, votive kylix, cup with high handles, jug and jar, basin with horizontal handles. Decorative motives in addition to over-all coating: horizontal wavy bands, reversed N, spiral, arcs, parallel chevrons, dots along rim, stippling, panel.

THE POTTERY

THE classification of the pottery presented in this volume is not a general treatise on Mycenaean ceramics: it is based altogether on the material recovered from the Palace of Nestor, and it deals with the large collection of pots and pans that happened to be standing on the wooden shelves in many pantries or were left scattered about on tables or floors in numerous rooms on the day the entire complex of buildings was demolished in a devastating fire. All the fittings, furniture, and other contents of perishable nature were consumed by the flames, but the pots, tablets, and sealings made of clay, though often more or less damaged, withstood the ordeal remarkably well, if they did not indeed actually profit from it.

This first discovery of what appears to be virtually the whole stock of ordinary dishes and crockery in a Mycenaean palace is worthy of more than a passing glance. Nothing comparable is known from Mycenae, Tiryns, and Gla, not to mention the Minoan palaces in Crete. Something analogous was encountered by Professor A. D. Keramopoullos at Boeotian Thebes, where he found a mass of several hundred plain kylikes in the House of Kadmos.[1] Further exploration there may yet bring to light a larger stock of pottery. At Englianos upwards of 7,000 vessels of 80 shapes and some variations have been tabulated. Almost all were cracked, broken, or shattered, but distinctive parts, such as the foot of a kylix, the handle of a dipper, or the neck of a jug, permitted the compilation of a tolerably close count of the total numbers and types represented.

All the vases from the pantries appear to be in mint condition, presumably stored on the shelves awaiting their turn to be taken into use. With the exception of a few small jugs, decorated with horizontal bands, and some scanty examples of other forms, bearing painted lines or blobs, these many pots are plain and unadorned, and relatively few have a smoothly polished surface. It is obvious that they could have been no more than the ordinary everyday earthenware utensils required for the needs of the large staff that surely composed the household, retainers, servants and slaves in the palace. The king and his family no doubt had their gold and silver services as well as a collection of specially decorated china, all of which must have been safeguarded in a royal storeroom. The intruders who destroyed the palace evidently looted it first and carried away most of the articles of intrinsic value.

Professor Keramopoullos, believing that each Mycenaean king held a monopoly on commerce and trade in his realm, suggested that this huge stock of pots stored in the Palace of Nestor was made for sale in behalf of the royal exchequer. It seems to me somewhat unlikely that a monarch who possessed the wealth necessary to occupy and maintain a palace so large as this one would have found it profitable to

---

[1] *EphArch* 1909, 71. Keramopoullos collected more than 100 bases which had been recovered and thrown away by an earlier excavator and he found 240 additional kylix bases in the same quarter.

retain exclusive rights to the sale of such common utensils of infinitesimal value.

Evidence observed during the excavations indicates that on the contrary these plain undecorated vessels were used in abundance in the palace itself. Hundreds and thousands of kylix stems were recovered everywhere in a widespread distribution throughout most of the rooms and strewn about the outside of each building. This vast quantity of broken and discarded pottery, representing many of the shapes that occur in the pantries, demonstrates that there must have been a constant heavy demand for replacements to maintain in the various parts of the establishment an adequate supply of household crockery.

Five interconnecting pantries (Key Plan, Rooms 18, 19, 20, 21, and 22), occupied the western angle of the Main Building. They yielded more than ·6,500 pots of many different kinds. A single, fairly large room, No. 60, beside the ramp leading to the Southwestern Building, was found to contain a stock of approximately 800 vessels of various types; and in the Southwestern Building two small chambers, Nos. 67 and 68, were discovered to contain more than 200 jars, tripod-pots, and braziers. When the fire swept through the palace complex and burned away the shelving in the pantries these vessels were precipitated in heaps to the floor below. The evidence observed in the course of the excavations disclosed that—with few exceptions—each heap was normally made up of pots of like shape. We may consequently conclude that this assembly of pottery had been neatly arranged in an orderly series, shape by shape, throughout the storerooms. Large wide-mouthed "milk-bowls" and jars were stacked on the floor, one inside another, in Rooms 60 and 68; shallow bowls and cups were fitted one into another in rouleaux of ten or more on the shelves in Pantries 21 and 22, while small votive cups and miniature amphoras were apparently looped together on strings and suspended from pegs in Room 18. Despite the wreckage caused by the fire, traces of system and order in the arrangement of the pantries are unmistakable.

The five pantries (18 to 22) in the Main Building contained almost exclusively dishes and vases for eating, drinking, and pouring, all made of light yellowish-tan clay (e.g., Figs. 323-325, 328). They were well shaped, thin-walled, adequately fired, and in many instances attractive in appearance. It has been suggested that they were perhaps being held for decoration with painted patterns and a second firing. If that were a procedure customarily followed in the palace, we should expect to find among the discarded fragments strewn in and about the buildings many shattered remnants of such pots that had been properly finished. So far as has been observed during many years of excavation, however, few if any pieces of decorated examples representing the shapes found in the pantries have been recovered, though plain fragments, as mentioned above, occur by the thousands. This is strikingly illustrated if we look at the kylikes, the shallow cups, and the shallow bowls and basins with pinched-out handles. It is probably safe to conclude that the plain undecorated pots were provided for everyday domestic needs.

Pantry 60 offers a strong contrast in comparison with the foregoing group: here, with few exceptions, the vases are dark and smoky-looking. This difference cannot be attributed solely to local effects of the fire that wrecked the palace; it is manifest at the outset that the clay itself is not of the same fine kind as that used for the pots stored in Pantries 18 to 22. It is coarser in texture possibly because of admixture of different tempering matter. In general the pot-shapes from Pantry 60 (Fig. 340) are somewhat more heterogeneous than those found in Pantries 19, 21, and 22: kylikes, four different kinds of cups, basins, and shallow bowls appear along with pouring vessels such as spouted bowls, scoops or ladles, but they are accompanied also by coarser wares for storage and for cooking. Notable are the series of large handmade polished "milk-bowls" and small incense-burners in coarse ware. The utensils and the pots kept in Room 60 must surely have been made for other purposes and for other people than the types that were supplied from the five pantries in the Main Building.

Pantries 67 and 68 in the Southwestern Building present yet another kind of ware, mainly coarse crockery (Figs. 341, 342). Here storage vessels and small cooking pots standing on three legs are most numerous, presumably manufactured for still another class of users, evidently having some connection with cooking. Small braziers for carrying coals from one place to another are commonly represented along with two-handled and one-handled krater-like jars, but two or three flat circular baking-pans, each with two ring-handles, belong to a rarer type.

These many pantries in three separate quarters of the palace give evidence for at least three different pot factories or kilns, which apparently obtained their raw materials from different types of clay and met demands for different purposes. But other establishments must surely have existed in which fine Mycenaean pottery adorned with artistic decoration could be—and certainly was—produced. Western Peloponnesos, indeed, had a long earlier tradition of Mycenaean ceramic art. This is demonstrated by the series of magnificent jars, decorated in the Palace Style, first found by Dörpfeld at Kakovatos, then by Kourouniotis at Tragana, and later by Marinatos at Koukounara and elsewhere, and by the Cincinnati Expedition in a tholos tomb only some 200 m. to the south of the Palace of Nestor. All these pots are of early Mycenaean date (Late Helladic I and II), but the tradition was transmitted to the late Mycenaean Period also, as shown by a considerable group of large pithoid jars which were found in the palace, where they were in use in the final days of the establishment. Their makers copied with success the shapes of the jars created by predecessors many generations earlier and attempted—far less happily—to adapt some of the characteristic designs of the original Palace Style. This late class, which first makes its appearance at Englianos, is represented by a few pithoid jars. All seem to be made of clay containing mica, which is not present in any of the pots found in Pantries 18 to 22, but shows itself conspicuously in the capacious handmade "milk-bowls" from Pantry 60. Micaceous clay, which is not indigenous in Messenia, was evidently regarded as desirable or necessary for crockery vessels of considerable size. The mica, or clay containing it, may have been imported from the Aegean Islands or elsewhere, and mixed with local clay. In any event it is highly unlikely that these many unwieldy storage jars were themselves brought from a distance to Pylos: they betray all the signs of local manufacture.

Indeed, in the entire collection of pottery from the palace only a few pieces stand out as if they might have come from foreign factories, perhaps in Argolis. They comprise three or four small stirrup-vases and four or five pithoid jars of moderate size, all of which bear patterns, admirably executed in fine lines, in a style comparable with the best of the same period at Tiryns or Mycenae. But it is by no means impossible that fine ware of this kind was produced also in workshops at Pylos itself. Attention has been called to the fact that in the last phase of the palace at Englianos the vast majority of the pottery used in the establishment was plain unpainted ware. The contemporary chamber tombs in the neighborhood, however, have yielded abundant decorated pottery, as in other regions of the Mycenaean realm. This evidence indicates that the production of fine wares had not been abandoned. One may perhaps draw the conclusion that for economy or other reasons inexpensive cups, bowls, jugs, and jars were made to serve in the daily life of the palace, while much more elegant and costly vases were placed in the tombs as offerings accompanying the dead. Beautiful vessels created by real artists, moreover, must surely have found their place for decorative purposes in many of the principal apartments occupied by the royal family and its entourage.

The classification of shapes and the descriptive terms that we have adopted are our own, worked out in our study of the material from the palace. References to Furumark's work on Mycenaean pottery are given wherever we judged them applicable; but the Messenian repertory, which has only recently begun to be known, though generally similar to that of Argolis, displays many minor differences and variations, perhaps local peculiarities. Simple flat bottoms seem to be much more usual than the raised and ring bases of eastern Peloponnesos, as recorded by Furumark. But it must not be forgotten that we are dealing at Pylos mainly with the plain pots for daily use and not with choice pieces for tombs or for display.

It has often been pointed out that almost all ancient pots were shaped and finished separately as individual items and not turned out mechanically on an endless assembly line. Some little diversities owed in part to the idiosyncrasies of the particular potters and painters must therefore be expected, and there are consequently no exact duplicates. Other divergencies may have arisen from local customs and preferences. A few shapes or types of vessels, not hitherto known in Argolis, have been noted to

Messenia, such as the "milk-bowls." On the other hand "krater-bowls," also called "deep bowls," which occur in great profusion in Argolis and Corinthia and eastern Greece are extremely scanty in western Peloponnesos: not one pot nor even a fragment of a krater-bowl was found in any of the pantries and among the pottery collected from the floors in other parts of the Palace of Nestor only 12 deep bowls (Fig. 385) and fragments of a score or more have been recognized as compared with hundreds at Tiryns and Mycenae. A difference of this kind, if it is not merely the result of chance, may reflect variant habits in eating and drinking as well as perhaps in diet, in the widespread provinces and regions of the Mycenaean world.

A brief survey of the Mycenaean pottery which has recently been found in considerable quantities in chamber tombs in the neighborhood of Olympia reveals many characteristics similar to or identical with those that are observable in the material from the Palace of Nestor and elsewhere in Messenia. It looks as if a distinctive west Peloponnesian provincial style of late Mycenaean ceramics is beginning to emerge as excavations in that area continue. This school undoubtedly sprang from roots in an earlier period when the elegant Palace Style of decoration flourished.

In our catalogues inventory numbers have been given to all pots which were found intact or have been put together from fragments, or have been restored with plaster (Figs. 323-343). The estimates of the total number of vessels of the various shapes represented in the shattered material that has been found in all parts of the palace are based on a conservative count of distinctive fragments which could be recognized. Our figures are only meant as probable approximations, and when they err it is surely on the side of minimizing rather than exaggeration.

So far as possible, all the shapes that have been differentiated in the following classification are illustrated by sections drawn in profile by Mr. de Jong and Miss Athanasiades, by an elevation of at least one example of each shape made from those drawings, and by photographs.

The large number of pots available in intact or complete state of preservation, and others only slightly filled out with plaster, offered an opportunity to measure the capacities of 778 vessels of numerous different shapes. This work was carried out with great efficiency by Dionysios Androutsakis, our foreman, who used cracked and broken wheat grains as the filling material. All quantities were measured by the metric system in certified containers of 1,000, 500, 200, 100, and 50 grams. Absolute accuracy in the results cannot be claimed, for water could not be poured into the pots. Moreover, no measures for quantities smaller than 50 grams were available, and exact precision could not be attained. The results are nonetheless of interest and can be compared with the units of measurement of capacities recorded in the Linear B script, as pointed out in Professor Lang's analysis.[2]

[2] *AJA* 68 (1964), 99-105.

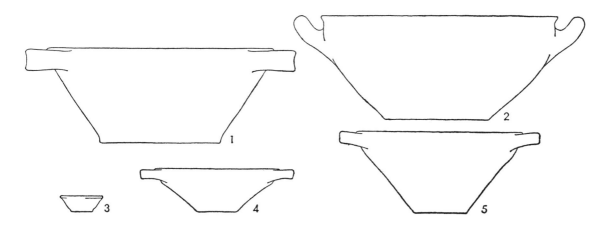

1. BASIN: TWO PINCHED-OUT HORIZONTAL HANDLES (*decorated and plain*) Figs. 349, 350

Large flat bottom or slightly raised base, somewhat concave underneath; flaring side, straight or with double curve; sloping rim; two broad flattened pinched-out handles set horizontally just below lip. Usually plain, one with traces of decoration.

Cf. *MP*, Type 295, p. 53 fig. 15. *BSA* xxv, fig. 33 b, d, from room west of northern portal at Mycenae. *Zygouries*, fig. 150 nos. 522, 123, with raised bases.

Examples: 18 counted, 14 numbered.

Size:	largest	smallest
height	0.138 m.	0.080 m.
diameter	0.400 m.	0.235 m.
diameter base	0.230 m.	0.077 m.
width handles	0.035 m.	0.019 m.
capacity[2]	9.500 liters	1.700 liters

Example with decoration:

No. 812. Surface badly damaged, decoration almost obliterated. Traces of dark red paint on pinkish-buff. Band above base, two below handles; one below, one on, another inside lip; one broad band on upper part of interior and ring around bottom. Stripe on outside of handles, their bases circled. In handle zone apparently a single thick wavy stripe with shallow waves (cf. *MP*, Motive 53: 20, 23; p. 373 fig. 65).

Distribution:

Throne Room: 1 numbered.
Room 18: 14 counted, 11 numbered.
Doorway Rooms 18-20: 1 numbered.
Room 20: 1 counted.
Area 102: 1 numbered.

2. BASIN: TWO HORIZONTAL ROUND LOOP-HANDLES Figs. 349, 350

Large flat bottom; convex side ending in plain or everted rim, flattened on top and sloping inward; two round loop-handles set horizontally on side below rim.

Cf. *MP*, Type 293, p. 75 fig. 21 with four handles instead of two and ring-base instead of flat bottom. *Zygouries*, fig. 151 nos. 496, 509, 518 with four handles.

---

[1] Drawings of the shapes, with numbers corresponding to those in the text, appear in sequence on the following pages.

[2] Of the inventoried examples no two pots have the same capacity: 9.500 liters, 5.700, 5.500, 5.200, 4.500, 4.300, 3.800, 3.700, 3.600, 3.400, 3.200, 2.900, 1.900, 1.700.

POTTERY

Examples: 76 counted and 4 numbered.

Size:	largest	smallest
height	0.139 m.	0.115 m.
diameter	0.325 m.	0.300 m.
diameter		
handles	0.020 m.	0.020 m.

diameter base 0.125 m.   0.119 m.
capacity[1]   6.500 liters   4.600 liters

Distribution:

Court 47: 1 numbered.
Room 60: 75 counted, 3 numbered.

3. BOWL: DIMINUTIVE; HANDLELESS, FLARING   Figs. 349, 350

Flattened bottom; flaring straight or slightly convex side, plain rounded rim, no handles.

No parallels found. Nothing so shallow or small.

Examples: 7 numbered, all from Room 18.

Size:	largest	smallest
height	0.025 m.	0.019 m.

diameter   0.065 m.   0.055 m.
diameter base 0.033 m.   0.030 m.
capacity[2]   0.025 liter   0.020 liter

4. BOWL: SHALLOW, ANGULAR; TWO PINCHED-OUT HORIZONTAL HANDLES   Figs. 349, 350

Flat bottom or, rarely, slightly raised base; side below angle, flaring, straight or slightly concave, above angle concave; everted rounded lip; two relatively broad, flattened, pinched-out handles set horizontally just below rim.

Cf. *MP*, Type 295, p. 53 fig. 15. *MV*, pl. XLIV, Shape 95. *ChT*, p. 183 and pls. XVII no. 29, XXXI no. 51. *Prosymna*, p. 425; figs. 176 no. 329, 206 no. 1184, 239 no. 1062, 296 no. 717, 305 no. 753, 307 no. 749, 353 no. 789, 356 no. 775, 396 no. 86, 425 no. 103, 530 nos. 1040, 1044, 532 no. 1039, 534 no. 1045. *Asine*, fig. 240 and p. 369 nos. 61, 62; p. 385 nos. 38, 39. *NT, Dendra*, p. 43 no. 4.

Examples: 1,382 counted, 103 numbered.

Size:	largest	smallest
height	0.081 m.	0.040 m.
diameter	0.225 m.	0.130 m.
width handles	0.016 m.	0.013 m.
diameter base	0.065 m.	0.040 m.
capacity[3]	1.400 liters	0.200 liter

Distribution:

Room 18: 2 counted.
Doorway Rooms 18-20: 2 counted.

Room 20: 75 counted, 7 numbered.
Room 21: 1,099 counted, 58 numbered.
Room 22: 147 counted, 30 numbered.
Room 43, in tub: 1 numbered.
Room 53, in drain: 1 numbered.
Room 55: 1 numbered.
Room 60: 51 counted, 2 numbered (less angular).
Room 98: 2 numbered.
Room 105: 1 numbered.

5. BOWL: DEEPER, ANGULAR; TWO PINCHED-OUT HORIZONTAL HANDLES   Figs. 349, 350

Like the preceding but more capacious and with angle rounded off.

[1] Of the inventoried examples one holds 6.500 liters, one 5.900, two 4.600.

[2] Six hold 0.025 liter, the other 0.02 liter.

[3] Of the inventoried examples one holds 1.400 liters, one 1.300, one 0.850, three 0.700, four 0.650, fifteen 0.600, one 0.570, eleven 0.550, twenty-five 0.500, eighteen 0.450, twelve 0.400, three 0.350, three 0.300, four 0.250, and one 0.200.

Example: 1 numbered, from Room 20.

Size:	No. 636	diameter rim	0.227 m.
		diameter base	0.06 m.
height	0.107 m.	capacity	1.750 liters

6. Bowl: small, shallow; one high side handle, open trough spout

Figs. 351, 352

Ring- or raised base; convex side curving in to spreading lip; relatively long open horizontal spout set at angle of 90° to a broad flattened handle from rim to side, forming an oval loop that rises obliquely above and away from the rim.[1] In undecorated ware typical of Room 60.

No parallels in plain ware from other sites, except at Prosymna where at least one somewhat similar was found. Decorated examples occur more frequently.

Cf. *MP*, Type 253, p. 48 fig. 13; handle lower in examples from Pylos. *ChT*, pl. LII no. 12 (higher handle, decorated). *Prosymna*, figs. 150 no. 350, 235 no. 476, 255 no. 688, 454 no. 121, 474 no. 866, 521 no. 444 (undecorated), 557 no. 638. *Asine*, p. 416 nos. 47, 48, 49 (fig. 271 nos. 12, 11, 14) are somewhat similar though more delicately shaped and with painted decoration.

Examples: 9 counted, 6 numbered, all from Room 60.		width handle 0.018 m.	0.022 m.
		length spout 0.045 m.	0.041 m.
Size:	largest	smallest	width spout
height over-all	0.100 m.	0.077 m.	at end 0.022 m.	0.022 m.
h. without			diameter base 0.053 m.	0.052 m.
handles	0.075 m.	0.047 m.	capacity[2] 0.550 liter	0.350 liter
diameter	0.173 m.	0.145 m.		

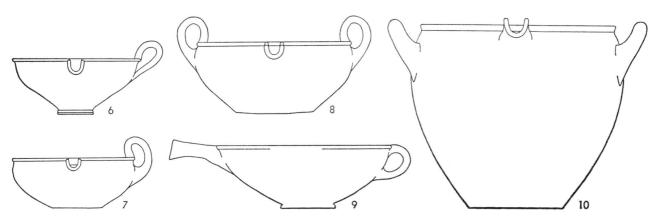

7. Bowl: small, shallow; one high side handle, open trough, bridged spout

Figs. 351, 352

Bottom flat; convex side curving in sharply to rounded lip; relatively long, open horizontal spout set at angle of 90° to a thick flattened grooved handle, extending

---

[1] Vessels of this and the following shape were evidently designed to be used by right-handed persons.

[2] Of the inventoried examples one holds 0.550 liter, three 0.500, two 0.350.

from rim to side, forming an oval loop that rises above the rim and inward;[1] lip bridges the spout.

Much like preceding shape but the bowl is more rounded and the base is flat instead of ringed or raised. Typical ware of Room 60.

Cf. *MP*, Type 253, p. 48 fig. 13. Somewhat similar but examples from Pylos have flat bottom in all instances when spout is bridged. *Prosymna*, figs. 178 no. 324, 184 no. 439, 235 no. 1077 (undecorated), 396 no. 85, 431 no. 168, 501 no. 52, 457 no. 135, 692 no. 135, 693 no. 169, 436 no. 169. *Ergon* 1963, fig. 84, shows a pot found by Professor Marinatos in Tomb 1 at Akona near Koukounara. Thanks to the courtesy of the Ephor, Dr. N. Yalouris, we are permitted to mention an example from Makrysia Chania in the storeroom of the museum in Olympia which is identical with those from our palace in every respect: shape to the last detail, size, clay, finishing of surface, etc.

Examples: 46 counted, 12 numbered, all from Room 60.			width handle	0.019 m.	0.017 m.
			length spout	0.035 m.	0.029 m.
Size:	largest	smallest	width spout		
height over-all	0.092 m.	0.087 m.	at end	0.024 m.	0.020 m.
height of bowl	0.072 m.	0.053 m.	diameter base	0.079 m.	0.057 m.
diameter	0.172 m.	0.152 m.	capacity[2]	0.950 liter	0.600 liter

8. BOWL: TWO HIGH HANDLES, OPEN BRIDGED SPOUT   Figs. 351, 352

Bottom flat; body semi-globular with rounded lip; open bridged spout; two broad flattened but slightly grooved handles rising vertically from rim and curving down to side in an oval loop. Typical ware of Room 60; like the foregoing but a little larger with two handles instead of one.

No parallels known to us from other sites.

Example: 1 numbered, from Room 60.		width handles	0.020 m.
Size:	No. 668	length spout	0.039 m.
height over-all	0.134 m.	width spout at end	0.026 m.
height without handles	0.096 m.	diameter base	0.090 m.
diameter rim	0.205 m.	capacity	1.550 liters

9. BOWL: LARGE, SHALLOW; ONE VERTICAL HANDLE OPPOSITE OPEN SPOUT (*decorated*)
Figs. 351, 352

Flat bottom or low ring base; convexly spreading sides with rounded or sloping lip; long narrow tapering open spout; opposite, flattened handle in low loop from rim to shoulder.

Cf. *MP*, Type 250, p. 48 fig. 13. Thebes, Kolonaki Tomb 25: *Deltion* 3, p. 193 nos. 38-39, fig. 138 nos. 2, 5 similar but smaller (height 0.05 m., diameter 0.19 m.) and much smaller (height 0.025 m., diameter 0.082 m.).

---

[1] See footnote 1, p. 357.
[2] Of the inventoried examples one holds 0.950 liter, three 0.850, two 0.800, two 0.750, three 0.700, one 0.600.

Examples: 5 numbered.

Size:	largest	smallest
height	0.077 m.	0.071 m.
diameter rim	0.290 m.	0.235 m.
width handle	0.022 m.	0.013 m.
length spout	missing	missing
diameter base	0.130 m.	0.068 m.
capacity[1]	2.700 liters	1.500 liters

Examples with decoration:

All five have horizontal bands on or just above base, around middle of body, on or just below rim which sometimes also bears transverse dashes; bands likewise on interior around center and higher up.

Distribution:
Room 18: 3 numbered.
Room 98: 2 numbered (both with spout missing).

10. BOWL: LARGE, DEEP; TWO HORIZONTAL HANDLES, BRIDGED SPOUT ("MILK-BOWL")

Figs. 351, 352

Thickened flattened bottom, high convex side ending in everted lip, flattened on top and sloping inward; two round loop-handles set horizontally high on shoulder and rising slightly above level of rim; large trough spout bridged by rim.

Nothing really comparable known to us from other sites.

Examples: 33 counted, 6 numbered, all from Room 60.

Size:	largest	smallest
height	0.270 m.	0.239 m.
diameter	0.264 m.	0.236 m.
diameter handles	0.022 m.	0.022 m.
diameter base	0.135 m.	0.138 m.
length spout	0.057 m.	0.052 m.
capacity[2]	13.400 liters	9.500 liters

11. CUP: CONICAL; HANDLELESS

Figs. 353, 354

Flat bottom, or slightly raised base; flaring side often slightly convex or with double curve; plain rounded rim. Wheel marks and grooves on side and on bottom distinctive string marks where cut off the wheel. Considerable variation in size and in details of shape.

Cf. *MP*, Type 204, p. 53 fig. 15. *BSA* xxv, fig. 33 c, p. 215, below floors of palace. *ChT*, pls. xxxiv no. 21, LH II; xliii no. 14, LH II; T520 no. 25, LH III; T521 no. 3, LH II-III. *Korakou*, fig. 81, LH II. *Prosymna*, pp. 413-414, 424; LH III—44 examples—shape goes back to LH I. *NT*,

[1] Of the inventoried examples one holds 2.700 liters, one 2.200, one 1.800, one 1.700, one 1.500.

[2] Of the inventoried examples one holds 13.400 liters, two 11.500, one 11.000, one 10.500, and one 9.500.

[359]

Dendra p. 43 nos. 5, 6, fig. 47 nos. 2, 3; p. 93 no. 48, p. 94 no. 49, fig. 104 nos. 3, 4; p. 99 nos. 14, 15, fig. 110 no. 5; p. 104 fig. 113 nos. 1-2. Persson thinks these handleless cups were also used as lamps with floating wicks. So too the shallow bowls found in great numbers in the underground spring-chamber of the "Caravanserai." *PM* II, pp. 123ff.; p. 548, fig. 348. *RT, Dendra*, p. 107 no. 61, fig. 81. *Asine*, p. 370 nos. 67-74, fig. 240, from Chamber Tomb 1:1; p. 385 nos. 40-46 from Tomb 1:2; p. 416 no. 51 from Tomb 1:7.

Examples: 16 numbered.

Size:	largest	smallest
height	0.060 m.	0.035 m.
diameter	0.124 m.	0.100 m.
diameter base	0.060 m.	0.040 m.
capacity[1]	0.300 liter	0.095 liter

Distribution:

Enclosure outside Corridor 52: 1 numbered.
Drain from Room 53: 2 numbered.

Drain 1: 4 numbered.
In jar under Room 55: 5 numbered.
Below floor-level of Room 65: 3 numbered.
Room 98: 1 numbered.
Probably not in general use at the time of the destruction of the palace as all but one of these examples were found in drains and under floors. Many other examples (e.g., Fig. 354 No. 981) came from various areas outside the palace where the deposit is earlier.

12. CUP: SHALLOW; ONE LOW HANDLE ("TEACUP")   Figs. 353, 354

Flat bottom or slightly raised base; flaring, convex or doubly curved side; plain rounded or spreading lip; one low, round or slightly flattened handle, attached on rim and lower part of side, forming an almost horizontal loop. Characteristic wheel marks on side and bottom. Endless variation in size, bottom, profile, rim, shape of loop of handle. One (from the aqueduct) shows remnants of what may be allover paint or stippling.

Cf. *MP*, Type 220, p. 48 fig. 13; Type 222, p. 53 fig. 15. *MV*, pl. XLIV Shape 87 from Mycenae. *ChT*, pl. XXXI no. 50. *Zygouries*, fig. 145 nos. 403, 450. *Prosymna*, figs. 305 no. 751, 521 no. 442, 557 no. 969, 565 no. 606.

Examples: 1,160 counted, 89 numbered.

Size:	largest	smallest
height	0.052 m.	0.032 m.
diameter	0.129 m.	0.104 m.
width handle	0.013 m.	missing
diameter base	0.050 m.	0.052 m.
capacity[2]	0.280 liter	0.130 liter

Distribution:

Room 20: 72 counted, 13 numbered.

Room 21: 1,024 counted, 62 numbered.
Room 22: 55 counted, 5 numbered.
Room 43, Pithos 2: 2 numbered.
Room 55: 3 numbered.
Room 60: 1 numbered.
Room 98: 1 numbered.
Terracotta water channel under Roadway 101: 1 numbered.
Aqueduct: 1 numbered.

13. CUP: ONE LOW HANDLE, RING-BASE (*plastic ornament*)   Figs. 355, 356

Ring-base, convex side and spreading lip; one flattened handle attached on rim and rising slightly above it then curving down in an oval loop to side. Plastic crescent-

[1] Of the inventoried examples one holds 0.300 liter, one 0.280, one 0.220, one 0.210, four 0.200, two 0.190, two 0.180, one 0.170, one 0.160, one 0.115, one 0.095.

[2] Of the inventoried examples one holds 0.280 liter, one 0.260, three 0.255, two 0.250, one 0.245, one 0.240, three 0.230, five 0.220, nine 0.210, four 0.200, seven 0.190, one 0.185, six 0.180, seventeen 0.170, two 0.165, ten 0.160, two 0.155, seven 0.150, two 0.145, two 0.140, three 0.130.

shaped ornament attached to each side closer to the handle than to the transverse axis. Bottom of the inside has a circle in its center marked off by a V-shaped groove. Lip not level and sides pinched-in, intentionally or warped by the fire.

Furumark illustrates nothing comparable. Cf. *MV*, pl. XLIV no. 89 from Ialysos (not really very similar because there are two little horizontal handles 90° from the vertical one and the cup is decorated). *Prosymna*, figs. 521 no. 443, 571 no. 1196 (without plastic decoration and not pinched).

Examples: 4 counted, 3 numbered, all from Room 18.

Size:	No. 241	No. 220	No. 242
height	0.062 m.	0.057 m.	0.056 m.
diameter	0.125 m.	0.143 m.	0.125 m.
width handle	0.012 m.	0.012 m.	0.012 m.
diameter base	0.043 m.	0.042 m.	0.043 m.
capacity	0.400 liter	0.350 liter	0.400 liter

14. CUP: SHALLOW; ONE HIGH LOOP-HANDLE Figs. 355, 356

Large, flattened bottom; side flares to rounded shoulder, then rises almost vertically to spreading lip; one flattened handle rises obliquely from rim and curves down to join side below at greatest diameter.

No parallels found.

Example: 1 numbered, from Room 55.

Size:	No. 717		
height over-all	0.065 m.	diameter rim	0.104 m.
height without handle	0.038 m.	width handle	0.014 m.
		diameter base	0.057 m.
		capacity	0.150 liter

15. CUP: SHALLOW; STRADDLE HANDLE Figs. 355, 356

Flat bottom; low rounded or somewhat angular side with plain or rounded rim; thick round handle attached on the interior and the exterior of the bowl and straddling the rim in a moderately high loop.

Similar straddle handles occur on diminutive kylikes (Shape 26, p. 366) that were found in considerable numbers in many rooms of the palace and rarely in the chamber tombs at Volymidia, but no examples from other Mycenaean sites are yet known to us. A much more ancient handle of the same type was found at Troy in the deposit of Phase IIf (*Troy* I, pp. 228, 306, fig. 379 no. 36.855).

Examples: 83 counted, 12 numbered, all from Room 60.

Size:	largest	smallest
height over-all	0.068 m.	0.068 m.
h. without handle	0.037 m.	0.035 m.
diameter	0.104 m.	0.100 m.
diameter base	0.049 m.	0.050 m.
diameter handle	0.014 m.	0.013 m.
capacity[1]	0.130 liter	0.100 liter

[1] Of the inventoried examples one holds 0.130 liter, four 0.120, three 0.110, four 0.100.

16. CUP: SHALLOW; ONE UPRIGHT ROD-HANDLE Figs. 355, 356

Flattened bottom; side flares widely to rounded shoulder then rises almost vertically to spreading rounded lip; handle, attached to and rising from rim, becomes
round in section and is crowned by a disk.

No ceramic parallel illustrated in *MP* but a handle of this upright type from Berbati (T 1:8)
is mentioned under Form 69: cylindrical cup with raised handle, Type 239 a, p. 625. The pot
can be seen in the Museum at Nauplia. A somewhat similar shape in bronze is relatively well
known (*Prosymna*, fig. 159; *RT, Dendra*, pl. XXXII; *Prehistoric Tombs at Knossos*, p. 39, pl.
LXXXIX; *MonAnt* XIV, p. 94, fig. 55).

Examples: 2 numbered, from Room 60.

Size:	No. 664	No. 665	diameter		
height over-all	0.104 m.	0.098 m.	handle	0.016 m.	0.021 m.
h. without			d. disk on		
handle	0.040 m.	0.038 m.	handle	0.026 m.	0.035 m.
diameter rim	0.112 m.	0.112 m.	capacity	0.180 liter	0.150 liter

17. CUP: BELL-SHAPED; ONE HANDLE, LOW FOOT Figs. 355, 356

From ring-base, side flares in concave curve to sharp angle and then splays out
broadly in concave curve to plain rim; one flattened handle makes wide horizontal
oval loop from rim to middle of side.

Cf. *MP*, Type 231, III B, p. 53 fig. 15. *MV*, pls. XLIV Shapes 99, 100; IX no. 51 XXVII from
Ialysos. *ChT*, pl. XXII no. 8 "bell-shaped cup." *Prosymna*, pp. 430-431; figs. 167 no. 1134 (yellow
Minyan), 206 no. 1172 (decorated), 227 no. 435 (decorated), 235 no. 470 (gray Minyan), 260
no. 625 (flaring, decorated), 274 no. 519 (allover paint), 293 no. 722 (decorated), 478 no. 937
(decorated), 530 no. 1032 (gray Minyan), 281 no. 597 (flaring, yellow Minyan), 571 no. 807
(shallow, yellow Minyan).

Examples: 4 numbered, all from Room 60.

Size:	largest	smallest	diameter base	0.044 m.	0.033 m.
height	0.067 m.	0.057 m.	width		
diameter rim	0.114 m.	0.123 m.	handle	missing	0.011 m.
			capacity[1]	0.230 liter	0.210 liter

18. CUP: SHALLOW; TWO HIGH HANDLES, RAISED BASE (*fine*) Figs. 355, 356

Very small raised base, concave underneath; low convex sides with spreading lip;
two flattened handles rise vertically from rim and descend in close loop to join lower
part of side. In the bottom of the inside a circle made by a V-shaped incision, and
in one instance a countersunk circular area instead.

Cf. *MP*, Type 236, p. 48 fig. 13 which is somewhat similar but has only one handle instead
of two and is deeper. *MV*, pl. XLIV Shape 93. *Prosymna*, figs. 240 no. 1092 (plain), 354 no. 779
(decorated).

[1] Of the inventoried examples one holds 0.230 liter, one 0.220, two 0.210.

Examples: 5 numbered, all from Room 18.

Size:	largest	smallest
height over-all	0.099 m.	0.087 m.
h. without		
handles	0.040 m.	0.045 m.

diameter	0.125 m.	0.105 m.
width handles	0.013 m.	0.013 m.
diameter base	0.030 m.	0.032 m.
capacity[1]	0.220 liter	0.160 liter

19. CUP: TWO HIGH HANDLES, RING-BASE (*decorated and plain*)   Figs. 355, 356

Convex side with spreading lip; two thick flattened handles rise almost vertically from rim and curve down in oval loop to side. Similar to the preceding but deeper and the handles make a wider loop.

Cf. *MV*, pls. XLIV Shape 93, XXXII no. 305 from Mycenae (our handles higher).

Examples: 7 counted, 4 numbered.

Size:	largest	smallest
height over-all	0.113 m.	0.103 m.
h. without		
handles	0.063 m.	0.052 m.
diameter rim	0.135 m.	0.120 m.
width handles	0.013 m.	0.014 m.
diameter base	0.050 m.	0.045 m.
capacity[2]	0.420 liter	0.280 liter

Example with decoration:

No. 246 (Fig. 355). Brown paint on buff. Countersinking in bottom of inside outlined by painted band with trace of another higher up on side. Band along rim, narrow bands around lower part of side and base, and longitudinal stripe on each handle.

Distribution:

Room 18: 4 counted, 1 numbered.
Room 60: 3 numbered.

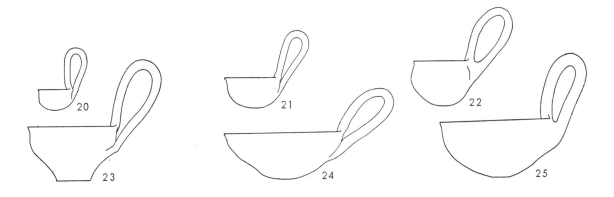

20. DIPPER: DIMINUTIVE; ONE HIGH HANDLE (*decorated and plain*)   Figs. 357, 358

Rounded bottom with no real standing surface; fairly straight, rounded or convex-concave side ending in rounded lip; one high flattened handle forming oval loop from lip to side just below; width of handle varies from one example to another.

Parallels for this size are not known to us.

[1] Of the inventoried examples two hold 0.220 liter, one 0.200, one 0.180, one 0.160.

[2] Of the inventoried examples one holds 0.420 liter, one 0.400, one 0.300, one 0.280.

Examples: 24 counted, 14 numbered.

Size:	largest	smallest
height over-all	0.073 m.	0.063 m.
h. without		
handle	0.033 m.	0.020 m.
diameter rim	0.059 m.	0.043 m.
width handle	0.012 m.	0.010 m.
diameter body	0.053 m.	0.042 m.
capacity[1]	0.037 liter	0.015 liter

Decoration:

Usually decorated in red on pinkish or brown on buff with daubs or strokes on out-turned part of lip and outer surface of handle.

Distribution:

Room 18: 16 counted, 11 numbered.
Doorway Rooms 18-20: 1 numbered.
Room 20: 7 counted, 2 numbered.

21. DIPPER: SMALL, SEMI-GLOBULAR; ONE HIGH HANDLE (*decorated and plain*)

Figs. 357, 358

Like the preceding but larger: slightly flattened bottom or no standing surface; semi-globular with rounded lip; one high flattened handle forming oblique oval loop from lip to side just below; handles vary in width.

Nothing exactly similar in *MP*. Cf. *Prosymna*, figs. 125 no. 235, 534 no. 1046. *Asine*, p. 304 no. 21, ladle, fig. 209 no. 1.

Examples: 37 counted, 14 numbered.

Size:	largest	smallest
height over-all	0.120 m.	0.094 m.
h. without		
handles	0.051 m.	0.033 m.
diameter rim	0.100 m.	0.070 m.
width handle	0.013 m.	0.011 m.
diameter body	0.094 m.	0.067 m.
capacity[2]	0.230 liter	0.070 liter

Decoration:

Some examples (6) have daubs or transverse strokes on lip and outer surface of handle. Paint red on pinkish, brown on buff, red-brown on pinkish-buff.

Distribution:

Room 18: 35 counted, 12 numbered.
Doorway Rooms 18-20: 1 numbered.
Room 98: 1 numbered.

22. DIPPER: SMALL, ROUNDED; ONE HIGH HANDLE

Figs. 357, 358

Deep globular bowl with spreading rim; high, thick, broad, flattened handle rising in wide oblique oval from rim and attached just below. Like the preceding but a little heavier, and more globular.

No exact parallels found.

Example: 1 numbered, from Room 43, found next to step of tub.

Size:	No. 590		
height of bowl	0.057 m.		
height handle			restored
width handle			0.016 m.
diameter rim			0.072 m.
capacity			0.150 liter

[1] Of the inventoried examples one holds 0.037 liter, two 0.035, one 0.030, two 0.027, three 0.025, four 0.020, one 0.015.

[2] Of the inventoried examples one holds 0.230 liter, one 0.165, one 0.150, one 0.140, one 0.135, one 0.120, two 0.100, two 0.090, three 0.080, one 0.070.

23. DIPPER: BROAD HIGH HANDLE, RAISED BASE OR FLAT BOTTOM   Figs. 357, 358

Raised base or flat bottom; moderately deep rounded or angular body with spreading or rounded lip; broad, thick flattened handle rises high from lip and curves down in oval loop to join body at its widest dimensions.

Cf. *MP*, Type 236, pp. 48, 49, figs. 13, 14. None of the shapes Furumark illustrates under this number is like the shape from Pylos, although he classifies under this type some examples that are almost identical with ours. *MV*, pl. XLIV Shape 102. *ChT*, pl. XXXI no. 14. *Zygouries*, Potter's Shop, fig. 144 nos. 87, 88. *Prosymna*, figs. 256 no. 677, 375 no. 905 (fragment); shallower and more bowl-like.

Examples: 426 counted, 39 numbered.

Size:	largest	smallest
height over-all	0.190 m.	0.109 m.
h. without handle	0.095 m.	0.061 m.
diameter rim	0.141 m.	0.107 m.
diameter body	0.136 m.	0.109 m.
width handle	0.023 m.	0.020 m.

diameter base	0.052 m.	0.040 m.
capacity[1]	0.700 liter	0.250 liter

Distribution:

Room 18: 13 counted, 1 numbered.
Room 20: 7 counted, 2 numbered.
Room 21: 7 counted, 1 numbered.
Room 22: 399 counted, 35 numbered.

24. DIPPER: ONE HIGH HANDLE, ROUNDED BOTTOM; PERFORATED BOWL ("STRAINER")   Figs. 357, 358

Shallow spreading bowl with rounded bottom; convex below concave above rounded shoulder; rounded lip; broad, thick flattened handle rises from rim obliquely and curves down to shoulder and below in a narrow loop. A hole (diameter 0.015 m.) cut through center of bottom surrounded by five additional holes (diameter 0.007 m. to 0.01 m.), irregularly spaced, 0.03 m. to 0.04 m. higher up. The five clumsily cut; central hole more regular in shape.

No parallels found.

Example: 1 numbered, from Room 20.

Size:	No. 639
height over-all	0.125 m.

h. without handle	0.056 m.
diameter rim	0.171 m.
width handle	0.027 m.

25. DIPPER: LARGE; ONE HIGH HANDLE, ROUNDED BOTTOM   Figs. 357, 358

Semi-globular bowl with spreading lip; one broad, high, thick, flattened handle rises in an oval loop from rim and curves down to side just below. One example (Fig. 358 No. 194) has neatly cut hole in its bottom widening in diameter from 0.014 m. on inside to 0.021 m. on outside. One (Fig. 357 No. 624) differs from the rest in having its bottom elongated almost to a point.

---

[1] Of the inventoried examples one holds 0.700 liter, one 0.600, four 0.550, two 0.500, one 0.470, seven 0.450, six 0.400, eight 0.370, five 0.350, one 0.330, two 0.300, one 0.250.

Cf. *Zygouries*, fig. 133 no. 312, smaller than ours.

Examples: 9 counted, 5 numbered.

Size:	largest	smallest
height over-all	0.180 m.	0.147 m.
h. without		
handle	0.096 m.	0.074 m.
diameter rim	0.157 m.	0.160 m.

diameter body	0.152 m.	0.146 m.
width handle	0.036 m.	0.035 m.
capacity[1]	1.000 liter	0.750 liter

Distribution:
Room 20: 8 counted, 5 numbered.
Doorway Rooms 18-20: 1 counted.

26. KYLIX: DIMINUTIVE; TWO HIGH STRADDLE HANDLES   Figs. 359, 360

Conical foot, slightly convex on top, flat underneath, always bearing fine marks of separation from wheel; stem generally very thick; bowl conical or slightly convex ending in plain rim; two thick round or flattened handles attached on the inside below the rim rising vertically and descending in a loop to the outside. Shape rather clumsy and awkward for practical use. One may wonder if these cups were not made as votives or possibly as playthings for children.

Shape not mentioned by Furumark and no example from Argolis is known to us. Perhaps a western Peloponnesian specialty, for votives of the same kind have been found by Professor Marinatos in chamber tombs at Volymidia. Similar straddle handles occur on cups of Shape 15 from Room 60 (p. 361).

Examples: 163 counted, 38 numbered.

Size:	largest	smallest
height over-all	0.091 m.	0.072 m.
h. without		
handles	0.059 m.	0.037 m.
diameter rim	0.073 m.	0.045 m.
diameter stem	0.016 m.	0.013 m.
width handles	0.012 m.	0.012 m.
diameter base	0.045 m.	0.033 m.
capacity[2]	0.035 liter	0.009 liter

Distribution:
Throne Room: 3 numbered.
Room 7: 12 counted, 11 numbered.
Doorway Rooms 18-20: 43 counted, 20 numbered.
Room 20: 19 counted, 1 numbered.
Room 24: 2 counted.
Drain 2: 2 numbered.
Room 60: 82 counted, 1 numbered.

27. KYLIX: SMALL, ANGULAR; ONE LOW HANDLE   Figs. 359, 360

Foot conical or rounded, flat or hollowed out underneath, sometimes hollowed into the stem; fairly low relatively thick stem; angular bowl, lower part of side

[1] Of the inventoried examples two hold 1.000 liter, one 0.950, one 0.750; No. 194 with hole in bottom holds 0.700 when hole is stopped up.

[2] Of the inventoried examples one holds 0.035 liter, one 0.031, two 0.025, two 0.022, four 0.020, four 0.018, two 0.017, two 0.016, six 0.015, three 0.014, one 0.013, four 0.012, two 0.010, one 0.009; three are too fragmentary to measure.

conical, upper part above shoulder vertical or concave, ending in spreading or rounded lip; handle flattened, extending in almost horizontal loop from rim to point below angle of body and occasionally rising slightly above lip.

Cf. *MP*, Type 267, p. 61 fig. 17, III B. The shape is common at almost all Mycenaean sites, e.g.: *MV*, pl. XLIV Shape 85; *ChT*, pls. XII no. 15, XVI no. 27, XXXI no. 52, LII nos. 6, 15; *BSA* xxv, p. 149, fig. 33 a, from west lobby of palace at Mycenae; *Zygouries*, Potter's Shop, p. 153, fig. 143 nos. 185, 91, 214; *Prosymna*, p. 432, figs. 125 no. 238, 134 no. 411, 206 nos. 1175, 1185, 235 nos. 471, 1076, 1073; *Asine*, p. 369 nos. 50-60 (fig. 235) from Chamber Tomb I:1; p. 416 nos. 44 (fig. 271 no. 10), 45 from Chamber Tomb I:7; *RT, Dendra*, p. 83 no. 13, figs. 57, 59; *NT, Dendra*, p. 98 nos. 7, 8, fig. 109 nos. 2, 3, from Chamber Tomb No. 11.

Examples: 209 counted, 35 numbered.

Size:	largest	smallest
height	0.110 m.	0.098 m.
diameter	0.116 m.	0.100 m.
width handle	0.013 m.	0.011 m.
diameter base	0.063 m.	0.059 m.
diameter stem	0.025 m.	0.018 m.
h. stem and		
base	0.041 m.	0.037 m.
capacity[1]	0.300 liter	0.150 liter

Distribution:

Room 20: 174 counted, 8 numbered.
Room 21: 12 counted, 4 numbered.
Room 43: from Pithos 1, 7 numbered; from Pithos 2, 7 numbered.
Drain from Room 53: 1 numbered.
Room 55: 2 numbered.
Drain 2: 1 numbered.
Room 60: 3 numbered, each with a rudimentary pour-channel at 90° to left of handle.
Room 98: 1 numbered.
Room 105: 1 numbered.

28. KYLIX: SMALL, SQUAT; TWO VERTICAL HANDLES ON SIDE, LOW STEM Figs. 359, 360

Solid foot flat on bottom, conical or slightly concave on top; thick low stem; semi-globular, bowl tapering toward stem and closing slightly toward spreading lip; two thick rounded handles set vertically on side looping from below rim to below greatest diameter. Height approximately equal to diameter.

Cf. *MP*, Type 269, III A, p. 60 fig. 16. *Prosymna*, fig. 127 no. 259, similar but more elegant. Ialysos, Tomb 5: *BMC* I, 1, pl. X A 860 (stemmed goblet, height 0.145 m. painted all over red-black), A 861 fig. 205 (similar with shorter stem).

Examples: 5 numbered, all from Room 60.

Size:	largest	smallest
height	0.118 m.	0.106 m.
diameter rim	0.115 m.	0.110 m.
diameter		
handles	0.013 m.	0.012 m.
diameter stem	0.024 m.	0.025 m.
diameter base	0.066 m.	0.056 m.
h. stem and		
base	0.040 m.	0.020 m.
capacity[2]	0.450 liter	0.400 liter

[1] Of the inventoried examples five hold 0.300 liter, twenty-two 0.250, one 0.230, four 0.200, one 0.180, two 0.150.

[2] Of the inventoried examples two hold 0.450 liter, one 0.430, two 0.400.

29. KYLIX: TWO LOW FLATTENED LOOP-HANDLES FROM RIM TO UPPER PART OF SIDE

Figs. 359-364

Many variations in size, proportions, and in details of foot, stem, bowl, handles, and rim but shape essentially the same. Foot conical, or flattened and somewhat convex on top with vertical edge, flat or hollowed underneath with a central circular depression extending up to or into stem; stem straight-sided, tapering, varying in height; bowl conical or flaring to rounded shoulder; plain or spreading lip; handles form flattened loops, varying in detail but usually oblique and oval in shape.

Cf. *MP*, Type 274, p. 61 fig. 17 (III B), Type 265, fig. 17 (III A). *ChT*, pl. xxvii no. 11. *Zygouries*, Potter's Shop, figs. 141, 142. *Korakou*, p. 66, figs. 94, 95. *Prosymna*, figs. 124 no. 268, 235 nos. 1066, 1068, 296 no. 720, 425 no. 104 (allover paint).

Examples: 3,278 counted, 90 numbered which have been divided into the following categories on the basis of size and the relative height of the stem. It was not possible to differentiate the various categories as the pots were being removed and counted:

	Numbered
a. small, squat; stem of medium height	2
b. small; high stem	7
c. standard size; mostly high stem	24
d. "outsized" standard	12
e. somewhat larger; low stem	18
f. still larger; stem low or of medium height	8
g. approximately of same capacity as f.; high stem	7
h. very large; stem high or of medium height	6
i. giant size; stem high or of medium height	6
	—
	90

29a. KYLIX: SMALL, SQUAT; STEM OF MEDIUM HEIGHT

Figs. 359, 360

Conical foot, flat or hollowed underneath; thick stem; conical bowl flaring to rounded shoulder, ending in spreading lip; two flattened handles extending in wide loop from lip to just below shoulder. Height slightly less than diameter.

No exact parallel in *MP*. Cf. *ChT*, pl. lvii no. 11. *Asine*, p. 369 no. 47 (fig. 235), p. 414 no. 40 (fig. 271 no. 6). *Prosymna*, figs. 151 no. 351, 173 no. 302, 237 nos. 1080, 1082, 296 no. 715, 305 no. 750, 329 no. 735, 415 no. 60, 433 no. 185, 435 no. 184, 472 no. 963.

Examples: 2 recognized and numbered.

Size:	No. 721	No. 701
height	0.135 m.	0.104 m.
diameter rim	0.140 m.	0.109 m.
width handles	0.014 m.	0.012 m.
diameter base	0.066 m.	0.058 m.
diameter stem	0.025 m.	0.021 m.
h. stem and base	0.052 m.	0.042 m.
capacity	0.550 liter	0.250 liter

Distribution:

Drain from Room 53: 1 numbered.
Room 55: 1 numbered.

29b. KYLIX: SMALL; HIGH STEM

Figs. 361, 362

Foot flat with vertical edge and hollowed underneath; relatively slender stem; conical or slightly rounded bowl; spreading or plain lip; two flattened handles from rim to just below shoulder forming horizontal oval loop.

Cf. *MP*, Type 259, p. 61 fig. 17. *MV*, pl. xliv Shape 84. *Zygouries*, fig. 142 no. 463. *Prosymna*, figs. 296 no. 720, 235 no. 1066.

Examples: 7 numbered.

Size:	largest	smallest
height	0.156 m.	0.133 m.
diameter	0.140 m.	0.135 m.
width handles	0.015 m.	0.016 m.
diameter base	0.070 m.	0.074 m.
diameter stem	0.021 m.	0.020 m.
h. stem and base	0.070 m.	0.080 m.
capacity[1]	0.500 liter	0.300 liter

Distribution:
Room 18: 5 numbered.
Room 19: 1 numbered.
Drain 2: 1 numbered.

29c. KYLIX: "STANDARD" SIZE; MOSTLY HIGH STEM   Figs. 361, 362

So called because the enormous stock of more than 2,853 vessels stored in Room 19 and many from other rooms appear to be of this category. Occasional shorter variations.

Cf. *Asine*, pp. 368f. nos. 43, 44, 45, 47 (fig. 235); pp. 414f. nos. 38, 39 (fig. 271 nos. 4, 5). *NT, Dendra*, pp. 71f. no. 14 (fig. 85 no. 2).

Examples: 24 numbered.

Size:	largest	smallest
height	0.174 m.	0.170 m.
diameter	0.190 m.	0.155 m.
width handles	0.014 m.	0.012 m.
diameter base	0.077 m.	0.078 m.
diameter stem	0.023 m.	0.024 m.
h. stem and base	0.080 m.	0.094 m.
capacity[2]	1.200 liters	0.750 liter

Distribution:
Room 18: 2 numbered.
Room 19: 11 numbered.
Room 20: 2 numbered.
Room 43: 5 numbered.
Room 98: 4 numbered.

29d. KYLIX: "OUTSIZED" STANDARD   Figs. 361, 362

Appreciably larger than foregoing standard size but in general of same shape and with same variations in detail, height of stem, profile of bowl, breadth of handles, etc.

[1] Of the inventoried examples two hold 0.500 liter, two 0.400, one 0.350, one 0.300; one is incomplete. four 1.100, three 1.050, one 1.020, one 1.000, one 0.950, seven 0.900, one 0.850, one 0.820, one 0.800, one 0.750.

[2] Of the inventoried examples three hold 1.200 liters,

Examples: 12 numbered, all from Room 20.

Size:	largest	smallest
height	0.197 m.	0.180 m.
diameter	0.216 m.	0.195 m.
width handles	0.021 m.	0.018 m.

diameter base	0.090 m.	0.085 m.
diameter stem	0.031 m.	0.028 m.
h. stem and base	0.045 m.	0.050 m.
capacity[1]	2.100 liters	1.400 liters

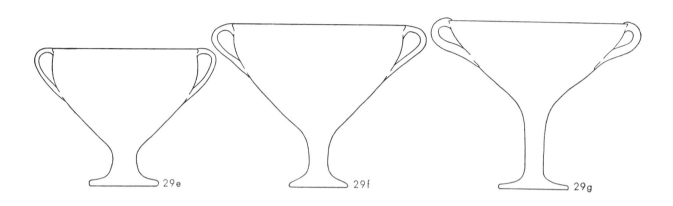

29e   29f   29g

29e. KYLIX: SOMEWHAT LARGER; LOW STEM

Figs. 361, 362

Slightly larger and more capacious than Class d.

Examples: 18 numbered, all from Room 20.

Size:	largest	smallest
height	0.197 m.	0.195 m.
diameter	0.225 m.	0.219 m.
width handles	0.020 m.	0.017 m.

diameter base	0.092 m.	0.086 m.
diameter stem	0.032 m.	0.027 m.
h. stem and base	0.035 m.	0.050 m.
capacity[2]	2.800 liters	1.900 liters

29f. KYLIX: STILL LARGER; STEM LOW OR OF MEDIUM HEIGHT

Figs. 361, 362

Examples: 8 numbered.

Size:	largest	smallest
height	0.203 m.	0.197 m.
diameter	0.240 m.	0.240 m.
width handles	0.024 m.	0.020 m.
diameter base	0.096 m.	0.091 m.
diameter stem	0.033 m.	0.032 m.

h. stem and base	0.040 m.	0.035 m.
capacity[3]	3.500 liters	2.700 liters

Distribution:

Room 18: 2 numbered.
Room 20: 6 numbered.

[1] Of the inventoried examples two hold 2.100 liters, three 2.000, two 1.800, one 1.600, one 1.500, three 1.400.

[2] Of the inventoried examples one holds 2.800 liters, five 2.500, three 2.400, three 2.200, four 2.100, one 1.900, and one is incomplete.

[3] Of the inventoried examples one holds 3.500 liters, one 3.400, two 3.200, two 3.000, one 2.800, one 2.700.

29g. KYLIX: APPROXIMATELY OF SAME CAPACITY AS PRECEDING; HIGH STEM Figs. 363, 364

Examples: 7 numbered.

Size:	largest	smallest
height	0.261 m.	0.223 m.
diameter	0.262 m.	0.240 m.
width handles	0.019 m.	0.015 m.
diameter base	0.110 m.	0.092 m.
diameter stem	0.031 m.	0.028 m.

h. stem and base	0.090 m.	0.095 m.
capacity[1]	3.200 liters	2.200 liters

Distribution:
Room 18: 4 numbered.
Room 20: 3 numbered.

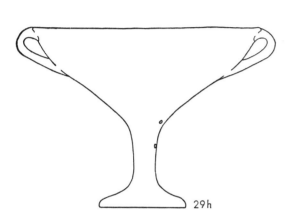

29h

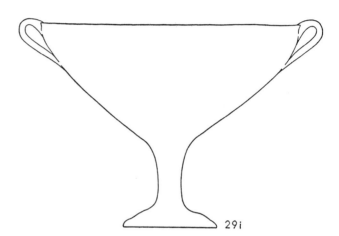

29i

29h. KYLIX: VERY LARGE; STEM HIGH OR OF MEDIUM HEIGHT Figs. 363, 364

Examples: 6 numbered, all from Room 20.

Size:	largest	smallest
height	0.231 m.	0.219 m.
diameter	0.303 m.	0.290 m.
width handles	0.022 m.	0.020 m.

diameter base	0.095 m.	0.101 m.
diameter stem	0.025 m.	0.026 m.
h. stem and base	0.065 m.	0.110 m.
capacity[2]	4.000 liters	2.700 liters

29i. KYLIX: GIANT SIZE; STEM HIGH OR OF MEDIUM HEIGHT Figs. 363, 364

Examples: 6 numbered.

Size:	largest	smallest
height	0.269 m.	0.248 m.
diameter	0.363 m.	0.320 m.
width handles	0.028 m.	0.035 m.
diameter base	0.128 m.	0.100 m.
diameter stem	0.032 m.	0.034 m.

h. base and stem	0.105 m.	0.070 m.
capacity[3]	7.000 liters	4.700 liters

Distribution:
Room 18: 1 numbered.
Room 20: 5 numbered.

[1] Of the inventoried examples one holds 3.200 liters, one 2.600, two 2.500, one 2.400, two 2.200.

[2] Of the inventoried examples one each holds 4.000,

3.800, 3.500, 3.300, 3.000, 2.700 liters.

[3] Of the inventoried examples one holds 7.000 liters, one 5.500, two 5.000, one 4.700; the sixth is incomplete.

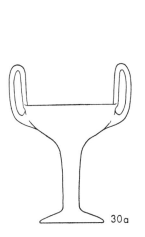 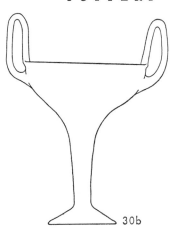 

30a   30b   30c

30. KYLIX: TWO HIGH HANDLES   Figs. 365, 366

Great variations in size, proportions, profile, and details, but shape essentially the same. Foot conical or rounded on top, rarely with vertical edge, concave underneath, sometimes with central circular hole carrying up to or into the stem; stem cylindrical, straight, tapering or slightly bulging; bowl most commonly fairly deep, conical, curving to rounded shoulder then rising to spreading lip; handles round or flattened, rising vertically or obliquely from rim and forming oval loop varying from narrow to wide to or below shoulder.

Cf. *MP*, Type 273 p. 61 fig. 17. *ChT*, pls. XII no. 26, XVI no. 31. *Asine*, p. 368 nos. 39, 40, 42 (fig. 235); p. 414 no. 35 (fig. 271 no. 1). *NT*, *Dendra*, p. 98 nos. 5, 6 (fig. 109 nos. 1, 2). *Prosymna*, figs. 239 no. 1089, 297 no. 712, 353 nos. 786, 787, 788, 532 no. 1013, 533 no. 1020.

Examples: 262 counted, 32 numbered. Divided into following categories depending on size and height of stem: 30a. small with shallow bowl, high stem (fine); 30b. exactly like the preceding but considerably larger; 30c. medium size, deep bowl, stem of medium height.

30a. KYLIX: SMALL; SHALLOW BOWL, HIGH STEM (*fine*)   Figs. 365, 366

Conical foot convex on top, concave underneath; high stem; relatively shallow bowl; two high handles rise vertically from rim and, making a close loop, join the side at greatest diameter.

Examples: 3 numbered, from Room 18.

Size:	No. 240	No. 237	No. 279
height over-all	0.223 m.	0.212 m.	0.199 m.
h. without handles	0.167 m.	0.156 m.	0.147 m.
diameter rim	0.140 m.	0.132 m.	0.115 m.
width handles	0.013 m.	0.014 m.	0.013 m.
diameter stem	0.025 m.	0.022 m.	0.023 m.
diameter base	0.085 m.	0.084 m.	0.082 m.
h. stem and base	0.105 m.	0.095 m.	0.100 m.
capacity	0.400 liter	0.350 liter	0.300 liter

30b. KYLIX: EXACTLY LIKE PRECEDING BUT MORE THAN TWICE AS CAPACIOUS

Figs. 365, 366

Examples: 3 numbered, from Room 18.

Size:	No. 235	No. 236	No. 266
height over-all	0.287 m.	0.280 m.	0.277 m.
h. without handles	0.219 m.	0.217 m.	0.210 m.
diameter rim	0.170 m.	0.167 m.	0.173 m.
width handles	0.020 m.	0.018 m.	0.020 m.
diameter stem	0.026 m.	0.026 m.	0.029 m.
diameter base	0.105 m.	0.094 m.	0.100 m.
h. base and stem	0.135 m.	0.130 m.	0.135 m.
capacity	0.900 liter	0.900 liter	0.900 liter

30c. KYLIX: DEEP CONICAL BOWL, STEM OF MEDIUM HEIGHT

Figs. 365, 366

Foot convex on top, concave underneath, with countersunk hollow of varying depth, sometimes shallow, in some instances deep, extending into stem; bowl conical curving in from rounded shoulder to spreading lip; two thick flattened handles rising obliquely outward and curving down in fairly wide loop to join body at shoulder or below. Sometimes handles rise vertically with narrow loop as in preceding class. Considerable variation in size.

Cf. *MP* Type 277, p. 61 fig. 17. *Prosymna*, figs. 254 no. 686, 305 no. 754, 530 no. 1030.

Examples: 256 counted, 26 numbered.

Size:	largest	smallest
height over-all	0.265 m.	0.220 m.
h. without handles	0.199 m.	0.157 m.
diameter rim	0.158 m.	0.135 m.
width handles	0.016 m.	0.013 m.
diameter stem	0.027 m.	0.024 m.
diameter base	0.085 m.	0.071 m.
height foot	0.069 m.	0.065 m.
capacity[1]	1.050 liters	0.550 liter

Distribution:

Room 18: 2 numbered.
Room 55: 1 numbered.
Room 60: 253 counted, 23 numbered.

[1] On the basis of capacity they fall into several series: the largest holds 1.050 liters, one 0.950, two 0.900; one 0.850, eight 0.800, two 0.780; two 0.750, one 0.700, one 0.650, four 0.600, two 0.550; one is incomplete.

31. KYLIX: ONE HIGH HANDLE, SHALLOW BOWL, HIGH STEM (*fine*) Figs. 365, 366

In shape exactly like the corresponding two-handled variety.

Cf. *Prosymna,* figs. 239 no. 1091, 351 no. 776, similar but larger.

Examples: 2 numbered.			diameter stem 0.024 m.	0.024 m.
Size:	No. 238	No. 269	diameter base 0.083 m.	0.084 m.
height			h. base and	
over-all	0.213 m.	0.217 m.	stem 0.095 m.	0.095 m.
h. without			capacity 0.400 liter	0.350 liter
handles	0.163 m.	0.156 m.	*Distribution*:	
diameter rim	0.139 m.	0.128 m.	Doorway Rooms 18-20: 1 numbered.	
width handle	0.013 m.	0.014 m.	Room 18: 1 numbered.	

32. KYLIX: ONE HIGH HANDLE, DEEP CONICAL BOWL, STEM OF MEDIUM HEIGHT Figs. 365, 366

In shape exactly like the corresponding two-handled variety. Some variation in size.

Cf. *Prosymna,* figs. 294 no. 710, 307 no. 727, 356 no. 791. *Asine,* p. 368 no. 41 (fig. 235), p. 414 nos. 36, 37 (fig. 271 nos. 2, 3).

Examples: 6 numbered, all from Room 60.			width handle 0.012 m.	0.012 m.
Size:	largest	smallest	diameter base 0.073 m.	0.070 m.
height			diameter stem 0.023 m.	0.024 m.
over-all	0.194 m.	0.167 m.	h. base and	
h. without			stem 0.055 m.	0.055 m.
handles	0.145 m.	0.126 m.	capacity[1] 0.500 liter	0.350 liter
diameter rim	0.122 m.	0.117 m.		

33. TANKARD: LARGE; ONE HANDLE (*plain and decorated*) Figs. 365, 366

Flat or slightly convex bottom; deeply concave high side; plain rim; one relatively small flattened handle making smallish oval loop attached vertically to side above or at minimum diameter of body.

Cf. *MP,* Type 226, III A:2 1 — C:1, p. 53 fig. 15. *MV,* pls. XLIV Shape 96, IX no. 56 XXXV from Ialysos, XXI no. 150. Examples from Prosymna are all smaller. Ours have a more strongly concave side with diameter of rim greater than height.

Examples: 3 numbered.				width			
Size:	No. 234	No. 233	No. 336	handle	0.023 m.	0.023 m.	0.023 m.
height	0.160 m.	0.155 m.	0.150 m.	diameter			
diameter				base	0.150 m.	0.138 m.	0.140 m.
rim	0.193 m.	0.177 m.	0.167 m.	capacity	1.950 liters	1.600 liters	1.600 liters
diameter							
waist	0.124 m.	0.120 m.	0.120 m.				

[1] Of the inventoried examples one holds 0.500 liter, two 0.450, two 0.400, one 0.350.

Examples with decoration (Fig. 365):

No. 234. Brown to reddish-brown paint on buff. Bands at irregular intervals around edge of bottom, two below handle, one straddled by handle, one above handle. Also one covering rim and one well down on interior. Handle edged with color and its lower attachment irregularly encircled.

No. 336. Dark brown to reddish-brown paint on buff. Four bands below handle, three above; one covering rim and extending down on interior, two more below on inside. Remnant of transverse line on handle.

Distribution:
Doorway Rooms 18-20: 2 numbered.
Room 20: 1 numbered.

---

34. JUG: SMALL; ONE HANDLE, NARROW NECK (*decorated*)   Figs. 367, 368

Flat or flattened bottom, "depressed ovoid" body; fairly narrow concave splaying neck; plain or rounded lip; one flattened handle coming off rim almost horizontally then curving down abruptly in a wide loop and joining body at its widest diameter (similar to Furumark's perpendicular handle).

Cf. *MP*, Type 112, p. 30 fig. 5 (II B — III A2). *ChT*, pls. XIX no. 2, LI no. 17. *Prosymna*, figs. 261 no. 696 (painted bands), 297 no. 716 (allover paint), 455 no. 124 (patterns), 516 nos. 11 (bands), 19 (allover paint). Argos, Skhinokhori-Lyrkeia, Tomb Γ: *BCH* 17 (1923), p. 208, fig. 18.

Examples: 19 numbered.

Size:	largest	smallest
height	0.099 m.	0.082 m.
diameter rim	0.049 m.	0.043 m.
diameter neck	0.033 m.	0.030 m.
diameter body	0.091 m.	0.077 m.
width handle	0.017 m.	0.017 m.
diameter base	0.043 m.	0.043 m.
capacity[1]	0.210 liter	0.115 liter

Decoration:

In brown paint on buff to greenish-buff, reddish on pinkish-buff, red on light red: irregular bands, one at or just above greatest diameter and carrying over base of handle, a second around base of neck and a third on lip; careless dashes or stripes on exterior of handle.

Distribution:

Room 18: 15 numbered.
Doorway Rooms 18-20: 10 counted,[2] 1 numbered.
Room 20: 2 numbered.
Room 23: 1 numbered.

---

35. JUG: SMALL; ONE HANDLE, WIDE NECK (*decorated*)   Figs. 367, 368

Exactly like preceding in shape and decoration except for proportionately wider neck.

For Shapes 34 and 35 compare *MP*, Types 112, 113, 114, 115, pp. 30f. figs. 5, 6 (II B - III A - III B-III C). There are many minor variations in all details; no precise duplicates.

[1] Of the inventoried examples one holds 0.210 liter, one 0.200, two 0.195, one 0.180, one 0.175, one 0.170, four 0.165, three 0.160, one 0.140, two 0.135, one 0.125, one 0.115.

[2] When counted before removal it was impossible to tell which of these were of Shape 34 and which of Shape 35.

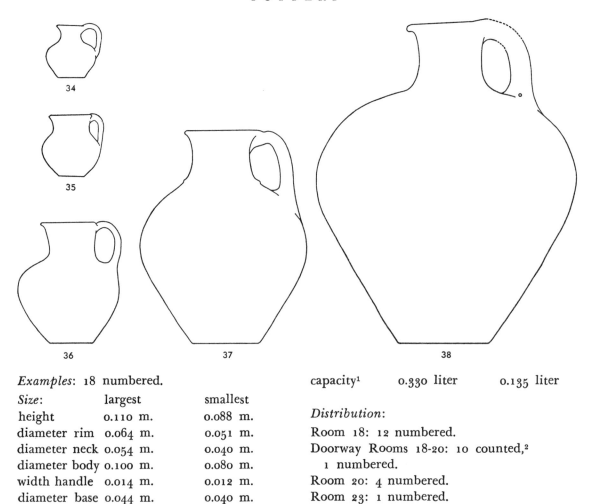

34

35

36   37   38

Examples: 18 numbered.

Size:	largest	smallest
height	0.110 m.	0.088 m.
diameter rim	0.064 m.	0.051 m.
diameter neck	0.054 m.	0.040 m.
diameter body	0.100 m.	0.080 m.
width handle	0.014 m.	0.012 m.
diameter base	0.044 m.	0.040 m.

capacity[1]   0.330 liter   0.135 liter

Distribution:

Room 18: 12 numbered.
Doorway Rooms 18-20: 10 counted,[2]
   1 numbered.
Room 20: 4 numbered.
Room 23: 1 numbered.

36. JUG: ONE HANDLE, RELATIVELY WIDE NECK   Figs. 367, 368

Flat bottom; fairly squat "globular-biconical" or "ovoid" body; moderately high, relatively wide, concave splaying neck with rounded rim; one flat or flattened arched handle from rim to shoulder. Sometimes rim is cut away above top of handle, apparently a Messenian feature, since it occurs also on jugs from chamber tombs excavated by Professor Marinatos at Volymidia.

Cf. *MP*, Type 109, p. 35 fig. 7; similar except that all Pylian examples of this type have flat bases. There are many similar jugs from other sites but references are given only to those that appear to have flat bases. *Zygouries*, p. 169 and fig. 165 nos. 355, 348. *ChT*, pls. XLII no. 10, XLIV no. 3, LI no. 18, LVII no. 15. *Prosymna*, figs. 315 no. 507, 476 no. 961, 483 no. 930, 516 no. 16, 571 no. 765, 572 no. 1191.

[1] Of the inventoried examples one holds 0.330 liter, one 0.250, two 0.200, one 0.190, one 0.185, two 0.175, three 0.170, two 0.165, two 0.160, one 0.155, one 0.145, one 0.135.

[2] See footnote 2, p. 375.

Examples: 8 counted, 6 numbered.

Size:	largest	smallest
height	0.224 m.	0.190 m.
diameter rim	0.094 m.	0.095 m.
diameter neck	0.078 m.	0.071 m.
diameter body	0.185 m.	0.167 m.
width handle	0.020 m.	0.023 m.
diameter base	0.071 m.	0.070 m.
capacity[1]	2.500 liters	1.850 liters

Distribution:

Room 18: 3 counted, 1 numbered.
Room 20: 5 counted and numbered.

37. JUG: TALL; ONE HANDLE, RELATIVELY NARROW NECK
(*decorated and plain*)   Figs. 367, 368

Flat bottom; ovoid body; (usually) tall, relatively narrow, concave or splaying neck with rounded lip; one thick rounded or flattened loop-handle from rim to shoulder. Sometimes rim is cut away above handle. In two instances there is a barely perceptible raised ridge at junction of neck and body.

No exact parallel illustrated by Furumark but his Type 105, *MP* p. 35 fig. 7 is similar, although type from Palace of Nestor has more ovoid body and flat base.

Examples: 5 numbered.

Size:	largest	smallest
height	0.335 m.	0.260 m.
diameter rim	0.117 m.	0.095 m.
diameter neck	0.089 m.	0.074 m.
diameter body	0.273 m.	0.195 m.
diameter handle	0.030 m.	0.022 m.
diameter base	0.115 m.	0.073 m.
capacity[2]	9.800 liters	3.300 liters

Example with decoration:

No. 676 (Fig. 367). Black paint on gray discolored by fire. Single bands around rim, neck, base of neck; paired bands on shoulder, below greatest diameter, and just above base. Wavy stripe on handle, band around its lower part.

Distribution:

Room 43: 1 numbered (rim cut away above handle, slight ridge at junction of neck and body).
Room 46: 2 numbered (one with painted bands; cut away rim).
Corridor 59: 1 numbered.
Corridor 95: 1 numbered (slight ridge at junction of neck and body).

38. JUG: LARGE; ONE HANDLE, RELATIVELY NARROW NECK
(*decorated and plain*)   Figs. 369, 370

Similar to the preceding but much plumper and with thick horizontal rounded lip, and thick handle extending in short loop from rim to upper part of shoulder.

No exact parallel to this shape illustrated by Furumark nor recognized from any other site.

[1] Of the inventoried examples one holds 2.500 liters, one 2.400, one 2.250, one 2.100, two 1.850.

[2] Of the inventoried examples one holds 9.800 liters, one 5.950, one 4.300, one 3.300, the fifth cannot be measured.

Examples: 2 numbered, both from Room 105 (on No. 1087 rim cut out above handle).

Size:	No. 858	No. 1087
height	0.510 m.	0.438 m.
height neck	0.105 m.	0.094 m.
diameter rim	0.140 m.	0.124 m.
diameter neck	0.100 m.	0.099 m.
diameter body	0.416 m.	0.361 m.
width handle	0.040 m.	0.032 m.
diameter base	0.144 m.	0.132 m.
capacity	cannot be measured	

Example with decoration:

No. 1087 (Fig. 369). Blackish paint on light brown to gray. Two horizontal bands only a little above bottom, two just below greatest diameter, three high on shoulder, one at base of neck, and another along the lip. Handle edged with paint and probably bore diagonal cross stripes. Irregular ring around base of handle and two stripes curve down below it crossing the shoulder bands.

39. JUG: ONE HANDLE, WIDE MOUTH, ROUNDED BOTTOM
(coarse handmade) Figs. 369, 370

Ovoid body with no standing surface; low concave neck, rounded rim; one thick, heavy, round handle rising very slightly above rim and curving in a loop from rim to shoulder. Two examples have approximately circular mouths, the third somewhat elliptical.

Examples: 3 numbered.

Size:	No. 1174	No. 829	No. 830
height	0.260 m.	0.238 m.	0.218 m.
diameter rim	0.145 m.	0.130 m.	0.125 m.
diameter body	0.203 m.	0.190 m.	0.186 m.
diameter handle	0.040 m.	0.032 m.	0.027 m.
capacity	4.000 liters	3.600 liters	3.200 liters

Distribution:

Room 98: 2 numbered.
Room 99: 1 numbered.

40. JUG: DIPPER-LIKE; ONE HIGH HANDLE, WIDE MOUTH *(coarse)* Figs. 369, 370

Flattened bottom; ovoid body; low, wide concave neck with plain rim; one thick high flattened handle springing from rim and neck in high oblique loop to shoulder.

No parallels found.

Example: 1 numbered, from Room 98.

Size:	No. 802			diameter rim	0.115 m.
height with handle	0.246 m.			width handle	0.030 m.
height body	0.170 m.			diameter base	0.090 m.
				capacity	1.900 liters

41. JUG: BASKET-HANDLE, TUBULAR SPOUT ("TEAPOT," *in heavy domestic plain ware*) Figs. 369, 370

Flat or flattened bottom; ovoid body; fairly wide, low, upright neck with plain rim; thick flattened basket-handle attached on each side to rim and rising in fairly high arch across mouth; straight tubular spout slanting outward from shoulder in line with handle.

Cf. *MP*, Types 159, 160, 161, 162, pp. 30f. figs. 5, 6. Furumark shows no exact parallel. The tombs at Prosymna yielded 21 examples of variant types (*Prosymna*, p. 444). The examples from the palace at Englianos and one from Chamber Tomb K 1 are obviously late clumsy descendants of the earlier types.

Examples: 21 counted, 5 numbered.

Size:	largest	smallest		width handle	0.023 m.	0.023 m.
				length spout	0.038 m.	0.038 m.
height with handle	0.230 m.	0.210 m.		diameter spout inside	0.017 m.	0.013 m.
height of body	0.173 m.	0.161 m.		diameter base	0.090 m.	0.080 m.
diameter rim	0.090 m.	0.089 m.		capacity[1]	1.700 liters	1.250 liters
diameter neck	0.088 m.	0.081 m.				
diameter body	0.150 m.	0.146 m.				

Distribution:

Room 60: 20 counted, 4 numbered.
Room 105: 1 numbered.

[1] Of the inventoried examples one holds 1.700 liters, one 1.500, two 1.350, one 1.250.

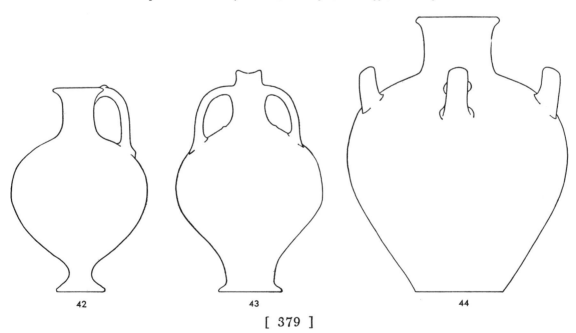

42 43 44

42. JUG: ONE HANDLE, NARROW NECK, LOW STEM *(decorated)* Figs. 369, 370

Disk-like foot with vertical edge, hollowed somewhat deeply underneath, sloping upward to narrow stem; body ovoid, almost globular; neck tall, straight, relatively narrow with horizontal beveled lip; handle flattened, arching down from rim to shoulder; boss on top above junction with rim and a knob at base of handle.

Cf. *MP*, Type 120, p. 31 fig. 6 (III B). No exact parallel known to us but some distant relatives may be recognized: e.g., *ChT*, pl. xlv no. 1 (similar except for foot, neck and neck-molding, and handle); *Prosymna*, fig. 150 no. 1049.

Example: 1 numbered, from Room 18.

Size: No. 245

height	0.269 m.
height neck	0.061 m.
diameter rim	0.070 m.
diameter neck	0.043 m.
diameter body	0.180 m.
width handle	0.021 m.
diameter stem	0.030 m.
diameter base	0.062 m.
capacity	2.000 liters

Example with decoration:

No. 245 (Fig. 369). Brown to red paint on buff, no slip. Band on lip, ring around base of handle; slanting strokes on handle; three pairs of elongated reversed S-shaped stripes extending from neck band to band or bands around stem which may have extended over entire foot. No doubt related to Furumark's Motive 67, Curved Stripes (*MP*, p. 403 fig. 70). Two stirrup-vases (No. 401, first in second row, Fig. 329 right and No. 595 Fig. 391) from the palace and a pedestaled jug (No. 766) from Chamber Tomb K 1 have the same type of decoration. Cf. also two pedestaled jugs from Tragana Tholos Tomb (*EphArch* 1914, p. 112, figs. 23, 24).

43. JUG: TWO HANDLES, NARROW NECK, DOUBLE SPOUT *(decorated)* Figs. 369, 370

Pedestal base with splaying foot, hollow underneath; piriform body, spreading sharply from pedestal; relatively high narrow neck marked off from body by low raised ridge; neck prolonged into two upward slanting, shallow, broad open spouts; separating spouts, one on each side, two broad flat perpendicular handles extending from top of neck to shoulder.

This is clearly a descendant of a long series of vessels comprised in Furumark's Form 42, exemplified by Types 150, 151, 152, 153, and 154. The types nearest to the Pylian Shape 43 are *MP*, Types 151 and 152 of Mycenaean III B and III C, represented by *ChT*, pls. xvii nos. 19, 21, liii no. 14, all of which, however, have a single and not a double spout. Several jugs of comparable shape were found in chamber tombs at Prosymna (*Prosymna*, pp. 440f.).

Examples: 2 numbered, both from Room 32.

Size:	No. 404	No. 405
max. height	0.313 m.	0.300 m.
diameter neck	0.043 m.	0.043 m.
diameter body	0.215 m.	0.230 m.
width handles	0.020 m.	0.023 and 0.025 m.
diameter pedestal	0.056 m.	0.069 m.
diameter base	0.082 m.	0.083 m.
capacity	3.680 liters	2.850 liters

Decoration: black to brownish-black paint on greenish-buff.

No. 404 (Fig. 369). Trace of color on edge of spout, stripes along each edge of handles, ring around base of neck. Remnants of horizontal bands on body; as discerned by Mr. de

Jong just below handles two broad bands enclosing two narrow stripes between them, demarcating bottom of shoulder zone; lower down two broad bands with a narrow one between, marking the under limit of the middle zone; one wide band round stem and one on top of spreading foot. No decoration visible in middle and upper zones.

No. 405 (Fig. 369). Trace of color on edge of spout, stripes along each edge of handles connected by irregular transverse blobs, ring around base of neck; shoulder zone marked off by bands above and below; two bands lower down on body; remains of paint on foot. Details difficult to determine.

44. JUG: THREE HANDLES ON SHOULDER, TWO HORIZONTAL, ONE VERTICAL; NARROW NECK (*decorated*)   Figs. 369, 370

Large flattened bottom; ovoid body, concave neck, rolled rim; two large flattened horizontal loop-handles set opposite each other rising vertically from shoulder; midway between, on one side, also on shoulder, a flattened vertical loop-handle.

No parallels to this shape found; unique among pots from the palace.

Example: 1 numbered, from Room 39.

Size:	No. 544
height	0.364 m.
diameter rim	0.118 m.
width rim	0.008 m.
diameter neck	0.095 m.
diameter body	0.309 m.
diameter base	0.125 m.
w. horizontal handles	0.037 m.
w. vertical handle	0.025 m.
capacity	12.100 liters

Decoration:

Paint black; slipped but original color has turned smoky gray from effects of fire. Solidly coated 0.035 m. deep inside mouth, extending over lip and 0.025 m. below rim on exterior; band around base of neck, another between neck and handles forming top of shoulder zone, which is bordered below by three bands. It contains the vertical and two horizontal handles and bears pattern of connected arches, five in panel opposite vertical handle, two in each panel between the vertical and horizontal handles; longitudinal stripe on each handle. Between bottom of shoulder zone and base two horizontal bands. Perhaps related to some descendant of Furumark's Arcade Pattern (*MP*, Motive 66:1 and 2, p. 403 fig. 70). Or possibly it is nearer Furumark's Isolated Semicircles (*MP*, Motive 43:15, p. 343 fig. 57) in an inverted form and clearly belonging to the end of Mycenaean III B and the beginning of III C.

45. AMPHORA: LARGE; TWO HANDLES (*decorated and plain*)   Figs. 371, 372

Flat or flattened bottom or raised base; ovoid body; concave neck varying in height and diameter; rounded horizontal or sloping lip; two perpendicular, thick, rounded or flattened handles from rim or just below rim to shoulder.

Cf. *MP*, Type 69, p. 35 fig. 7. *Zygouries*, Potter's Shop, fig. 158 no. 375.

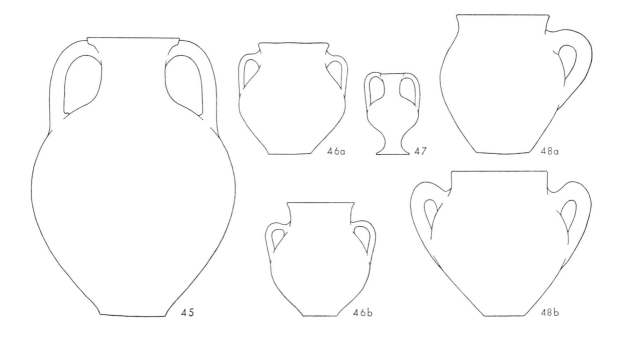

Examples: 7 numbered.

Size: largest   smallest
height
  over-all   0.404 m.   0.370 m.
height body   0.290 m.   0.310 m.
diameter rim   0.128 m.   0.112 m.
diameter neck   0.095 m.   0.087 m.
diameter body   0.326 m.   0.288 m.
diameter
  handles   0.032 m.   0.029 m.
diameter base   0.130 m.   0.116 m.
capacity[1]   15.100 liters   10.500 liters

Examples with decoration:

No. 806. Paint as preserved is grayish-white. Uncertain whether slipped or not. Very badly damaged by fire and decoration difficult to distinguish. Apparently had three white bands on upper part of body and three at or below widest diameter delimiting a zone. The latter may have been divided by vertical stripes into panels, perhaps three on each side. Impossible to determine whether panels contained patterns.

No. 1138 (Fig. 371). Vessel very badly damaged, warped and blackened by fire. Black paint; dark greenish-gray slip. Single band at one third of height of pot, two bands forming lower border of shoulder zone which extends to band around base of neck. Probably had stripe on handle and ring around rim.

No. 1175 (Fig. 371). Bands in almost obliterated dull white paint: two below greatest diameter of body, three on shoulder below handles, one around base of neck. Each handle has ring around bottom and bears diagonal stripes on exterior.

Distribution:
Room 38: 1 numbered.
Room 46: 2 numbered (one with handles from neck).
Corridor 59: 1 numbered.
Room 98: 2 numbered.
Room 99: 1 numbered.

---

[1] Of the inventoried examples one holds 15.100 liters, one 12.800, one 10.900, one 10.500; the other three are not measurable.

46. AMPHORA: SMALL; WIDE MOUTH

Figs. 371, 372

Flattened bottom; squat, rounded biconical body; splaying neck ending in plain rounded rim; two relatively narrow flattened loop-handles set vertically either extending from neck (type a) or from base of neck (type b) to body above greatest diameter.

Cf. *MP*, Type 67, p. 36 fig. 8 which occurs frequently in Argolis and is approximately like shape from the Palace of Nestor except that it has raised base. *Prosymna*, figs. 166 no. 330, 167 no. 332, 315 no. 510. *ChT*, pl. XLV no. 3.

Examples: 4 numbered, 2 of each kind.

Size:	largest	smallest
height	0.162 m.	0.142 m.
diameter rim	0.110 m.	0.090 m.
diameter neck	0.090 m.	0.080 m.
diameter body	0.148 m.	0.132 m.
width handles	0.015 m.	0.012 m.

diameter base 0.064 m. 0.053 m.
capacity[1] 1.350 liters 0.980 liter

Distribution:
Room 20: 2 numbered, both of type a.
Doorway Rooms 18-20: 1 numbered, type b.
Room 18: 1 numbered, type b.

47. AMPHORA: SMALL; NARROW NECK, PEDESTAL-BASE

Figs. 371, 372

Conical foot, flat underneath, slightly convex on top; relatively thick high stem; globular body; tall, straight, narrow neck (approximately same diameter as stem) splaying to plain rim; two perpendicular handles from rim to side above greatest diameter. Four examples have elliptical mouths, the rest circular.

Cf. *ChT*, pl. XLV no. 8, which has been restored with a spout.

Examples: 29 counted, 22 numbered.

Size:	largest	smallest
height	0.127 m.	0.105 m.
diameter rim	0.031 m.	0.033 m.
diameter neck	0.020 m.	0.021 m.
diameter body	0.080 m.	0.061 m.
width across handles	0.065 m.	0.065 m.
width handles	0.010 m.	0.010 m.

diameter
pedestal 0.022 m. 0.022 m.
diameter base 0.053 m. 0.037 m.
capacity[2] 0.115 liter 0.055 liter

Distribution:
Room 18: 23 counted, 22 numbered.
Room 20: 6 counted.

48a. JAR: DOMESTIC; ONE HANDLE ON SIDE, WIDE MOUTH, LOW NECK (*coarse*)

Figs. 371, 372

Flattened bottom or slightly raised base (six instances); thick-walled ovoid body; wide, low, splaying neck with rounded rim; one thick round loop-handle attached on shoulder below neck making fairly wide loop to body below widest diameter.

Cf. *MP*, Type 65, p. 36 fig. 8. *Zygouries*, Potter's Shop, fig. 153 no. 225, p. 159.

[1] Of the inventoried examples one holds 1.350 liters, one 1.070, two 0.980.

[2] Of the inventoried examples one holds 0.115 liter, one 0.110, three 0.095, two 0.090, one 0.087, two 0.085, seven 0.080, one 0.075, three 0.060, one 0.055.

Examples: 51 counted,[1] 20 numbered.

Size:	largest	smallest
height	0.206 m.	0.175 m.
height neck	0.026 m.	0.023 m.
diameter rim	0.138 m.	0.119 m.
diameter neck	0.133 m.	0.107 m.
diameter body	0.195 m.	0.166 m.
diameter handles	0.021 m.	0.019 m.

	largest	smallest
diameter base	0.075 m.	0.068 m.
capacity[2]	3.100 liters	1.900 liters

Distribution:

Doorway Rooms 66-67: 1 numbered.
Room 67: 10 counted,[1] 8 numbered.
Room 68: 41 counted,[1] 11 numbered.

48b. JAR: DOMESTIC; TWO HANDLES ON SIDE (*coarse*)   Figs. 371, 372

Exactly similar to preceding except that it has two handles of same kind set opposite each other on side of jar.

Examples: 51 counted,[1] 12 numbered.

Size:	largest	smallest
height	0.213 m.	0.193 m.
height neck	0.026 m.	0.028 m.
diameter rim	0.140 m.	0.123 m.
diameter neck	0.137 m.	0.116 m.
diameter body	0.200 m.	0.177 m.

	largest	smallest
diameter handles	0.019 m.	0.019 m.
diameter base	0.069 m.	0.069 m.
capacity[3]	3.300 liters	2.450 liters

Distribution:

Room 67: 10 counted,[1] 1 numbered.
Room 68: 41 counted,[1] 11 numbered.

[1] This figure represents the total number of domestic jars counted since the difference between the one-handled and the two-handled was not obvious when the broken pots were removed.

[2] Of the inventoried examples one holds 3.100 liters, one 3.000, two 2.750, one 2.700, one 2.650, one 2.600, two 2.500, three 2.400, one 2.250, one 2.120, one 1.900; five were too incomplete to be measurable.

[3] Of the inventoried examples one holds 3.300 liters, one 3.150, one 3.100, one 2.800, one 2.750, one 2.650, one 2.600, three 2.500, one 2.450, one is incomplete.

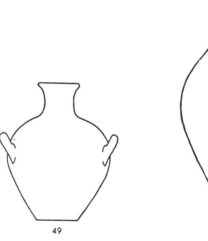

49

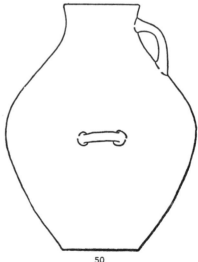

50

49. JAR: LARGE; TWO HORIZONTAL HANDLES; HIGH NECK (*decorated and plain*)

Figs. 373, 374

Large flat bottom; ovoid body; relatively high, narrow, concave neck; thick horizontal rim rounded on top; two round loop-handles set horizontally at greatest diameter of body and slanting obliquely outward.

Nothing exactly similar in Furumark's *Mycenaean Pottery*. The shape is something like his later Type 58 (*MP*, p. 36 fig. 8, III C:1-2), except that ours has flat bottom. Similar, except that they have a raised base, are: *BSA* xxv, pl. x d, e, f, from east basement at Mycenae; *Prosymna*, fig. 16 no. 1213, from a Late Helladic house.

Examples: 3 numbered, essentially same shape but differing greatly in size. The two smaller have painted band decoration.

Size:	No. 467	No. 1141	No. 818
height	0.585 m.	0.394 m.	0.384 m.
h. neck and rim	0.135 m.	0.082 m.	0.090 m.
diameter rim	0.215 m.	0.110 m.	0.120 m.
diameter neck	0.140 m.	0.082 m.	0.085 m.
diameter body	0.465 m.	0.304 m.	0.300 m.
diameter handles	0.031 m.	0.020 m.	0.025 m.
base	0.160 m.	0.150 m.	0.120 m.

Examples with decoration:

No. 1141 (Fig. 373). Black to brownish paint on gray, mottled by fire. Three horizontal bands, one just below handles, one above handles, one at junction of body and neck spreading a little up on the latter; ring around lip, stripe on handle carried down on each side to band.

No. 818 (Fig. 373). Reddish-brown brightening to red paint; creamy buff to tan slip. Band on lip, a single band around base of neck. Another above handles and one below. Careless stripe along top of handle.

Distribution:

Room 32: No. 467.
Room 46: No. 1141.
Room 97: No. 818.

50. JAR: VERY LARGE; THREE HANDLES, TWO HORIZONTAL NEAR GREATEST DIAMETER, ONE VERTICAL FROM NECK TO SHOULDER; RELATIVELY NARROW NECK (*decorated*)

Figs. 373, 374

Large flattened bottom; biconical body; fairly narrow splaying neck with rounded slightly everted lip; at greatest diameter of body two projecting round loop-handles set horizontally and opposite each other; at 90° to their axis round vertical handle loops down from neck to upper part of shoulder.

No real parallel is known to us but the general shape with its arrangement of handles recalls a Middle Helladic water jar found at Korakou (*Korakou*, p. 23 fig. 32).

Examples: 2 numbered, both from Room 38. Decorated with linear patterns in dull paint, they look like Middle Helladic products.

Size:	No. 597	No. 598
height	0.683 m.	0.660 m.
height neck	0.090 m.	0.090 m.
diameter rim	0.217 m.	0.162 m.
diameter neck	0.195 m.	0.147 m.
diameter body	0.543 m.	0.473 m.
diameter handles	0.026 m.	0.036 m.
diameter base	0.225 m.	0.160 m.

Examples with decoration:

No. 597 (Figs. 330, 373). Paint blackish and mat; no slip apparent. Band around rim, another near bottom of neck. In middle of shoulder broad zone bordered above and below by single broad band. The zone contains continuous zigzag running around entire vessel, passing below vertical handle. On latter stripe ·of paint which continues on down across shoulder zone and well below it to widest part of body.

No. 598 (Figs. 330, 373). Paint blackish

and mat; no slip visible. Single bands around rim, base of neck, middle and lower part of shoulder. In each of the two zones thus outlined continuous zigzag running around vessel, lower one interrupted by the vertical handle. On latter broad stripe which continues down to widest diameter. One curving stripe extends from rim to bottom of neck; whether this is intentional or a drip is uncertain. What is surely a drip appears below to left of vertical handle.

51. JAR: PITHOID, SMALL; THREE HORIZONTAL HANDLES ON SHOULDER, WIDE MOUTH, PEDESTAL-BASE (*decorated and plain*)　　　　　Figs. 375, 376

Spreading conical foot, hollowed underneath, with low thick splaying stem; ovoid body; low, concave or splaying neck; wide mouth; sloping or horizontal rounded lip; three round arched handles set horizontally on shoulder rising almost vertically or obliquely. Minor variations.

Cf. *MP*, Type 28, p. 22 fig. 3. The small pithoid jar with three horizontal loop-handles on shoulder is one of the favorite Mycenaean shapes but no exact parallel to the Pylian type with stemmed foot is known to us from other regions. *MV*, pl. XLIV Shape 28.

Examples: 4 numbered.

Size:	largest	smallest
height	0.131 m.	0.131 m.
diameter rim	0.096 m.	0.095 m.
diameter neck	0.090 m.	0.083 m.
diameter body	0.113 m.	0.108 m.
diameter handles	0.007 m.	0.007 m.
diameter stem	0.028 m.	0.029 m.

diameter base 0.055 m. 　0.053 m.
capacity[1]　0.600 liter　0.450 liter

Distribution:
Room 20: 3 numbered.
Room 32: 1 numbered, possibly once decorated with painted bands but arrangement not discernible.

52. JAR: PITHOID, SMALL; THREE VERTICAL HANDLES SPANNING SHOULDER ZONE; WIDE MOUTH (*decorated*)　　　　　Figs. 375, 376

Pedestal-foot with low stem or torus or ring-base; piriform or ovoid body; relatively wide, low, concave or splaying neck with sloping or horizontal, rounded lip; three flattened vertical loop-handles from top of shoulder zone to greatest diameter of body. Painted band decoration. Considerable variation in details of size, shape, and proportions.

Cf. *MP*, Types 42 and 49, p. 23 fig. 4. The examples from the palace are of Messenian style lacking the elegance usually noted in the best examples found in tombs. All seven differ in some re-

[1] Of the inventoried examples one holds 0.600 liter, two 0.500, one 0.450.

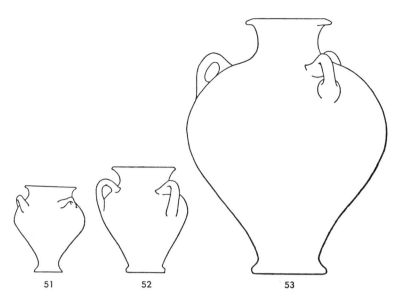

spects from the types common in Argolis and they probably represent a Messenian ceramic tradi-tion. *Prosymna*, figs. 141 no. 152 (plain, handles lower on shoulder), 167 no. 631, 178 no. 317 (plain, handles lower), 454 no. 125 (handles lower), 516 no. 15 (shorter handles). *ChT*, pl. xvi nos. 7, 14. Pylos: Chamber Tomb K1, nos. 761, 763.

Examples: 7 numbered.

Size:	largest	smallest
height	0.222 m.	0.157 m.
diameter rim	0.100 m.	0.092 m.
diameter neck	0.076 m.	0.072 m.
diameter body	0.172 m.	0.134 m.
width handles	0.018 m.	—
diameter		
pedestal	0.054 m.	0.034 m.
diameter base	0.077 m.	—
capacity[1]	1.750 liters	0.850 liter

Examples with decoration (Fig. 375):

No. 413. Light red to brown paint on buff slip. Inside of mouth coated; stripe along outer edge of lip; neck coated solidly down to junction with body. Narrow bordering band just below neck, three similar bands at widest part of body; two wider bands near foot; broad band on latter. Broad stripe en-circles each handle. Top of latter painted but whether all over or with stripes uncertain.

No. 419. Brown paint; greenish-buff slip.

Lip and neck solidly coated inside and out; one band just above handles, three below handles, one near bottom, one at junction with foot and one along edge of foot. Stripe on each handle which is framed by a loop. In each panel between handles a row of seven double arches (cf. U-pattern, *MP*, Motive 45:4, p. 345 fig. 58) placed alternatingly with curve up and down.

No. 460. Brown paint on greenish-buff clay. Band on inside of mouth, on top of lip, two bands on neck, one just below, two bands at greatest diameter, one at junction of body and foot. Stripe on handles.

No. 461. Brown paint lightening to red on buff clay. Band over lip, careless band at junction of neck and body; at greatest diam-eter three bands which split into five in one panel; one band on foot; stripe on each han-dle and loop enclosing handle.

No. 471. Dark brown paint lightening to red on clay varying from gray to red. Decora-tion practically identical with that of No. 413.

---

[1] Of the inventoried examples one holds 1.750 liters, one 1.700, one 1.400, two 1.100, one 0.850; the seventh is incomplete.

No. 521. Orange-red paint on buff clay. Band along lip, around base of neck, two bands around body below handle, one band at junction of body and foot. Broad stripe on handles and careless stripe on each side of handle.

No. 1028. Red-brown paint; grayish-tan clay. Paint almost obliterated on two thirds of the jar. Band over lip extending down on interior and exterior. One band around base of neck, another above handles, three below, one broad between two narrower, one at junction of body and foot (foot itself miss-

ing). Stripe on each handle and ring around bases of handles. In the panel that is preserved between handles a thick, continuous wavy line with relatively deep waves (cf. *MP*, Motive 53, p. 373 fig. 65). *Prosymna*, fig. 97 no. 203. *ChT*, pls. XXII no. 5, XLIV no. 2 (on which the wavy line is broken).

Distribution:

Room 32: 2 numbered.
Corridor 59: 3 numbered.
Room 60: 1 numbered.
Room 67: 1 numbered.

53. JAR: PITHOID; THREE VERTICAL HANDLES ON SHOULDER, NARROW NECK
(*decorated*)
Figs. 377, 378

Pedestaled foot with ring-base, hollow underneath; low stem; piriform or ovoid body; relatively narrow, concave neck, set off from body by very slight ridge; broad, horizontal beveled lip; three flattened or ridged loop-handles set vertically in shoulder zone dividing it into three approximately equal panels; painted decoration: bands with pattern in shoulder zone.

The five jars from Room 32 stand out sharply from almost all of the other pots found in the palace. We were led to wonder if they might not be importations from the Argolid.

Cf. *MP*, Type 35, p. 23 fig. 4 (III B). *MV*, pl. XLIV Shape 25. *ChT*, pl. XVII nos. 16, 24. *Prosymna*, figs. 305 no. 701 (bands only), 351 no. 790, 357 no. 769, 425 no. 157, 529 no. 1024. *RT*, *Dendra*, p. 107 nos. 54, 55, 56 (fig. 81). *NT*, *Dendra*, p. 67 no. 5 (fig. 79); p. 68 no. 6 (fig. 80); p. 70 no. 11 (fig. 83). *Asine*, p. 359 no. 1 (fig. 233 no. 1); pp. 378 and 380 nos. 5, 6 (fig. 248 nos. 2, 3), 7 (fig. 249 no. 1).

Examples: 5 numbered (minor variations in size and details), all from Room 32.

Size:	largest	smallest
height	0.448 m.	0.370 m.
diameter rim	0.165 m.	0.133 m.
width rim	0.020 m.	0.015 m.
diameter neck	0.109 m.	0.090 m.
diameter body	0.381 m.	0.300 m.
width handles	0.040 m.	0.025 m.
diameter stem	0.128 m.	0.106 m.
diameter base	0.157 m.	0.130 m.
capacity[1]	22.000 liters	10.200 liters

Examples with decoration (Fig. 377):
No. 403 (Fig. 378). Brownish-black ranging to reddish-brown paint on greenish-buff slip. Paint of good quality. Interior and exterior of neck coated solidly; narrow reserved strip along inner edge of lip, painted band covering outer edge; shoulder zone bordered above by two narrow, below by three broader horizontal bands, neatly painted while the pot was revolving; each handle bears stripe and is framed by loop; in each panel conventionalized nautilus (cf. *MP*, Motive 22, Argonaut, p. 307 fig. 50, not exact parallel) in linear style, the three tentacles being represented by spirals with central dot and the shell by five, six, or seven parallel loops. Low down on body two further bands; pedestal and foot coated over-all.

[1] Of the inventoried examples one holds 22.000 liters, one 14.250, one 11.250, one 11.000, one 10.200.

No. 406 (Fig. 378). Brownish-black ranging to brown paint on greenish-buff slip. Neck inside and out coated over-all; reserved strip along inner edge of lip; painted band around outer edge; shoulder zone marked off above by two narrow bands, below by one broad bordered by two narrow. Handles surrounded by oval frames and painted over-all on tops and edges; each panel filled with scale-pattern (*MP*, Motive 70:1, p. 403 fig. 70), seven rows of somewhat carelessly made scales, open end up; below greatest diameter another broad band bordered above and below by narrow one; near bottom yet another broad band, then narrow one just above pedestal, which is coated solidly.

Cf. *Asine*, p. 407 no. 4, fig. 268 no. 4. *NT, Dendra*, p. 67 no. 5, fig. 79; p. 70 no. 11, fig. 83. *ChT*, pl. xxviii no. 1. One from Schliemann's excavations at Mycenae in storeroom of National Museum. *Prosymna*, figs. 260 no. 621, 402 no. 813, 456 no. 111.

No. 407. Light brown shading to blackish-brown paint on greenish-buff slip. Almost identical with No. 406. Neck inside and out coated over-all; reserved strip on inner side of lip, painted band over outer edge. Shoulder zone demarcated by two narrow bands above and below by broad bordered by narrow band. Handles framed by wide loops and coated all over on top and edge. Each panel filled with scale-pattern (*MP*, Motive, 70:1, p. 403 fig. 70). Here again there appear to be seven rows of scales with convex end down. Two broad bands just above pedestal, latter coated.

No. 408 (Fig. 378). Brownish-black, brown, reddish-brown lustrous paint on gray to creamy buff slip. Interior and exterior of neck coated over-all; reserved strip along inner edge of lip, painted band around outer edge; shoulder zone bordered above by three narrow, below by three broad bands; each handle with longitudinal stripe on top framed by oval loop; each panel filled by motive of quintuple spirals (cf. *MP*, Motive 47, p. 357 fig. 60 which illustrates only double and triple spirals), a large one in center from which branch out two on each side. The two on right

in each panel send off stems that meet in frame of handle. Near bottom a fairly broad and a narrow band, and whole pedestal is coated over-all. This motive has no doubt grown out of or been influenced by the conventionalized spiraliform representation of the argonaut (*MP*, Motive 22, p. 307 fig. 50).

No. 409 (Fig. 378). Brownish-black ranging to mostly dark red paint on buff slip. Interior and exterior of neck coated over-all; broad reserved strip on lip, painted band over outer edge; shoulder zone bordered by two bands, narrow and broad, above, three below; handles, framed in very broad oval loop and coated over-all on top, mark off three decorated compartments or panels. Each contains large squid, body of which, heart-shaped at top, narrow in middle and broadening out below, hangs down across and beyond lower border of zone. Eyes represented by two reserved circles each with dot in the middle. A central spike and four tentacles spring out of top of head, two curving to right, two to left. In one panel outer tentacle is short, curving down to end just below narrowest part of body; the inner one swings down beyond waistline then curves outward in broad loop which bends back again and continues on down across the three bands of border ending in an open curl. In another panel the arrangement is reversed: the inner tentacle is short, stopping in a little curl below waist of squid while the outer tentacle, reaching top band of lower border, swings outward and up again before turning once more downward across the triple bands to end in a curl (this section shown in the water color by Mr. de Jong, Fig. 378). The third panel is not well enough preserved to determine the exact arrangement but both inner and outer tentacles seem to be equally large and long and end on top band without crossing the triple border. Suckers are represented by short strokes or blobs jutting out from tentacles. Details vary from panel to panel: in one the outer tentacles have suckers while the inner have none until they make their broad outward turn; in another both inner and outer tentacles have suckers; in the third, the inner has none but the outer has. Two bands above pedestal; latter and top of foot coated over-all.

The cuttlefish, illustrated in *MP*, Motive 21, pp. 303, 305 figs. 48, 49 offer no exact parallel to the Pylian examples.

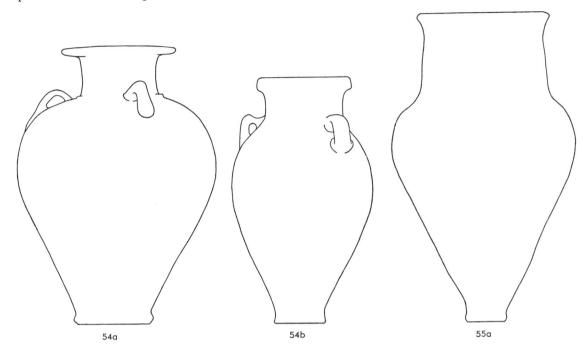

54a.   54b   55a

54a. JAR: PITHOID, LARGE; THREE VERTICAL HANDLES ON SHOULDER. PLUMP TYPE, MODELED AFTER A SHAPE OF PALACE STYLE (*decorated*)   Figs. 379, 380

Disk-base with projecting angular edge; plump ovoid body; relatively high, slightly concave neck set off from body by sharp neck-molding; broadly projecting horizontal lip; three wide flattened ridged or grooved handles set high on shoulder. Micaceous clay. Allover decoration in an imitation of Palace Style.

Cf. *MP*, Type 15, p. 22 fig. 3, Late Helladic II A. *ChT*, pl. L no. 21, Late Helladic II, smaller but similar. It is obvious that the jars from Pylos were definitely modeled after prototypes that go back to Mycenaean II A. The decoration too imitates the Palace Style of that earlier age. These late pots therefore actually represent an efflorescence of a revived local Palace Style. The potters were certainly more successful in reproducing the shapes than the vase painters were in adapting the decorative motives.

Examples: 4 counted, 3 numbered.

Size:	No. 418	No. 610	No. 612
height	0.875 m. pres.	0.804 m. pres.	0.748 m.
height neck	0.135 m.	0.118 m.	0.154 m.
diameter rim	0.383 m.	0.370 m.	0.480 m.
width rim	0.077 m.	0.060 m.	0.069 m.
diameter neck	0.240 m.	0.263 m.	0.312 m.
diameter body	0.690 m.	0.620 m.	0.662 m.
width handles	0.043 m.	0.040 m.	0.045 m.
diameter base	0.262 m.	missing	missing

[390]

Examples with decoration (Fig. 379):

No. 418. Entire exterior of jar was apparently coated with creamy slip which also extended well down inside neck. Latter then coated with red paint, and decoration in same paint was applied to the slip on exterior. On top of broad flat rim seven large spirals connected by tangents (*MP*, Running Spiral, Motive 46:54, p. 357 fig. 60). Space below tangents in each interval filled with irregular dots; space above empty. On neck continuous Rock Pattern 1 (*MP*, Motive 32:5, p. 323 fig. 54). Horizontal band coats molding at base of neck. Upper half of body divided by double bands into two zones, the upper containing the three handles, each edged with paint framing multiple chevrons pointing downward (cf. *MP*, Motive 75:8, p. 414 fig. 72). Around attachment of handles the usual border of paint. Each zone decorated with continuous Rock Pattern 1, the humps formed by concentric arcs all bordered above, as on the neck, by row of dots. The humps are not altogether uniform in size and shape, one being pointed instead of rounded on top. Below rock pattern three groups of three bands forming zones without decoration. Band of paint around base. The pattern has been almost obliterated and many details are difficult to determine. Cf. *NT, Dendra*, p. 41 no. 2 (fig. 46), somewhat similar.

No. 610. Entire exterior and interior of neck coated over-all with creamy slip. Inside neck traces of red paint which is likewise used for decoration of outside. Flat rim bears irregular crosshatching. Band along outer edge of lip. On neck continuous Rock Pattern 1 (*MP*, Motive 32:5, p. 323 fig. 54). The humps are carelessly painted in solid color and in some places corresponding but smaller humps hang down from above. No uniformity in size or shape. Band along molding at base of neck. Entire surface of jar divided into three vertical panels by broad irregular stripes descending from handles to bottom of vessel. One panel is not subdivided, upper two thirds of it filled with scale-pattern (*MP*, Motive 70:2, p. 403 fig. 70) of wildly irregular design, no two scales of the same shape but

all marked with one to eight dots, blobs, or dashes. Into lower part of this panel, but not separated from it, a grasslike plant pushes up with many branches spreading to right and left to the vertical stripe bordering the panel. In panel next to right, the upper half is divided by single horizontal bands into three zones; the topmost contains wiggly or straight parallel lines running up and down (*MP*, Motive 53:37, p. 373 fig. 65), the spaces between being filled with dashes. The middle zone is of same general type with wiggly irregular lines at right and careless arcs at left all running up and down. No dots. The third zone which is narrower is occupied by multiple irregular lunate lines. Beneath in lower half of panel is a much larger space filled with grasslike plant with upright stem from which innumerable curving blades spread out to right and left. The third panel is less well preserved and almost nothing of its lower half can be clearly made out, except a small area of crosshatching. The upper half is divided by single bands into six narrow horizontal zones, each filled with crudely drawn but roughly parallel, curving or lunate lines all with convexity to left. The second zone from top is marked off from rest by row of dots along its upper border. Two of the handles bear multiple chevrons pointing downward (*MP*, Motive 75:8, p. 414 fig. 72). The third has same pattern but was executed so carelessly as to appear to have a central stem. Bottom of jar missing.

The whole scheme of decoration is characterized by a crude undisciplined exuberance almost unparalleled in Mycenaean pottery decoration. The motives seem to be derived from antecedents in the Palace Style of Late Helladic II from which the shape of the jar itself was no doubt borrowed, but the careful craftsmanship of the painters of that earlier period is wholly lacking.

No. 612. Like the foregoing this too was first coated with a creamy slip on which decoration was applied in light red. Interior of neck painted in solid color. Top of broad flat lip bore pattern of crosshatching arranged in separated sections of different sizes probably six in number (though part of lip is missing). Edge of lip, under part, and top of neck coated. Lower part of neck decorated with Rock Pattern 1 (*MP*, Motive 32:5, p. 323 fig. 54), humps high and rounded and of nearly uniform size. Band along raised molding at base of neck. No panels marked off but whole upper two thirds of body filled with checkerboard pattern (*MP*, Motive 56:1, 2 Chequers, p. 383 fig. 67; also Motive 75:7, 19, 34, p. 414 fig. 72) comprising five rows of approximately equal "squares" running all the way around vessel. Alternate "squares" are filled with cross-hatching, decorated and undecorated thus falling into diagonal rows. Handles fitted without special reference to squares in two upper rows. Two carried pattern of parallel chevrons

springing from central stem with points upward (*MP*, Motive 58:30, p. 383 fig. 67). The third was probably similar but surface is missing. Edges of handles painted and irregular stripe circled place of attachment to jar. Below the checkerboard design three horizontal bands, somewhat lower a pair of bands. Bottom of jar missing.

The craftsmanship in the decoration of this jar is much better than that on No. 610 and somewhat better than that on No. 418. All alike were based on the older Palace Style.

Distribution:
Room 32: 1 numbered (No. 418).
Room 38: 2 counted, 1 numbered (No. 610).
Room 43: 1 numbered (No. 612).

54b. JAR: PITHOID, LARGE; THREE VERTICAL HANDLES ON SHOULDER. SLENDER TYPE
   (*decorated and plain*)   Figs. 379, 380

Thick disk-base with slight projecting edge; somewhat elongated ovoid body; relatively high neck with slightly concave profile; broad horizontal lip; three wide ribbed, grooved or flattened handles set vertically on shoulder. Minor variations in detail. Similar to preceding shape but much more slender and smaller. Three jars bear decoration of painted patterns in shoulder zone with a stripe continuing below each handle.

Furumark illustrates no exact parallel to this Pylian shape. These jars like those of the preceding category are clearly adaptations of types that go back to early Mycenaean times. The potters succeeded in evolving an attractive shape. The decorators seem to have used late Mycenaean motives (III A and on) rather than those of the older Palace Style, but they applied the patterns aesthetically and produced pleasing effects.

Examples: 7 counted, 6 numbered.

Size:	largest	smallest
height	0.782 m.	0.570 m.
height neck	0.140 m.	0.100 m.
diameter rim	0.300 m.	0.217 m.
width rim	0.045 m.	0.036 m.
diameter neck	0.235 m.	0.148 m.
diameter body	0.450 m.	0.387 m.
width handles	0.055 m.	0.040 m.
diameter base	0.165 m.	0.154 m.

Examples with decoration (Fig. 379):
   No. 542. Very faint traces of parallel chev-

rons on flat top of lip and of band below base of handles.

No. 600 (Fig. 330). Decorated mainly in two-color technique, white superposed on red. Red stripe along inside of mouth. On flat top of lip pattern of parallel chevrons in white on red. Broad horizontal red band, bearing narrower white band, running around middle of neck, divides latter into two narrow zones, each of which carries wavy band, white on red. Bottom of neck marked by similar white on red band which also forms upper limit of shoulder zone. The latter is bordered below by much wider red band extending around jar just under handles and carrying superposed running spiral in white. Handles mark off three panels on shoulder, each of which is decorated by upright groups of irregular parallel S-shaped lines in white on red, four groups in one panel, three in the others. Broad red stripe descends from each handle toward bottom of jar; it bears multiple upward-pointing parallel chevrons in white. In one instance pattern continues on up handle. The other two handles carry each two longitudinal stripes; all three handles are framed within usual surrounding border in same technique.

No. 604 (Fig. 330). Whole exterior of jar seems to have been coated with creamy slip now in part turned gray. On it were painted bands, stripes, and motives in dark—whether black or brown or red is uncertain, but probably the latter—bearing white lines and chevrons in same technique as seen on No. 600. On flattened top of lip red band bearing wavy stripe in white. Below rim and around base of neck broad red bands, with superposed narrow bands in white. At level of bottom of handles similar two-colored band forms lower border of the three shoulder panels in the handle zone. Each is decorated with groups of triple S-shaped lines in sharply curved form, two groups in one panel, three in another, and the number doubtful in the third—all in red paint apparently without applied white. The handles, surrounded by usual border in the red-and-white technique, bear multiple chevrons pointing upward; they continue down on a broad stripe descending to a red band, carrying a superposed white one just above foot.

No. 606 (Fig. 330). Like Nos. 600 and 604, decorated in same technique of white superposed on red. Top of flat lip painted reddish; a red band around bottom of neck and spreading somewhat below junction with body; on upper part of shoulder a fairly broad zone in similar reddish paint, and on each handle a wide stripe of same color continuing on down below to bottom of jar. On this under layer of red are painted in white broadly splaying multiple chevrons (*MP*, Motive 58:32 or 33, Parallel Chevrons, p. 383 fig. 67) on lip; a white band at base of neck; white bands bordering the red zone above and below and in the shoulder panels a running spiral (*MP*, Motive 46:54 p. 357 fig. 60) interrupted by the handles. Four spirals appear in two of spaces between handles, only three in the third. On each handle two longitudinal white stripes. Two similar white lines border the vertical red stripe below handles and between them two wavy white lines running down to base. Among Furumark's motives straight bordering lines and wavy lines are numerous but no combination of the two exactly like that here described is shown.

These three jars, Nos. 600, 604, and 606, are much alike and presumably came from the same atelier. The painters were somewhat more conservative than the exuberant artists who decorated the jars numbered Nos. 418, 610, 612, and they seem to have been satisfied with adapting motives of their own time rather than going back into the past.

Distribution:
Room 23: 1 numbered.
Room 38: 6 counted, 5 numbered.

55a. Pithos: handleless, high neck (*coarse*)   Fig. 382

Very small torus base; tall ovoid body sloping in to high, wide, tapering neck ending in thick everted rim, flat on top.

Cf. *MP*, Type 13, p. 75 fig. 21.

Examples: 2 numbered, No. 416 (Fig. 329) from Room 32, No. 602 (Figs. 330, 382) from Room 38.

Size:	No. 416	No. 602
height	1.40 m.	0.97 m.
diameter rim	0.48 m.	0.419 m.
width rim	0.045 m.	0.050 m.
thickness rim	0.023 m.	0.016 m.
d. neck below rim	0.415 m.	0.393 m.
max. d. neck	0.50 m.	0.460 m.
diameter body	0.720 m.	0.628 m.
diameter base	0.178 m.	0.132 m.

55b. PITHOS: VERY LARGE; RIBBED (*coarse*)   Fig. 381

Thick walls made of clay containing mica. Flat base, piriform body, relatively narrow high neck of concave profile splaying outward to thick broad flattened rim. Body decorated (and perhaps strengthened) by 42 encircling horizontal molded "rope-bands" of clay, each bearing numerous transverse impressions made by fingernail or implement. Two broad handles set horizontally opposite each other just below junction of neck and body; at same level two narrow vertical handles also set opposite each other in axis at right angles to that of horizontal handles. Two further rather small vertical handles attached opposite each other 0.305 m. above bottom of jar, exhibiting no recognizable relation to the handles above.

Example: 1 numbered, from Room 7.			
Size:	No. 1147	diameter	1.075 m.
height	1.64 m.	d. across horizontal handles	1.05 m.
diameter rim	0.61-0.64 m.	d. across vertical handles	1.06 m.
width rim	0.08-0.09 m.	diameter base	0.38 m.
thickness rim	0.03 m.	width lower handle	0.045 m.
min. diameter neck	0.47 m.	width horizontal handles	0.06 m.
from top of rim to first rib	0.21-0.22 m.	width vertical handles	0.045 m.

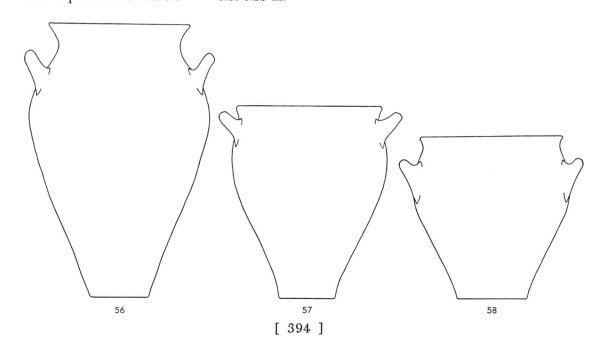

56   57   58

[394]

56. STORAGE JAR: LARGE, VERY DEEP; TWO HORIZONTAL HANDLES, LOW NECK, WIDE MOUTH (*plain and decorated*)   Figs. 382, 383, 384

Flattened bottom or torus base; tall ovoid body; very low splaying or tapering neck ending in thick everted rounded lip flat on top; two round or grooved loop-handles set horizontally high on shoulder. Plain or with painted decoration on shoulder. Variations in type of base, shape of body, angle of handles, neck, and decoration.

No real parallels of this size.

Examples: 3 numbered, all from Room 38 (Fig. 330).

Size:	No. 607	No. 601	No. 611
height	0.930 m.	0.883 m.	0.760 m.
diameter			
rim	0.505 m.	0.465 m.	0.423 m.
width rim	0.045 m.	0.045 m.	0.035 m.
diameter			
neck	0.491 m.	0.402 m.	0.374 m.
diameter			
body	0.700 m.	0.630 m.	0.675 m.
diameter			
base	0.185 m.	0.195 m.	0.238 m.

Example with decoration:

No. 607 (Fig. 383). Reddish paint on reddish-buff clay. Flat top of lip bears diagonals in alternating groups of three, right to left, left to right, almost a zigzag. Broad band around exterior of lip overlapping top of neck. Another broad band at level of handles. Space between divided by narrower horizontal band into two zones, each bearing highly irregular zigzag or wavy band. Cf. *MP*, Motive 53:18, 19, 20, p. 373 fig. 65. Handles have stripe along each edge and one in groove. Rings around bases of handles from which paint has dripped down. May have had painted band on edge of base but not certain.

57. STORAGE JAR, KRATER-LIKE: LARGE, DEEP; TWO HORIZONTAL HANDLES, WIDE MOUTH (*decorated and plain*)   Figs. 382, 383, 384

Flat bottom; tall piriform body; wide mouth with thick horizontal lip; two round loop-handles set horizontally and obliquely high on shoulder.

Furumark illustrates no parallels nor have we found any from other sites.

Examples: 2 numbered.

Size:	No. 599	No. 820
height	0.653 m.	0.620 m.
diameter rim	0.474 m.	0.455 m.
width rim	0.043 m.	0.033 m.
d. beneath		
rim	0.460 m.	0.438 m.
diameter body	0.500 m.	0.505 m.
diameter base	0.213 m.	0.185 m.

Example with decoration:

No. 599 (Fig. 383). Badly injured by fire. Lip may have had decoration but no recognizable remains of it. From lip to level of handle attachment a fairly broad zone, coated over-all in paint, probably originally reddish, ran around vessel. On it are faint traces of a broad irregular wavy line or zigzag in grayish-white. A band in similar white marks lower border of zone and continues across outer surface of handle. A narrow loop apparently framed bases of handles on each side.

Distribution:

Room 38: No. 599.
Room 98: No. 820.

[395]

58. KRATER: LARGE; TWO HORIZONTAL HANDLES, WIDE MOUTH (*coarse*)

Figs. 382, 383, 384

Flattened bottom; deep ovoid or rounded biconical body with wide mouth; spreading rounded lip; two round loop-handles set horizontally and obliquely on shoulder. Diameter close to or greater than height.

Cf. *MP*, Type 280, p. 75 fig. 21. *Zygouries*, Potter's Shop, pp. 161-162, fig. 157 no. 530.

Examples: 4 numbered.

Size:	largest	smallest
height	0.515 m.	0.439 m.
diameter rim	0.498 m.	0.449 m.
diameter body	0.520 m.	0.491 m.
diameter		
handles	0.032 m.	0.028 m.
diameter base	0.232 m.	0.189 m.

Distribution:

Room 32: No. 417. Lip pulled out on one side to form little pour-channel. Allover light grayish paint.
Room 34: No. 400.
Room 38: No. 609.
Room 98: No. 839.

59. KRATER: SMALL; TWO VERTICAL HANDLES ON SIDE

Figs. 383, 384

Flattened bottom or raised base sometimes slightly hollowed underneath with or without hump at center of interior; semi-globular or globular-biconical body, diameter greater than height; splaying or spreading lip with rounded or beveled edge; two relatively large thick round or flattened handles set vertically from top to middle of side making a wide loop. Between handles high on each side occasionally a carelessly made, angular, elongated boss set vertically.

Cf. *MP*, Type 288 (not illustrated). *Zygouries*, Potter's Shop, cooking pots, p. 157 no. 9, fig. 152 nos. 126, 127. Ours very similar.

Examples: 66 counted, 21 numbered.

Size:	largest	smallest
height	0.304 m.	0.138 m.
diameter rim	0.214 m.	0.140 m.
d. below rim	0.204 m.	0.134 m.
max. diameter	0.310 m.	0.154 m.
diameter		
handles	0.023 m.	0.016 m.
diameter base	0.138 m.	0.075 m.
capacity[1]	12.800 liters	1.550 liters

Distribution:

Exterior Propylon: 1 numbered.
Room 23: 1 numbered.
Room 60: 31 counted, 3 numbered.
Room 68: 30 counted, 13 numbered.
Room 97: 1 numbered.
Room 98: 2 numbered.

[1] The pots inventoried are of three more or less standard sizes: in the first group one holds 12.800 liters, one 12.700, one 10.950, one 10.200, one 9.000, one 8.400, one 8.300. In the second group one holds 3.950, one 3.600, two 3.500, two 3.350, two 3.300, one 3.200, one 2.500. In the third group one holds 1.650, two 1.550. One cannot be measured.

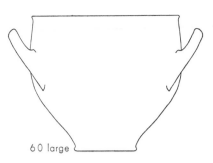
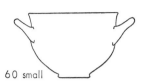

59   60 large   60 small

60. KRATER-BOWL ("DEEP BOWL"): SMALL; TWO HORIZONTAL HANDLES (*decorated*)

Figs. 385, 386

Ring-base; convex side flaring to widest diameter then closing slightly to spreading rounded rim (maximum diameter somewhat greater than height); two relatively large round arched handles set horizontally and obliquely above or at greatest diameter of body; coated in solid color all over or with patterns in shoulder zone.

Cf. *MP*, Type 284, pp. 48, 49 figs. 13, 14. Many examples cited. Hard to recognize variations or to see difference between what Furumark calls III B (Type 284) and III C (Type 285). *ChT*, pls. XXXI no. 59 (Granary Class), XLV no. 5. Mycenae, *BSA* XXV, fig. 9a, b, e, f (Granary Class), fig. 12 b (Granary Class), pls. V (LH III), X b (Granary Class), XI m, n (Granary Class). *MV*, pl. XLIV Shape 76. *Prosymna*, this shape is rare; figs. 206 no. 1166, 236 no. 451, 252 no. 861, 719 no. 153, pp. 450-451 kraters. *Korakou*, figs. 83, 85, 103; pp. 61-63, Shape 1. *Asine*, p. 302 nos. 6 (fig. 207 no. 6), 8, 9 (fig. 208 nos. 1, 2); p. 368 no. 36 (fig. 237); p. 398 no. 12 (fig. 260 no. 5), no. 15 (fig. 260 no. 8). *Ergon*, 1955, fig. 26; 1960, fig. 24 no. 768; 1961, fig. 13 no. 837; 1962, fig. 25 no. 1032: all from chamber tombs at Perati. *Ergon*, 1961, fig. 58, from Iolkos. *Ergon*, 1958, fig. 134, krater-bowls (III B) from first room of Sector Γ at Mycenae.

Examples: 10 numbered. Variations in size, profile, shape of base, rim and slope of handles.

Size:	largest	smallest
height	0.183 m.	0.093 m.
diameter rim	0.199 m.	0.115 m.
diameter body	0.215 m.	0.114 m.
diameter handle	missing	missing
diameter base	0.085 m.	0.052 m.
capacity[1]	3.800 liters	—

Examples with decoration (Fig. 385):

No. 576. Dark brown lightening to reddish-brown paint on greenish-buff. Band on plain rim; wider band just below forming upper limit of decorated zone; lower limit marked by two bands which pass just under handles; handles coated over-all. Band around base. Decorated zone occupied by multiple zigzag of five, six or seven lines. At the bottom some of the lines run over the bordering bands. Though not identical, pattern is much like Furumark's Motive 61:17 Zigzag (*MP*, p. 383 fig. 67).

No. 593. Black lightening to brown paint; gray to buff slip. Band about half way down around interior, broad ring around bottom; band around inside of lip continuing outside and below; two bands below shoulder zone passing underneath handles; band around ring base and broad stripe on exterior of handles. Daub of paint around upper part of each handle attachment. On each side in

---

[1] Of the inventoried examples that can be measured no two hold the same amount: 3.800 liters, 1.700,

1.450, 1.150, 0.850, 0.750, 0.600.

shoulder zone central triglyph enclosing parallel chevrons pointing upwards; from triglyph springs to right and left long curving stem that ends in spiral, winding down to right (only one preserved), up to left (both preserved). Triglyph on one side of pot fringed on its left edge (its right edge missing). Triglyph in other panel not fringed.

No. 594. Coated over-all, inside and out, in reddish-brown paint mottled by the fire.

No. 677. Brownish-black paint on greenish clay. Coated over-all inside and out except for reserved handle zone. The handles themselves painted on exterior. In reserved zone, decoration consists of floral motive with central bud and long pointed leaf spreading to right and left, outlined and hatched; or it may be meant for bird with outstretched wings. Above head or bud group of seven irregular short vertical lines of unknown meaning. No comparable motive illustrated by Furumark. Possibly a remote variant of his Antithetic Spiral Pattern (*MP*, Motive 50:22, 31, p. 366 fig. 63).

No. 808. Brownish-black to reddish-brown paint on grayish slip. Fairly wide band half way down on interior, narrow one on rim, inside and out. Handle zone bordered by broad band above, two narrow bands below. Stripe on handles and on each side of attachment. Main decoration consists of central panel filled with crosshatching (cf. *MP*, Motive 75:23, p. 414 fig. 72) bordered laterally by three upright lines beyond which Antithetic Spiral Pattern (cf. *MP*, Motive 50:24, 29, 32, p. 366 fig. 63) extends out right and left to handles. Fairly broad band at junction of body and base. *Prosymna*, fig. 236 no. 451 has comparable pattern.

No. 813. Brownish-black to reddish-brown paint on greenish-gray to buff slip. Five concentric circles on bottom of interior. Bands inside and on rim. Six fine horizontal lines mark bottom of handle zone. Latter contains handles with blobs on top and big smear at junction with body and between handles panel decoration: central "triglyph," bordered on each side by four upright lines, enclosing four units of triple concentric half

circles arranged in two groups, one with convexity upward and one above inverted (cf. *MP*, Motive 43:22, p. 343 fig. 57). Toward each extremity of panel near handle two fine upright bordering lines enclosing vertical zigzag (cf. *MP*, Motive 75:10, 22, 38, p. 414 fig. 72). Band around top of base. Horizontal lines, neatly and delicately executed, carefully drawn while pot revolved on wheel, Cf. *BSA* xxv, pl. v c, e from Mycenae. *MV*, pl. vi no. 31 xii, from Ialysos.

No. 862. In very badly damaged state, most of surface worn away. Remnants of brownish-black paint on creamy buff slip. Traces of concentric circles around bottom of interior and band along inside and outside of rim. Faint suggestions of band forming lower border of handle zone, remnants of paint on handle but nature uncertain. In each field between handles there were apparently three upright "triglyphs" consisting of two vertical bordering lines containing a column of parallel chevrons pointing upward (*MP*, Motive 75:9, 20, p. 414 fig. 72) arranged with one unit centered and one far to each side close to the handles. Vestiges of band around top of base.

No. 1150. Reddish-brown paint. Narrow band along rim inside and out; shoulder zone bears pattern of Triglyph and Half Rosette (cf. *MP*, Motives 74 and 75, p. 414 fig. 72, combined with some elements of Motive 43, Multiple Semicircles, *MP*, p. 343 fig. 57, p. 345 fig. 58; but not exactly duplicating the Pylian composition) on one side formed by ten vertical lines flanked to right and left by triple concentric arcs (cf. *MP*, Motive 43:43, p. 345 fig. 58); on the other side of vessel similar design but with only eight vertical lines forming triglyph. In the spaces between triglyphs and handles an upright column of overlapping chevrons (cf. *MP*, Motive 58:17 p. 383 fig. 67).

No. 1172. Coated solidly inside and out with streaky grayish-black paint, showing reddish blotches.

No. 1176. Surface badly worn; apparently once coated in reddish-brown paint. May in part have had patterned decoration.

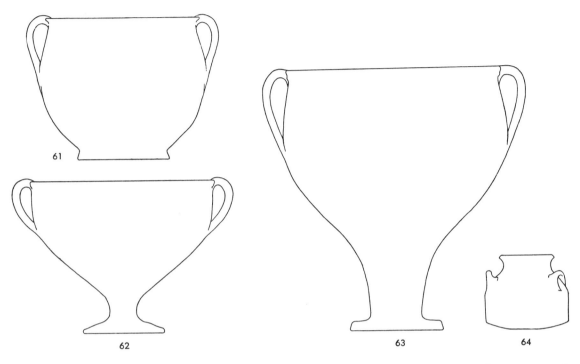

61. KRATER: TWO FLAT VERTICAL HANDLES FROM RIM TO SIDE   Figs. 387, 388

Disk-base with projecting angular edge; fairly deep bowl spreading widely from base to greatest diameter then curving slightly inward to rounded everted lip; two broad flat handles extending from rim to widest part of body.

No near analogy found in Furumark's illustrated examples but the bowl with its flat handles is much like that of the two following stemmed and pedestaled types.

Example: 1 numbered from Room 46.

Size:	No. 1131	diameter neck	0.216 m.
height	0.188 m.	diameter body	0.244 m.
diameter rim	0.221 m.	width handles	0.033 m.
		diameter base	0.128 m.

62. STEMMED KRATER: TWO FLAT VERTICAL HANDLES FROM RIM TO SIDE

Figs. 387, 388

Large splaying foot with rounded or straight edge, concave underneath with deep central countersunk hollow; stem relatively thick, very short; deep bowl spreading widely from foot to greatest diameter then curving slightly inward to rounded

[399]

everted rim; diameter greater than height. Two broad flat handles coming out almost horizontally from rim and looping down to body at greatest diameter.

Korakou, fig. 91 is somewhat similar except for its massive foot. The short-stemmed kraters from Pylos, which have no real parallels in the Mycenaean III B Period at other sites, look as if they are descended from much earlier Mycenaean types (*Korakou*, figs. 58, 59). The potters who worked for the palace seem to have had archaizing antiquarian tastes.

Examples: 24 counted, 8 numbered, all from Room 20.

			diameter		
			pedestal	0.059 m.	0.041 m.
Size:	largest	smallest	width handle	0.040 m.	0.030 m.
height	0.261 m.	0.203 m.	diameter base	0.115 m.	0.115 m.
diameter rim	0.300 m.	0.250 m.	capacity[1]	9.500 liters	4.000 liters

63. Pedestaled krater: high; two flat vertical handles from rim to side (*decorated*)
Figs. 387, 388

Broad thick disk-like foot, hollow underneath; fairly high thick cylindrical pedestal spreading out on interior as well as exterior to deep rounded bowl that narrows slightly to everted lip, flat on top and sloping inward (diameter of rim is approximately the same as the greatest diameter of the bowl); two broad, flat handles coming out almost horizontally from lip and looping down to body at greatest diameter.

Cf. *MP*, Type 9, p. 23 fig. 4 (III B). *MV*, pl. xxxi no. 297 from Mycenae has same decoration as No. 826 but higher stem; pl. xliv Shape 48; pl. vi no. 32 xii from Ialysos has more rounded bowl; pl. xv no. 93 from Nauplia. *Korakou*, pp. 63-64, fig. 91 (LH III).

Examples: 5 numbered.

Size:	largest	smallest
height	0.355 m.	0.290 m.
diameter rim	0.355 m.	0.307 m.
diameter body	0.353 m.	0.320 m.
width handles	0.040 m.	0.043 m.
diameter stem	0.070 m.	0.066 m.
diameter foot	0.130 m.	0.120 m.
capacity[2]	14.600 liters	11.000 liters

Examples with decoration (Fig. 387):

No. 596. Blackish-brown to brown paint on greenish-buff. Band on inside of lip spreading out over rim to upper part of body; three broad bands mark lower limit of handle zone. Handles, framed by widely curving stripe on each side, bear broad stripe along edges which is continued across horizontal bands and curves outward in spreading loop that turns up again to lowest band. In field on each side of bowl two broad, more or less parallel, wavy bands (cf. *MP*, Motive 53:9, 11, 21, p. 373 fig. 65; *Asine*, p. 302 no. 8, fig. 208 no. 1 for similar pattern on krater-bowl). Stem and top of base coated over-all. Execution careless: paint applied rather thickly and has dripped down in several places.

No. 810. Black to brownish-black lightening to reddish on gray to buff slip. Continuous band inside, on top of and outside rim; two bands just below handles forming lower border of decorated zone. Handles, framed within broad curving stripes, bear two wide longitudinal bands which continue far down on body then bend widely upward again to lower of two bordering bands. In spacious field on each side between handles a more or less nearly symmetrical composition. At center a

[1] Of the inventoried examples one holds 9.500 liters, one 8.500, one 7.800, one 7.700, two 7.000, one 6.500, one 4.000.

[2] The third measurable example holds 13.500 liters.

highly conventionalized Mycenaean III Flower (cf. *MP*, Motive 18:27, p. 287 fig. 42). Stem represented by six upright lines, three curving sharply to right, three to left, and hanging down almost parallel to main stem. In one panel a short curving leaf springs out from bottom on each side of stem. The flower above, supported by stem, is made of irregular concentric arcs (six on one face, nine on the other) bordered above by row of dots; two stamens (?) flare out widely to right and left. Flanking central motive on each side, between it and handle, are three (in one instance four) stiffly made murex shells (*MP*, Motive 23, Whorl-shell, p. 311 fig. 51) standing upright side by side, all turned in same direction. Each is attached to rim-band by a straight line which turns at right angles and makes four narrow parallel loops to represent upper part of shell. Lower part, triangular in shape, is long and narrow, terminating in a sharp point at bottom border of zone; each contains central column of dots that continues to lower border. Three bands run around lower part of body; stem and upper part of base coated over-all.

No. 826. Brownish-black to red paint on greenish-gray to pinkish-buff. Band covers inside and outside of lip forming upper border of handle zone, lower limit of which marked by two neatly drawn horizontal bands. Handles, framed by widely curving stripes, bear two longitudinal bands which continue far down below zone curving out broadly to right and left and swinging up again to lower of two bordering bands. Each field between handles is sparingly decorated with three "antithetic" pairs of murexes (cf. *MP*, Motive 23:19, 20, Whorl-shell, p. 311 fig. 51) all attached to the upper border by a line descending in slight curve to two circles, the inner presumably representing the mouth. Three narrow loops below, each filled with row of dots or dashes render upper part of shell. Lower part tapers to point resting on upper bordering stripe, a central column of dots in each extending down to the bottom. Much lower on body two horizontal bands,

just above stem and foot which were coated over-all.

Cf. *Eutresis*, House v, fig. 263 no. 5. *MV*, pl. xxxi no. 297 found by Schliemann at Mycenae (NM. 1148).

No. 1090. Brownish-black paint on greenish-buff. Band covers inside, top and outside of lip and slightly lower forming upper border of handle zone which is delimited below by three horizontal bands. Each handle bears two broad stripes overlapping at top and spreading out to right and left below, across lower border of zone and curving slightly upward ending midway between handle zone and stem. Decorated field, relatively narrow, bears on one face five widely spaced single murexes in upright position (cf. *MP*, Motive 23 Whorl-shell, p. 311 fig. 51). Other face too badly damaged to preserve arrangement but it was probably the same. Each murex is suspended from upper band by a straight or slightly curving line (perhaps its proboscis). A circle with central dot may indicate mouth; below it are three narrow loops filled with dots representing upper part of shell. Lower part is shown by two lines that taper gradually to a sharp point reaching middle line of the triple border below. A central column of dots extends down to uppermost band of border. A broad band encircles stem and spreads down over top of foot.

Cf. Stubbings, *Mycenaean Pottery from the Levant*, pl. v no. 3 (British Museum A 875 [*CVA. BM* 5, p. 3.8]) from Ialysos, Rhodes.

No. 1151. Brownish-black paint (which has lost its luster) on greenish-gray clay. Foot and stem coated all over to height of 0.08 m.; just above are three broad horizontal bands forming lower limit of wide undecorated zone, separated by three similar bands from upper or handle zone. Latter bears on each side, between the two flat vertical handles, a fairly symmetrical composition. At center a figure similar to Furumark's Motive 18:27 or 28 (*MP* p. 287 fig. 42) but somewhat more elaborate: upper part is shaped by three groups of concentric arcs: large one underneath, bordered below by horizontal line, and smaller one superposed and splaying outward to left and right. Triple vertical lines form stem below, stopping when they reach the horizontal line; the latter at each end bends downward in sharp curve and descends to lower limit of zone. About midway between main design and handles to right and left is a subordinate motive, a double, joined murex, Furumark's Motive 23:21 or 22 (*MP*, p. 311 fig. 51). In most interspaces between central figure and twin murex, and between latter and handles is small subsidiary ornament: a dotted circle surrounded by dots. By exception, on one side near handle a more complex device comprising three or four small circles with lines and dots above and below. Band of paint along rim inside and outside; edges of each handle similarly marked. Broad stripe borders handles on each side, running from rim to and across the three bands forming bottom of decorated zone.

Most remarkable feature of vessel is burned and twisted projecting section of lower part of one side which was melted and almost vitrified by intense heat of fire.

All five of the numbered examples from the palace bear painted decoration in the shoulder zone. In four instances the motive is the murex or Whorl-shell (*MP*, Motive 23, p. 311 fig. 51) in a variety of arrangements, paired, triple, quadruple, once at least with a floral design in the center of the composition. In a deposit apparently of Mycenaean III A was found a pedestaled krater of approximately the same shape but with an altogether different pattern.

Distribution:

Inner Stoa of Propylon: No. 1151.
Room 38: No. 596.
Room 64: No. 826.
Corridor 95: No. 810.
Room 99: No. 1090.

64. SQUAT JAR OR ALABASTRON: ANGULAR PROFILE; THREE HORIZONTAL HANDLES
(*decorated*)   Figs. 385, 386

Flat or flattened bottom; straight vertical sides, sloping rounded shoulder, low concave neck splaying to sloping rim. Three round loop-handles set horizontally and rising vertically from low on shoulder.

Cf. *MP*, Type 94, p. 44 fig. 12 (III A:2 — B). *MV*, pls. XLIV Shape 34, XV no. 95 from Nauplia. Pylos Chamber Tombs E 6 and Kokkevis 3, nos. 734, 954. *Prosymna*, figs. 97 no. 201, 194 no. 452, 564 no. 993; 357 no. 771 and 572 no. 1188 have crosshatching on the shoulder. *BCH* 17 (1923), p. 218, fig. 31 from Skhinokhori-Lyrkeia, Tomb E: angular albastron, crosshatching on shoulder. *Deltion* 3, p. 83, fig. 59 from Thebes, Ismenion, Tomb 2: angular alabastron, crosshatching on shoulder.

Examples: 2 numbered.

Size:	No. 410	No. 464
height	0.098 m.	pres. 0.055 m.
diameter rim	0.075 m.	—
diameter neck	0.063 m.	0.050 m.
diameter body	0.113 m.	0.080 m.
diameter handles	0.008 m.	0.005 m.
diameter base	0.045 m.	0.075 m.
capacity	0.500 liter	—

Examples with decoration (Fig. 385):

No. 410. Paint now black on dark gray clay; original color uncertain. Band around inside, top and outside of lip, another at base of neck which marks upper limit of shoulder zone. Latter bordered above and below by a horizontal band, the lower at angle of body. Handles painted on top. The three panels between handles occupied by diagonal crosshatching (*MP*, Motive 57:2, Diaper Net, p. 383 fig. 67); one horizontal band around bottom of body.

No. 464. Reddish paint on grayish-tan. Lip and most of neck missing. Horizontal band just below angle and two just above bottom. Upper zone bears some trace of decoration but design cannot be recognized.

Distribution:
Room 32: No. 410.
Room 60: No. 464.

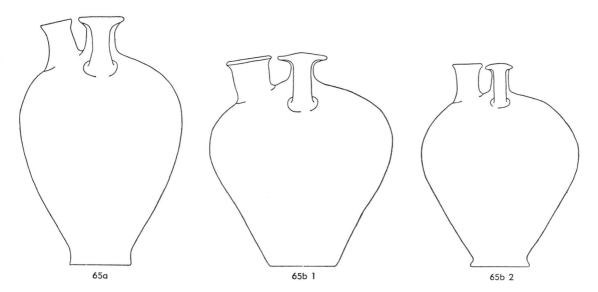

65a   65b 1   65b 2

65. STIRRUP-VASE OR FALSE-NECKED AMPHORA   Figs. 389-394

One of the most popular and most distinctive shapes of all those created by Mycenaean potters is the stirrup-vase or false-necked amphora as it has been variously and not too happily called. Great numbers have been found especially in tombs and less frequently in settlements throughout the whole extent of the Mycenaean world. The Palace of Nestor yielded 45 examples which have been numbered and many more incomplete. Numerous variations in size, proportions, details of shape of base, body, spout, neck, disk, and handles. All but one decorated. The following descriptions deal successively with the chief sub-varieties of the stirrup-vase that we have ventured to differentiate:

      a. slender   d. small, high shouldered
      b. plump   e. pedestaled
      c. globular   f. unclassified

65a. STIRRUP-VASE: SLENDER TYPE (*decorated and plain*)   Figs. 389, 390

Flat base with slightly splaying edge; tall, elongated piriform body; concave neck; flat disk somewhat larger than neck with sloping edge; thick flattened perpendicular handles; slightly slanting spout.

In form this type is similar to the stirrup-vases found in the House of the Oil Merchant at Mycenae (*BSA* XLVIII [1953], pl. 7 c, d); also closely resembles the inscribed jars from Tiryns,

Mycenae, and Orchomenos as well as those found in the Kadmeion at Thebes (*PM* IV, pp. 739ff., figs. 723, 726). Cf. *MP*, Type 164, p. 37 fig. 9. *Prosymna*, p. 451 type a, fig. 529 no. 1025. *BSA* XXV, p. 80, fig. 19 a and pp. 20f., fig. 5, from Ramp House at Mycenae.

Examples: 2 numbered.

Size:	No. 402	No. 1142
height		
over-all	0.438 m.	—
height of		
body	0.375 m.	0.315 m.
diameter		
spout	0.046 m.	—
diameter		
rim spout	—	—
diameter neck	0.055 m.	—
diameter disk	0.075 m.	—
width handles	0.032 m.	—
width across		
handles	0.190 m.	—
diameter body	0.298 m.	0.295 m.
diameter base	0.110 m.	0.111 m.

Example with decoration:

No. 1142 (Fig. 348 Nos. 1-4). Brownish paint; tan "oatmeal fabric." Band around base, another just above base; at about one fourth of height of vessel two more bands forming the lower border of a broad decorated field; it probably extended all the way up to just below spout and neck (only fragments of which are preserved). In this extensive field on each side of vessel is painted a very large squid with heart-shaped upper part of body connected by spindly line with sacklike lower end. Great eyes represented by two concentric circles enclosing dot. From top of head between eyes a pair of tentacles spring to right and left. On better preserved side upper tentacle waves its way along upper part of shoulder in compressed convolutions to end in a loop below handle. The lower tentacle drops down to bottom border of field and, bending sharply, rises up and descends again and again and finally terminates in curl below that of upper tentacle and above terminal loop of corresponding tentacle from other side of jar. The pair to left was similar but lower tentacle ended near lower border, under loop formed by tentacle of other group. Opposite side of jar is to a considerable extent missing but what has been preserved indicates an arrangement similar to that already described. Ring of paint about bottom of handle on each side. Fragment of disk decorated with two concentric circles.

No exact parallel for the decoration appears in *MP*, but cf. Motive 21:5 Cuttlefish, p. 303 fig. 48 which might perhaps be a remote ancestor of the squid from the palace. A vase of the same general shape and with a strikingly similar decoration appears in *MV*, p. 24, pl. XIV no. 88. It is said to have been purchased from a Cretan. Cf. also *PM* IV, fig. 720 a and b.

Distribution:

Room 32: No. 402.
Area 101: No. 1142 (fragment).

65b. STIRRUP-VASE: PLUMP TYPE, COMMONEST SHAPE (*decorated*)   Figs. 389, 390, 393

Flat bottom or ring-base, piriform body convex or flattened on top; relatively slender slightly concave false neck surmounted by flat or flattened projecting disk, some slightly concave some slightly convex on top; sloping or perpendicular handles; cylindrical slightly concave vertical spout with everted lip rounded or flattened on top; disk and rim of spout approximately level. All decorated with horizontal bands.

Examples: 44 counted, 30 numbered.

65b 1. The three largest examples have flat bottoms and relatively large spouts set with a slight outward slant. On one handles slope outward to join shoulder (Figs. 389, 390).

Examples: 3 counted, 2 numbered.

Size:	No. 807	No. 817
height		
over-all	0.404 m.	0.370 m.
height of		
body	0.350 m.	0.320 m.
diameter		
spout	0.072 m.	0.065 m.
diameter rim		
of spout	missing	0.084 m.
diameter neck	0.047 m.	0.039 m.
diameter disk	0.080 m.	0.083 restored
width handles	0.037 m.	0.030 m.
width across		
handles	0.200 m.	0.210 m.
diameter body	0.352 m.	0.326 m.
diameter base	0.140 m.	0.125 m.

Examples with decoration:

Unrestorable example (Fig. 345 No. 1). Although most of jar is vitrified and completely out of shape it is possible to reconstruct decoration which was in reddish-brown paint on buff. Two broad bands around lower part of body, two below handles; bands around rim and base of spout. Wide stripes on handles, bases of which seem to have been circled. Disk edged with paint enclosing two opposed arcs backed up to each other forming a kind of cross or wheel pattern.

No. 807 (Fig. 389). Blackish paint on gray. Stripes on handles and border around handle attachments, also around base of spout. Scanty remnants of bands around body but surface too damaged to make clear arrangement of decoration.

No. 817 (Fig. 389). Red to red-brown paint on tan to gray. Trace of color on remnant of disk, band around bottom of neck, stripes on handles and around base of attachment; bands around rim and base of spout. Three horizontal bands high on shoulder, two lower on body carelessly drawn, the lower one separating into two through part of circuit.

Distribution:

Room 38: 1 counted; too badly vitrified to be restorable.
Room 96: No. 817.
Room 99: No. 807.

65b 2. Thirteen somewhat smaller are of approximately uniform size: all have a ring-base and perpendicular handles; seven are convex on top, six are flat (Figs. 389, 390, 393).

Cf. *MP*, Type 164, p. 36 fig. 8.

Examples: 17 counted, 13 numbered.

Size:	largest	smallest
height		
over-all	0.357 m.	0.327 m.
height body	0.300 m.	0.269 m.
diameter		
spout	0.043 m.	0.041 m.
diameter		
rim spout	0.057 m.	0.056 m.
diameter neck	0.028 m.	0.026 m.
diameter disk	0.050 m.	0.054 m.
width handles	0.025 m.	0.023 m.
width across		
handles	0.097 m.	0.103 m.
diameter body	0.291 m.	0.263 m.
diameter base	0.109 m.	0.103 m.

Examples with decoration:

No. 682. Black paint brightening to red in many places; probably on light buff slip. Broad band on foot spreading a little way up on body; two bands just below middle of body, three bands on shoulder; stripes around each base of stirrup-handle, stripe along each edge; cross within broad circle on disk (Fig. 393); necks of false spout and real spout ringed at base, stripe around lip.

Nos. 686 and 1140. Altogether similar to No. 682. No. 1140 has suffered severe damage from fire and paint has turned black on greenish-gray.

No. 684 (Fig. 393). Exactly similar to No. 682 except no cross in circle on disk.

No. 685 (Fig. 393). Similar to No. 682 but it has spiral within circle on disk.

No. 689 (Fig. 389). Similar to No. 682 in having two and three bands on body but top of base is painted over-all spreading up onto body. False neck, disk and spout show some traces of paint, although exact arrangement is not certain.

No. 681. Brown paint lightening to red in a few places, probably applied on creamy buff slip. Stripe on top of base encroaching on body. Three bands below greatest diameter, three high on shoulder. Stripes around bases and along edges of handles, spiral on

top of disk; ring around base of false spout as well as spout; top of lip also painted.

No. 683 (Fig. 393) and No. 690 (Fig. 389) are like No. 681.

No. 687 is similar to No. 681 except that its spiral ends in a central blob (Fig. 393).

Nos. 678 (Fig. 393), 679, 680 are similar to No. 681 except that base is wholly coated.

Distribution:
Outer Stoa of Propylon: 1 counted.
Room 46: 1 numbered.
Court 47: 2 numbered.
Room 53: 13 counted, 10 numbered.

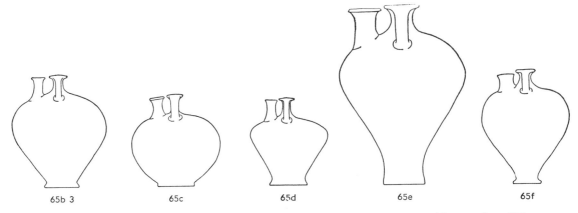

65b 3   65c   65d   65e   65f

65b 3. Fifteen examples form group of much smaller, almost uniform size. They are similar to those in foregoing group with minor variations. The top of the spout is slightly lower than that of disk (Figs. 389, 390).

Cf. *Prosymna*, p. 451, figs. 471 no. 940, 530 no. 1026. *Zygouries*, pp. 149-151, 4: ten large stirrup-vases, fig. 139 no. 370.

Examples: 24 counted, 15 numbered.

Size:	largest	smallest
height with		
handles	0.221 m.	0.190 m.
height body	0.180 m.	0.155 m.
diameter spout	0.017 m.	0.015 m.
diameter rim		
of spout	0.025 m.	0.023 m.
diameter neck	0.025 m.	0.015 m.
diameter disk	0.035 m.	0.032 m.
width handles	0.018 m.	0.013 m.
width across		
handles	0.093 m.	0.069 m.
diameter body	0.185 m.	0.168 m.
diameter base	0.062 m.	0.072 m.

Examples with decoration:

No. 414. Brown lightening to red paint; probably buff slip. Band on top of base spreading slightly up adjacent part of body. Two bands just below greatest diameter; two bands above shoulder zone, the lower splitting into two to make the number three on one side. Ring on base of, and stripes on outer surface of handles, spiral on disk; ring around lower part of false neck and also on lower part of spout connected by a blob with upper band. Top of spout missing.

Nos. 688, 1169. Brown paint; greenish-buff slip. Like No. 414 in all details except that upper part of bands splits into four on one side of vessel. Rim of spout painted.

No. 691 (Fig. 389). Brown lightening to red paint; probably pinkish-buff slip. Band around base spreading onto body; two horizontal bands just below widest diameter, three bands on shoulder. Ring around bases of, and stripes on upper surface of handles; crude spiral on disk; ring around base of false neck, also around base of spout and around rim.

Nos. 692, 693, 694, 1164-1168 are like No. 691.

No. 695 (Fig. 389) is similar to No. 691 except that disk has circle on top and is edged with paint.

No. 696 is also similar to No. 691 except that disk is decorated with three concentric circles (Fig. 393).

No. 459 is similar to No. 691 except that it has four bands on shoulder, two broad with two narrow between.

Distribution:

Outer Propylon: 11 counted, 6 numbered.
Room 32: 1 numbered.
Court 47: 7 counted, 6 numbered.
Room 53: 4 counted, 1 numbered.
Room 60: 1 numbered.

65c. STIRRUP-VASE: GLOBULAR (*decorated*) Figs. 391, 392

Low ring-base; "depressed-globular" body; slender, relatively high false neck, large projecting disk, convex on top with diminutive central knob; flat perpendicular handles; spout with concave profile, everted round lip; spout a trifle short of height of disk.

Cf. *MP*, Type 171, p. 31 fig. 6. *ChT*, pls. XIX nos. 3, 7, XLV no. 4, LI no. 15, LII nos. 10, 11. *Prosymna*, p. 451, figs. 720 no. 38, 721 no. 130. *MV*, pls. XLIV Shape 50, VII no. 37. *RT, Dendra*, fig. 57. *Asine*, fig. 234. This shape appears frequently in tombs in Argolis. In Messenia too it seems to have been often placed in chamber tombs but only a single example was recovered in the palace: Pylos, Chamber Tomb Kokkevis 3: nos. 942, 953; Chamber Tomb K 1: nos. 753, 757.

Example: 1 numbered, from Room 32.

Size:	No. 411
height over-all	0.162 m.
height body	0.125 m.
diameter spout	0.017 m.
diameter rim spout	0.027 m.
diameter neck	0.012 m.
diameter disk	0.033 m.
width handles	0.015 m.
width across handles	0.079 m.
diameter body	0.160 m.
diameter base	0.066 m.

Example with decoration:

No. 411 (Fig. 391). Dark brown paint with red blushes; smooth buff slip. Band on base spreading somewhat upward on body. Exterior of vessel from bottom to circle on top decorated by horizontal bands and groups of fine lines, the bands dividing surface into four main zones of unequal breadth. Lowest and broadest bears—somewhat below middle of area—three thin parallel horizontal lines. Next succeeding zone, which is narrow, contains seven fine horizontal lines which fill space between bordering bands. Shoulder zone, third in order and fairly wide, carries near its middle two parallel horizontal lines fringed above and below by attached Joining Semicircles or Arcs (cf. *MP*, Motive 42:6, III B, p. 343 fig. 57), running around the pot, with short interspaces, in six groups, ranging from 13 to 19 semicircles in each. Fourth zone is filled with six fine lines between the framing bands. The circle forming top of vessel and containing handles, false neck and spout, is decorated with a floral motive (*MP* Mycenaean III Flower, Motive 18:128, III B, p. 293 fig. 45), one flower on each side of spout, and two on opposite side of handles, which are edged and almost coated with paint on top; top of disk bears stripe along edge enclosing four concentric circles. Base of false neck and that of spout, as well as rim of latter, ringed.

Workmanship admirable, decoration executed with neatness and care in all details. Possibly an import from Argolis.

65d. STIRRUP-VASE: SMALL; HIGH SHOULDER (*decorated*) Figs. 391, 392, 394

Ring-base; body flares outward to shoulder then curves sharply to convex top from which rise handles, false neck, and spout. In three examples top of spout is approximately level with that of disk; and in four slightly lower. The nine examples numbered differ somewhat in proportions; seven belong to what may be called a high type, two to a squat type, one being very small. Band decoration and pattern on shoulder.

Cf. *MP*, Types 182, 179, p. 44 fig. 12. *RT, Dendra*, fig. 57. *Prosymna*, figs. 722 no. 149, 723 no. 84. *Asine*, fig. 234.

Examples: 9 numbered; considerable variation in size and details.

Size:	largest	smallest
height		
over-all	0.170 m.	0.120 m.
height body	0.131 m.	0.085 m.
diameter		
spout	0.016 m.	0.014 m.
diameter rim		
spout	0.024 m.	0.024 m.
diameter neck	0.013 m.	0.027 m.
diameter disk	0.032 m.	0.028 m.
width handles	0.013 m.	0.012 m.
width across		
handles	0.070 m.	0.070 m.
diameter body	0.151 m.	0.125 m.
diameter base	0.071 m.	0.062 m.

Examples with decoration:

No. 412 (Fig. 391). Dark brown paint lightening almost to reddish; buff slip. Band on base spreading slightly up on body and bordered by two fine lines; two broad horizontal bands just below greatest diameter enclosing between them fine lines, four or five in number; two more broad bands above shoulder zone also with four fine parallel lines between them (missing in water color). In shoulder zone narrow decorative band of Running Zigzag (*MP*, Motive 61:2, 3, 4, p. 383 fig. 67) bordered above and below by two fine lines. Stripe on stirrup-handles, spiral with central blob on disk, ring around bot-

tom of false neck, spout missing. Handle zone decorated with Mycenaean III Flower (cf. *MP*, Motive 18:127, 129, p. 293 fig. 45, but in reverse). Three flowers on half opposite spout; to right of spout between latter and handle another form of Mycenaean III Flower (cf. *MP*, Motive 18:136, p. 293 fig. 45), but on No. 412 the flower has double curved lines bordered by dots at top. Area to left of spout missing.

No. 412 was made and decorated with skill and delicacy, more or less in same style as No. 411.

For similar Running Zigzags compare: *BSA* xxv, fig. 6 a, from Lion Gate, and *Ergon*, 1961, fig. 161 right, from outside citadel at Mycenae; *Prosymna*, fig. 124 no. 267.

No. 809 (Fig. 391). Paint brown deepening almost to black, greenish-buff slip; surface of pot badly worn and paint almost obliterated in some places. Band on base spreading onto body, bordered above by two fine lines; just below angle two broad bands enclosing five fine horizontal parallel lines; similar pair of broad bands with seven fine lines between in shoulder zone (Fig. 394). Only decoration within it consists of two fine parallel lines. Longitudinal stripes on top of handles; disk decorated with seven neatly drawn concentric circles; ring around base of false neck and of spout; lip probably also edged with paint. Handle zone decorated with Mycenaean III Flower (somewhat like *MP*, Motive 18: 113,

114, p. 293 fig. 45, but reversed and with an open curl instead of a closed loop), three flowers on the half opposite spout, one on each side between spout and handle.

This pot too was painted with great delicacy and precision.

No. 613 (Fig. 391). Brown paint turning reddish here and there; greenish-buff slip. Surface badly worn; paint obliterated in some places. Only remnant of base preserved; probably covered by band of paint spreading up on body. Two broad horizontal bands just below greatest diameter. Two broad bands enclosing fine lines on shoulder zone; difficult to count exact number of fine lines, at least three possibly five. Handles bear stripes on top; ring around base; spiral ending in blob on disk (Fig. 394); ring around bottom of false neck and spout. Band along rim of spout. Decoration in handle zone: two units of Mycenaean III Flower in half opposite spout and one each between spout and handles. Not well enough preserved to identify with any of the variations illustrated by Furumark (*MP*, Motive 18, p. 293 fig. 45), though similar.

No. 699 (Fig. 391). Brown paint lightening to red; buff slip. Band on base spreading a little on body. Two bands somewhat below greatest diameter. Shoulder zone bare, bordered above by two broad horizontal bands enclosing four to five lines. Bottom of handles, false neck and spout, and rim of latter ringed with paint; band on surface of handles, spiral on disk. Simple decoration in handle zone (Fig. 394): an arc of 14 parallel strokes in the half opposite spout; between spout and stirrup-handle seven strokes on one side, eight on the other. These parallel strokes are not illustrated as a separate pattern by Furumark but they might well be a last survival in the evolution of the Mycenaean III Flower (cf. *MP*, Motive 18, handle zone examples, p. 293 fig. 45).

No. 697 (Fig. 391). Brown to brownish-black paint; buff slip. Decoration virtually identical with that of No. 699 except that motive ornamenting handle zone (Fig. 394) is different consisting of U-Pattern (cf. *MP*,

Motive 45:4, p. 345 fig. 58) in interlocking pairs of U's one right side up the other upside down. Half of zone opposite spout contains a curving row of five pairs; between spout and handle on each side are two pairs.

No. 698. Brown paint turning red; buff slip. Band around top of base spreading up on body. Two horizontal bands just below widest diameter. At top of shoulder two broad bands with lines between them, three to four in number. Stripe on handles. Ring around bottom of handle, false neck and spout. Spiral on disk, lip of spout painted. Decoration in handle zone (Fig. 394): graduated chevrons pointing upward (cf. *MP*, Motive 58:17, 18, Parallel Chevrons, p. 383 fig. 67), two units in half opposite spout, one on each side between spout and handle (only one preserved).

No. 674. Reddish-brown changing to red paint; buff slip. Large part of vessel missing but sufficient remains to indicate decoration (Fig. 394) which is almost identical with that of No. 698, save that it is executed with less precision.

No. 614 (Fig. 391). Brown paint with ruddy tinge in some places; greenish-buff slip. Foot missing but traces of band spreading slightly up on body. No bands below greatest diameter. On shoulder are two broad bands enclosing six lines (Fig. 394). Upper part, handle circle, similar to that of Nos. 674 and 698, except that parallel chevrons are somewhat shorter.

No. 1149 (Fig. 391). Red to brown paint on buff slip which has turned pinkish in places. Band on base spreading onto body. Two bands below greatest diameter, three on shoulder. Handle zone not decorated. Fine spiral on disk.

Distribution:

Outer Propylon: 1 counted.
Room 32: 1 numbered (No. 412).
Room 38: 2 numbered (Nos. 613, 614).
Court 47: 4 numbered (Nos. 674, 697, 698, 699).
Room 96: 1 numbered (No. 809).
Room 99: 1 numbered (No. 1149).

65e. Stirrup-vase: pedestal base (*decorated*)   Figs. 391, 392

Relatively small flat bottom, well-shaped thick stem, piriform body, convex top, fairly large false neck topped by flattened disk; round, or flattened handles; relatively large concave spout, broadening to everted rounded or sloping lip. Top of spout not so high as disk.

Cf. *MP*, Type 165, p. 22 fig. 3. *Prosymna*, figs. 357 no. 772, 174 no. 307.

Examples: 2 numbered.

Size:	No. 595	No. 401
height		
over-all	0.363 m.	0.317 m.
height body	0.320 m.	0.270 m.
diameter		
spout	0.053 m.	0.037 m.
diameter rim		
spout	0.078 m.	0.060 m.
diameter neck	0.037 m.	0.037 m.
diameter disk	0.071 m.	0.062 m.
width handles	0.025 m.	0.022 m.
width across		
handles	—	0.153 m.
diameter body	0.288 m.	0.229 m.
diameter base	0.100 m.	0.078 m.

Examples with decoration:

No. 401 (Fig. 329 at right, first in second row). Brownish-black paint; buff slip with slightly greenish tinge. Broad band around bottom of jar bordered above by two narrower ones. Another broad band at about one third of height of vessel. From this level to base of false neck a single zone or field, decorated by broad sweeping snakelike bands curving in an S-like formation, 18 all told, some beginning at ring around base of spout or of handles, others springing from band around false neck. Handles, bordered by stripes, bear slanting transverse curving dashes. Band at middle height of spout and around lip. False neck banded half way up. Faint trace of circle on disk.

No. 595 (Fig. 391). Brown paint with reddish tinge in some places; buff slightly greenish slip. Very broad band around bottom bordered by a narrower one. Two broad bands at about one third of height of vase and, as on No. 401, zone or field of decoration extending up to double band around bottom of false neck. Decoration similar to that of foregoing: broad stripes swinging down from above in curving S-shaped formation; five spring from band around spout, the other 14 from handle or bottom of false neck. Band around middle of false neck and spout and around rim of latter. Disk has two concentric circles. Traces of diagonal stripes on handles.

The decoration on these two pots is very striking and uncommon. No example from Argolis is known to us. Indeed the only comparable pieces that we have seen—jugs not stirrup-vases—come from western Messenia, two from the tholos tomb at Tragana excavated by Kourouniotis in 1912 (*EphArch* 1914, p. 112 figs. 23, 24), one from the Palace of Nestor (Room 18, Fig. 369 No. 245) and one from Chamber Tomb K 1 (no. 766). Perhaps all were made in the same Pylian workshop.

Distribution:

Room 32: 1 numbered (No. 401).
Room 38: 1 numbered (No. 595).

65f. Stirrup-vase: unclassified (*decorated*)   Figs. 391, 392

Relatively high projecting ring-base with vertical edge and sloping top; piriform body uncommonly narrow at bottom, flaring in a slightly concave and then convex curve to relatively broad high convex top. Narrow concave false neck crowned by flat disk with slight sinking at its center; flat perpendicular handles; concave spout, fairly broad, widening to thin plain lip; top of spout ca. 0.005 m. lower than rim of disk. Center of top enclosed within a slightly raised flat ridge which probably marks the opening into which the disk with its support was fitted by the potter.

We have been unable to find any real parallels.

Example: 1 numbered from Corridor 59.

Size:	No. 545
height over-all	0.205 m.
height body	0.168 m.
diameter spout	0.026 m.
diameter rim spout	0.030 m.
diameter neck	0.018 m.
diameter disk	0.036 m.
diameter body	0.159 m.
diameter base	0.050 m.
width handles	0.014 m.
width across handles	0.076 m.

Example with decoration:

No. 545 (Fig. 391). Surface badly damaged; paint faded, but apparently brown, red in some places; buff slip discolored through the effects of fire. Band on foot extending upward a little on body. Traces of broad band somewhat higher. Three bands, not very wide, around greatest diameter, three narrower bands bordering upper circle. Band around bottom of false neck, bottom of spout, and rim of latter. Longitudinal stripes on handles; ring around top of disk, perhaps enclosing spiral. No trace of decoration in shoulder zone nor in upper circle.

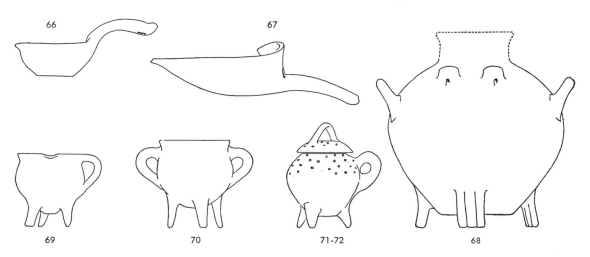

66. LADLE OR SCOOP (*coarse*) Figs. 395, 396

Flattened bottom; shallow rounded or slightly angular bowl; rounded rim pinched out to form a small pour-channel opposite a long, thick, flattened grip-handle that curves up and away from rim then becomes almost horizontal or bends down slightly; a large suspension hole near its end. Handle so heavy that it tips bowl off its bottom and not long enough nor curved sufficiently to serve as prop to keep bowl in horizontal position. In coarse ware typical of Room 60.

Cf. *MP*, Type 311, p. 75 fig. 21: ladle or brazier of this type is common in Argolis. All examples from Messenia differ from foregoing in not having handle curved so as to support vessel on its base. *BSA* xxv, p. 53, Granary at Mycenae (a large example height 0.085 m.; diameter 0.20 m.). *ChT*, p. 57 nos. 12, 13, 15, pl. xxvii nos. 12, 13; p. 80 and pl. xliii no. 13. *Zygouries*, Potter's Shop: 10 scoops of coarse fabric, fig. 155 nos. 186, 413. *Prosymna*, figs. 203 no. 433, 433 no. 188. *NT, Dendra*, fig. 28; p. 24 no. 2, p. 29 no. 17; pp. 103f., fig. 113; Persson calls them "scoop-lamps." *Asine*, fig. 240 no. 66, p. 370; fig. 271 no. 15, p. 416 no. 52. *Deltion* 3, p. 193 nos. 40-42, fig. 138 no. 4, Thebes, Tomb 25 Kolonakion.

Examples: 40 counted, 19 numbered.

Size:	largest	smallest
height	0.052 m.	0.052 m.
diameter rim	0.130 m.	0.122 m.
diameter base	0.071 m.	0.058 m.
length handle	0.123 m.	0.114 m.
width handle	0.034 m.	0.033 m.

d. hole in handle	0.013 m.	0.011 m.
capacity[1]	0.330 liter	0.220 liter

Distribution:

Room 43, tub: 1 counted and numbered.
Room 60: 39 counted, 18 numbered.

67. BRAZIER (*coarse*)   Figs. 395, 396

Rounded or flattened bottom; shallow bowl, flaring to rounded or slightly spreading beveled rim; where handle joins body, side of latter is bent up sharply, presumably to protect hand from heat; thick heavy horizontal grip-handle, flattened and bending down slightly to support vessel. One suspension hole near end of handle; either two holes in body, one on each side of handle, or rarely (in four examples) a single hole above handle. Vessel was undoubtedly designed for carrying glowing coals.

Cf. *MP*, Type 312, p. 75 fig. 21. *Zygouries*, fig. 156 nos. 407, 410. *Prosymna*, fig. 176 no. 319. *NT, Dendra*, p. 109.

Examples: 52 counted, 24 numbered.

Size:	large[2]	small[2]
height at back	0.100 m.	0.090 m.
height at front	0.074 m.	0.044 m.
width	0.278 m.	0.235 m.
length handle	0.155 m.	0.135 m.

width handle	0.050 m.	0.047 m.
d. hole in handle	0.015 m.	0.020 m.

Distribution:

Room 39: 1 numbered.
Room 67: 51 counted, 23 numbered.

68. TRIPOD-JAR (*decorated*)   Figs. 395, 396

Flat bottom; globular-conical body (probably had low collar-neck which is missing); two round loop-handles set horizontally at greatest diameter; between these on each side two pairs of elongated lugs set horizontally high on shoulder and pierced vertically; legs, made of three strips of clay pressed together and flattened, are relatively short and attached well up on body raising bottom of vessel 0.015 m. above ground.

---

[1] Of the inventoried examples one holds 0.330 liter, one 0.300, one 0.285, two 0.280, three 0.275, one 0.270, one 0.265, two 0.260, four 0.250, one 0.240, one 0.230, one 0.220.

[2] Not actually the largest and smallest but well enough preserved to be measurable.

No parallel found and the pot is unique in the Palace of Nestor, although Professor Wace informed us that he had found fragments of a somewhat similar vessel at Mycenae. Cf. *MP*, Type 63, p. 37 fig. 9, which has a similar body but no legs. The same is true of pots illustrated in *Asine*, figs. 233 nos. 2, 3, 268 no. 6. Cf. also *Korakou*, p. 68 fig. 98. Except for the lack of legs, all these pots are comparable to Shape 68 and all seem assignable to Mycenaean III C.

Example, from Room 39.

Size:	No. 457
height pres.	0.260 m.
diameter neck	0.120-0.125 m.
diameter body	0.293 m.
diameter bottom	0.120 m.
height legs, front face	0.055 m.
height legs, back face	0.027 m.
width legs at bottom	0.043 m.
thickness legs at bottom	0.012 m.
capacity	8.950 liters

Example with decoration:

No. 457. Brownish-black paint; slipped. Surface worn and damaged; decorative pattern extremely difficult to determine. Stripe on each of triple strips of legs; horizontal band around body at top of legs; two bands at greatest diameter forming lower limit of decorated zone which is bordered above by broad and narrow bands below neck. Traces of stripes around lugs. Design in fine lines on each face (approaching if not actually of the "close style") consists of composite figures. On one face (see Mr. de Jong's water color, Fig. 395) the left and central figures are formed each by two groups of triple concentric half circles side by side with graduated multiple chevrons pointing upward between them (*MP*, Motive 43:32, 33, Isolated Semicircles, p. 345 fig. 58); spiral inside inner half circle of each group and a free spiral rises on each side of chevrons. Farther to right, just below lug, filling motive appears consisting of triple spiral, one large and two small rising from stem. Beyond it twin spirals, both large, branching from one stem with multiple chevrons pointing upward between them. Traces of free spiral rising beside chevrons. On opposite side of jar, which is very badly preserved and to a considerable extent missing, it looks as if arrangement was somewhat more regular comprising three units like the two at left and center in the other panel without intervening filling motive.

69. TRIPOD-CUP: ONE HANDLE (*coarse*)   Figs. 395, 396

Flat bottom; globular-conical body; spreading lip pinched out slightly to form small pour-channel about 90° to left of handle; the latter, thick, heavy, round or slightly flattened, forms loop extending from rim or below rim to below widest diameter of body; three slightly splaying legs raise bottom of cup from 0.011 m. to 0.03 m. above ground. Legs flattened on outside and taper behind: when seen from side they look almost pointed. Toes turn out slightly. Variations in size, proportions, form of lip, position of handle. Though small these vessels were presumably made to be set over a fire for cooking purposes.

No good parallels found. *Asine*, fig. 250 no. 3, p. 385 no. 48 is larger but somewhat similar in shape.

Examples: 34 numbered.

Size:	largest	smallest
height		
over-all	0.135 m.	0.110 m.
h. bottom above		
ground	0.023 m.	0.023 m.
height neck	0.017 m.	0.009 m.
diameter neck	0.112 m.	0.096 m.
diameter rim	0.113 m.	0.095 m.
d. rim with		
spout	0.122 m.	0.102 m.
diameter body	0.133 m.	0.110 m.
diameter handle	0.018 m.	0.016 m.
diameter bottom	0.034 m.	0.020 m.
capacity[1]	0.850 liter	0.450 liter

Distribution:

Doorway Rooms 66-67: 1 numbered.
Room 67: 33 numbered.

70. TRIPOD-CUP: TWO HANDLES (*coarse*)   Figs. 395, 396

Similar in all respects to the preceding type except that it has two handles set opposite each other and has no pour-channel in the lip.

Examples: 18 numbered.

Size:	largest	smallest
height	0.172 m.	0.120 m.
bottom above		
ground	0.015 m.	0.026 m.
height neck	0.021 m.	0.013 m.
diameter neck	0.122 m.	0.110 m.
diameter rim	0.127 m.	0.118 m.
diameter body	0.157 m.	0.120 m.
diameter handles	0.017 m.	0.015 m.
diameter bottom	0.041 m.	0.028 m.
capacity[2]	1.650 liters	0.600 liter

Distribution:

Doorway Rooms 66-67: 1 numbered.
Room 67: 17 numbered.

71. TRIPOD "INCENSE-BURNER": SMALL PERFORATED CUP; ONE HANDLE (*coarse*)

Figs. 395, 396

Flattened bottom; compressed globular or globular-conical body; hole-mouth with plain rim; large thick round vertical handle springing from just below rim, forming loop that sometimes rises higher than rim before swinging down to lower part of body and being attached above one leg; three relatively tall splaying tapering legs, flattened on outside, attached to lower part of side just above flattened bottom; upper part of body pierced by many holes arranged in irregular horizontal rows: three examples have two rows, one has four, one has five.

Cf. *MP*, Type 315, p. 75 fig. 21. *ChT*, p. 184; Tomb 502 nos. 18, 19, p. 8 fig. 3; peculiar raised bases on pl. LIV nos. 10, 11. *Prosymna*, figs. 368 no. 852 (pot), 375 no. 906 (perforated lid). *NT, Dendra*, p. 28 no. 12 (fig. 28:2).

[1] Of the inventoried examples four hold 0.850 liter, one 0.800, seven 0.750, two 0.700, one 0.670, three 0.650, one 0.600, two 0.570, one 0.550, two 0.450; ten were too fragmentary to be measurable.

[2] Of the inventoried examples one holds 1.650 liters, one 1.300, two 1.200, one 1.150, one 1.100, one 1.050, one 1.000, one 0.900, three 0.850, one 0.780, two 0.750, one 0.700, one 0.650, one 0.600.

Examples: 5 numbered, all from Room 60.

Size:	largest	smallest
height with		
handle	0.117 m.	0.081 m.
height without		
handle	0.115 m.	0.071 m.
diameter		
mouth	0.065 m.	0.045 m.

maximum		
diameter	0.120 m.	0.098 m.
h. bottom above		
ground	0.015 m.	0.013 m.
diameter		
handle	0.015 m.	0.015 m.

72. LID FOR "INCENSE-BURNER": SMALL, PERFORATED; ONE HIGH LOOP-HANDLE (*coarse*)   Figs. 395, 396

Convex with carelessly made perforations through its central part, arranged with a bare suggestion of concentric rings; roughly flattened loop-handle attached to top rising high in a pinched loop.

Cf. *MP*, Type 335, with perforated vessel Type 315, p. 73 fig. 21. *ChT*, pl. LIV nos. 10, 11. *Prosymna*, fig. 375 no. 906.

Examples: 6 numbered, all from Room 60.

Size:	largest	smallest
height with		
handle	0.047 m.	0.044 m.

height without		
handle	0.018 m.	0.018 m.
diameter	0.093 m.	0.066 m.
width handle	0.014 m.	0.015 m.

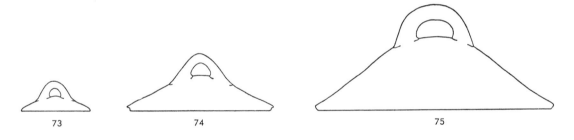

73   74   75

73. LID: CONVEX, SMALL; ONE HANDLE (*domestic ware*)   Figs. 397, 398

Slightly convex on top, concave underneath; plain rim; approximately across the top a thick arched handle.

Cf. *MP*, Type 335, B. handled, Shape b. *Zygouries*, Potter's Shop, fig. 154 nos. 586, 585. *BSA* XLIX (1954), pl. 37 a (right), from House of the Sphinxes at Mycenae.

Examples: 2 numbered, both from Room 32.

Size:	No. 470	No. 469			
height	0.027 m.	0.025 m.	diameter	0.122 m.	0.122 m.
			handle	missing	missing

74. LID: CONVEX, CONSIDERABLY LARGER; ONE HANDLE (*coarse*)   Figs. 397, 398

Convex on top spreading broadly to flattened grooved rim; one flattened grooved arched handle on top.

No parallels found.

Examples: 2 numbered, both from Room 67.

Size:	No. 1022	No. 899			
			diameter at rim	0.289 m.	0.266 m.
height with handle	0.106 m.	0.103 m.	diameter handle	0.016 m.	0.021 m.
height without handle	0.066 m.	0.065 m.			

75. LID: CONVEX, VERY LARGE; ONE HANDLE (*coarse*)   Figs. 397, 398

Convex top, sloping sides flaring slightly to flattened plain rim; on top one thick round arched handle.

No parallels found.

Examples: 3 numbered.

Size:	No. 543	No. 1137	No. 586				
				diameter rim	0.545 m.	0.520 m.	0.440 m.
height with handle	0.223 m.	0.212 m.	0.180 m.	diameter handle	0.031 m.	0.030 m.	0.025 m.
height without handle	0.163 m.	0.155 m.	0.115 m.				

Distribution:
Room 23: Nos. 586, 1137.
Room 24: No. 543.

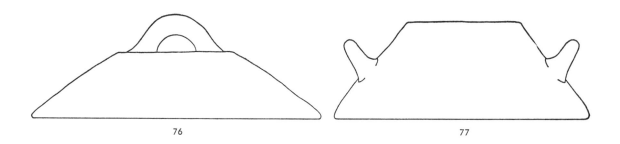

76   77

76. LID: BASIN-LIKE, LARGE; ONE CENTRAL HANDLE (*coarse*)   Figs. 397, 398

Flat top; side spreads sloping down in convex curve to slightly grooved rim; large thick round arched handle on top.

No parallels found.

Examples: 2 numbered.			diameter flat		
Size:	No. 1136	No. 1132	top	0.210 m.	0.200 m.
height with			diameter		
handle	0.210 m.	—	handle	0.032 m.	—
height without			*Distribution*:		
handle	0.150 m.	0.117 m.	Room 23: No. 1136.		
diameter rim	0.564 m.	0.534 m.	Room 24: No. 1132.		

77. LID: BASIN-LIKE, VERY LARGE; TWO HANDLES ON SIDE (*coarse*)   Figs. 381, 397, 398

Flat top, straight or concave or slightly convex slanting side, ending in plain or grooved rim; two round horizontal arched handles set obliquely opposite each other about half way down side.

No parallels found.

Examples: 7 numbered.			*Distribution*:
Size:	largest	smallest	Room 7: 1 numbered
height	0.200 m.	0.142 m.	Room 21: 1 numbered.
diameter flat			Room 23: 3 numbered.
top	0.256 m.	0.150 m.	Room 46: 1 numbered, apparently used as a
diameter rim	0.670 m.	0.474 m.	cover for the chimney above the hearth (Fig.
diameter			333).
handles	—	0.026 m.	Room 105: 1 numbered.

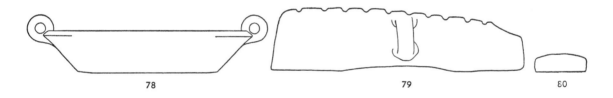

78   79   80

78. PAN: CIRCULAR, SHALLOW; TWO RING-HANDLES ON RIM (*coarse*)   Figs. 397, 398

Large flattened bottom, convex on the interior; low slightly convex flaring sides; thick flattened outward sloping lip; two round or flattened ring-handles fitted over rim opposite each other.

No close parallel is given by Furumark nor is the shape known to us from any other site.

Examples: 3 counted, 2 numbered, all from Room 68.			width handles	0.030 m.	0.028 m.
			diameter rim	0.403 m.	0.396 m.
Size:	No. 547	No. 331	thickness rim	0.015 m.	0.014 m.
height with			diameter		
handles	0.127 m.	0.100 m.	bottom	0.282 m.	0.260 m.
height without					
handles	0.079 m.	0.072 m.			

[417]

79. Broiling-pan (*coarse*)   Figs. 397, 398

Long, shallow, approximately rectangular pan: flattened bottom; one end open; the other end and sides rise vertically to thick plain rim; sides slightly higher than closed end, toward which they slope down; two flattened handles looping out from rim almost to bottom, set vertically opposite each other in middle of long sides; 10 roughly V-shaped notches in rim of each long side,[1] apparently arranged to hold spits laid across the pan above hot coals, clearly a grilling pan for making *souvlakia*.

Not listed by Furumark and no analogies from other places known to us.

Examples: 1 numbered, from Room 105; fragments of several others from various parts of the palace.

		width	0.325 m.
		height on long sides	0.095 m.
		height on end	0.070 m.
Size:	No. 861	width handles	0.030 m.
length	0.460 m.		

80. Disk-shaped pot   Figs. 397, 398

Flattened bottom; slightly convex vertical sides; top also very slightly convex, curving to central hole in top, finished with a plain rim; interior hollow. Purpose unknown; possibly a lid or stopper of a jar.

No parallels found.

Example: 1 numbered, from Room 55.

Size:	No. 706	height	0.033 m.
diameter	0.102 m.	diameter central hole	0.023 m.

[1] One side is complete; part of the other with four notches is missing.

CHARACTER, DATE, AND IDENTIFICATION
OF THE PALACE

IN THE period when pottery of Mycenaean III B was still being used and wares of Mycenaean III C had begun to be made, the establishment on the hill now called Englianos was unmistakably a capital, a center of government. Situated in a dominating position which commanded a broad view in all directions, it comprised a citadel serving as the royal seat and residence of a Mycenaean king, and, clustered on the descending slopes around it to the northwest, southwest, and southeast, a lower town of considerable extent in which the ordinary people dwelt in houses built on stone foundations.

That it was definitely an administrative center of government is abundantly demonstrated by the numerous tablets, inscribed in the Linear B script, which have been found in the Archives Rooms (7 and 8 on Key Plan) and in many other parts of the building complex. These records, which, as convincingly established by Michael Ventris, were written in an early form of Greek, are mainly concerned with economic and related affairs of bureaucratic administration. They deal with many cities, towns, and places—some perhaps far away. Authority seems clearly to be exercised over two groups of what appear to be subordinate dependencies, one comprising nine different communities, always listed in the same perhaps hierarchical order, the other composed of seven, apparently likewise enumerated in a fixed order. This division of subject towns or places into two groupings of nine and seven vividly recalls the list of the nine towns tabulated in the Catalogue of Ships (*Iliad* II, 591-602) as ruled by King Nestor, and the group of seven towns situated along the Gulf of Messenia on the outermost border of Pylos which Agamemnon tendered to Achilles as a peace offering to settle their feud at Troy (*Iliad* IX, 149-153).

The name Pylos occurs—sometimes often repeated—on more than 50 tablets of those found in the palace at Englianos, and this must surely be the designation of the capital city itself. It is true that the names of the nine and the seven towns, as given in the *Iliad*, actually correspond clearly in only one or two instances with those that have been preserved on the tablets; but the agreement in the two sources of identical numbers for the components of the two groupings must surely spring from the same tradition rather than from fortuitous coincidence. The discrepancy in the names themselves might have been brought about by the vicissitudes and disturbances that followed the Mycenaean era and the Dorian Invasion. This was a long period—sometimes called the Dark Age, since so little is known about what was happening in those three or four turbulent centuries of movement and change which passed before the Homeric epics were somehow molded from the ballads and songs, sung and transmitted by generations of troubadours, into a more or less fixed form and order. It was a time when migrant peoples were spreading over the land, causing shifts and changes in the population. Many of the old towns and occupied places were destroyed and abandoned and new settlements built, while the old toponyms no doubt suffered numerous alterations and displacements. The frequent appearance of the name of Pylos on the tablets in any event offers decisive evidence for the identification.

The general design of the principal unit in the complex of buildings forming the palace is closely similar to the plans of the megara at Tiryns and Mycenae: a propylon gives access to an inner court beyond which a two-columned portico, a vestibule, and a throne room of generous proportions follow one after the other along the same longitudinal axis. Though not exactly identical in size, these apartments in all three instances were laid out on a spacious scale. The palatial architecture represented at Mycenae, Tiryns, and Pylos shows considerable variety in details, as for example in the numbers of columns, their flutings and bases, in the stairways, bathrooms, corridors, wall-construction, hearths, and floors, but similar workmanship of comparable quality is recognizable at all three sites. The patterns of the painted decoration on the stucco floors, and the style as well as the subjects of the frescoes from the walls display close kinship from one region to the other. In all these respects the palace at Englianos holds its place beside the contemporary palaces at Tiryns and Mycenae. Only the Cyclopean fortification walls of the strongholds so conspicuous in Argolis are lacking at the Messenian capital. Why this western citadel was left without a corresponding defensive wall remains unknown.

The palace at Englianos is the only one of its size, administrative character, and date that has yet been discovered in western Peloponnesos. Scanty ruins of buildings that might have been palatial structures have been noted at various places here and there in a range extending from the Alpheios on the north to Cape Akritas and the Gulf of Messenia on the south, but none is sufficiently well preserved to give any indication of its plan or to demonstrate that it was a center of administration. In the light of recent exploration and research it appears that this western region flourished in the early Mycenaean Period, LH I and II, with many strongholds, each no doubt ruled by its local king; but in late Mycenaean times, when pottery of the III B category was in use, consolidation into a larger kingdom seems to have been effected, with more widespread authority exercised from a capital center. The western coastal strip and south Messenia could easily be controlled and governed from the site at Englianos, the only such establishment which is yet known; and it is not likely that a rival of the same size could have been supported in this part of Greece, which is not overly rich in agricultural productiveness.

The date of the catastrophe that destroyed the palace at Englianos is clearly indicated by the vast quantity of distinctive pottery which was found almost everywhere throughout the entire complex of buildings. From eight pantries came more than 7,000 pots of many different shapes which chanced to be standing in good order on wooden shelves on the day of the destructive fire that left the whole site in ruins. Many vessels were also recovered from the floors in almost all parts of the palace, where they were in use on that same ill-fated day. The collection as a whole reflects chiefly the latest stage in the style of Mycenaean III B. The vast majority of these vessels fall into the category of plain undecorated ware, but painted patterns are not altogether lacking; the pots of this kind bear simple designs: horizontal bands, arcs, wavy lines, spiraliform survivals, and the like, all pointing to the very end of the III B ceramic style. Along with the late III B types in a good many rooms were found examples which, if recovered by themselves alone, would be unhesitatingly attributed to the succeeding style of III C. This judgment applies notably to a series of distinctive krater-bowls (Fig. 385), as we call them, though they are also known in some places as "deep bowls." One was found on the floor of the "Queen's Room" (No. 677), two came from the Bathroom (Nos. 593, 594), one, badly broken, was recovered from Pithos 13 in Room 27 (No. 862), part of another from Ramp 59 (No. 576), one from Room 12 (No. 1172) and one from the Main Drain (No. 1150), two from Corridor 95 (Nos. 808 and 1176) and one from Room 98 (No. 813) in the Northeast Building. All were in use before the fire and were buried underneath the debris of the catastrophe. Several might confidently be ascribed to Mycenaean III C, and some of them, e.g., Nos. 593, 594, 677, and 862, appear to belong not to the very earliest products of that period. Many pots of other shapes may also plausibly be assigned to the early phases of the III C style.[1] It is therefore obvious that the palace came to its end at a time when pottery of Mycenaean III C was beginning to be made and to displace the wares of III B.

After a thorough scrutiny of the evidence available, Furumark in his great work on Mycenaean pottery reached the conclusion that the change from the III B to the III C ceramic style began about 1230 B.C. This was the most likely approximation possible at the time on the basis of the comparisons with pottery found in Egyptian, Palestinian, Syrian, and Cypriote contexts which, however, were not adequate to give pin-point precision in dating. Until these connections have been more widely extended and more fully established, it might be safer to regard the last three decades of the thirteenth century, 1230-1200 B.C., which Furumark calls Mycenaean III C:1 e, as a period of transition from III B to III C. This is the period to which the bulk of the pottery recovered in the palace at Englianos must surely be attributed.

---

[1] E.g., Shape 52, pithoid jars: Fig. 375 Nos. 460, 461, 521; Shape 63, pedestaled kraters: Fig. 387 Nos. 596, 1151; Shape 65a, stirrup-vase: No. 1142, Fig. 348 Nos. 1-4; Shape 68, tripod-jar: Fig. 395 No. 457.

The latest vessels in the entire collection were all found lying on the floors, broken by the weight of the debris that fell upon them, for the most part blackened and somewhat warped by the heat of the fire which reduced the entire establishment to ruins.

No evidence whatever of a reoccupation in Mycenaean times after the catastrophe has been observed. The site was obviously abandoned and thenceforth left deserted, the crumbling walls overlaid by falling stones and masses of dissolving clay from the superstructure of crude brick. In the course of time vegetation spread its mantle over the whole area. Ultimately, apparently in the seventh century B.C., an olive press was evidently set up on the hill, which had perhaps already been converted into an olive grove. From the seventh century—and probably much earlier—only scanty vestiges of the palace buildings remained visible above ground, though not impressive enough to be recognized as the surviving landmark of the onetime seat of a king who reigned over western Messenia.

The identification of the citadel at Englianos as Nestor's Pylos surely requires no long argumentation and discussion. In the preceding paragraphs we have called attention to the general character of the royal establishment: its files of bureaucratic records demonstrate plainly that it was an administrative center of government ruling over many subordinate towns and places. In its size, architectural quality, in the decorative style of its frescoes and its floor paintings—in all these features it holds its own in comparison with the contemporary palaces at Tiryns and Mycenae; its chronological range clearly extends from the beginning to the end of the ceramic period of Mycenaean III B and probably a little beyond that, in an era more or less nearly equated with the thirteenth century B.C. to which the strongholds of Argolis also belong.

That is surely the era in which the Achaean coalition carried out the expedition against Troy. The results of the excavations conducted at Troy from 1932 to 1938 by the University of Cincinnati have demonstrated, we believe, that if there ever was a Trojan War—and we have no doubts about that—it must have been waged against Settlement VIIa which was utterly destroyed by a catastrophic fire, accompanied by some indications of violence, about the middle of the thirteenth century, if not a trifle earlier. Tradition held that the Descent of the Herakleidai—or the Dorian Invasion—rolled over mainland Greece two generations after the fall of Priam's capital. Ancient historians variously calculated the length of a generation, ranging from 30 to 35 and 40 years. Thucydides apparently accepted the highest figure in his conclusion that there was an interval of 80 years between those two events. Other writers of later antiquity vary greatly in their computations to fix the year when Troy was sacked, spanning some two centuries from 1334 to 1135 B.C. when their results are translated into the modern system of reckoning. In any event Nestor played a distinguished role in the Trojan Expedition, serving mainly as the trusty counsellor and confidant of King Agamemnon. The palace at Englianos was burned down at the end of the thirteenth century, some 50 or 60 years after the destruction of Troy VIIa. In this chronological problem archaeological evidence seems to us to fit tidily with the general, if not precise, dating handed down by Greek tradition.

That tradition records only one royal dynasty domiciled in southwestern Peloponnesos which politically, economically, and in general rank and standing could associate on terms of more or less equality with the lords of Mycenae, Tiryns, and Sparta. That was the Neleid family, founded by Neleus who came down from Thessaly and took or otherwise acquired Pylos. He was succeeded by his son Nestor, the most famous member of the family and the most respected of all the heroes who took part in the expedition against Troy. He had a long reign, living through three generations of men. Nestor was followed on the throne by a nephew and by other Neleids to the third and fourth generation. Then Pylos was captured and destroyed by the Herakleidai of the Dorian Invasion.[2] The Neleids fled from the country, some going to Athens where they became the founders of four eupatrid families which in classical times took pride in their origin; others sailed on across the Aegean to set themselves up in Ionia. The citizens and commoners who lived in the lower town are also said to have departed, some moving down to the shore of the sea at the foot of Koryphasion where the name of Pylos lingered on into classical times.

As it has been revealed by the excavations, the history of the palace at Englianos fits admirably with this traditional account in all essential details. The destruction by burning of the earlier settlement, which at the end of the ceramic phase III A occupied the hill and the slopes below, might be taken to indicate that Neleus conquered the place with violence, which an alternative tradition mentions as a likelihood. It is not impossible that the Southwestern Building was the actual palace existing at the end of the fourteenth century and was then demolished in the struggle for domination. The re-erection of that unit in a different style of architectural technique and the razing of all other residences on the citadel might perhaps be ascribed to the victorious Neleus, while the larger Main Building could perhaps represent the work of Nestor. The Wine Magazine, evidently a necessity in a Mycenaean palace, was presumably built at the same time as the Main Building. It is difficult to determine the place of the Workshop in the building sequence; it too was an indispensable element from the beginning in such a palace. So far as the evidence goes, it might be a construction of the early part of the thirteenth century B.C., or a supplement of a later stage. The addition of the North Oil Magazine could perhaps, but not necessarily, be attributed to one of the successors to the throne. The repair of the western angle and the enclosing of Courts 42 and 47 are, however, surely structures of the final phases.

2 *Pausanias* IV, 3, 3.

In any event it is clear that the entire complex of buildings was in use and fully occupied until the end. Looting may presumably have preceded the destruction by fire, but an examination by an anthropologist, Dr. J. C. Trevor, of numerous bones recovered in many parts of the palace disclosed not a single identifiable human element. The people of the palace and town seem therefore to have escaped; but the furniture, equipment, and other contents not carried off by the plunderers, remained in various states of damage and disintegration, buried in the ruins under the debris of walls, floor, and roof. This was the end of human occupation of the site.

INDEX